COMPUTER INFORMATION SYSTEMS DEVELOPMENT:
Analysis and Design

Michael J. Powers
The Country Companies
Bloomington, Illinois

David R. Adams
Associate Professor, Computer Information Systems
Northern Kentucky University
Highland Heights, Kentucky

Harlan D. Mills
IBM Fellow
Professor, Computer Science
University of Maryland
College Park, Maryland

Published by

J82 **SOUTH-WESTERN PUBLISHING CO.**

CINCINNATI   WEST CHICAGO, ILL.   DALLAS   PELHAM MANOR, N.Y.   PALO ALTO, CALIF.

ISBN: 0-538-10820-7

Library of Congress Catalog Card Number: 82-62635

　　　　　4　5　6　7　8　K　7　6　5

Printed in the United States of America

CONTENTS

Preface   xi

I. OVERVIEW   1

Purpose   1
Achievements   1

1. The Systems Development Environment   4

Learning Objectives   4
Systems and Subsystems   5
Business Systems and Information Systems   7
The Systems Approach   14
Systems Analysis   22

2. The Systems Development Life Cycle   28

Learning Objectives   28
CIS Development—A Complex Process   29
The System Life Cycle   38
The Systems Development Life Cycle   40
Project Control Structure   47
The Process of Systems Analysis   51

II. THE INVESTIGATION PHASE   60

Objectives 60
Activities 60
Process 62
End Product 62
Decision 62

3. Initial Investigation   64

Learning Objectives 64
Activity Description 64
Objectives 65
Scope 66
End Products 71
The Process 72
Personnel Involved 77
Cumulative Project File 78

4. Information Gathering   83

Learning Objectives 83
Importance of Information Gathering 84
Categories of Information 85
Sources of Information 94
Methods for Gathering Information 95

5. Feasibility Study   120

Learning Objectives 120
Activity Description 121
Objectives 131
Scope 131
End Products 132

The Process   134
Personnel Involved   138
Cumulative Project File   141
Cumulative Documentation   141

6. The Process and Products of Analysis   **148**

Learning Objectives   148
The Goals of Analysis   148
Systems Models   151
Logical and Physical Models   160
The Analysis Process   167
The Products of Analysis   179

7. Cost/Benefit Analysis   **184**

Learning Objectives   184
The Nature of Cost/Benefit Analysis
Value/Cost Relationships in Information Systems   188
Evaluating Costs and Benefits   193
Analyzing Costs and Benefits   199

8. Communication   **214**

Learning Objectives   214
The Need   215
Identifying Audiences   216
Problem Solving Sessions   217
Technical Reviews (Walkthroughs)   221
Reporting   225

III. ANALYSIS AND GENERAL DESIGN PHASE   238

Objectives   238
Activities   238
Process   238
End Product   240
Decision   240

9. Existing System Review   242

Learning Objectives   242
Activity Description   242
Objectives   243
Scope   244
End Products   245
The Process   250
Personnel Involved   253
Cumulative Project File   253

10. System Modeling Tools   256

Learning Objectives   256
Modeling in Systems Analysis   257
Constructing Data Flow Diagrams   257
Hierarchical (Top-Down)
   Partitioning of Data Flow Diagrams   269
Developing the Initial Diagram 0   277
Defining Data—The Data Dictionary   285
Specifying Processing Rules—Processing Descriptions   294
Use of Modeling to Support the Analysis Process   308

11. New System Requirements   323

Learning Objectives   323
Activity Description   323
Objectives   325

Scope   325
End Product   328
The Process   332
Personnel Involved   354
Cumulative Project File   354
Case Scenario   354

12. Output Design   **367**

Learning Objectives   367
The Output Design Task   367
Purposes of System Outputs   368
Output Media and Devices   373
Output Evaluation Criteria   378
Output Design   380
Case Scenario   383

13. Input Design   **398**

Learning Objectives   398
The Task of Input Design   398
Input Alternatives   399
Input Equipment   404
Evaluation of System Input Options   411
Input Design   417
Case Scenario   420

14. Logical Data Analysis   **426**

Learning Objectives   426
Analyzing Data Stores   426
Logical Data Structure Criteria   428
Normalization of Data Stores   429
Data Structure Diagrams   445
Advantages of Third Normal Form   450

15. New System Design   457

Learning Objectives 457
Activity Description 458
Objectives 459
Scope 460
End Products 462
The Process 466
Personnel Involved 479
Cumulative Project File 479
Case Scenario 480

16. File Design   489

Learning Objectives 489
File-Related Design Decisions 489
Application Support Files 490
File Organization and Access 492
File Equipment and Media 494
Sequential File Organization 498
Direct File Organization 501
Indexed-Sequential File Organization 506
File Design Trade-Offs 515
Case Scenario 519

17. Control and Reliability Design   529

Learning Objectives 529
The Need for Controls 529
Types of Controls 530
Responsibility for Defining Controls 540
Case Scenario 540

18. Implementation and Installation Planning   550

Learning Objectives 550
Activity Description 550

Objectives   551
Scope   551
End Products   552
The Process   554
Personnel Involved   556
Cumulative Project File   556

IV. **IMPLEMENTATION, INSTALLATION,
AND REVIEW PHASES**   558

Purpose   558
Achievements   560

19. **Detailed Design and Implementation Phase**   561

Learning Objectives   561
Phase Description   561
Objectives   564
Scope   564
End Products   565
The Process   569
Personnel Involved   576

20. **Installation**   579

Learning Objectives   579
Phase Description   579
Objectives   581
Scope   582
End Products   582
The Process   582
Personnel Involved   589
Cumulative Project File   589

21. Review 593

Learning Objectives   593
Phase Description   593
Objectives   596
Scope   596
End Products   596
The Process   598
Other Systems Development Options   600

22. Project Management 613

Learning Objectives   613
Nature of Project Management   613
Applying Project Management   615
Project Management Techniques   616
Planning and Scheduling Networks   619
Gantt Charts   629

APPENDIX A: Systems Analysis Project 636

Introduction   636
1. System Selection and Feasibility Study   637
2. Existing System Review   640
3. New System Requirements   641
4. New System Design   643
5. System Presentation   645
Project Evaluation Form   646

APPENDIX B: A Case Scenario 647

Existing System Overview   647
Input for New System Requirements   652

Glossary 654

Index 678

PREFACE

PERSPECTIVE

This book, in part, represents an implementation of the *Model Curriculum for Undergraduate Computer Information Systems Education* of the Data Processing Management Association-Education Foundation (DPMA-EF). Specifically, the information presented in this book meets or exceeds the content called for in the suggested outline for course *CIS-4—Systems Analysis Methods*. Correspondence between this book and the course specifications is assured by the fact that the text was developed under the oversight of the DPMA-EF, with content appropriateness and technical accuracy validated through independent review.

The DPMA-EF curriculum specifies a structured approach to systems development through use of structured analysis methods within an established life cycle. The curriculum is aimed at graduating students qualified as entry-level programmer/analysts in business-oriented computer facilities.

CONTENT LEVEL

This text is designed to support an undergraduate course. It is assumed that students using this text will have completed an introductory course in computer information systems (CIS). Students should also have completed—or be enrolled concurrently in—a sequence of instruction in structured programming designed to impart skills in the development of COBOL programs that solve business problems. Students should be familiar with the terms and techniques of program development to gain full value from a course based on this book.

The approach taken to systems development in this book is compatible with that of the companion texts, *Computer Information Systems: An Introduction,* by Adams, Wagner, and Boyer, as well as with *Programming Principles With COBOL I,* by Medley and Eaves.

This book provides the instructional content for a first semester in a two-semester sequence for the building of understanding and competence in systems analysis and design. A companion text, *Computer Information Systems Development: Design and Implementation,* provides a basis for the work of the second semester. At the conclusion of the first semester, students should be able to analyze existing information processing systems and prepare user specifications for improved systems.

CONTENT HIGHLIGHTS

The book uses a basic, easily taught systems development life cycle as a framework. This life cycle divides a typical systems development project into five phases and 15 activities. The first two phases, dealing with the analysis and design aspects of systems development, are covered in depth in this book. The remaining three phases, which form the basis for the second semester of instruction in systems development, are treated at an overview level only.

In this way, a student who is able to have only one semester of instruction in systems development will gain the maximum benefit in building analysis and design skills. These are the most-used skills demanded of entry-level systems analysts. On the other hand, students moving ahead to a second semester of instruction in systems development will have a solid basis on which to build advanced skills in detailed design and implementation of new systems.

This book makes heavy use of case methods for illustration and instruction. A single case is introduced in the third chapter and carried throughout the book. Students move incrementally through the processing of a request for systems development, analysis of opportunities and needs, and the design of a new system. The case used is universal in nature and fully understandable for undergraduate students. It deals with a request to expand an existing water billing system for a small city to encompass billing for waste disposal services from a local sanitary district.

In addition to the continuity of this underlying case, other cases are introduced as appropriate throughout the book. Though these other cases are not developed as fully as the water billing system, they do provide the basis for illustrating and teaching specific principles or skills for which the water billing case could not provide an ideal vehicle. Finally, there are two appendices that establish content and mechanisms for supplementary case studies in systems development that can be assigned to students—individually or as project team members.

The chapters of this book are divided into two categories:

- Phases and activities of the systems development life cycle.

- Skills applied in systems analysis and design.

'Activities' Chapters

These chapters deal with the individual activities of the first two phases of the life cycle and with the activities that make up the final three phases. These activity chapters use standard subject headings and follow a common presentation pattern. Within each of these chapters, there are standard sections on:

- Activity Description
- Objectives
- Scope
- End Products
- The Process
- Personnel Involved
- Cumulative Project File.

For each activity, two of these areas are treated as keys to a student's understanding of the analysis process. They are the objectives of each activity and its end products. The other areas tend to be natural consequences of these two.

'Skills' Chapters

The second series of chapters deals with the individual skills applied in analysis and design of computer information systems. These chapters cover:

- Information Gathering
- The Process and Products of Analysis
- Cost/Benefit Analysis
- Communication
- System Modeling Tools

- Output Design
- Input Design
- File Design
- Logical Data Analysis
- Control and Reliability Design
- Project Management.

ACKNOWLEDGMENTS

To assure accuracy and appropriateness for the content of this text, a highly experienced, objective group of persons was asked to review the manuscript during development. The careful readings and thoughtful comments of this group represented, cumulatively, an important contribution to the soundness of this text. Their contributions are acknowledged with sincere thanks.

Terrence J. Boyer, Mercantile Trust Co., N.A., St. Louis, MO
Prof. Hollis Latimer, Tarrant County Junior College, Hurst, TX
V. Arthur Owles, Wang Laboratories, Inc., Lowell, MA
Dr. Blair Stephenson, Pegasus-Basis Software, Inc., Richardson, TX

In addition to the in-process reviews, final evaluations of the manuscript were provided independently to the DPMA-EF by the following persons, whose contributions are hereby acknowledged:

Dr. Coleman Furr, President, Coleman College, San Diego, CA
Dr. Beverly B. Madron, Texas Instruments, Dallas, TX
Stan Piercefield, Public Service of Indiana, Plainfield, IN

In addition, a special note of thanks is extended to V. Arthur Owles, who participated in development of some of the concepts that distinguish the content of this book.

OVERVIEW I

PURPOSE

The two chapters in this initial part are designed to build an understanding that encompasses both the need for a formal approach to systems development and a method for developing systems.

Chapter 1 establishes some basic definitions of what systems are and how they are developed. This chapter also describes the environment in which systems development takes place.

Chapter 2 introduces a process for systems development, known as the systems development life cycle. A systems development life cycle provides a tool for managing complex processes by breaking them down into a series of phases and activities with well-defined products or objectives. The five-phase life cycle introduced is diagrammed in Figure I-1.

Also discussed in Chapter 2 are the relationships among the phases of a systems development life cycle and the flow of information that takes place within a systems development project. These aspects are represented in the data flow diagram of Figure I-2.

ACHIEVEMENTS

On completing your work in this part of the book, you should have the background necessary to proceed with specific study of systems development activities and to build your skills through a series of later chapters designed to help build systems analysis skills.

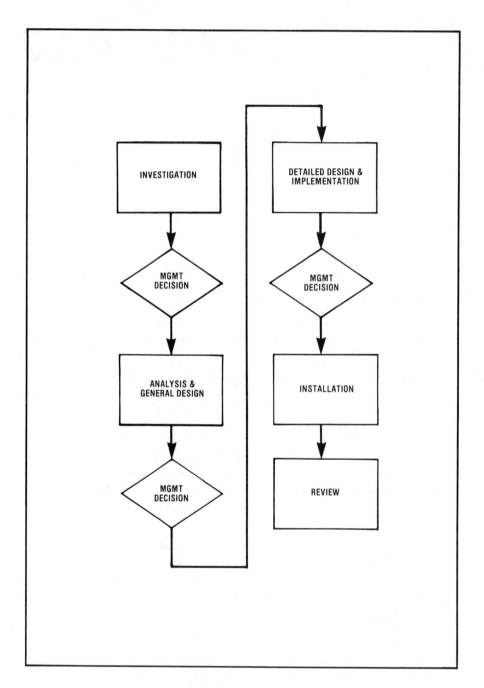

Figure I-1.   The systems development life cycle—a control-oriented view.

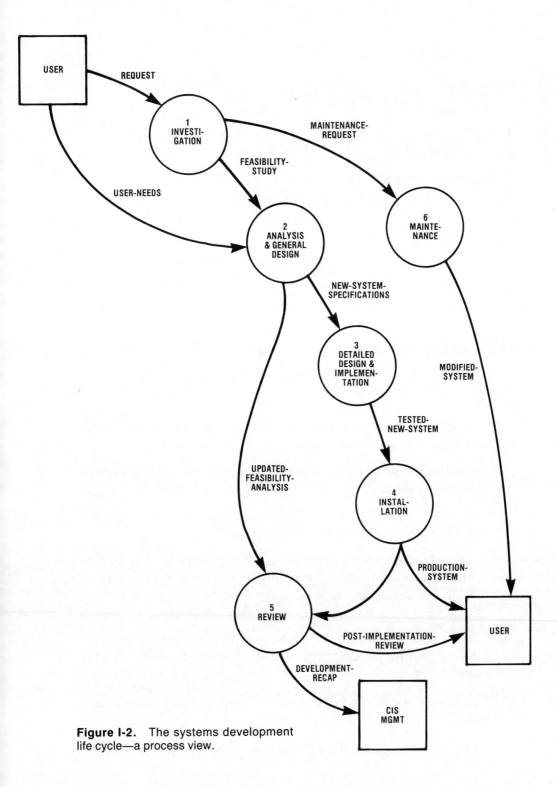

Figure I-2. The systems development
life cycle—a process view.

3

1 THE SYSTEMS DEVELOPMENT ENVIRONMENT

LEARNING OBJECTIVES

On completing the reading assignments and practice exercises for this chapter, you should be able to:

☐ Define the terms system and subsystem and explain the similarities and differences between them.

☐ Describe the role of organization structures as implementations of business systems.

☐ Describe the role of information as an integrating force within organizations and as a corporate resource.

☐ Describe the functions and purposes of three types of computer information systems—data processing, management information, and decision support—as well as the relationships among these systems.

☐ Identify and describe the components of information systems, including input, processing, output, feedback, control, and adjustment.

☐ Describe methods and values of the systems approach to problem solving.

☐ Define and describe the purposes and values of systems analysis.

SYSTEMS AND SUBSYSTEMS

This book is about computer information systems (CIS). The text deals with analysis, design, and development of computer information systems. Thus, a good place to start is to identify what a computer information system is.

Definition of System

As a general definition, a *system* is any set of interrelated, interacting components that function together as an entity to achieve specific results. The components, or elements, that make up a system are closely interdependent; actions or conditions that affect any one element will also affect all others within the system. An effective system will be *synergistic*. This means, simply, that when a system is functioning as it should, it produces results with a value greater than the total value produced by its separate, individual parts.

Identification of Systems

Identification of systems lies in the viewpoint and experience of a trained observer. To illustrate, the earth and the sun can be looked upon as separate entities. However, a person with a systems perspective notes that the earth is dependent on the sun for heat, light, and other characteristics without which the earth could not exist in its present form. Therefore, the earth and the sun can be regarded as elements of a single system. The sun, in turn, has a similar relationship to Mercury, Venus, and other planets. Thus, the earth can be seen as one component, or element, of a solar system.

The solar system can be identified, or classified, as a natural, physical system. Humanity, a species that is part of the synergism of that system, is, in turn, part of what can be identified as a biological system of the earth. The biological system, in proper perspective, is related to and dependent upon an ecological system. The point is, systems are built upon relationships, and upon the recognition that complex activities are dependent upon one another.

The same is true for other types of systems. For example, in addition to natural systems like those cited above, there are also many human-made systems. These can be thought of as either abstract or physical. Examples of abstract systems include languages, systems of numbers (mathematics), systems of thought (philosophy, religion), and systems of logic (laws). Physical systems can take many forms. There are mechanical systems, such as automobiles, trains, and aircraft. There are social systems organized around geography or heritage (cities, states, nations). And there are organizational systems, which are commonly broken down according to public and private sectors.

Businesses fit into the picture right about here. A business, as a system, is composed of people, facilities, equipment, materials, and methods of work that function together to provide goods or services.

Definition of Subsystems

Individual systems can have different degrees, or levels, of complexity. As systems become increasingly complex, a series of smaller systems can be identified within larger ones. These smaller systems are known as *subsystems* of the systems that contain them. A subsystem, in turn, has its own interacting elements that function together to produce identified end products. However, these end products are related to and become part of the result produced by the larger system of which the subsystem is a part. Thus, both subsystems and their products become part of more complex, total systems.

Relationships of Systems and Subsystems

Subsystems, in effect, are identified by the relationships that exist within larger systems. For example, a family is a social system on its own. But a family is also a subsystem of its local neighborhood. The neighborhood, in turn, is a subsystem of a larger entity called a community. The community is a subsystem of a city, and so on.

The same is true for business organizations. Virtually any large business organization is a complex system made up of a number of subsystems. Subsystems are defined by the way in which a business organizes itself. Typical designations include production, marketing, accounting, and distribution. Each of the subsystems has individual purposes and produces measurable results. The results of the subsystems, however, serve primarily to contribute to the goals and the products or services of the organization as a whole.

Again, recognition of systems and subsystems is a matter of perspective. For example, a large business organization may be regarded as a subsystem of an overall system of free enterprise. The free enterprise system, ultimately, can be regarded as a subsystem of an economic system that takes in elements of governmental and social subsystems as well.

BUSINESS SYSTEMS AND INFORMATION SYSTEMS

The identification of any system—including a business—lies in the perception of the people who look at it. This perception of a business as a system is implemented through the organization of that business. Thus, the *organizational structure* of a business represents a formal recognition by its management of the subsystems from which it is composed. An *organizational chart* is, in effect, a graphic representation identifying the subsystems of a business and portraying their relationships.

The partial organization chart in Figure 1-1 represents typical departmental designations, lines of authority and responsibility, and reporting for a large organization. Looking at this chart, it becomes obvious that people are departmentalized according to certain criteria. These criteria include such considerations as function performed, the process involved, relationships with customers, geographic territories, products produced, and services rendered. The weighting of such criteria in the building of individual business structures will vary widely with the type and nature of the organization involved, as well as with the background of its top managers.

In the process of identifying subsystems within an organization and representing them graphically, managers seek several important results, including:

- People are grouped according to working relationships and functional subsystems within which they perform their jobs. The subsystems identified are typically called departments of the organization. Departmentalization of an organization, then, is management's way of establishing subsystems that build the overall system's identity.

- In the process of identifying departments or other organizational groupings, management also sets up relationships in terms of authority and responsibility for performing the tasks within the subsystems and also for delivering the end results of those subsystems.

- The authority and responsibility identifications, for their part, serve as the basis for establishing work responsibilities and work flows throughout an organization. These work flows and their task definitions serve to determine the methods and procedures

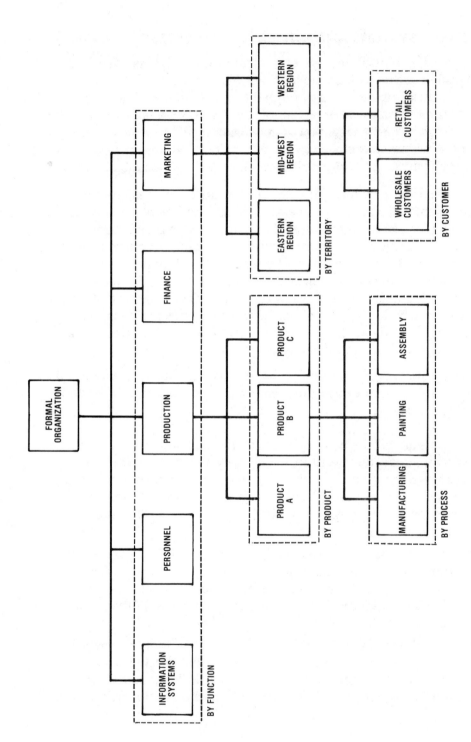

Figure 1-1. Organization structure chart showing breakdown of business system into subsystems.

through which people, equipment, materials, and other resources are brought together and applied to produce the end-product goods or services of an organization.

Information as an Integrating Force

Any complex system, and any organizational structure that implements a complex system such as a business entity, is made up of parts that are interrelated, that function together. The interrelationships among the parts of the system lie in the sharing of the resources used. One of the resources that must be shared by viable systems is *information*.

Information is an essential resource for any functional system that delivers planned results. Therefore, any functional system, within any organization, should encompass methods and procedures for developing and delivering information. This is known as an *information system*.

An information system is formed through the coordinated functioning of people, equipment, procedures, data, and other resources to provide uniform, reliable, accurate information. In effect, an organizational system is tied together by its informational elements. Putting it another way, information can be seen as the bonding agent that permits systems to function cohesively. Because information is a universal tool for the operation of any organization, information systems are, typically, not confined within individual departments. Rather, information systems tend to involve persons in multiple parts of an organization, cutting across departmental boundaries.

Types of Information Systems

For business organizations, information needs exist at a number of organizational levels. Informational support is needed in controlling the day-to-day operations of the business, in ongoing management, and also in strategic planning for what the business will look like in the future. Each of these levels of information need has, over the years, evolved its own types of information delivery tools. Three types of closely interrelated information processing systems are implemented to meet specific areas of management need:

- Operational controls over the day-to-day activities of business organizations are established by *data processing systems (DPS)*.
- Managerial control over the ongoing functions of a business is maintained with the aid of *management information systems (MIS)*.

- Strategic planning is supported by the results of *decision support systems (DSS)*.

Data processing systems.   This type of information system supports the functional subsystems of a business. Emphasis is on record keeping—on the recording of basic operational details and on the production of paperwork associated with business transactions. Thus, data processing systems concern themselves with such tasks as the generation of invoices, the production of shipping documents, the preparation of payrolls, and the creation of other documents that integrate the work flows of organizational subsystems.

To illustrate, an invoice prepared in response to a customer order serves to authorize removal of merchandise from a warehouse, to generate manufacturing and materials plans for replenishment of the merchandise sold, to pay sales commissions, to collect bills from customers, and so on. The information flow, as represented by the captured data and generated outputs, serves to tie together all of the related functions associated with the normal conduct of business.

The data processing system captures the basic operational data and creates the documents and information outputs necessary for this support. In addition, the data processing system often creates information files that, in turn, support the managerial and planning function of the business. In essence, the information produced by the processing of data concerning business transactions can serve to establish an information base for all of the integrated functions of a business.

Management information systems.   The outputs of a data processing system, though they stand on their own, are also essential components of an MIS.

A management information system, basically, involves procedures for reviewing the results of day-to-day operations and calling attention to situations that require special concern or decisions. In any given operating organization, perhaps 90 percent or more of all day-to-day operations function routinely. As long as things are normal, no special management attention is required.

For example, it is common to establish stock quantity limits for merchandise held in inventory. As long as the inventory quantity for each item remains between established upper and lower limits, a normal condition exists.

Suppose that a large organization had 1,000,000 separate items in inventory and that, at any given moment, some 970,000 were within normal supply limits. It would be extremely time-consuming for the buyers within that organization to have to review information about the large majority of items for which the status was normal. Instead, it is far more efficient for the buyers to focus their attention on the 3 percent of the items that are not in normal status.

A management information system applies the power of computers to review information records on the basis of their data content. Managers establish the standards, or boundaries, that separate normal conditions from those requiring attention. The system then calls management attention to these *exception* conditions that require human intervention and decision making.

In addition to capabilities for exception reporting, an MIS provides a resource for the answering of management questions about the status of a business. MIS files can be used, for example, to develop responses to information requests about individual segments of a business, such as materials costs, sales of product lines, or other management information requirements. The ability of an MIS to summarize information to help managers derive the meaning they need quickly and accurately adds to the value of this type of system.

Thus, data processing systems provide detailed information, whereas management information systems provide selective information through further processing of detailed information. The systems relationship involves further processing to add value to the information for purposes of organizational management.

Decision support systems. Data processing and management information systems both focus upon the functions of an operational organization, as it actually exists. Both of these are important dimensions of management. A third important dimension of management lies in looking ahead to set long-term goals and to envision and plan for the structure and functions of the business entity in the future. This planning dimension of management uses information generated by decision support systems.

Decision support systems utilize the results of DPS and MIS operations. In addition, further data content may be brought in from external sources. For example, a DSS could incorporate, in addition to data on the operations of the sponsoring company, information files on the state of the economy, on market share, on government policies, and on the company's own future capabilities. With such data components, a DSS can, in effect, look ahead and project operating results based upon given conditions supplied by planners. Thus, a DSS becomes a tool for producing a *model* or *simulation* of the future state of the business—based upon sets of assumptions or conditions supplied by managers.

Computer information systems.   These interrelated subsystems—DPS, MIS, and DSS—all fall within an overall systems capability known as a *computer information system (CIS)*. As the term is used in this book, a CIS is a total system that includes the use of computers and encompasses all computer-related—people-designed and people-controlled—information processing within an organization.

Organizational Goals and Information Systems

Organization plans are built for achievement of each entity's goals and objectives. These plans and their implementing structures may vary widely, depending upon management goals. Thus, some organizational approaches may stress achievement of targeted profit margins on investments. Others may use market share or sales volumes as their criteria. Still others may adopt societal-based goals as part of their business philosophy and organization plan. In all cases, however, an effective organization must have a clear idea of what is to be accomplished within a particular time frame. These accomplishments represent the measure of success that is to be applied to the company's performance.

Seen in this light, the organizational structure becomes a plan for achieving an organization's goals and objectives. Since the various components of a business organization are integrated and coordinated by means of information, the organization's information system implements the organizational plan. Thus, an information system exists primarily to further the goals of the organization and to meet objectives that contribute to achievement of these goals.

The technology of information systems makes possible the achievement of organizational goals. At the same time, however, technology can obscure the essential relationship between information resources and company objectives. Computerized methods can generate a fascination—or a degree of complexity—that comes to overshadow, for persons who don't understand computer technology, the value of the information and the purpose for which it is being developed. This pitfall must be carefully avoided. The purpose of an information system is to help achieve organizational goals and objectives. Technology can either contribute to or detract from this purpose. The overriding concern for business managers or for users of information should be the ability of information systems to meet the goals of the organization.

Components of Information Systems

Information systems, regardless of whether they use computers, all perform certain basic tasks. Systems are assembled from arrangements of these tasks, or functions, into processing sequences. The basic components of any information system are:

- *Input* consists of the data that serve as the raw material for processing or that trigger processing steps.
- *Processing* includes the activities that transform input data into useful information.
- *Output* is the product, or result, of processing. Outputs are either delivered to specific, authorized persons with a need for the information or are incorporated in files for later reference and use.
- *Feedback* is a specially designed output used for verification, quality control, and evaluation of results.
- *Control* consists of any function that tests system feedback to determine if performance meets expectations.
- *Adjustments* are the products of the control process that bring system input or processing back into line with expectations.

All of these systems elements work in unison, as shown in Figure 1-2, to transform input data into output information and to maintain system processing at acceptable levels of quality.

As an example of a business information system that includes all of these components, consider a typical utility billing system. Use of electric current in homes or business facilities is recorded on meters. Periodically, say monthly, these meters are read by personnel who record the current figures in a meter book. These data become input to the process of producing monthly bills (output) that are sent to customers as requests for payment. Feedback is provided in listings of delinquent accounts—that is, in reports on customers who have failed to pay their bills. Control processing then produces utility shutoff notices (adjustments) informing customers that service will be discontinued unless payment is received. The purpose of the shutoff notices is to bring system processing back into line with expectations. The flow of processing in this electric billing system is shown in Figure 1-3.

THE SYSTEMS APPROACH

The *systems approach* is a perspective—a way of identifying and viewing complex, interrelated functions as integral elements of systems. Although there is concern for the individual parts of a system, emphasis is on the integration of components to produce the end products of the systems themselves.

Because of the way components, or elements, are viewed as parts of an integrated whole, the systems approach provides an effective method for analyzing and developing solutions to complex problems.

Characteristics of the Systems Approach

The systems approach to problem solving is effective because of the kind of thinking that it promotes. With the systems approach, problem solving efforts are first organized, then broken into logical patterns for analysis and solution.

Organization of problem elements under the systems approach is according to their *hierarchical* function. In establishing a hierarchy, the idea is to review the entire problem—one that is normally too complex to be understood as a whole—and to break it down into a series of understandable, workable subproblems with recognizable relationships. The subproblems, in turn, are subdivided successively until elements, or components, of the overall problem are defined in understandable, soluble modules. At each succeeding, lower level, the components of the problem can be viewed in relative isolation. However, with the relationships established by a hierarchical structure, the overall problem can be kept clearly in sight.

To illustrate, consider the problem-related hierarchy, illustrated in Figure 1-4, associated with building a successful professional football franchise. The overall goal is straightforward: Each organization sets

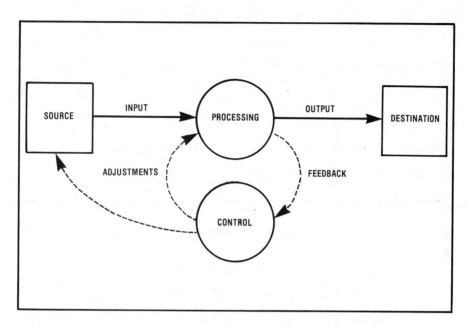

Figure 1-2. Process diagram showing interaction of system elements.

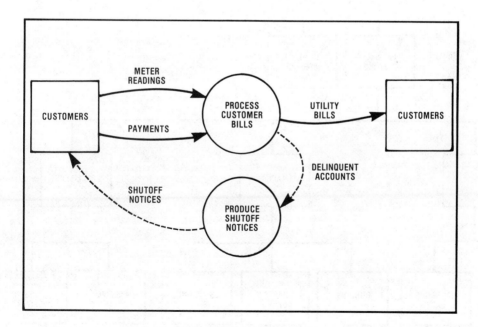

Figure 1-3. Flow of processing for system that issues bills for electric service.

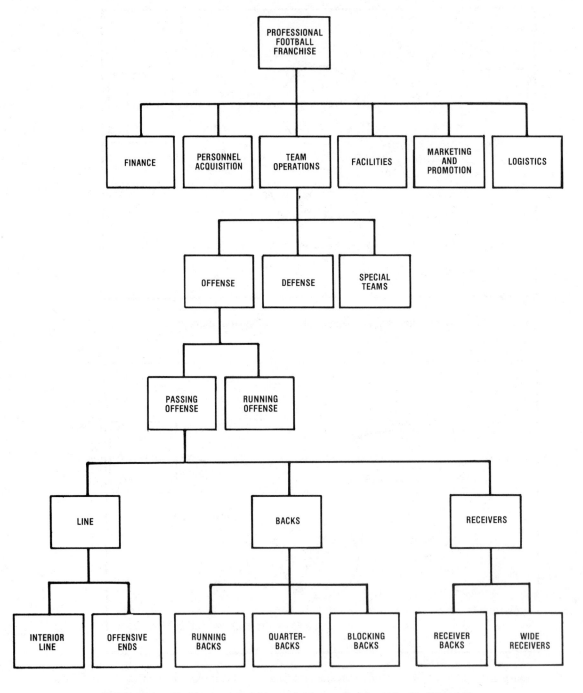

Figure 1-4. Problem-related hierarchy for professional football franchise.

out to provide an entertainment service and to generate revenue to make the service worthwhile to owners, investors, and employees. Fielding a professional team is a business proposition with many dimensions, all of which must work together to further the goals of the franchise.

The organization (system) itself has several interacting components (subsystems) that have objectives which contribute to the overall goals of the franchise. Thus, there are problem-related functions centered upon acquisition of personnel (players), team operations (coaching) to produce a winning team, facilities management to make the stadium available and attractive, logistic considerations involved in equipping the team and moving it to its games, marketing and promotion activities necessary to fill the stadium with paying customers, and financial dealings to underwrite the cost of the team. Thus, realization of the overall goals of the franchise depends on the ability of management to recognize and provide for realization of several contributing objectives of franchise subsystems.

Each of the major subsystems of a professional football franchise has its own realm of problems and its own specific objectives. To illustrate, consider the area of team operations. A football team is a composite of several specialized teams. There is an offensive team, a defensive team, and specialty teams for kickoffs and kick returns. Each of these teams has certain objectives that, when met in combination with the objectives of the other teams, contribute to the larger objective of winning games.

At the next lower level in the functional hierarchy are even more highly specialized teams that are fielded according to specific game conditions, field positions, and strengths and weaknesses of opponents. Within each team are individual positions—such as offensive linemen, backs, and receivers—each of which have specific objectives on every play. Thus, the objective of a player in a particular position contributes to the objective of the team for each individual play. Each play, in turn, contributes to the success or failure in meeting the objectives of the team for the entire game. The performance in each game, of course, contributes to the meeting of or failure to meet objectives for an entire season of games. Overall season performance determines whether the franchise has a winning team. This, in the final analysis, helps to establish the level of success for the entire franchise.

The components of the franchise are organized into a hierarchy in which, at each level, there are functions to be performed that, in combination, further the goals of the organization. The value of the hierarchy rests in this functional *partitioning* of effort. Levels of objectives range from the overall goal of the organization through to specific objectives for individual players.

The value of this hierarchical approach lies in a perspective that forces problem solvers and managers to deal with problems at different levels of *abstraction*. That is, goals and objectives are formulated with increasing levels of detail from the top to the bottom of the hierarchy. At the top of the organization, goals are described functionally, in terms of the overall mission. At the bottom level, the objectives are clearly operationalized in terms of specific actions that must be taken or specific results that must occur.

At each level and for each function, the objectives are within the realm of capability of the person charged with meeting them. Through this abstraction hierarchy, the complexities of running an organization are more easily managed. Although all organizational components are related in some fashion, specialization of function permits somewhat independent consideration of each function.

Thus, in the professional football franchise example, the team owner does not have to be concerned with blocking schemes for the offensive line. Neither does the offensive lineman have to be concerned with ticket sales. Each individual problem area is a concern of the organization as a whole. Yet each can be dealt with in a specific way by specific components of the organization.

Problem Solving with the Systems Approach

The systems approach to structuring an organization is applied to problem solving as well as to the processing of information. Two major problem solving strategies can be identified:

- *Analysis.* With a systems perspective, a problem is partitioned, or factored, into component parts. Subproblems are identified at a level that promotes understanding and makes possible a solution. The partitioning process, in effect, isolates subproblems and their relationships with one another, facilitating individual study and solution.

- *Synthesis.* The systems approach provides a structure for bringing all the parts together into a related, functional whole. As subproblems are solved, the solutions can then be combined into a remodeled system in which existing problems have been eliminated. A series of subproblems that have been solved go back together again as an altered, improved total system.

The development of information systems is a form of problem solving. Whatever the specifics of the situation, the underlying problem is to provide the right information, to the right person, in the right form, and at the right time. This type of problem is generally too complex to be solved in its entirety, all at once, by a single individual. The solution is likely to entail many different computer programs, processing several streams of input data and producing a number of forms of output and feedback. All these processes must be integrated, along with control and adjustment functions. Clerical, managerial, and training procedures must be established. Given this level of complexity, the systems approach becomes essential to the development of information systems.

The first step is analysis of the problem, partitioning it into smaller, manageable parts. In this way, a large problem is decomposed into successively detailed levels of subproblems. These subproblems can then be brought into focus and dealt with individually, without the distraction and confusion of trying to juggle all the components of the original problem at the same time. With the hierarchical structure of the problem clearly established, the problem solver can now develop subproblem solutions in relative isolation, without losing overall perspective.

Once solutions have been developed for the identified subproblems, the second step is to synthesize, or integrate, all these solution components into a complete problem solution. At this stage, the hierarchical structure established during problem analysis becomes a point of departure for structuring the solution components as an integrated whole. In this way, the systems approach—with its twin strategies of analysis and synthesis—ensures that the overall solution fits the original problem.

Figure 1-5 illustrates the application of analysis and synthesis in the solution of problems:

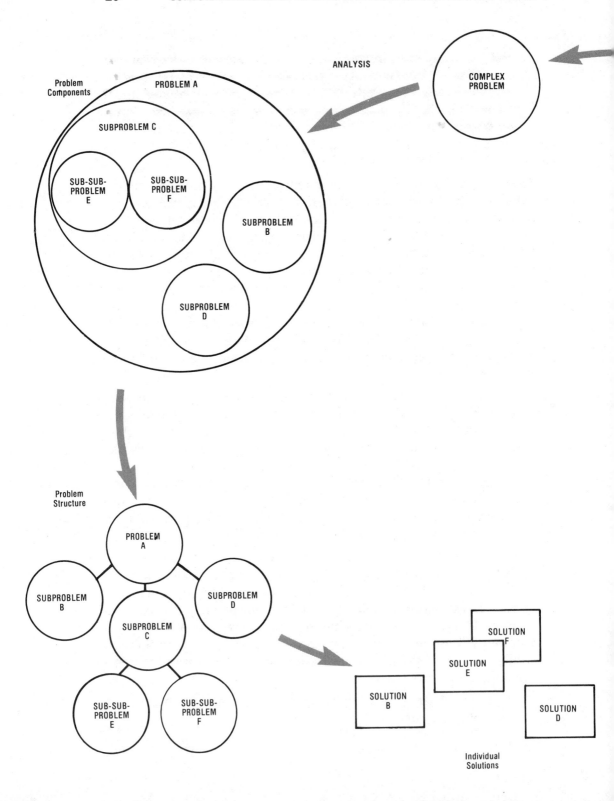

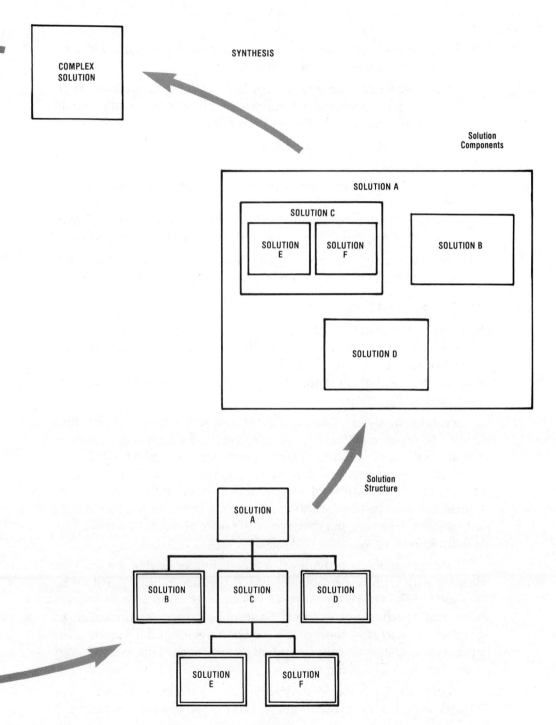

Figure 1-5. Application of analysis and synthesis in the solution of problems.

- First, the problem is analyzed. The problem is partitioned into its component parts, or subproblems.

- Second, the relationships among the subproblems are identified. The result is a hierarchical structure that isolates the components of the problem and establishes their relationships to one another.

- Third, solutions are developed for each of the identified subproblems.

- Fourth, these solution components are synthesized, or meshed together, into an overall problem solution. This process of synthesis, in effect, reconstructs the hierarchy of the original problem, so that the structure of the solution matches that of the problem.

- Fifth and finally, the synthesized, structured collection of solution components is now a complete solution to the original problem.

SYSTEMS ANALYSIS

Systems analysis is the application of the systems approach to the study and solution of problems. Within a CIS environment, systems analysis is applied to business problems that require development of computer information systems. Systems analysis makes it possible to understand problems and to shape solutions.

Systems analysis, then, is a mental process—a way of thinking about a problem, analyzing its components, and structuring a solution. It is also a perspective. The systems approach, as applied to business problems, means seeing the business organization itself as a system, analyzing its goals and objectives, and understanding uses for the information that will be the end product of the problem solution. Seeing the problem from the perspective of the user of information is a central dimension of systems analysis.

Systems analysis provides a set of strategies and techniques for dealing with complex problems, based on hierarchical partitioning methods applied through various levels of abstraction to analyze problems and synthesize solutions. Systems analysis is supported by graphic and narrative tools that have been developed to facilitate the process and systematically document its approach. This methodology is discussed in Chapter 6.

Within the CIS field, systems analysis also refers to a certain type of work assignment. Systems analysis is the job of a *systems analyst*. A systems analyst is a problem solving specialist who brings a systematic perspective to the analysis of information processing needs and the design and development of computer-based solutions to these problems.

Systems analysts are usually assigned to the CIS function, department, or group within an organization. In large organizations, particularly, computers have become sufficiently important that they are integral components of the organizational structure of their companies. CIS responsibilities may be at the departmental level, or a CIS group may be regarded as a division of a company. The function may be headed by a vice president, an assistant vice president, or a department head. The role and responsibilities of the CIS function will vary according to the size of the organization, its goals, and the way in which its resources have been allocated. Figure 1-6 shows a typical organization chart and the placement of the systems analysis function.

Again depending upon company size, goals, and allocation of resources, systems analysts may also be assigned to portions of an organization other than the CIS function. Almost any group within an organization—marketing, accounting, production, distribution, and so on—may have its own systems analysts. In all cases, however, the systems analyst is a specialized CIS professional who brings technical skills and a systems perspective to the analysis and solution of business problems.

Summary

A system is a set of interrelated, interacting components that function together as an entity to produce a predictable end result.

A business is a system composed of people, facilities, equipment, materials, and methods of work that function together to provide goods or services.

Components of a system can be seen as subsystems. Subsystems, in turn, may have smaller components, or elements, within them. By the same token, any system may be a subsystem of some wider system.

The organizational structure of a business represents a formal recognition by its management of the subsystems from which it is composed. An organizational chart identifies these subsystems (divisions,

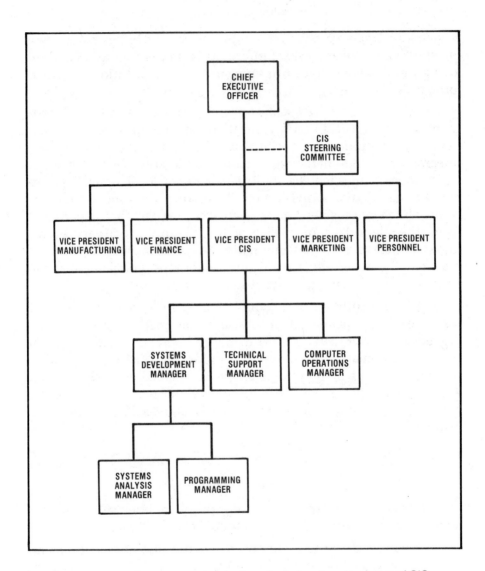

Figure 1-6. Typical corporate organization chart showing placement of CIS.

departments) and shows their relationships (lines of authority and responsibility).

For a system to function effectively, all its components should generate and communicate information. An information system is that subsystem primarily responsible for enabling all other components of the system to develop and deliver information.

Within business organizations, the three basic types of information systems are: data processing systems (DPS), which control day-to-day operations; management information systems (MIS), which support organizational management; and decision support systems (DSS), which facilitate future planning. These three interrelated subsystems together make up the organization's computer information system (CIS).

The basic components of any information system are: input, processing, output, feedback, control, and adjustment. These systems elements work together to transform input data into output information and to maintain processing at acceptable levels of quality.

The systems approach is a way of identifying and viewing complex, interrelated functions as continuous elements of systems. An organization is seen as a hierarchy, with functions partitioned into subsystems that pursue assigned portions of the organization's goals.

The systems approach provides a valuable tool for problem solving. First, the problem is analyzed, or broken down, into a hierarchy of component subproblems that can then be studied and solved in relative isolation. Then, component solutions are synthesized, or recombined, within a single hierarchical structure. This systems approach is critical to the development of information systems.

The systems approach, as applied to the development of information systems, is known as systems analysis. Systems analysis, in turn, provides a basic perspective on systems-related problems and a specific methodology for analyzing and solving them.

Systems analysis is the job of a systems analyst. A systems analyst is a specialized CIS professional who brings a systems perspective to the analysis of information processing needs and the design and development of computer-based solutions to these problems. Systems analysts are usually assigned to the CIS function, department, or group within an organization.

Key Terms

1. system
2. synergistic
3. subsystem
4. organizational structure
5. organizational chart
6. information
7. information system
8. data processing system (DPS)
9. management information system (MIS)
10. decision support system (DSS)
11. exception
12. model
13. simulation
14. computer information system (CIS)
15. input
16. processing
17. output
18. feedback
19. control
20. adjustment
21. systems approach
22. hierarchical
23. partitioning
24. abstraction
25. analysis
26. synthesis
27. systems analysis
28. systems analyst

Review/Discussion Questions

1. What is a system? Give one or more examples of: a natural system; an abstract system; an organizational system. Describe these entities as systems, identifying their subsystems, the individual goals or purposes of the subsystems, and the relationships among the subsystems.

2. What does an organizational chart tell you about a business organization?

3. Describe the role of information in a business organization.

4. Name the three basic types of information systems, and explain how they relate to one another.

5. Why does an MIS emphasize reporting of exception conditions? Describe a business situation in which this type of system would be particularly useful.

6. Computer technology can be a help or a hindrance to a business organization. Explain.

7. Name the six basic elements of an information system. Describe their functions and interrelationships.

8. What is meant by a systems approach? How does this approach make possible the solution of complex problems?

9. Why is the concept of hierarchy, or hierarchical structure, essential to the analysis and solution of problems?

10. What is systems analysis? What is its function in the CIS environment?

11. What is a systems analyst? Describe the job function, and its place within a business organization.

12. Consider a catalog ordering system for a large merchandiser. Give examples of each of the six elements of a system in this setting.

2 THE SYSTEMS DEVELOPMENT LIFE CYCLE

LEARNING OBJECTIVES

On completing the reading and other learning assignments for this chapter, you should be able to:

- [ ] Explain the need for and value of a step-by-step, process approach to the analysis, design, and implementation of computer information systems.

- [ ] Describe the need for computer information systems development in terms of the identification and solution of business problems.

- [ ] Describe the work of systems analysis and the role of the systems analyst.

- [ ] Describe the stages in a system life cycle.

- [ ] Identify and describe the five phases of the systems development life cycle used as the basis for instruction in this book.

- [ ] Describe the work units or structure of a project in terms of tasks, activities, and phases, and establish the relationship of these work units to the control of systems development projects.

- [ ] Describe the process of systems analysis, including the use of data flow diagrams as a tool for the modeling of systems.

CIS DEVELOPMENT—A COMPLEX PROCESS

Computer information *systems development* is a lengthy and complex process that includes identifying information needs, designing information systems that meet those needs, and putting those systems into practical operation. Development of a CIS involves the services and participation of many different people, with many different types of skills, performing literally thousands of separate tasks.

Given the sheer number and diversity of people, skills, and tasks involved, some type of control and coordination is clearly needed. In an environment filled with specialists, the tendency is for each individual to focus exclusively on his or her own area. The result can be work that is fragmented, off the track, and possibly useless. If a systems development project is to proceed in a rational and orderly fashion, someone needs to be responsible for keeping track of the overall system and keeping its development on course. This is a major part of the work of the systems analyst.

Briefly, the systems analyst helps to give a systems development project its meaning and its direction. Computer information systems meet needs and solve problems. These needs may be so complex that they are hard to understand, even for the people who have the problems. Yet, needs cannot be met and problems cannot be solved unless they are understood thoroughly and stated clearly. This, basically, is the function of systems analysis. The results of systems analysis include:

- A thorough understanding is established and a clear statement is developed of needs and problems.

- A viable solution is developed for these problems.

- The proposed solution is communicated clearly.

Systems analysis is a *service function*. Computer information systems provide information to users within the organization who need this information to carry out their own functions. These user information needs establish one of the primary reasons for the systems analysis function to exist. Therefore, user involvement is critical to the systems analysis function.

Information systems frequently cut across formal organizational boundaries. For example, an order entry and billing system may involve users in the sales order department, the merchandise warehouse, the credit department, the invoicing department, and the accounting department. To be sure that all user needs and perspectives are represented, a *project team* is usually formed to carry out a systems development project. This team is usually headed by a senior systems analyst and includes other information system specialists. Of equal importance, the team also includes representatives from each of the functional areas impacted by the system. The systems analyst brings a specialized systems development perspective to the project, but applies these skills in the service of user needs.

A user-based systems perspective in meeting information needs should also be present at the highest levels of the organization. In large organizations, there is often a *steering committee* composed of top management personnel representing all user areas. When it exists, such a committee sets organizational priorities and policies concerning CIS support. New computer information systems are major capital investments that require top management authorization and commitment. Decisions on which systems development projects are to be supported should rest with this steering committee.

The specific framework and methodology of systems development projects may vary from one organization to another. The skills of the systems analyst, however, are broadly transferable. That is, the underlying skills for identifying needs and solving problems transcend specific methodologies and industries. These skills will be useful within any organization and under any systems development methodology.

This book deals with some specific, proven tools for performing systems analysis. This chapter introduces a framework, or methodology, within which these tools may be applied. This framework will then be used consistently throughout the rest of this book.

The CIS Need—An Example

To illustrate, consider a typical systems development problem. A national hotel chain franchises a number of local hotels. A typical local hotel has about 150 rooms and operates its own restaurant, bar, and banquet facility.

A local hotel can gain some important advantages by associating with the national chain. One of the most important is an international reservations system. Travel agents located anywhere, and individuals using an "800" number anywhere in the United States, can make reservations through the chain's computerized system. Reservation inquiries to the computerized network create exposure and generate many reservation opportunities for the local hotel.

Each morning, the computerized national system delivers a printed list, via teletypewriter, to the front office of every local hotel. This list includes the names, addresses, and payment guarantee information for all guests holding reservations that day. The hotel acknowledges receipt of this information and also transmits information to the central computer about the availability of its own rooms.

Once the computerized reservation information has been delivered, however, processing is still manual in the local hotels in this example. Individual cards must be created for guests holding reservations. Managers of the hotels must match reservations against available rooms, determining which guests are staying over, which ones are leaving, and so on. As rooms become available, reservation cards are dropped into racks with slots for each room in the hotel. When guests arrive, they must fill out complete registration forms. These forms are then used to create individual ledger cards for each room. The ledger cards, in turn, must be posted manually on bookkeeping machines.

Each transaction between a guest and the hotel—whether it be nightly room rent or purchases of food, beverages, or souvenirs—must be recorded individually through keyboard entries on the ledger machine. Opportunities for error are great. Sometimes guest charges are lost altogether. For example, many guests make telephone calls right up to the time of departure. Many of the charge slips filled out by telephone operators do not get posted to the ledger cards in time for collection before checkout.

Even in the typical 150-room motor hotel, there are continuing problems with overselling or underselling facilities. If some guests leave early and their rooms become available, it may be too late to sell those rooms for the coming night. On the other hand, if unexpected numbers of people extend their stays at the hotel, there may not be enough room to handle all of the reservations. Because of problems that can occur when a hotel is "oversold," most local hotel managers sell fewer rooms than they think they will have available. Typically, they "undersell" by as much as 10 percent of their available rooms, just to make sure that all reservations can be accommodated. If empty rooms result, this can be costly. A hotel room is an extremely perishable item of merchandise.

If it is not used tonight, the revenue opportunity it represented is lost forever.

These problems are classic for small and medium-sized hotels:

- Opportunities to rent rooms are lost for lack of information about what is available.
- Bookkeeping procedures are cumbersome and costly. Guests often have to wait at checkout time for their bills to be computed. Some charges made by guests are never collected by the hotel.

These situations represent needs that could be met by the development of a new computer information system. A local hotel could install a minicomputer to handle its "front office" accounting. This system could tie into the national reservation system. That is, when data are transmitted each morning on current reservations, these would go right into the local hotel's own computer. The hotel computer would then preprint registration cards which would be ready when the guests arrived. Instead of having to wait in line and fill out all registration information, each guest would simply verify existing information, then sign his or her name.

The computer within the hotel would show the exact status of rooms at all times. As vacated rooms were cleaned, the housekeeping department, working from its own terminal, would input this information and the master file would be updated immediately. Instead of having to sift through racks full of cards to find available rooms, desk clerks could simply access room status data at a terminal to see what was available, making assignments without having to leave the guests. Throughout a guest's stay, charges could be entered into terminals as they occurred. There would be no need to batch charge tickets to handle postings on machines during off-hours. Instead, when a guest was ready to check out, the computer could be instructed simply to generate a bill, which would be ready in a matter of 10 or 15 seconds.

This example illustrates the three basic types, or aspects, of computer-based systems that comprise the overall CIS field. As introduced in Chapter 1, these are data processing systems (DPS), management information systems (MIS), and decision support systems (DSS).

A DPS is basically a set of procedures used to process transactions and to produce reports or documents necessary to the current day-to-day operations of a business. An example of a DPS in the local hotel would be the procedures used to record room rents and guest purchases and to produce bills rendered to guests on checkout.

An MIS derives input from data processing systems. The MIS then monitors the continuing operation of an organization and identifies situations requiring management attention. To illustrate, the home office of a hotel chain might assume that local facilities are doing well as long as 80 percent of available rooms are sold and occupied. As long as occupancy rates meet this standard, operations are considered normal. However, if vacancy rates are more than 20 percent, for more than two or three days in a row, managers might want to know about this situation. One function of an MIS, then, would be to report only on local hotels with vacancy rates of more than 20 percent for three days or more. Managers would not have to sift through large volumes of routine reports to identify problems. Rather, this output from the system would help to focus attention on business problems that need to be solved.

A DSS, basically, uses accumulated information to help managers project future expectations or objectives for an organization. DSS reports are used to direct efforts toward future improvement or continued profitability of a venture. For example, management of a local hotel might analyze files of information on guests to find out what areas or regions most of the clientele come from. This information could then be used to direct advertising or promotional efforts.

Obviously, these three types of systems are closely interrelated. In fact, data processing systems often supply most of the basic data on which the other two systems are based. Because of these interrelationships, it is common to view these three types of systems as simply three aspects of a larger system. For example, a "hotel registration and billing system," designed for local hotels, may be thought of as encompassing data processing, management information, and decision support functions, or subsystems.

An individual hotel, with few management personnel, would find it difficult, and probably unfeasible economically, to develop a system for itself. Yet, should such a system be readily available so that it could be installed routinely, the results would be profitable. Both the hotel chain and the owners of the local hotel have a mutual stake. The hotel chain operates the franchise on a percentage basis. The more money the local hotel makes, the greater the fees collected by the hotel chain. Obviously, the owners of the local hotels also increase their profits as the hotel chain expands its earnings.

This type of thinking has led a number of national hotel organizations to develop ''packaged'' computer systems that can be installed in local hotel or motel properties quickly and profitably. The chain undertakes all of the systems development and installation responsibilities. Local hotels and motels do not need data processing professionals on their own premises.

At the central office of the hotel chain, this type of system represents a logical expansion—and an excellent opportunity—for the CIS department. Management at every level—both at the local hotel and at the central office of the chain—will get better information, on a more timely basis.

Role of Systems Analysis

Note the nature of this system description and of the systems development opportunity introduced. There has been no mention of programming or of program needs. There has been no description of computer hardware other than to indicate a minicomputer is being considered. Those things will come. But first the challenge lies in identifying business needs and problems and turning them into opportunities. This is the real crux of systems analysis work.

Systems analysts must be problem solvers. They must combine a strong technical background with well-developed interpersonal skills. They must have the imagination and the flexibility to develop CIS solutions to problems regardless of the tools or the equipment available to them.

Systems analysis begins with building a detailed understanding of the business and of the objectives of its managers. To illustrate, look at the types of systems analysis considerations listed below. These relate to a project to develop an operations and information reporting system that could be installed readily at local hotels. Again, note that these considerations do not yet contain any definition of computer processing. Some of the systems analysis tasks to be undertaken in such a situation would include:

- First, it is necessary to understand the expectations that managers both at the local hotel and at the chain have for the computer system being considered. These concerns are not expressed in terms of computer programs or hardware. Rather, managers interested in having computer systems developed think and speak in terms such as cash flow, return on investment, rate of occupancy for available rooms, and ratios of payroll to revenue.

- An understanding of the basic business objectives or problems should then lead to a determination of whether the functions involved lend themselves to computer processing. Is the computer the right tool for a stated problem? In a hotel, for example, the systems analyst must consider whether a computer could fit physically into the hotel facility, whether its operation could be mastered by the employees, and whether the cost would be in line with the revenues expected from its operation. In addition to being able to function at a business level, the systems analyst must also be well grounded in computers. In this case, he or she must be able to make relatively quick, preliminary judgments about whether a computer "belongs" in an application under consideration. Later, if a new system is to be implemented, it will be necessary for the analyst to develop full specifications for the computer and communications equipment that will be needed.

- A systems analyst must be (or must become) familiar enough with existing methods in a business to determine whether and how a computer can do the job better. In a hotel system, for example, the analyst would have to visit one or more local facilities and "walk through" existing systems to understand what is being done physically and how these methods support the overall business objectives of both the hotel and the chain. To understand the reservation process, the analyst would need to know how cards were being processed in racks. The analyst does not need to know how to fill racks, but must understand what information is being created and how it is being used. Thus, the racks are seen as a means of presenting information on room availability. The analyst would then understand that, somehow, the computer system must be able to present better information, on a more timely basis, about the availability of rooms. What is happening, in effect, is that the analyst is considering the physical reality of the present system, then deriving a logical model that emphasizes the handling of data and its transformation to information that supports the business objectives of the organization.

- Once the logical, or business, purpose of an existing system is understood, systems analysts can begin to look for opportunities for improvement. These opportunities exist at two levels—logical and physical. At the logical level, opportunities are sought either to add useful data to the system or to make better use of available data. For example, suppose a hotel does a considerable part of its business with tours. Under the existing reservation system, tours are booked as a unit. When reservations are reported to the local hotel, however, cards are broken out in the names of individual guests. The fact that these guests are tied to a single tour is lost, creating a gap in information that might be useful to management. For example, suppose a hotel in southern Florida learns that a snowstorm has caused cancellation of all flights from Pittsburgh. Suppose further that the hotel had 20 guests in a single tour scheduled to arrive from Pittsburgh. If the cards had already been broken out by guest name, it would be difficult to locate the unavoidable cancellations. However, a computer system could quickly search for and report the names of all guests who would not be arriving. The added dimension of information made available to management represents a system improvement achieved at a logical level. Timely information about business problems makes it possible to understand, anticipate, and react to situations that would not come to light under present methods. The ability to get information into a computer immediately represents a substantial improvement at the physical level. Rooms status is more current, by hours, than was possible under the manual system.

- Identified opportunities for improvement can then be used to create a model for a new system that will incorporate these improvements. The new system would replace the current manual systems at the local hotels. At a logical level, the model will stress the new information capabilities designed to enhance the basic business objectives of both chain and local hotel management. At a physical level, the model will specify the manner in which this information will be provided.

- All of this analysis, definition, and design work takes place before a decision is made about whether to go ahead with the implementation of a new computer system. In other words, managers of both the local hotel and the chain must be able to visualize the results they will get before they decide whether the investment is worthwhile. After that, the systems development project can concentrate on designing the computerized portion of the system. Hardware can be specified. Software can be selected. Application programs can be developed. Systems can be tested and implemented. But, in a well-run organization, nothing happens until after systems analysts have defined plans to meet needs and solve problems.

Based on this description, systems analysis is a methodology for applying computer technology to solve business problems. Computers are tools for dealing with change. Therefore, systems analysts can be seen as specialists in dealing with and managing change.

Dealing with change and creating opportunities for improvement is exciting. Systems analysis is both a challenging and an exciting field. For those who accept the challenge, systems analysis can be a highly interesting and rewarding field of work.

The Importance of Communication in Systems Analysis

The previous discussion makes it clear that the systems analyst is a key person who imparts continuity to a systems development project. The analyst must work with user personnel who have widely varying backgrounds to gain an understanding of the business objectives of the organization, to understand how these objectives are supported by the present system, and to identify needs for the proposed new system. To fulfill this role, effective communication between analyst and users is vitally important.

Eventually, if the project moves into implementation, the analyst will have to communicate user objectives and needs—as well as a general design for a system to support those needs—to systems designers and programmers. Here, too, effective communication is of utmost importance.

Systems analysis builds a bridge from the user to the detailed design. The systems analyst is the key communication link in the development process.

THE SYSTEM LIFE CYCLE

This book is about the development of computer information systems. To understand systems development, it is necessary to establish some perspective on where development fits in the life of a computer information system.

Development is only one part of the overall *system life cycle* of a CIS. It is an important part, to be sure. But it still remains only a part. In looking at the total scope of a CIS, it is possible to identify several major stages:

- *Recognition of need.* Before anything happens, a need or problem must be recognized as existing. The requirement could result because a company is growing and transaction volumes are swamping current processing capabilities. At other levels, needs might emerge from increasing sophistication in the use of computers. Management, aware of the accumulation of information in files through a data processing application, may recognize the potential of, and ask for, MIS capabilities. Similarly, top management, aware of the value of MIS outputs, may ask for DSS-type support. The need must be defined clearly. Without clearly stated needs, attempts at systems development lack direction and effectiveness.

- *Systems development.* A process, or set of procedures, is followed to analyze needs and develop systems to meet them. The rest of this book deals with the process of systems development.

- *Installation.* After development, a system comes into use. Installation is that important milestone in the system life cycle at which a transition takes place from development to ongoing operation. Installation, therefore, is actually the last step in systems development.

- *System operation.* The programs and procedures that comprise a CIS are static. However, the organization served by the system continues to change. Changes may be motivated by growth of the business, new procedures or policies, or technological advances.

To cope with these changes, the system must be maintained, or updated, throughout the course of its useful life. This process of *maintenance,* or enhancement, enables the system to accommodate change.

- *System obsolescence.* Eventually, the rate of change overpowers capabilities for maintaining or updating operational systems. A time comes when it is both desirable and economical to replace existing systems with new ones.

Computer information systems, then, go through a continuing life cycle. They are born to meet a need. They adapt to changes in their dynamic environment. Ultimately, they are overpowered, growing old and going into a decline. New systems are continually replacing old ones that decline for reasons that can include increasing user sophistication, changes in business structures or functions, or advances in technology.

Of the five stages in the system life cycle identified above, two are critical in terms of incurred cost. These are systems development and system operation. Too often, system cost considerations are focused exclusively on developing new or replacement systems. This obscures the fact that system operation, through periods of growth, maturity, and decline, represents a major ongoing expense. Development decisions, in fact, should always involve a weighing of ongoing maintenance or enhancement costs for the current system against the option of total replacement through creation of an entirely new system.

Consider the chart in Figure 2-1. This chart assumes an overall life cycle for a moderate-sized CIS of 10 years. Of this total, the first two years are spent in development. The remaining eight years represent the useful life of the system. For a moderate-sized system (by standards within large organizations), total expenditures might be $5 million. Some $2 million might be spent on development of the system. During its ensuing useful life, another $3 million might be spent to enhance or update the system through maintenance. Typically, as a system becomes more mature, it costs more to maintain. Of course, as a system becomes obsolete and replacement is anticipated, less effort and expense will be justified for maintenance. Only essential changes will be made. As a result, the annual maintenance costs may level off near the end of the operational life of the system. The system life cycle, then,

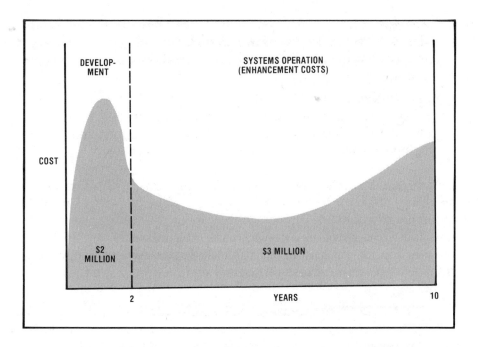

Figure 2-1. Enhancement costs are a major factor for an ongoing information system.

involves a continuing need for system maintenance and an eventual need for new systems development to replace those systems that have come to the end of their useful life.

The nature of this life cycle also points up some of the important challenges that should be incorporated into the goals and methods of the systems development process. Maintenance must be recognized as part of system requirements. Systems should be designed for flexibility and maintainability, thereby extending the useful life of the system and reducing its maintenance costs. In other words, systems should be developed with an eye toward the total requirements of their normal life cycle.

THE SYSTEMS DEVELOPMENT LIFE CYCLE

A *systems development life cycle* provides a methodology, or an organized process, that can be followed in developing any CIS. Emphasis is on organization. In developing a CIS, thousands of separate, individual tasks must be completed. Some of these must be performed in a certain given order. Many people are involved. Their efforts must be coordinated. By organizing all of these efforts, the systems development life cycle fulfills its main purpose: It provides a basis for *control*.

Any systems development effort will be too large to proceed without control. The controls needed are in the areas of:

- Functions
- Budgets
- Schedules
- Quality.

To make sure that a system is being developed with the proper and necessary functions, within budget, on schedule, and up to quality expectations, a number of checkpoints are needed. These checkpoints are important for assuring that work is reviewed and decisions are made on a timely, organized basis. In other words, checkpoints hold the key to control in systems development.

The relationship of work flow to major management checkpoints in a systems development life cycle is illustrated in Figure 2-2. This flowchart shows the breakdown of the overall systems development effort into a series of five phases. After each of the first three phases— critical points in the systems development process—a management review and decision is scheduled. It is assumed that these reviews and commitment decisions are made by a top-level steering committee empowered to authorize the overall process of systems development within an organization or by senior management within the user area if there is no steering committee.

Another way of representing the systems development life cycle is shown in Figure 2-3. This presentation method is more process- and product-oriented than the one in Figure 2-2. Stress is on products produced and the interrelationships of efforts with one another. The emphasis here is on the flow of work, rather than on step-by-step control.

Figures 2-2 and 2-3 show one method for structuring the systems development life cycle. There are many other ways of organizing systems development life cycles, and variations in life cycle structures exist in almost all large CIS organizations.

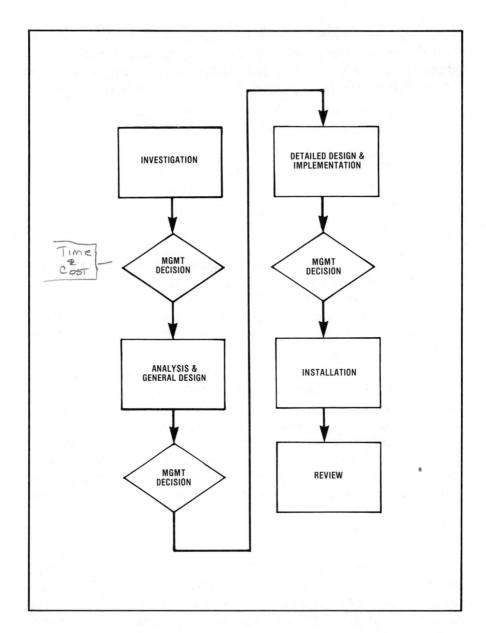

Figure 2-2. Overview of systems development life cycle shows relationships of major phases and management checkpoints.

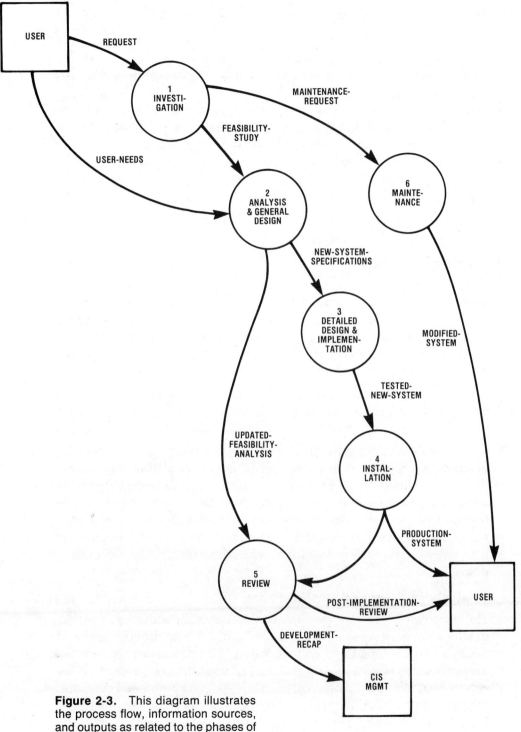

Figure 2-3. This diagram illustrates the process flow, information sources, and outputs as related to the phases of the systems development life cycle.

No matter how methodologies are individualized, the principles remain the same. A systems development life cycle is a means of organizing the thousands of individual, interrelated tasks that must be completed in the building of an information system. Further, the life cycle provides a means for control—to assure that the development of the system remains within approved budgets and time schedules, that the final product is of high quality, and, most important, that the resulting system meets the needs of the organization.

The five phases of the systems development life cycle are described briefly in the sections that follow.

Investigation Phase

The chief purpose of the *investigation phase* is to determine whether a problem or need requires a full systems development effort or whether another course of action is appropriate. One alternative course of action may be to do nothing, to leave operations as they are. Another alternative may be to undertake a project to upgrade, or maintain, the existing system rather than to develop a new one.

CIS users and systems analysts together look at both the existing system and the proposed changes, determining whether development of a new, computerized system will be feasible and economical.

If a systems development project seems appropriate, a feasibility evaluation is done. At any given time, an organization will have a number of CIS projects proposed or under development. Priorities must be established among these projects to determine both the allocation of funds and the allocation of time of both CIS and user personnel. These decisions, as indicated in Figure 2-2, are made by the steering committee on the basis of feasibility evaluations undertaken during this phase.

Analysis and General Design Phase

The *analysis and general design phase* encompasses the activities and tasks in which the existing system is studied in depth and the concepts and designs are developed that will ultimately become the new system. By the end of this phase, as much as half of the total time and effort involved in systems development may have been expended. Therefore, the project plan used to guide the work performed during this phase is vital in maintaining control and assuring the appropriateness of the analysis and design work that takes place. An approved project plan is, in effect, an allocation of assets and authorization to perform certain work, within stated boundaries. Project leaders and systems analysts are responsible for making sure that work progresses according to the established plan, with any significant variances reported to management as potential problems are noted. The major emphasis of this book is on the analysis and design activities of this phase.

One major purpose of this phase is to establish definitions and descriptions of existing systems. Current procedures are documented from the point of view of their users. Thus, users become involved in understanding their own problem(s) and in determining the value of proposed new methods.

Users and systems analysts also work closely to define requirements for, and design the features of, the new system that will replace the existing one. In the process, costs and benefits of the new system are identified more closely than was possible during the investigation phase. Users understand what to expect and what savings they should achieve. Users and systems analysts, together, then present a recommendation to the steering committee based on the refined feasibility evaluation and the expected results for the new system. At this point, a major decision is made on whether to proceed with implementation of the new system or to take another course of action.

Detailed Design and Implementation Phase

Most of the computer-oriented work of systems development takes place during the *detailed design and implementation phase*. Hardware and software specifications, possibly begun in the previous phase, are refined. Programming plans are established. Programs are actually written and tested. A core group of users is trained. Then, with user participation, the system goes through testing that is extensive enough to result either in acceptance or in specifications for further modification. When users are ready to accept the system on the basis of this testing, the steering committee is asked for approval to proceed with the installation that will begin the useful life of the new system. The approval, at this point, is based chiefly on user confirmation of acceptability of the design and operating features of the new system.

Installation Phase

The main achievement of the *installation phase* is conversion from the existing procedures to the new ones. The remaining users are trained.

The old system is phased out. At the conclusion of this phase, the new system has been implemented and is in ongoing use.

This is the point in the life cycle when the impact of change is felt fully by the organization and its people. Thus, the work of this phase can involve considerable human discomfort and myriad organization problems. These problems can be both extensive and serious. However, advance planning and sensitivity in execution of plans can avoid or minimize problems.

Depending on the nature of the system, extensive user training may be required during this phase. It may be necessary or beneficial to conduct special demonstrations, briefings, and continued consultations that help users to understand the full potential of their system. This is especially true if a system includes MIS or DSS features. The prospective management potential of these tools will have been identified during systems analysis. Once these tools are actually available, however, extended potential values may be uncovered—values not anticipated during development. In such situations, an investment of time in user training may produce high yields by enhancing the value of the new system.

Note that no specific management review is called for at the end of this phase. At this point, results speak for themselves. The implemented system now belongs to its users, and user acceptance constitutes some measure of success. This success will be more precisely evaluated in the activities of the ensuing phase.

Review Phase

The *review phase* of a systems development project is devoted to learning. Considerable effort and money have been expended to develop a new system. Considerable experience has been gained, and, hopefully, considerable learning has taken place. Now it is time to review what has been accomplished.

Two reviews are useful for each project. The first should take place shortly after the system has been implemented, while the project team is still together and can share experiences that are still fresh in their memories. The purpose of this review is to recap the successes and failures that occurred during the systems development project. Although nobody enjoys discussing failures, this type of review should help the organization to improve the systems development skills it brings to future projects.

A second review takes place perhaps six months after implementation. The purpose of this review is to measure results of the new system to see how they compare with projections at the outset of the project. The emphasis is on determining whether the new system has, in fact, fulfilled its promises of benefits and savings.

The relative amount of time spent on each of the four main development phases—investigation, analysis and general design, detailed design and implementation, and installation—will vary greatly for individual projects. An idealized percentage distribution of effort among the phases might be 10, 40, 40, and 10. If a packaged software system is purchased, however, the percentage for the third phase might be close to zero. On the other hand, the third phase could represent as much as 60 to 70 percent of the project if the system is to be programmed internally and presents complex challenges in the areas of communications and response time.

The key to understanding how much time should be spent on a particular phase is to understand the objectives of that phase and the products it must produce. These objectives and products, together with the processes used to achieve them, are stressed in the chapters that follow.

PROJECT CONTROL STRUCTURE

The main idea behind the systems development life cycle is to provide a means of establishing control over a complex process that can involve literally thousands of different work assignments and end products that have to be integrated into a single entity. Work units within a systems development project need to be structured, or related to one another, to make control possible.

Control itself, in anything as complicated as a systems development project, has to be structured at several levels. At the lowest level are the controls over day-to-day work assignments. Many people are involved in systems development. Some of these people may be unfamiliar with the particular business operation, while others may know little about data processing. Therefore, at this lowest level, it is necessary to break down work assignments into relatively small, manageable units. For example, a rule of thumb on many projects is that each project team member reports to a supervisor to review progress at least once every three or four days. The idea is to make it difficult, if not impossible, for people to go off on tangents and work unproductively.

At a middle level, work assignments are greater in scope and are designed to produce substantial end products. These end products might include models of current systems, designs for new systems, test plans, or tested programs. The definition of this level of activity is that a series of individual work assignments culminate in a defined, documented result.

The highest level of control is the point at which enough work has been done to present a progress report to management and to go through a full-scale review and decision about whether to proceed with the project.

These three levels of control are clearly distinguished within the systems development framework. Although individual methodologies may use varying terms, three standard terms have been selected for use throughout this book. These terms are:

- Tasks
- Activities
- Phases.

Tasks

A *task* is any unit of work that can be performed by an individual person, usually in a maximum of one week. A number of tasks make up an activity. A number of activities, in turn, make up a phase, as diagrammed in Figure 2-4.

A task is the smallest unit of work that can be assigned and controlled through normal project management techniques. Control, as discussed earlier, consists of functional, budgeting, scheduling, and quality reviews.

Suppose, for example, in developing a system for hotels, a systems analyst is assigned to study registration procedures under existing systems. Suppose this task is budgeted for two working days, with an end product to consist of a model that documents what happens in the course of guest registration. This task is readily and easily budgeted because it is small enough to define and assign. Tasks are also relatively easy to schedule because the assigned individuals can complete these work units independent of other assignments and of other project team members. Functional and quality controls are implicit because each task has an end result that can be checked readily by a user or by peer review. If rework is necessary, losses are minimal because tasks are relatively small.

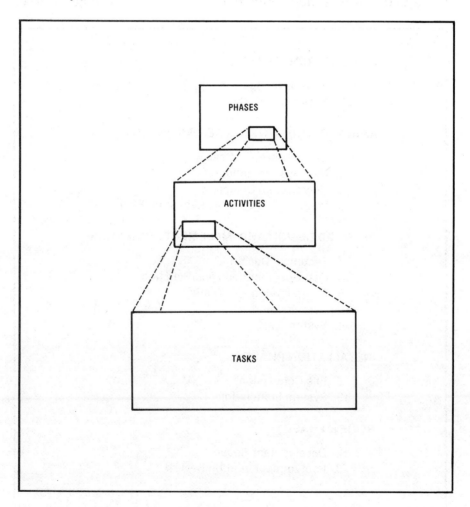

Figure 2-4. Phases of the systems development life cycle consist of activities which, in turn, are made up of tasks.

Activities

An *activity* is a group of logically related tasks that, when completed, lead to accomplishment of a specific objective. Activities are defined by the specific end products that are produced. Quality control is applied formally and carefully at the activity level.

Figure 2-5 is a table listing the activities that make up the systems development life cycle. Note that each activity falls within a specific phase of the systems development process. Activities do not overlap

INVESTIGATION PHASE

    1. Initial Investigation
    2. Feasibility Study

ANALYSIS AND GENERAL DESIGN PHASE

    3. Existing System Review
    4. New System Requirements
    5. New System Design
    6. Implementation and Installation Planning

DETAILED DESIGN AND IMPLEMENTATION PHASE

    7. Technical Design
    8. Test Specifications and Planning
    9. Programming and Testing
   10. User Training
   11. System Test

INSTALLATION PHASE

   12. File Conversion
   13. System Installation

REVIEW PHASE

   14. Development Recap
   15. Post-Implementation Review

Figure 2-5.   Phases and activities of the systems development life cycle.

phase boundaries. They all begin and end within the phase of which they are part. However, the activities themselves can be carried out in parallel. For example, in phase 2 (analysis and general design), tasks that involve modeling the existing system could be going on in parallel with tasks designed to document requirements for the new system. In fact, work could be progressing on Activities 3 through 5 concurrently.

Phases

A *phase* is a set of activities that brings a project to a critical milestone. In most cases, the milestone is accompanied by a management review and decision about whether to proceed with the project. Phases exist to assure that, at several points in the course of systems development, each project has the necessary management support and backing in terms of money and personnel.

THE PROCESS OF SYSTEMS ANALYSIS

Systems analysis activities include, but go far beyond, computer and program specifications. Analysis deals with the realities of the world of business transactions and management results.

An often-raised challenge centers around why systems analysts are needed at all. The reasoning goes this way: The people who do a job are more familiar with it than an outsider, such as an analyst, could possibly be. Why don't these people just get together, think about the problem, and come up with a solution based on their own intimate knowledge of the situation?

The answer, quite simply, is that a systems analyst has at least three advantages over the people who actually work at the job in question. The first is a broad perspective based on general experience with many business situations. The second is an objectivity that seldom exists among people who are immersed in a given job, day in and day out. The third is professional expertise and experience in the analysis and design of systems. These, then, are the essential contributions of systems analysts: perspective, objectivity, and professionalism.

Despite these invaluable advantages, it is still necessary to understand a system and its immediate problems before improvements can be devised. Thus, systems analysts need a process, or a set of procedures, that can be followed in identifying and solving problems or meeting stated objectives. A later chapter of this book describes a process for systems analysis in some depth. However, certain broad, common characteristics of that process can be introduced now. These characteristics include:

- Iteration
- Hierarchical decomposition
- Use of graphic tools
- Use of models
- Understanding, imagination, and creativity.

Iteration

One important characteristic of the systems analysis process is *iteration*. No outsider should expect to learn all there is to know about a business or a job with a single review of what is happening. Rather, a process of decomposing the problem into its component parts may be repeated, or iterated, to reach increasing levels of understanding. Systems analysis begins by overviewing the business procedures and policies that comprise a system. Then, following a structured, analytic process that can involve use of models representing the system, a deeper look is taken. As needed, the analyst repeats the process, probing ever deeper until a thorough understanding is built—and until agreement about purposes, functions, and procedures exists between the systems analyst and users.

Hierarchical Decomposition

Hierarchical decomposition is the breaking down, or partitioning, of a large problem, or project, into a series of structured, related, manageable parts. This decomposition goes hand in hand with the iterative process described above. For example, the first iteration in studying a system might identify the major constituent parts, or subsystems. Subsequent iterations then take closer looks at the individual system parts that have already been identified. Each part of the system is defined in terms of its relation to the other parts and is, itself, decomposed further into a series of constituent parts. Decomposition continues until a level is reached at which the functions and requirements of the individual system parts are understood clearly.

Use of Graphic Tools

A range of graphic presentation techniques is available to help the systems analyst. These tools can help to build an understanding about what the current system is and what the future system should be. The graphic presentations that result can provide a basis for agreement between systems analysts and users about expectations for systems under development.

One method for achieving this analysis and documentation of a system is the *data flow diagram*. Data flow diagrams are both analytic and communication tools. They provide a means of visualizing how data elements flow through a system and are transformed into information.

A relatively simple data flow diagram, describing the processing involved in a student registration system, is shown in Figure 2-6. Note the similarity between this illustration and Figure 2-3 overviewing the relationship of phases within the systems development life cycle.

Use of Models

Data flow diagrams meet an important requirement of systems analysis: They provide a universal, clear method for describing systems and for establishing agreement on the basis of these descriptions. It is a well-known phenomenon that a dozen people witnessing an accident will all describe the event differently. Systems cannot be built around vague descriptions or opinions. Rather, a specific understanding must exist about what is to be accomplished and how the work is to be done. To achieve this understanding, analysts use data flow diagrams as part of a technique known as modeling.

Models, in this sense, are graphic and written representations of what systems are and how they work. For projects on which they are applied, data flow diagrams can become part of a uniform modeling tool. The diagrams themselves are supplemented by *data dictionaries* and *process descriptions.* Both of these supplementary documents add clarification to the data flow diagrams they accompany. A data dictionary describes the content of data items that flow through a system. Process descriptions, in turn, are narratives explaining the handling and transformation of data at identified processing points within the system. Together, the data flow diagrams, data dictionaries, and process descriptions form models that describe and represent systems under study or development.

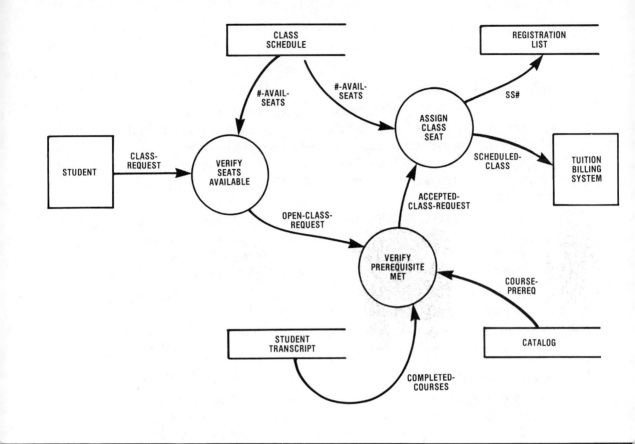

Figure 2-6. Data flow diagram for simplified student registration system.

Consider an analogy: When an architect develops a home for a client, a process takes place that begins with a description of the lifestyle to be supported and special features desired. From this description, the architect visualizes a way to meet the client's needs. Before breaking ground to construct a building, however, some modeling must take place. This is done with blueprints, detailed drawings, and, in some cases, actual miniature models of the buildings. In the same way, data flow diagrams and the supporting data dictionary model a system conceived in the mind of a systems analyst for a user. Models, then, are tools for communication and understanding.

Understanding, Imagination, and Creativity

To model effectively, a systems analyst must start with an understanding of the true business objectives to be met. Once again, consider the hotel reservation and accounting system described earlier in this chapter. An analyst talking to a cashier involved in the present system might be told that the purpose of the system is to prepare bills so that charges can be collected from guests. In talking with the president of the company, however, a different picture might emerge. At this level, the proposed system is seen as a way of providing information that will help management fill its rooms more completely and effectively. Thus, the business problem is to fill hotel rooms, not to generate bills. An analyst who sets out to support the filling of rooms will be more successful than one who concentrates simply on printing bills quickly.

Having understood the objectives or the problem to be solved, the analyst must then have the imagination to look for the best solution without being inhibited by things as they are. Existing organizational structures and methods should not be accepted as constraints upon analysis and design. They are simply a starting point. The job of the systems analyst is to figure out the best way of meeting the objectives or solving the problem.

To illustrate this caliber of thinking, consider a recent trend in the processing of transactions at supermarket checkstands. The supermarket industry was caught in a bind. Competition was keeping prices down, while costs of real estate and of labor were going up. Under these pressures, levels of customer service were becoming a problem. People were having to wait too long in checkout lines.

One way of approaching this problem would have been to search for ways of getting checkers to key data more rapidly. Another solution tried in many outlets was to add another person to the checkout line to bag or box groceries, increasing productivity without adding equipment. The most creative—and effective—solution was the universal product code. Under this system, the checker simply passes the label over a scanner and computers enter product and pricing information automatically. The keying of prices is reduced to a small fraction of the effort needed when products do not have machine-readable labels. The resulting increases in productivity were made possible because, at some point on the leading edge of all of this activity, some systems analyst refused to have his or her imagination constrained by procedures for entering information into keyboards. Instead, somebody looked for a more creative way to record sales.

The process of systems analysis supports creative thinking and the achievement of deeper levels of understanding. The modeling process begins with the existing system as it physically exists. From this physical model, a more logical model is derived, one that emphasizes the true business objectives to be met. Then, as key business objectives for the new system are understood, they are used to create a model for the new system. This modeling process is iterated as understanding gradually increases.

No process, of course, can guarantee creative solutions to all problems. However, a process can create opportunities and assure thoroughness in the search for improvement. The process approach to systems development incorporates analytic methods that accomplish these purposes. A major portion of this book is concerned with understanding this process and the tools that support it.

Summary

Systems development is a complex process involving many different kinds of people, skills, and tasks. The systems analyst is responsible for coordinating all these elements and keeping the systems development project moving in the right direction.

It is the job of the systems analyst to gain a thorough understanding of the needs to be met or the problem to be solved, to devise the best possible solution, and to communicate that solution as clearly as possible. In performing this job, the systems analyst works closely with system users, often through a systems development project team, and reports the results to top management.

The real challenge of systems analysis work is to identify business needs and problems and turn them into opportunities. The successful systems analyst combines a strong technical background with well-developed interpersonal skills, and has the imagination and flexibility to develop creative solutions.

The process of systems analysis involves understanding the basic business objectives or problems; determining whether the situation lends itself to a CIS solution; developing a logical model of the existing system, whether manual or computerized; identifying opportunities for improvement; creating a model for a new system that will incorporate these improvements; and communicating this model effectively to the responsible decision makers.

Any CIS goes through a life cycle that can be divided into five stages: recognition of need, systems development, installation, system operation, and system obsolescence. When needs are no longer being met, or system maintenance becomes too expensive, the old system is replaced by a new one.

The overall framework, or structure, of a systems development project is known as the systems development life cycle. The life cycle structure to be used in this book has five phases: investigation, analysis and general design, detailed design and implementation, installation, and review. This structure provides a basis for control of the project, ensuring that the system is being developed with the needed functions, within budget, on schedule, and up to quality expectations.

Control of a systems development project is structured at three levels: task, activity, and phase. A task is any unit of work that can be performed by an individual person, usually in a maximum of one week. An activity is a group of tasks that together produce a major systems-related end product. A phase is a set of activities that brings the project to a critical milestone, usually accompanied by a management review and decision about whether to proceed with the project.

One effective tool used by systems analysts for analysis and documentation of a system is the data flow diagram. These diagrams provide a means of visualizing how data elements flow through a system and are transformed into information.

Data flow diagrams are used as part of a technique known as modeling. Models, in this sense, are graphic and verbal representations of what systems are and how they work. As the analyst probes deeper into a problem, the model is refined, and this process is repeated, or iterated, as necessary. Used in this way, models are powerful tools for understanding and communication.

Key Terms

1. systems development
2. service function
3. project team
4. steering committee
5. system life cycle
6. maintenance
7. systems development life cycle
8. control (systems development)
9. investigation phase
10. analysis and general design phase
11. detailed design and implementation phase
12. installation phase
13. review phase
14. task
15. activity
16. phase
17. iteration
18. hierarchical decomposition
19. data flow diagram
20. model
21. data dictionary
22. process definition

Review/Discussion Questions

1. What are the basic functions of a systems analyst in a large-scale systems development project?

2. Describe the role of system users in the systems analysis process.

3. Name three skills or qualities needed by a systems analyst, and explain why each is important.

4. Why does a systems analyst need to understand the old system before starting to design a new one?

5. Explain the role of interpersonal communication in the job of the systems analyst. With whom does the analyst need to communicate, and why?

6. Describe the life cycle of a CIS. What factors determine the useful life of a system?

7. Name the five phases of the systems development life cycle, as used in this book, and briefly describe the purpose and results of each.

8. The steering committee has just suggested that the Investigation phase be dropped from the systems development life cycle to save money and get projects done sooner. Committee members argue that the work is repeated in the Analysis and General Design phase. Present reasons why this should not be done.

9. During which phase of systems development does the project team focus on computer hardware, software, and programming? Why are these not dealt with earlier in the systems development process?

10. What are the three levels of control in a systems development project, and how do they relate to one another?

11. What is a data flow diagram, and what is its role in systems analysis?

II | THE INVESTIGATION PHASE

OBJECTIVES

This part of the text covers the first phase of the systems development life cycle. The main objective in working through this phase is to look at and evaluate a request for systems development. At the conclusion of the work in this phase, one of four courses of action is recommended:

- Carry systems development efforts into the next phase of the life cycle. The recommendation would be to continue efforts toward development of a new system.

- Enhance an existing system through a maintenance project that modifies and extends procedures already in place rather than developing a new system.

- Use an alternate approach in which new processing procedures are implemented through use of sophisticated software in a facility known as an information center. The result is a set of reporting capabilities developed directly by the user with the aid of analysts assigned to the center.

- Do nothing, tabling or rejecting the request. Inaction is frequently an open option in systems analysis.

ACTIVITIES

The activities that make up the first phase of the systems development life cycle are given in the exploded view of the flowchart in Figure II-1.

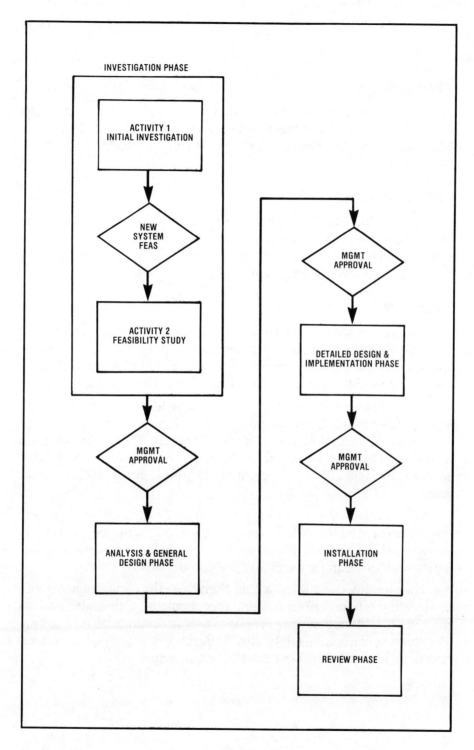

Figure II-1.   Investigation phase in relation to rest of systems development life cycle.

61

PROCESS

A process view of the steps in the first phase of the systems development life cycle is given in the data flow diagram presented in Figure II-2. Step 1 corresponds with Activity 1, while steps 2 through 6 constitute Activity 2.

END PRODUCT

The end product of the first phase of the systems development life cycle is a feasibility report. This contains a recommendation on whether the system can, potentially, be developed and implemented profitably. Included is a review of benefits and costs.

DECISION

Decisions are made at two levels. At the first level, the team performing the investigation makes a recommendation on the handling of the request to the management steering committee. At the second level, the steering committee decides on the disposition of the recommendation.

If the recommendation of the investigation team is to develop a new system, the feasibility report would normally suggest completing the next phase in the systems development life cycle. The feasibility report would also include a general, nondetailed description of a possible system that will solve the problem identified in the initial service request.

If the initial decision is to maintain the existing system or to refer the request to the information center, there might not be a feasibility report. Instead, there would be a joint recommendation on a course of action concurred in by users and the CIS department.

The steering committee would then have the choice of accepting or rejecting whatever recommendation is made. Other alternatives might be to table or delay the proposed action, or simply to do nothing. The steering committee might also request further study or consideration of an alternative other than the one recommended.

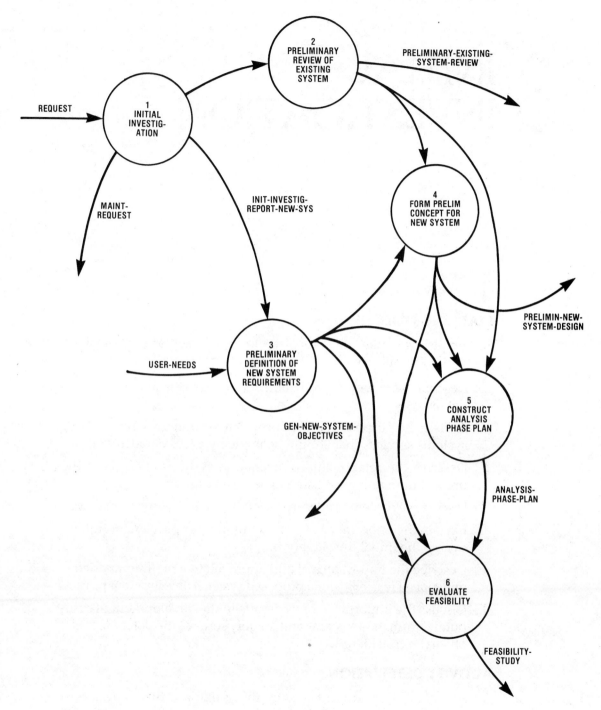

Figure II-2. A process view of the Investigation phase.

63

3 INITIAL INVESTIGATION

LEARNING OBJECTIVES

On completing reading and other learning assignments for this chapter, you should be able to:

☐ Describe the extent, content, and objectives of the initial investigation activity.

☐ Explain the purpose of and appropriate responses to requests for systems services that should be made by a CIS department.

☐ Describe the relationship of users and systems analysts in the presentation and processing of service requests.

☐ Discuss the contents and purpose of the initial investigation report.

☐ Explain the importance of and techniques for problem definition during the initial investigation.

☐ Describe the importance of and approach to a preliminary determination of feasibility for a proposed systems development project.

☐ Discuss the importance of trade-offs in the development of computer information systems and identify some of the potential trade-offs to be considered.

ACTIVITY DESCRIPTION

An active CIS department is something like a utility that serves subscribers or customers. Someone always wants to change the kind of service being delivered or to improve or enhance existing systems. There is a continual traffic in new ideas or suggestions for developing new systems or modifying those that already exist.

Because there tends to be a steady stream of requests for new or improved services, it makes sense to establish standard procedures for dealing with these requests. The *initial investigation* activity is a way of handling this service.

Suggestions or ideas for new or improved systems are received, examined, and evaluated at a preliminary, exploratory level. The work performed is somewhat superficial—just enough to be able to define and come to agreement upon what is being requested. The end result is an understanding of the service request—at least to a level that makes it possible to evaluate, on a preliminary basis, what is to be done next.

At the conclusion of this activity, the initial request for systems work has been processed and the person handling the request is able to make a preliminary recommendation about a course of action to follow. Alternative recommendations may be to do nothing, to refer the request to a system maintenance team, to refer the user to an information center, or to move on into the next activity within the systems development life cycle.

Three of these four alternatives—doing nothing, maintaining the existing system, or developing a new system—are self-explanatory. The option of referring the request to an information center is limited to companies that pursue this alternative approach to CIS support. An *information center* is a specialized entity within the CIS department that assists users in developing certain applications through use of sophisticated software tools and necessary databases. For some development requests, it is possible to bypass the extensive analysis and design steps and allow the user to fill the request directly. Descriptions of information centers, along with a discussion of their advantages and disadvantages, are presented in Chapter 21.

OBJECTIVES

The objectives of this activity are, first, to determine whether the request is both valid and feasible and, then, to arrive at one of the following recommendations:

- A new system is required.

- The work can be handled through expansion and/or better use of existing systems.
- The user could satisfy the request by applying the tools and services of an information center.
- It is best to do nothing.

An underlying objective is to provide enough documentation to serve as a basis for a decision on how to handle the request.

SCOPE

This activity may involve anywhere from two or three days' work by a single analyst up to several months' effort by a team of users and analysts. For small changes in an existing system, one person can often conduct an initial investigation in a few days. But for the development of a new information system of considerable scope, it might take several months of team effort, all dedicated to studying the impact of requested changes upon the operations of the business.

A systems service request may be motivated by a wide variety of considerations. Many of these considerations are external to the organization. For example, if there is a change in social security or other tax deduction rates, payroll systems must be modified to conform to the law. The post office may reassign ZIP code numbers, requiring extensive changes to name-and-address files. A government agency may require an entirely new kind of report for a specific type of business. Trucking and transportation companies, for example, are now required to file mileage reports as part of their tax reporting on the use of roads.

Often, requests for systems development or improvement respond to forces in the marketplace. An organization can use information systems to increase market penetration, to lower production costs, or for other purposes. In the future, flexible, responsive information systems will be key ingredients in an organization's ability to increase revenues and profits.

Business decisions can also trigger systems development requests. A company may decide to bring out an entirely new product line or to go into an entirely new field. CIS support may be needed for the new venture.

Another business consideration would be that existing systems are simply being outmoded, either for technological or transaction volume reasons. There is a rule of thumb in the CIS field: If a system has been in place for more than five to seven years, some type of major system change is probably indicated. The reason for the change may lie either in electronic technology or in the dynamics of the business itself. For example, as users become more experienced and sophisticated, new opportunities will come to mind. These new opportunities might be associated with better use of information to run the business or with better ways of delivering current information to system users. For whatever reason, most business systems need major revision or replacement in the course of time.

Improvement of customer satisfaction can also be an important factor in motivating requests for systems service. If a company's competitors announce improved management or service techniques, this, in itself, can be cause enough to trigger an interest in systems improvements. Opportunities to improve services or reduce the costs of dealing with present customers may also be identified. An example of this type of development can be seen in the automatic teller machines installed outside many banks and in a number of large shopping centers. Service is improved because the machines can be made available in locations and at hours that are more convenient to customers than traditional, in-bank tellers. Costs are reduced because the customers, in effect, are doing work normally performed by tellers.

No matter what the cause of a systems service request, the initial investigation activity begins when a request is initiated and ends, often in a matter of days, after the request has been evaluated and a course of action has been recommended.

Case Scenario

Throughout this book, the process of systems development is illustrated with appropriate examples. The idea is to provide a means for understanding and applying knowledge, as well as for learning procedures and techniques.

A typical case, based on a real systems development project, occurred in a small city in the Midwest. For purposes of illustration, the name Central City will be used. Central City has a population of approximately 75,000.

The city operates its own water utility, the Central City Water Department. The water department is a major user of the city's CIS installation. Water bills are mailed every two months to approximately 20,000 customers. Bills are processed on a cycled basis, with approximately 5,000 bills going out every two weeks. This spreads the work load in the computer center. The cycling of bills also spreads the work for the department's meter readers, who walk through the neighborhoods and note current readings of the water meters by hand in logbooks set up according to route.

In the computer center, these logbooks become input documents for the punching of cards containing two data elements: customer number and current reading. The cards are then verified and entered into a minicomputer. The input data are processed against customer files. The figures for the current reading are entered into files maintained by the computer for each customer. Then, in a separate billing run, the computer processes these files. During this operation, the figure for the previous reading is deducted from the current reading to establish water usage. The resulting figure is then multiplied by the appropriate billing rate, which is combined with other charges to produce a customer bill.

Figure 3-1 shows some of the features of this water billing system in the form of a data flow diagram. Each circle, or *bubble,* in the diagram represents a point within the system at which data are processed, or *transformed,* in some way. The open rectangles represent *data stores,* or collections of data records for use by the system. The squares are for *external entities*—people or organizations outside the system that are involved in the handling or use of data. The emphasis is on the processing performed at each of the bubbles:

1. Preparation of meter books
2. Updating of meter status information for customers
3. Preparation of bills
4. Crediting of customer payments to account files and depositing of funds in the bank
5. Accounting procedures for reporting on cash receipts.

This water billing system has been in place for a few years. There have been some complaints from the finance department about difficulties

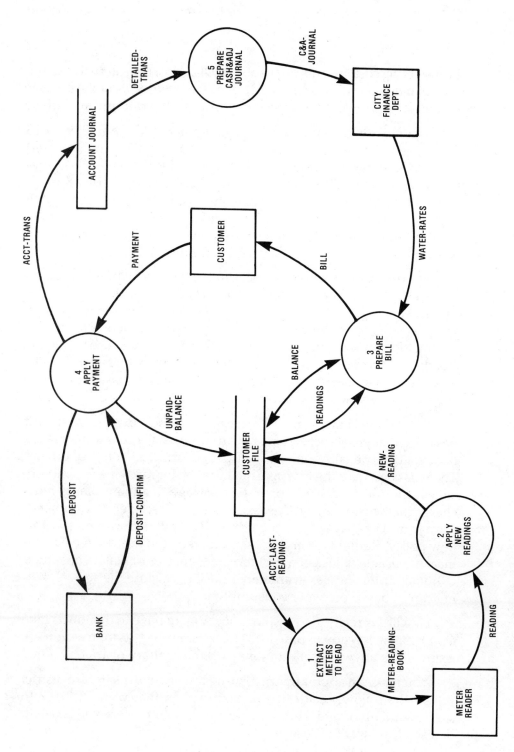

Figure 3-1. Simplified data flow diagram of the existing water billing system.

in answering customer questions about bills. Also, the external auditors have expressed some dissatisfaction about the *auditability* of the system. By and large, however, the system appears to be running smoothly.

Assume you are the analyst/programmer in Central City's CIS department. Your phone rings one day and a frantic person named Howard Rogers introduces himself. He explains that he is the operations manager for the Midstate Sanitary District, which serves most of the residents in your city, as well as many customers from surrounding suburbs and rural areas. Howard is friendly as well as excited. He puts your relationship on a first-name basis immediately, explaining that he was referred to you by the city manager, Susan Garcia.

As you interpret the conversation, Howard has a problem. As he describes it, you have an opportunity. Until now, the revenue requirements of the sanitary district have been taken care of automatically. District operations have been supported by property taxes. The commissioners of the district could simply get together once a year and decide what tax rate to apply against the property in their area. The city and county agencies then collected the money and passed it along to the sanitary district.

Now, things have changed. An agency of the federal government has ruled that property taxes are not an equitable way of raising money because they penalize one class of people at the expense of others. There has been a ruling that, as a qualification for receiving federal subsidies and grants, districts operating sewage treatment plants must charge their customers on the basis of services received. A number of sewage districts have gotten together and asked for clarification of this new policy. Rather than trying to put meters into the sewage lines to measure usage, it has been decided that, since most water consumed in homes or businesses eventually finds its way into the sewers, billing can be based on water consumption.

Howard is really glad he met you. All you have to do now is take a rate that he is ready to plug into your system and, as long as you are issuing bills anyway, collect money for the sanitary district.

You make an appointment to visit Howard at the sanitary district offices the following afternoon. You explain that you will have to understand his organization's needs a little better before you can help devise an answer to those needs.

Right after you hang up from this call, your phone rings again. It is Susan Garcia, the city manager. She explains that she has offered the sanitary district full cooperation by all city agencies. Susan explains that she really believes in efficiency in government through this type of cooperation. Then she adds that this looks like a good opportunity to gain some revenue by charging the sanitary district for the service, thus recovering some of the costs of running your computer center.

Your job is, very quickly, to figure out the scope of the problem:

- Find out about the customer base and billing needs of the sanitary district under the new regulations.

- Compare these needs with the existing billing system for the water department.

- Determine just how big a job it will be to merge the two systems.

- Come up with a recommendation about what has to be done and approximately how much it will cost.

You recognize also that you have to get all this work done in a day or two. Yours is a small department. Your job is service. But you have many services to worry about.

END PRODUCTS

Each activity within the systems development life cycle has defined end products that result from the specific tasks performed. These end products, in turn, are added to the cumulative documentation for the project. At the end of a phase, the end products of all the activities are used to produce a consolidated document that serves as a basis for decision making and direction setting.

The initial investigation activity has two end products. One is an *initial investigation report* that documents the work done, the findings, and the recommendations. The second end product is an oral report by the systems analyst that explains and, in effect, lobbies for the recommended action.

Although the extent of documentation in response to a particular request will vary, certain basic elements should be included in any initial investigation report:

- A brief narrative statement should outline the basic objectives behind the service request, the stated needs, the projected achievements, the impact upon the organization, and other pertinent considerations.

- There should be a description of major desired outputs from the requested system.

- There should be a list of transaction or data sources for key systems inputs.

- The relationship between existing systems and procedures and those included in the new request should be described.

- Any operational problems or policy questions that have surfaced during the initial investigation should be identified and explained.

- There should be a rough, preliminary estimate of cost and of projected benefits that could be anticipated if the request for service is approved and the proposed changes are implemented.

- A recommendation should be stated concerning the request. Again, the options are systems development, system maintenance, referral to an information center, or rejection of the request.

- If the recommendation is for development of a new system, the initial investigation report should contain an estimate of the amount of time and money that would be involved in moving ahead to the feasibility study, which would follow. This plan for the next activity is critical, as it becomes the basis for allocating time and money. The feasibility study cannot be completed successfully unless there is a commitment to provide the necessary personnel by both CIS and user management.

- If the recommendation is for maintenance of existing systems, a brief document must be prepared describing what is to be done and the amount of time and money that would be involved.

THE PROCESS

As explained in the previous chapter, an activity consists of a number of separate tasks. A task is a unit of work that can be performed by an individual, usually in a week or less.

A basic principle of systems project management is that the systems development life cycle should be a guide, not a cookbook. Thus, this book will not list mandated or rigid groups of tasks within each activity. Rather, the content of the activity, or the work to be performed, will be described and discussed. In practice, these work units would then be broken down into tasks, depending upon the size of an individual project and the complexity of any given system.

Define the Problem

One of the first things that should be done in any initial investigation is to define the problem that led to the request. This definition should be stated in such a way that it is clearly understood and agreed to by both the user and the systems analyst doing the initial investigation. Sometimes, the definition arrived at will differ from the initial description by the user. Analysis separates symptoms from causes of problems. In so doing, the actual problem may be found to differ from the perceived problem, leading to a restatement.

The definition of the problem should begin with statements of the business objectives of the user area for which the systems request has been made, the responsibilities of the area, and the decisions that must be made by its managers. Ultimately, all systems modifications and improvements that are recommended will have to be justified on the basis of these business objectives.

Next, the problem definition should contain statements of systems objectives—the results the user wants to see. These objectives should be stated precisely, but in business terms. Emphasis should be on the logical requirements—the business solutions—to the problem or request. Physical requirements, such as how the processing will occur, should be minimized or eliminated at this point.

To illustrate the difference between logical and physical requirements connected with a service request, consider the sanitary district situation. During an initial investigation, objectives would be stated in terms of a need for preparing and mailing bills to customers. It would not be important, at this point, that Howard Rogers wants to have the work done on the city's computer. The need to issue bills is a logical requirement. The option of processing the bills as part of the city's water billing system is a physical consideration.

At this level of problem definition, system details should be minimized. However, certain details may need to be included because of their overriding importance. For example, in the initial investigation of the sanitary district request, a detail that should be included involves the nature of the customer base. Although most people in your area receive both water and sanitary services, there are some who are water customers only and some who are sanitary district customers only. From your own experience, you know that homes in some parts of the city have septic tanks and are not connected to the sewers. You also know that some rural housing developments on the outskirts have their own wells and do not subscribe to water services, even though they are connected to sewers. This kind of detail may be important because it could have a direct impact on the ultimate design and resulting feasibility of the system.

On the other hand, you would not have to include, at this point, the fact that there are different classes of customers for both water and sanitary district services. That is, different rates apply for household, commercial, and industrial users. You don't need this level of detail to come up with an initial estimate of feasibility.

Describe Existing Procedures

At a relatively high, logical level, the initial investigation report should describe briefly the operation of existing systems or procedures. A listing of major outputs and input sources would normally be included. The major manual and computerized functions that are a part of the current system would also be reviewed.

Generate Possible Solutions

The initial investigation report should identify the major options that have been considered. If a feasibility study is to be recommended, one or two general approaches to solving the problem should be described here for further review during the feasibility study activity. The description of each approach should indicate the business functions or processes that are to be reviewed—especially the additions to or modifications of the existing system—as well as initial suggestions for physical solutions.

Classify the User Request

The purpose of this set of tasks is to come up with a recommendation on whether the request should be handled through development of a new system or whether another alternative is appropriate. This determination depends chiefly on the knowledge and judgment of the person conducting the investigation.

In considering the sanitary district request, for example, it is evident that the job can be handled by computers. In fact, the water district CIS is handling a similar job already. The question, then, centers around whether the existing system can be modified to handle the sanitary district billing or whether a new system will be needed to handle billing for both water and sanitary services.

This determination depends upon the characteristics of the existing system and the service requirements involved in the new request. In the actual city on which this case is based, it proved impractical to try to add sanitary services billing to the existing water system. The data files and programs simply couldn't be expanded to meet the dual needs. Thus, if the request were to be met, a new system would be needed. Consideration of the practicality of the new system involved other, nontechnical but highly practical considerations to be discussed below.

Evaluate Feasibility

At this stage, a preliminary determination of feasibility must be made. This decision should be based upon business considerations. That is, a determination should be made about the urgency of the need or the economies to be realized through the proposed system. It is usually not necessary to get into computer hardware or software considerations at this point.

For example, feasibility of the sanitary district request is easily determined on a business basis. At the moment, the sanitary district has no billing or collection costs. However, these costs are unavoidable in the future. All you have to do in a case of this type is look at the alternatives to the proposed system. Suppose the water department and the sanitary district each had separate billing operations. Each entity has about 20,000 customers. Suppose you estimate that about 17,500 customers use both water and sanitary services. By combining the systems, a single bill can do the work of two. In other words, the sanitary district eliminates the prospective cost of issuing 17,500 bills every two months. In the course of a year, the cost of issuing 105,000 bills is avoided. Between the postage and the billing forms alone, savings through elimination of duplication will come to more than $20,000 annually. You don't have to go any further than this to determine that development of a combined system is very probably feasible.

Consider Trade-Offs

Throughout the systems development process, the systems analyst is called upon to make difficult decisions—difficult because there is no single right or wrong answer, but rather several possible options. Each option may offer certain advantages and certain disadvantages that are in competition with those presented by other choices.

For example, in the hotel reservation system, how should room status be reported to the manager on duty? There are two principal options: First, a printed report can be supplied each morning and updated manually throughout the day. Second, an on-line inquiry capability can be provided.

Which option is better? The first is inexpensive but awkward and potentially inaccurate. The second provides timely information—but at a substantially higher cost. It is impossible to give a blanket answer to the question about which is better. The choice depends on the situation at a particular hotel, its volume of business, and the activity level of registration processing.

The process of evaluating two or more possible responses to a given situation and selecting the best solution is referred to as making a *trade-off* decision. The decision process involves identifying possible responses or options and then selecting the one that maximizes the advantages and minimizes the disadvantages for that specific situation.

Throughout this text, trade-off decisions are discussed in context within systems development situations. At this point, one straightforward situation will serve to illustrate the principles involved.

After a new system has been developed and tested, an installation approach has to be chosen. Three options, each with its own advantages and disadvantages, can be identified:

Option 1.   Cut over abruptly at a given point. Simply stop operating the old system and begin using the new one. Advantages are that this approach is fast, inexpensive, and avoids confusion as compared with the other choices. Disadvantages include a high level of risk because, with the old system discontinued, there is nothing to fall back on. Also, the setting up of files to support a sudden conversion can be difficult.

Option 2.   Use parallel processing, running both systems side by side for a certain length of time. During this period, results of the two processing methods are compared and balanced. Advantages include low risk and an opportunity to operate the new system for some time before relying on it. Disadvantages include comparatively high costs and many possible logistical problems. (Duplications may be involved both in computer processing time and in manual procedures.)

Option 3. Follow a plan of gradual implementation. New and old systems are run in parallel, with the volume handled by the new system gradually increasing. For example, one region (or branch office) at a time may be converted to the new system. Advantages are moderate risks and expenses. Disadvantages might include possible confusion of personnel from having two systems in use, as well as possible technical feasibility problems.

Each of these options has advantages and disadvantages. There is no clear-cut best choice among them. Rather, the option that is best for any given situation is the one that maximizes advantages and minimizes disadvantages.

A systems analyst must develop the ability to view most decisions in terms of their trade-offs. Choices are made by identifying viable options and then evaluating those options as they apply to the situation at hand. This evaluation can be made by following a series of orderly steps:

- Determine first that the decision actually does involve choices, or trade-offs.
- Identify all viable options.
- List the major advantages and disadvantages of each option.
- Evaluate these advantages and disadvantages with respect to the particular situation.
- Select the option that maximizes the advantages and minimizes the disadvantages for the given situation.

PERSONNEL INVOLVED

From the outset, a systems development project is a team effort. Even at the initial investigation stage, the systems analyst cannot do the job alone, but must work closely with at least one user. Often, the systems analyst, together with the person initiating the request, can do most of the work involved in this initial activity. Sometimes, however, the analyst will need to interview several user personnel to build even an initial understanding of existing procedures.

The point is that some form of teamwork must be present right from the start, even though the formal formation of a project team will not come until later in the systems development life cycle.

CUMULATIVE PROJECT FILE

An important principle of the process approach to systems development is that of *cumulative documentation*. Relevant analysis and design information is committed to paper as it is discovered or created, thus avoiding end-of-project documentation crises. The cumulative project file consists of a growing collection of documents that will help to support later stages of the development process.

At the conclusion of the initial investigation activity, the major documentation within the project file will be the initial investigation report. Other accumulated documents may include:

- Interview schedules
- Written notes gathered during interviews
- An organization chart for the user function
- The beginnings of a glossary of terms that are central to understanding the user's business activities.

Summary

The initial investigation activity is an established, standardized way of handling requests for new or improved CIS services. The end result of this activity is an understanding of the request at a level sufficient to make a preliminary recommendation on a course of action to be followed.

Recommendations that may result from the initial investigaton are: to do nothing; to handle the request through maintenance of existing systems; to refer the request to an information center; or to proceed to the next activity in the systems development life cycle.

A systems service request may be motivated by a wide variety of considerations. External considerations include changes in government reporting or tax withholding requirements. Internal business considerations might include the introduction of new products, the outmoding of existing systems by transaction volume or by new technology, or the perception of a new opportunity to reduce costs or improve customer services.

A data flow diagram shows how data move through and are transformed by a system. Circles are used to represent processes within the system that transform data in some way. Open rectangles represent data stores, or collections of data files, used by the system. Squares are used for external entities—people or organizations outside the system involved in the handling or use of data.

The findings and recommendations of the initial investigation activity are documented in an initial investigation report. This report should include a brief statement of objectives, needs, and projected achievements; a description of major desired outputs from the new system; a list of transaction or data sources for key system inputs; an outline of the relationships among new and existing systems; a discussion of any operational problems or policy questions that may have surfaced during the initial investigation; a very rough, preliminary estimate of costs and benefits anticipated for the new system; and a recommendation for dealing with the request.

If the recommendation is for development of a new system, one or two general approaches to solving the problem should be described, along with an estimate of the amount of time and money required for a feasibility study. If the recommendation is for maintenance of existing systems, a brief document should be prepared describing what is to be done and the amount of time and money that would be involved.

The first step in any initial investigation is to define the problem that led to the request. This definition should include statements of underlying business objectives and of systems objectives at a nontechnical, business-oriented level. The problem should be defined clearly and the description should be understood and agreed to by both the user making the request and the systems analyst doing the initial investigation.

The ultimate recommendation on how the request should be handled depends chiefly on the knowledge and judgment of the person conducting the investigation, based upon the characteristics of the existing system and the service requirements involved in the request. If a new systems development project is to be recommended, a preliminary determination of feasibility must be made from a business point of view, based upon the urgency of the need or the economies to be realized through the proposed system.

Throughout the systems development process, the systems analyst is called upon to make choices among various options, each of which has advantages and disadvantages. These trade-off decisions can only be made based upon the particular situation, by identifying all viable options, identifying the advantages and disadvantages of each, evaluating them with respect to the situation at hand, and selecting the option that maximizes the advantages and minimizes the disadvantages.

Cumulative documentation of a systems development project commits relevant information to paper as it is recorded, helping to support later stages of the development process. The major documentation of the initial investigation activity is the initial investigation report. Other documents produced during this activity may include interview schedules, written notes gathered during interviews, an organization chart for the user function, and the beginnings of a glossary of terms used in the user's business activities.

Key Terms

1. initial investigation
2. information center
3. bubble
4. transform
5. data store
6. external entity
7. auditability
8. initial investigation report
9. trade-off
10. cumulative documentation

Review/Discussion Questions

1. Describe the purpose and end results of the initial investigation activity.

2. What are the four basic types of recommendations that may result from an initial investigation?

3. What kinds of circumstances might give rise to a systems service request? Give several examples.

4. List at least five items that should be included in an initial investigation report.

5. Why is it important to estimate the cost, in time and money, of a feasibility study?

6. What are the essential elements of a problem definition? What should be included in such a definition? What should be excluded?

7. How does the systems analyst decide which course of action to recommend?

8. What is meant by "feasibility" at the initial investigation stage? What kinds of considerations are involved?

9. Describe the basic methodology, or series of steps, involved in making trade-off decisions.

10. What is meant by cumulative documentation, and why is it important?

Practice Assignments

1. You are conducting an initial investigation for the Central City water billing/sewage system. You have to identify options or alternatives for providing customer status information to be used in responding to inquiries. Two identified options are the printing of status reports periodically and on-line inquiry. What are the trade-offs between these options? Can you identify other options?

2. You are working on a system for billing guests on checkout from a motel. You are interested in determining the best and most cost-effective way of making sure that all charges are included on bills of guests who are checking out. These can involve charges for telephone calls or purchases at the restaurant, bar, or gift shop. Options already identified are on-line entry of charges from the points at which they are incurred or a plan under which desk clerks call the charge points at the time of checkouts. What are the trade-offs between these options? Can you identify other options?

INFORMATION GATHERING 4

LEARNING OBJECTIVES

On completing the reading assignments and practice exercises for this chapter, you should be able to:

- ☐ Explain the importance of information gathering in a systems development project.

- ☐ Identify four categories of information that should be gathered and describe the relevant types of information within each category.

- ☐ List several types of existing documentation that may be important sources of information.

- ☐ Name four basic methods of information gathering and state the advantages and disadvantages of each.

- ☐ Describe the steps involved in preparing for and conducting interviews.

- ☐ Describe the characteristics of a good questionnaire.

- ☐ Identify five basic types of questionnaire items and explain how each is used.

- ☐ Describe the observation method of information gathering.

- ☐ Explain the meaning of work sampling and its use in systems analysis.

IMPORTANCE OF INFORMATION GATHERING

The first four of the 15 activities in the systems development life cycle are aimed primarily at building an understanding of the business problem to be solved and of the nature and content of the business operations themselves. In other words, the early part of a systems development project is devoted to studying and learning about particular portions of a business and about the information processing systems that currently support that business activity.

Tasks connected with these analysis activities, therefore, involve special challenges in gathering necessary information. There are no books or road maps to lead you to perceived business problems or opportunities. There is probably very little in the way of documentation to tell you what is happening within a current information system. Those documents that do exist are probably spread out across the length and breadth of the organization, with some additional items tucked away in desk drawers of persons doing the work. The point is that, before any studying or learning can take place, the information itself has to be assembled.

Even after existing documentation has been located, the information gathering job may have just begun. It is common for systems analysts to collect complete sets of documentation for existing systems and procedures, only to find that they are out of date—that people don't do things that way anymore. The information gathering task then extends to making the contacts and observations necessary to update information on what really is happening. Locating and putting together the needed information is often likened to the pulling of teeth.

In summary, information gathering during the early activities of a systems development project is neither routine nor easy. At the same time, however, the job of information gathering is absolutely vital. Without an understanding of the business and its present activities, design and development of new computer information systems simply cannot go forward.

This chapter overviews some of the basic sources of information about existing systems as well as some rudimentary techniques for gathering that information.

CATEGORIES OF INFORMATION

One of the first requirements in the gathering of information about systems is to figure out what you are looking for and where to find it. In starting this search, it can be invaluable to have a checklist covering the types of documentation needed and some possible locations. Such a checklist, annotated with descriptions of the documents involved and their importance in systems analysis, is provided below.

Information About the Organization

- *Goals of the company.*   Most large companies, and many medium-sized organizations, have formal statements about their reason for being in business and the goals of their management. Goals are long-term in nature and are often covered by formal statements of company strategy. These statements of goals represent management's image of what the organization should look like in the long-term, such as five to seven years into the future. Such statements may be contained in orientation pamphlets given to new employees or in annual reports. In other cases, there may be a less formal, typewritten list of management goals. The value of having such a statement of goals is that it sets the tone and direction for much of the systems analysis and development work that will follow. An information system supports an organization. An organization is a group of people and resources headed in a known direction. These goals orient the organization—and may also provide a frame of reference for the systems development project.

- *Organizational structure.*   A company's organizational structure, like its statement of goals, is an indication of management intentions and directions. It is a basic principle of management that goal setting comes first. Then the company is organized to meet those goals. In many companies, formal organization charts will be available for the asking. If they don't exist, less formal, but perhaps more accurate, charts should be drawn on the basis of inputs from top-level managers. If actual lines of communication and responsibility differ from those shown on existing documents, the actual situations should be noted. An organization chart is an achievement-oriented structure. An information system is a tool for supporting that organization. Therefore, an understanding of the organization is a prerequisite to information systems development. This understanding should encompass the workings of the organization as an integrated, high-level system. In the course of gathering information, one thing to watch for is a correspondence between statements of goals and organizational structures. If the organizational structure does not appear to support the top-level goals of the enterprise, some further data gathering and clarification of intent are indicated.

- *Objectives and purposes of functional units.*   Functional units are subsystems of the overall organization. As such, each separately identifiable group, division, or department of an organization should have its own objectives and purposes. Logically, these should match and support the goals of the organization as a whole—though this is not always the case. Again, it is important to understand how the objectives established for subsystems mesh with—or fail to mesh with—those of the overall system. Information systems very frequently cross organizational lines. Therefore, an understanding of the purposes established for the parts of the organization will help direct the content and flow of information.

- *Policies.*   Policies are rules or guidelines for the conduct of business. These policies should implement overall goals and objectives. Again, it is important to find out how policies mesh with—or fail to mesh with—goals and objectives. An information system is a direct implementation of policies. Therefore, policies and the relationships of policies to goals and objectives represent the prospective needs that an information system should be meeting. Any exceptions to policies that are encountered in the course of information gathering should be noted, along with the impact of these special conditions on the conduct of the business.

Goals, objectives, and policies are closely interrelated, expressing the direction of the organization in increasingly specific terms. Goals are broad statements of the purposes of the organization. Objectives are milestones of accomplishment along the way toward those goals. Policies are specific rules or procedures for reaching those objectives. Since an information system implements policies, and policies, in turn, implement objectives and goals, the basic purpose of a CIS is to facilitate achievement of the organization's misson.

Therefore, any request for systems services must be evaluated in light of its contribution to company goals and objectives.

Information About the People

- *Authority and responsibility relationships.* In some cases, this information will simply fill out and enlarge upon existing organization charts. In many cases, however, actual working relationships will be vastly different from those represented in organization charts. Individuals with natural leadership may have assumed responsibility or taken on authority simply because others to whom it was assigned were too hesitant or timid. In other words, the idea at this point is to learn how an organization actually operates at the people level, rather than the view presented by an organization chart. The information gathered, which may be kept confidential, should provide the project team with an understanding of who really makes the decisions and who can be enlisted to help when it is really important to get something done. The success of any systems development project ultimately depends on management support. Therefore, it is important to identify leaders who can and will make the commitment of company resources necessary to guarantee success of the project.

- *Job duties.* In reviewing existing methods and procedures, it is important to understand what each person actually does in connection with the ongoing operation of the existing system. Available documentation, including manuals or formal procedures for task performance, should be collected. Gathering documents, however, may not be the same as pulling together information and understanding what is really going on. There are frequently differences between formal, written procedures and the way the work is actually done. Several of the information gathering methods discussed later in this chapter provide techniques for uncovering work procedures that have not been formally documented. Here, as throughout the systems development process, the job of information gathering is to learn what is really going on.

- *Interpersonal relationships.* Again, this information gathering effort serves either to validate or to correct impressions established by formal organization charts. Within any organization, informal, personal relationships will be built. People take shortcuts. People prefer to deal with their friends. People do whatever they have to do to get the job done most conveniently for them, in the least time. In the process, the actual flow of information may differ both from organization charts and from systems designs. The systems analyst needs to find out what is really happening, rather than simply collecting documents about what is supposed to be going on. Another reason for studying interpersonal relationships is to identify key people who can assist in "selling" the new system to their peers. Many people resist change, and a new system introduces changes that may be unsettling to them. If influential persons can be identified and convinced of the value of the new system, their peers can be more easily influenced to accept the necessary changes.

- *Information needs.* For each person, in every job, information requirements should be assessed. This assessment should include a study of what information is actually being received. Frequently, there will be shortfalls: People need more information about the organization than they are actually getting if they are to do their jobs efficiently. The converse may also be true: People may be so swamped with unneeded information that much time is wasted. The purpose, at this level, is to find out what each person really needs. Then, systems analysis techniques can be applied to compare information requirements with information received. These results will be used later to evaluate and balance the flow of data through the system.

Information About the Work

- *Tasks and work flows.* The objective here is to find out how data flow through the system and are transformed by the functions of the system. In part, this information can be gathered by collecting forms that include actual entries made at each point in the system. Note that the emphasis is on processing points, rather than on individual persons. There may be processing steps that center around the personalities, skills, or experience of individuals. If this is the case, information gathering should uncover those situations in which existing systems are personality-dependent. In general, however, the focus is on the data and content changes within data structures. One graphic means of capturing this type of information, shown in Figure 4-1, is a document flowchart.

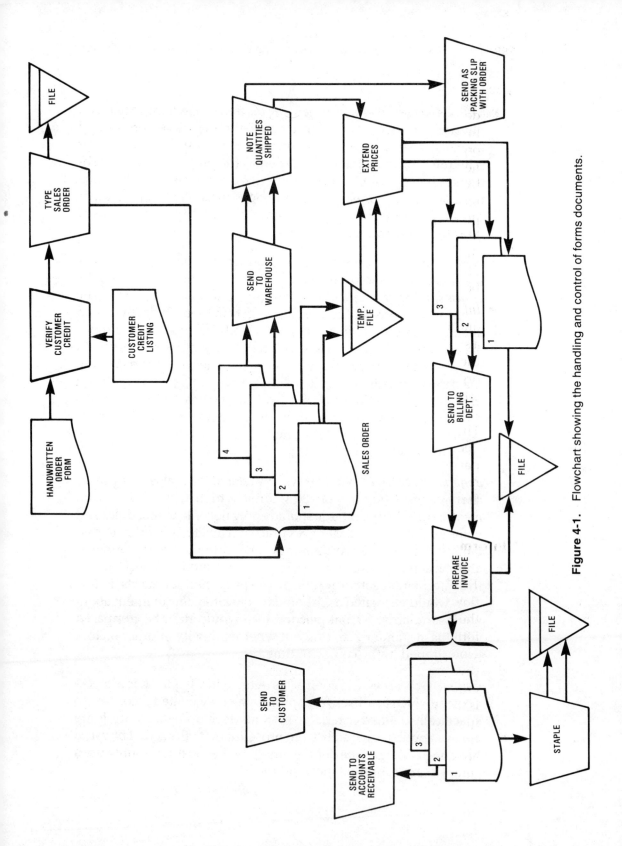

Figure 4-1. Flowchart showing the handling and control of forms documents.

- *Methods and procedures for performing the work.* Here the focus is on physical processes. The information gathering job centers around learning what is done, by whom, with what equipment, on what schedules, under what rules. Whereas the previous task concentrated upon data and data content, this one focuses closely on actions and procedures. A frequently encountered document that can help supply needed information of this type is a system flowchart, illustrated in Figure 4-2.

- *Work schedules and volumes.* This information—the amount of work that needs to be accomplished in a given period of time—can be critically important in building computer information systems. The value of computers, of course, lies largely in their productivity and speed. Therefore, realistic ideas of schedules and work volumes are essential information to support the development process. In this area, it is particularly important to gather realistic data from the people actually doing the work. If an existing system has been in place for some time, actual work volume has probably far surpassed the estimates made at the time the system was instituted. Also note variations—peaks and valleys—in work loads for the areas under study.

- *Performance criteria.* For any system-related job that is performed, there should be standards against which the work can be measured. These standards should apply not only to schedules and volumes, but also to quality, accuracy, reliability, and other expectations of information processing work. Both the stated standards and the actual performance being realized should be included in this information gathering effort. The published standards, in this case, would be treated as "shoulds," or statements of intent about work standards. Actual performance would then be compared with these standards to find out whether quality or other factors have slipped in the course of time.

- *Control mechanisms.* A control, as defined in Chapter 1, is a checkpoint at which feedback from processing is evaluated according to specifically defined criteria. In systems development, controls are always applied separately from procedures for the actual physical handling of data. For example, possibly the most commonly used controls are input balances or totals.

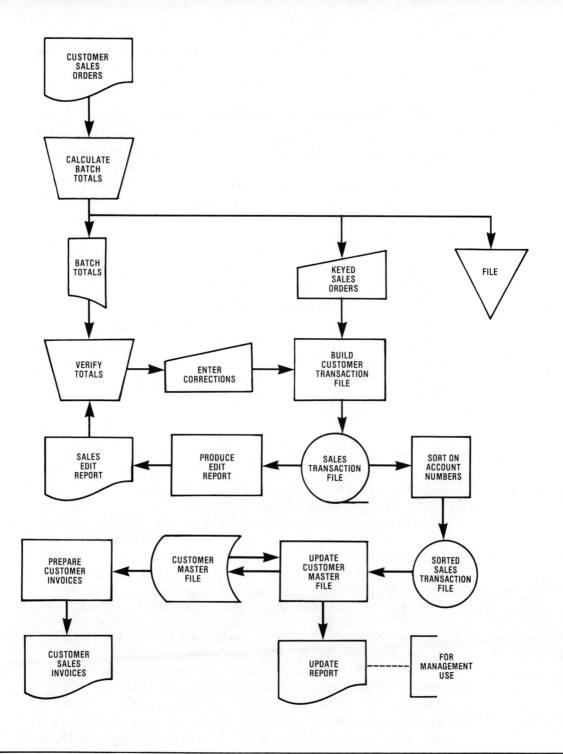

Figure 4-2. System flowchart.

Information About the Work Environment

- *Physical arrangement of work areas.*   This category of information provides additional physical details associated with work flows and job performance. The information gathered describes the physical movement of documents, forms, people, or transmitted data within the offices where work is done. Figure 4-3 illustrates a method for capturing and presenting such information—a flow diagram for a work area. The result will generally be a floor plan indicating desks and work positions, with a series of arrows showing where and how data move in the course of processing. This information will be used in evaluating the efficiency, effectiveness, and degree of control within the existing system.

  Any new system is likely to disrupt existing work flows and the human contacts connected with them. As a result, social relationships and comfortable work patterns may be upset. Information gathered at this stage will also help the project team to understand these problems and to anticipate and deal with them as new systems are evolved.

- *Resources available.*   This category of information focuses on the specific items of physical equipment in use, along with their costs. At each work station, notes should be made about the kinds of equipment and facilities available, such as desks, files, business machines, computer terminals, or other items. These task-specific resources are generally supplemented by other, general systems resources. For example, copying machines may be available for use in a central location. An organization's computer system may also be an available resource, even if it is not being used in the existing system for this functional area. All of these items should be included in the inventory of available resources.

The discussion above covers the categories of information to be gathered during the early activities of a systems development project. This checklist and accompanying explanations are intended to serve as general guidelines only. No attempt has been made to assign relative importance to the various categories or to suggest the amount of effort that should be devoted to each. Nor should it be assumed that each category of information will necessarily be required in all cases. These decisions are judgmental, varying with the nature and complexity of the individual system. One of the basic challenges of information

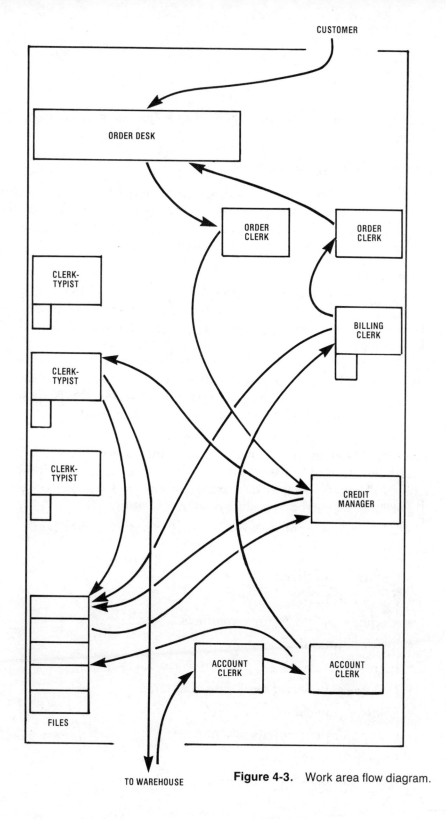

Figure 4-3. Work area flow diagram.

gathering lies in determining where to look, how much is enough, and when to stop.

SOURCES OF INFORMATION

If needed information already exists in written form, existing documents are collected, either within the organization or externally. Where reliable documentation does not exist, the information gathering effort must create the necessary documents.

Existing Documentation

Any business operation that has reached the point of needing an information system probably already has a considerable amount of documentation. Typically, there will be a regular flow of paperwork dealing with customers, vendors, and other outside agencies, as well as a flow of accounting, management, and other reports internal to the organization. This collection of documents can be an extremely valuable source of information because, for better or for worse, this is the set of sources on which the business has been operating to date.

In gathering this type of documentation, try to assess its completeness based on your knowledge of the business operation. If there are evident gaps or ''missing links,'' see if these can be filled in by existing documents that may have been overlooked. Do this before moving on to other methods of information gathering.

Existing documents to be gathered during the early activities of a systems development project may include:

- Organization charts
- Policy manuals
- Methods and procedures manuals
- Job descriptions
- Forms and reports
- Document flow and work flow diagrams
- Systems flowcharts
- Computer program documentation
- Data dictionary listing
- Computer operations manuals.

System Users and Managers

Information can be gathered from people as well as from documents. Techniques for gathering information through personal contacts with users and managers are identified and described below.

External Sources

For some systems, it will be necessary to gather information from outside the organization itself. In particular, in examining alternatives for new systems, analysts may have to consult external information sources to find out what is available and, if appropriate, how well individual methods are working elsewhere. These external sources include:

- Other companies
- Equipment and software vendors
- Business publications, seminars, workshops, or visits to showrooms or other companies for demonstrations.

METHODS FOR GATHERING INFORMATION

Four representative, commonly used methods for gathering information through contacts with people have been selected for discussion in this chapter:

- Interviews
- Questionnaires
- Observation
- Work sampling and measurement.

The interview method involves interaction between an interviewer and a subject. The questionnaire method involves development of a written instrument that encourages the subject to present information independently of any external prompting. In the observation method, data are also gathered unilaterally, this time by the collector rather than the subject. Work sampling involves statistical techniques for gathering information about a large work volume by studying a carefully selected portion of the total. Other methods can be used, including combinations of these, but these four represent a basic cross section of methodologies.

Interviews

An *interview* is a planned meeting between a data gatherer and one or more subjects for the express purpose of identifying information sources and collecting information. Interviews are used to gather information in situations in which it is particularly valuable to allow a systems analyst or other team member to apply judgment and to respond to observed situations. This is because, with the interviewing technique, the data gatherer is on the scene and can respond to situations as they arise. Interviews are also interactive. The interviewer has an opportunity to guide the efforts and contributions of information providers. Further, an interviewer can probe, as necessary, to seek out needed information.

Identifying information sources.   The first step in an interview program for information gathering is to identify the sources of information. During the early stages of a project, interviews will typically concentrate on managers and supervisors who have an overview perspective on the business, its problems, and its information needs. As the project moves on, more detailed information may be needed on operational functions. As these needs arise, the emphasis will probably shift from managerial people to operational personnel. A further advantage of this top-down approach is that the project gains top management support before interviews are conducted at lower levels of the organization. Thus, people at the operational level know that their supervisors and managers have already lent their support to the study by participating in it.

No matter at what level the interviews are conducted, advance identification of sources makes it possible to allocate the time and other resources to be expended in information gathering. Without advance planning, there is no way of knowing the extent of the information to be gathered or its projected cost. Thus, planning includes both identification of subjects and allocation of interviewer time and other costs.

Preparing for the interview.   To prepare for the interview, the interviewer must have an idea of exactly what this interview is to accomplish. The interviewer should begin by writing down one or two basic objectives for the interview. These objectives should be explained to the subject when making an appointment for the interview and again at the start of the interview session.

Next, the interviewer should prepare a written outline of points to be covered in the interview. This will not be a formal list of questions, since all possible questions cannot be anticipated, but should be an outline of topic areas to be discussed. Often, in following up points raised by the interviewee, an interview will move in unexpected directions. The outline of topics helps to keep the interview discussion in perspective and on target, and lets the interviewer fit the responses into the framework of what needs to be known. An outline that can serve as an interview guide is shown in Figure 4-4.

Once sources have been identified and the objectives and interview topics have been established, the next step is to contact prospective interview subjects to set up appointments. These contacts can be handled by phone or in writing. If all of the parties work for the same company, telephone contacts are usually adequate. If the organization or the study is relatively large, however, it is often desirable to follow up with a written outline of the information to be gathered. Source personnel should always be advised, either orally or in writing, about the objectives of the interview, the topics to be covered, and the types of documents that might be needed. An example of a memo requesting an interview appointment and outlining the purpose and topics of an interview is shown in Figure 4-5.

Sufficient lead time should be allowed to enable subjects to prepare themselves. An unprepared subject greatly diminishes the value of an interview. Similarly, it is crucial that needed documents or other information be on hand at the time of the interview to avoid the necessity of additional visits to cover the same topic.

An effective interview program involves mutual cooperation. Cooperation, in turn, is improved through understanding and preparation. The interviewer should prepare by learning about the person to be interviewed and his or her responsibilities. Preparation should also include a review of any existing documentation about the system or portion of the business being surveyed.

Conducting the interview.   Staging can be important to the success of an interview. If at all possible, the interview should be held in the subject's own office or department. It is best that the subject be on familiar ground, where reference materials or support personnel are available as needed. To the extent possible, time should be blocked so

Interview Subject

   Cliff Mason, Office Manager, Sales Order and Billing Department

Objectives

The purpose of this interview is to determine the current procedure for processing customer sales orders. The need is to confirm that the procedures followed parallel those documented in the procedures manual. Also, it will be determined whether the current system is adequate for the volume and nature of orders received and for management reporting.

Topics

1. Nature of orders. Methods for original writing of orders that are placed through standard order forms, over the telephone, or in person. Estimates of the proportions of orders taken via these methods. Number of orders processed daily and staffing required to handle the orders.

2. Credit procedure. Estimated proportion of orders that require credit verification or approval. Time spent on credit approval and availability of credit evaluation sources. General policy on credit sales. Proportion of credit-approved orders that result in bad debts.

3. Sales volume. Estimated dollar average of sales orders. Proportions of sales volume accounted for by ordering methods. Percentage of volumes resulting in bad debts.

4. Inventory checking. General procedures for checking stock availability. Availability of up-to-date stock lists. Estimated proportion of back-ordered items per order.

5. General satisfaction with order entry procedure. Problem areas.

6. Management reporting. Availability of reports to facilitate management of order entry procedures.

Figure 4-4. Outline of interview objectives and topic areas.

Date: February 15

To: Cliff Mason, Office Manager, Sales Order and Billing

From: Bob Underwood, Systems Analyst, CIS

Re: Interview Appointment

This memo will confirm our phone conversation of last Monday regarding the interview scheduled for next Tuesday, February 22. I will be at your office at 9:30 a.m. We should plan on spending no more than an hour on the topics listed below.

As you are aware, the CIS Department is responding to a request from Diane Morris, Administrative Assistant, to look into the sales order processing system. It has come to her attention, primarily through customer letters and phone calls, that delays in processing and delivering orders are becoming a real problem. It is likely that the growth we have experienced over the past two years has placed a burden on our current manual order processing system. There is interest in investigating the possibility of implementing automated procedures to support these increased sales volumes.

Over the next two-and-a-half weeks, I will be speaking with most of the managers and supervisors who oversee the various aspects of order processing and delivery. The purpose of these interviews is to gain a basic understanding of the current procedures that are followed and to uncover any problems that might account for delays in processing orders.

Your assistance is needed in the following areas. Please give some thought to these topics prior to our meeting and, if possible, bring along any documentation and statistics relevant to them.

1. Order writing procedures, including staffing levels and volumes of orders.

2. Credit verification procedures, including delays caused by the procedures and problems in controlling bad debts.

3. Inventory verification. Problems with stock-outs and backorders.

4. Management reporting procedures pertaining to above areas.

Figure 4-5. Memo confirming interview appointment and outlining topics to be covered.

as to avoid interruptions during the interview. Also, to the extent possible, interviews should be conducted one-on-one. Unless additional parties have specific roles to play, their presence should not be encouraged.

As a general rule, the best interview will be one in which the interviewer says the least. At the very most, an interviewer should not talk more than perhaps 15 or 20 percent of the time. The interviewer can't learn anything as long as he or she is talking. Therefore, to the extent possible, interviews should be devoted to listening. Comments or questions should be limited to those specifically designed to get the subject to provide information.

Listening tactics should be responsive. That is, as the subject talks, the interviewer should make it clear that he or she understands what is being said. An effective technique is simply to restate, or paraphrase, what the subject has just said. Thus, the interviewer might say, ''Just to make sure I understand the point you are making, let me give you my understanding of what you have said.'' The restatement that follows should simply paraphrase the information provided, in neutral terms and from the subject's own point of view.

Above all, the interviewer's comments should be noncommittal. They should express neither approval nor disapproval of what is being said—only comprehension. As long as the purpose is information gathering, the interviewer should not argue with the subject. Nor should facial expressions or tone of voice betray strong positive or negative reactions. Because the interviewer's own reactions can have the effect of distorting the information presented, interviewers must try to be as unobtrusive as possible.

Because of the overriding need to be noncommittal, many inexperienced interviewers go to the other extreme and say nothing at all. They just listen, making notes as appropriate. Total silence from the interviewer, however, can be intimidating in itself. It is far better to acknowledge what is being said and to provide some indication of comprehension. Responsive listening of this type encourages the presentation of more information.

Note taking during the interview should be kept to a minimum. Extensive note taking or recording of the interview can be intimidating to the subject, who may not be willing to speak as freely as in informal discussions. Summary or reminder notes are usually sufficient to help the interviewer recall the information obtained during the interview. Immediately following the session, these summary notes should be fleshed out to capture all of the important information gathered during the interview.

To the extent possible, the subject should be able to set the pace and pattern of the interview. The interviewer should be careful not to ask questions that seem argumentative or that break the subject's train of thought. Remember, the subject has had advance notice and knows what the interview is expected to accomplish. He or she has prepared, mentally at least, the information to be presented. Any question that interrupts or upsets this established thought pattern may be resented or simply ignored. It is far better to let the subject go ahead and make the statements he or she has prepared. After that, probing questions can be asked. To the extent possible, these should be referenced within the framework of statements already made by the subject. If a question must be asked that is totally unrelated to the subject's previous statements, the interviewer should make it clear that this question represents a change of subject and content.

Above all, the interviewer should never forget that the interviewee is the one providing the information. It can be tempting to get into a discussion with the person being interviewed, making comments or asking questions that demonstrate the interviewer's own command of the subject. Remember that this doesn't collect any information—it just slows the process down. Comments by the interviewer should be limited to whatever is needed to encourage the presentation of information by the person being interviewed.

The following is a checklist of potential pitfalls to be avoided, along with some suggestions for avoiding them:

- Beware of leading questions. Leading questions can bias an interview by establishing expectations that can influence responses. Avoid questions that begin with "Isn't it true that . . ." or "Don't you agree that . . ."

- Avoid premature conclusions. If a subject makes a positive statement, it can be tempting to draw a conclusion, thus closing off further discussion of the topic. On each topic, be sure to give the subject a full hearing.

- Be careful, conversely, not to accept negative responses too readily. Particularly in situations in which change is anticipated, people are bound to be upset. Change, by its nature, begets resistance. Accept and understand negative responses, but don't overreact to them.

- Don't be so impressed or overawed by a person such as a top-level manager that the interview loses its objectivity. Interviews associated with systems development projects frequently involve persons at the top levels of their organizations. A "halo effect" can easily set in. The interview, even the entire project, can be distorted in an effort to please a top-level executive, rather than to identify facts needed to solve a problem.

- Beware of interview subjects who try too hard to please. Many people in large organizations become politically motivated. They may be tempted to say what they think the interviewer wants to hear, rather than to analyze what is really happening and to present relevant information. By the same token, the interviewer should avoid stereotyping interview subjects. Remember, the purpose of the interview is to gather information. This purpose is thwarted if the interviewer is thinking: "He's just a clerk," or "She's only a secretary."

In summary, the interviewer must maintain control over the interview. A balance must be struck between letting the subject do the talking and ensuring that relevant and useful information is obtained. Maintaining this type of balance and control is the basic challenge involved in conducting a successful interview.

Follow-up.   Persons who cooperate by participating in interviews should receive the courtesy of some follow-up that acknowledges the productivity of the time and effort they have expended. One simple method of follow-up is to send information collection summaries to interview subjects. Another practice, as time permits, is to send thank-you notes or memos to those who have been interviewed. A memo recapping an information-gathering interview is shown in Figure 4-6.

If formal summaries of individual interviews are prepared as part of systems documentation, these should be shared with interview subjects. Interviewees should be encouraged to comment on drafts of these

Date: March 1

To: Cliff Mason, Office Manager, Sales Order and Billing

From: Bob Underwood, Systems Analyst, CIS

Re: Interview Summary

Thank you for sharing your time and expertise during these opening phases of the
systems study on the order processing systems. Your insights will be valuable in our
efforts to improve customer service and to provide you with information needed to
manage the order processing function.

Below are listed the main points that I was able to glean from our conversation.
Please take a few moments to review this listing for accuracy and to check that these
statements represent your general viewpoint. If I have misstated or misinterpreted
your ideas, call and we can discuss any discrepancies.

1. The current procedure has been in place for approximately 7.5 years. During this
    time, sales volumes have risen from an average of 80 to an average of nearly 150
    orders per day. Orders themselves have increased from an average of 4 items per
    order to 10 per order. Most orders (about 60%) are mail orders, with the
    remaining order methods being nearly equally divided between phone and in-person
    orders. The average order amount is $265, up from $58 7.5 years ago.

2. Regular order writing staff include 7 full-time clerks. Their job is primarily to
    transcribe orders onto standard order forms. This is done manually. Checking of
    stock availability is done by having the clerks reference an inventory list during
    order writing. This list is shared by the clerks and is updated every few days as
    time becomes available in the warehouse.

3. Credit checking is performed by the credit officer. All orders not accompanied by
    payment are forwarded to this person, who checks the credit status against a
    listing of customers provided by the accounts receivable area. Approximately
    three-quarters of all orders are from repeat customers with established credit
    ratings.

4. The staff of order writers is pressured by the volume of orders to be processed.
    Errors result from hurried transcription of orders and from inaccessibility of
    up-to-date inventory lists.

5. There is a general feeling that backorders are excessive. However, there are no
    data available to support this assumption and there is no general policy on
    acceptable volumes of backorders. It is difficult to anticipate stock-outs in
    advance, since inventory lists may be outdated.

6. The credit officer spends most of her time checking credit status of customers
    with acceptable credentials and track records of on-time payment. Bad debts are
    almost nonexistent among repeat customers and are even very low among new
    customers. Processing delays occur because of excessive credit check efforts.
    Orders stack up on the credit officer's desk (delays run as long as two days)
    awaiting checks. The company would be better served by accepting a higher level
    of bad debts in exchange for expedited orders.

7. No regularly scheduled reports are provided.

Figure 4-6.   Memo following up on interview includes a summary of findings.

summaries. They may have additional information to add or points to clarify or correct. Remember, the idea is to gather information. Information acquired as a follow-up to an interview is just as valuable as data from any other source.

Advantages of interviews. The principal advantage of interviews lies in the personal contact involved. A person gathering data face-to-face from another person can be flexible and adaptive. This is bound to produce more information of higher quality than alternate, impersonal methods.

Interviews can probe to greater depths than is possible with any other information gathering method. Conversely, if an interview subject is not sufficiently informed or is hostile, the interview can be terminated quickly with relatively little time wasted. In other words, the interview provides a controlled opportunity for information gathering.

Disadvantages of interviews. Interviews are time-consuming. For this reason, they are generally the most costly means of information gathering.

Evaluation of the information gathered through interviews may be more difficult than the tabulation of comparable results produced by questionnaires or other more highly structured methods.

Interviews carry with them the danger of a biased interviewer. If the interviewer has made up his or her mind in advance about the results to be derived, the resulting information will be biased.

Questionnaires

A *questionnaire* is a special-purpose document that requests specific information from respondents. As compared with an interview, a questionnaire is an impersonal, often mass-production, method for gathering the same information from many people. Questionnaires are particularly appropriate in information gathering situations involving large populations of source people whose responses can be tabulated quantitatively. A questionnaire is best suited to situations in which respondents are asked to make limited numbers of factually oriented contributions.

Characteristics of good questionnaires.   To be an effective information gathering instrument, a questionnaire should have certain basic characteristics, including:

- *Validity.* This means, simply, that the questionnaire does the job it was intended to do. The validity of a questionnaire can be difficult to judge. The usual means of determining validity is to compare the tabulated results of the questionnaire with other known measurements. For example, the results of a questionnaire can be compared with the findings of interviews, with the results of observation, or with predetermined expectations of managers and systems analysts.

- *Reliability.* Measures of reliability are built into the structure of questionnaires themselves. That is, the same information is sought in different ways through the use of multiple questions. Then, the responses to these redundant questions are compared for consistency of information. In some questionnaire situations, inconsistent responses on key questions can result in a downgrading of the confidence placed upon individual responses or even on the survey as a whole.

- *Face validity.* In appearance and content, a questionnaire must establish credibility with the respondent. That is, on reviewing a questionnaire, the respondent should get the feeling that the persons who developed the instrument knew what they were doing and had a valid purpose for including the items they did. Given the stated purpose of the questionnaire, the questions should appear to the respondent to be authentic and purposeful.

- *Ease of administration and scoring.* Directions to respondents should be stated clearly and should be easy to follow. Questions should be arranged in logical order, according to subject matter. The physical appearance of the questionnaire should be orderly—it should not appear difficult to follow or to complete. Questions should be as simple as possible to answer, and the length of the questionnaire should be manageable. If appropriate, and if the numbers are great enough, the questionnaire may be structured for machine scoring.

Planning for a questionnaire.   In considering the use of a questionnaire, the first planning step is to determine the exact purpose of the information gathering activity. Once this purpose has been clearly defined, a decision should be made about whether a questionnaire is the best tool to use.

Questionnaires are effective means of identifying specific facts, opinion choices, perceptions of a subject on a multiple-choice basis, or respondent attitudes. In general, a questionnaire will be most useful if:

- The number of respondents is large.
- The same information is required from all respondents.
- It is impractical to gather the information by any other means.
- A mechanism exists to count and tally responses.

The next step is to identify the *respondents*—those who will receive questionnaires. The total group of persons who are potential information providers is known as the *population* to be surveyed. In some cases, it will be both practical and desirable to provide questionnaires to all members of this population.

If the number of potential respondents is very large, however, some subset of the total group must be chosen to receive questionnaires. This group is known as the *sample*. Selection of a sample must be made using special techniques to assure that the responses of the sample group accurately represent those of the entire population.

Next, a decision must be made on how the questionnaire is to be administered. The basic choices are personal delivery with scoring done by interviewers, mail distribution, or telephone survey. Each of these alternatives has its own productivity and cost trade-offs.

Finally, decisions must be made about the form of the questionnaire and the methods to be used in analyzing the results. Again, a number of options are available. If extensive use is to be made of a questionnaire, qualified specialists should be consulted.

Writing questionnaire items.   A number of choices are available in the types of questions that can be written and the types of responses that can be solicited:

- *Open-ended* questions offer no response directions or specified options. A question is asked, and space is provided for writing in any answer the respondent wishes. This type of question can be used only if a questionnaire has extremely limited distribution, or if it is to be used as an interview guide. Large numbers of questionnaires with open-ended questions would be impossibly time-consuming to score. For examples of such items, see Figure 4-7.

- *Fill-in-the-blank* questions are generally used to solicit specific facts. This type of question seeks specific, finite, factual answers. But responses are not restricted to a given set of choices. Numeric responses are often totaled and divided by the number of respondents to determine an average response. See Figure 4-8.

```
a.  What one specific improvement would you seek to improve the flow of
    paperwork across your desk?

b.  What do you feel is the major reason for the increased number of product
    returns that has occurred during the past six months?

c.  Describe briefly your opinion of the proposed policy changes concerning the
    accounts receivable discount rates and periods.
```

Figure 4-7. Examples of open-ended questionnaire items.

```
a.  What is the name of your immediate supervisor?

    _____

b.  How many sales orders do you write on the average day? _____

c.  What is your estimate of the percentage of invoices that are paid in full
    within the first 10 days?

    _____ %
```

Figure 4-8. Examples of fill-in-the-blanks questionnaire items.

- *Multiple-choice* questions provide the respondent with a series of specific choices. These choices are finite and limit the response content. Often, one response is provided that permits the respondent to disqualify himself or herself if the question is inappropriate to his or her specific situation. See Figure 4-9.

- *Rating scales* are a type of multiple-choice question. Rather than providing a series of different answers, however, the rating scale offers a range of responses along a single dimension. For example, a user might be asked to rate the satisfaction level of an existing system on a scale of 1 to 5. Alternatively, a series of satisfaction ratings might be provided, offering a number of choices ranging from completely satisfied to completely unsatisfied. See Figure 4-10.

- *Ranking scales* ask respondents to rank a number of items in order of preference or in order of their importance. For example, users might be asked to rank a list of suggested improvements in the order in which they would find them most helpful. See Figure 4-11.

```
     a.  How many customers do you service on an average day? (Check one.)

         []   0-5
         []   6-10
         []   11-15
         []   More than 15

     b.  What is your opinion of computer automation?

         []   It should be avoided at all costs.
         []   It should be used only if people's jobs are not threatened.
         []   It should be used if costs are reduced, regardless of job losses.
         []   It should always be used.
         []   No opinion.

     c.  What is your annual salary range?

         []    $5,000 -  $9,999
         []   $10,000 - $14,999
         []   $15,000 - $19,999
         []   $20,000 - $24,999
         []   $25,000 or more
```

Figure 4-9. Examples of multiple-choice questionnaire items.

a. What is your general level of satisfaction with each of the following aspects of your job? (Circle your response.)

		Very Dissatisfied					Very Satisfied	
1.	Salary	1	2	3	4	5	6	7
2.	Co-workers	1	2	3	4	5	6	7
3.	Work environment	1	2	3	4	5	6	7
4.	Supervisor	1	2	3	4	5	6	7

b. Rate your supervisor along the following dimensions by placing an (X) along the scale.

1. Helpful ___:___:___:___:___:___ Unhelpful
2. Well organized ___:___:___:___:___:___ Disorganized
3. Decisive ___:___:___:___:___:___ Indecisive
4. Friendly ___:___:___:___:___:___ Unfriendly

Figure 4-10. Examples of questionnaire items using rating scales.

a. Rank each of the following aspects of your job in order of importance to your satisfaction with your work. (1 = most important, 5 = least important)

_____ Salary

_____ Benefits

_____ Co-workers

_____ Work environment

_____ Supervisor

b. What proportions of your time are spent on the following activities during a normal working day. (Percentages should total 100%.)

_____% In meetings

_____% On the phone

_____% Answering correspondence

_____% Meeting with subordinates

_____% On break

_____% Other duties

Figure 4-11. Examples of questionnaire items using ranking scales.

109

No matter which types of questions are used, certain rules must be followed in the preparation of questionnaire items:

- Each item on a questionnaire should be limited to a single topic.
- Each item should be appropriate for the respondents who will receive the questionnaire. Relevant considerations include the educational level of the respondents, the special jargon of their industry, their area of work, and the ready availability of the information requested.
- Items should be designed for easy scoring, in keeping with the method of analysis to be used.
- Questions should be worded precisely and accurately. Simple sentence structures that avoid biased or negative wording should be used. Any alternatives given should be mutually exclusive. That is, there should not be two overlapping response choices for a single question.
- Items should be grouped on the questionnaire for similarity of information content, with some logical order among groups of questions.

Advantages of questionnaires.   Questionnaires are generally the most economical method of gathering data from large groups of people. A questionnaire program can be implemented and administered quickly and easily. Results can be tabulated rapidly and analyzed readily.

Disadvantages of questionnaires.   Effective questionnaires can be difficult to construct. If the subject matter is complex, several drafts, and possibly trial mailings, may be necessary before the final instrument is ready to be administered.

Questionnaires produce only specific, limited amounts of information in direct response to the questions that are included. There is no mechanism for adapting to a subject's responses or for probing more deeply as answers are received.

Observation

Observation is a method of information gathering in which a qualified person watches, or walks through, the actual processing associated with a system. Data are gathered based on what is seen, without discussing the operation with users.

For example, in studying the flow of work through an office, a trained observer might follow the paperwork from the time a source document is created, through the various work stations where data are added to or gathered from the document, until the document is finally filed away permanently. The work flow would be documented on special forms, which could then be studied for possible improvements in the physical layout of the office.

Observation programs can be structured to varying degrees. A highly structured program would use specialized data gathering instruments similar to questionnaires as tools for observing and noting specific data about a given operation. Only predetermined functions within the system would be reviewed and recorded.

A semistructured approach can also be used. Under this method, an observer does not make any notes during the observation. Rather, the observer watches what is happening for a specified period of time, such as one hour. Notes are then recorded on a special form after the observation has been completed.

An important characteristic of observation as an information gathering method is that highly trained people are needed. Observers usually have to be experienced systems analysts, or in some cases industrial engineers.

Advantages of observation.   A major advantage of observation is that the information gathered relates directly to observed performance of system-related tasks. That is, the observer sees firsthand just what is happening in the operation of a system. Thus, information obtained by observation can be of much higher quality than is possible through secondhand reports gathered from interviews or questionnaires.

Another advantage is that data are collected on a real-time basis. Information is generated in the process of observation. There are no instruments to be evaluated or reports to be prepared, as is the case when questionnaires or interviews are used.

Finally, data gathered by observation are highly believable; they have a high face validity.

Disadvantages of observation.   Observation techniques can present logistical problems. For example, the observer must be on the scene when a specific function is being performed. Thus, if an operation takes place only on an overnight basis, observation could become highly inconvenient.

Another potential disadvantage is that the performance of people being observed may be affected by the very presence of an observer. People may not perform the same when they are being watched as they do in the normal course of system processing activities.

A final disadvantage is that specially trained people are needed for observation assignments. These people may not be readily available. Even if they are available, the need for specialists may limit the extent of observation that can be conducted.

Work Sampling and Measurement

Sampling is a methodology used to gather information about a large population of people, events, or transactions by studying some subset of the total. For example, before an election, a sample of voters will be questioned about their preferences. These data are then projected to predict the outcome of the election.

Similar methods can be used to gather information about the operation of an existing system. Representative transactions are selected and studied, and statistical methods are used to infer characteristics of the entire population of transactions from which the sample was drawn.

One sampling technique, for example, is simply to write a program that causes the computer to select a sample of transactions or file records. Another sampling technique might be to select random batches of manually processed transactions or to select, say, one transaction document out of every 20 or 30 processed.

These methods produce limited, specific, but potentially valuable results. One application for sampling techniques is a review of error rates and error distributions. All clerical functions within all information systems are subject to errors. In establishing controls and exception handling procedures for computer information systems, it can be important to derive a reasonably accurate estimate of the rate and distribution of errors. This information makes it possible to design control and corrective procedures, to identify the points at which controls must be established, and also to estimate the cost of corrections.

Another potential use of sampling techniques is to study transaction distributions. For example, a company may want to know where transactions will originate for a given system. This distribution may be geographic, or it may be departmental within the organization. In either case, the information is needed as a basis for specifying the location and number of terminals to be installed, the types and capacities of communication lines, and other system elements.

Sampling programs require the services of highly qualified individuals with experience in research design and statistics. These specialties are beyond the scope of this book. If sampling activities are contemplated, appropriate qualified persons should be consulted.

Summary

An information system exists to support a specific organization. To understand an existing system or to develop a new system, the systems analyst needs to gather information about the organization itself, the people who make up the organization, the work that they do, and the environment in which they work.

Essential information about the organization includes its goals, its organizational structure, the functional objectives that support its goals, and the policies and procedures designed to achieve those objectives. Important information about people includes their authority and responsibility relationships, their job duties, their interpersonal relationships, and their information needs. Information about the work of the organization includes a description of tasks and work flows, methods and procedures for performing the work, work schedules and volumes, performance criteria, and control mechanisms. Information about the work environment includes the physical arrangement of work areas and the resources available to those who work there.

Information can be gathered from existing documents, including organizational charts, policy manuals, methods and procedures manuals, job descriptions, forms and reports, document flow and work flow diagrams, systems flowcharts, computer program documentation, data dictionary listings, and computer operations manuals. Information can be gathered from people by means of interviews, questionnaires, and observation. Information, particularly on new systems, can also be gathered from sources external to the organization, including other companies, equipment and software vendors, business publications, seminars, and workshops.

The most common methods of gathering information that have not already been documented are interviews, questionnaires, observation, and work sampling.

An interview is a planned, face-to-face meeting between a data gatherer and one or more subjects for the express purpose of collecting information. Interviews have the advantage of personal contact, enabling the interviewer to probe for information. Disadvantages include the time and expense of interviewing, difficulty of evaluation, and possible bias of the interviewer.

Steps in preparing for an interview include identifying the subjects to be interviewed, preparing a list of objectives and an outline of topics to be covered, and setting up appointments. In conducting the interview, the interviewer should listen responsively, indicating interest and comprehension, while remaining as noncommittal and unobtrusive as possible. The interviewer should let the subject do the talking, yet maintain control over the interview to ensure that relevant and useful information is obtained.

A questionnaire, a document that solicits specific responses, is an impersonal, often mass-produced, method for gathering the same information from many people. Questionnaires have the advantages of low cost, ease of administration, and rapid tabulation when collecting data from large groups of people. Disadvantages include the difficulty of constructing effective questionnaires and the inability to adapt to or probe responses as they are received.

The characteristics of a good questionnaire are validity, reliability, face validity, and ease of administration and scoring. Questionnaire items may include open-ended questions (for a questionnaire of limited distribution), fill-in-the-blank items, multiple-choice questions, rating scales, and ranking scales. The questionnaire should be logically organized, appropriate to the respondents who will receive it, and designed for easy scoring and analysis.

Observation is a method of information gathering in which a qualified person watches, or walks through, the actual processing associated with a system. Data are gathered based on what is seen, without discussing the operation with users. The major advantage of observation is that the observer sees firsthand what is actually happening, thus obtaining information of the highest quality, on a real-time basis, and with maximum credibility. Disadvantages include inconvenience, the possibility that people may perform differently under observation, and the need for specially trained observers.

Work sampling is a method of gathering information about a large number of transactions by studying a small subset of the total. Sampling techniques are used to select representative transactions for study, and statistical methods are used to infer characteristics of the entire population of transactions from which the sample was drawn. In systems development work, sampling techniques can be used to study the geographic or departmental distribution of transactions or the rate and distribution of transaction errors. Use of these techniques requires the services of specialized personnel with experience in research design and statistics.

Key Terms

1. interview
2. questionnaire
3. validity
4. reliability
5. face validity
6. respondent
7. population
8. sample
9. open-ended
10. fill-in-the-blank
11. multiple-choice
12. rating scale
13. ranking scale
14. observation
15. sampling

Review/Discussion Questions

1. What is the role of information gathering in systems development?

2. What kind of information does the systems analyst need about the organization with a CIS problem or requirement? Why?

3. Name the three major sources of information in a systems development project.

4. What are the advantages of interviews over questionnaires as a means of gathering information? What disadvantages do interviews have?

5. Why is it generally a good idea to interview managers and supervisors before interviewing operational personnel?

6. How does an interviewer go about preparing for a series of interviews?

7. Describe the basic rules and tactics for conducting a successful interview.

8. Under what circumstances is a questionnaire likely to be the most appropriate method for gathering information?

9. What are the four basic characteristics of a good questionnaire?

10. What are the main advantages of observation as a method of information gathering? What are the main disadvantages?

11. Under what circumstances is work sampling likely to be a useful technique? What are the advantages and disadvantages of this methodology?

Practice Assignments

1. For each of the following information needs, suggest an appropriate data gathering technique and describe how and why it is suitable. Also, identify a second source of information that could be sought if the primary source is not available.

   a. The formal structure of responsibility and authority within a major department of a large organization.

   b. The company policy on assignment of credit ratings to new customers.

   c. The job duties of an accounts receivable clerk within a small company that has only one accounting staff member.

   d. The amounts of time spent by a secretary on various job duties.

   e. The average number of errors made by a billing clerk in calculating invoice totals.

   f. The reason for preparing a three-part purchase order form to buy merchandise to replace inventory stocks.

   g. The best arrangement of desks and other fixtures within an office.

   h. The difficulty in modifying a computer-generated management report by rearranging the columns of information.

   i. The general level of satisfaction among 50 employees in the warehouse.

   j. The computerized procedure for selecting suppliers and producing purchase orders for merchandise.

   k. The type of information collected about job applicants.

   l. The cost to the company of having the office manager spend time in responding to customer complaints.

2. Figure 4-12 is a memo that was sent to the head of the accounting department as an interview request. Critique this memo.

```
Date:      March 14

To:        Dennis Warren, Accounting Supervisor

From:      Anne Paige, Analyst

Re:        Interview

I would like for you to come to my office next week sometime to
discuss the very serious problems that you have in your department.
It seems that many of the other managers are upset that their reports
are late and never up-to-date.

I will be discussing the following topics:

1.  How many people work for you?  What are their salaries?

2.  What are the exact duties of each of your employees?

3.  Why do they make so many errors?

4.  What procedures are followed by the data processing department to
    keep your files up to date?

5.  What kinds of reports do the other managers need?

6.  How will your staff feel if we automate the entire accounting
    function and have to lay off the unproductive workers?

I will use this information in coming up with some better ways of
doing the work in your area.  I already have some idea of the
changes I would like to see and hope you will agree with them.
If I am not in my office when you come by, please wait, as I will
probably return soon.
```

Figure 4-12. Sample interview appointment memo for review and comment.

3. Construct questionnaire items to solicit the following information items. The gathered information should be easy to tabulate.

   a. The amount of time an office worker spends: 1) answering the phone, 2) filing, 3) typing correspondence, 4) typing reports, 5) writing memos, and 6) other duties.

   b. The degree of importance each of the following job dimensions plays in the job satisfaction of an average worker: 1) salary, 2) fringe benefits, 3) co-workers, 4) work environment, 5) amount of supervision, 6) amount of work, and 7) other factors.

   c. The salaries of workers paid between $10,000 and $25,000.

   d. The relative importance of each of the following reasons for customer complaints: 1) late deliveries of orders, 2) stock-outs, 3) damaged merchandise, 4) misbillings, 5) discourteous service, and 6) high prices.

5 FEASIBILITY STUDY

LEARNING OBJECTIVES

On completing reading and other learning assignments for this chapter, you should be able to:

☐ Define the term feasibility study.

☐ Explain the need for, tasks included in, and objectives of the feasibility study activity.

☐ Define and describe the considerations associated with financial feasibility, operational feasibility, technical feasibility, schedule feasibility, and human factors feasibility.

☐ Describe the feasibility report, its contents, and the decisions that will be based upon it.

☐ Describe the purpose, value, and contents of a project plan.

☐ Describe the role of application software packages and explain their potential value within the systems development life cycle.

☐ Explain the concept and importance of the layering of work in succeeding activities and phases of the systems development life cycle.

☐ Describe the principle of cumulative project documentation and explain its value.

☐ Describe the decision alternatives open to the steering committee at the end of the feasibility study activity and explain the significance of a decision approving continuation of the project into the analysis and general design phase.

ACTIVITY DESCRIPTION

Something that is *feasible* can be done. There is also an implication of practicality associated with feasibility. A systems development project that is feasible, can be done within boundaries considered to represent good business practices.

The term *feasibility study* implies some additional meanings:

- When a feasiblity study is completed, it is assumed that the original problem or need has been understood and that alternative solutions to the basic need or problem have been considered. The feasibility lies in the solution, not in the problem itself.

- It is assumed that a feasibility study will encompass at least two, perhaps more, prospective solutions to the stated need or problem. This does not mean that two or more separate systems are designed, then the best one is selected. Rather, it means that several alternatives will be considered before a project focuses on the one that appears best for the situation under study.

- Where an information system is concerned, a feasibility study involves a number of separate, related considerations. These include financial, technical, and people factors. It is assumed that all appropriate factors connected with any given system will be evaluated.

- A feasibility study should conclude with a clear-cut recommendation. That is, a definite course of action should be proposed. At a minimum, this recommendation will indicate whether the project should be continued or abandoned. Feasibility study recommendations also establish dollar values for systems development projects. One of the results of the feasibility study will be a projected budget indicating the cost of developing the new system. Thus, the recommendations imply that a project is feasible and also indicate the associated cost and potential payback of proceeding with the development project.

Feasibility Study Considerations

Feasibility considerations covered during this activity should include:

- Financial feasibility
- Operational feasibility
- Technical feasibility
- Schedule feasibility
- Human factors feasibility.

Financial feasibility.   *Financial feasibility* is a classic, and probably the most often used, method for evaluating proposed computer information systems. The result is usually called a *cost/benefit analysis.* Since Chapter 7 is devoted to this type of study, there will be no detailing here. Briefly, however, the idea is to determine savings and other benefits that would result from implementation of a new system. These benefits are then compared with costs. If the benefits come out far enough ahead, the decision is positive. If not, there must be other compelling reasons for development of a new system to be justified. Financial considerations are only one aspect of feasibility—but they are important.

Financial considerations relate to an organization's normal investment practices. Most organizations have some standards that are applied in determining whether a *capital investment* (a purchase of equipment or facilities) is worthwhile.

Often, the financial feasibility of a proposed investment is determined by the projected *payback period*—the length of time it will take to pay back the investment. For example, suppose a company is paying $2,000 a month in rent for an office and factory building. Suppose management finds that a similar building can be purchased for $100,000. The payback period, for the purposes of this example, would be 50 months. Even considering building maintenance, it might turn out that the company could own its own building (rather than paying rent and having nothing to show for it) within seven or eight years. This could justify a purchase, as long as the money was available to buy the property.

Another way of measuring financial feasibility is to consider the *return on investment*. This term refers to the amount or percentage of monetary gain (profit) derived from investment of funds. Suppose a company has $100,000. Invested in securities, this capital sum might return an income of, say, $16,000 a year. If purchase of a building for the same $100,000 would save $24,000 a year in rent, this would be an improved return on investment.

Where computer information systems are concerned, costs can be infinitely more difficult to calculate. Benefits can be even harder to determine than costs. However, the same basic principles apply. That is, a computer information system represents an investment. Managers of the organization should base systems development decisions at least partly upon the projected payback period and return on this investment.

Operational feasibility. An operational CIS should meet business needs or solve business problems. Therefore, one of the considerations in evaluating the feasibility of a proposed system is whether the organization can gear up to handle the manual processing efficiently. In other words, the question centers on whether the system will work from a people processing—rather than from a computer processing—point of view. This is known as *operational feasibility*.

For example, consider the case of adding the sanitary district billing to the water department system. One of the operational considerations is that substantially more money will be handled if a combined system is undertaken. Further, the flow of money will follow closely behind the billing cycles established for the system. Itemizing and accounting for all of these receipts—and responding to the increased level of customer questions and complaints—could become a major undertaking. Further, while the checks or other payments are being tallied, the money is not earning anything.

Rather than add a major cashiering operation within the city's water department, it might be best simply to have all of the payments, for both water and sanitation, mailed directly to a bank. Bank personnel would open all the envelopes and deposit the money to an account, which would begin paying interest on the funds the same day they were received. The bank would then provide enough detailing about receipts so that the data could be processed routinely, after the fact, within the city's computer system.

The point is that, under one approach, one aspect of a proposed system could be operationally difficult. Under another approach, the potential problem is turned into an advantage. Operational feasibility evaluations should look at proposed systems and their potential problems in this way.

Technical feasibility. Considerations of *technical feasibility* center around the existence of computer hardware and software capable of supporting the system being studied. The concern is whether the equipment and software that an organization has, or can justify financially, are capable of processing the proposed application. Although financial considerations are related, this concern is primarily technical.

Suppose, for example, that Central City finds it would need a much bigger computer to handle the combined water and sanitary billing application. The larger computer may be more than the city can afford or more than its personnel are capable of operating. If this is the case, the new application could be considered unfeasible on technical grounds.

One frequent reason for technical unfeasibility lies in unreasonable suggestions received from users who are not acquainted with the limitations of computers. When people see computers doing complex things, such as sending people to the moon and back or looking for income tax evaders, they get the idea that computers can do almost anything. In particular, since people can read natural language, puzzling out incomplete sentences and fragments of handwriting, they may see this as an easy task for computers.

However, computers are most efficient at handling algorithmic processes when all data are given. Problems of incomplete information, such as recognition of partial patterns, are extremely difficult for computers to handle. Such tasks can be programmed only with a great deal of effort and require much computer time. To achieve recognition processing, it is necessary to apply trial-and-error methods by looking at low-level details over and over again to eliminate the many possibilities that humans never even consider in their personal reasoning processes. Without an understanding of the limitations involved, users may request services that are inappropriate for computers to deliver.

To deal with such situations, it is extremely important that systems analysts themselves have a background in computer programming. Systems analysts who are not experienced in computer programming may come up with ideas and suggestions that are technically unfeasible for computer application. This can diminish the credibility of systems analysis and also waste time and opportunity costs that could be allocated to other, more productive projects.

Schedule feasibility.   The question of *schedule feasibility* arises when a systems development request is accompanied by a specific, possibly inflexible, deadline. The question then becomes: Can the proposed system solution be implemented in the time available?

For example, the sanitary district billing application may be perfectly feasible on all counts—until you learn that the system has to be in operation within 90 days. Looking around, you find that you just don't have the people or the skills within the city's staff to handle this job in the time available. Under these circumstances, you might contact independent software development companies to see if you can find an outside supplier who can do the work in the time available, even though costs might be greater.

This concern with scheduling and deadlines points up once again the importance of in-depth knowledge on the part of the systems analyst about the problems of software development, particularly the programming and computer-related concerns involved in detailed systems design and implementation. If the analyst is well acquainted with the programming process, he or she can provide at least gross estimates for how long it will take to develop certain kinds of software. If the software is particularly difficult, the analyst will recognize that potential schedule delays may be encountered.

By the same token, the systems analyst who knows what software really does may find ways to modify and reuse existing software. This can lead to a proposed solution that saves both time and money through utilization of existing resources rather than from-scratch development of entirely new programs.

The question of schedule feasibility highlights one of the important, intangible factors associated with a feasiblity study. That is, each of the feasibility considerations may affect others. As a result, trade-offs may be required in evaluating the feasibility of a new system.

In some situations, scheduling or deadlines may not be a factor. However, it always pays to look and ask, just to be sure.

Human factors feasibility.   New or modified computer information systems are vehicles of change. People are, by nature, resistant to change. Thus, there is always a potential for conflict to arise in the development and implementation of a computer information system. For this reason, a feasibility study should evaluate the dimension of *human factors feasibility.* An estimate should be made as to whether the reactions of people to a new system might impede or obstruct its development or implementation. If so, an evaluation should be performed to determine the extent of such obstructions and to devise measures for dealing with them.

It is commonplace, for example, for implementation of major computer information systems to trigger extensive employee turnover. The classic example is a person who has been doing one job, one way, for perhaps 20 years. Under a proposed computer information system, the tasks that this person will perform are to be changed significantly. This can create severe trauma—possibly resulting in an inability or unwillingness to perform at all.

Such reactions should be anticipated and plans should be made for dealing with them. In fact, systems have been delayed or not developed at all because of the prospect of human trauma. This type of decision may be a sound one. People who are afraid of or resistant to change may actually—though perhaps unwittingly—work actively to sabotage any system that appears to threaten them.

Evaluating Feasibility

The responsibility of the project team that performs a feasibility study is to make a recommendation to the steering committee. It is important that this responsibility be clearly understood. The project team does not make the feasibility decision. Rather, the project team makes recommendations and lives with decisions made by others.

At some point during the feasibility study activity, project team members will have to think about the needs and decision processes of the steering committee. Some management level groups have a natural tendency to emphasize cost/benefit analysis over all other feasibility considerations. Some steering committee members may put operational concerns at the head of the list. In other cases, steering committees may be intrigued by the technical sophistication of proposals. While presentations should address the interests of members of the steering committee, professional objectivity should be evident in the wording and content of the *feasibility report,* the chief end product of this activity.

Enthusiasm for new projects can be contagious. If the project team is enthusiastic about going ahead with systems development, strategies for presentation of the feasibility report to the steering committee should be reviewed carefully. In general, responsibility for "selling" a project should be carried by the senior user member of the project team. Systems analysts or project leaders from the CIS function should avoid being advocates for user benefits that justify the system. Systems professionals can attest to the operational and technical feasibility of a proposed system. But they should not present themselves as experts on its impact upon user departments.

An Example

In the examples cited so far, feasibility considerations have been relatively simple and decisions about whether to proceed with the development of a system have been readily apparent. However, actual systems decisions are not always that clear-cut.

Assume, for example, that you are in charge of systems development at State University. It is just a few days before the beginning of the fall semester. You get a call from Ian McNamara, the university's registrar. Except for Ian's office, the campus is relatively calm, since students aren't due to arrive for a few days. Ian, however, is going through the busiest few days he will experience throughout the school year. He and his staff are getting ready for final registration for fall classes.

At your university, a two-tier registration system is used. Departing students are permitted to register in advance for fall classes before they leave at the end of May. Data on this advance registration have already been processed, partial class lists have been delivered to faculty members, and preregistering students have received copies of their class schedules. Thus, perhaps 60 to 65 percent of the spaces in this fall's classes have already been allocated.

The remaining registration, to begin in a few days, will involve entering freshmen and transfer students. Theoretically, fall registration should pose only minor problems. Preregistration documentation shows how many places are available, in which classes. It should be possible, therefore, to allocate these available places on a first-come-first-served basis. For many years, this has been done simply by punching cards to represent available places in classes still open. These cards are then made available at departmental desks in the field house, where fall registration takes place. Advisors or faculty members can then hand these cards out as students apply for classes. Qualifications or course prerequisites can be checked right on the spot, as the cards are distributed.

This system, however, suffers from a common problem shared by many systems: Severe difficulties can arise in the handling of relatively few exceptions. Ian explains that he expects that some 10 percent of the students who preregistered in June will not return in September. Further, of those that do return, probably 15 percent will want to change their schedules in some way. The result: chaos.

Over the summer, Ian attended a meeting of university administrators. At this meeting, he spoke with a registrar from another university, who told him that these problems had been substantially reduced by developing an on-line registration system. Under this system, registration workers could look up the exact status of registrations, adjusting enrollments for nonreturning students and for those who wished to change their schedules. The whole process of registration was calmer and more efficient.

Ian knows that your university's computer system has on-line capabilities. He wants to know if, perhaps, you can handle this fall's registration through on-line procedures. You explain patiently that systems development takes more time than two or three days. At his insistence, however, you do agree to meet with him and to conduct an initial investigation.

Your initial investigation uncovers some interesting possibilities. For one thing, if total student information files did exist in an on-line system, at least 15 departments on your campus could profitably use these files. Another thing you learn is that the benefits to be derived from a system of this type do not present clear-cut savings. It will actually cost quite a bit more to set up and operate an on-line system than it does to punch cards and handle them on a batch basis.

To evaluate the feasibility of such a system, then, you are going to have to talk to a number of department heads and get them to assign values to the benefits, if any, that they foresee. For example, Ian believes the system would enable him to do a better job of allocating existing course openings to the student body. The work load among the faculty could be distributed more efficiently and equitably. Overcrowding of some classes could be eliminated.

In talking to student advisors, you find that they could do a better job of guiding students if they had access to on-line files containing information on courses completed by individual students, as well as seats available in classes for the coming semester. The office that certifies the meeting of graduation requirements by seniors could do its work much more efficiently. Similar savings could be realized in grade reporting and standardized testing functions. The placement office could do a better job of matching students with job interview opportunities if available information was more current. However, none of these potential users would realize enough savings to establish the financial feasibility of the new system for any single application. Even with all these applications combined, the cost savings would still not be great enough to justify development of the new system. Yet, you can see clearly that departments all over the campus will benefit from this system if it is developed.

In a situation of this type, a feasibility study can become quite involved. A major complication is the need to establish values for intangible benefits. How much is it worth, for example, to provide better registration services to students? Clearly, a feasibility study for this type of request will be far more complex than for the water/sanitary billing system.

Feasibility Report Expectations

The feasibility study is a relatively brief activity. Actual time spent on this activity varies widely for individual projects. Typically, however, the feasibility study accounts for less than 10 percent of a systems development project. Obviously, then, the results cannot be sufficiently complete or detailed to be considered totally reliable and accurate. The purpose of a feasibility report is simply to provide a basis for a decision on whether more work is justified.

Once a project team gets going, it may be tempting to try to design the finished system right on the spot. This temptation must be resisted.

Team members should keep in mind that the structure of a systems development project involves a layering of effort. In the feasibility study activity, the idea is to overview the prospects for the proposed system, going only far enough to make a recommendation about the commitment of corporate funds to the next phase of the system development life cycle. Feasibility studies are funded by user and CIS departments out of normal operating budgets. If efforts at this level are overextended, the departments involved will suffer elsewhere.

Another temptation to be resisted during the feasibility study activity is the urge to gather enough information so that costs of installing and operating a new system can be pinpointed with great accuracy. Such accuracy takes time and costs money. It is acceptable during this first phase of a project to present rough estimates only, as long as the quality of the estimates and reservations about their acccuracy are made clear to the steering committee. Many organizations, for example, are willing to accept estimates that may be off by 75 to 100 percent—as long as the evidence indicates a good potential for success. Feasibility is evaluated again at the end of the analysis and general design phase, providing an opportunity for more accurate estimates.

In summary, the feasibility report should be structured—and limited—to conform to the scope and objectives of this activity.

Case Scenario

The awareness of this need to limit the feasibility study activity hits you hard as you, Howard Rogers, the chief accountant of the sanitary district, and the city clerk, and the head of your own department's data entry section review possible methods for capturing data for the proposed combined system. Since the water billing system is to be expanded, the data entry supervisor, Shizu Matsumoto, suggests that advanced data capturing methods may now be affordable.

She explains that, rather than keypunching all meter reading entries, as is now done, it may be possible to input data directly from meter reading tickets prepared in the field by using optical character recognition equipment. Shizu also points out that there are automatic meter reading systems now available. Customer meters are equipped with small radio transmitters. Meter reading personnel simply drive through the neighborhood slowly, activating the meter transmitters with small transponders that they carry with them. This triggers the transmission of reading information and the recording of data on tapes within the transponders. The tapes can then be read directly into the computer.

As an experienced systems analyst, you are prepared for this type of suggestion. You explain that this kind of consideration belongs in the next phase, where you will take a deeper look at the proposed new system. During the feasibility study, the project team does not yet need to get into this level of detail because it isn't necessary to consider such possibilities to determine general feasibility. You ask Shizu to give you information on current keypunching costs. Your reasoning is: If it looks feasible to implement the new system with existing keypunching techniques, enhanced methods can only improve the picture.

OBJECTIVES

The objectives of this activity are:

- Establish the overall scope and approximate costs and resource commitments for the proposed project.
- Recommend a decision and a course of action to the steering committee.
- If a "go" decision is recommended, include project schedule and priority suggestions in the report to the committee.

SCOPE

The feasibility study activity begins with a review of the initial investigation report and other documentation produced during the first activity. In a global sense, this activity is a preview of the activities and tasks of the next phase in the project—analysis and general design. This activity should cover essentially the same ground as the analysis and general design phase, but in far less depth. Setting the scope for this activity is a good exercise in establishing the layering approach to project management. As the work is done, team members will recognize the need to go deeper and to probe further. But they will be constrained by the budgets and schedules they have agreed to.

END PRODUCTS

The principal end products of this activity are:

- A feasibility report to the steering committee
- A project plan to be implemented if the steering committee authorizes continuation of the project
- A preliminary set of working papers for the next phase of the project.

Feasibility Report

The feasibility report contains:

- A narrative explanation of the purpose and scope of the project, including the reason the project is being undertaken, which areas of the organization and which functions are included, and how the project contributes to the objectives of the organization
- A brief description of the existing system, anticipated changes, and expected results, including evaluations of technical and operational feasibility
- A concise, specific statement of anticipated benefits—including dollar values for these benefits wherever possible
- Preliminary cost estimates for both development and ongoing operation of the system
- A return on investment (ROI) analysis of the project
- An impact statement describing any changes in equipment or facilities that will be needed—either in the computer center or in the user areas
- A proposed schedule indicating both time and people to be involved in the project—comparatively detailed for the second phase of the project, less detailed for succeeding phases
- A list of policy level decisions that cannot be made by the project team and must be resolved by management.

Note the last item above. Any systems study is bound to uncover situations that cannot be resolved by the project team—that require management to set policies concerning how work will be done or information will be handled. In the sanitary district study, for example, one such question might involve how partial payments from customers are to be allocated. Suppose a customer owes $62 and pays only $50. Should the water bill be paid in full first and the remainder allocated to the sanitary district? Should the money be divided equally between the two collecting authorities? Should the money be divided proportionally according to the amount owed to each authority? Systems analysis can only pose such questions, not answer them.

Project Plan

The *project plan* prepared in connection with a feasibility study lays out detailed scheduling and staffing—to the task level—for the second phase of the project. This plan should list all of the people involved, either by individual names or by skill requirements, along with work-hour estimates for each task. For succeeding phases of the project, the plan is more general—and also more approximate.

Working Papers

In keeping with the layering principle, *working papers* provide start-up guidance for work in the next phase of the project. These documents include:

Preliminary review of new system requirements. This presentation takes an overview look at the requirements for the proposed new system. Included are statements of minimum business objectives to be achieved, descriptions of both required and desired outputs, identification of input data sources, and special processing requirements. This set of documentation will be enlarged and detailed further in Activity 4—New System Requirements.

Preliminary review of the existing system. This documentation includes relevant organizational charts (showing both formal and informal relationships), a glossary of terms used within the existing system, and overview-level data flow diagrams (both physical and logical) for manual and computerized portions of existing systems. Also provided are estimates of current operating costs, transaction volumes, and operating schedules. These documents will be expanded during Activity 3—Existing System Review.

Possible system solutions.   This documentation includes descriptions of techniques and equipment that could be used to implement the new system. If appropriate, data flow diagrams are included, as are hardware and software specifications. Any solutions put forward at this point should be qualified with explanations that they are suggestions only. Further study will be given to this topic during Activity 5—New System Design.

THE PROCESS

This feasibility study activity is a classic, though miniature, systems analysis study. To the extent needed for an evaluation of feasibility, all of the same methods and procedures used in the analysis and general design phase of the systems development life cycle are undertaken. Since these activities are discussed in future chapters, they are not reviewed here.

In addition to previewing the analysis and general design phase, the feasibility study builds on the results of the previous activity. One result of the initial investigation activity is a clear definition of the problem or opportunity that prompted the request. This definition establishes the scope of the project. Most development projects have a tendency to grow in scope. As project team members and users reach deeper levels of understanding, they see new opportunities to add features to the system or to move into related areas not covered in the original request. This tendency toward project expansion must be controlled. Any significant change in project scope should require steering committee approval.

A long-standing guideline for systems development is known as the *80-20 rule*. This suggests that 80 percent of the benefits of a system can be achieved for 20 percent of the cost. The remaining 80 percent of the cost goes into providing the last—possibly unnecessary—20 percent of the benefits. The point is that, as a result of the feasibility study, the scope of the project should be firmly established in terms of the business objectives to be met, the major outputs to be produced, and the main processing functions to be included. These objectives, outputs, and processing functions encompass the requirements—the 80 percent of benefits. Once this clear understanding of scope is established, it is possible to resist the temptation to enlarge the scope by adding nonessential "bells and whistles" that can increase complexity and costs disproportionately.

It becomes important, during this activity, for all members of the project team to begin to differentiate between the logical and physical aspects of the system. The logical aspects stress the business objectives of the system, what the system is to do with what data. The physical aspects stress the mechanics of how data are provided and processed. Separate logical and physical documentation should be established during this activity.

This activity begins with a review of the initial investigation report. This input serves as a basis for establishing a plan that includes a list of tasks, personnel assignments, time allocations, and a calendar for completing the assignments.

The primary study method involves interviews with users and managers associated with the current system. For the most part, the feasibility study interviews will be with upper- and middle-level managers who can explain the system to the necessary level of understanding. It would be an exception for team members to interview personnel at operating levels during this activity.

Based on interviews and other data gathering activities, a preliminary picture of potential benefits and possible cost savings is developed. In the course of these studies, any situations requiring policy decisions are identified and listed.

Proposed solutions or approaches to new systems are reviewed with managers of user and CIS departments. Persons who would be involved in recommending implementation of the new system must agree to its feasibility and desirability.

Once this base of knowledge has been built, work can proceed on preparation of a cost/benefit analysis, a project plan, and a feasibility report for presentation to the steering committee.

Three special considerations should be taken up during a feasibility study and applied to later project activities as well:

- Packaged application software
- Layering
- Project management tools.

Packaged Application Software

High quality *application software packages* are becoming available for increasingly wider ranges of applications. This option should be considered in any systems development effort. A package may well exist that meets all or a substantial portion of the users' needs.

It is too early, during the feasibility study, to make a software purchase decision. Needs are not yet fully understood. However, potential packages should be identified and solutions should be defined that integrate these packages. A closer evaluation of potential packages and integration problems can be made during the analysis and general design phase.

Layering

Systems analysis activities during the early stages of a project cover the same general concerns and areas several times, moving to increasing depths of knowledge and understanding with each iteration. This concept of adding to the depth of knowledge through successive iterations is known as *layering*.

In this respect, the systems development life cycle resembles the process approach to structured programming. In programming, people have a tendency to get restless, to push to begin coding as soon as possible. Experience has shown, however, that it is better to take the time to understand and define the problem before beginning to write the program code. The same principle applies in the systems field. It can be tempting to begin designing a new system based on past experience, or on a cursory understanding of what currently exists and what is wanted. The danger lies in the possibility that a systems analyst may begin to design a new system before he or she fully understands what is needed or what actually exists at present.

The layering approach avoids this type of pitfall. Phases and activities in the systems development life cycle are structured so that the necessary base of knowledge is built, step by step, before extensive commitments are made to changes that might not work. For example, in the analysis and general design phase, emphasis is on user needs and overall technical solutions rather than on detailed technical design considerations. A complete understanding between systems analysts and users should be a prerequisite before the project moves into detailed technical design and program development.

The analysis and general design phase is actually at the second level in project layering. Because this phase represents a major commitment of time and money, the investigation phase, concluding with the feasibility study covered in this chapter, serves as a first layer. A general understanding of project needs and possible new system solutions is achieved during the investigation phase. This provides a firm base of understanding upon which the systems analyst can build during the analysis and general design phase.

Actually, each phase is composed of a number of layers of understanding. This layering structure has been likened to the process of peeling an onion. The new system is at the center of the onion. Each layer of the onion represents an increasingly detailed understanding of the organization's needs and of the new system possibilities. The center is revealed by peeling the outer layers away one at a time.

The controls built into the systems development life cycle help maintain the necessary order in the development of the needed level of understanding. Each activity and each phase has its own specific objectives. Each of these objectives should be met. However, work should not progress beyond the objectives of any given activity or phase before the appropriate decisions and commitments have been made. This ensures that commitments are made on the basis of adequate information. The probability of project success is increased by this layering approach to systems understanding and project management. At the same time, layering minimizes the rework required on any given project.

Project Management Tools

Specific tools used in project management are described and analyzed in the final chapter of this book. At this point, it is important to be aware of the need for these tools and the functions they perform:

- A *project plan*, described earlier, includes lists of tasks and schedules for their performance.

- A *staffing plan* encompasses personnel assignments for the project and includes estimates of days or hours to be worked.

- A *time reporting* system keeps track of work completed and scheduled to be done, with controls applied at the task level.

- *Status reporting* must be carried out periodically, on a scheduled basis, throughout the project. Status reports should include information on tasks completed (with both estimated and actual hours reported), tasks in process (with estimated hours, actual hours to date, and estimated remaining hours reported), future tasks (reported in terms of estimated work to be done), and overall project status. Overall project status should be reported on the basis of both budgeted hours and a calendar schedule.

One tool that is commonly used to control schedules as a part of project management is the *Gantt chart.* This is a well-established tool in the industrial engineering field. The purpose of the Gantt chart, as illustrated in Figure 5-1, is to show the start, elapsed time, and completion relationships of work units that make up a project or a part of a project. A Gantt chart does not show the intensity of work or level of effort being applied to a work unit at any given time.

The time dimension of a Gantt chart reads from left to right, following normal calendar divisions, such as days, weeks, or months. The vertical dimension deals with content, such as phases, activities, or tasks. The Gantt chart is updated as work is completed. Looking at the entire chart makes it possible to identify points at which work is ahead of schedule, on schedule, or behind schedule.

Another key tool for project management is some type of *project planning sheet,* such as the one shown in Figure 5-2. This is a simple work sheet used to identify work units, to assign persons to handle them, and to keep track of planned hours for each assignment, actual hours worked, and planned and actual dates for the beginning and conclusion of work on each assignment. Typically, planning sheets of this type are used at the task level. All of the tasks are listed as a basis for allocating and monitoring completion of work.

PERSONNEL INVOLVED

The feasibility study activity marks the formation of a systems development project team. Thus, one of the challenges of this activity lies in building teamwork, as quickly and effectively as possible. Team members may be strangers to each other at the outset. Very quickly, a sense of purpose and a spirit of cooperation must be established.

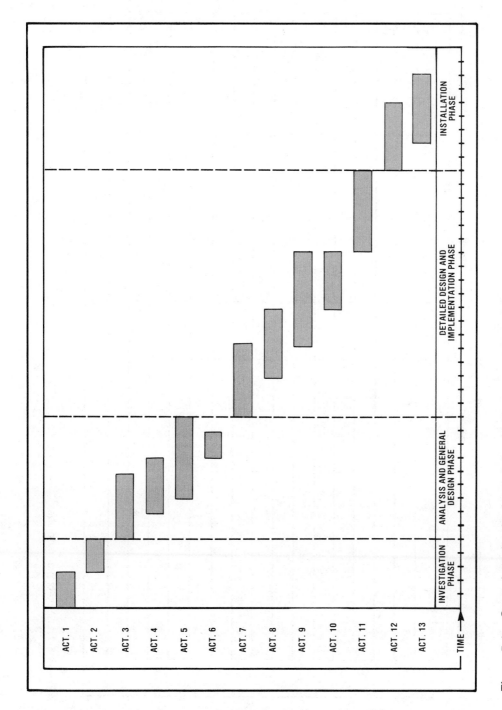

Figure 5-1. Gantt chart showing interrelationships among activities of the systems development life cycle.

PROJECT PLANNING SHEET

Project _____   Date Prepared _____

☐ Activity List

Leader _____   Prepared By _____

☐ Task List

Task/Act.	Task/Activity Description	Individual Assigned	Planned Hours	Actual Hours	Planned Date		Actual Date	
					Begin	End	Begin	End

Figure 5-2. Project planning sheet.

Team members need each other. Except in rare instances, users cannot develop systems by themselves. Systems people cannot develop systems unless users want them and will apply them. Thus, a mutual dependence exists and must be recognized at the outset of a project.

The project team leader is usually an experienced systems analyst from the CIS department. However, in some organizations, qualified user personnel act as team leaders. If this is the case, a systems analyst is assigned as the senior CIS member of the team. Other team members, at this stage of the project, will be middle managers from the user groups and additional systems analysts. Over the life of the project, the composition of the project team will change. The size of the team will depend on the complexity of the project.

CUMULATIVE PROJECT FILE

At the conclusion of this activity, the cumulative project file will include:

- The project plan, which will be revised continually throughout the systems development life cycle
- The initial investigation report
- The feasibility report
- A list of policy decisions that must be addressed before design of the new system can be completed
- A schedule of interviews conducted and summaries of findings
- A glossary of terms, which will be updated continually
- Preliminary documentation for the existing system, to serve as a basis for Activity 3—Existing System Review
- Preliminary documentation of new system requirements, to be enlarged during Activity 4—New System Requirements
- Descriptions of possible system solutions, to be considered and expanded upon during Activity 5—New System Design.

CUMULATIVE DOCUMENTATION

Closely related to the layering concept for building knowledge— discussed above—is the idea of *cumulative documentation*. This technique calls for the building of systems documentation gradually, keeping pace with the accumulation of information and ideas. A systems development project produces two separate, equally important types of documentation—final and interim.

Final documentation describes the system after the development project is completed. Included are all the required types of documentation of programs, processing, procedures, forms, and files that are critical working tools for an operational system.

All too often, these end products are regarded as the only documentation required. There is a temptation to wait until the system is developed completely before documentation begins. This end-of-project approach to documentation can be costly because a crash program is usually required to meet all of the documentation needs. Further, procrastination can lead to oversight—things are left out simply because they aren't remembered during the last-minute rush.

A better approach is through *interim documentation,* building a working base for systems development as the project goes forward. Each activity and phase within the systems development life cycle has well-defined document outputs. These are identified in the End Products section of each activity chapter in this book. These documentation requirements have been built into the systems development life cycle for some very important reasons: Documentation is, fundamentally, a way of organizing thinking and applying discipline to be sure that all key points are considered. Documentation is also an essential means of communication. The makeup and nature of a project team change as the development life cycle progresses. If systems are to meet user needs, system specifications must be clear about what is wanted. You can't design and implement systems first, and prepare specifications later. Thus, documentation provides an orderly, cumulative dimension to the systems development process.

Requirements for system documentation and for communication among project team personnel are built into the systems development life cycle. Documentation is prepared on a dynamic basis. The documentation created in one activity or phase is analyzed, revised, torn apart, and added to in the course of creating the documentation for successive activities or phases. The documentation evolves as understanding increases. In this way, cumulative documentation promotes creative thinking and supports the layering process.

Finally, when the project is concluded, the required end product documentation has already been assembled, ready for final editing and production. Last-minute crises are rare in projects that have been documented cumulatively.

Summary

Feasibility means that a project is possible, practical, and realistic. Factors to be considered in evaluating feasibility are financial, operational, technical, scheduling, and human.

Completion of a feasibility study means that the original problem or need has been understood, alternative solutions have been considered, and the best one has been recommended for evaluation. A feasibility study should conclude with a clear-cut recommendation as to whether the new system should be developed, along with a projected budget for the systems development project.

An evaluation of financial feasibility results in a cost/benefit analysis, weighing projected benefits against costs of developing the new system. As with any other capital investment, development of an information system must be justified in terms of its projected payback period and return on investment.

Operational feasibility involves the question of whether the organization can gear up to handle the manual processing involved in a given systems operation efficiently.

Technical feasibility involves the availability of computer hardware and software capable of supporting the proposed system. A related concern is whether the equipment and software that an organization has, or can justify financially, are capable of processing the proposed application.

The question of schedule feasibility arises when a systems development request is accompanied by a specific, possibly inflexible, deadline. If the proposed system solution cannot be implemented in the time available, alternative solutions may need to be considered.

An evaluation of human factors feasibility involves estimating the reactions of people within the organization that might impede or obstruct development or implementation of the new system. Human factors considerations may be important in the planning process, and even in the decision on whether or not to proceed with development.

Evaluating the feasibility of a proposed system can be complex, depending on the factors involved. A major complication can be the need to establish values for intangible benefits.

The principal end products of this activity are: a feasibility report to the steering committee, a project plan to be implemented if the steering committee authorizes continuation of the project, and a preliminary set of working papers for the next phase of the project.

The feasibility report should contain: a narrative explanation of the purpose and scope of the project; a description of the problem and proposed solution, including evaluations of technical and operational feasibility; a statement of anticipated benefits, including dollar values wherever possible; preliminary cost estimates for development and ongoing operation of the system; a return on investment (ROI) analysis of the project; an impact statement describing any changes in equipment or facilities that will be needed; a proposed schedule for succeeding phases of the project; and a list of policy-level decisions that need to be resolved by management.

The project plan prepared in connection with a feasibility study lays out detailed scheduling and staffing for each activity and task in the second phase of the project. For succeeding phases of the project, the plan is more general.

The working papers prepared in the course of a feasibility study provide start-up guidance for work in the next phase of the project. These documents include a preliminary review of new system requirements, a preliminary review of the existing system, and suggestions for possible system solutions.

Information gathering for the feasibility study is generally limited to interviews with upper- and middle-level managers associated with the existing system. Available application software packages should be identified so that proposed solutions can incorporate them wherever possible.

The layering approach to systems development means, in part, that each activity and phase of the project has its own specific objectives. Work should not proceed beyond these objectives until the appropriate decisions and commitments have been made. This ensures that commitments are made on the basis of adequate information while minimizing wasted effort.

Project management tools help keep the systems development project on course and on schedule. The project plan lists tasks and schedules for their performance. A staffing plan lists personnel assignments and estimates of time involved. A time reporting system keeps track of work completed and scheduled work still to be done. Status reports, issued periodically throughout the project, summarize tasks completed, tasks in process, future tasks, and overall project status.

Gantt charts can be used to show start date, elapsed time, and completion date relationships among the various work units that make up an activity, a phase, or an entire project. Project planning sheets keep track of individual tasks, the persons assigned to handle them, and planned and actual start and completion dates.

The feasibility study activity marks the formation of the systems development project team. The project team leader is usually an experienced systems analyst from the CIS department, but may be a qualified user. Other team members, at this stage of the project, will be middle managers from the user groups and additional systems analysts. Team members, who may never have worked together before, must establish an atmosphere of teamwork and cooperation.

At the conclusion of this activity, the cumulative project file should contain: the project plan, the initial investigation report, the feasibility report, a list of policy decisions to be made, a schedule of interviews conducted and summaries of findings, a glossary of terms (continuously updated), preliminary documentation for the existing system, preliminary documentation of new system requirements, and descriptions of possible system solutions.

Each activity and phase has defined document outputs. The documentation created in one activity or phase is analyzed, revised, torn apart, and added to in the course of creating the documentation for successive activities. This process of cumulative documentation is a reflection of the layering approach to systems development, helping to organize thinking and ensure effective communication. At the conclusion of the project, new system documentation is ready immediately, preventing last-minute crises and omissions.

Key Terms

1. feasible
2. feasibility study
3. financial feasibility
4. cost/benefit analysis
5. capital investment
6. payback period
7. return on investment
8. operational feasibility
9. technical feasibility
10. schedule feasibility
11. human factors feasibility
12. feasibility report
13. project plan
14. working papers
15. 80-20 rule
16. application software package
17. layering
18. staffing plan
19. time reporting
20. status reporting
21. Gantt chart
22. project planning sheet
23. cumulative documentation
24. final documentation
25. interim documentation

Review/Discussion Questions

1. What is the purpose of a feasibility study?

2. Name the five types of feasibility considerations that should be taken into account, and give a brief explanation of each.

3. Before making a recommendation on whether to invest in a new system, what two measures of financial feasibility should be applied? Why?

4. Under what circumstances might a systems development project be terminated despite strong evidence of financial feasibility? When might a project be continued despite poor or uncertain financial feasibility? Explain.

5. Why is it important for a systems analyst to have a solid understanding of computer software and programming? How is this knowledge helpful in the early stages of systems development?

6. How would you describe the relationship between the project team and the steering committee? What is the role of each in the systems development process?

7. Name the three end products of the feasibility study activity, and explain why each is important.

8. How does the feasibility study relate to the initial investigation activity? How does it relate to the analysis and general design phase?

9. What is the 80-20 rule, and what is its importance in systems development?

10. What is the purpose of a status report, and what information should it contain?

11. What is a Gantt chart, and how can it help in project management?

12. What are the contents and purpose of the cumulative project file at this point in the life cycle?

6 THE PROCESS AND PRODUCTS OF ANALYSIS

LEARNING OBJECTIVES

On completing reading and other learning assignments for this chapter, you should be able to:

- [ ] Describe the process and the results of systems analysis and explain the role of systems analysts in the development of computer information systems.
- [ ] Explain the demands for and importance of interpersonal communication within the process of systems analysis.
- [ ] Describe system modeling procedures and documentation.
- [ ] Describe logical and physical models, their purposes, and the differences between these two types of models.
- [ ] Describe the contents and purposes of user specification and new system design specification documents.

THE GOAL OF ANALYSIS

Systems analysis is the key component of the first two phases of the systems development life cycle. In Phase 1: Investigation, systems analysis techniques help to build an understanding of existing systems, of the need that has brought about a request for change, and of the potential solutions to identified problems. In Phase 2: Analysis and General Design, systems analysis is used to further this understanding and to produce specifications for a new system that will meet user needs and requirements. The completion of these specifications is the central goal of systems analysis.

These new system specifications can be challenging to produce, in part because of the critical communication links involved. Systems analysis is, in large part, a communication process. The specifications for the new system must be understandable to the user, who must verify their accuracy and completeness. The same document must also be understandable to the designer, who must use it as a basis for an accurate, detailed design. Thus, the systems analyst is the key communication link between users, who generally have a business outlook, and designers, with their computer orientation and outlook.

The tools and processes introduced in this chapter and described further throughout the book are important techniques used in working toward accuracy, completeness, and effective communication during the analysis process.

Communication Alternatives

Communication, a key ingredient of systems analysis, is the act of imparting information that is understood by its intended receiver. In other words, communication has two parts: explanation and understanding. If either ingredient is missing, there is no communication. Explanation alone is not enough. The real challenge in communication lies in assuring that understanding takes place. The easier an analyst can make it for both users and designers of systems to understand each other, the better the newly developed system will be.

In fulfilling the role of communication link between user and designer, the analyst has some basic choices to make concerning the communication methods to be used:

- One widely used, time-honored method for communicating information about analysis and design of information systems is narrative description. Needs, data content, procedures, and design results are all described in words. When a large, complex system is involved, narrative descriptions can become extremely lengthy and hard to understand. System narratives that incorporate as many as eight or 10 volumes of text materials are not uncommon.

- As an alternative, narrative descriptions can be augmented with graphic presentation tools. That is, rather than writing about what is happening, the analyst constructs diagrams to show what is going on. The graphic symbols used are simple and easily understood. The result is that the documentation can be absorbed by users and designers in a fraction of the time that would be required to read through the equivalent narrative descriptions. At the same time, the possibility of errors because of misunderstandings or omissions is greatly reduced.

Accuracy and Completeness in Communication

The challenge in communicating system specifications lies in developing documentation that is both accurate and complete and also in transmitting its content from the user to the designer. Using words alone, achieving the necessary degree of accuracy and completeness can be extremely difficult. In some situations, it is virtually impossible.

To illustrate, consider the following short, accurate description of a procedure to be applied within a computer information system. The system processes billings for the Associated Grocers of America. AGA is a grocery warehouse operation selling to retailers—both AGA members and nonmembers. The following description involves AGA's discount policy:

> A minimum 5 percent discount applies for all purchases. If the retailer maintains an average monthly purchase volume of at least $100,000, a 15 percent discount applies, provided the retailer is an AGA member. When the retailer's purchase volume is under $100,000, the discount rate is 12 percent for AGA members and 7 percent for nonmembers. Retailers who are not AGA members, but who maintain a $100,000 monthly purchase volume, qualify for a 10 percent discount, unless the purchase totals less than $35,000.

Now, imagine yourself as the designer reading a few hundred, or even a thousand, pages of this kind of narrative. Even after a thorough reading, would you feel comfortable writing program specifications and coding if this was the only documentation you had to work with? Could you be sure that the explanations and documentation contained in these narratives were accurate and complete? Would you be able to maintain objectivity—an understanding of the major components of the system and their interrelationships—without becoming lost in the hundreds of pages of details? This book stresses a set of tools and an analysis process that can help assure understanding, as well as completeness and accuracy, of system requirements and specifications.

SYSTEMS MODELS

A primary method for representing and communicating systems information clearly is through the use of models. As described in Chapter 2, a model is a graphic representation of the system and the processing that takes place.

One modeling tool, introduced in Chapter 2 and used thoughout this book, is the data flow diagram. A data flow diagram provides a special way of looking at a computer information system, emphasizing the flow and transformation of data. The data flow modeling process and graphic techniques used in this book are well established and widely used. These methods have been popularlized by a number of writers and researchers, including Glenford Myers, Victor Weinberg, Thomas DeMarco, Chris Gane, Trish Sarson, and Edward Yourdon. Techniques for development of data flow diagrams are covered in Chapter 10. This chapter concentrates on the role of data flow diagrams in presenting and conveying information.

Context Diagram

Data flow diagrams can be constructed at several levels, each delving deeper into the content of the system. The first level of modeling is known as a *context diagram*. As the name suggests, it defines the context, or scope, of the system under study.

A context diagram for the existing water billing system in Central City is shown in Figure 6-1. Typically, this type of diagram might serve as a starting point in a review of existing procedures between a systems analyst and management of the city's water department.

The entire water billing system is represented by a single circle in the center of the context diagram. The diagram simply shows the flow of data and information between the system itself and the *external entities* with which it interacts. Note that the flow lines in this diagram are labeled to show the data content moving to and from the system. Data

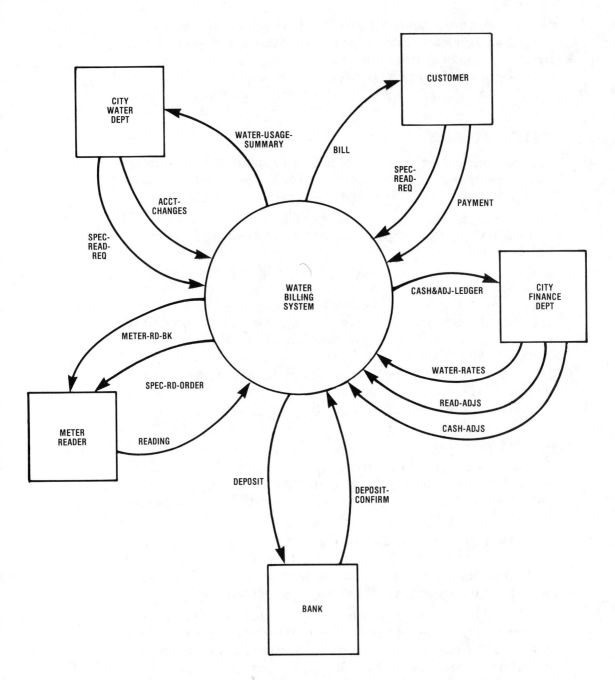

Figure 6-1. Context diagram for current Central City water billing system.

flows are always uniquely and specifically identified in data flow diagrams.

A context diagram delineates the scope of the system being analyzed or designed. Establishing the scope of the project is an important aspect of systems analysis. Early in any project, it is important to identify what is included in the system under study—and what is excluded.

The scope of a system is determined, in effect, by the data it receives and the information it produces. To illustrate, the context diagram in Figure 6-1 shows the flow of data between the system and the city finance department. The data flows relate to water billing matters only. Despite the fact that the water billing system is administratively housed in the finance department, there is no attempt to cover all of the procedures for financial accounting within the scope of this system. Even the accounting entries for water billing revenues are not included in the system.

The context diagram is a useful communication tool. It fits easily on a single sheet of paper. Information is conveyed in a way that can be understood by accountants and public officials on the one hand and by computer professionals on the other. All of the information is relevant and specific. Each party involved in the system can see what his or her organization or department provides to or receives from the system. This graphic communication vehicle is simple and comprehensible.

Diagram 0 (Zero)

The next step in modeling a system is to *partition* the central circle in the context diagram to show the major processes—perhaps subsystems—and the flow of data among them. This level of data flow diagram, shown in Figure 6-2, is known as *Diagram 0*. This diagram provides an overall perspective on the system, identifying only the main processing functions, data flows, external entities, and data storage points. This diagram—like all data flow diagrams—uses a limited number of symbols. The symbols used in this book are illustrated and identified in Figure 6-3.

The graphic nature of data flow diagrams is one of their major strengths. In effect, the four symbols shown in Figure 6-3 constitute a full, easily understood vocabulary. The meanings of these symbols, which can be learned in a matter of minutes, are used to establish and

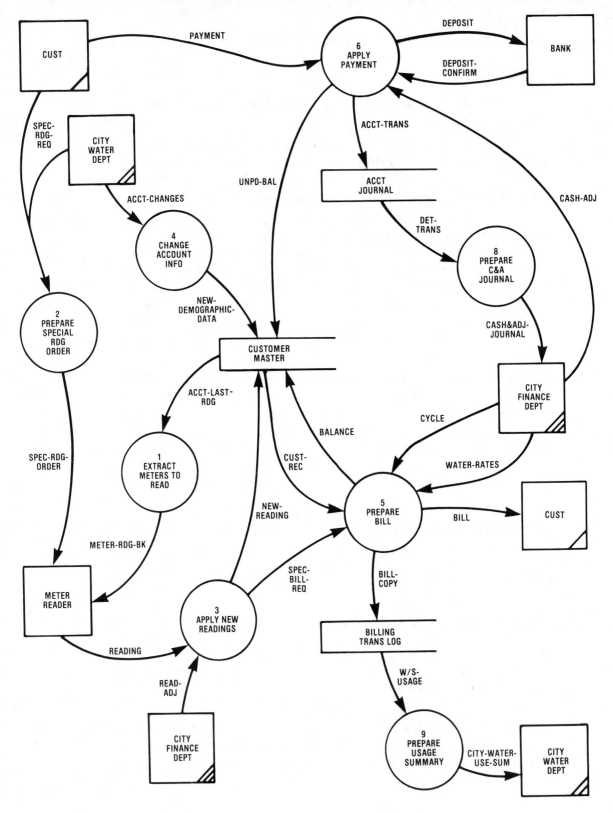

Figure 6-2. Diagram 0 for current Central City water billing system.

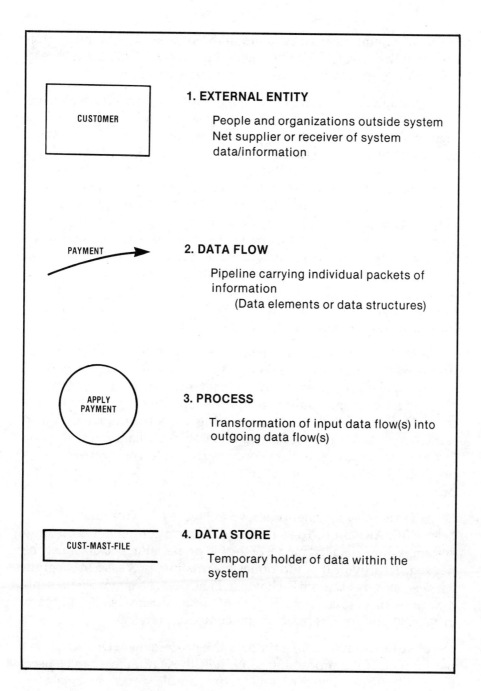

Figure 6-3. Data flow diagram components.

maintain communication throughout the systems development project. Even the least technically oriented user can quickly learn to read and follow presentations based on data flow diagrams.

Although the data flow diagram does not show processing controls, it can be interpreted in an orderly sequence. For example, the meter reader is given route assignments that include lists of customers prepared by the computer, as well as special reading orders. Within a utility operation, special reading orders might be required when a user is terminating service or questions the accuracy of a reading. The meter reader, then, goes into the field with a combination of a computer-prepared meter reading book and a series of special orders. The actual meter reading procedure is not part of the defined scope of the system. The meter reader returns readings to the system. The data from these new readings are applied against a customer master file, represented in the data flow diagram as a *data store*. By simply following the direction of the data flow arrows, it is possible to trace the movement and transformation of data through to the outputs.

Even though a Diagram 0 depicts the complete system, the description is still a long way from being detailed to the level needed for systems analysis and design. With a Diagram 0, however, the stage has been set for building additional information into the graphic presentation. Note that each of the processing steps is numbered. These numbers can be used to identify further data flow diagrams that, in effect, *explode,* or partition, the processing to whatever level of detail is needed. The numbers do not imply an order or sequencing of the processes.

For example, consider process 5 in Figure 6-2. This function is labeled PREPARE BILL. To analyze and design a computer information system, a more detailed model of the bill preparation will obviously be needed. To provide this additional information, process 5 in Diagram 0 is described by Diagram 5, shown in Figure 6-4. Diagram 5 represents a partitioning of process 5 in Diagram 0. Process 5 has been split apart, or partitioned, into its basic, major components.

Note the number convention for the processing in Diagram 5. As partitioning of the processing continues, these numbers can be used to identify further levels of detail. For example, process 5.2, labeled PRODUCE INCYCLE BILL, can be partitioned further into a set of more

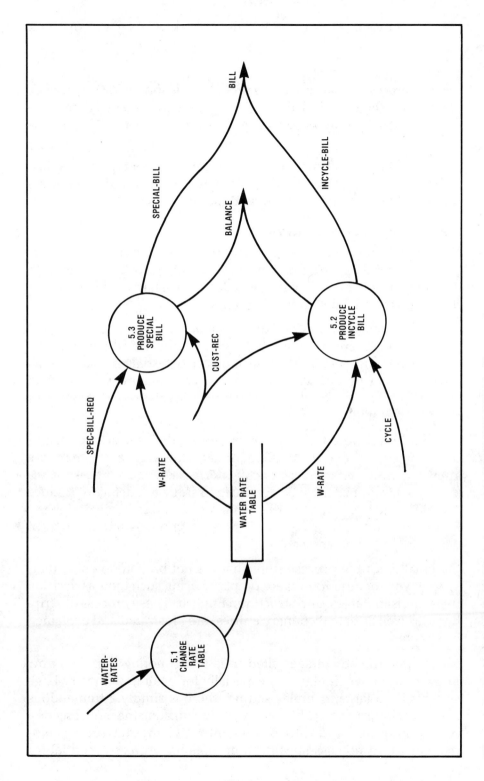

Figure 6-4. Diagram 5, a partitioning of process 5 (PREPARE BILL) in Diagram 0 (Figure 6-2) for current Central City water billing system.

detailed processes. Partitioning of process 5.2 is shown in Diagram 5.2, illustrated in Figure 6-5. This further detailing indicates all of the processing and data components that go into calculating a regular, incycle water bill.

This type of top-down, or hierarchical, partitioning of data flow diagrams can be continued to the point at which the resulting processes can be defined by brief process descriptions.

Supporting Documentation

Data flow diagrams, in effect, present a graphic model of processing, the storage of data, and the movement of data through a system. In building this model, the analyst uses descriptive names to identify the components of the data flow diagram.

For the data flow diagram to do its job, there must be additional, reference documents that clarify the meaning of all of the terms used to name the components. Thus, in addition to the data flow diagrams, the analyst must prepare a *data dictionary*. This contains the terms and their definitions, encompassing all of the data flows and data stores within the system.

In addition to a data dictionary, one other set of supporting documents is needed to supplement data flow diagrams. These are known as *process descriptions*. The principle is that each process *bubble* (circle) in Diagram 0 must be described in sufficient detail to produce complete understanding on the part of users and systems designers. Partitioning into lower level data flow diagrams is one method of describing these processes.

Finally, for the process steps that are not broken down further, special types of descriptions are prepared using such tools as decision trees, decision tables, and structured English. These process descriptions, as well as data dictionary entries, are illustrated and explained in Chapter 10.

Despite the advantages cited, it is worth noting that data flow diagrams do have limitations, especially for dealing with very large systems. In a large, complex setting, there is simply a tremendous amount of information to be communicated, making the modeling process complicated and difficult to control. Computerized system-modeling and process-specification tools have great potential for

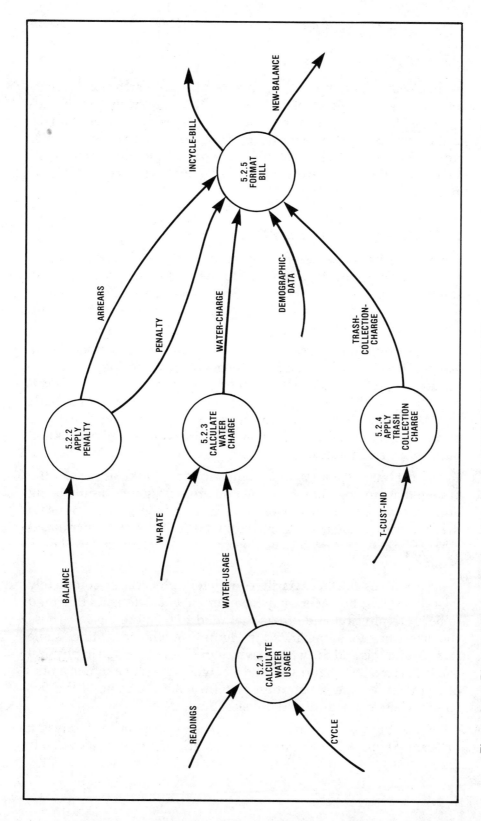

Figure 6-5. Diagram 5.2, a partitioning of process 5.2 (PREPARE INCYCLE BILL) in Diagram 5 (Figure 6-4) for current Central City water billing system.

dealing with such complex assignments. Major research and development efforts have been applied, for several years, to creating such computerized tools. These computerized techniques may lead to changes in the form and methods for developing models and specifications. However, the principles that apply are basic—and are effectively illustrated by the data flow diagrams and the analysis process presented in this book.

LOGICAL AND PHYSICAL MODELS

A model is a graphic representation of a system. Models using data flow diagrams represent the system in terms of data flows, processing shown in bubbles, and data stores. These modeling tools are applied to represent different aspects, or dimensions, of the system being analyzed or developed.

One dimension of a system that can be shown in a model is the essential business, or logical, processing. As used here, logical processing does not refer to detailed computer program logic. Rather, a *logical model* presents the data content and handling, regardless of methods used to provide them. Thus, the logical aspects of a system are those elements that are the same whether the work is done with pencils and paper or by a computer.

By contrast, a *physical model* tends to identify the aspects of the system that are dependent on how the processing is currently being done—the people who are involved in the processing, the forms used, the computerized processing, and so on. Logical models, then, concentrate on *what* the system does, while physical models stress *how* the job is done.

A model is not necessarily completely physical or completely logical. Models, however, may have certain characteristics that tend to be more physical and others that tend to be more logical. These characteristics are summarized in Figure 6-6, which identifies some traits of systems and the ways in which they are presented in physical and logical models. Figures 6-7 and 6-8, which present a simple model of a student course registration system, illustrate some of the differences between logical and physical models.

Notice the sequential nature of the processing in the more physical diagram, Figure 6-7. The processes to check prerequisites, available

MAJOR CHARACTERISTICS OF MODELS		
	Physical	**Logical**
Viewpoint	How processing is done	What the system does
Processes	Sequential	Often parallel
Names	Documents, people, forms	Underlying data and processes
Data flows	Excess (tramp) data	Only data used or produced by the process
Controls	Includes controls for crossing man-machine boundaries	Limited to essential business controls

Figure 6-6. Summary of key differences between physical and logical models.

seats, and student credit are presented in sequence. There is no organizational—or logical—rule that specifies this order. This diagram is merely a presentation of the way processing happens to be done currently. The more logical view, in Figure 6-8, shows these processes occurring in parallel. A model that shows processes occurring in parallel when there is no logical, or business, reason that the processes must occur in a specific sequence stresses what the system does and leaves flexibility for the designer to match the sequencing to the design approach to be used.

The names in the more physical diagram tend to refer to actual, physical objects and records while the names in the more logical diagram refer to the actual data, with no implication about physical packaging. Moreover, the data flows in the logical diagram transport only the data actually used or produced by the processes covered. By contrast, the entire course request is drawn through the sequence of processes in the physical diagram, with each process using only that part of the request that pertains to its operation. Again, the more logical diagram stresses what the system does and leaves flexibility for the

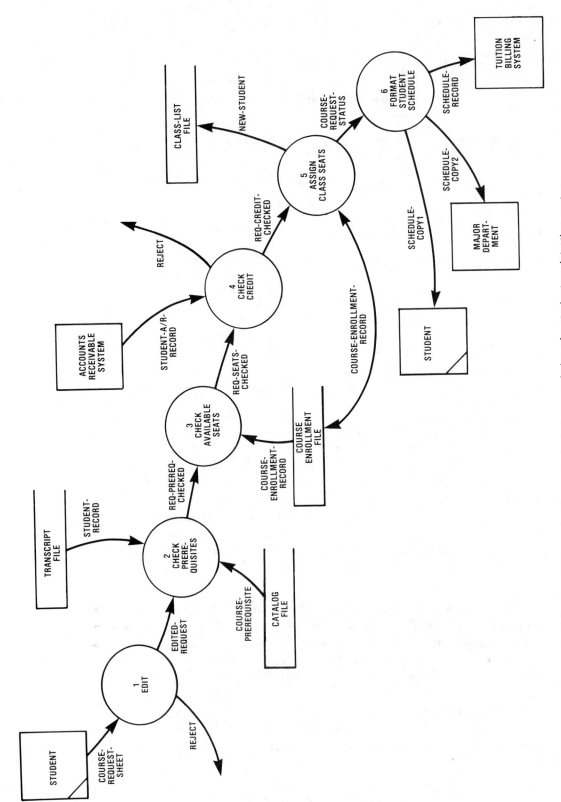

Figure 6-7. Data flow diagram that emphasizes physical characteristics of a student registration system.

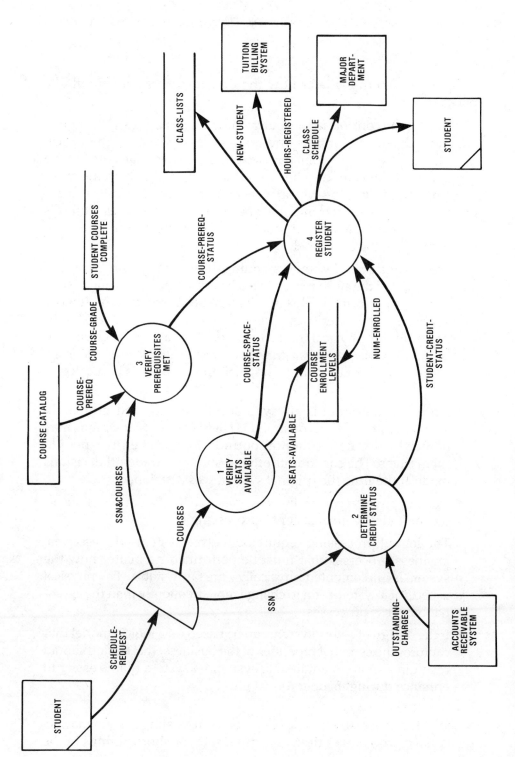

Figure 6-8. Data flow diagram that emphasizes logical characteristics of a student registration system.

designer to determine later how the data and processes should be packaged.

Finally, the controls in the logical diagram, processes 1 through 3, are critical business controls and are a necessary part of the logical model. The physical diagram has two other controls—the edit and the formatting of the student schedule—that pertain strictly to the man-machine boundary. If the system were implemented physically in a different way, these controls might not be necessary. Since these controls are not concerned with the essential rules of the business, they are not included in the logical model.

The starting point for understanding the existing system is to construct a model of the system based on a physical understanding of how processes are performed. This initial model will tend to exhibit more of the physical characteristics of data flow diagrams. The reason for moving from this physical model to a more logical one is simple, but crucial: *A logical model provides a firmer foundation on which to base the design of a new system.* The key points on which this concept is based are:

- An existing system is always bound, limited, and ultimately shaped by its physical constraints. These physical constraints may be hardware, departmental boundaries, or even the people themselves. The constraints often result from trade-off decisions made at the time the original system was developed.

- Existing physical constraints may result in inefficient—even incorrect or logically inconsistent—processing.

- The logical processing requirements of a system—the essential business processes that must be performed no matter how the system is implemented physically—are fairly stable. The physical aspects of a system tend to change more frequently than the essential business processes.

- If the design of a new system can be based on a logical model that captures the essential processes of the business, that design should result in a more maintainable system—a system that is easier to enhance during its operational life.

Much of the processing that takes place in an existing system may actually have grown over time to compensate for shortcomings in the physical system. It may not be at all essential to the business being con-ducted. As a dramatic example, consider an actual finding at a large government agency in Washington.

Analysts were studying a paperwork processing system throughout this large bureau to determine manpower and equipment needs of a major business data processing system. On the basis of a purely physical study, it was determined that the request from one of the departments to expand its personnel by 20 percent was probably justified.

As the next step in the project, however, the analysts converted this physical model into a logical one, and another group of analysts re-viewed the flow of data on a logical basis. This analysis revealed that the overworked department did not have to be expanded; in fact, it wasn't needed at all. It turned out that the functions of this department were redundant with operations being performed elsewhere. Under a strictly physical review, there was no way of telling what was hap-pening, logically, to the data. Under a logical review, physical duplica-tion came quickly to light.

Practice Assignment

A data flow diagram need not be exclusively physical or logical. Rather, diagrams often include both physical and logical characteristics. Consider the diagram in Figure 6-9, modeling a simplified catalog ordering process.

1. Which elements of this diagram are particularly logical?
2. Which elements of this diagram are particularly physical?
3. How might this diagram be modified to make it as logical as possible?

Certainly, a more detailed knowledge of the business is re-quired to be able to answer these questions fully. However, a great deal can be inferred from the diagram alone.

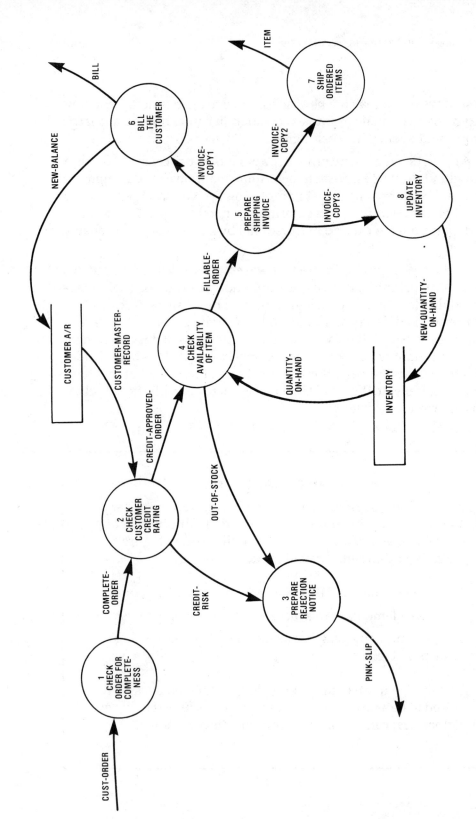

Figure 6-9. Simplified data flow diagram containing both physical and logical aspects of a catalog ordering process. (For use with exercise.)

THE ANALYSIS PROCESS

Within a CIS context, systems analysis is a process that involves repeating, or iterating, a series of process steps to build an understanding of current systems and procedures and to define new systems.

The questions, or challenges, faced by systems analysts include:

- How do you get started in systems analysis? How do you begin to understand the current system?

- How do you break through the current physical restrictions of a system to an understanding, or model, of the underlying business functions and transactions?

- How do you identify and evaluate potential alternatives for improved systems?

- How do you guide your work naturally from analysis of existing systems into design of new ones?

Functionally, systems analysis is a technique for building models by using a clearly defined process. The models created are represented through data flow diagrams and accompanying support documentation. The process that systems analysts follow involves three basic steps that are repeated, or iterated, as part of virtually every activity in the first half of the systems development life cycle. The skill of systems analysis lies in knowing how far to go—how much work is enough—at any given point. The basic idea is to start at a comprehensive level, then probe to increasing depths each time the process is applied.

Process Steps

The basic process of systems analysis itself involves three straightforward steps for the construction and use of models. These steps are:

1. Understand the existing system.

   - Construct a model of the physical system.
   - Derive a logical model from the physical model.

2. Identify changes in user requirements.

   - Document business processing (logical) requirements.
   - Document physical processing requirements.

3. Specify a new system solution.

- Create a logical model for the new system. Use the logical model of the existing system and the changes in processing (logical) requirements.

- Create a physical model for the new system. Use the logical model for the new system and the changes in physical requirements.

To illustrate how this systems analysis process is applied in the development of a new system, consider the series of illustrations beginning in Figure 6-10.

Figure 6-10 shows an abstract, idealized, data flow diagram. Assume that it represents a logical model of an existing computer information system. A systems analyst would use this type of data flow diagram to establish agreement about the essential business processing in an existing system. That is, user managers would be asked to review this type of data flow diagram and to agree that it does, in fact, represent what is happening now.

Once the model is *signed off,* or agreed to formally, the analyst modifies the existing model to reflect the changing business situation. The result is a marked up version of the data flow diagram of the existing logical system, as shown in Figure 6-11. In effect, the analyst has added a series of notations that will be used to update the model in designing a system that will meet new and future business needs.

As a next step, the analyst develops a data flow diagram that reflects these business changes. This produces a logical model of the new system, as shown in Figure 6-12. This logical model of the new system is then the basis for planning the new physical system, as shown in Figure 6-13.

Note that the designation of physical aspects of the new system has been accomplished by overlaying processing boundaries on the logical data flow diagram. The effect is to separate the model into physical components on the basis of equipment and timing. Portions of the data flow diagram in Figure 6-11 fall outside the human-machine or computer boundaries that have been drawn. The portions of the system external to these boundaries are the manual functions. The overall data flow diagram in Figure 6-11 illustrates that a system is an entity that includes both manual and computerized elements. Computer processing is only part of any computer information system.

These diagrams are oversimplified for purposes of illustration. An actual system would involve an entire set of diagrams modeling complex processing. Nonetheless, it is instructive to note the order in which the diagrams for the new computer information system have been derived. At the outset, the analyst begins with the physical model and builds an understanding of the logical system from that base. A logical model becomes the working base for the identification of requirements and the design of a new system. That is, the logical model of the existing system is updated and used as a basis for a logical model of the new system. In the final design of the new system, work progresses from the logical to the physical. Thus, the initial process of analysis has been reversed. At the outset, the transition was from physical to logical. As systems analysis proceeds, the progression is from logical to physical.

This basic three-step process of systems analysis is repeated, or iterated, throughout the first two phases of the systems development life cycle, becoming increasingly deeper at each iteration. By the time the full, iterated process has been completed, users have a graphic model of the new system as they will see it. This model then becomes the basis for understanding, and for agreement on how the new system should function.

Applying the Analysis Process

As the systems development life cycle progresses, this same basic process of analysis produces results that differ in form, but that are really deeper, more detailed views of what the new system will look like.

Initial investigation. The iteration process begins with the initial investigation activity. Based on a request for a new or improved system, the analysis process is used to probe for just enough information to establish the scope of the project. The analyst's documentation identifies some important aspects of what the new system will look like if it is developed. These include:

- Major outputs
- Major inputs
- Major processing functions
- Relationships to other computer information systems.

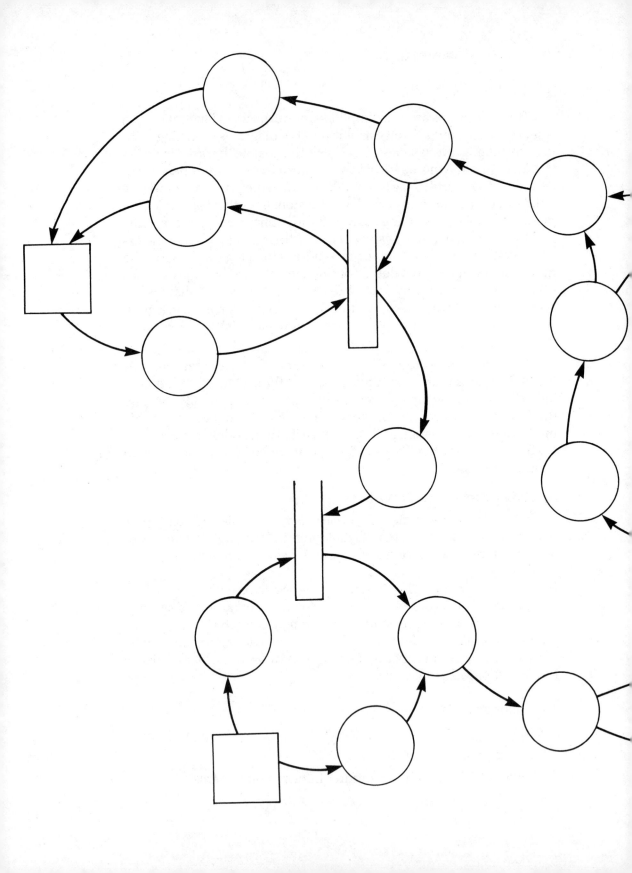

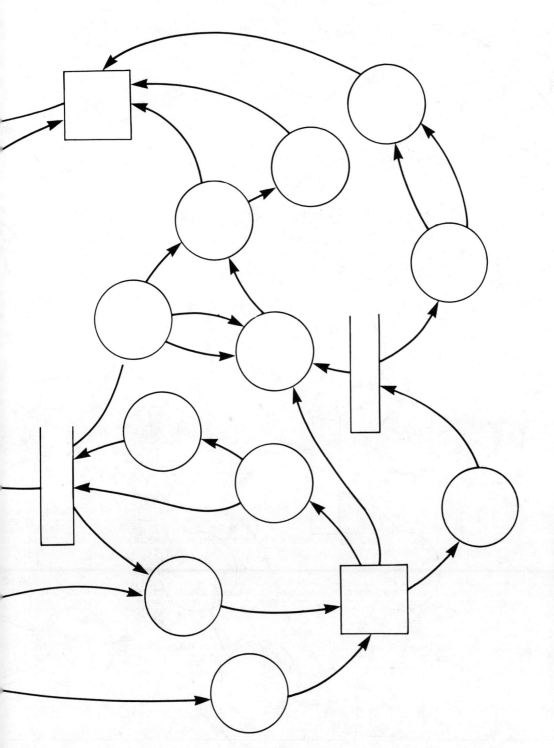

Figure 6-10. Logical model of an existing system.

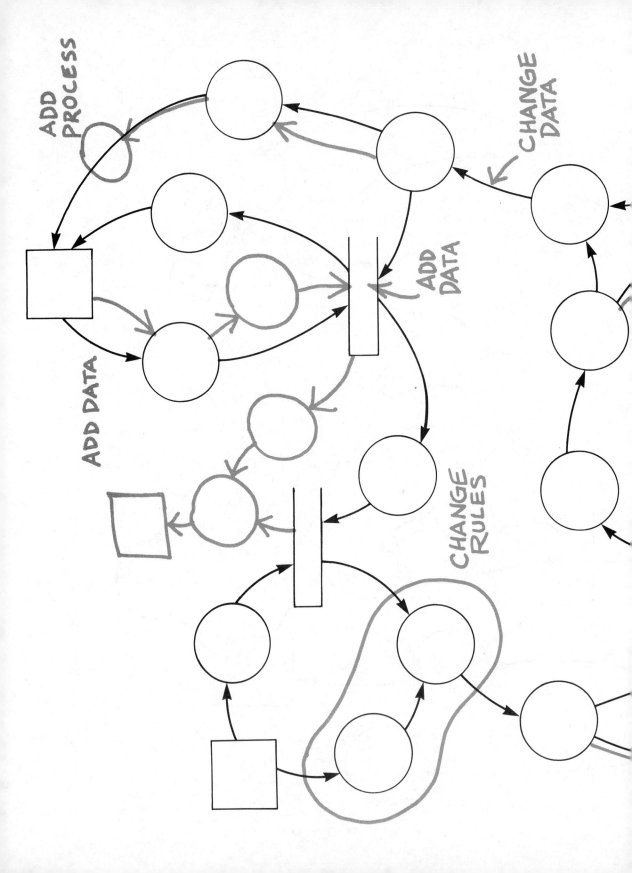

ADD PROCESS

CHANGE DATA

ADD DATA

ADD DATA

CHANGE RULES

ADD DATA

CHANGE RULES

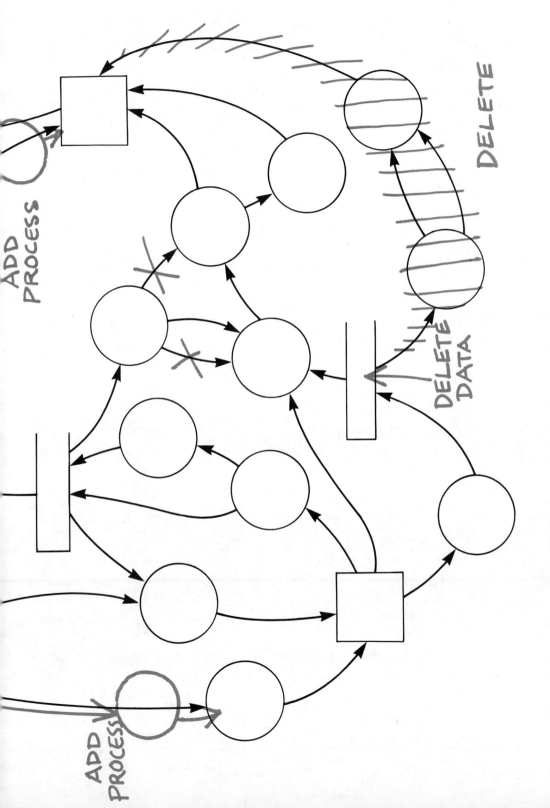

Figure 6-11. Logical model of an existing system—as modified by business requirements.

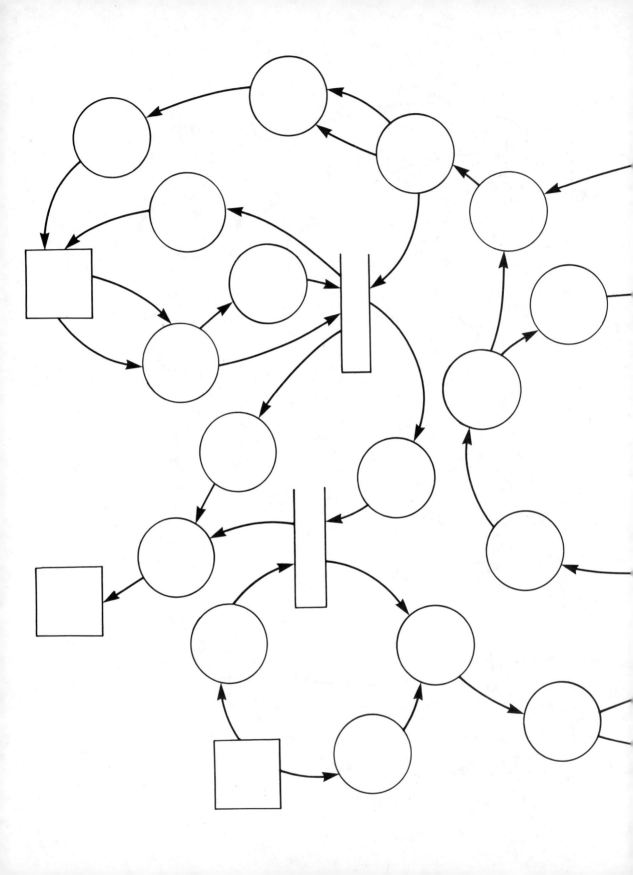

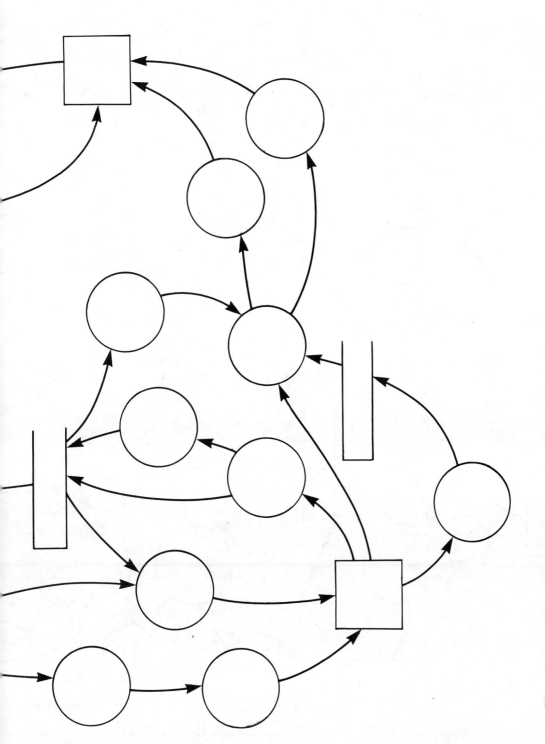

Figure 6-12. Logical model of new system—derived from logical model of existing system and new business requirements.

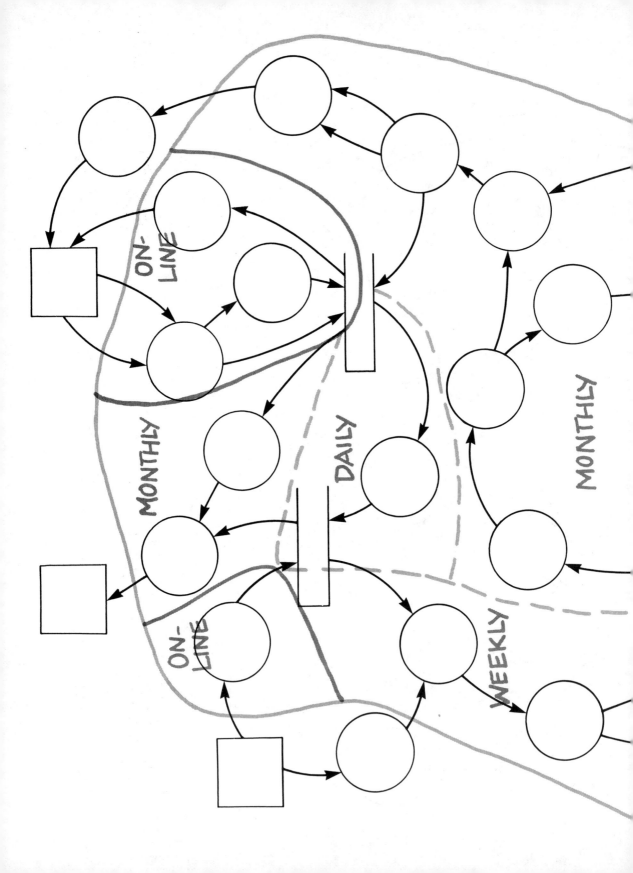

ON-LINE

MONTHLY

DAILY

MONTHLY

ON-LINE

WEEKLY

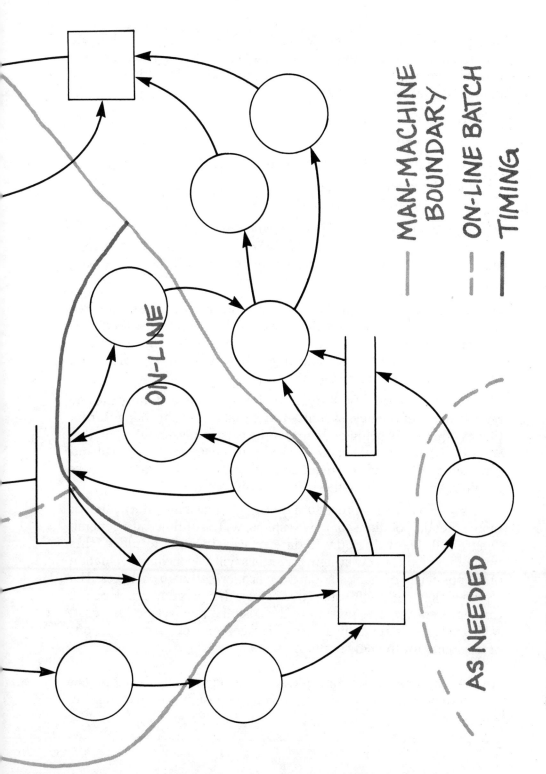

Figure 6-13. Physical model of new system—derived from logical model of new system and new physical (delivery-oriented) requirements.

MAN-MACHINE
BOUNDARY

ON-LINE BATCH

TIMING

Along with gathering this information, the analyst also builds an understanding of the objectives that lie behind the request for new system development. In a short time, the analyst should be able to answer several key questions:

- What do we have?
- What is needed?
- What could we deliver with the resources available to us?
- Does the project have sufficient potential to justify further investigation and development?

Modeling is minimal at this stage. During the initial investigation, the primary modeling result will probably be a context diagram. Depending on the size of the project, there may or may not be a need to take the time or to go to the effort necessary to develop a Diagram 0.

Feasibility study.   During the feasibility study activity, the same three steps in the analysis process produce a result drawn to greater detail. Typically, the analyst will develop a Diagram 0 for the current system and will make some attempt to distinguish between the logical and the physical aspects of the system.

Within the feasibility study, also, the analyst will identify the key requirements of the new system—those that represent changes from the way things are being done under the existing system. Within this context, the analyst will begin to distinguish between the logical and physical aspects of the new requirements—between the actual business requirements and the methods for delivering them.

As a final analysis procedure during the feasibility study, one or more potential solutions, or new systems, will be outlined at a general, Diagram 0, level. In today's data processing marketplace, this preliminary look at new system potentials will also include evaluation of the possibility of using standard application software packages. The reason for looking at software at this point is that program development can represent up to 50 percent of the cost of a new system. If a cost-saving solution is apparent at an early stage, this can affect projections of feasibility for the new system.

Analysis and general design phase.   As the systems development project moves into the analysis and general design phase, increasing levels of detail are added. By the time this phase of the project is completed, modeling techniques will have unfolded minute details about the new system and the steps that will be required for its implementation. This detailing will be established in a multiple series of layers of data flow diagrams and their accompanying documentation.

THE PRODUCTS OF ANALYSIS

Graphic models of computer information systems are, basically, analytic and communication tools. But they also provide an added bonus. Modeling techniques make it possible to identify the end products of systems analysis and design.

Within the overall systems development life cycle, there are two important end products of systems analysis. These are:

- User specification
- New system design specification.

User Specification

The *user specification* is the major end product of Activity 4: New System Requirements. This report presents a complete model of the new system as the user will see it—including enough detailing so that the user can stipulate that the system will meet all previously stated requirements and objectives. Within this report, processing is described by means of data flow diagrams. In addition, there are complete descriptions of system outputs, inputs, performance requirements, security and control requirements, design and implementation constraints, and any unresolved policy considerations that must be dealt with before the system can be implemented.

This type of predefined structure for documentation provides a built-in answer to the question of when systems analysis is complete. The project has a complete user specification when users are ready to ''buy'' the system on the basis of the evidence they see. At this point, the system has reached an important juncture—without overstepping the technical depth appropriate at each activity or phase. However, even though the user may have agreed to specifications from his or her perspective, many questions are still unanswered, left for the next product of systems analysis.

New System Design Specification

Questions that remain unanswered in the user specification include overall internal design for computer processing, file or database design, hardware specifications, and internal controls. These levels of detail are dealt with in the final product of the analysis and general design phase, the *new system design specification.*

In creating this final product, systems analysis is carried far enough so that:

- Final specifications are developed in sufficient detail to assure all dimensions of feasibility for the new system, including technical, financial, operational, scheduling, and human factors.
- The communication responsibility of systems analysis in bridging the gap between users and technicians is fulfilled.

The new system design specification is the major end product of Activity 5: New System Design. It is a comprehensive document, encompassing both the user specification and all additional specifications for hardware, software, procedures, and documentation needed for actual design and implementation of the new system. This specification can then be used as the basis for two key sign-off commitments. One is from the user, indicating that the system specified will meet the identified needs. The other is from the CIS design group, signifying that the system specified can and will be designed and implemented within the stipulated budget and schedule constraints.

Summary

The central goal of systems analysis is the development of specifications for a new system that meets user needs. These specifications are the primary results of systems analysis.

The analyst uses graphic representations known as models. One modeling tool, used to meet needs for communication between users and designers, is the data flow diagram. The most general level of modeling is the context diagram, which defines the scope of the system under study. This diagram shows the flow of data and information between the system and the external entities with which it interacts.

The next level of modeling is the Diagram 0, which shows the main processing functions, data flows, external entities, and data storage points.

Data flow diagrams use four basic symbols: external entity (rectangle), data flow (arrow), process (circle), and data store (open rectangle).

Within Diagram 0, each processing step is numbered. These numbers are then used to identify more detailed representations of each step in subsequent data flow diagrams. This process can be continued until each step is broken down into all of its component parts.

Supporting documentation for data flow diagrams includes a data dictionary and individual process descriptions.

A logical model is a general, overview presentation of what the system does, regardless of the methods used. A physical model focuses on how the processing actually takes place, in sequence. Included are people, forms, and manual or computerized processing. To understand an existing system, a systems analyst begins by building a physical model. The next step is to derive a logical model of the existing system and from that to develop a logical model of the new system. A logical model provides a firmer foundation on which to base the design of a new system, unhindered by the physical constraints and assumptions of the existing system. Finally, a physical model of the new system is created.

Systems analysis as a process involves three steps that are repeated, or iterated, at levels of increasing detail and deeper understanding. These steps are: 1) Understand the existing system. 2) Identify changes in user requirements. 3) Create a new system solution.

The principal end products of systems analysis are user specifications and new system design specifications.

A user specification presents a complete model of the new system as the user will see it. A new system design specification encompasses both the user specification and all additional specifications of hardware, software, procedures, and documentation needed for actual design and implementation of the new system.

Key Terms

1. context diagram
2. external entity
3. Diagram 0 (Zero)
4. data store
5. explode
6. data dictionary
7. process description
8. bubble
9. logical model
10. physical model
11. starving the process
12. sign off
13. user specification
14. new system design specification

Review/Discussion Questions

1. Why is communication so important in the work of systems analysis? With whom must the analyst communicate?

2. What are some of the advantages of graphic presentations over narrative descriptions in systems analysis work?

3. Describe the four basic symbols used in data flow diagrams, and explain how each is used.

4. What does a context diagram tell you about the system under study?

5. What is the relationship between a context diagram and a Diagram 0? What does Diagram 0 show?

6. How does Diagram 0 relate to all subsequent data flow diagrams? Explain.

7. In addition to data flow diagrams, what types of documentation does the systems analyst need to prepare? Why?

8. What is the difference between a physical model and a logical model? How do data flow diagrams reflect these differences?

9. Describe the use of logical and physical models in understanding the existing system, and in designing a new system.

10. Why is it important to develop a logical model of the existing system before starting to design a new system?

11. What is a user specification, and what is its function in systems development?

12. What is a new system design specification? How is it related to the user specification? What role does it play in the overall systems development life cycle?

7 COST/BENEFIT ANALYSIS

LEARNING OBJECTIVES

On completing reading and other learning assignments for this chapter, you should be able to:

- [ ] Describe the nature of cost/benefit analysis and explain its role in systems development.

- [ ] Describe the relationships among quality, value, and cost in the development of computer information systems and analyze the trade-offs involved.

- [ ] Identify the types of costs and benefits associated with computer information systems and give some examples of each.

- [ ] Distinguish between developmental and operational costs.

- [ ] Define payback period, present value, and net present value and explain their use in cost/benefit analysis.

- [ ] Evaluate a proposed system or compare alternative systems by discounting future costs and benefits to their present dollar values.

THE NATURE OF COST/BENEFIT ANALYSIS

Costs and benefits, within a systems development context, are offsetting factors that figure in many trade-off decisions. The trade-off is straightforward: Identifiable benefits must equal (or preferably exceed) identified costs.

Implicit in applying this trade-off is the need to determine both costs and benefits. Exact cost and benefit figures can be elusive to identify and difficult to compile.

Costs and benefits are studied and quantified separately, then compared with one another as a basis for decision making, during feasibility studies. Costs and benefits are identified for both existing and proposed replacement systems. The cost/benefit analysis is often a deciding factor in the selection of methods or equipment to be used in newly designed systems. Remember, it is a common practice to outline general specifications for two or more new systems during feasibility studies, leaving the decision about which one will be implemented for the second phase in the project life cycle.

Systems development projects encounter two types of costs and benefits:

- Tangible
- Intangible.

Tangible Costs

Tangible costs include the cost of new equipment, stated either in terms of purchase price or payout over the useful life of the system. Tangible costs are often converted to operational terms. For example, if a piece of equipment that costs $1 million will handle 10 million transactions over a five-year period, the tangible cost is 10 cents per transaction.

Human factors are also measured in terms of their tangible costs. Payroll costs associated with developing or using systems are examples of tangible costs.

Tangible Benefits

Tangible benefits are realized when a new system is projected to make money or save money for its organization. Computer information systems make money by producing outputs with measurable values. Tangible benefits through the saving of money can be realized by reducing the expense of delivering results from a system. For example, a change that required fewer personnel to operate a new system could lead to a reduction in tangible payroll costs.

Intangible Costs

Intangible costs are those that cannot be easily pinpointed in terms of money. However, intangible costs often are readily identifiable. For example, because of apprehensions about the changes in job content, employees may produce a lower level of output than initially expected. Recognition of this decreased output would then be noted as an intangible cost of converting from the old system to a new one.

In the early phases of conversion from an old system to a new one, error rates are likely to be higher than they will be once employees have overcome their initial fears or uncertainties. During these periods, disgruntled employees are likely to blame the computer (rather than themselves) for delays or incorrect outputs delivered to customers. A loss of customer confidence could result. This is a potentially dangerous intangible cost of the new system.

In dealing with intangible costs, the feasibility study will be more realistic if an attempt is made to assign dollar values. This is normally done through a combination of analysis and executive judgment. Often, there is an attempt to offset intangible costs with intangible benefits.

Intangible Benefits

Intangible benefits are those delivered, identifiable improvements for which values can be elusive. One of the challenges of systems analysis is to identify these benefits well enough to ascribe a value to them in offsetting the cost of a new system.

For example, assume that a particular department converts from the typing of source documents to the use of terminals. Employees report that their jobs are more pleasant since they have eliminated the noise of the typewriters. Further, the terminals provide a status symbol, giving the operators added respect among their peers.

In such an environment, employee turnover will probably decrease. If employees stay longer, the cost of training new employees is reduced. To calculate the value of these benefits, an estimate (based on experiences with similar systems) can be made of the decrease in turnover. Savings in the training of new employees can then be calculated and applied to the cost/benefit analysis.

Improvements in customer services are particularly important in evaluating intangible benefits. For example, suppose a supermarket switches from cash registers to terminals that read the universal product code tags on merchandise. Average checkout time for customers may be reduced by 30 seconds or even one minute. As a result, the time each customer spends waiting in line might be reduced by three or four minutes. These benefits are intangible, as compared with such benefits as the improvement of transaction volumes that results from installing the computer terminals. However, customer convenience—and the potential loyalty that results—is definitely a benefit to the business. A value can and should be placed on such benefits.

In cases of this type, as is the case with intangible costs, benefits often have to be valued judgmentally. A systems analyst might simply ask the merchandising manager of the supermarket chain, "How much is it worth to reduce customer waiting time by two minutes?" Very often, however, this type of open-ended question does not produce results. The manager will simply indicate that he or she doesn't know the value of reducing customer waiting time. A better approach is to ask for a judgment between specific alternatives. For example, if the manager is asked whether it is worth $10,000 or $20,000 to reduce customer waiting time, the response received has the effect of assigning a judgmental value to the intangible benefit. If the manager says that the improvement is worth $10,000 but not $20,000, he or she has estimated the value of that improvement to the business.

In studying feasibility, and also in other areas of systems analysis, cost/benefit decisions are ruled by the alternatives available. An ideal alternative may not exist. The ideal, in most instances, would be a clear-cut situation in which affordable costs produced identifiable benefits that far outweighed these costs. For example, suppose that purchasing three new computer terminals at $1,500 each would eliminate the need to hire an additional clerk at an annual salary of $10,000. The economic benefit in the first year can be readily set at $5,500, the difference between the two costs.

In practice, however, the equipment or methods available may not fit exactly into the identified requirements. For example, it may be that the only equipment available for a specific job is a large, expensive device that involves costs far greater than the identified benefits to be delivered. The trade-off, then, could lie in determining whether it is better to struggle on with existing methods or to spend more money than is currently justified in the expectation that processing volumes will grow to justify the expense.

The point is that systems analysts must learn to work with the tools and situations as they find them. Cost/benefit analysis, more often than not, involves trade-offs among less than ideal alternatives.

Within the context of the feasibility study, cost/benefit analysis focuses on the financial, or economic, aspects of proposed systems. This emphasis is limited by practical considerations, such as the availability of cost figures and the time constraints imposed on the study itself. A cost/benefit analysis represents just one dimension of a feasibility study. In the final analysis, projects are evaluated on all dimensions of feasibility, not solely on financial considerations.

VALUE/COST RELATIONSHIPS IN INFORMATION SYSTEMS

The end product of a computer information system is information, delivered to those who need it. That product has a value to the users of information—a value that depends on the quality of the information received. The quality of information, in turn, involves such factors as completeness, correctness, timeliness, accuracy, and availability. The extent to which these criteria are met determines the quality of the information, and hence its value to the user. It is this value that must be balanced against the cost of developing the system that will produce the information.

Relationship Between Quality and Value

The relationship between the quality of information and its value is illustrated in Figure 7-1. Generally speaking, as the quality of information increases, so does its value—but only up to a point. Eventually, the law of diminishing returns sets in and additional increases in quality produce only negligible increases in value.

For example, consider one dimension of quality—timeliness. In an on-line system, where response times are critical, the value of the information received increases as response times become shorter. Thus, information received in one second is more valuable than information delivered in five seconds, which is more valuable than information with a response time of 15 seconds. Possibly, information that took as long as one minute to deliver might be nearly worthless.

Beyond a certain level of quality, however, the value of timeliness decreases. Thus, as response time is reduced from one second to one-half second, to one-fourth second, the increase in value might be negligible.

In an airline reservation system, for example, it is vital that processing be completed and information be delivered while the customer is still standing at the counter. In this situation, a one-minute response time would have a very low information value. A one-second turnaround would have a high value, represented by a high point on the graph. However, if the response time could be reduced to one-tenth of a second, the value would not increase commensurately—at least not in this particular situation.

The same general relationship between increases in quality and increases in value applies to accuracy, completeness, and all other measures of information quality. Higher quality produces higher value. However, at some point—depending on the situation—the increases in value become insignificant.

Relationship Between Quality and Cost

Obviously, there are costs associated with increasing the quality of information. As a general rule, the quality of information increases with increasing costs, but at a declining rate. The nature of this relationship is illustrated in Figure 7-2.

Consider, once again, the on-line system described above. As greater efforts, and increasing costs, are applied to development of the system, the quality of information will increase. That is, increasing costs would be associated with improvements in response time from one second to one-half second, one-fourth second, and so on. A point would be reached, however, at which additional money, time, and effort would produce insignificant gains in quality. It might even be impossible to improve the quality of information regardless of how much money was poured into the project.

Value/Cost Trade-Offs

As the graphs in Figures 7-1 and 7-2 suggest, the quality of information received from a system is a trade-off between the cost of the system and the value of the information received for that cost. This cost/benefit relationship is illustrated in Figure 7-3, which combines the two earlier graphs.

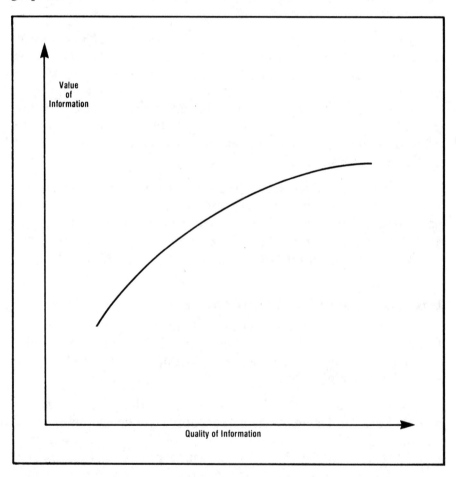

Figure 7-1.   General relationship between quality and value of information.

In a sense, the intersection of the two curves in Figure 7-3 represents the "best" system the organization can afford. That is, it represents the highest quality of information that can be justified financially. In fact, however, this is probably *not* the best or *optimum* solution from a business point of view. The reason can be seen most easily by studying the shape of the two curves.

The level of information quality at which this gap between the two curves is widest is—theoretically speaking—the optimum system solution. The value received is not as great as it would be at a higher level of quality. However, any increase in quality beyond this point would

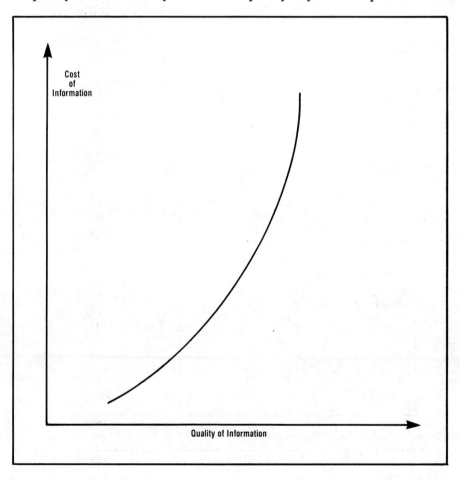

Figure 7-2. General relationship between cost and quality of information.

increase costs more than it would increase value. Therefore, this is known as the most *cost-effective* solution.

Whether the most cost-effective solution is, in fact, the best solution for any given organization or need is another question entirely—and is dependent on other considerations. Many other factors and trade-offs will enter into this decision. The point here is simply that the highest quality that could be achieved is not necessarily the best solution from an economic point of view. Another way of saying the same thing is the 80-20 rule, discussed earlier. Beyond a certain point, that

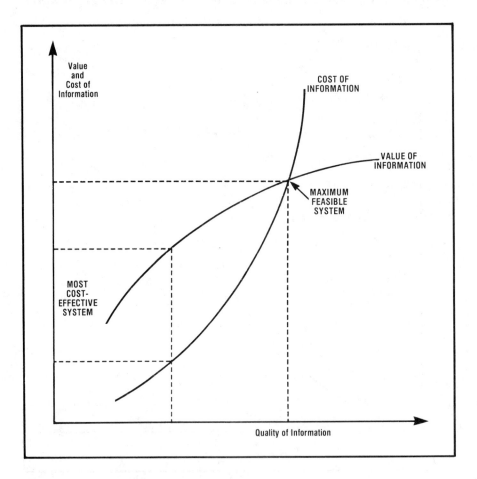

Figure 7-3.   The optimum, most cost-effective system produces the most favorable ratio of information value to information cost.

is, improvements in quality may not be worth the increased cost of achieving them.

EVALUATING COSTS AND BENEFITS

One of the major tasks of a systems analyst in connection with feasibility studies is to identify potential costs and benefits, and also to assign values to them. Trade-off decisions made as a result of these analyses are only as good as the reliability of the values assigned.

There are so many sources of costs and benefits—and so many methods for analyzing them—that it would be impossible to discuss all appropriate sources and categories of this type of information. Relevant areas of study will depend on the particular project under development. However, the discussions that follow cover some typical methods for identifying and evaluating costs and benefits. Developmental costs and benefits are distinguished from operating costs and benefits.

Evaluating Developmental Costs

Developmental costs are one-time expenses necessary to establish a new system and bring it into operation. The cost categories covered in the following discussion are typical:

Company personnel. The salaries of people assigned to a systems development project normally are a large percentage of developmental costs. These costs include salaries for the analysts, programmer/analysts, programmers, users assigned to the project, and any other internal people assigned to a project.

Cost estimates are based on the proportion of time these people devote to a project. The rate of error in estimates of such costs can become a major problem simply because the working times of staff members are difficult to project. The most appropriate method for projecting staff personnel costs is usually to base projections upon working-hour results of previous, similar projects. The time required for training project team members should also be factored into such estimates. If no experience-based figures are available, industry statistics or educated guesses may have to suffice.

Consultants.   In some cases, independent consultants may be engaged to work on projects. Cost figures on use of consultants are generally easy to estimate because fees are usually negotiated in advance. If the work of consultants is not contracted on a fixed-fee basis, it is still possible to secure relatively reliable estimates of the total time required to complete an engagement.

Developmental system.   On major, large-scale projects, it is common for analysts, designers, and programmers to use special developmental computer systems. Such systems, for example, can include programmer work stations through which a new system is developed and tested before it is put into operation. In other instances, computer terminals or other devices may be purchased specifically for use in systems development.

The point is that special hardware and software used in building a new system must be factored into the developmental costs. If these special systems are used for one project only, the total cost is absorbed. If recurring use is made of developmental systems, costs should be proportioned as equitably as possible.

Computer processing.   This is the cost of using a computer, particularly for the development of programs and for installation preparation for a new system. Billings for these computer services are typically generated by accounting routines within system software. Fee schedules for these services, along with experiences on past systems, can be used to estimate costs. During the initial feasibility study, it is possible to produce only rough estimates of these costs. As program development, software specifications, and file designs take shape, estimates can be refined continually.

Supplies.   This cost includes computer printout paper, coding forms, documentation forms, input/output media, and other nonreusable resources that support the development project. Again, cost estimates can be based reasonably on those experienced for other projects.

Overhead.   Overhead costs are administrative expenses associated with a project. Included are the costs of office space, record keeping, lighting, electricity, telephone service, and other utilities. Often, administrative expense is calculated as a percentage, say 15 percent, of the total of other developmental costs.

Start-up costs. The expenses of installing a new system and bringing it into use are often considered as part of developmental costs. Included could be the cost of new hardware and software, costs of converting from the old system to the new one (especially in the case of changing from manual to computer-maintained files), user training costs, system testing costs, and the costs of supplies and overhead necessary to convert to the new system. Estimates of these costs can be developed from comparisons of plans for the new system and the existing methods, with estimates made on the costs of implementing the new requirements.

Evaluating Developmental Benefits

Developmental benefits are those dollar amounts that represent revenues or savings that result from a systems development project. These savings occur one time.

One obvious source of revenue is the sale of obsolete equipment. Within a cost/benefit analysis, these revenues can be considered separately or may be factored into the cost of new equipment, especially if a trade-in is involved.

Another appropriate revenue category is the value of investment credits that lead to tax breaks. That is, part of the cost of equipment purchased may be usable as direct tax deductions. There may be other, similar incentives as well. For example, tax deductions may be available in recognition of personnel retraining that takes place as part of a systems development project.

Most of these types of benefits can be forecast accurately with the help of qualified tax accountants.

Evaluating Operating Costs

Operating costs recur over the life of a system. These are subdivided into *fixed costs*, which do not vary with activity or volume, and *variable costs*, which fluctuate to reflect activity or volume.

Determination of operating costs depends on whether expenses are incurred exclusively to meet the needs of a single system or whether the items are shared with other systems. If sharing takes place, costs should be prorated equitably among systems. In each case, however, a specific effort should be made to identify the operating costs in the categories identified below that apply to an individual system.

Hardware and software.   The major fixed-cost category will probably be hardware and software expenses. If the computer equipment is purchased outright, these costs are represented by the depreciation expense assigned by accountants. Otherwise, the cost of leasing the hardware and fees charged for the software become operating costs. Expenses associated with peripheral equipment to handle input, output, storage, and communications are also fixed costs. Total or prorated charges should be made to reflect purchase prices, lease payments, or depreciation expenses. Included also should be the ongoing costs of contracts for maintaining equipment and software.

Overhead.   Administrative expense is an ongoing, fixed cost. Most companies have established procedures for applying overhead costs to internal operations.

Personnel.   The largest category of variable costs is for personnel. People are required to operate and maintain information systems. Projections for such costs are readily available from references to historic data on system operation and maintenance.

Computer processing.   The new system will require CPU cycles, disk accesses, disk storage space, and other processing resources to support continuing operations. Estimates should be made on the frequency and volume of use projected for applications under development. These projections come from discussions with users on their needs. Initially, processing costs are estimated on the basis of resource usage by comparable systems. Later, estimates can be refined when the size and resource demands of the software portion of the new system are better known.

Supplies.   Operation of the new system will require forms, reports, input and output media, and other expendables. Volume and frequency estimates on usage can serve as the basis for projections of these variable costs.

Communications. If a projected system is to provide on-line service, there usually will be telephone or leased-line charges. These costs will vary with volume and the length of time over which connections are maintained. As with most variable costs, the accuracy of estimates for these expenses will depend on the accuracy with which demand and usage can be forecast. Representatives of communication utilities should be asked for estimates based on their experiences with other, similar installations.

Evaluating Operational Benefits

Operational benefits are favorable recurring results from day-to-day use of a system. These benefits usually will be in the form of ongoing cost reductions. These indirect contributions to revenues often serve as the primary justification for undertaking a systems development project.

Depending on the nature of the system, the operating benefits may be tangible and easily measured or intangible and difficult to identify.

An obvious example of a tangible benefit would be a reduction in staff size. Cost savings would be the differences in salaries paid before and after the implementation of the new system.

An intangible benefit might lie in a decision support system that improves management capabilities at forecasting sales or other business functions. In such cases, it can be more difficult to assign values to operational benefits.

Potential operational benefits that should be reviewed as part of a cost/benefit analysis are described below.

Reduced operating expenses. There are several potential sources of reduced operating costs. One would be reduction in paperwork. A system that introduced on-line terminals in place of printed forms and reports would generate savings equal to the difference between current costs of producing, distributing, and using these documents and the expenses associated with delivering the same information through the proposed methods.

Another cost saving might come from the streamlining of business processes. For example, assume that a current, nonautomated system makes it possible for a salesperson to process an average of 25 orders a day. If that person earns $25 per day, the cost of processing a single order averages $1. A new system might make it possible for the same person to process 50 orders daily. This would reduce the cost for processing an order to 50 cents. Since the salesperson's output has doubled, it could be possible to reduce staff by as much as 50 percent.

This, of course, is a simplified example. There will, however, be many opportunities to trace the impact of proposed new systems upon company operations. The principle remains the same: Compare current productivity and operational costs with those projected for the new system.

Improved cash flow.   Because automated systems can make it possible to collect money sooner and spend it later, an organization's cash position can represent important potential benefits.

One area that often delivers improved cash flow is accounts receivable. Computerized systems can make it possible to send notices sooner to customers with past-due accounts. Also, management reports can lead to earlier collection efforts. The earlier a company can collect its outstanding accounts, the smaller will be the outstanding balance of receivables. Early collection, in turn, means that the money is received and available sooner. This earlier availability of money can represent a significant operational benefit.

To illustrate, assume a company is carrying an average past-due amount of $300 for 100 accounts for which balances are outstanding for an average of 75 days. With closer, faster follow-up, assume that these accounts will be paid in 45 days. This means that the company will receive $30,000 one full month earlier than is done under an existing system. If accounts receivable are valued at 20 percent annually, this improvement delivers an operating benefit of almost $600 per month.

Another example of improved cash flow is inventory control. Computerized systems check on-hand inventory levels with the processing of each order. Because of this timeliness, inventory quantities can often be reduced. Reorder points for inventory items can be reset at lower levels because the system notifies management more promptly when new purchases should be made. Reduced also is the amount of money tied up in inventories.

Increased revenues.   Although increased revenues can be more difficult to estimate and measure than improved cash flow, this benefit area does have potential worth examining. For example, suppose better inventory information and faster order processing improved customer service. Because service was improved, the business might attract new customers, or might increase business volumes with existing customers.

Users of systems under development should be asked to estimate such potential operating benefits and to assign values to them.

Improved decision making.   Because of appropriateness and timeliness of information provided, managers may improve their effectiveness as decision makers. This capability has a definite—though hard to pinpoint—value to a company.

Managers may decline to attach specific dollar values to such capabilities. However, managers are in the best position within any given company to appreciate the potential of such support. A good strategy, therefore, may be to refrain from assigning specific dollar values to decision support services. Instead, note these capabilities as an adjunct to other economic factors dealt with under cost/benefit analyses and let managers apply their own weighting to these capabilities.

Within the framework and timing of a cost/benefit analysis, it will usually be impossible to provide all of the answers about financial impacts of a proposed system. There are simply too many information sources that are too vague at this stage of a project.

Nonetheless, a cost/benefit analysis will always be critical to a decision on whether a new system is to be developed. Therefore, a cost/benefit analysis is normally required on each system development project. The greater the skill an analyst brings to this activity, the more information he or she will produce—and the more believable the estimates will be. Further, the cost/benefit analysis offers a prime opportunity to make users and managers aware of the potential for a new system—and to maintain or build enthusiasm for and support of a systems development project.

ANALYZING COSTS AND BENEFITS

After costs and benefits have been identified and their values estimated, several methods can be used to support decisions on the financial feasibility of proposed systems. Recall that systems development projects are viewed as capital investments. That is, information systems are expected to produce revenues or to reduce costs as a basis for justifying their development. Thus, most of the methods used in evaluating general capital budgeting alternatives apply equally to systems development decisions. Although many methods are used, two common techniques are described below:

- Payback
- Net present value (NPV).

Payback Analysis

Payback analysis is a technique for determining the length of time it will take for a new system to generate cost savings great enough to cover its development, or investment, expense. The length of time required to "pay back" the original investment is known as the *payback period*. This time span can also be referred to simply as *payback*.

A straightforward method for determining payback is to apply the cost savings anticipated each year against outstanding investment costs. For example, assume a new system requires a one-time investment of $100,000 and is expected to producing savings of $20,000 a year in operating costs. The payback period is calculated by dividing the investment by the yearly returns:

$$\text{Payback} = \frac{\text{Investment}}{\text{Yearly savings}}$$

$$= \frac{\$100,000}{\$20,000}$$

$$= 5 \text{ years}$$

Therefore, it will take five years for the savings produced by the system to cover its development costs. This example is simpler than those encountered in actual systems development projects. It is more typical for the investment in a new system to be spread across two or more years. Also, operational savings usually vary from year to year over the life of a system.

To illustrate a more typical application of payback analysis, assume that a proposed system will require an initial investment of $153,500 in the current year and an additional $32,600 during the system's first year of operation. Projected operating costs will vary over the expected five-year life of the system, as shown in Figure 7-4.

In this example, annual cost savings are calculated by subtracting the operating costs of the proposed system from those of the current system. Payback is determined by applying the savings against any remaining development costs during each year and noting the year in which net savings are first produced.

As shown in Figure 7-5, cost savings are applied totally against development costs during each of the first three years. At the end of the third year, there is still an unrecovered balance. During the fourth year savings reach a level sufficient to cover the remaining development costs and to produce net returns above the cost of the system. In this example, payback occurs 4.8 years after the start of the development project.

Knowing the payback of a project may have little meaning in itself. It can be valuable to have standards or comparisons against which anticipated paybacks can be compared. Such comparisons make for meaningful evaluation of cost/benefit criteria.

In some instances, there will be general company guidelines covering decision rules on payback. For example, there may be a policy requiring payback within 4.5 years as a criterion for approving development of optional systems. (These rules, of course, will not necessarily apply in the case of mandatory new systems.) In such instances, the period incorporated within the policy statement becomes a threshold. If payback takes longer than the stated time and there are no other compelling reasons to develop the system, the proposal is rejected and the existing system is retained.

In other instances, payback analyses may serve as the basis for choosing between two or more alternatives for proposed new systems. Differing investment policies may apply. One alternative would be to allow users and systems personnel to choose any design they prefer

	Current Year	+1	+2	+3	+4	+5
NEW SYSTEM COSTS						
Developmental Costs:						
Personnel	85,000	18,000				
Hardware/software	40,000	5,000				
Training	18,000	9,000				
Supplies	2,500	600				
Overhead	8,000	–				
Total Development Costs	153,500	32,600				
Operating Costs:						
Personnel		37,500	26,000	16,750	17,500	18,300
Hardware/software		34,000	24,000	25,000	26,000	27,000
Supplies		3,200	3,400	3,600	3,800	4,000
Overhead		2,500	3,000	3,500	4,000	4,500
Total Operating Costs		77,200	56,400	48,850	51,300	53,800
CURRENT SYSTEM COSTS						
Personnel	50,000	52,500	54,125	58,000	61,520	64,000
Hardware/software	25,000	27,000	28,000	29,000	31,000	33,000
Supplies	10,000	12,000	15,000	18,000	20,000	24,000
Overhead	5,000	5,500	6,000	6,500	7,000	8,000
	90,000	97,000	103,125	111,500	119,520	129,000
NET OPERATING BENEFITS		19,800	46,725	62,650	68,220	75,200

Figure 7-4. Comparative cost figures for current and proposed system over useful life of proposed system.

	Current Year	+1	+2	+3	+4	+5
Operating Costs:						
Current System	–	97,000	103,125	111,500	119,520	129,000
Proposed System	–	77,200	56,400	48,500	51,300	53,800
Savings		19,800	46,725	62,650	68,220	75,200
Developmental Costs:						
Previous Years	–	153,500	166,300	119,575	56,925	(11,295)
Current Year	153,500	32,600				
Total	153,500	186,100	166,300	119,575	56,925	(11,295)
Applied Savings	–	19,800	46,725	62,650	68,220	75,200
Unrecovered Costs	153,500	166,300	119,575	56,925	(11,295)	(86,495)

$$\textbf{Payback} = 4 + \frac{56,925}{68,220} \text{ Years} = 4.8 \text{ years}$$

Figure 7-5. Payback analysis shows the number of years required to recover development costs.

as long as the threshold payback requirements are met. Other policies may mandate choice of the alternative with the shortest payback period.

The payback method was among the first techniques applied to cost/benefit analyses of information systems. This approach is still popular. Its attraction stems from the fact that it is easy to compute, has a straightforward interpretation, and is conceptually easy to understand. These same characteristics, however, can also limit the value of the payback method. Drawbacks include the fact that the payback method is applied to one opportunity at a time; it does not compare the profitability of multiple investment alternatives. Another limitation is that the payback method does not consider the time value of money.

The Time Value of Money

The value of money today is not the same as the future value of that same money. Consider a simple example. You deposit a dollar in a bank account today at 7 percent interest. One year from today, that same dollar has a value of $1.07. On this basis, the dollar would have a value of $1.07 if it were to be invested in a one-year program for development of an information system.

Now, consider the converse situation. You put your dollar bill away in a drawer instead of depositing it in a bank. When you remove the bill after a year, it is worth less than when you put it away. Inflation may have deprived your dollar bill of some of its purchasing power. At the very least, you have missed an opportunity for a 7 percent growth. Putting it another way, you have experienced the cost of a missed opportunity.

Thus, no matter what course you take in applying available funds, the value of money changes over time. Money has a time value that should be considered in guiding investment decisions.

The time value of money can be an important factor in considering investments in systems development projects. As a capital investment, a systems development project competes with other financial alternatives. For example, assume that a new system will cost $60,000 to develop and is expected to save $20,000 annually for a three-year anticipated life.

Is this a good investment as compared with 8 percent interest from depositing the same amount in a bank? At first glance, the investment in the system might seem sound. However, $60,000 left in a bank account at 8 percent for three years would grow to $75,583. On this basis, the investment is not cost effective—unless there are other pressing reasons for developing the system.

Because the value of money changes over time, it is desirable to establish some common denominator for comparison—a factor that makes it possible to state values in constant dollars. The most commonly used point of reference for comparing values over time is the present year. That is, future economic values are *discounted* backward in time at given rates to arrive at their *present values*. The discounted rates represent projected interest earnings, inflation losses, or other meaningful changes in the value of money over time.

	Discount Rate		
Year	8%	10%	12%
1	.926	.909	.893
2	.857	.826	.797
3	.794	.751	.712
4	.735	.683	.636
5	.681	.621	.567

Figure 7-6. A portion of a present-value table with factors for selected discount rates and years.

Any future value can be discounted to its *present value* through multiplication by a *present value factor (pvf)*. The appropriate factor is extracted from present value tables that provide discount coefficients for different discount rates for different time periods. A portion of a present value table is shown in Figure 7-6. This table covers discount rates of 8, 10, and 12 percent for periods of one through five years.

As an example of how a discount table is used, assume that a new system has a development cost of $19,000 and is expected to produce a savings of $20,000 at the end of one year. Assume also that the money could be invested in securities that will earn 10 percent interest over the same period. If the discounted value of the $20,000 savings is less than the required investment of $19,000, the project will not produce returns comparable to the investment in securities. In financial terms alone, the discounted value of $20,000 at 10 percent over one year represents the maximum amount that should be spent on the project.

The calculation of the present value is straightforward. The present value factor (.909) is found at the intersection of the 10 percent column and the one-year row of the table. The factor is then multiplied by the principal amount:

$$\$20,000 \times .909 = \$18,180$$

On financial grounds, therefore, the project would be rejected because the required investment of $19,000 is greater than the present value of $18,180. The company would do better to invest its $19,000 at 10 percent.

Net Present Value

Use of present values of future amounts recognizes the time value of money and equates different investment opportunities with differing costs, benefits, and discount rates. One important application of this concept is known as *net present value (NPV)*.

The net present value of an investment alternative is defined as the sum of the present values of the benefits, minus the sum of the present values of the investments. NPV, therefore, is measured in dollars. The value stated can be positive, zero, or negative. The algebraic sign of the value reflects the rate of return of the investment with respect to a given discount rate.

As an example, reconsider the costs and benefits given for the proposed system in Figure 7-5. This table is used earlier in the chapter to illustrate application of the payback technique. Development costs for the system are $153,500 in the current year, with an additional $32,600 to be spent during the first year of operation. Savings produced by the system are projected over five years as $19,800, $46,725, $62,650, $68,220, and $75,200.

The net-present-value technique discounts the costs and benefits to the present year, then compares them. Assuming that an alternative investment opportunity is available that can earn 10 percent, the calculations are shown in Figure 7-7.

The positive NPV ($13,803) indicates that the project's rate of return exceeds the 10 percent benchmark figure. Therefore, investment in the system will produce greater returns than the alternative investment—by a total value of $13,803. Note that the NPV calculation does not indicate the exact rate of return on the investment—only the dollar amount by which it exceeds the benchmark rate. A positive NPV indicates that the return on the project investment is greater than for the alternative considered. A zero NPV indicates equality between the system and the comparative investment. A negative NPV indicates that the projected return for the investment in a project is less than the comparative value. Note that a negative NPV does not mean that the project is unprofitable. It means only that the rate of return is less than the amount used for comparison.

NPV can also be used to compare two or more alternative proposed systems. For example, assume systems development project A costs $10,000 and will produce savings of $4,000 a year for five years. Project B costs $100,000 and returns savings of $30,000 a year for five years. Assuming a minimum acceptable rate of return of 12 percent, which project should be accepted? The net-present-value calculations are shown in Figure 7-8.

	Investment Costs			Savings		
	Investment Cost	10% Present Value Factor	Present Value of Investment	Savings	10% Present Value Factor	Present Value of Savings
Year 0	$153,500		$153,000			–
Year 1	32,600 ×	.909 =	29,633	$19,800 ×	.909 =	$ 17,998
Year 2				46,725 ×	.826 =	38,595
Year 3				62,650 ×	.751 =	47,050
Year 4				68,220 ×	.683 =	46,594
Year 5				75,200 ×	.621 =	46,699
			$183,133			$196,936

NPV = $196,936 − $185,133

    = $13,803

Figure 7-7. Net-present-value analysis equates present values of development costs and returns from investment in development.

	Project A					Project B			
	Investment	Returns	12% pvf.	Present Value of Returns		Investment	Returns	12% pvf.	Present Value of Returns
Year 0	$10,000		1.000		Year 0	$100,000		1.000	
Year 1		$4,000 ×	.893 =	$ 3,572	Year 1		$30,000 ×	.893 =	$ 26,790
Year 2		4,000 ×	.797 =	3,188	Year 2		30,000 ×	.797 =	23,910
Year 3		4,000 ×	.712 =	2,844	Year 3		30,000 ×	.712 =	21,360
Year 4		4,000 ×	.636 =	2,544	Year 4		30,000 ×	.636 =	19,080
Year 5		4,000 ×	.567 =	2,268	Year 5		30,000 ×	.567 =	17,010
	$10,000			$14,416		$100,000			$108,150

NPV = $14,416 − $10,000 = $4,416   NPV = $108,150 − $100,000 = $8,150

Figure 7-8. Net-present-value calculations for alternate projects.

Project A	Project B
NPV Coefficient $= \dfrac{\text{Net-present-value}}{\text{Investment}}$	NPV Coefficient $= \dfrac{\text{Net-present-value}}{\text{Investment}}$
$= \dfrac{\$4,416}{\$10,000}$	$= \dfrac{\$8,150}{\$100,000}$
$= .44$	$= .08$

Figure 7-9. Calculations of net-present-value coefficients for two projects.

The net present values of both projects are positive, indicating that the returns on both are above the minimum required rate of return of 12 percent. Thus, both projects qualify. To determine which is best, the returns must be related to the dollar investments involved. This is done by determining the *net-present-value coefficient* for each project. The NPV coefficient is the ratio between the net-present-value and the amount of the investment. The coefficient becomes a percentage figure that can be used to compare projects. Calculations of the coefficients for the two projects are presented in Figure 7-9.

The results indicate that project A has a higher return on its initial investment than project B. Although the coefficients do not represent the actual percentage rate of return for the projects, they provide a basis for comparison that recognizes the investment costs as well as the returns.

Summary

Costs and benefits are trade-offs used in deciding whether to proceed with a particular systems development project or in deciding which of two or more systems to implement.

In evaluating costs and benefits, the quality of information produced by a system has a bearing on the value of that information. Generally speaking, as the quality of information increases, so does its value. Beyond a certain level of quality, however, the value of the information received increases at a decreasing rate. Also as a general rule, the higher the quality of information desired, the higher will be the cost of developing a system to produce that level of quality.

Tangible costs and tangible benefits are those that can be measured readily in terms of money. Intangible costs and benefits are just as real, but it is harder to assign them a direct dollar value.

Developmental costs are the costs associated with establishing a new system and bringing it into use. These include the costs of new equipment, software packages, and facilities expansion, as well as the time of systems analysts and others involved in development and implementation of the new system. Developmental costs are one-time-only capital investments. They are considered assets of the company and are depreciated over the anticipated useful life of the system.

Developmental benefits are the income items realized as a result of a decision to implement a new system. Included are the sale of equipment that is no longer needed and other revenues that may result from the project itself.

Operational costs are the costs associated with using a system. These are the ongoing costs of doing business. The existing system has operational costs that need to be compared with those of any new system(s) under consideration. This comparison leads to identification of operational benefits for the new system. The operational benefits, in turn, are the basis for deciding whether it will be profitable to proceed with development of a system.

Payback analysis is a method for determining how long it will take for the new system to generate operational cost savings great enough to cover its developmental costs. A straightforward technique for determining the payback period of any new system is simply to apply the cost savings anticipated each year against any remaining investment cost.

Other methods for evaluating proposed systems consider the value of money over the period of investment and also provide a basis for comparison of multiple system development opportunities.

In regarding a new systems development project as a capital investment, it is a good practice to consider the time value of money. That is, money has earning power that should be considered in evaluating investments. Techniques are available to discount projected savings from a new system back to their present value. These present value figures can then be compared with investment requirements to develop new systems.

Discounted values are used in determining the net present value (NPV) of a project investment. The NPV system can be used to compare systems development results with other investment opportunities. Total discounted costs of development are subtracted from the total discounted amounts for projected returns. The result is a figure that is positive, zero, or negative. A positive figure indicates a more profitable return than the other investment opportunity; zero indicates a situation in which the two provide the same rate of return; and a negative result means that the return from the proposed system is not as good as the investment on which the present value factor is based. The method can also compare alternative systems being considered for development.

Key Terms

1. cost	11. operational benefit
2. benefit	12. payback analysis
3. optimum	13. payback period
4. cost-effective	14. payback
5. tangible cost	15. time value
6. tangible benefit	16. discount
7. intangible cost	17. present value
8. intangible benefit	18. present value factor (pvf)
9. fixed costs	19. net present value (NPV)
10. variable costs	

Review/Discussion Questions

1. What is cost/benefit analysis, and how is it used in systems development?

2. What is meant by the quality of information? What are some of the considerations involved?

3. Describe the general relationship between the quality of information and its value to the user. Give an example, using some measure of quality other than timeliness.

4. What is the nature of the relationship between quality and cost? Why do you suppose this is true?

5. What is meant by cost-effectiveness? How does this concept enter into systems development decisions?

6. Why might a project team recommend development of an "inferior" over a "superior" system, in terms of accuracy level? Think of a situation in which this type of recommendation might be appropriate.

7. How might the so-called 80-20 rule be applied to the trade-offs between cost and value?

8. Give one or more examples of: a tangible cost; an intangible cost; a tangible benefit; an intangible benefit.

9. Explain the difference between developmental costs and operational costs, and give some examples of each.

10. What is meant by a system's payback period? How might this concept be used in making a systems development decision?

11. Why is it necessary to discount all future costs and benefits to their present dollar values?

12. How would you calculate the net present value of an investment in a proposed new system?

Practice Assignments

1. Payback analysis is to be applied to a systems development project to determine the number of years required to recover investment costs. The projected costs and benefits are given in the table in Figure 7-10. Determine the payback period.

2. A company has an established policy that all investments should earn a return of at least 8 percent to be considered as acceptable funding alternatives. Given the projected costs and benefits for a proposed system shown in Figure 7-11, determine whether the project qualifies. Use the present value factors given in Figure 7-6 in making this determination.

3. Two systems development projects are being considered for funding. Project A has a development cost of $90,000 and will return savings of $40,000 a year over three years. Project B has a development cost of $150,000 and would return $55,000 a year over four years. If company policy requires a minimum return of 10 percent annually, should the projects be considered for development? If so, which one should be selected?

		System Costs (000)			
	Current Year	+1	+2	+3	+4
Operating Costs:					
Current System	–	$57	$65	$70	$80
Proposed System	–	40	30	20	20
Development Costs	$100	20	5	5	

Figure 7-10. Projected operating and development costs for use in Practice Assignment 1.

	Current Year	System Costs +1	+2	+3
Operating Costs:				
Current System	–	$50,000	$60,000	$70,000
Proposed System	–	20,000	20,000	20,000
Development Costs	$75,000	30,000		

Figure 7-11. Projected operating and development costs for use in Practice Assignment 2.

8 COMMUNICATION

LEARNING OBJECTIVES

On completing reading and other learning assignments for this chapter, you should be able to:

- [ ] Explain the importance of communication in a systems development project.

- [ ] State the basic principles of audience identification and effective communication.

- [ ] Identify the primary interests and the major information needs of different groups involved in the systems development process.

- [ ] Use the five basic steps in problem solving as a basis for management-type presentations on information systems.

- [ ] Describe a walkthrough, including personnel, procedures, and end products, and explain its role in systems development.

- [ ] List and describe briefly the steps involved in preparing a written report or an oral presentation.

- [ ] Explain the purpose and organization of a management summary.

- [ ] State the principles involved in creating an effective procedures manual.

- [ ] Explain the purpose of a training manual.

THE NEED

A CIS project enlists participation of a broad range of individuals, including multiple levels of management, a wide range of user personnel, and an equally wide range of CIS professionals. These people have different backgrounds. They come from different disciplines. They may speak virtually different languages and use widely varying jargons.

A CIS project may be so extensive, in terms of the number of people involved and the elapsed time required, that all of the people who work on a project may not even get the chance to meet one another. In effect, a group of total strangers may be asked to produce a coordinated, integrated, responsive system. To pull all of these diverse people and interests together, a CIS project needs effective communication programs directed to the specific information requirements of all involved parties. Identifying some of these people may help to illustrate the problem:

- Users participate in a project because they have business problems to solve. They may have little or no knowledge of computers or of the process involved in developing information systems. But users need to understand the process of systems development at least enough to appreciate the application of this process to their own requirements.

- Computer professionals, including systems analysts, programmers, and technical support personnel, may be knowledgeable about systems development but have limited knowledge of how the business functions. They need to gain an understanding of organizational objectives and business functions, as well as of the specific problems they are being asked to solve.

- Computer professionals must also be able to communicate meaningfully with each other. In particular, systems analysts must be able to present information so that designers and programmers can work quickly and effectively and so that technical support personnel will understand hardware and systems software requirements.

- Top level managers, including members of the CIS steering committee, need to look at a project in terms of the importance to the business objectives to be met and also in terms of the investments that must be made and the projected returns on these investments.

- All parties associated with a systems development project must gain an understanding of top level corporate policies and guidelines that apply to their efforts.

Although communication needs are diverse, responsibilities are clear. The project leader must create a communication structure that delivers information people need to do their jobs. Systems analysts are at the hub of this communication network. They are positioned as a vital communication link between users on the one hand and designers, programmers, and technical support staff on the other. Because of their role, systems analysts must be aware of the communication needs of all the people with whom they deal.

IDENTIFYING AUDIENCES

A key responsibility of the systems analyst in any systems development project is to identify the audiences to whom messages must be communicated—as well as the information needs of these audiences. If communication is to be effective, messages must be shaped to meet the specific information needs of selected individual persons or groups. This principle of audience identification is illustrated in the case of the water billing system. Consider the separate audiences interested in this project and the individuality of their needs:

- Management of the city administration wants to know about the opportunity to realize economies by sharing expenses with the sanitary district.

- Management of the water department is motivated by an interest in maintaining support for their own customer billing operations. They need assurances that service will not be interrupted or degraded through the cooperative effort. They really don't want to learn too much about how they can help the sanitary district.

- Management at the sanitary district is under pressure. They are doing something they really don't want to do and probably don't believe in. They need to comply with the federal ruling—and they want to do so as easily, inexpensively, and painlessly as possible. They probably have little interest in the computer methodology that will be applied on their behalf. Rather, their concerns are likely to center around cash flows and the meeting of their own budget commitments.

- The CIS director for the city is, in effect, being forced to go through an equipment and possibly a software conversion that was not planned or even anticipated. The concern here may be to get as much technical enhancement as possible from this effort, while maintaining the quality of service to current users.

- Systems analysts responsible for developing the new system will find themselves trying to be many things to many people. They have direct responsibility for helping each of these individuals and groups to understand the total picture well enough to cooperate with the others. At the same time, they must be realistic enough to recognize that each of the participants will place his or her own needs ahead of those of the others.

- Designers, programmers, and technical support personnel must be sure that they understand the specifications for their work. They must also understand how the products they will produce will meet the needs of their diverse audiences.

Communication needs of individual audiences are easy to recognize, once the matter is given some thought. The point to be made here is that the needs of the audience must determine the content of the message. All effective communication is, first and foremost, *to* an audience. The content of messages delivered *about* a subject must be tailored to the audience that is to receive it.

The principles involved are logical and straightforward: Know your audience; understand their interests or motivation, as well as their information needs; then shape your message to meet those needs. Following this simple approach will result in more efficient and more effective communication in any systems development project.

The communication activites of systems development projects fall into three broad categories:

- Problem solving work sessions
- Technical reviews (walkthroughs)
- Reports (written and oral presentations).

PROBLEM SOLVING SESSIONS

Systems analysis is problem solving. A computer information system solves a business problem. This is a basic definition of why systems are developed and what they do. In practice, the overall problem being solved consists of scores, probably hundreds, of smaller subproblems. Members of the project team, particularly systems analysts and user managers, will typically address one or more of these problems during each working day.

The main requirement in dealing with and defining potential solutions for problems lies in being objective. Problem solvers should avoid being drawn into the details or personal frustrations of information system problems. In looking at a problem objectively, the analyst can separate symptoms from fundamental causes, moving logically toward identifying alternatives, or logical cures.

Objectivity will also save time. An objective problem solver will not become swamped in irrelevant details that prevent identifying solutions.

Objectivity in problem solving can be assured by following a relatively simple process:

- State the problem clearly, separating large problems into individual, smaller ones.

- Analyze the problem for its probable cause.

- Identify alternatives for eliminating the cause.

- Consider the consequences of these alternatives.

- Choose the best alternative.

This problem solving model is simple and direct. The best way to apply it is simply to remember the steps, then follow them when problem solving or decision making situations arise. To illustrate how this model works, consider a situation that arose in developing the water billing system on which the example in this book is based.

The city finance department presented this problem: The level of customer complaints is too high. The situation was studied by a systems analyst, a clerk in the city finance office who handled customer payments, and a service representative from the water department. As the first step in the process, the initial statement of the problem was accepted; the group set out to deal with the problem of excessively high levels of customer complaints.

As the process continued into its second step, the clerk in the finance office was asked about the basis, or cause, for typical customer complaints. It turned out that complaints reached a peak after each billing cycle. Fortunately, the clerk had kept a log of the complaints. Copies of the customer bills associated with the complaints were made and studied. In reality, it turned out that the volume of complaints was not very high at all. On the highest day logged, there were 12 complaints. However, these 12 complaints took a total of slightly more than four hours to process. Total complaints averaged less than 100 per month—not an excessive number at all in a system serving 20,000 customers.

Analysis then focused on why it took so unreasonably long to handle what seemed like relatively simple complaints. The problem was that the clerk in the finance office did not have convenient information access. For each complaint, it was necessary to wade through at least two extensive printouts. These were transaction logs for the billing operation and also for the meter reading inputs and associated calculations. In between, there were inevitable phone calls, interruptions to accept payments for other bills, and so on. Thus, the extensive reference work could never be completed in a single operation. During interruptions, other people would refer to the documents, causing the clerk to lose track of where the reference stood.

Based on analysis of the cause, it became apparent that the original statement was not an accurate description of the problem. So, as part of the analysis step, the problem was restated: Find a better way to handle customer inquiries. With this new orientation, the process was ready to move forward into its third step.

To find alternative problem solutions, project team members should think as creatively as possible. Alternatives offered as possible solutions should not be restricted to capabilities of current systems or even to technologies that have been discussed. For example, in the water billing situation, one possibility might have been simply to take customer names and complaint descriptions, with a promise to call back after the information had been found. The reference functions could then have been handled at slack times or possibly after hours. Other alternatives might have been on-line file inquiry, inclusion of more information on the customer bills to eliminate inquiries, preparation of simple, consolidated reports arranged alphabetically by billing cycle, and other information sources or references.

A significant feature of the problem solving process is that solution alternatives are generated initially without consideration of their consequences. Consideration of the consequences of each alternative as it is listed introduces inhibitions. Emphasis will be on acceptance or rejection without full consideration. Concentration of participants is interrupted, and creativity is diminished.

At the next step, when consequences are considered, the job should be done thoroughly. For each alternative, both advantages and disadvantages should be identified. A scenario should be played out under which it is assumed that the solution has been implemented. The projected system solution should then be compared with current methods to identify possible improvements or new problems. Consideration of consequences, in effect, makes it possible to model the results of potential solutions before time and money are expended to implement them.

In the water billing situation, the potentially workable alternatives were narrowed down rapidly to a choice between on-line inquiry and the production of special, consolidated reports with customer account information spanning several months. It was recognized that file content lay at the heart of the inquiry processing problem. Thus, emphasis was placed on studying account information needs. Based on this study, it was determined that clerks in the finance office should have a six-month history available for each customer. This history, it was decided, should include meter reading information, usage data, and a billing/payment history. The contents of this record became the focal point of the study as analysts realized that the same information would be needed whether it were delivered in a printed report or on a display screen.

The choice of which alternative to implement was relatively easy to make, in the end, on the basis of cost/benefit analyses. The point is that this process led to identification of a clear-cut need that could be reported to management in easily understood terms. There was no need to involve managers, or even other members of the team, in the details of how the finance clerk looked up account information. Rather, the problem was identified, its cause was pinpointed, and logical alternatives were made available for decision making by managerial and technical personnel.

TECHNICAL REVIEWS (WALKTHROUGHS)

A *walkthrough* is a quality review applied to such systems development products as data flow diagrams, program structure charts, pseudocode listings, collections of proposed input documents, collections of proposed output documents, test plans, and others.

A walkthrough of a systems development product can be compared to a quality inspection of a manufactured product. At manufacturing plants, there are points at which inspectors review all of the work done in a given department or set of work stations. They make sure that wires are connected correctly, that the parts of the product actually function, and so on. A manufactured product is a system made up of parts that have to work together. With computer information systems, the component parts are analysis, design, and implementation products.

As is the case with a manufactured product, the people doing the walkthrough simply identify problems. There is a separation between quality inspection and actual production. Inspectors don't fix things, they just find errors or problems. People who conduct walkthroughs are not expected to conduct detailed analyses of the errors or to fix them. Their job is simply to identify any errors or problems where they exist, referring the work back to the responsible developer.

Within a systems development project, a technical review, or walkthrough, should be conducted any time a product is developed. For this purpose, a product is any portion of the system that can be identified as a separate unit and that has the capability of introducing errors into the system. Project management procedures should be set up to check each such product with a walkthrough by qualified personnel.

Walkthrough Participants

A walkthrough is conducted by enough people to do the job thoroughly, but not so many that it will become bogged down. Typically, three to five persons will be involved in reviewing any particular product. The key person is the *author*, or developer, of the product. The author must decide when the product is ready for a walkthrough. The nature of the product will shape the selection of other members of the review team.

If the project is relatively large, one or more experienced systems analysts may be appointed as *administrators* of walkthroughs. The administrator schedules walkthroughs as requested by authors and monitors their progress. It is part of the administrator's job to make sure that all reviewers have copies of the document to be examined in advance of the meeting. During the meeting, the administrator resolves any conflicts or disputes that may arise. The administrator must keep in mind that the purpose is to identify errors, not to correct the errors nor to argue about matters of personal approach or style. Thus, the administrator has the authority to cut off any discussion that is no longer productive, moving the group on to its next topic.

The administrator also checks the document itself to make sure that the walkthrough job will be manageable. Product reviews should be relatively small tasks, short enough so that a walkthrough can be completed in a concentrated period, unsually 30 to 60 minutes.

Each walkthrough should have someone appointed as secretary. This individual's job is to write down a summary of identified errors or questions that are raised. From these notes, the secretary prepares a walkthrough report that is distributed, promptly, to members of the walkthrough team. A separate, abbreviated version is distributed to project management. The secretary must have a thorough understanding of the product being examined. The secretary, therefore, is not a clerical person, but a professionally qualified member of the project team.

Two or more persons serve as reviewers of the technical document during a walkthrough. Their job is, clearly and simply, to spot problems or errors in the product under review.

Walkthrough Structure

A walkthrough is not a general, informal meeting, but rather a constructive analysis session in which all parties should participate as equals. The plan for a walkthrough should recognize that the participants are busy people. For a walkthrough to be productive, the rule about simply identifying problems, not solving them, should be strictly enforced. Ideally, the walkthrough will trace through the product from beginning to end, completing this task in a short, concentrated effort. Participants should complete their work without interruption.

The session should be planned so that all members of the review team receive copies of the product to be reviewed a sufficient time in advance. At the session itself, the author should describe the product. Reviewers should then present their concerns and questions. After all these questions have been identified, the author traces through the document. Starting at the beginning, each question or criticism is addressed. Some questions may be resolved with on-the-spot answers. Others, however, may be identified as requiring further work by the author. In addition, the discussions may raise new questions. All problems, together with their resolution or agreement that further work is needed, should be noted and described by the secretary.

Walkthroughs should be conducted in a businesslike way. Personal remarks or personal criticisms of team members are counterproductive. If such statements are made, the discussion should be brought back into its main channel immediately. Comments should focus on questions of accuracy, conformance to standards, following of specifications or objectives, maintainability of software being reviewed, and general quality of work. Ideally, minor mechanical errors should be covered in separate written comments submitted before the walkthrough takes place. This will improve the efficiency and productivity of the walkthrough session.

To the extent possible, members of a walkthrough team should have different experience levels. Junior members have the opportunity for a valuable learning experience as they work with more experienced people. At the same time, junior personnel can bring fresh approaches into these sessions.

If rework requirements are identified, additional walkthroughs may be scheduled. The review process is continued until all identified problems have been fixed.

Walkthrough End Products

As indicated, a walkthrough produces two end-product documents:

- Walkthrough report
- Management report.

Walkthrough report.   This is a brief, factual document. It should identify the product involved, the author, the date, and the names of all persons who participate.

The outcome of the walkthrough should be noted. The three possible outcomes are:

- The product is accepted.
- The product will be considered accepted when specific, identified revisions have been made.
- Another walkthrough will be necessary after identified problems have been corrected.

The main report content consists of any concerns raised during the walkthrough or submitted in writing. This report should be completed and submitted to walkthrough participants as soon as possible after the session.

Management report.   This report summarizes the walkthrough report. It contains the identifying information and walkthrough outcome, but not the detailed list of errors or concerns.

The management report is submitted to the CIS supervisor responsible for the project and also becomes part of the permanent documentation about the product. If the outcome is full or conditional acceptance, participants sign the report to indicate acceptance of the product reviewed. By signing, the participants share responsibility for the quality of the product they have certified.

Avoiding Common Pitfalls

When walkthroughs are conducted expertly and professionally, they can serve a valuable quality control purpose. They can help to mold a highly professional team committed to producing a quality system. For success in the conduct of walkthroughs, however, it is important to recognize that they will not be successful automatically. Potential problems and pitfalls exist that should be anticipated and avoided.

One common problem is that a walkthrough team is given too large a product to review. The session takes too long. People lose their concentration and begin to worry about other things they should be doing. The administrator should apply his or her experience to assure that the products selected for review can be covered in a relatively short time.

Another problem can occur if participants do not receive copies of the document to be reviewed in time to prepare themselves. Of course, no matter how much time is allowed, it is possible that participants will be unprepared. An atmosphere should be created in which reviewers understand the necessity to prepare themselves for a walkthrough session. At minimum, each participant should have read through the document being reviewed carefully before the walkthrough takes place.

Constructive criticism should be encouraged and supported. However, care must be taken to avoid letting criticism deteriorate into arguments or personal attacks. The product must, at all times, be separated from its author. At the same time, people should not be so inhibited that they are afraid to criticize anything. Solid, professional criticism helps improve a product. It takes judgment and experience to know the difference between professional comments and personal insults. Professional criticism is necessary. Dwelling on personalities is unacceptable.

REPORTING

The reporting function is a major component of any communication structure for a systems development project. Reports deliver messages to identified audiences. Each message must be:

- To an audience
- About a clearly identified subject.

The needs of the audience shape the content of the message.

Organizing a Message

To help assure that written reports or oral presentations meet the needs of their audiences, a relatively simple process, or set of steps, can be followed:

- *Collect all information first.* Relevant information should be gathered and reviewed first. This becomes the basis for the content of the message. Thus, information gathering is a key first step.
- *Identify audience needs.* Given a body of information that is ready for presentation, the needs of the audience or audiences should be identified and defined. On the basis of these needs, priorities should be established that rate the importance of the information items to the audience. On a relatively long document, information items can be listed, then numbered in order of their priority.

- *Start the presentation with the most important item, then support this initial statement.* The beginning statement in any report or message should contain the information most important to the identified audience. After that, information items should be arranged in the order of their importance. At the same time, the ordering of information items should be logical. That is, if a recommendation or finding is presented at the beginning of the message, the items that follow should support the initial statement. These items should follow a logical progression.

- *Analyze and criticize the content of the message.* If the full message seems incomplete or doesn't make sense in its entirety, it may be necessary to review the initial statement or even, possibly, to gather more information.

- *Use only enough time or words to deliver a message that meets the information needs of the audience.* It is not necessary to put all available information into every message. Part of the skill of efficient writing or presentation lies in deciding what to leave out. Again, the needs of the audience should shape the message.

This approach to organizing and preparing messages works equally well in either of the two main types of reporting that occur within a systems development project: written reports and oral presentations.

Written Reports

To the extent possible, documents produced in a systems development project use graphic techniques or are structured to meet specific communication needs. Examples include data flow diagrams, structure charts, process specifications, and data dictionaries.

Each of these structured documents, however, requires at least a brief narrative description as an overview. Further, management reports that serve as the basis for project decisions require carefully prepared management summaries.

In addition to these basic working documents, systems development projects are expected to produce considerable volumes of written documents in the form of procedures manuals and training manuals.

In each case, thought must be applied to tailor the information content of the written messages to the needs of its audiences.

Management summaries.   Managers use summary reports as a basis for making resource decisions. From the manager's point of view, this is a problem solving situation. A sound technique for organizing management summaries, therefore, is to follow a problem solving model.

Earlier in this chapter, a methodology for problem solving is reviewed. In writing a summary report to managment of technical people, assume that they will be going through this problem solving process as they review the information presented in your report.

A good way to begin a management summary, then, is to describe the problem being solved. This description should make it clear that the problem or decision situation has been analyzed and that causes have been identified. That is, reporting should be done as though the problem solving process had already been applied successfully, without having to pause for each analytical step.

The next portion of a management summary should identify the alternatives that were considered. Those that obviously didn't fit can be discarded with brief explanations about why they were rejected. The consequences of the most likely alternatives can then be reviewed in somewhat greater depth.

Obviously, since management summaries are recommendations, no decision can actually be made. Rather, the summary should end with a recommendation to the management group. If the presentation has been structured carefully, the recommendation should come as a logical conclusion to the report. If, for any reason, the conclusion does not seem fully supported by the presentation, revision should be considered.

This type of structuring is basic to management reporting. Managers don't want to be presented with problems. They want recommendations for solutions and for actions. By structuring reports in this way, members of the project team make it clear that they have thought about the situation and are ready to make a commitment to deliver results if they receive management support in the form of a favorable decision.

Some report writing guidelines suggest that management summaries begin with a recommended decision, then support the recommendation with factual presentations. This type of format is used and can work. However, the report structure suggested here, which follows the decision making process, seems to relate more closely to the requirements and thought processes of this particular audience: Identify the problem, briefly state and evaluate the potential solutions, and recommend a course of action. In oral presentations to management groups, discussed later in this chapter, the situation is somewhat different. In this environment, after the group has seen the documentation, the opposite approach can be used: Begin with a recommendation, then go through the written report in support of the recommendation.

In following the problem solving model for management reporting, remember the basic principle of problem solving: Large problems are solved by partitioning them into a collection of smaller problems. The problem solving process should then be applied separately to the individual subproblems, no matter how closely related they may be to one another. Thus, if a management summary covers a complex situation involving multiple problems or decisions, each should be summarized individually. A collective summary on the total recommendation can then be placed in the report, either at the beginning or at the end, depending on the length of the document and the nature of the group that will receive it.

In general, a management summary should be limited to a one- to two-page typewritten presentation. If the summary is longer than that, it defeats its own purpose. Any further detailing required to support the recommendation should be contained in separate sections of or appendices to the management summary.

Procedures manuals.   *Manuals,* as the term is used here, are documents that direct people in performing manual procedures within a computer-based system. In effect, manuals do for people what programs do for computers. However, people and computers are different. Manuals should reflect these differences.

The guiding principle in developing a manual should be that people are in the system because they are able to apply judgment. Any functions that can be automated completely would be done by a computer. Thus, emphasis in the procedures manual should be on those points in the system at which people assure quality or apply judgment. Care should be taken to explain the reasons for doing things in the ways that have been specified.

This type of presentation helps to convince people that the jobs they are doing are worthwhile. A well-executed procedures manual should have the effect of selling the person doing the work on the value and importance of his or her job. Unfortunately, many procedures manuals give the impression of talking down to the people who actually do the work—of emphasizing the steps taken rather than the importance of the results. Such manuals, rather than guiding and helping people, encourage feelings of boredom and futility. Thus, they defeat their own purpose, contributing to a lack of quality rather than assuring that standards are met.

Some content items within procedures manuals that can help build human understanding and interest are:

- Explain the purpose and value of the overall system of which the individual is a part.

- Identify the customer, or user, of the outputs produced by each task.

- Describe, specifically, what successful performance will look like and what will be expected from the person handling each task.

- Describe any and all quality standards that should be met within the context of the job description itself.

- In describing procedures, cover each step to be taken in sequence. Be sure to identify the starting and completion points for each step, as well as the overall continuity between steps.

- Whenever a judgment or decision is to be made by a human operator, emphasize the value of this judgment and its contribution to the success of the system. Follow the decision making model in identifying what is to be decided, what alternatives are available, and the conditions under which each alternative should be selected.

- Encourage people to apply judgment. That is why they are part of the system. Include instructions on how individuals can make suggestions to improve the system or to streamline the work flow.

The same guidelines apply in developing procedures manuals for computer console operators. The more a manual can do to help make an operator feel important because of his or her ability to apply judgment, the more effective that manual will be. Conversely, the more a manual tends to treat a person as an attendant waiting upon a machine, the less effective that manual will be.

Training manuals.   The job of training operators and users for installation and use of a new system should be approached with some humility. When it comes to using computer information systems, experience is still the best teacher. There is no way that a trainer, no matter how skilled, can impart all of the knowledge and experience needed for smooth, continuous operation of a computer information system. This kind of skill and experience can only be built on the job.

Therefore, materials and presentation programs for training sessions should be prepared with the full knowledge that it will be almost impossible to complete the job of training personnel during the brief classroom sessions that are made available. Recognizing this, the training program should concentrate on teaching people to meet needs or solve problems on the job. This is a more practical approach than undertaking a probably impossible task of teaching all of the operations, functions, and skills that will be needed on a relatively complex job.

Training materials have a different purpose than procedures manuals. Training manuals should be designed as easy-to-use references. Thus, for example, it is perfectly acceptable to have a reference in a training manual that simply tells an operator what page of the procedures manual to turn to for instructions on a given job. The training manual can then offer hints aimed at helping the operator to master the functions described in the procedures manual. It is not necessary to duplicate all of the procedures manual content in a training manual. Rather, the idea is to help the operator feel comfortable with the procedures manual so that it can be used as a job aid.

In a CIS environment, there are many opportunities to use the computer itself as a training aid. This is particularly true in the training of operators working at video display terminals. Many ''user friendly'' systems build in options in which operators can ask for prompting or help from the computer itself. Under one option, for example, the operator simply enters a question mark at the beginning of a line on the terminal, then presses the return key. The computer is directed to display a menu of assistance routines that the operator can call up.

Another common technique, used in data entry systems, is to display blocks of data at the top of the screen. These identify the codes or formats to be used by the operator. As the operator learns the job, this display on the screen can be eliminated.

Above all, effective training programs *teach operators to learn*. A training effort should never downgrade people to the level of machines by attempting to simply ''program'' them to make the correct responses.

Oral Presentation

There are many points within any systems development project at which complete sets of information must be considered, organized, assembled, and presented orally rather than in written reports. The process of organizing information for oral presentation is much the same as that described above for written reports. However, the emphasis or pattern of presentation may differ.

Oral presentation situations that arise in systems development projects fall into three broad categories:

- *Project management reviews.* These sessions involve reports by members of the project team to team leaders or project managers. The content of the reports may be either technical or general, depending on whether the work is done by computer professionals or user members of the team. Usually, these meetings are held periodically, as often as the project manager considers necessary to manage or control the development process. Topics for these meetings may include reports of progress during the current week, completion of tasks, time remaining for tasks in process, reviews of particular problems encountered, or tasks that are about to begin.

- *Status reviews.* These meetings are conducted periodically, usually weekly or biweekly, throughout a project. Their purpose is to keep user management current on the progress of the project. Status reviews are information sessions, not sales meetings. They do not necessarily culminate in approval or acceptance of work done. Rather, they are a means of achieving communication, of keeping project management and key user managers in touch with each other to assure a continuity of understanding. Participants in these meetings are usually the project leader, key user managers, and, possibly, members of the project team with special contributions to make.

- *Acceptance reviews.* These are sessions in which the project team goes before some management group to present information on a phase, activity, or interim product for which approval is needed. One of the most important types of acceptance review during a project is the phase report presented to the steering committee, recommending commitment to the next phase of the system development life cycle. In addition to the steering committee sessions, acceptance reviews may be held with user managers who are asked to review a set of output reports, business forms, data entry formats, a model for the new system, or some other product of the systems development process. Meetings of this type may also be held with auditors who review the reliability and auditability of procedures being designed. The common denominator of such meetings is that brief, formal documents are usually prepared in advance and provided to the decision makers. The oral presentation then explains and supports the written document, with the intent of securing approval for recommendations made.

As stated above, many of the guidelines for preparing written reports apply equally to oral presentations. However, certain special considerations also apply in the case of oral presentations. These include visual support and certain questions of organization.

Visual support.   Wherever possible, an oral presentation should be supported by visual aids of some sort. The number and type of visual materials used will depend on the situation. At a management review, for example, the visual focus may be on the forms or products being analyzed. A programmer reviewing the design of a module might provide copies of his or her structure charts for all persons attending the meeting. The same would be true for systems analysts presenting data flow diagrams for analysis of existing or proposed systems.

At larger meetings, different types of visuals might be appropriate. For example, if 10 or more persons are attending an acceptance review, it could be distracting if each of them was expected to leaf through a set of loose pages. It is more effective, in a case like this, to use slides or overhead transparencies to project summary notes onto a screen. In this way, the attention of participants is focused on one specific topic at a time.

Whatever method is used, the principle is the same: Meetings devoted to reviews of project content should be supported by some sort of visual device that focuses the attention of participants on the topics being discussed. Further, each participant should be able to take away a set of notes that will serve as reminders, or reinforcement, of the discussions held.

Organizing oral presentations. As is the case with written messages, a safe practice for oral messages is to structure information content according to the decisions to be made. However, some modification may be necessary to cover situations in which participants have already seen the summary report on which the oral presentation will be based. It certainly is not acceptable simply to stand up and read a report that people already hold in their hands.

Thus, if the audience has already seen the report, it is best to begin with a statement of the recommendations. Then, brief references can be made to the content of the report in support of the recommendation.

In oral reports associated with written summaries, interaction with the audience is essential. Listeners should be left with the feeling that a thorough job has been done of analyzing the topic. They should feel that the decision that they make is soundly supported. Audience participation is essential to establishing this feeling.

Provision should be made for dealing with questions from the audience. If no questions materialize during the presentation, two techniques may help. One is to identify, before the presentation, questions that members of the audience ought to have. Then, during the presentation, these questions can be raised and answered on the spot. Another, somewhat more aggressive approach is to ask questions and require answers from members of the audience. In any case, audience participation should be encouraged throughout the presentation, rather than waiting until the end to invite questions.

To illustrate how participation can be stimulated at an acceptance review, suppose a group of top level users is checking out a training plan for a new system. The person presenting the plan sees nothing but nodding of agreement from the audience. To stimulate participation, some priming questions are in order. For example, as a summary point during the presentation, the speaker might ask: "As you can see, we are planning to train four people at a time from your department. Can you spare this number of people at any given time? Will this rate of training keep up with the installation program you have planned?"

At a steering committee meeting, priming questions might deal with interdepartmental interfaces in a system under development. Assuming that the heads of two or more departments that will use the system are present, it is always a good tactic to ask these individuals whether the planned interfaces within the system reflect their ideas of how the system should work.

In summary, systems development work is done by project teams. Teams, in turn, are bound together by common commitments and common understandings of a shared purpose. The development of this singleness of purpose and unity of effort among the many and diverse people involved in a systems project does not happen automatically. It requires a carefully defined communication structure, made up of many elements and serving a wide range of information needs.

Summary

A CIS project may involve many people, with widely varying backgrounds and interests. Communication with all of these individuals and groups must address the specific requirements of each. The systems analyst is responsible for filling these information needs. The systems analyst must identify each audience, its primary interests or motivation, and its information needs. Messages, or communications, can then be shaped to meet the specific interests, as well as the information needs, of selected individuals or groups.

The communication activities of systems development projects fall into three broad categories: problem solving work sessions; technical reviews or walkthroughs; and reports, both written and oral.

Effective problem solving requires objectivity. This objectivity can best be assured by following a step-by-step problem solving process.

First, state the problem clearly, separating large problems into individual, smaller ones. Then, analyze the problem for its probable cause. Next, identify as many alternatives as possible for eliminating the cause. Then, after all alternatives have been identified, consider the consequences of each. Finally, choose the best alternative.

A walkthrough is a quality review applied to such systems development products as data flow diagrams, program structure charts, pseudocode listings, collections of proposed input documents, collections of proposed output documents, test plans, and others. The purpose of a walkthrough is to identify errors or problems, which are then referred back to the responsible developer for analysis and correction.

All members of the review team should receive copies of the product to be reviewed at least one day in advance. The review session itself should be focused, businesslike, and brief—a maximum of 30 minutes or so. Constructive criticism should be encouraged, but personal remarks or arguments are out of place. A walkthrough report should be prepared and delivered to all participants as soon as possible after the review session. A separate management report should state the outcome but omit the detailed list of errors or concerns.

In preparing written reports or oral presentations, it is best to follow an established, step-by-step process. First, collect all relevant information. Next, identify and define the needs of the audience and establish information priorities. Then, prepare the presentation, starting with the item most important to the identified audience and arranging other items in their order of importance. Next, analyze and criticize the content of the message, making sure that the presentation is orderly, logical, and complete. Finally, be sure you have included enough information—but not too much—to meet the specific needs of this audience.

Management summaries are used as a basis for decision making, which is a form of problem solving. Therefore, management summaries are most effective if they follow the basic problem solving model reviewed earlier. Procedures manuals are documents that direct people in performing manual procedures within a computer-based system. Care should be taken to explain the reasons for following established procedures and the importance of quality information to the organization as a whole.

Training materials should be aimed at teaching people to meet needs and solve problems on the job. With appropriate software, the computer itself can also be used as a training aid.

Oral presentations are often required in connection with project management reviews, status reviews, and acceptance reviews. Wherever possible, oral presentations should be supported by visual aids to help focus the attention of participants. Members of the audience should be encouraged to ask questions and participate actively in the discussion.

Key Terms

1. walkthrough
2. author
3. management summary
4. procedures manual
5. training manual
6. project management review
7. status review
8. acceptance review

Review/Discussion Questions

1. Why are communications skills and techniques so important to the systems analyst?

2. What is meant by audience identification, and why is it important?

3. List the five basic steps in problem solving. Use a sample problem to illustrate how these steps might be applied.

4. What is the role of walkthroughs in a systems development project?

5. If you were responsible for organizing a walkthrough, how would you go about it?

6. What are the three possible outcomes of a walkthrough? How, and to whom, is the outcome reported?

7. Describe the basic steps involved in preparing a report, whether written or oral.

8. What is a management summary, and how should it be organized?

9. What are the basic guidelines or principles for creating an effective procedures manual?

10. What is the purpose of a training manual? How does it relate to the relevant procedures manual(s)?

11. How does an oral presentation differ from a written report?

12. What is the purpose of visual aids in an oral presentation? What types of aids might you use for meetings of various sizes?

III ANALYSIS AND GENERAL DESIGN PHASE

OBJECTIVES

The objectives in this phase are:

- Define and analyze current systems and procedures.
- Establish a general design for the new system.
- Establish user acceptance of and concurrence in the design.
- Secure a commitment from the CIS department that the design of the new system can be implemented within the established time dollar limits.
- Develop a plan for carrying out the next phase of the project.
- Present sufficient information so that the steering committee can reach a decision on whether to continue or abort the project.

ACTIVITIES

The continuity of activities within this phase is shown in the flowchart in Figure III-1.

PROCESS

The process of systems development during this phase is shown in the data flow diagram in Figure III-2. Note that this data flow diagram indicates a number of processes performed within the activities identified

238

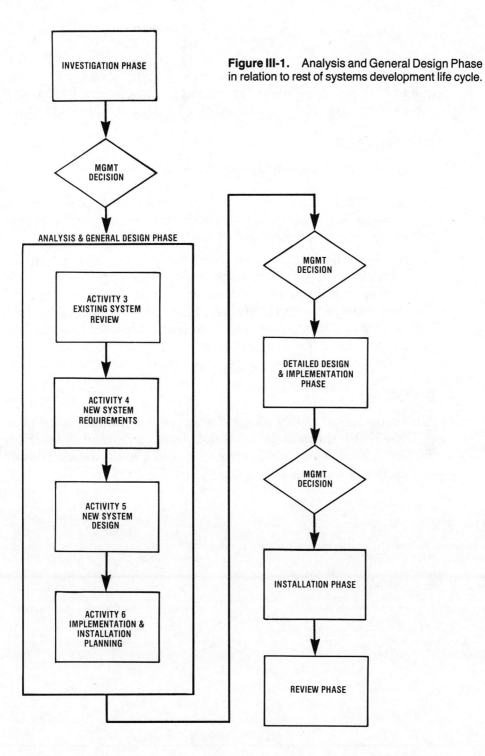

INVESTIGATION PHASE

MGMT DECISION

ANALYSIS & GENERAL DESIGN PHASE

ACTIVITY 3
EXISTING SYSTEM
REVIEW

ACTIVITY 4
NEW SYSTEM
REQUIREMENTS

ACTIVITY 5
NEW SYSTEM
DESIGN

ACTIVITY 6
IMPLEMENTATION &
INSTALLATION
PLANNING

MGMT DECISION

DETAILED DESIGN
& IMPLEMENTATION
PHASE

MGMT DECISION

INSTALLATION PHASE

REVIEW PHASE

Figure III-1.   Analysis and General Design Phase in relation to rest of systems development life cycle.

239

in Figure III-1. Processes 1 and 2 correspond to Activity 3: Existing System Review; processes 3 through 5 to Activity 4: New System Requirements; processes 6 and 7 to Activity 5: New System Design; and process 8 to Activity 6: Implementation and Installation Planning.

END PRODUCT

This phase has two major end products:

- *User specification.* This presents a physical model of the new system from the user's point of view. Included is a commitment by the user to accept and support implementation of the new system.

- *New system design specification.* This introduces technical design considerations for the new system, building upon the content of the user specification. The added detailing updates the feasibility evaluation performed in the first phase and serves as a basis for the detailed design activities of the next phase. Included here is a commitment from the design staff within the CIS area to implement the system within the budget and time schedule specified.

DECISION

At the conclusion of this phase, the steering committee is asked to decide whether the new system should be implemented. A favorable decision authorizes the project to go forward into the detailed design and implementation phase.

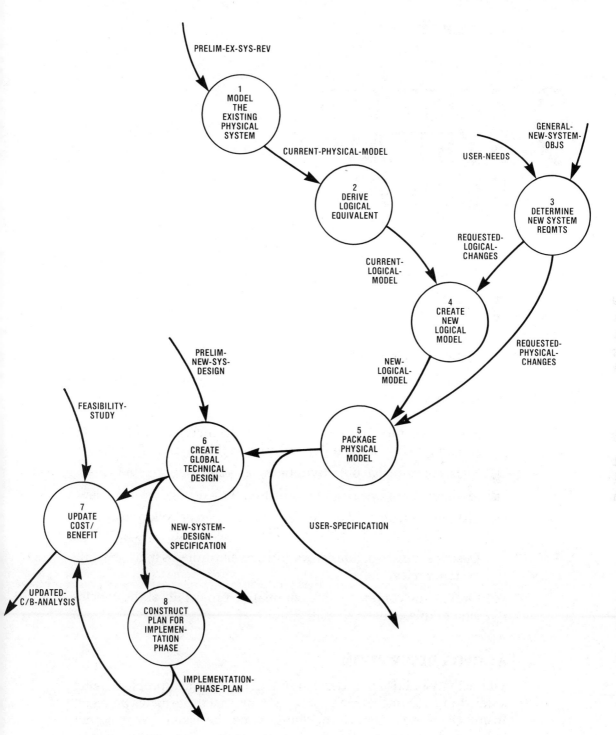

PRELIM-EX-SYS-REV

1
MODEL
THE
EXISTING
PHYSICAL
SYSTEM

CURRENT-PHYSICAL-MODEL

2
DERIVE
LOGICAL
EQUIVALENT

USER-NEEDS

GENERAL-
NEW-SYSTEM-
OBJS

3
DETERMINE
NEW SYSTEM
REQMTS

REQUESTED-
LOGICAL-
CHANGES

CURRENT-
LOGICAL-
MODEL

4
CREATE
NEW
LOGICAL
MODEL

REQUESTED-
PHYSICAL-
CHANGES

PRELIM-
NEW-SYS-
DESIGN

NEW-
LOGICAL-
MODEL

FEASIBILITY-
STUDY

6
CREATE
GLOBAL
TECHNICAL
DESIGN

5
PACKAGE
PHYSICAL
MODEL

7
UPDATE
COST/
BENEFIT

NEW-SYSTEM-
DESIGN-
SPECIFICATION

USER-SPECIFICATION

UPDATED-
C/B-ANALYSIS

8
CONSTRUCT
PLAN FOR
IMPLEMEN-
TATION
PHASE

IMPLEMENTATION-
PHASE-PLAN

Figure III-2. Process view of the Analysis and General Design phase of systems development life cycle.

9 EXISTING SYSTEM REVIEW

LEARNING OBJECTIVES

On completing reading and other learning assignments for this chapter, you should be able to:

- ☐ Explain the importance of the existing system review and describe its relationship to the other activities in this phase.
- ☐ State the principal objectives of the existing system review.
- ☐ Identify the two major end products of the existing system review.
- ☐ List the main types of documents that need to be collected and explain their role in building a model of the existing system.
- ☐ Describe the use of interviews and of walkthroughs in the existing system review.
- ☐ Outline the contents of the cumulative project file at the conclusion of this activity.

ACTIVITY DESCRIPTION

This activity builds an understanding of the business problem being studied and documents the existing systems that relate to this problem. In any given project effort, the question may be asked: "Why bother to look at the existing system?" As long as the existing system is to be replaced, there seems to be little or no value in detailing and documenting established procedures. Because of this reasoning, the study of existing systems is often shortchanged. As a result, many systems development efforts start with insufficient or inadequate information concerning the business problem that is being attacked and solved.

The reason for studying and documenting the existing system, plainly stated, is that this is where an understanding of business problems and needs is built. Without this understanding, it would be difficult, perhaps impossible, to build an adequate replacement system.

The project team may apply systems analysis methods to build a model of the existing system. Tools for this modeling include data flow diagrams, data dictionaries, and process descriptions. This activity is not concerned with precise documentation of current procedures, files, programs, and so on. The point is to understand the business objectives and business functions of the existing system. This can be a difficult job because these basic business considerations are probably not well documented. But the payoff in terms of understanding is great. For, even though the physical system may change drastically as a result of the development project, the underlying business objectives and the logical functions of the system generally will not change all that much. It is this logical understanding that carries forward and serves as an important underpinning for the design of the new system.

As a further value, the understanding that leads to a working rapport among members of the project team begins with a sensitivity to things as they are. From this basis, users can better articulate their own needs and systems professionals can better understand the business needs that the new system should be meeting.

OBJECTIVES

The primary objective of this activity is to build an understanding of the business goals, objectives, and functions involved in the application areas encompassed by the project.

The actual study of the existing system and its results form the secondary objective. That is, as a working tool, the project team should develop documentation at a general level for the existing system. This documentation is not usually important for its own sake. Rather, it provides a basis for understanding key business objectives and functions and for identifying improvements in the new system.

SCOPE

The feasibility report launches this activity with documentation that provides an overview of what happens within the existing system. The project team has a rough idea of the major functions of the system and, particularly, of its key deficiencies in terms of current business needs. Also known at the outset is the extent to which computers are used, as well as the approaches taken in computer processing, such as batch, on-line, centralized, distributed, or other options.

At the conclusion of this activity, the project team should know all that it needs to know—and probably all that it will ever know—about the existing, in-place system and procedures. The study of the existing system should go to great depth in building an understanding of the logical aspects of the system. In most cases, less depth and detailing are needed in reviewing physical processing—particularly in documenting physical procedures that are going to be abandoned. However, the physical review of existing systems should contain enough details to support the updating of the cost/benefit analysis at the end of this phase. Results should include an understanding of any procedures that could profitably be carried forward into the new system.

For example, in the Central City water billing system, at a logical level it is necessary to recognize that preparation of customer bills based on water consumption is a key business function. It is necessary to understand the nature of the water rates—the fact that the cost per unit varies by customer type and level of usage. Also relevant is the business policy on applying penalties to past due accounts: A 10 percent surcharge is assessed on any balance unpaid at the time the next bill is processed, despite the fact that the bill itself states that the penalty will be assessed after 10 days. It is necessary to document the basic characteristics of the computer job stream that produces the bills. However, it is not necessary to document the individual programs that make up this job stream.

A heavy overlap exists between this activity and Activities 4 and 5. As data on the current system are gathered, they form input to the design of new system elements in Activity 4: New System Requirements and the specification of new procedures or operational details in Activity 5: New System Design. The continuity lies in the modeling that takes place. The logical model of the existing system feeds the logical model of the new system which, in turn, feeds the physical model of the new system. Thus, there is a sequence as well as an overlapping. Activity 3 begins first. The next two activities have some concurrent overlapping. But Activity 5 concludes last.

END PRODUCTS

The end products of this activity are documents that build, cumulatively, upon portions of the feasibility report.

Functional (Logical) Model

The model constructed for the existing system should stress the business objectives that the system supports, the main functions that the system performs, the management decisions that the system supports, and the affected decision makers (identified by department and position).

This particular end product emphasizes logical aspects of the existing system, rather than physical details. For example, in reviewing the water billing system, the writing of customer bills would be recognized as important business functions and included as logical system content. By contrast, the editing of inputs to be sure that all keypunched meter readings were numeric and reasonable would be part of the physical model and would be of relatively minor interest at this point.

The focus here is on the key business features of the system—the data and the policies or organizational rules by which they are transformed. These are rules for operating the business and will need to be included in the revised system. Therefore, these policies or processing rules should be documented carefully and in some detail. Failure to do so at this point may result in the omission of required data elements and data relationships among functions, causing rework and delays later in the project.

Physical Documentation

One reason for avoiding extensive depth in documenting the physical details of the existing system is that there are apt to be so many details that the project could lose its perspective. In practice, a relatively small percentage of all the documents and procedures control most of the services within any given system. Here again, the 80-20 rule is a handy guideline. In other words, perhaps 20 percent of the documents represent 80 percent of the value in any given system, including transaction documents, management reports, and decision support outputs.

Thus, systems analysts must develop judgment about what is really important. This judgmental skill can be difficult to achieve. Among the 80 percent of the less critical documents may be reports that are no longer used, processing controls that no longer apply, and even source input forms that are no longer necessary. But beware. A portion of this 80 percent may deal with how to handle certain processing exceptions. An example in the water billing system would be the special documents and processing that allow a landlord to receive a composite bill covering all properties, rather than directing individual bills to each of the tenants. While the documents themselves are low volume and of relatively little interest as part of the physical documentation, their existence discloses an important business policy—the willingness of the city to provide this special service to landlords. Such a policy must be reflected in the logical model of the system.

Documentation of the existing system is usually guided by some sort of checklist of the kinds of forms or records to be collected. A typical checklist of this type is shown in Figure 9-1. Guidelines for using this type of checklist in gathering information on the existing system are:

- To the extent possible, collect forms or documents that have actually been used for input and output. Do not collect only blank forms

---

CHECKLIST OF INFORMATION CATEGORIES VALUABLE FOR USE IN ANALYSIS PROCESS

A. ORGANIZATION

Organization charts
Objective/purpose of each functional unit
    Why is it necessary?
    How does it overlap other units?
    Are there conflicting purposes within the unit or among units?

B. POLICIES AND PROCEDURES

Copies of existing policies and procedures
Current use
    Followed?
    Maintained?
    Method of distribution?

Used by?
When used?
Inconsistencies and current problems

C. CURRENT SYSTEM OUTPUTS

Typical copies
  Manual
  Computerized
Purpose/use
Problems with accuracy and use

D. CURRENT SYSTEM INPUTS

Typical copies (actually filled out)
Purpose/use
Problems with accuracy and use

E. DESCRIPTIONS OF CURRENT PROCESSING

Physical system
  Overall work flows
  Volume and timing considerations
  System performance statistics
  Man/machine boundaries
  Control points and control mechanisms
  Work scheduling and priority handling
  Current bottlenecks and other procedural problems
Logical system
  Flow of data through the system
  Required transformation of data by the system
  Inconsistencies, unnecessary or missing flows

F. DATA FILES (MANUAL OR COMPUTERIZED)

Description of contents
Samples of manual data records
Methods for updating/maintaining files
Problems with currency, accuracy, redundancy

G. PERIPHERAL SYSTEMS

Other systems that must interface with this system
Nature of intersystem dependencies
  Data flows
  Shared files

Figure 9-1. Checking of categories of physical documentation to be collected during Existing System Review activity.

or form layouts. Actual examples of entries on the forms hold the key to evaluating the system. From these entries, an analyst can tell what is really happening in the system, as distinct from what was originally meant to happen when the forms were designed. Also, actual entries may show situations in which data are needed that are not called for on the form and might have been missed had a blank form been used. Bear in mind that all of this data gathering is of temporary interest only. Forms and other documents do not have to be picture-perfect. Rough entries are sufficient.

- As appropriate, supplementary explanations should be added to input and output forms to document where they are prepared and how they are used.

- All file structures should be documented with file definitions and record layout forms. Any manually maintained files should be described, with all data and information content identified.

- Collect any existing documentation of systems or procedures. These may include manuals, flowcharts, or possibly data flow diagrams. However, do not place heavy reliance on existing documentation. There is a high likelihood that the system has been modified and that documentation prepared when the system was developed is obsolete. Thus, any documentation collected should be used primarily as a basis for studying the system further to find out what is actually happening.

- Controls or timing requirements incorporated in the physical system to comply with business processing needs should be noted and described.

- Organizational charts for all departments or groups affected by the existing system should be collected. These should be supplemented with descriptions of the identified jobs.

- Enough data on current operating costs should be collected to support an updating of the cost/benefit analysis.

- Review the documentation on the maintenance history of the existing system. Maintenance efforts can tell a lot about a system. For example, if one portion of the system has been modified frequently, this could point either to volatile business conditions or to an inadequacy in the original design. Conversely, stability in a portion of the system could indicate satisfaction. Or, it could indicate that these procedures are of little importance and may actually have fallen into disuse.

- Informal or "off the books" records kept by system users should be noted and described. These could point to deficiencies in the existing system.

Current System Deficiencies

Throughout the review of the existing system, members of the project team should work actively to identify system deficiencies. This goes beyond the routine guidelines for a systems study. If the study is confined to actual, documented procedures, deficiencies may never be uncovered. Instead, if a systems analyst pays attention to user complaints about things that aren't happening or services that are unsatisfactory, this information could lead to substantial improvements in the design of the new system.

Some deficiencies in the existing system will be readily apparent to users. These will tend to be physical problems. For example, because of increased business activity, the existing system may be unable to process the current volume of transactions. Or, if users are compiling operating statistics by hand, this could be a sign that an additional report should be added to the new system.

Logical deficiencies might be less apparent to users. For example, if overlapping responsibilities existed in two or more departments, none of the users involved might know about it. This is the type of deficiency that should show up in effective systems analysis. Also, users may be doing things routinely and be unaware that the computer—or improved manual methods—can help them by doing the same work more efficiently. For example, the water department may have people checking through miles of copies of water bills for follow-up on late payments. The person doing this work may be unaware that the computer could do the same thing in a small fraction of the time now being spent on the job.

Interface Points With Other Systems

Most operational systems receive inputs from and deliver outputs to other systems. This is true for both manual and computer-based systems. Information on all such interfacing relationships should be gathered during this activity. The critical information includes the timing, volume or amount, and timeliness requirements for data and information passed among these systems.

Management Policy Decisions

As the project team digs deeper into the procedures of the existing system, additional situations requiring policy guidance may be uncovered. These situations may result from a lack of existing policies, from existing policies that conflict with one another, or from failure to adhere to established policies. These situations should be noted and documented carefully. Management decisions may be needed before work can proceed on design of the new system.

THE PROCESS

This activity builds on the preliminary existing system review produced during the feasibility study. Through extensive use of interviews and other data gathering techniques, information is collected for the documentation end product, defined above. Techniques for this type of information gathering are covered in Chapter 4.

Concurrent with these data collection tasks, the system modeling process begins. This process is overviewed in Chapter 6 and covered further in Chapter 10. Early in this activity, construction may begin on a model consisting of a set of (physical) data flow diagrams that show how data flow through and are transformed by the system. Such a physical model can tie together and give meaning to the physical documentation elements.

There is no lasting interest in the physical model itself. The desired end product is a logical model of the existing system. The physical model is, however, a natural starting point. It emphasizes *how* processing is currently done—modeling the system from the user's point of view. This enables the user to verify the accuracy of the model being created. Since the desired end product is a logical model, however, care should be taken from the very beginning to base even the physical model on the major business activities of the organization, rather than on particular people or departments.

As understanding of the existing system improves, analysts begin to develop a logical model. This process is described in Chapter 10, which includes modeling examples. The key point to understand here is that physical aspects of the system such as editing, backup, auditing, and processing security are downplayed. Emphasis is placed on the essential business functions that are important to the system no matter how it is physically implemented. For the water billing system, this would include such things as preparing bills, processing payments, and responding to customer queries.

The emphasis throughout is on understanding. The analyst should continually ask, "why?" An understanding is needed of why each step in the process is performed, why each data element is necessary, why each output is produced, and even why certain things are not of interest. The answers to these questions should be consistent with the objectives of the organization and the system under study. This type of questioning may well turn up current practices that are unnecessary or that are not supportable in terms of organizational objectives. In any case, it will ensure an intimate knowledge and understanding of the existing system.

Understanding here and in all phases of analysis is greatly improved if the analyst attempts to view the system through the eyes and mind of the user. For example, suppose the analyst is working with a middle level manager and is attempting to discover what information that manager uses from the current system. The inexperienced analyst would simply ask—and would accept the response at face value. The experienced analyst, viewing the system through the eyes and mind of the user, would first think, "If I were in that manager's position, with the decisions she must make and the pressures she faces, I would need to know . . ." The experienced analyst would then be prepared to follow up the original question, pushing the user to be complete and very probably to identify deficiencies in the existing system.

Two standard systems analysis tools are used heavily during this activity: interviews and walkthroughs. These methods are described in Chapters 4 and 8. The important points to understand here are the areas of emphasis and the projected results anticipated from the use of these methods.

Interviews

During this activity, interviews are conducted at every level of the organization. However, the sessions should be oriented toward the building of knowledge about business considerations, business decisions, and business objectives. This kind of information, by its very nature, comes primarily from top and middle managers. Thus, while interviews with clerical-level personnel are important for understanding how the system works, special emphasis should be placed on management interviews.

Recognize also that, while the main purpose for the interviews is to gather information to use in modeling the current system, users will be far more interested in discussing complaints and frustrations they have with the current system. Exposure to user complaints or problems is an opportunity that should be exploited. Turn the complaints into positive statements of what the user would like. Then, as these interview notes are carried forward into the requirements and design activities that follow, these suggestions can be studied and, if appropriate, incorporated. Such a show of responsiveness can build enthusiasm and support for a systems development project. This illustrates the way in which the several activities of the analysis and general design phase overlap. While attempting to model the current system, the analyst is beginning to identify requirements for the new system and is probably forming preliminary ideas for potential solutions to meet these requirements.

Walkthroughs

A walkthrough is, by nature, a troubleshooting technique. It is designed to identify errors in a product. Many CIS professionals are sold on the value of program design and code walkthroughs. But the products of analysis benefit just as much from the walkthrough process as do programming products.

Particular attention should be given to walkthroughs of sets of data flow diagrams and process descriptions on which the model of the existing system is based. Emphasis should be on the completeness as well as on the accuracy of these model components. Obviously, knowledgeable users are key participants in these walkthroughs.

Caution

In studying the existing system, many users, and some systems analysts, find themselves using the terms "system" and "department" interchangeably. These are not the same. A given department may use several data processing systems. A given individual may have several responsibilities and may perform tasks connected with several systems. In working through this activity, and particularly in conducting interviews, care should be taken to focus on the system under study. Extreme confusion can result from describing overall jobs or responsibilities of department personnel rather than describing the processing steps or the way the system under study is used.

PERSONNEL INVOLVED

Members of the project team during this activity will include:

- The project leader
- Systems analysts
- User managers
- User operating personnel (as appropriate).

CUMULATIVE PROJECT FILE

At the conclusion of this activity, the project file should contain:

- An updated project plan
- The initial investigation report
- The feasibility report
- A list of management policy decisions that must be made to enable the project to continue
- An interview schedule and interview summaries, updated to reflect interviews conducted during this activity
- An updated glossary of terms
- A logical model of the existing system
- Additional physical documentation of the existing system
- A preliminary overview of new system requirements, prepared during the feasibility study activity
- A description of possible new system solutions, also prepared during the feasibility study activity.

Summary

The existing system is studied and documented to build an understanding of its underlying business goals, objectives, and functions. A logical model of the existing system is created as a basis for this study. Physical processing need not be emphasized.

In gathering documentation on the existing system, systems analysts should include forms or records related to organization, policies and procedures, current system outputs, current system inputs, description of current processing, data files, and peripheral systems.

Existing documentation, which is frequently out of date, should be used as a basis for studying the system to find out what is actually happening. Interviews with top and middle managers should be emphasized.

Throughout the review of the existing system, members of the project team should work actively to identify system deficiencies. User complaints aired during this activity can lead to substantial improvements in the design of the new system.

The information gathered on the existing system is used to construct a physical model of the system. Based on this physical model, the systems analyst builds a logical model of the existing system which, in turn, will become a basis for designing the new system. Walkthroughs help ensure the completeness and accuracy of data flow diagrams and process descriptions on which the model of the existing system may be based.

Members of the project team during Activity 3 will include the project leader, systems analysts, user managers, and user operating personnel (as appropriate).

At the conclusion of this activity, the project file should contain an updated project plan, the initial investigation report, the feasibility report, a list of policy decisions that must be made by management, an interview schedule and interview summaries, an updated glossary of terms, a logical model of the existing system, and additional physical documentation on the existing system. It should also contain a preliminary overview of new system requirements and a description of possible new system solutions, both prepared during the feasibility study activity.

Review/Discussion Questions

1. Why is it important to study the existing system?

2. What is the principal objective of the existing system review?

3. Describe the relationship of this activity to Activity 4: New System Requirements and Activity 5: New System Design.

4. What are the two major end products of the existing system review?

5. How does the 80-20 rule apply to documentation of the existing system?

6. Why can't the systems analyst simply build a model of the existing system based on existing documentation?

7. What is the advantage of studying actual input and output entries, rather than blank forms? What can be learned from these entries?

8. What can be learned by reviewing the maintenance history of the existing system?

9. Why do systems analysts first build a physical model of the existing system before constructing a logical model?

10. What is the role of walkthroughs in the existing system review?

10 SYSTEM MODELING TOOLS

LEARNING OBJECTIVES

On completing reading and other learning assignments for this chapter, you should be able to:

- [ ] Describe the role that modeling, and data flow diagrams, can play in systems analysis.
- [ ] Use and interpret the basic symbols of data flow diagrams.
- [ ] Assign meaningful names to the components of a data flow diagram.
- [ ] Construct simple data flow diagrams and spot obvious errors.
- [ ] Use and interpret the notation used in hierarchical data flow diagrams.
- [ ] Explain the relationships among a context diagram, Diagram 0, and child diagrams.
- [ ] Describe the steps involved in moving from a context diagram to Diagram 0, or from a parent bubble to a child diagram.
- [ ] Identify data structures according to their composition—sequence, iteration, and/or selection.
- [ ] Specify processing rules by means of narratives, decision trees, decision tables, and/or structured English.

☐ Review the main steps in systems analysis and relate them to activities in the systems development life cycle.

☐ Convert a physical model of an existing system into a logical model of the same system.

MODELING IN SYSTEMS ANALYSIS

Modeling can be a key tool of systems analysis. Models can help to accomplish one of the basic goals of systems analysis—establishing a clear communication link between nontechnical users and technically oriented systems designers. Through modeling, it is possible to build an understanding of and modify existing systems to meet new organizational and operating needs. As a communication tool, modeling makes it possible to go from existing systems to new systems with good understanding of user needs and expectations.

CONSTRUCTING DATA FLOW DIAGRAMS

A number of tools and techniques may be used by analysts to model systems. One proven approach, the one followed in this book, is to use data flow diagrams as the basic model building tools. These diagrams represent computer information systems in a way that stresses the flow of data through and their transformation by the system. Emphasis is on data flow and processes, rather than on the control or timing of events. Data flow diagrams can be used to represent portions of systems or entire systems.

Using Data Flow Diagram Symbols

Data flow diagrams are based on a set of simple, standard symbols. Some of these symbols are introduced in Chapter 6. These and two additional symbols are shown in Figure 10-1. Since you will be using these symbols to construct your own data flow diagrams as you work through this chapter, their meaning and use are reviewed briefly below.

External entity. A rectangle indicates any entity external to the system being modeled. The entity represented by a rectangle can be a person, an organization, or even another system. The function of an external entity is to supply data to or receive data from the system.

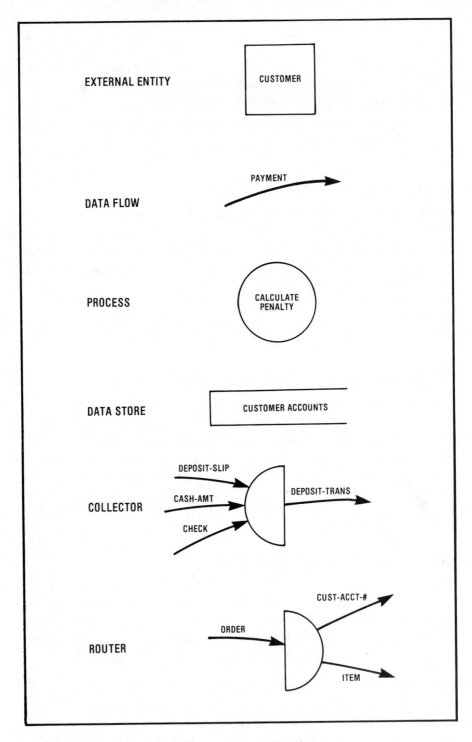

EXTERNAL ENTITY — CUSTOMER

DATA FLOW — PAYMENT

PROCESS — CALCULATE PENALTY

DATA STORE — CUSTOMER ACCOUNTS

COLLECTOR — DEPOSIT-SLIP, CASH-AMT, CHECK → DEPOSIT-TRANS

ROUTER — ORDER → CUST-ACCT-#, ITEM

Figure 10-1. Data flow diagram symbols and meanings.

Data flow. Data flows are indicated by arrows marking the movement of data through the system. A data flow can be thought of as a pipeline carrying individual packets of data from an identified point of origin to a specific destination.

Process. Bubbles, or circles, are used to indicate those points within the system at which incoming data flows are processed or transformed into outgoing data flows.

Data store. Open rectangles are used to identify temporary holding points for collections of data. Processes can add data to or retrieve data from these stores.

Collector. *Collectors* are points within the system at which separate, more detailed data flows are brought together; packaged as a single, more general or higher-level flow; and forwarded. No processing or transformation other than this packaging takes place. Therefore, collectors are unlabeled. A half circle is used to note that this function has taken place. The separate, detailed data flows enter the collector on the curved side and the packaged, higher-level data flow exits on the flat side.

Router. A *router* serves the reverse function of a collector. Thus, a reverse-facing half-circle symbol is used to indicate points at which packets of data are disassembled. The higher-level data flow enters the router on the flat side and the separate, detailed data flows exit from the curved side. A router is often used in a second way. A data flow may represent a transaction that can be one of several types, with each type to be sent to a different process. The router, in this case, would not break an incoming packet of data into several parts, but would direct the entire packet to the appropriate process, depending on its type.

An Example

Consider the data flow diagram shown in Figure 10-2. This is a Diagram 0 for a simplified course registration system for college students.

The external entities in the diagrammed system are a student (STUDENT), faculty (FACULTY), and the university's accounts receivable system (A/R SYSTEM).

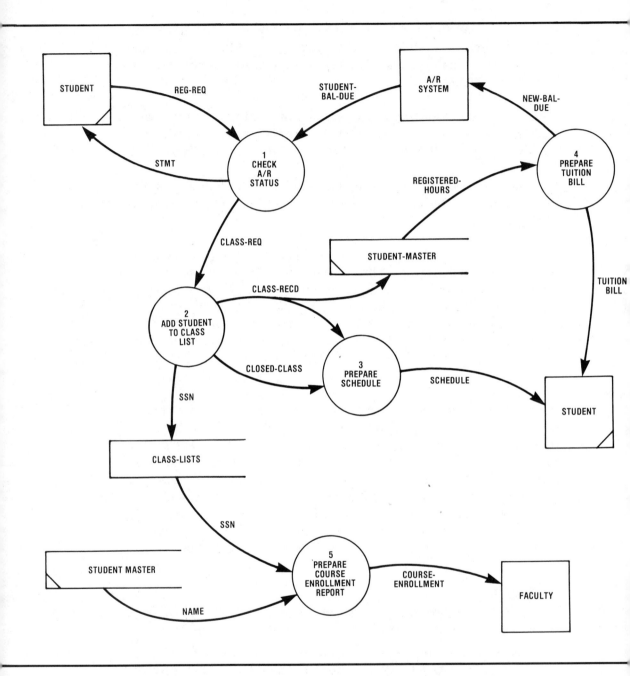

Figure 10-2.   Data flow diagram for simplified course registration system.

The data flow diagram shows that the student submits a registration request (REG-REQ) to the system. As part of the processing, the registration system accesses the balance due for the student (STUDENT-BAL-DUE) from the accounts receivable system. If the student still owes money to the university, the system prepares and delivers to the student a statement for this balance due (STMT). If there is no balance due, the transaction is considered to be a "clean registration," and process 1 sends each individual class request (CLASS-REQ) on to the next process.

For each class request, a test of available space is made. If the class assignment is received, the student's social security number (SSN) is added to the data store for that class (CLASS-LISTS). At the same time, an entry (CLASS-RECD) is made to indicate a completed class registration in the record for this student within the student master (STUDENT-MASTER) data store.

Next, the classes received (CLASS-RECD) and classes denied (CLASS-CLOSED) are compiled on a schedule of classes (SCHEDULE) sent to the student.

The data store of student master information is used to issue a tuition bill (TUITION-BILL) that is sent to the student and also to update the accounts receivable system (NEW-BAL-DUE).

Finally, the STUDENT-MASTER data store is used, together with the CLASS-LISTS data store, to prepare lists of students registered in the various classes (COURSE-ENROLLMENT) for delivery to the faculty.

Note that both the external entity STUDENT and the data store STUDENT-MASTER appear twice in this diagram. The reason for this repetition is to avoid crossing data flow lines. A special convention has been established for handling this type of situation. If an external entity must be repeated, each occurrence is marked with a single slash in the lower right-hand corner. If a second external entity is repeated, a double slash is used for each occurrence of that entity, and so on. A similar convention is used when data stores are repeated, with the slashes appearing in the lower left-hand corner.

Assigning Names

The data flow diagram symbols identify relationships among components of a system. For a data flow diagram to complete its mission as a communication vehicle, these components must be given clear and meaningful names that support the description of the system. The naming of system components should follow these clear, simple rules:

- Data flows and data stores should receive names that describe the composition of the data flowing through the system.

- Process bubbles should be named with strong verbs to indicate the basic transformation or process that is taking place.

Care must be taken to find names that accurately reflect the data and the processing involved. Difficulty in finding names is often a sign of a more serious problem: It may indicate a lack of understanding about what is happening. More detailed information may be necessary before the diagram can be completed.

Construction Hints

The basic purpose of a data flow diagram is to convey an understanding of the system, and to communicate this understanding to users, analysts, and designers. Success in achieving this purpose can be enhanced by avoiding certain common pitfalls. Use these hints as a guide in constructing your own data flow diagrams:

- *Use bubbles only to show processing or transformation of data.* Avoid thinking of computer program commands as processing steps. For example, look at the two data flow diagrams in Figure 10-3. Figure 10-3A includes a process bubble for the reading of an order from a transaction file. The data themselves have not been processed or transformed in any way. Therefore, this process bubble is not necessary, and the diagram should be revised as shown in Figure 10-3B.

- *Data flows must begin and/or end at a process bubble.* That is, there must be a processing function associated with each data flow. Data flows may not begin *and* end at data stores or external entities. As an example, compare the two diagrams in Figure 10-4. This partial system is designed to provide a daily report about inventory status to a purchasing office. Data on parts received daily update an inventory file. The inventory file then serves as the basis for the purchasing office report content. The data flow diagram in Figure

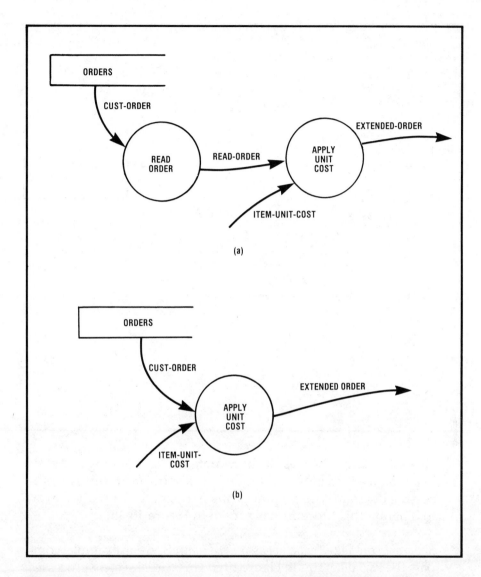

Figure 10-3. Drawing (a) contains an incorrect data flow diagram component: READ ORDER is not a process. Drawing (b) is the correct method for presenting the same procedure.

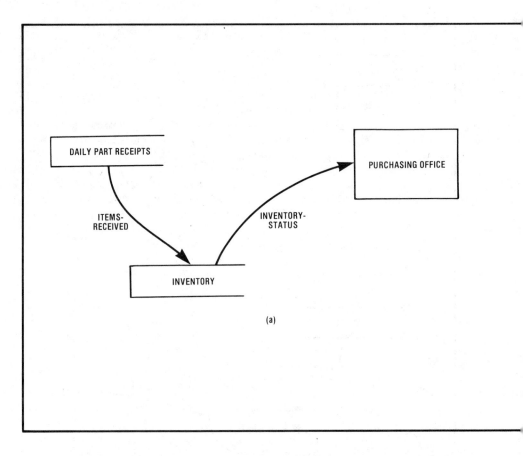

(a)

10-4A is incorrect because it shows data flows beginning and ending at data stores and/or external entities. In effect, this is a processing diagram with no processing happening. The correct way to diagram this procedure is shown in Figure 10-4B.

- *Show only the flow of data, not associated controls.* As an example, compare the two diagrams in Figure 10-5. This partial system processes three types of transactions, identified by the numbers 1, 2, and 3. Corresponding processing steps applied to these transactions are identified as A, B, and C. In Figure 10-5A, all of the program control logic has been diagrammed. This diagram does not really show the flow of data, but instead shows the flow of program processing. The correct way to represent this partial system in a data flow diagram is shown in Figure 10-5B.

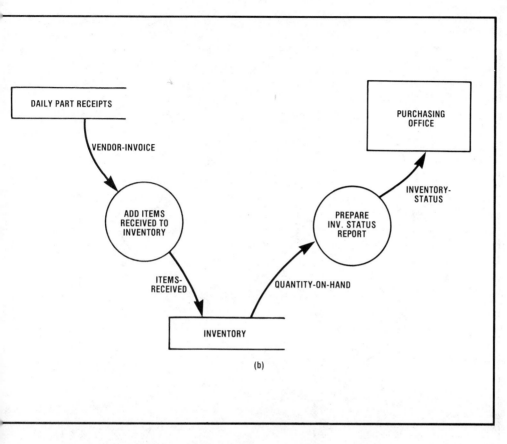

Figure 10-4.   Drawing (a) is incorrect because processing bubbles have been omitted. Drawing (b) shows a correct approach.

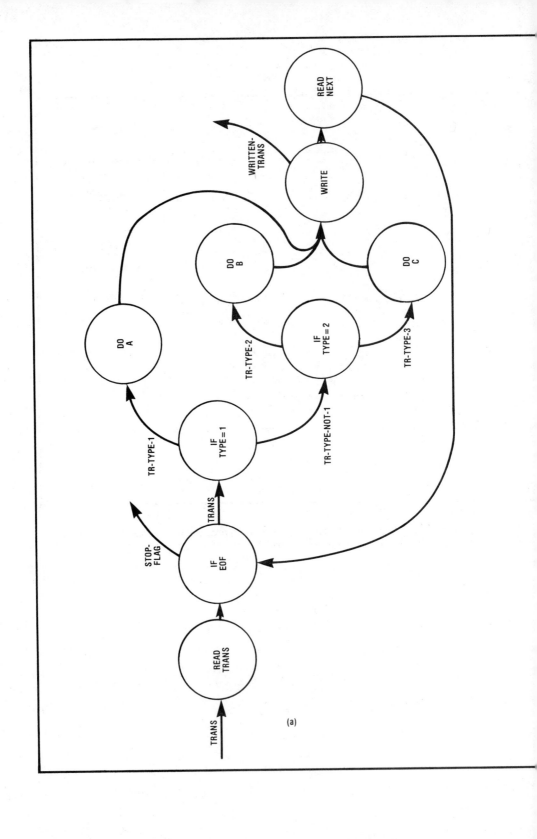

(a)

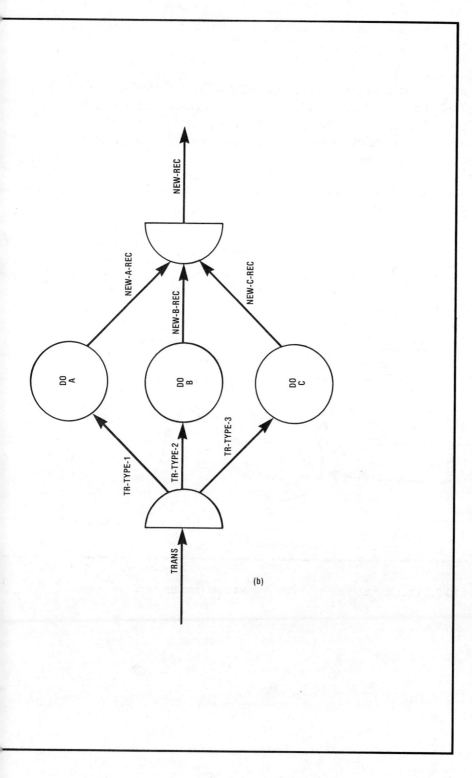

Figure 10-5. Drawing (a) is correct, providing an extreme example of overemphasis of control in a data flow diagram. Drawing (b) is a correct presentation for this procedure.

- *Data flow diagrams can be given a quick visual check to identify obvious errors.* For example, look at the abstraction of a data flow diagram shown in Figure 10-6. Note that the first processing bubble, P1, receives three inputs but does not put out any data. Something is obviously wrong.

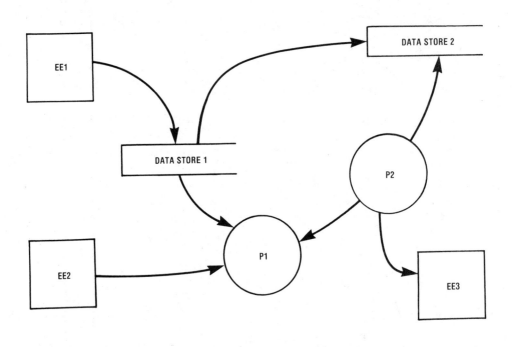

Figure 10-6. Locate the six errors in this abstract data flow diagram.

Practice Assignments

1. The diagram in figure 10-6 has six errors. One of these errors was identified in the discussion above. What are the remaining errors?

2. Critique the three data flow diagram segments shown in Figure 10-7.

3. Draw a data flow diagram to represent a simplified inventory system whose main processing is described as follows: When parts are received from VENDORS, they are accompanied by an INVOICE. The invoice is first checked against the ORDER file to verify that the parts were actually ordered. (Unordered parts are returned.) If they were ordered, the PART-QUANTITY for those particular parts is updated in the INVENTORY file. For accepted parts, a PAYMENT is sent to the vendor, and the payment transaction is entered in the GENERAL LEDGER file. To check parts out of inventory, people on the shop floor submit a REQUISITION. This requisition form is used to update the inventory file. Each week, the complete inventory file is processed to identify parts whose part-quantity has fallen below the REORDER-POINT. For each such part, a PURCHASE-REQUEST is sent to the PURCHASING OFFICE.

(handwritten margin note: P2 NO INPUT / DIS 1 TO DS2 / DS 1 TO P1)

HIERARCHICAL (TOP-DOWN) PARTITIONING OF DATA FLOW DIAGRAMS

The purpose of data flow diagrams is to communicate—to make the relationship among system components clear. One of the basic requirements for effective communication is simplicity. If data flow diagrams become too complex, it becomes difficult to trace data flows and transformations—and their purpose is defeated.

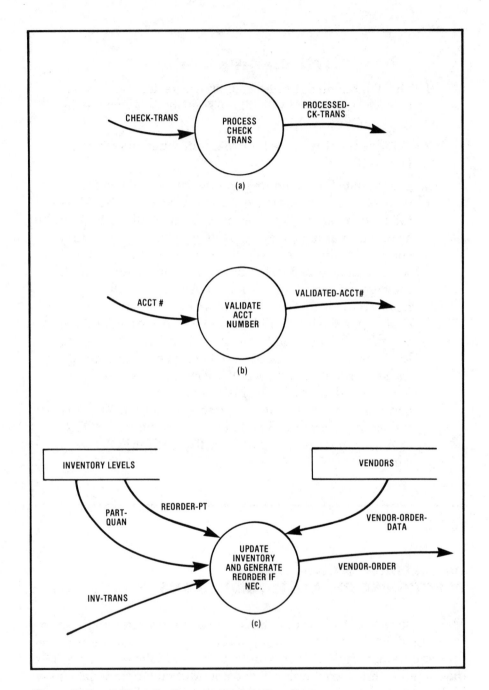

Figure 10-7.   Critique the three partial data flow diagrams.

The mechanism used to keep data flow diagrams simple and understandable is a technique known as *hierarchical* or *top-down partitioning*. Partitioning of data flow diagrams means breaking out details associated with individual processing bubbles to create new diagrams that show data flows and transformations in greater detail.

Even a moderate-size computer information system, if it were to be represented in a single data flow diagram, might require as many as 200 separate process bubbles. With this degree of complexity, data flows and transformations would be extremely difficult to follow, and the diagram would be hard to understand. The same amount of information can be presented, instead, using multiple levels of relatively simple data flow diagrams. With a structured system of identification and numbering, increasing levels of detail can be added without creating confusion. This is possible because the degree of complexity of the diagrams at each level of detail is no greater than at the next higher level.

The starting point is the context diagram, which, in effect, defines the scope of the system. The context diagram highlights the net inputs and sources as well as the net outputs and destinations of data for the system.

A Diagram 0 is used to describe, at a high level, the overall processing in the system. The scope of the system presented in Diagram 0 remains the same as in the context diagram. Consider the abstract context diagram in Figure 10-8. The Diagram 0 shown in Figure 10-9 still contains all of the same inputs and outputs as the context diagram. The only difference is that the single, central bubble in Figure 10-8 has been partitioned into a series of components. At the Diagram 0 level, the process bubbles represent major system components, or major subsystems within an overall system.

Since simplicity promotes understanding, partitioning should never become overly complex or confusing. A good general rule of thumb is that data flow diagrams, at any level of detail, should be limited to between five and 10 process bubbles. This is by no means a hard and fast rule, however. The number of process bubbles can vary depending on the situation and the use to which the diagram will be put. For example, as a working document for systems analysts and designers, it will often be desirable to create a considerably larger and

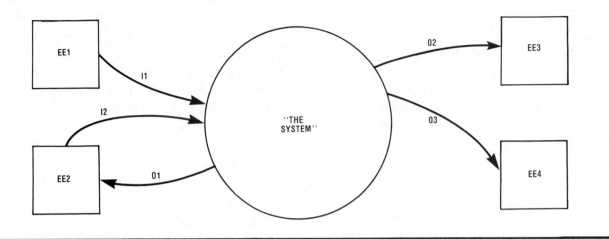

Figure 10-8. This is an abstract context diagram.

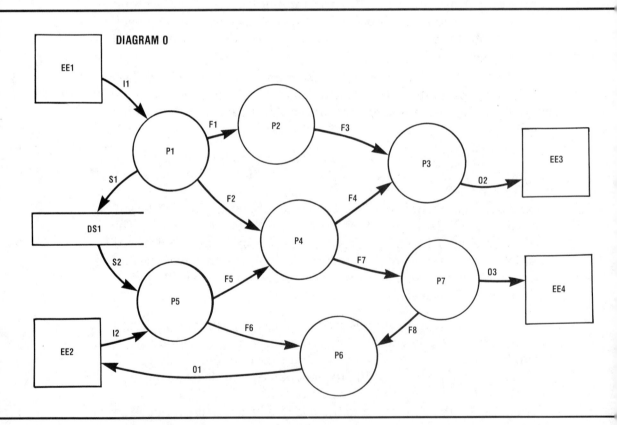

Figure 10-9. This is an abstract Diagram 0 corresponding with the context diagram in Figure 10-8.

more complex data flow diagram, possibly mounted on a wall. This provides a more detailed look at major portions of the system—often a necessity for a full understanding of the impact of proposed changes on solution alternatives.

Individual data flow diagrams can be kept relatively simple because of the ease with which additional levels can be added. At any point, a single process bubble can be exploded into a separate, lower level data flow diagram. The products of this partitioning process are often referred to as *parent* and *child*. Thus, in comparing Figures 10-9 and 10-10, the process bubble P5 in Figure 10-9 would be considered the parent, and the exploded, lower-level diagram shown in Figure 10-10 would be the child.

Note that a clear, hierarchical structure has been established by labeling the child Diagram 5 to correspond with the number of the process bubble that has been exploded. The same type of identification relationship is maintained at each succeeding level of data flow diagrams.

DIAGRAM 5

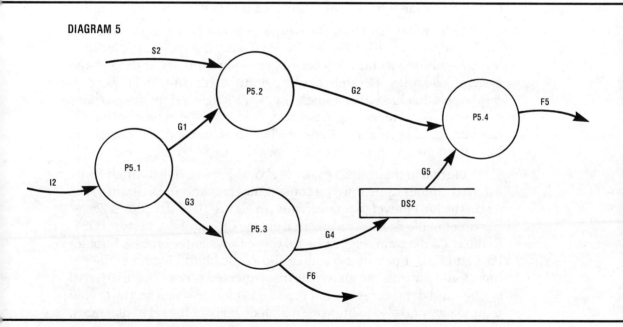

Figure 10-10. This is an abstract Diagram 5 corresponding with process P5 of the Diagram 0 in Figure 10-9.

Thus, for example, if a child diagram were to be prepared for the processing represented by bubble P5.3 in Diagram 5, it would be called Diagram 5.3 and its processing bubbles would be numbered P5.3.1, P5.3.2, and so on.

As succeeding levels of data flow diagrams are developed, it is important to maintain a *balance* in content. This balance has two dimensions:

First, the flows in and out of the parent bubble should be the same as the *net* flows in and out of the child diagram. For example, look at the diagrams in Figures 10-9 and 10-10. The inputs to Process 5 are I2 and S2. In Figure 10-10, these inputs are directed to different process bubbles. However, they are the net inputs to the child Diagram 5. Similarly, outputs from Process 5 are F5 and F6. These are also the net outputs of the child Diagram 5.

The second balance requirement is that the functions accomplished by both the parent bubble and child diagram must be the same. This is not apparent from the abstract illustrations provided here. However, it is up to the analyst to make sure that this balance is maintained.

A determination of how far to explode a data flow diagram is based on the judgment of the systems analyst. Generally speaking, partitioning is continued as far as necessary to assure understanding of the system. Two rules of thumb may be helpful in this context: First, a process bubble that has either a single input or a single output has probably been partitioned far enough. Second, the lowest-level process bubble diagram should perform a single, well-defined function. If these criteria have been met, partitioning has probably been carried far enough.

Note that in the abstract example above, Figures 10-8 through 10-10, external entities appear in the context diagram and in Diagram 0, but not in the lower level diagram. Thus, in Figure 10-9, data flows I2 and S2 enter bubble P5 from an external entity, EE2, and a data store, DS1. In the child diagram, Figure 10-10, these flows enter process bubbles P5.1 and P5.2, but with no source shown. In child diagrams, the net inputs and outputs are shown as disconnected flows. These external entities and data stores are not repeated at lower levels so as to avoid redundancy and also to improve maintainability of the set of diagrams.

Also note the placement of data stores within this hierarchical set of data flow diagrams. Data store DS1 appears in Diagram 0, but not in the lower level Diagram 5. Data store DS2, which did not appear in Diagram 0, is shown in Diagram 5. The convention is that each data store appears once in a hierarchical set of data flow diagrams, at the first level where it is needed by two or more processes. In Diagram 0 (Figure 10-9), both processes P1 and P5 must reference data store DS1; therefore, DS1 appears in Diagram 0. Data store DS2, on the other hand, is internal to process P5. It is used by processes within P5, but not by any of the other processes. Hence, DS2 appears in Diagram 5 (Figure 10-10) and not in Diagram 0.

The hierarchical partitioning of data flow diagrams for the Central City water billing system is illustrated in Chapter 6. The context diagram for the existing system is shown in Figure 6-1 and Diagram 0 in Figure 6-2. Process 5, PREPARE BILL, is shown in Diagram 5, Figure 6-4. Finally, Figure 6-5 shows the child decomposition of Process 5.2, PRODUCE INCYCLE BILL.

Practice Assignment

1. An abstract hierarchical set of data flow diagrams is shown in Figure 10-11. How many errors can you find in Diagram 1 and Diagram 1.2?

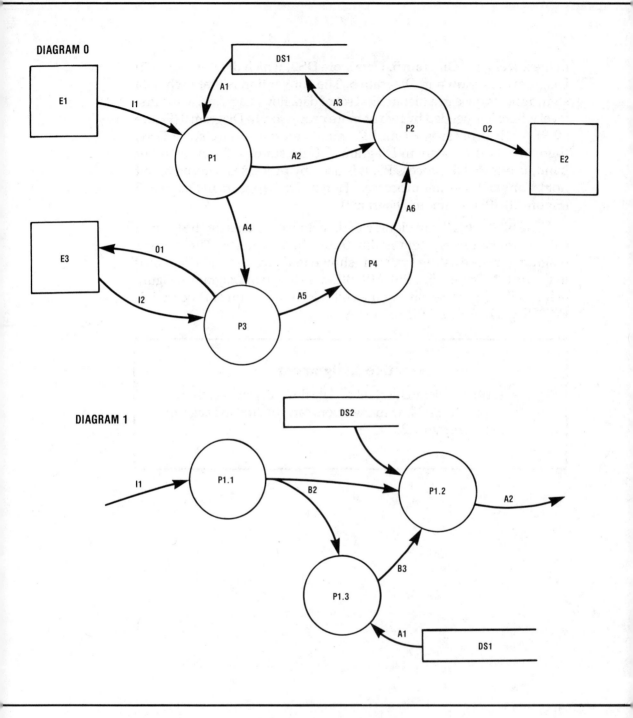

Figure 10-11. Critique this set of abstract, leveled data flow diagrams.

276

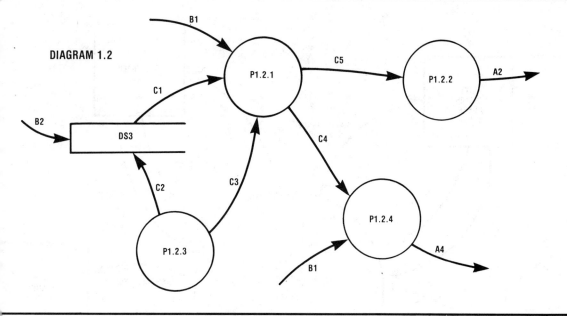

Figure 10-11. Continued.

DEVELOPING THE INITIAL DIAGRAM 0

Possibly the single most difficult task in developing data flow diagrams is determining where and how to start. The context diagram presents no great difficulties, since the entire system is represented by a single circle, the external entities are readily identifiable, and the major inputs and outputs can be listed.

Before getting started on Diagram 0, remember the need to focus on major business operations or occurrences rather than on specific, narrow, physical processing functions. A physical processing function, as it presently exists, may be tied to a procedure that is outmoded and will be discarded. However, long after the new system has been developed and installed, the organization will still be in the same business, performing the same services and conducting the same basic transactions. Concentrating from the beginning on key business occurrences or events will establish a good basis for creating a logical model.

Starting with this basic orientation, the development of Diagram 0 should proceed in a series of logical steps. Since the Central City water billing system will be used as an example throughout this discussion, the context diagram for the existing system is repeated in Figure 10-12 for ease of reference.

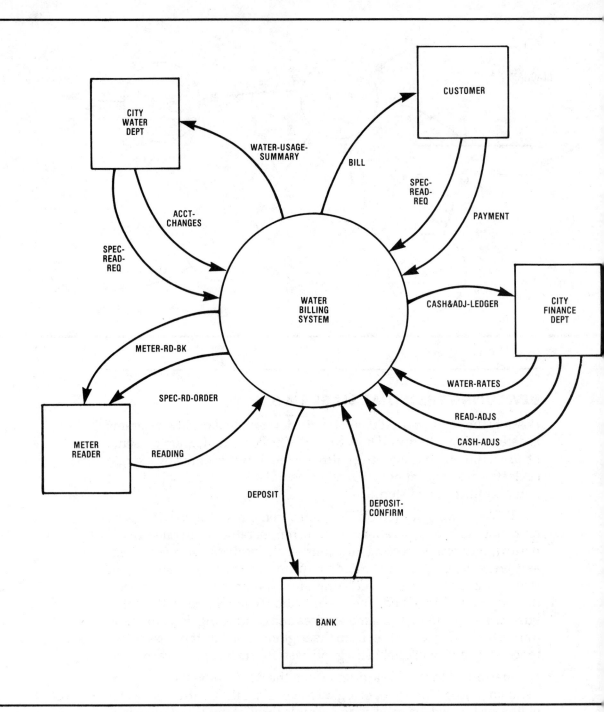

Figure 10-12. The context diagram for the current Central City water billing system is repeated here for reference.

The first step is to note and list the major data stores currently in use. For example, in studying the water billing system, an analyst would quickly recognize three important, existing data stores:

- The customer master file
- The account journal, which lists payments received from customers and any adjustments made
- The billing transaction file, which contains records of all bills issued.

The second step is to list the major business occurrences or events within the system. To identify these, look for three important indicators:

- *Acceptance of a major input to the system.* In the water billing system, a customer payment would be a major input.
- *Production of a major output by the system.* In the water billing system, a customer bill is certainly a major output.
- *Any function triggered by timing.* In the water billing system, one of the requirements is an annual report of water consumption by customer type to be used in the calculation of new water rates. Other, admittedly physical, events within the system that are triggered by time are the annual purgings of old records from the account journal and the billing transaction file.

In the water billing application, 10 major business occurrences have been identified. These are listed in Figure 10-13. This list then becomes the basis for the process steps to be included in Diagram 0.

The building of this list is, to some extent, judgmental, depending on what the particular analyst considers to be the major business events within the system under study. In fact, each analyst is likely to develop a list that differs slightly from the list that would have been formed by another analyst.

The third step is to draw a segment, or fragment, of a data flow diagram for each of the identified events. Each segment will usually contain a single process bubble covering that event. As the data flow diagram is developed, this bubble will become a high-level parent with

---

Events tied to production of major outputs

    1. Prepare customer bill

    2. Extract meters to read

Events tied to application of major inputs

    3. Apply customer payments

    4. Apply new readings

Additional events—tied to minor outputs

    5. Prepare cash and adjustment journal

    6. Prepare special reading orders

Additional event—tied to minor inputs

    7. Modify customer account information

Events triggered by timing

    8. Prepare annual water usage summary

    9. Perform annual archiving of account journal transactions

   10. Perform annual archiving of billing transactions

Figure 10-13. These are the key business events in the existing Central City water billing system.

---

relatively large numbers of inputs and outputs. A series of fragments corresponding with the list in Figure 10-13 is shown in Figure 10-14.

In developing the diagram fragments, consider and identify the outputs produced as well as the events, or necessary inputs, that cause the processing to take place. In identifying inputs and outputs, be sure to note the source and destination of each. These sources and destinations may be external entities, data stores, or other processes. Specifying inputs and outputs in this way establishes the scope of the process, in effect, producing a clear definition of what the process does.

The fourth and final step in the preparation of a Diagram 0 is to assemble the fragments into a single data flow diagram. The first attempt will be rough. It will undoubtedly be necessary to rearrange or

1. Prepare customer bill

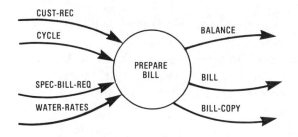

CUST-REC

CYCLE

SPEC-BILL-REQ

WATER-RATES

PREPARE BILL

BALANCE

BILL

BILL-COPY

2. Extract meters to read

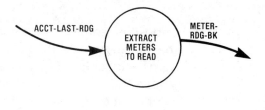

ACCT-LAST-RDG

EXTRACT METERS TO READ

METER-RDG-BK

3. Apply customer payments

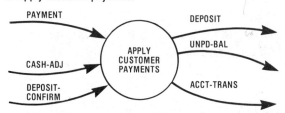

PAYMENT

CASH-ADJ

DEPOSIT-CONFIRM

APPLY CUSTOMER PAYMENTS

DEPOSIT

UNPD-BAL

ACCT-TRANS

4. Apply new readings

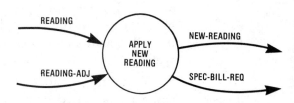

READING

READING-ADJ

APPLY NEW READING

NEW-READING

SPEC-BILL-REQ

5. Prepare cash and adjustment journal

DET-TRANS

PREPARE C&A JOURNAL

CASH&ADJ-JOURNAL

6. Prepare special reading order

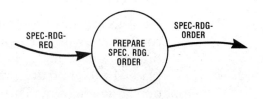

SPEC-RDG-REQ

PREPARE SPEC. RDG. ORDER

SPEC-RDG-ORDER

7. Modify customer account information

ACCT-CHANGE

CHANGE ACCT INFO

NEW-DEMOGRAPHIC-DATA

8. Prepare annual water usage summary

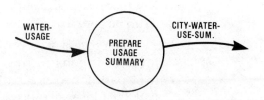

WATER-USAGE

PREPARE USAGE SUMMARY

CITY-WATER-USE-SUM.

9. Perform annual archiving of account journal transactions

Infrequent housekeeping process—omit from DFD

10. Perform annual archiving of billing transactions

Infrequent housekeeping process—omit from DFD

Figure 10-14. These data flow diagram fragments correspond with the key business events of the Central City water billing system.

reposition some of the components of the diagram to improve its appearance. As explained earlier, it may help to repeat data stores or external entities to avoid having data flows cross one another. Figure 10-15 shows the kinds of problems to be expected in preparing a first, rough draft of a data flow diagram. Figure 10-16, then, shows a finished diagram with these problems eliminated.

In this example, two attempts were needed to develop a finished data flow diagram. In practice, there may be many more. Data flow diagrams are so simple to prepare that they should not intimidate anyone. It's easy enough to throw one away and draw a new one. It may take several drafts, particularly during the initial attempts, to come up with documents that are clear and attractive enough to communicate well.

Two different analysts may well come up with two different versions of Diagram 0 for the same system. Following the steps outlined above, if they do not agree on the major business occurrences, the Diagram 0 processes will differ. Differences should not be extreme, however, since major business events should be clear.

A technique often employed when an analyst does not feel totally comfortable with the organization of a Diagram 0 is to explode the entire diagram at once. That is, each process bubble in Diagram 0 is replaced by its child diagram, and all the child diagrams are joined into one large diagram. This partitioning process may be repeated, as necessary, incorporating additional levels of detail and forming a very large and complex data flow diagram. Work with this diagram may suggest more natural groupings of processes from which a revised Diagram 0 can be constructed.

The process of constructing child diagrams is much the same as that involved in constructing a Diagram 0. Simply treat the parent bubble to be partitioned as a context diagram for a small system and proceed with the four-step process outlined above. When constructing data flow diagrams at any level, it is good practice to name the data flows first, then to name the processes. This helps to keep the concentration on the flow and transformation of the data.

One final hint, which applies at all levels of data flow diagram construction, is to concentrate first on the major data flows and processing, ignoring exceptions until a clear understanding of the main processing steps is achieved. Also, it is good practice to name the data flows

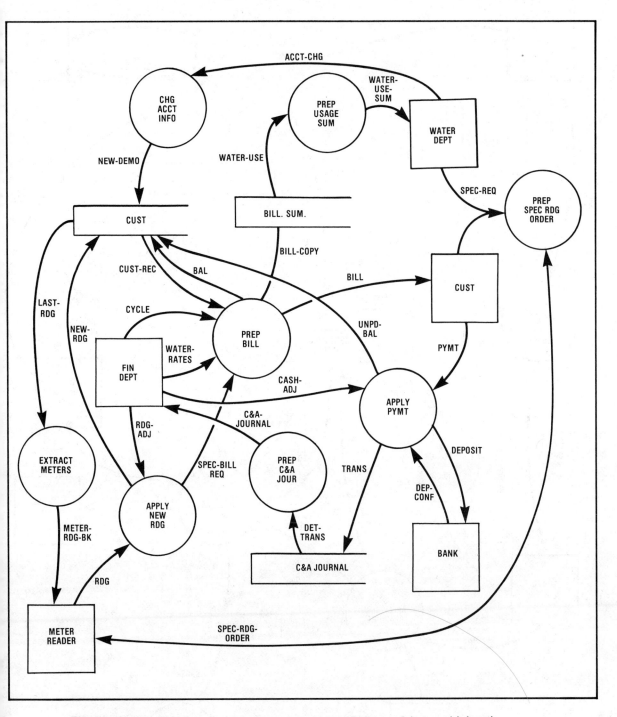

Figure 10-15. This is a first attempt to develop a Diagram 0 by combining the fragments shown in Figure 10-14. The most complex fragments, prepare bill and apply payment, were drawn first. The remaining processes were then appended.

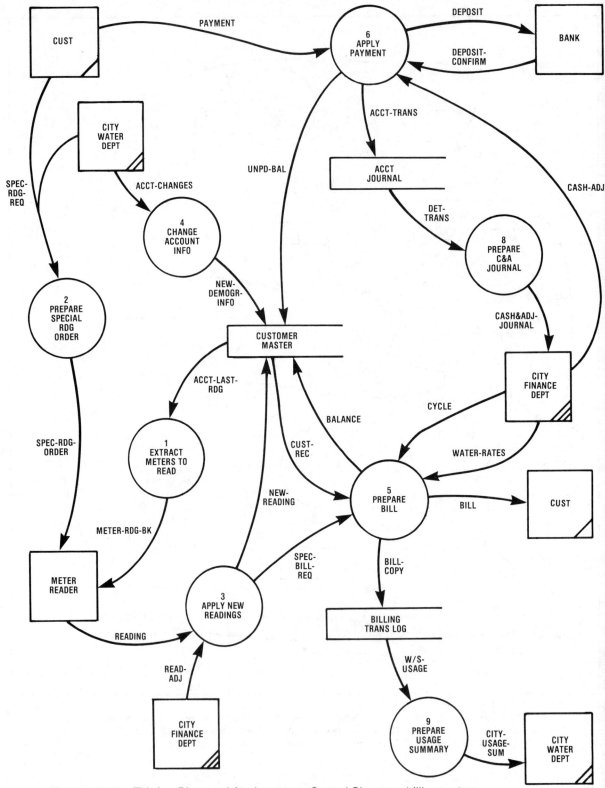

Figure 10-16. This is a Diagram 0 for the current Central City water billing system.

first, then to name the processes. For example, in the course registration system depicted in Figure 10-2, there will undoubtedly be problems with registration requests. Students will request classes that do not exist or that have a time conflict with one another. In the first attempt to construct data flow diagrams for this system, it is a good idea to ignore these exception situations. At the most, they should simply be noted as *stubs* until the first, global understanding is achieved. In Figure 10-2, for example, Process 2, which adds students to a class list, might produce a flow labeled ''invalid-class-request'' with no destination specified.

It is important to remember that data flow diagrams are supported by further documentation that serves to:

- Define data flows

- Define data store contents

- Define the processing that takes place in bubbles that have not been partitioned

- Add the needed control functions that are omitted from data flow diagrams

- Document necessary user access to data.

The first four of these additional systems analysis requirements are covered in the remainder of this chapter. Discussion of the final item is delayed until Chapter 14.

DEFINING DATA—THE DATA DICTIONARY

One of the requirements in the development of data flow diagrams is the naming of components. Among the components that must be named are data flows and data stores. The names that are assigned must then be used consistently throughout system documentation and in the programs that are developed to implement the system. Therefore, it is necessary to establish a common vocabulary, or *data dictionary*, that contains the names assigned to all data flows and data stores, with exact and complete definitions for each term.

Data Elements and Data Structures

Data flows have been likened to pipelines carrying packets of data. Each packet may contain several elements of data. In building a data dictionary, both individual elements and packets of data need special identities and definitions of their own.

A basic unit, or piece, of data that is not broken down into more detailed units is known as a *data element*. Examples of data elements within systems illustrated so far include customer account number, student social security number, balance due, and billing amount.

Packets of data that are broken down are known as *data structures*. A data structure consists of two or more data elements that are logically related. Data structures can be made up of other data structures, as well as of individual data elements. To illustrate, in the student registration system shown in Figure 10-2, the data structure for a registration request would include the student's social security number plus an iteration of course requests. This data structure consists of one data element and a series of other data structures. The social security number, which cannot be broken down meaningfully, is a data element. Each course request, however, consists of several data elements, including department number, course number, section number, and credit hours to be awarded. Thus, each course request is a data structure composed of four data elements.

Powerful techniques are available for describing data structures through use of techniques similar to those of everyday English syntax and grammar. For example, rules of normal English grammar require that a sentence contain two basic parts, a subject and a predicate. These basic sentence parts are, in turn, broken down into parts that can include nouns, verbs, adjectives, adverbs, articles, etc.

In the same sense, data structures can be identified in terms of three basic structures, or rules of grammar. These rules establish structures using *sequence, selection,* and *iteration*. For example, consider a file made up of a sequence of three items, a header record, the body of the file, and the trailer record. The header record may contain information on how to process the body of the file. The trailer record may contain control information such as instructions for cross-checking calculations. In other words, the file, as a whole, is described simply as a sequence of three items—header, body, and trailer.

Next, consider the body of the file. In its own right, the body can be considered a file, itself made up by an iteration of a variable number of records. In an iterated file, each record may be of the same type and follow the same format. But, as another option, a file may have records of several different types, such as a personnel record, a skill-experience record, a salary-history record, and so on. This option constitutes a use of the selection rule. That is, each record is of one type or another, depending on a selection indicator contained in the record. Continuing to a more detailed level, a personnel record might be considered a sequence of things like name, address, phone number, marital status, and so on, together with a sequence of subrecords. One of those subrecords might be a list of children—an iteration of zero or more names.

Specific notations are used to implement syntax rules. These notations are illustrated in Figure 10-17. Within data structures, a sequence is simply a linking together of data elements or data structures. Components that are joined together in a sequence are grouped into a single data structure by means of plus signs (+), which assume the meaning of "and." The use of the plus sign in this situation indicates a joining together, or grouping, rather than an arithmetic operation.

Iteration of data elements or structures within larger data structures is normally indicated by braces ({. . .}). The data element or structure enclosed within the braces is iterated, or repeated, within the data structure. Thus, for example, within a student record, the iterated course requests would be enclosed in braces. Optional data elements can also be considered as iterations because an optional item may be used either zero times or once. Thus, optional data items may be enclosed in braces or, alternatively, may be indicated by parentheses.

The third operation for building data structures is selection. Selection, in this context, refers to a group of data elements or structures out of which one, and only one, item may be selected for use. This is indicated by bracketing. The example in Figure 10-17c illustrates the data structure for a checking account transaction in a bank. An occurrence of the data structure CK-TRAN will be selected from a check, a charge for a check, a deposit, or an overdraft. Each of these four possibilities is itself a data structure.

Figure 10-18 illustrates the data dictionary syntax applied to the example of an EMPLOYEE-FILE. Note the similarity of the concept of

DATA STRUCTURE NOTATION CONVENTIONS

SEQUENCE
EX:

          COURSE = DEPT-NUM
                    + COURSE-NUM
                    + COURSE-TITLE
                    + CREDIT-HOUR-RANGE
                    + TERMS-OFFERED
                    + DESCRIPTION

REPETITION

EXACTLY N ITERATIONS	$_N\{\text{---}\}$
ONE TO N ITERATIONS	$_1^N\{\text{---}\}$ OR $\{\text{---}\}_{CONDITION}$
UNLIMITED ITERATIONS	$\{\text{---}\}$
OPTIONAL	$_0^1\{\text{---}\}$ OR (---)

EX: REGISTRATION-REQUEST =

STUDENT RECORD =
     SOC-SEC-NUM   SOC-SEC-NUM

$$+ \begin{Bmatrix} \text{DEPT-NUM} \\ +\text{COURSE-NUM} \\ +\text{YEAR-TERM} \\ +\text{CREDIT-HOURS} \\ +\text{GRADE} \end{Bmatrix}_{\substack{\text{ALL COMPLETED} \\ \text{COURSES}}} \qquad + \,_1^{10}\begin{Bmatrix} \text{DEPT-NUM} \\ +\text{COURSE-NUM} \\ +\text{SEC-NUM} \\ +\text{CREDIT-HOURS} \end{Bmatrix}$$

SELECTION—EXACTLY ONE OF SEVERAL OPTIONS
EX:

$$\text{COURSE-CHANGE-REQUEST} = \begin{bmatrix} \text{ADD-COURSE} \\ \text{DROP-COURSE} \end{bmatrix}$$

Figure 10-17.   These are illustrations of data structure notation conventions.

EMPLOYEE-FILE =   HEADER-RECORD
                 + BODY
                 + TRAILER-RECORD

BODY = {BODY-RECORD}

$$
\text{BODY-RECORD} = \begin{cases} \text{PERSONNEL-RECORD} \\ \text{SKILL-EXPERIENCE-RECORD} \\ \text{SALARY-HISTORY-RECORD} \end{cases}
$$

PERSONNEL-RECORD =   NAME
                    + EMPLOYEE-NUMBER
                    + BIRTH-DATE
                    + HOME-ADDRESS
                    + PHONE
                    + (SPOUSE-NAME)
                    + $_0^{10}${PREVIOUS-EMPLOYER + DATES}
                    + $_0^{15}${CHILD-NAME}

Figure 10-18.   These notations show different, increasing levels of detail for data dictionary syntax.

hierarchical partitioning of data flow diagrams to the partitioning illustrated by the increasing levels of detail shown in Figure 10-18. As a general rule, the data structures that define the data flows of higher-level data flow diagrams will tend to be higher-level data structures. As the data flow diagrams are partitioned into child diagrams, the corresponding data structures tend to be decomposed on the same basis—though this is not a hard and fast rule.

Building and Maintaining The Data Dictionary

The accompanying examples represent a manual method for establishing and maintaining control over a data dictionary. Included are three types of forms—for data elements, data structures, and data stores. In reviewing these forms, consider their content and what they accomplish, rather than their specific formats.

Figure 10-19 shows a form used to define data elements, in this case for the water billing system. The first part of the form names the data element, READING-DATE. The data element is then described: It indicates the date on which the meter was read, and it consists of six digits, representing the month, day, and year of the reading. The source, data store, and uses for this data element are also given.

For each data element, the analyst also assigns value limits and edit checks that will be applied in processing. Data elements can assume values that are either continuous or discrete. In Figure 10-19, the values are *discrete*, or confined to specific items. Values for months of the year, for example, can only be one of 12 specific options—the whole numbers 01 to 12. By contrast, values such as temperature readings or dollar amounts are *continuous* in that they can vary over a wide range of possible values.

Figure 10-20 shows a form used to define data structures. Heading content is similar to that on the data element form. Note the *alias* entry, which represents an alternate name that can be used to represent the same data structure. The composition of the data structure is described, using the notation explained earlier.

The form in Figure 10-21 is used to specify the content of a data store. This form can be used for manual as well as computer files. The final section describes, in data structure notation, the composition of a typical record in the data store.

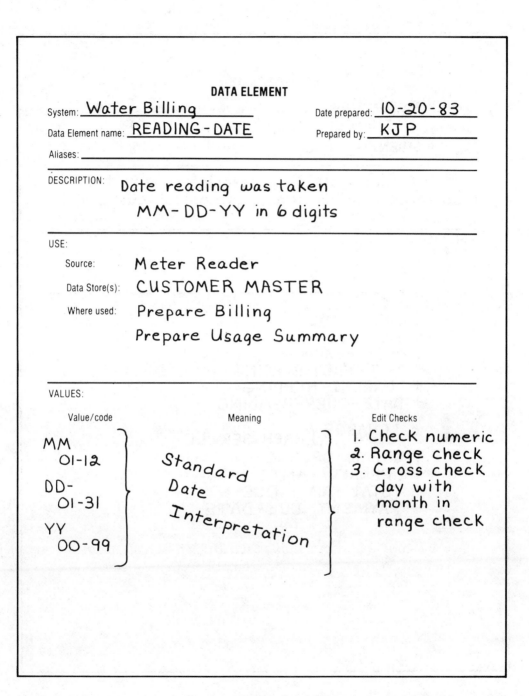

DATA ELEMENT

System: Water Billing   Date prepared: 10-20-83

Data Element name: READING-DATE   Prepared by: KJP

Aliases:

DESCRIPTION: Date reading was taken
               MM-DD-YY in 6 digits

USE:

Source: Meter Reader

Data Store(s): CUSTOMER MASTER

Where used: Prepare Billing
               Prepare Usage Summary

VALUES:

Value/code	Meaning	Edit Checks
MM 01-12 DD- 01-31 YY 00-99	Standard Date Interpretation	1. Check numeric 2. Range check 3. Cross check day with month in range check

Figure 10-19.   Form used for defining values of data elements.

DATA STRUCTURES

System: **Water Billing**   Date prepared: **10-27-83**

Data Structure name: **INCYCLE-BILL**   Prepared by: **KJP**

Aliases: **RESIDENTIAL-BILL**

DESCRIPTION: **Contains all data associated with the bill produced for an individual residential cust. acct.**

WHERE USED:

COMPOSITION: **ACCT #**
+ CUST-NAME
+ BILL-ADDR
+ PREV-READING
+ DATE-PREV-READING
+ CURRENT-READING
+ DATE-CURR-READING

+ { CHARGE } EACH SERVICE
+ UNPAID-BALANCE
+ (PENALTY-AMT)
+ TOTAL-AMT-DUE
+ PAYMENT-DUE-DATE

Figure 10-20. Form used for defining data structures.

DATA STORE

System: Water Billing   Date prepared: 12-7-83

Data Store name: CUSTOMER-MASTER   Prepared by: TAP

Aliases: _____

ORGANIZATION:

_____ Sequential   X Indexed   _____ Direct   Keys:

Number of records: 20K   Primary ACCT #

Expected rate of growth: 500/yr   Secondary _____

Approximate record size: 200 byte   _____

PRIMARY PURPOSE/USE: Used for preparing bills
Also-to prepare meter reading book & accept
      new rdgs

RECORD COMPOSITION: Approx.
   Data Structure/element name   Length
        ACCT #   6
      + CUST-NAME   25
      + SERVICE-ADDR   40
      + BILLING-ADDR   40
      + USER-CLASS   1
      + READING-SEQUENCE   4
      + METER-TYPE   2
      + (METER-READER-MSG)   30
      + CURR-BAL *   35
      + 6{READING}*   90

              *These are data structures

Figure 10-21. Form used to specify content of a data store.

294 OLD MAN INFORMATION

These forms illustrate the main content that is useful in a data dictionary. It is possible to maintain a manual data dictionary for a small system by creating three files—one for each type of form—with sheets in each file stored in alphabetical order by name. For most systems, however, this soon becomes unwieldy. A slightly better approach might be to implement a data dictionary using a word processing package. This would make available on-line inquiry and maintenance, as well as the ability to search text for key words. A still better approach is to use special-purpose data dictionary software. This type of software typically controls uniqueness of names, allows for easy updating, and provides definition lists and query capabilities. More advanced software systems exist that will create data flow diagrams, maintain the accompanying data dictionary, and link the two by automatically verifying balancing.

Practice Assignments

1. A budget record consists of the fiscal year, division and department numbers, number of line-items budgeted, and, for each line-item budgeted, the line-item number and budget amount. Prepare a data structure notation for this budget record.

2. A checking account master record contains the account number, customer name, home address, and perhaps a business address. It also contains the average daily balance for each month in the current calendar year. Further, it contains the account numbers of any related accounts held by the individual or members of his or her immediate family. Finally, if the person has opted for a special service—automatic loan on overdraft—there will be an indicator to this effect. Prepare a data structure for the checking account master record.

SPECIFYING PROCESSING RULES—PROCESSING DESCRIPTIONS

Process descriptions are sets of rules, policies, and procedures associated with process bubbles, specifying the data transformations. Process descriptions, like the data dictionary, support data flow diagrams. They state organizational policy, not the method of implementation.

The way in which processing within a given bubble is identified depends on the level of the data flow diagram. The usual method of describing upper level processes is to partition them into lower level processes through the use of child data flow diagrams. Ultimately, this brings the majority of processes down to a level at which there is either one data flow in and multiple data flows out or multiple data flows in and a single data flow out. It is not always necessary to partition this far. In practice, judgment may indicate that there is no point in partitioning to this level if the process is fairly straightforward and can be described completely in a single page of specifications. Tools for specifying these lowest level processes are presented in the sections that follow.

Occasionally it may be necessary to prepare process descriptions for intermediate level bubbles affected by conditions that cannot be shown on data flow diagrams. Typical examples include processes that have critical timing considerations or special procedural relationships within the system. In these cases, even though the intermediate level bubbles are partitioned further, it still may be desirable to prepare brief process descriptions.

Although process descriptions can be prepared in any form or format that provides the needed information, it usually helps to have a printed form available. This form serves both to guide the preparation of specifications and also to assure completeness of entries. A typical process description form is shown in Figure 10-22.

The principal tools used to communicate process descriptions are:

- Brief, explicit narratives
- Decision trees
- Decision tables
- Structured English
- Combinations of these methods.

Process Narratives

Process narratives are, basically, verbal descriptions of processes. Words, by their nature, are inexact ways of describing specific events or conditions. Thus narratives should be used only in situations in which

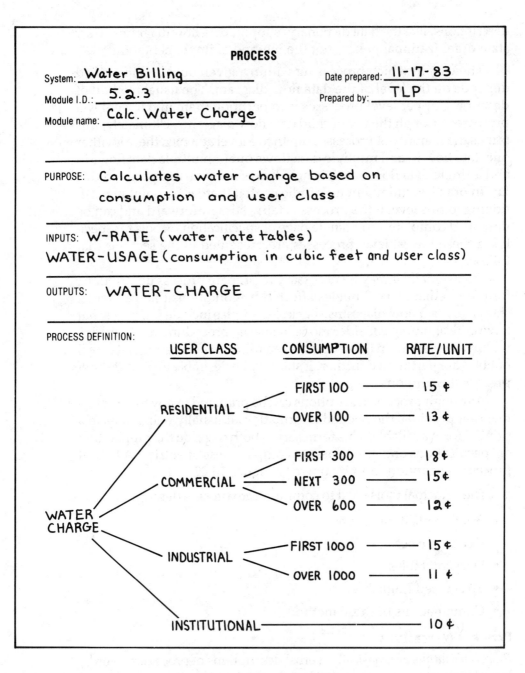

PROCESS

System: __Water Billing__   Date prepared: __11-17-83__

Module I.D.: __5.2.3__   Prepared by: __TLP__

Module name: __Calc. Water Charge__

PURPOSE: Calculates water charge based on
          consumption and user class

INPUTS: W-RATE (water rate tables)
WATER-USAGE (consumption in cubic feet and user class)

OUTPUTS: WATER-CHARGE

PROCESS DEFINITION:

USER CLASS	CONSUMPTION	RATE/UNIT
RESIDENTIAL	FIRST 100	15 ¢
	OVER 100	13 ¢
COMMERCIAL	FIRST 300	18 ¢
	NEXT 300	15 ¢
	OVER 600	12 ¢
INDUSTRIAL	FIRST 1000	15 ¢
	OVER 1000	11 ¢
INSTITUTIONAL		10 ¢

WATER CHARGE

Figure 10-22.   Process forms can use graphic notations or narratives for processing
definitions. This example uses a decision tree.

other tools are not appropriate. Process narratives should be as brief and as specific as possible. They may be used to describe special timing requirements, system constraints, or relationships among processes. An example of the use of a narrative within the water billing system is given in Figure 10-23. This description covers timing requirements for an intermediate-level process. The actual calculations are described in specifications for lower-level processes.

Some process descriptions require the communication of policy involving a number of different conditions that may occur in different combinations, with each combination producing a specific outcome. These differing combinations of conditions can be difficult to represent in narrative form. It is difficult to verify that all combinations of conditions have been covered without contradictions. It is even harder to modify this type of narrative specification once it has been written.

Two tools are available to represent combinations of conditions:

- Decision trees
- Decision tables.

Decision Trees

A *decision tree* gets its name from the fact that it develops a series of branches representing conditions or processing alternatives. Each condition to be dealt with during processing is represented by a separate set of branches, one for each value associated with the condition. Outcomes are listed, foliage style, at the ends of the branches.

To illustrate the development of decision trees, study carefully the process diagram and the narrative description in Figure 10-24. Note that the process diagram has three input data flows and one output data flow. Thus, the process meets the test of being at the lowest level of decomposition.

From the process description in Figure 10-24, three conditions can be identified. These are listed below, with their possible values:

- Checking account balance—values $>= 1000$ or < 1000
- Number of overdrafts—values $<= 2$ or > 2
- Average savings balance—values $>= 500$ or < 500.

PROCESS

System: Water Billing   Date prepared: 11-15-83

Module I.D.: 5.2   Prepared by: TLP

Module name: Prep. In-cycle Bill

PURPOSE: Batch run to prepare all water bills
          for a specified cycle

INPUTS: W-RATE (water rate tables)   CUST - REC
         CYCLE (cycle to be billed)

OUTPUTS: IN-CYCLE BILL and COPY
          BALANCE (new balance updates CUST-MAST)

PROCESS DEFINITION:

There are four residential cycles which are billed
bimonthly according to the following schedule:
        Cycle 1 - 2nd week (Jan, Mar, May, July, Sept, Nov)
          2 - 4th week   "
          3 - 2nd week (Feb, Apr, June, Aug, Oct, Dec)
          4 - 4th week   "
There is a 5th cycle consisting of all commercial,
industrial, and institutional accounts. They are billed
using the same process as for residential — except that
they are billed the 1st week of <u>each</u> month

Figure 10-23. This process form uses a narrative for a process definition.

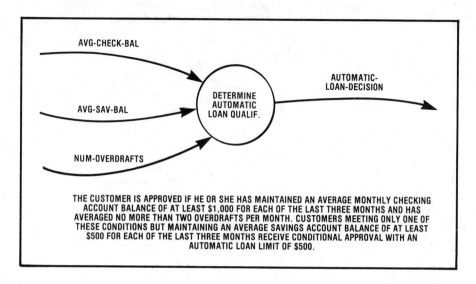

THE CUSTOMER IS APPROVED IF HE OR SHE HAS MAINTAINED AN AVERAGE MONTHLY CHECKING ACCOUNT BALANCE OF AT LEAST $1,000 FOR EACH OF THE LAST THREE MONTHS AND HAS AVERAGED NO MORE THAN TWO OVERDRAFTS PER MONTH. CUSTOMERS MEETING ONLY ONE OF THESE CONDITIONS BUT MAINTAINING AN AVERAGE SAVINGS ACCOUNT BALANCE OF AT LEAST $500 FOR EACH OF THE LAST THREE MONTHS RECEIVE CONDITIONAL APPROVAL WITH AN AUTOMATIC LOAN LIMIT OF $500.

Figure 10-24.   Translation of bank loan-qualification policy into a data flow diagram.

The three possible outcomes for this process are:

- Approval (no limit)
- Conditional approval ($500 limit)
- Rejection.

A decision tree representing the processing of these conditions to produce the identified outcomes is shown in Figure 10-25.

The principles for development of decision trees are relatively straightforward. Identify all conditions, the values these conditions may assume, and all possible outcomes. Each condition gives rise to a set of branches—one for each value the condition may assume. Figure 10-26 illustrates this process in a universal, generic way. This decision tree assumes that there are three possible conditions, identified as C1, C2, and C3. Two possible outcomes are identified as O1 and O2. The conditions may assume the following values:

- C1 may assume values of V11, V12, or V13.
- C2 may have values of V21 or V22.
- C3 may have values of V31 or V32.

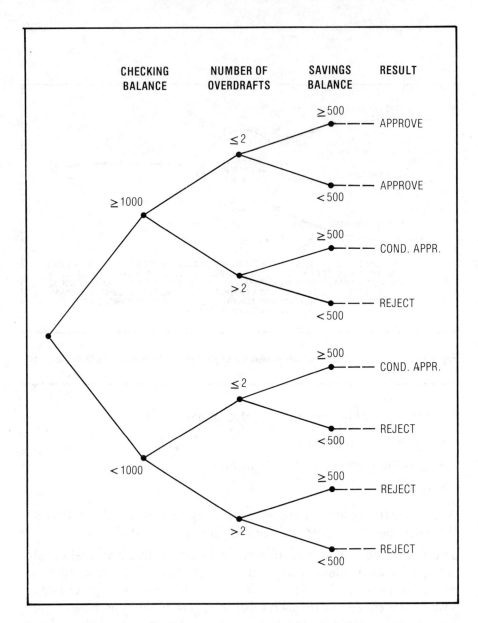

CHECKING BALANCE **NUMBER OF OVERDRAFTS** **SAVINGS BALANCE** **RESULT**

≥ 500 — APPROVE
≤ 2
< 500 — APPROVE
≥ 1000
≥ 500 — COND. APPR.
> 2
< 500 — REJECT

≥ 500 — COND. APPR.
≤ 2
< 500 — REJECT
< 1000
≥ 500 — REJECT
> 2
< 500 — REJECT

Figure 10-25. This is a decision tree expressing a bank's policy about loan qualifications.

Note that all of these conditions, outcomes, and values are logically interrelated in the decision tree shown in Figure 10-26. The power of a decision tree is twofold: It is easy to verify that all combinations of conditions have been covered, and changes are easy to make.

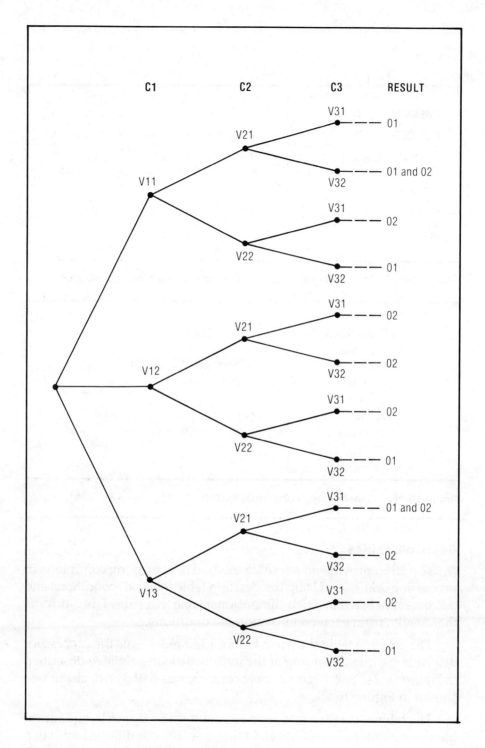

Figure 10-26. General format of a decision tree.

AVG CK BAL $\geq$ 1000	Y	Y	Y	Y	N	N	N	N
NUM OVERDRAFTS $\leq$ 2	Y	Y	N	N	Y	Y	N	N
AVG SAV BAL $\geq$ 500	Y	N	Y	N	Y	N	Y	N
APPROVE	X	X						
COND. APPROVE			X		X			
REJECT				X		X	X	X

Figure 10-27. Decision table covering policy for automatic loan qualification.

THE GENERAL FORM OF A DECISION TABLE IS

LIST OF CONDITIONS	COLUMNS REPRESENTING LOGICAL COMBINATIONS OF CONDITION VALUES
LIST OF OUTCOMES	X'S INDICATING RESULTING OUTCOME(S) FOR EACH SET OF CONDITIONS

Figure 10-28. General format of a decision table.

Decision Tables

Decision tables provide an alternate method of specifying conditions or processing branches. Using the decision table method, conditions and outcomes are listed in a two-dimensional table that shows the outcome that results from each combination of conditions.

The decision table shown in Figure 10-27 represents the process for determining qualifications for the automatic loan privilege described in Figure 10-24. This decision table corresponds with the decision tree shown in Figure 10-25.

The table is divided into four quadrants. The upper left quadrant has one row for each condition. In this case, the conditions have been stated so that the values will be either yes or no. The lower left quadrant

C1	V11	V11	V11	V11	V12	V12	V12	V12	V13	V13	V13	V13
C2	V21	V21	V22	V22	V21	V21	V22	V22	V21	V21	V22	V22
C3	V31	V32	V31	V32	V31	V32	V31	V32	V31	V32	V31	V32
01	X	X		X					X	X		X
02		X	X		X	X	X			X	X	X

Figure 10-29. This decision table corresponds with the decision tree in Figure 10-25.

contains one row for each possible outcome. The upper right quadrant contains the values associated with each of the conditions. There is one column for each combination of values. Finally, in the lower right quadrant, an ''X'' mark is used to designate each outcome that may result from the combination of values in the column above. These quadrants are depicted generically in Figure 10-28.

To provide a further illustration, the decision table in Figure 10-29 conveys the same conditions, values, and outcomes as the decision tree in Figure 10-26. Note that the columns and rows of data in the decision table convey all of the possible combinations of outcomes and values for the conditions stated, thus providing the same documentation of processing rules as the corresponding decision tree.

Practice Assignments

1. The process bubble in Figure 10-30 calculates the discount to be applied to retailer purchases from the Associated Grocers of America (AGA) warehouse operation. The accompanying narrative, used in Chapter 6, specifies the processing rules that apply.

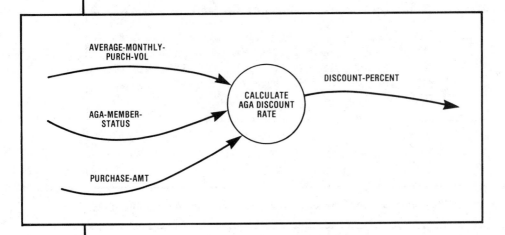

Figure 10-30. This partial data flow diagram implements the discount policy of AGA.

A minimum 5 percent discount applies for all purchases. If the retailer maintains an average monthly purchase volume of at least $100,000, a 15 percent discount applies, provided the retailer is an AGA member. When the retailer's purchase volume is under $100,000, the discount rate is 12 percent for AGA members and 7 percent for nonmembers. Retailers who are not AGA members, but who maintain a $100,000 monthly purchase volume, qualify for a 10 percent discount, unless the purchase totals less than $35,000.

Based on this narrative and diagram:
- a. List the outcomes.
- b. List the conditions.
- c. List the values that may be assumed by the conditions.
- d. Develop a decision tree relating these conditions, values, and outcomes.
- e. Develop a decision table relating the same conditions, values, and outcomes.

2. The following narrative describes a policy designed to balance demand and availability by specifying the number of CIS classes for which a student may register. Draw a

process bubble similar to the one in Figure 10-30 for this situation and follow the steps called for in Practice Assignment 1 above to construct both a decision tree and a decision table that expresses the policy:

CIS majors with below a 2.5 GPA may not register for CIS classes. Those above a 3.5 GPA may register for three CIS classes if they have completed at least 60 hours or two CIS classes if at least 30 hours or one CIS class if under 30 hours. Other CIS majors are limited to one CIS class unless they have more than 60 hours—in which case they may take two. CIS minors below a 3.0 GPA and students who are neither CIS majors nor minors may not register for CIS classes. CIS minors with at least a 3.0 GPA may register for one CIS class.

Structured English

Not all processes involve the consideration of multiple conditions and resulting outcomes like those considered above. Many processes lend themselves, instead, to a more straightforward sequence of steps or the iteration of smaller processes. In such instances, a series of formal English statements, using a small, strong, selected vocabulary, can be used to communicate processing rules. This tool is known as *structured English.*

One of the values of structured English is that verbal statements are a natural medium of communication between users and programmers. Users are generally comfortable with English statements. At the same time, the format of structured English is sufficiently precise so that it will not be misinterpreted by designers or programmers. To maintain the communication link with the user, however, care must be taken to avoid having structured English statements look like pseudocode.

Structured English uses three types of constructs:

- Sequence
- Selection
- Iteration.

SEQUENCE:

Set penalty of 10% of 90day-arrears.
Set net-bill to sum of curr-charge plus previous-balance plus penalty.

SELECTION (IF-THEN):

If 90day-arrears is over $50
    Then
        Set penalty to 15% of 90day-arrears.
    Otherwise
        Set penalty to 10% of 90day-arrears.
Set net-bill to sum of curr-charge plus previous-balance plus penalty.

SELECTION (CASE CONSTRUCT):

Select the appropriate case.
    Case1 (Customer-type is residential).
        .
        .
        .

    Case2 (Customer-type is commercial).
        .
        .
        .

    Case3 (Customer-type is industrial).
        .
        .
        .

    Case4 (Customer-type is institutional).
        .
        .
        .

ITERATION:

> For each account record in the customer-master-file:
>> Set consumption to the difference of
>>> Current-read less previous-read.
>> If consumption is positive,
>>> Then
>>>> Select the appropriate case.
>>>>> Case1 (Customer-type is residential):
>>>>> .
>>>>> .
>>>>> .
>>>>> Case2 (Customer-type is commercial):
>>>>> .
>>>>> .
>>>>> .
>>>>>
>>>>> .
>>>>> .
>>>>> .
>>> Otherwise
>>>> Write the account-number and service-address to the accts-not-billed report.

Figure 10-31. Samples of structured English statements.

Examples of structured English statements for these three constructs are shown in Figure 10-31. Note the major techniques of structured English used in these examples:

- Strong verbs are used to begin statements that describe initiation of an act or implementation of a decision.

- Statements are formatted with multiple levels of indentation. These indentations correspond with processing blocks.

307

As is the case with decision trees and decision tables, use of structured English statements is at the discretion of the analyst. These three tools can be used singly or in combination, depending upon the process being described. For example, Figures 10-32 and 10-33 show a situation in which a process is best described by a combination of structured English and a decision tree. Figure 10-32 provides the background information, while Figure 10-33 contains the actual process description.

USE OF MODELING TO SUPPORT THE ANALYSIS PROCESS

System modeling tools discussed in this chapter can play a vital role in the process of systems analysis. This last section of the chapter covers the way in which the modeling tools can be applied to the analysis process. This process, as described in Chapter 6, involves three main steps:

- Understand the existing system.
  - Construct a model of the existing physical system.
  - Derive from the physical model a logical model of the existing system.
- Identify changes in user requirements.
  - Document business processing (logical) requirements.
  - Document physical requirements.
- Specify a new system solution.
  - Create a logical model for the new system, using the logical model of the existing system and the processing (logical) requirements for the new system.
  - Create a physical model for the new system, using the logical model for the new system and the physical requirements for the new system.

This process is repeated, or iterated, throughout the first two phases of the systems development life cycle. With each iteration, work progresses to deeper levels of detail.

The analysis process extends across the activities of the analysis and general design phase. Activity 3: Existing System Review focuses on the first step of the process. Activity 4: New System Requirements aims

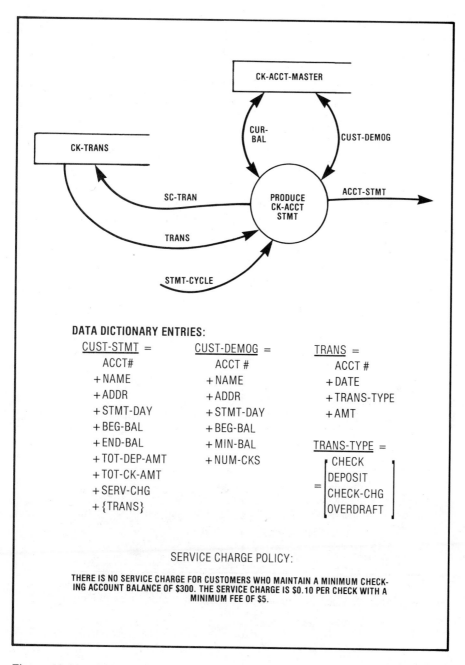

Figure 10-32. Background information needed to create a process description for development of monthly checking account statements.

PROCESS DESCRIPTION:

FOR EACH ACCOUNT IN THE CK-ACCT-MASTER FILE FOR THIS CYCLE:

FOR ALL TRANS RECORDS IN CK-TRANS FILE FOR THIS ACCT WHICH ARE DATED AFTER THE STATEMENT DAY (STMT-DAY)
TOTAL THE CREDITS (DEPOSITS)
TOTAL THE DEBITS (CHECKS, CHECK-CHGS, OVERDRAFT CHGS)

SET END-BAL = BEG-BAL + CREDITS − DEBITS

CACLUCLATE SERVICE CHARGE

RULE FOR SERVICE CHARGE CALCULATION:

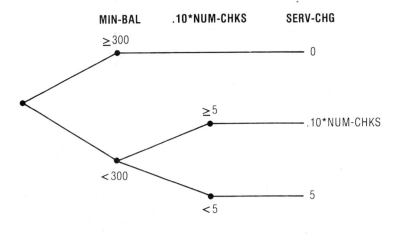

IF SERVICE CHARGE IS NOT ZERO,
THEN CREATE A SERVICE CHARGE TRANSACTION (SC-TRAN) TO BE PLACED IN THE CK-TRANS FILE

Figure 10-33. Process description developed from information in Figure 10-32.

to create a new system solution from the user's perspective. Thus, Activity 4 is involved in both the second and third steps of the analysis process. Activity 5: New System Design completes the last step in the process and begins the transition from analysis to design. Because of the iterative nature of the analysis process, these three activities overlap heavily.

The analysis process begins in Activity 3 with the construction of a physical model of the existing system. Then, as described in Chapter 9, a logical model for the existing system is derived from this physical model. This logical model, based on a set of logical data flow diagrams and supporting documents, is the end product of Activity 3. This product documents the understanding of the existing system and marks the completion of the first step in the analysis process.

Logical modeling can be a valuable part of systems analysis because it opens up important opportunities and insights. First, the building of a logical model may lead the systems analyst to uncover processes, outputs, or inputs that are part of the system but were omitted from the physical model. In providing information for the building of a physical model, users commonly forget one or more procedures or processes. The discipline of building a logical model almost invariably catches these problems by requiring analysis of business processes rather than system steps.

Second, this business emphasis also leads to a more specific understanding of why system functions are performed and what results are expected. With this understanding, it is often possible to simplify, even to eliminate, some existing processing steps that really aren't needed to conduct the business.

Third, the creation of a logical model forces the analyst to concentrate on the business objectives of the organization. A clear understanding of these objectives provides a basis for evaluating requirements for the new system, as they are identified during the second step of the analysis process.

Finally, the new system will be more flexible and maintainable if its design is based on a logical model. The logical model—concentrating on key business events—is not subject to frequent change. Thus, it provides a more stable basis for design than the more volatile physical aspects of the system and inhibits the carrying over of old biases from the previous implementation.

Discussions of the analysis process up to this point have reviewed the steps and procedures for developing physical data flow diagrams. The characteristics of logical data flow diagrams have been described, but methods for actually developing logical models have not yet been covered. The next section presents a process for deriving a logical model from a physical model.

Creating a Logical Model

As stated earlier, a logical data flow diagram models the data and the processing that are essential to the business. In other words, a logical model presents those features of the system that would have to exist no matter what physical processing methods were adopted. Given a physical model, the transition to a logical model can be accomplished by following a series of orderly steps:

Replace upper level parent bubbles with child diagrams.   Do this in one or more large, expanded data flow diagrams. As a general rule, lower level diagrams tend to be more logical. These very large diagrams, while not satisfactory for documentation and communication purposes, are very effective working models for team members who are deeply involved in the project.

Remove nonlogical processes.   These are the processes that:

- Edit data. Usually, edit functions are applied to data flows of manually captured input.
- Audit. Typically, data being output for users are audited through machine processes before reports or displays are generated.
- Move data within a system without transformation.

The reason for removing these processes is that they are entirely physical. They are totally dependent on how the system is implemented physically. They perform no logical function upon the data. (These processes will, of course, be replaced as necessary in the construction of the physical model of the new system.)

Remove nonlogical data stores.   These are data stores that exist as intermediate or holding files. They are not necessary to the logical processing of the data.

Connect system fragments.   Fragments resulting from the deletions in the previous steps will need to be reconnected.

Replace linear sequences of processes with parallel processes. This requirement does not apply if processing sequences are arranged in a certain order to meet business needs or policies. However, if processes are shown in linear order solely because of programming or execution needs, they should be replaced by parallel representations.

Remove excess data from data flows. The data flows in physical models tend to correspond with physical documents or records. Thus, the flows feeding or being produced by a lower-level process tend to carry extraneous data—data not needed or used by the process. This step in creating a logical model can be thought of as "starving" the process. Modify the data flows so that input flows contain only those data elements that are actually used by the process and output flows contain only those data elements that are a result of processing.

Reorganize and simplify data stores. Drop any data elements that are not used. Consider splitting large stores into smaller ones containing groups of logically related data elements. Chapter 14 discusses this topic in greater depth.

Regroup into a hierarchical set of data flow diagrams. Form a hierarchical set of data flow diagrams in which parent bubbles are defined in terms of key business events within the system. This final step forces the analyst to rethink how the system is partitioned, based on key business events rather than on current departmental boundaries or job descriptions. These existing physical constraints may actually be unnatural for the business functions being performed. The new system will be more reliable and more stable if these constraints are removed or, at the very least, recognized fully.

As an illustration of the process of deriving a logical model from a physical model, consider Figures 10-34 and 10-35. Figure 10-34 shows the portion of the expanded data flow diagram for the water billing system that processes new readings and produces incycle bills. This diagram is almost painfully physical. In creating the corresponding logical model, the nonlogical processes—bubbles 1, 2, and 3—and the update logs can be dropped. Figure 10-34 is the result. Fragments have been connected, parallel processes have been inserted where appropriate, and processes have been starved.

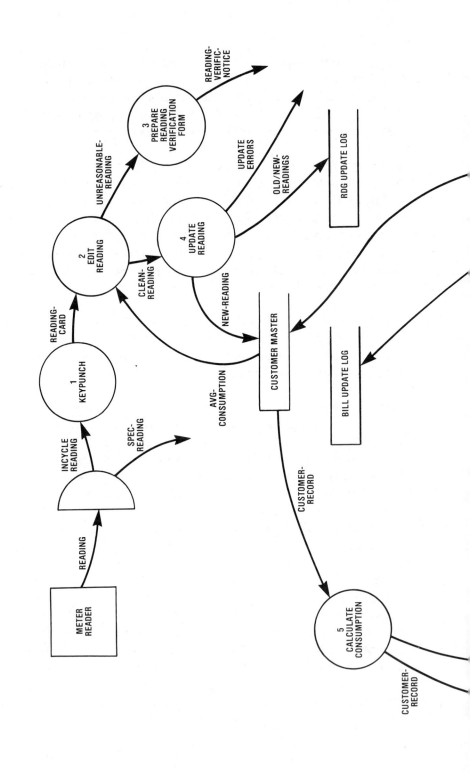

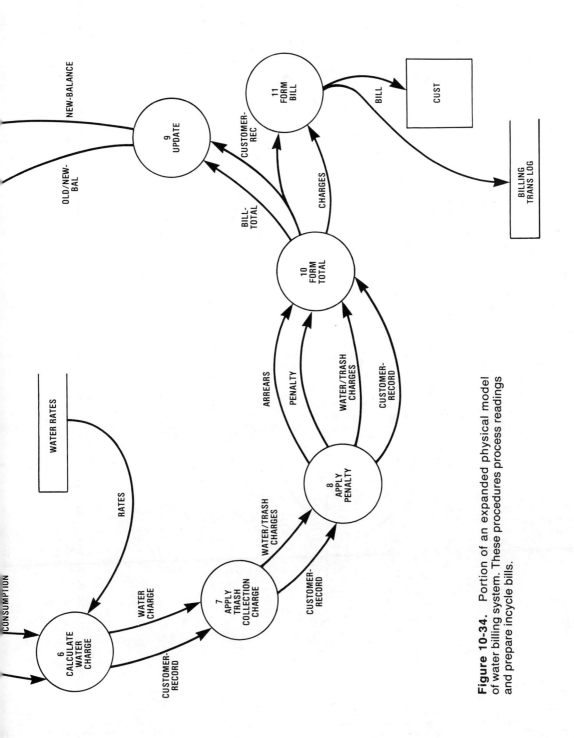

Figure 10-34. Portion of an expanded physical model of water billing system. These procedures process readings and prepare incycle bills.

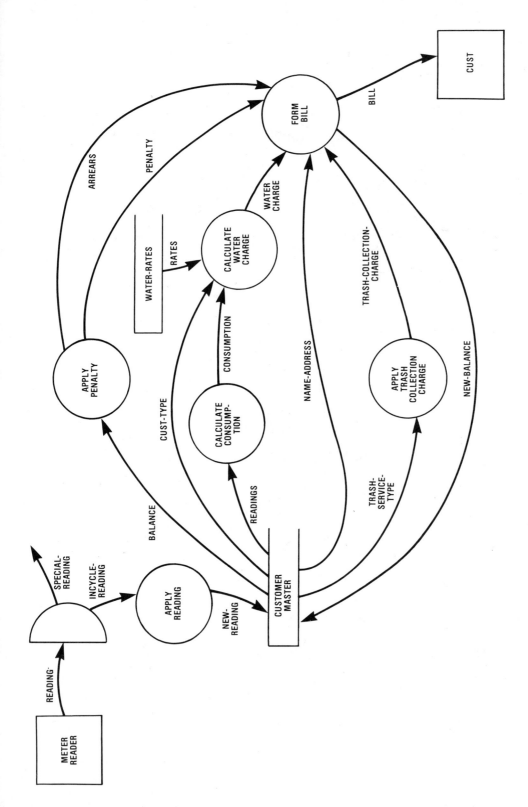

Figure 10-35. Portion of an expanded logical model of water billing system. These procedures process reading and prepare incycle bills.

Practice Assignment

The following narrative describes briefly the order entry processing for a small manufacturing company. Many details are omitted.

Sally opens the mail and checks orders for completeness. Incomplete orders are given to Nancy in Customer Relations. Complete orders are taken to Accounting by Pete, the messenger. Accounting checks the customer rating. If it is okay, the order is sent on to Sales, which checks to see if the item is in inventory. If it isn't, Sales backorders the item and informs Nancy. If it is, Sales prepares a three-part packing slip and sends it to Shipping. Shipping pulls the item and ships it to the customer with the first copy of the packing slip. The second copy of the packing slip goes to Accounting, which bills the customer. The third copy is used to update the inventory records.

Using this narrative:

1. Construct a physical data flow diagram modeling the order entry processing. Use questions marks to indicate those points where more detailed knowledge is needed.

2. Complete the physical model by making some reasonable business assumptions to answer the questions raised in the building of the physical data flow diagram.

3. Create a set of data dictionary entries for the data stores and major data flows, again making reasonable business asssumptions concerning content.

4. Derive a logical model from the physical model.

Defining User Requirements

The second step in the analysis process is to identify user requirements for the new system. These requirements will be used to derive a model for the new system, based on the logical model of the existing system developed in Activity 3. These models will become important end products of Activity 4: New System Requirements, discussed in Chapter 11.

User requirements should be divided into logical (business) and physical components. Logical requirements are found by identifying:

- New or changed organizational goals or objectives
- Changes or additions in data processed within the system
- Changes or additions in business policies that affect processes
- Changes in system scope.

Physical factors that should be considered include:

- Changes in timing or volumes of transactions within the system
- Changes in methods for delivery of results.

Throughout the gathering of information on user requirements, the analyst has to apply professional judgment. Determinations must be made as to whether a stated requirement represents a real need of the organization or simply a desire on the part of an individual. This distinction can be made by applying a simple principle: Compare each statement of user requirements with the overall goals and objectives of the organization. If a request falls within the organization's goals and objectives, it represents a need. If a request represents an interpretation of what the user feels should be included, this is a desire. Needs should always be covered by a new system. Desires should be evaluated on their merits.

Creating a New System Solution From the User's Perspective

The logical model of the existing system is modified on the basis of the business processing (logical) requirements identified in the second step of the analysis process. At this point, it is easiest to work with an expanded data flow diagram—adding, deleting, and changing both data and processes as necessary.

After the logical model has been developed, a new physical model is derived from it, using the physical requirements identified earlier. If there is some question of feasibility or of the level of user support that can be justified, it may be helpful to develop alternative physical models at this point. The physical model includes processing steps to show, specifically, the interactions between users and the computerized system in terms of inputs and outputs. This is the point at which the analyst inserts the nonlogical types of processes—edits, audits, logs, and so on—that were removed in the course of deriving the logical model of the existing system. The new physical model, in turn, forms the basis for the User Specification. This is the major end product of Activity 4: New System Requirements, described in Chapter 11.

The new physical model will ultimately be used as a basis for the design of the new system. During this requirements identification activity, however, the main purpose of the models produced is to build user confidence in and support for the new system that is evolving. The end result is user agreement, through formal sign-off, that the system defined in the User Specification is what the user wants to see developed.

Preparing Design Specifications

The ultimate goal of systems analysis is to prepare general design specifications for the new system. This is done during Activity 5: New System Design.

Input to this activity is the User Specification, built around a physical model for the new system that has been accepted by the user. This physical model serves as the basis for the technical design of the automated portion of the new system.

Sufficient work is performed in developing this design so that the feasibility evaluation for the proposed new system can be refined to reflect anticipated costs and benefits within 10 percent of those that will actually be experienced. Note, however, that the end products of Activity 5 represent a general technical design for the new system—not a complete set of technical specifications. Technical specifications are developed and implemented during later activities of the systems development life cycle.

Summary

Modeling can be an important tool of systems analysis, helping to establish a clear communication link between nontechnical users and technically oriented systems designers. Data flow diagrams, which can be used as modeling tools, are based on a set of simple, easily understood symbols.

The components of a system represented by a data flow diagram must be given clear and meaningful names. Guidelines are provided to help create clear and meaningful data flow diagrams. Hierarchical partitioning of data flow diagrams involves working in a top-down fashion to break out details associated with individual processing bubbles, creating new diagrams that show data flows and transformations in greater detail. These partial diagrams are tied together by means of a structured system of identification and numbering. Levels to which data flow diagrams are developed include the context diagram, Diagram 0, parent diagrams, and child diagrams.

The question of how far to partition a data flow diagram is largely a matter of judgment. Two general rules of thumb are: (1) A process bubble that has either a single input or a single output has probably been partitioned far enough. (2) A lowest-level process bubble ideally should perform a single, well-defined function.

Data flow diagrams must be supported by further documentation, including a data dictionary and process descriptions. The data dictionary includes the names assigned to all data elements, data structures, and data stores, with definitions for each. Process descriptions can use process narratives, decision trees, and/or decision tables.

Moving from a physical model to a logical model of the existing system involves a series of steps that are identified and described. User requirements must then be identified and used to derive a model for the new system. After a logical model has been developed, a new physical model is derived from it. The new physical model, in turn, forms the basis of the User Specification.

The main goal of systems analysis is to prepare general design specifications for the new system.

Key Terms

1. external entity
2. data flow
3. process
4. data store
5. collector
6. router
7. hierarchical partitioning
8. top-down partitioning
9. parent
10. child
11. balance
12. stub
13. data dictionary
14. data element
15. data structure
16. sequence
17. iteration
18. selection
19. discrete values
20. continuous values
21. alias
22. process description
23. process narrative
24. decision tree
25. decision table
26. structured English

Review/Discussion Questions

1. What are the six major symbols used in data flow diagrams, and what does each represent?

2. Name three types of obvious errors that can be spotted quickly through visual checking of data flow diagrams.

3. What is meant by hierarchical partitioning of data flow diagrams?

4. Explain the relationships among a context diagram, Diagram 0, Diagram 4, and Diagram 4.3.

5. Assuming that you have a context diagram for an existing system, how would you go about constructing a Diagram 0?

6. Describe the three basic types of data structures, including the notation generally used for each.

7. What do decision trees and decision tables have in common? How do they differ?

8. Make up a sample process description, and use three different methods—narrative, decision tree, and decision table—to communicate the same processing specifications. In the example you have chosen, which method seems to communicate most effectively? least effectively? Why?

9. Given a physical model of the existing system, how would you create a logical model of the same system?

10. What are the three main steps in the systems analysis process? How do these correspond with the three activities of Phase 2: Analysis and General Design in the systems development life cycle?

NEW SYSTEM REQUIREMENTS 11

LEARNING OBJECTIVES

On completing reading and other learning assignments for this chapter, you should be able to:

- [ ] Describe the reasons for involving users in preparing specifications for new systems, and also explain the contributions that users should be expected to make.
- [ ] Describe preparations for and conduct of effective data gathering interviews.
- [ ] Explain the value of models in systems analysis and describe the features and roles of logical and physical models.
- [ ] Describe the user sign-off process and tell why it is critical to the success of a systems development project.
- [ ] Explain the systems analyst's responsibilities in working with users to specify new system requirements.
- [ ] Describe how models are evaluated and how these models are used to gain user concurrence.

ACTIVITY DESCRIPTION

This activity marks a transition from the study of the existing system into the building of the new one. The purpose is to develop a description and statement of requirements for the new system in sufficient depth so that the user can evaluate and approve the new system from his or her own perspective.

The work in this activity includes further analysis, together with a synthesis process. The probing and information gathering undertaken to determine new system requirements is much like the work performed during the existing system review, and occurs at about the same time. As systems analysts are studying the existing system, the business functions and needs that must be met by the new system should be identified. In part, this involves investigating user descriptions of the inadequacies or problems of the existing system.

The main data gathering technique used at this point in the anlysis process is the interview. Interviews are conducted with both user management and operating personnel. These interviews are aimed at identifying logical and physical requirements.

Modeling techniques are used to begin a transition from the analysis of the existing system toward the design of the new one. Using both the logical model of the existing system and the logical requirements for the new one, analysts develop a logical model for the new system. Then, a physical model of the new system is prepared as a basis for user acceptance. Alternative physical models—representing various levels of service and cost—may be proposed.

Always remember that a computer-based information system consists of much more than a set of computer programs and processes. The system also involves people who accept input, process data themselves, turn some data over to computers for processing, prepare output, and so on. In a sense, the computer processing represents a subsystem within a larger system. The logical model of the current system concentrates on the flow and processing of data, no matter how it is accomplished—by computer or by manual processing. After modifying this logical model to accommodate the functional requirements for the new system, a new computer system within the overall information system is defined as part of the physical model for the new system.

This computer system is treated as a *black box* within the overall information system for purposes of user presentations. That is, the user has to know what goes into the subsystem and what comes out, but need not be concerned with how things happen inside the black box— the computer processing.

The result of this analysis activity is a specification for the new system from the user's perspective. This user specification defines the entire information system—both computerized and manual processing—from the user's point of view. The user specification covers the key processing functions, the degree of computerization required, the relative use of on-line and batch techniques, the business cycles and functions involved, and other user-oriented factors.

OBJECTIVES

This activity has two main objectives:

- Develop a complete definition of the necessary capabilities of the new system from the user's point of view. This definition should include descriptions of changes in processing capabilities (logical changes), and also descriptions of new methods of delivery (physical changes).
- Establish user concurrence that the capabilities described in the end-product documents of this activity contain a full and complete statement of user needs and that the solution is feasible, both from an operational and a human factors standpoint.

SCOPE

This activity, the determination of new system requirements, overlaps extensively with Activity 3: Existing System Review, and Activity 5: New System Design. Although schedules will vary for individual projects, the extent of overlap can be pictured as illustrated in the miniature Gantt chart shown in Figure 11-1. As indicated on this chart, work on new system requirements begins shortly after the initiation of Activity 3. In effect, then, reports of deficiencies or shortcomings in the existing system feed directly into the identification of requirements for the new system. However, systems analysts will generally stop short of trying to specify new system requirements until there is a satisfactory overall understanding of current processing methods. That is, the systems analysts will want to develop a comprehensive understanding of the existing system as a whole before serious consideration of new system requirements is begun.

The same type of overlap exists during the concluding tasks of this activity and those of Activity 5. That is, as analysts begin to build a solid

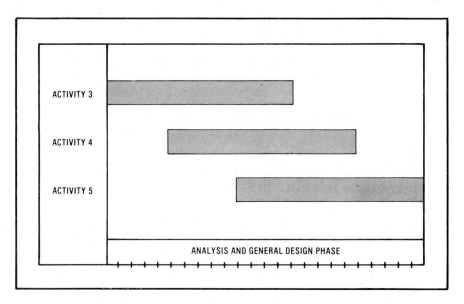

Figure 11-1.   Gantt chart for the Analysis and General Design phase illustrates the heavy overlap among analysis activities.

understanding of user requirements, possible design alternatives for the new system are worked out and may be reviewed with the users.

As discussed earlier, the layering concept is fundamental to the systems development life cycle in general and to the analysis process in particular. During analysis, layering is implemented by the iterative modeling technique—increasingly more detailed models of the existing system and the potential new system are constructed. Then, as understanding increases within Activity 4, analysts begin to look more closely at the feasibility of the new system. At this point, some doubts may arise about feasibility that were not present in earlier activities. If these doubts become serious, analysts may choose to develop multiple physical models for the new system. These models would represent varying levels of computerization and degrees of service to users. These variations would then be further described in the design tasks within Activity 5.

Another alternative, if feasibility seems doubtful, would be to limit design to a single new-system alternative, then move quickly into Activity 5 as a means of expediting the evaluation of feasibility. If feasibility then proves unacceptable, the work could be returned to Activity 4 for the development of other alternatives.

In some situations, the overlap between Activities 3, 4, and 5 may seem so extensive that it is tempting simply to fold them together. The problem with doing this is that a certain level of control over the project is lost. The key importance of the tasks that make up Activity 4 may be lost as concentration shifts to the design-oriented tasks necessary for implementing the new system. Bear in mind that the purpose of Activity 4 is primarily to build user understanding to a degree that permits acceptance, or sign-off, on the specifications for the new system. It is important to secure a sign-off before too much actual design takes place. The principle is straightforward: The later changes are permitted and made within the systems development life cycle, the more expensive they will be. Costs of changes actually increase rapidly as a project passes the New System Requirements activity. Thus, there are important values, in both organizational relationships and in project development costs, to be gained by retaining an activity dedicated to securing user sign-off.

It should be understood, of course, that user sign-off is a gradual process of commitment more than it is a single act at the close of an activity. True, there may be a formal statement of acceptance signed by the responsible user manager; and this acceptance may follow a formal overview presentation of the capabilities of the new system. But genuine user acceptance is built gradually throughout the process of Activity 4. Smaller groups of products will be developed with, and accepted by, appropriate users on the way toward building the User Specification that is the formal end product of this activity.

As a general rule, then, it is desirable to have users become serious about, and extensively involved in, a development project as early as possible. Yet, no matter how early user requirements are firmed up and no matter how committed a user may be, there will still be changes in the course of a systems development project. Changes are more easily handled if a mutual commitment between users and computer professionals is established early in the project. Remember: all systems ultimately belong to their users. The earlier this sense of possession can be established, the better a systems development project will proceed.

END PRODUCT

The end product of Activity 4 is an extensive document known as a User Specification for the new system. (In some CIS organizations, the same document may be called a Requirements Specification, or perhaps a Structured Specification.)

The user specification describes and documents all of the logical processing functions for the new system. Also included are one or more physical models that represent the user's view of the new system. These models will encompass the human-machine boundaries, batch and on-line processing, run cycles for batch processes, and user expectations for performance of the system.

The complete user specification document contains the following parts:

- *Overview narrative.* This document states the goals and objectives of the organization, presenting these goals as yardsticks against which new system requirements will be evaluated. Another portion of this narrative describes the purpose, goals, and objectives. Any background information that would help guide system designers should be included. There should also be a statement, at a general overview level, describing changes to be made between the existing system and the new one.

- *System function.* This is a brief, concise description of what the system will accomplish for the user. It is free of any description of physical processing functions and is written in user terminology, giving a black box description of the computer portion of the system.

- *Processing.* The processing to be completed under the new system should be modeled using a context diagram and a hierarchical set of data flow diagrams. A Diagram 0 should identify the major subsystems. Lower-level diagrams should indicate the physical packaging to be achieved—again, from the user's perspective. This physical packaging will identify manual and computerprocessing, batch and on-line functions, timing cycles, and performance requirements.

- *Data dictionary.* This document defines the components of the data flow diagrams.

- *Process descriptions.* These include narratives, decision trees, decision tables, and structured English descriptions of the lowest level processes within data flow diagrams.

- *Data structure and data access diagrams.* These diagrams document required access paths to various data elements within data stores from the user's perspective. This type of documentation is explained in Chapter 14.

- *Outputs for users.* An index is prepared listing all outputs to be delivered to users. This index is supported by a series of output documentation sheets like the one shown in Figure 11-2. Each output sheet is normally accompanied by a rough form layout.

- *Inputs to the system.* An index lists all proposed input forms or source documents. For each input, this index is accompanied by an input document specification form like the one shown in Figure 11-3. With each document sheet, there may be a rough format drawing for the proposed input form.

- *User interfaces with the system.* The more routine aspects of how user personnel work within the system and interface with the computerized portions of the system are included in process specifications for the manual procedures. This is a listing of any special considerations connected with the impact of the new system on job descriptions in the user area. If on-line processing is included, there should also be rough outlines of user-machine dialogues.

- *User-specified physical requirements.* For this specification, there should be descriptions of performance needs, such as response time, transaction volumes, and timing. Security and control considerations, as specified by the user, should also be listed, as should any new hardware or application software preferences or requirements. (These will be refined and extended in the next activity as design begins.)

- *Unresolved policy considerations.* Any policy considerations that still have to be resolved should be reported.

The user specification is a key product in the systems development process. The value of the user specification lies in these facts:

- The user can verify and subscribe to its contents.

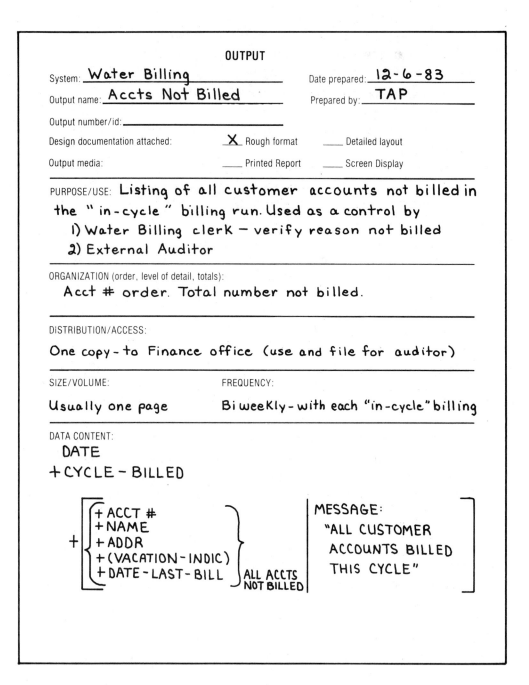

Figure 11-2. Sample output specification form.

INPUT

System: **Water Billing**   Date prepared: **12-13-83**

Input name: **Special-Reading**   Prepared by: **KJP**

Input number/id: _____

Design documentation attached: **X** Rough format   _____ Detailed layout

Input media: _____ Printed Report   _____ Screen Display

PURPOSE/USE: **To handle all special readings.**
A special reading is any reading that is not an "in-cycle"
reading. (In-cycle readings are entered in Meter-Reading-Book.)
Types: Final Reading (eg-customer moving)
Initial Reading (eg- new construction, new owner)
Problem with In-Cycle reading.

INPUT COMPLETED BY: **Meter Reader (usually)**
Water Department inspector (occasional)
Customer (rare)

COPIES/DISTRIBUTION: **One copy - to Water Billing clerk**

CONTROLS: **Final reading must be initialed by meter reader.**

ESTIMATED VOLUMES: **Very low**   TIME CONSTRAINTS: **Need rapid**
turnaround for special
billing if moving

DATA CONTENT:

ACCT #   **Note:**   ⌈ **CUSTOMER**
+NAME   **REQUESTOR =** | **WATER-DEPT**
+ADDR   ⌊ **FINANCE-DEPT**
+READING-DATE
+READING   ⌈ **FINAL-READING**
+REQUESTOR   **REASON =** | **INITIAL-READING**
+REASON   ⌊ **CORRECT-ERROR**

Figure 11-3.   Sample input specification form.

- Its content and format provide a natural starting point for system design, as well as a standard for comparison during the Implementation phase.
- The setting of user expectations at this point serves to establish the basis for measuring the ultimate success of the project.

THE PROCESS

During this activity, the systems analyst follows a sequence of tasks that are critical to the preparation of the User Specification. Involved are:

- Extensive interaction with and interviewing of users
- Extensive use of modeling
- Consideration of application software packages, if appropriate.

The Role of the Systems Analyst

Among the services rendered as part of the systems analyst's role during this activity are:

- *Analysis.* The analyst identifies, partitions, and studies the structure and anatomy of the existing system.
- *Criticism.* Constructive challenges are one of the mainsprings of effective analysis. The analyst must question why situations are the way he or she finds them and why changes have been requested or are needed. The analyst evaluates all such findings against organizational objectives.
- *Innovation.* The analyst is a change agent, or catalyst. He or she is expected to identify and suggest fresh approaches for dealing with problem situations.
- *Synthesis.* The analyst draws system elements together, creating solutions to replace problems.
- *Diplomacy.* The analyst must deal creatively with user uncertainties. It is necessary to guide persons who may be unsophisticated technically into a state of understanding and commitment. Analysts may also have to deal with—possibly to defuse—differences or conflicts among users or between users and others within an organization. Such activities may be needed to handle or overcome opposition to change or lack of needed cooperation.

Activities 4 and 5 are the points in the systems development life cycle at which systems analysis plays its most critical role.

Process Overview

Figure 11-4 gives an overview of that portion of the analysis process that is a part of Activity 4. Processes 1 and 2 are completed as part of Activity 3, giving rise to a logical model of the current system. Processes 3 through 6 are the heart of Activity 4:

- Determine new system requirements by analyzing requests for change.
- Modify the current model to incorporate these requests.
- Evaluate possible packaged application software.
- Create from all this a user specification document.

Analyzing Requests for Change

Most systems development projects are initiated as responses to requests from management or from user organizations. The request may result from a change in requirements or may represent an attempt to improve an existing system. Business changes may stem from external conditions, such as new or changed government regulations or competitive pressures. A request for change may also be motivated by the opportunity to do things more efficiently or to provide better service as a result of new technology. The nature or size of the business may have changed. Systems capabilities and methods may have to be modified or enhanced because an organization is expanding or redirecting its efforts. The use of new methods or technologies that are now feasible may make it possible to avoid increased costs.

In addition to these business changes, requests may arise from user frustration. Upper-level management may lack the information needed for effective planning. Middle-level management may not be receiving the support necessary to control operations of the business. Operating personnel may be forced to deal with procedures that have become obsolete or cannot handle increased processing volumes. Relationships among departments or areas of the business may be strained.

For whatever reason, initiators of change requests are often disappointed in, or frustrated with, things as they are. Requests for systems

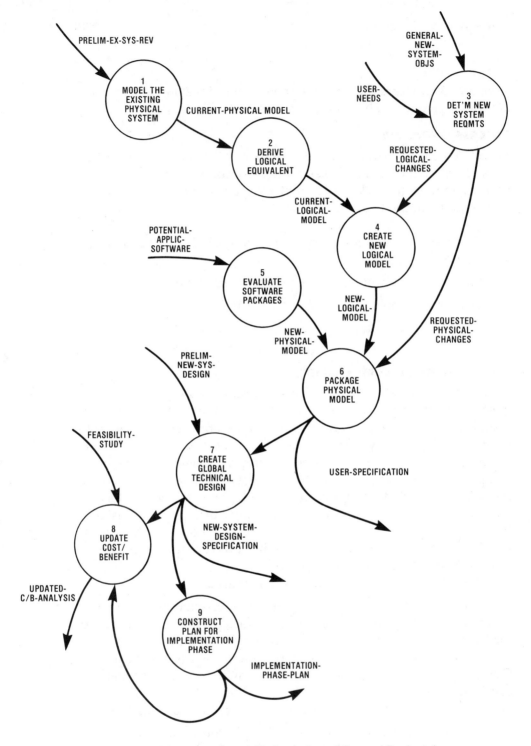

Figure 11-4. A process view of the Analysis and General Design phase.

development, almost invariably, seek some sort of improvement. Given these motivations, change requests represent opportunities for all parties.

An initial evaluation of the request is made in an earlier activity, during the Feasibility Study. However, now in Activity 4, probing and evaluation begin in earnest. In asking questions and reviewing existing practices, the analyst should be on the lookout specifically for:

- *New business opportunities.* If the organization or one of its departments has expanded rapidly in size or broadened its business scope, different or greater CIS support may be needed. On the other hand, a new development in computer technology may suggest improvement or enhancement of existing systems.

- *Forced business changes.* These are mandated reasons for systems development. Situations could include either regulatory requirements or decisions at the top level of the organization to meet competitive moves or to enhance market share.

- *Current system deficiencies.* The analyst should review existing systems with the users, and with the CIS staff. In addition to these reviews, it is a good practice to attempt to develop a maintenance history for the existing system. If a system has required frequent updating or maintenance, this could be a sign of possible problems. The updates may be the result of frequent changes in business needs or policies. On the other hand, if one portion of the system has had to be modified frequently, this could point to a basic design deficiency.

Part of the process of identifying and understanding requests for change includes categorizing each request as a logical request, impacting the new logical model, or a physical request, dictating the nature of the new physical model. Since logical requests relate to the processing that must occur, regardless of who does the processing or how, this new logical model may include new data elements used by or stored in the system, new processing or changed rules governing current processing, and new output information produced by the system. Physical requests involve the method of delivery as well as timing and processing volume constraints. For example, the users may request greater on-line processing capabilities or, perhaps, greater control over or responsibility for the processing.

In addition to the logical-physical categorization, another classification of requests is necessary. Since, in the final analysis, development costs may make it impossible to implement every request, some prioritization of requests is necessary. Possible priority categories might be:

- Changes that must be made because of government or management mandates. In these situations, system revision is a must.

- The next category would be for changes that are urgent but not mandatory. Reasons for such changes could include important competitive advantages, great cost savings, and so on.

- A third category would be for changes that can be described as highly desirable but possibly not urgent. Such changes would have to be clearly cost-effective. But the success of the business would not be as closely tied to their implementation as it is in the higher-priority categories.

- A final category might be set up for features or system refinements that would be useful as time and funding permit.

If a change is mandated, as in the first category, a deadline for implementation should be included in the evaluation. If not, a range of acceptable dates should be established for other categories.

Responsibilities of the analyst.   It is not enough for the analyst simply to process a request for change. Some user requests may be in the form of proposed solutions rather than functional business requirements. In these cases, the analyst must be sure the proposed solution represents a true statement of the problem.

In all cases, the analyst must understand the situation behind the request. Two things help in gaining this understanding: The analyst must put himself or herself in the user's place and must challenge each request. Rather than simply asking the user what he or she would like to have, the analyst must both anticipate requests that may not be expressed and determine why each requested change is needed.

It can be a tremendous challenge for the analyst to ''get inside'' the mind of the user. When dealing with a user manager, the analyst must think: "Given the objectives of my organization and things for which I am responsible, the following information will be critical for me to be able to do my job." When dealing with user operating personnel, the analyst must be aware of what motivates the staff and what support is required for an efficient and accurate job. This emphasis on viewing the system from the user's perspective will not only give rise to requests that the user may have overlooked, but it will also make it easier to evaluate actual user requests.

The basic goals and objectives of the organization, as they relate to the system under development, will have been identified as part of the Existing System Review. These goals and objectives are then used as a basis for evaluating the requests that have been made. The systems analyst is responsible for working with the user to relate each request to stated organization objectives or, if necessary, to point out that there is no basis for the request. The business need and business use of each requested output and process must be clear. This level of understanding also will be necessary to support the trade-off decisions that will arise in trying to create a feasible design for the new system.

In building an understanding of the business situation behind the request for change, the analyst will frequently enlarge or enhance the definition of needs. The request may have been triggered by what amounts to a symptom rather than by the root problem itself. "Fixes" that deal with superficial symptoms rarely solve problems. To isolate problems, the analyst has to examine the situation from the user's point of view.

Part of the analyst's contribution in evaluating requests may lie in the different perspective he or she brings to the scene. The analyst's expertise in information processing may lead to changes in the systems development request that enhance the value of the project.

Role of the user.   The user is a participant in systems development. A project cannot work effectively if the user expects simply to identify a problem, then step aside. Ultimately, the user will own the new system. The only way real ownership can be established is through continuing participation. Special areas for user participation lie in contributions to the design and development of system outputs and inputs, as discussed in Chapters 12 and 13.

The Modeling Process

In the course of this activity, the use of models proceeds through three stages:

- A logical model for the new system is created.
- The new logical model is evaluated and modified as necessary.
- One or more physical models are created for the new system.

Create a logical model of the new system.   Modeling, as explained earlier, begins with representations of the physical, then the logical, aspects of the existing system. The logical model of the new system then evolves from the logical model of the existing system. In beginning the modeling of the new system, the analyst concentrates on the areas of change:

- Determine whether each change represents a modification or an extension of capabilities.
- Determine the effect of each change in terms of processing activities, data flows, data store contents, data access capabilities, or process definitions.

During the process of identifying needs or requirements for the new system, individual changes may be modeled separately, in fragments, or mini-models. Each of the changes is then reviewed carefully in walkthroughs with the user. Next, the model fragments are incorporated into the logical model of the existing system, modifying that model to produce a logical representation of the new system. The new model is then used to communicate a complete understanding of what processing capabilities the user expects from the new system. This process is shown graphically in Figures 11-5 through 11-7. Figure 11-5 is a simplified, abstract logical model representing an existing system. Figure 11-6 shows how the concentration on specific areas of change between the existing and new systems leads to modification of the model. Figure 11-7 represents the resulting logical data flow diagram for the new system. This series of figures, of course, represents an idealized situation. In practice, the modifications will be performed on a set of large, expanded data flow diagrams representing the logical model of the current system.

The final step in creating the new logical model is to re-organize these diagrams by grouping logically related lower-level processes and forming a hierarchical set of data flow diagrams. Attempts should be made to create these logical groupings using some of the criteria identified for constructing the first model of the existing system. Identify key business events such as:

- The production of a major system output
- The acceptance of a major system input
- Major functional processes that occur within the system.

The resulting logical model, then, includes a hierarchical set of data flow diagrams, a complete data dictionary, a set of data access diagrams documenting required user access paths to different data elements, and a set of process specifications.

Evaluate the logical model of the new system. After the logical model of the new system has been constructed, a thorough set of walk-throughs should be conducted to assure the quality of this model. One review should test for simple mechanical correctness. Tests to be applied in this review could include:

- Are all components named?
- Are all of the names meaningful?
- Are the proper symbols used throughout?
- Are all levels of the data flow diagram consistent and balanced?
- Are the outputs from each process properly supported by the available input data?
- Are all data stores updated and also used as sources for data? Is there a balance between data accessed and data input to a data store?

In addition to mechanical checks, the model itself should be checked to be sure that it is an accurate and complete representation of the business. It should be verified that the model is clearly readable and understandable both to the user and to the analyst.

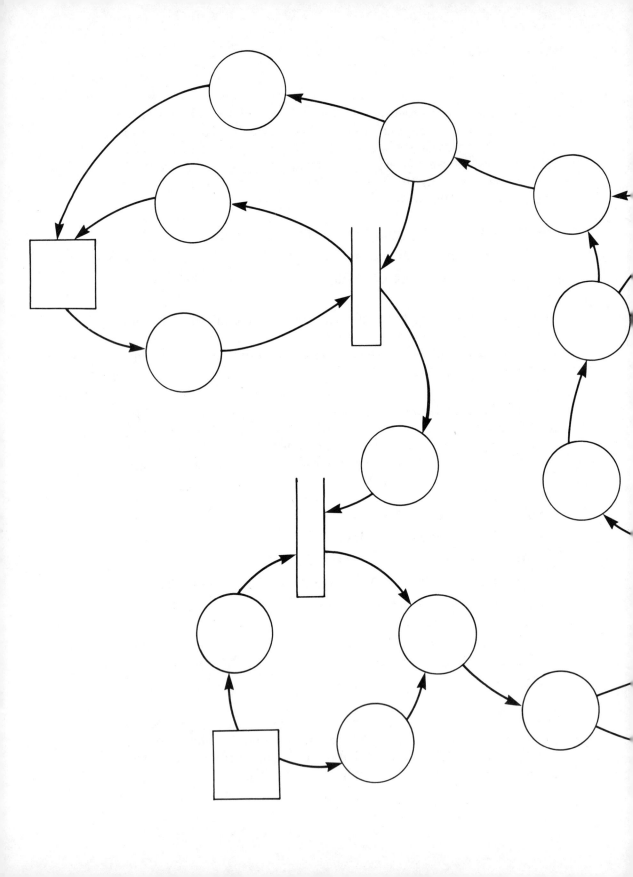

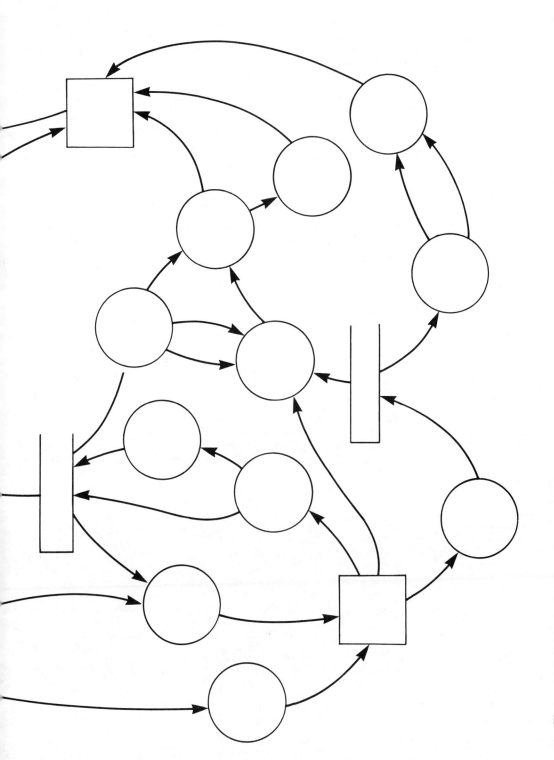

Figure 11-5. A logical model of an existing system.

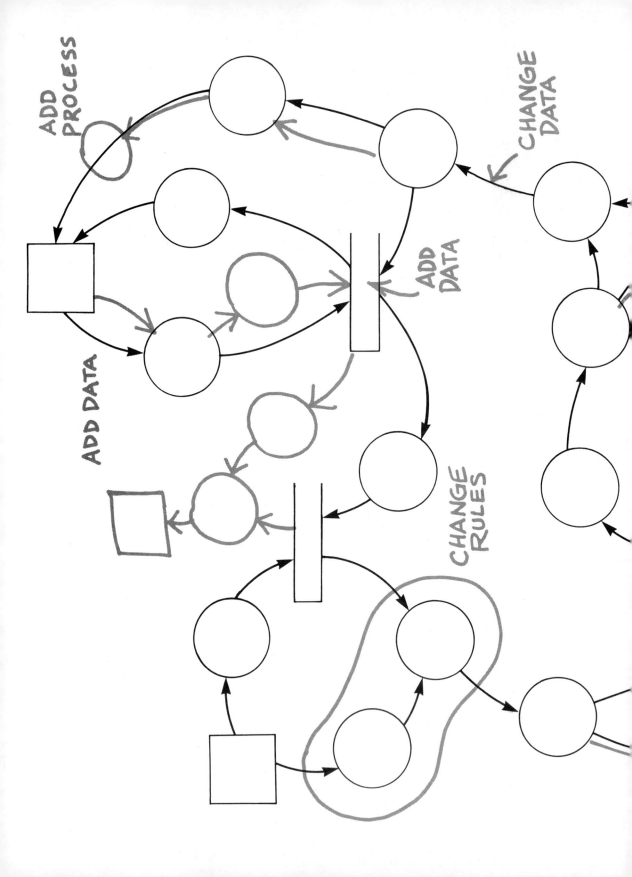

ADD PROCESS

CHANGE DATA

ADD DATA

ADD DATA

CHANGE RULES

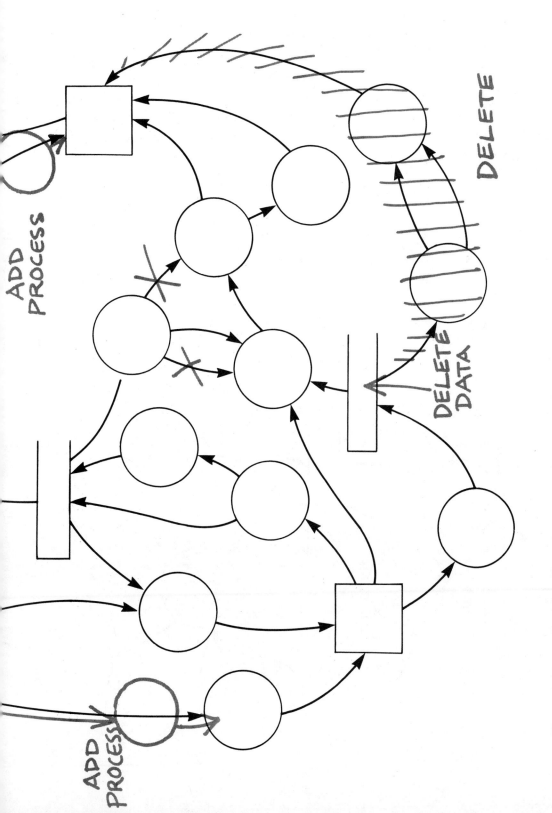

Figure 11-6. Annotated modifications of the logical model of an existing system to reflect new logical requirements.

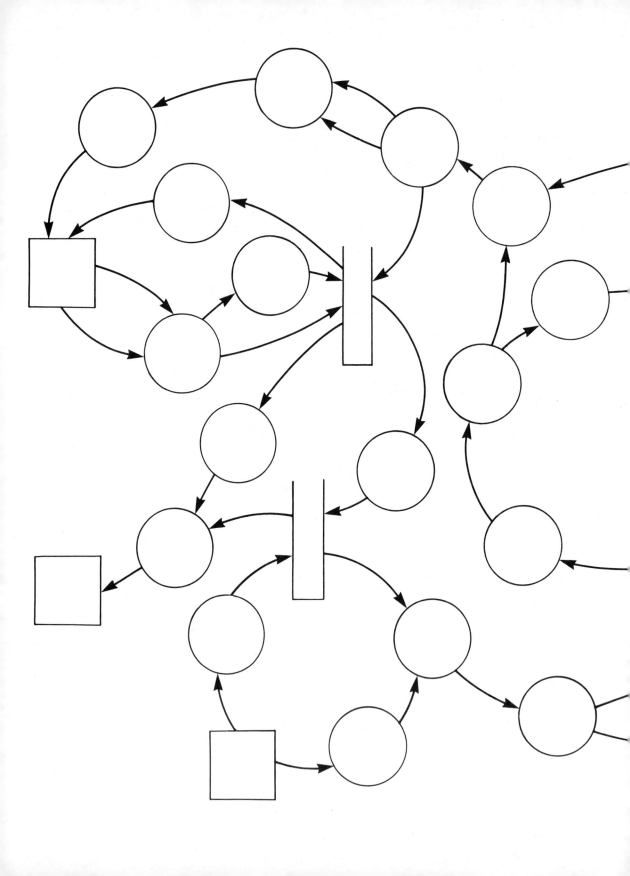

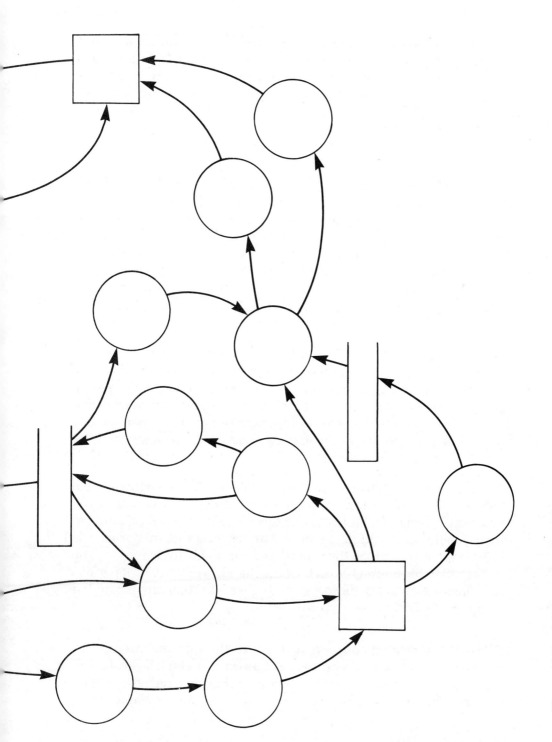

Figure 11-7. A derived logical model for a new system.

Finally, there can be at least an informal evaluation of the quality of the logical grouping decisions that evolved the hierarchical set of data flow diagrams from the large, expanded diagrams first produced. Two important design evaluations for higher-level processes criteria are:

- Coupling
- Cohesion.

Coupling refers to the number of data interfaces between the two higher-level processes, as represented by the number of data flows that connect them and the volume and type of data transferred. The goal is to minimize the coupling between the processes. This results in processes that are more independent and, hence, more easily maintained. With minimal coupling, a change to one process is less likely to affect other processes. Clearly, different decisions about how to group lower-level processes into parent processes will influence the degree of coupling between the parent processes.

For example, one common mistake is to create a parent process called UPDATE FILES within which is grouped all of the update processing for all input to the system. A similar error is to create a parent process labeled WRITE REPORTS. In both cases, many processes that have no particular business relationships are lumped together, thereby increasing the coupling of this parent process with a variety of other unrelated parent processes.

Consider, for instance, the abstract data flow diagram fragment in Figure 11-8, representing a portion of a "middle-level" diagram. The process P7, UPDATE FILES, is responsible for the actual updating of three totally unrelated data stores. The result is that this process is heavily coupled with all the others, and for no business reason. The organization in Figure 11-9, on the other hand, is preferable. It permits the construction of the more natural higher-level diagram illustrated in Figure 11-10.

Cohesion is a related concept. It refers to the internal strength or singularity of purpose of a process. A process has a high level of cohesion if it is directed toward achieving a single business purpose. A high level of cohesion is desirable and usually goes hand in hand with a

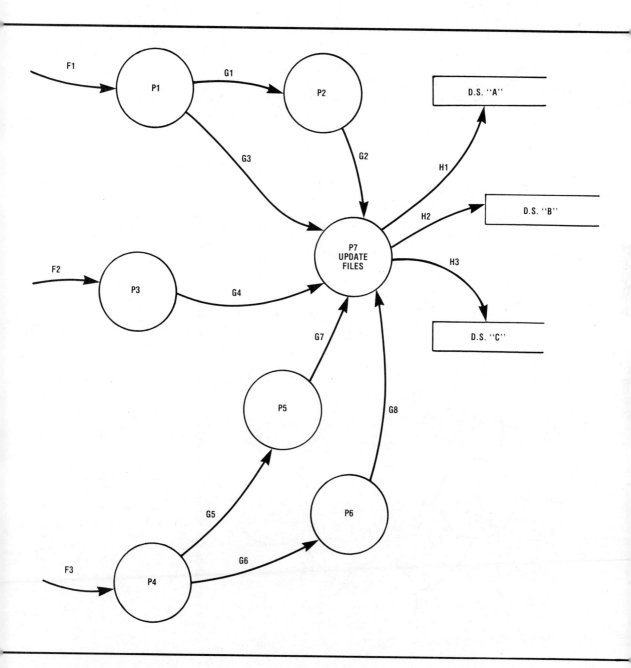

Figure 11-8.   Portion of data flow diagram illustrating heavy coupling—caused by a general update files process.

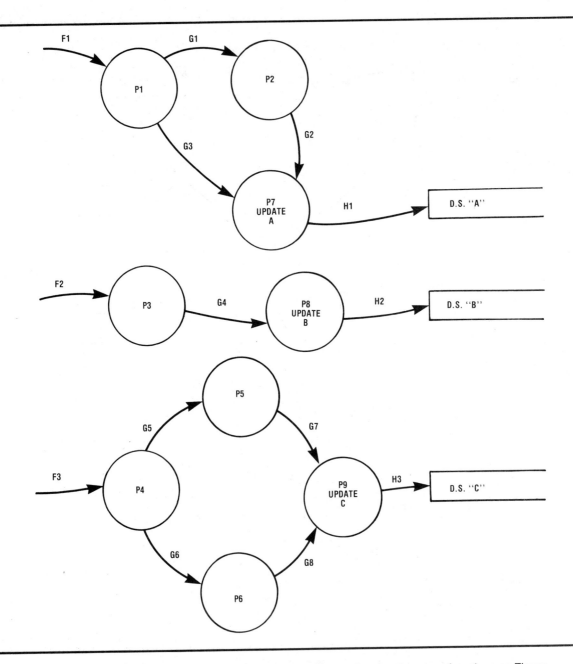

Figure 11-9.   Portion of a data flow diagram showing the same functions as Figure 11-8 with less coupling among processes.

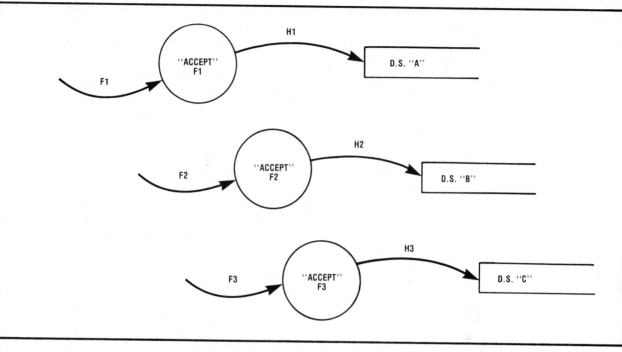

Figure 11-10. Portion of a Diagram 0 model corresponding with the intermediate-level models shown in Figure 11-9.

low level of coupling between processes. A process called WRITE REPORTS, for example, has a very low level of cohesion. It draws together a large number of lower level processes that have no business relationship to one another. On the other hand, a process such as PREPARE CUSTOMER BILL, while it may have 20 or more processes in an expanded child diagram, has a singularity of purpose—a high level of internal cohesion. There would be a minimal amount of coupling with other, outside processes.

As indicated above, the payoff for creating models with minimal coupling between higher-level processes and high levels of cohesion within these processes is greater system maintainability. If a system is designed based on a model with these characteristics and a change occurs, the change is likely to relate to only one or two of the high-level processes. Modifications can be made to the affected processes without impacting others.

Create a physical model of the new system.   In building the logical model of the new system, concentration is on what processing should be done. In creating the physical model, emphasis shifts to how these functions are to be performed. The physical requirements identified earlier are used to create the physical model from the logical model of the new system. These physical considerations will impact heavily the feasibility of the proposed system in every dimension—technical, financial, operational, scheduling, and human factors.

In building the physical model, it is necessary to deal with many trade-offs. Among these are determinations of the type of processing to be used. What portion of the processing should be computerized and what should remain manual? Within the computer processing, which processes should be interactive and which should be batch? What should be the basic nature of the human-machine interface? What are the critical performance requirements in terms of throughput, response time, and so on? Decisions on these questions will impact costs as well as other feasibility considerations.

Where users make requests about features of the system, trade-offs have to be evaluated in terms of importance of the request, cost, effectiveness, efficiency, and so on. It is often appropriate to develop multiple physical models representing different levels of user support.

The physical model constructed at this point must have sufficient detailing to show how the system actually will operate from the user's point of view. This level of understanding cannot be built with logical models alone.

Figure 11-11 illustrates a technique used in evolving from a logical to a physical model. The logical data flow diagram of Figure 11-7 is used as a basis for the building of a physical model. The basic technique is to "mark up" the logical model, showing the extent and type of computer processing. The resulting diagram indicates:

- The human-machine boundaries (identifying the computerized portions of the system)
- The nature of the computerized processing (batch and on-line)
- The timing cycles for the batch processing.

In addition to establishing processing boundaries, the new physical model must identify the control points within the system at which editing and auditing functions are applied. Recall that these control processes were dropped in creating the logical model of the existing system from the physical model. The most obvious, user-oriented input-output controls are added in Activity 4. Then, in Activity 5, a concentrated effort is made to specify all necessary system control processes—manual as well as computerized.

The new physical model is further supported by a statement of system performance requirements, including response time, transaction volumes, data store volumes, and anticipated growth patterns, and also rough formats for computer inputs and outputs.

Application Software Packages

Packaged software is becoming an increasingly important factor in the computer information system marketplace. The principle is straightforward: If a specialized organization can develop packages that meet the needs of many users, each user can acquire software at far less than the cost involved in developing the application programs from scratch. Further, the lead time in adapting packages may be significantly shorter than in doing the whole job.

If application packages are to be considered seriously, this is the point in the systems development life cycle at which they should be studied—objectively and carefully. The tool to use in studying application packages is the physical model for the new system. This new system model reflects careful consideration and agreement between users and systems analysts about what is needed. In effect, the model and its supporting documentation are on the way toward becoming specifications for application program development. It is just as straightforward and logical to use the model as a measure of how well a packaged software application meets the needs of the organization.

This is not to say that there must be a perfect fit between a potential packaged application and the physical model. A decision to accept and use a packaged application may include a commitment to compromise. By comparing the model with the software package, it becomes relatively easy to see what changes or adjustments will have to be made in the system or to the software package as a part of this compromise. Then the model can be used as a basis for evaluating the impact of the software package and the implications for its effective use. In effect, the physical model of a proposed new system can be an excellent shopping guide for consideration of application packages.

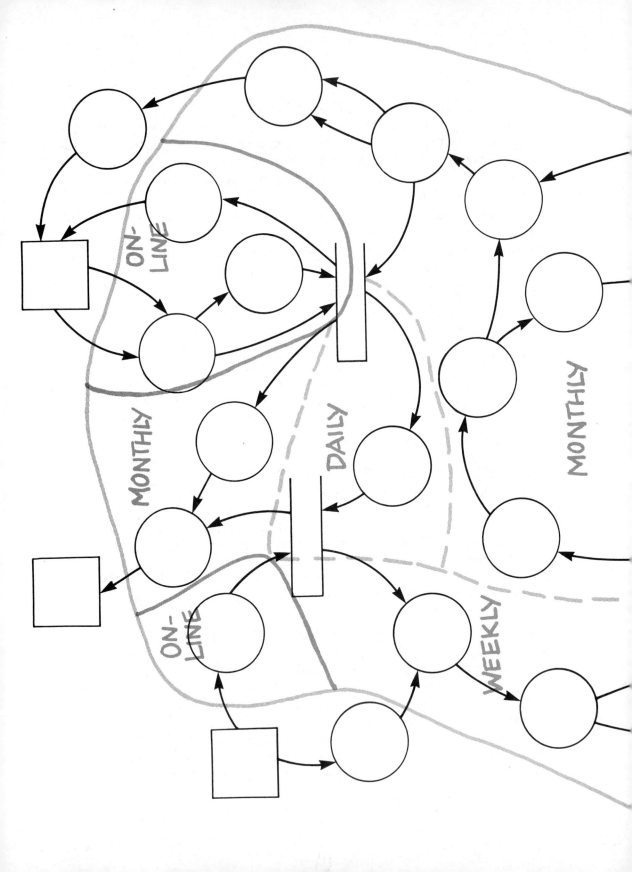

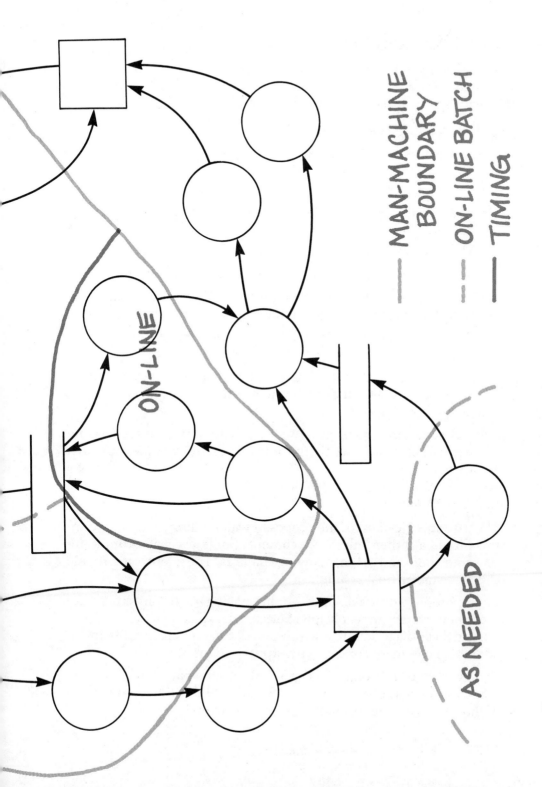

ON-LINE

MAN-MACHINE BOUNDARY

ON-LINE BATCH

TIMING

AS NEEDED

Figure 11-11. Notations on logical model of new system help to evolve a new physical model.

PERSONNEL INVOLVED

The makeup of the project team during this activity remains virtually the same as for Activity 3. In particular, team membership continues to have a strong user orientation.

CUMULATIVE PROJECT FILE

At the conclusion of this activity, the project file will encompass:

- An updated project plan
- The Initial Investigation Report (which is of historical interest only at this point)
- The Feasibility Report
- A list of management policy decisions that remain unresolved
- An interview schedule and interview summaries—updated to reflect interviews conducted during this activity
- A logical model of the existing system, including support documentation (of historical interest only)
- A User Specification (defined earlier) that includes a complete physical model for the new system and all required, supporting documentation
- A description of possible new system solutions, prepared during the feasiblity study activity for use in Activity 5: New System Design.

CASE SCENARIO

The user specification for the proposed water billing system for Central City is a rather lengthy document. Some excerpts from it are presented here and in the following chapters. The intent is to provide a glimpse of the final result.

A portion of the data flow diagrams making up the physical model of the new system appear below. Selected data dictionary entries supporting these diagrams are also presented. Chapters 12 and 13 contain additional comments on system outputs and inputs.

Figures 11-12 through 11-17 present selected data flow diagrams. For reference purposes, Figures 11-18 and 11-19 show the composition of the key data stores and selected data structures.

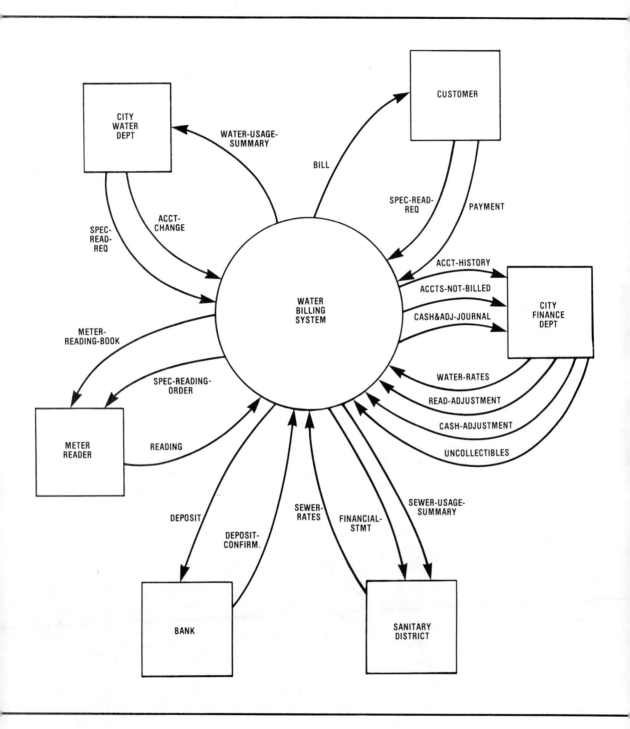

Figure 11-12. Context diagram for a new Central City water billing system.

355

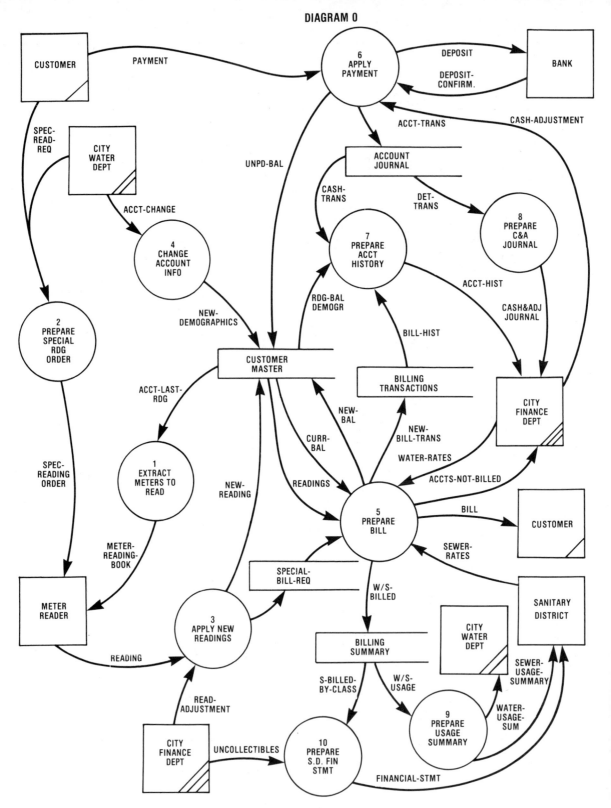

DIAGRAM 0

Figure 11-13. Diagram 0 for a new Central City water billing system.

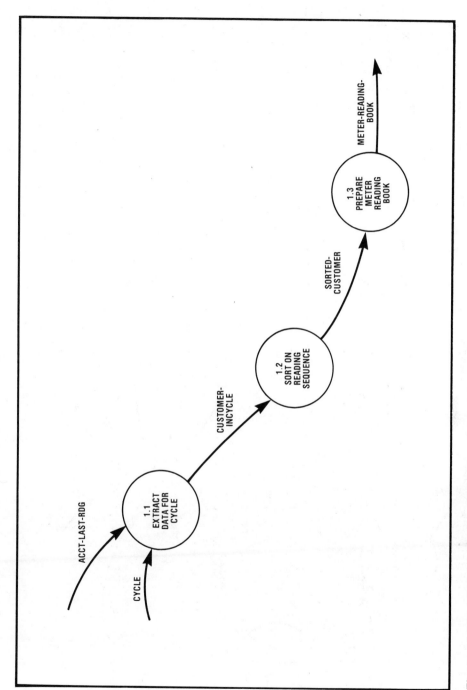

Figure 11-14. Diagram 1—Extract Meters to Read—corresponding with the Diagram 0 in Figure 11-13.

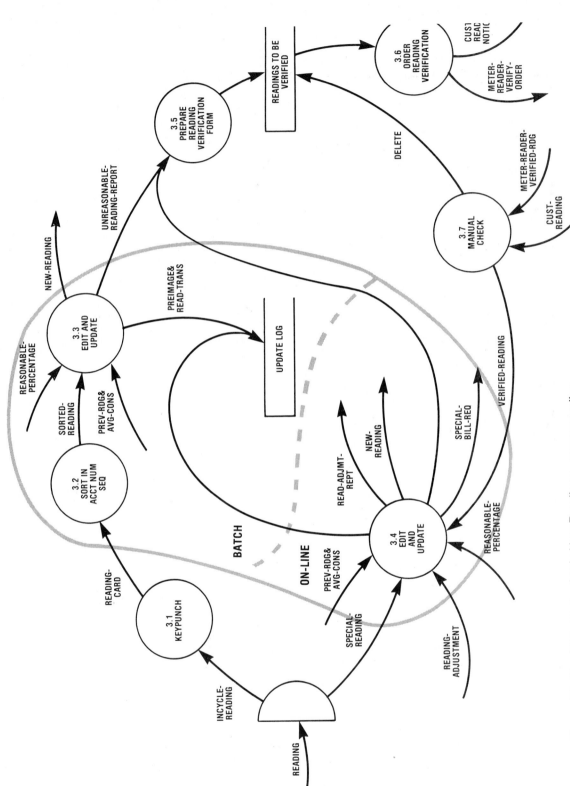

Figure 11-15. Diagram 3—Apply New Readings—corresponding with the Diagram 0 in Figure 11-13.

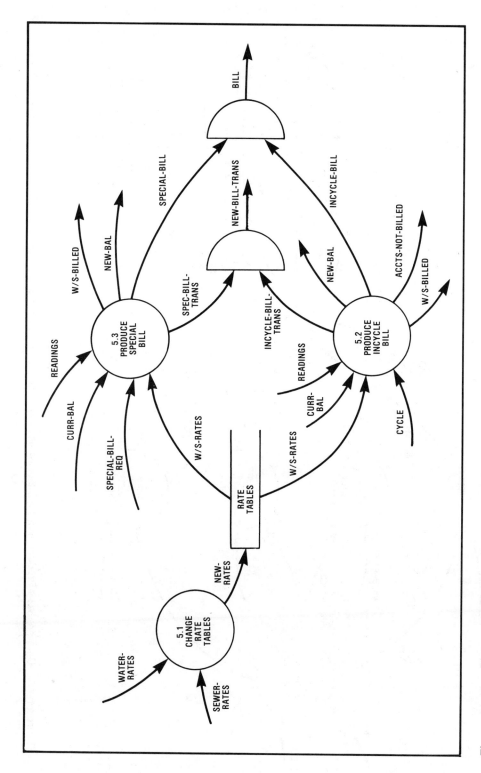

Figure 11-16. Diagram 5—Prepare Bill—corresponding with the Diagram 0 in Figure 11-13.

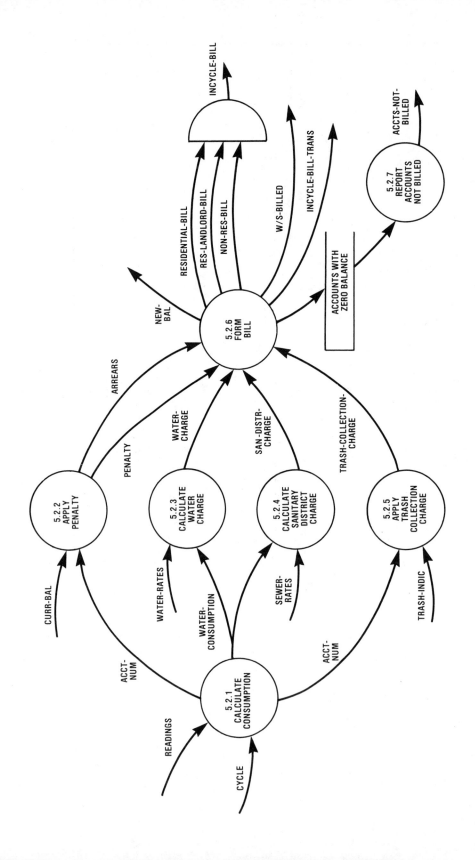

Figure 11-17. Diagram 5-2—Produce Incycle Bill—corresponding with the Diagram 5 in Figure 11-16.

ACCOUNT-JOURNAL

Each Trans $\left\{\begin{array}{l}\underline{\textbf{Acct-Num}}\\ +\text{User Class}\\ +\text{Transaction}\end{array}\right\}$ where TRANS = Date
$\qquad\qquad\qquad\qquad\qquad\qquad\qquad$ + Trans-type
$\qquad\qquad\qquad\qquad\qquad\qquad\qquad$ + Amount

BILLING-SUMMARY

4 $\left\{\begin{array}{l}\underline{\textbf{User-Class}}\\ +\text{Water-Consumption}\\ +\text{Sewer-Usage}\\ +\text{Water-Amt-Billed}\\ +\text{Sewer-Amt-Billed}\end{array}\right\}$ where USER-CLASS = $\left[\begin{array}{l}\text{Residential}\\ \text{Commercial}\\ \text{Industrial}\\ \text{Institutional}\end{array}\right]$

BILLING-TRANSACTIONS

All Accts $\left\{\begin{array}{l}\underline{\textbf{Acct-Num}}\\ +\text{User-Class}\\ +_8\{\text{Bill-Detail}\}\end{array}\right\}$ where BILL-DETAIL = Bill-Date
$\qquad\qquad\qquad\qquad\qquad\qquad\qquad\qquad$ + Bill-Water
$\qquad\qquad\qquad\qquad\qquad\qquad\qquad\qquad$ + Bill-San-Dist
$\qquad\qquad\qquad\qquad\qquad\qquad\qquad\qquad$ + Bill-Trash-Coll
$\qquad\qquad\qquad\qquad\qquad\qquad\qquad\qquad\quad$ + Arrears-Water
$\qquad\qquad\qquad\qquad\qquad\qquad\qquad\qquad\quad$ + Arrears-San-Dist
$\qquad\qquad\qquad\qquad\qquad\qquad\qquad\qquad\quad$ + Arrears-Trash-Coll
$\qquad\qquad\qquad\qquad\qquad\qquad\qquad\qquad\quad$ + Penalty

CUSTOMER-MASTER

All Accts $\left\{\begin{array}{l}\underline{\textbf{Acct-Num}}\\ +\text{User-Class}\\ +\text{Cust-Name}\\ +\text{Service-Addr}\\ +\text{Billing-Addr}\\ +\text{Meter-Read-Seq-Num}\\ +\text{Meter-Location}\\ +(\text{Meter-Reader-Msg})\\ +\text{Curr-Bal}\\ +_6\{\text{Read-Trans}\}\end{array}\right\}$ where

CURR-BAL = Cur-Water
$\qquad\qquad$ + Cur-San-Dist
$\qquad\qquad$ + Cur-Trash-Coll
$\qquad\qquad$ + Arr-Water
$\qquad\qquad$ + Arr-San-Dist
$\qquad\qquad$ + Arr-Trash-Coll
$\qquad\qquad$ + Penalty

READ-TRANS = Date
$\qquad\qquad\quad$ + Read-Type
$\qquad\qquad\quad$ + Reading-Value

READ-TYPE = $\left[\begin{array}{l}\text{Actual}\\ \text{Estimated}\\ \text{Self-Read}\end{array}\right]$

Figure 11-18. Notations for the content of the four main data stores of the new Central City water billing system.

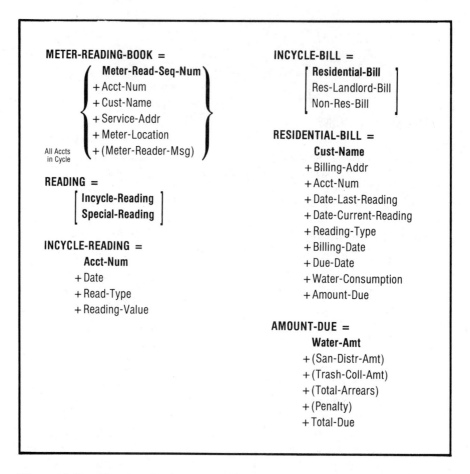

METER-READING-BOOK =

$$\left\{ \begin{array}{l} \textbf{Meter-Read-Seq-Num} \\ +\text{Acct-Num} \\ +\text{Cust-Name} \\ +\text{Service-Addr} \\ +\text{Meter-Location} \\ +\text{(Meter-Reader-Msg)} \end{array} \right\}$$

All Accts in Cycle

READING =

$$\left[\begin{array}{l} \textbf{Incycle-Reading} \\ \textbf{Special-Reading} \end{array} \right]$$

INCYCLE-READING =

   Acct-Num
   + Date
   + Read-Type
   + Reading-Value

INCYCLE-BILL =

$$\left[\begin{array}{l} \textbf{Residential-Bill} \\ \text{Res-Landlord-Bill} \\ \text{Non-Res-Bill} \end{array} \right]$$

RESIDENTIAL-BILL =

   Cust-Name
   + Billing-Addr
   + Acct-Num
   + Date-Last-Reading
   + Date-Current-Reading
   + Reading-Type
   + Billing-Date
   + Due-Date
   + Water-Consumption
   + Amount-Due

AMOUNT-DUE =

   Water-Amt
   + (San-Distr-Amt)
   + (Trash-Coll-Amt)
   + (Total-Arrears)
   + (Penalty)
   + Total-Due

Figure 11-19. Notations for the content of selected data flows of the new Central City water billing system.

Figure 11-12 is the Context Diagram of the new system. Diagram 0 is presented in Figure 11-13. Processes 1, 3, and 5 are partitioned here. A discussion of Process 6, which requires tighter control procedures, is presented in Chapter 17: Control and Reliability Design.

Diagram 1, shown in Figure 11-14, is straightforward. It does, however, illustrate two points. First, note the data flow—CYCLE—entering bubble 1.1. There is not a corresponding flow entering the parent bubble 1 in Diagram 0—an apparent violation of the balancing rule. Recall that CYCLE is simply a number, in this case between 1 and 4, that denotes a subset of the accounts located in one quadrant of Central City. Meter readings and billings are normally done by cycle. Thus CYCLE is merely a parameter input to process 1.1. To avoid cluttering data flow diagrams, parameter inputs are often shown only with the processes that use them and not with their parent processes. The second point to note about Diagram 1 is that it is "very physical." Processes 1.1 and 1.2, which extract and sort, don't really transform the data; they simply transport it. These processes would not have been included in a logical model for the new system; Process 1 on Diagram 0 would not have been partitioned at all.

The explosion of Process 3: Apply New Readings is presented in Diagram 3, Figure 11-15. As indicated, the majority of readings—the incycle readings—are keypunched and submitted to a batch updating process. Special transactions are entered on-line. A reading value is simply a six-digit number with no inherent meaning. As part of the edit process, then, the new and previous readings are used to compute a trial consumption. This is compared with a rolling average consumption for that account maintained in the CUSTOMER-MASTER data store. If the trial consumption varies from the average by more than the parameter REASONABLE-PERCENTAGE, the reading is rejected as unreasonable. Processes 3.5 through 3.7 are manual procedures to investigate these unreasonable readings.

The Prepare Bill process is partitioned in Diagram 5 of Figure 11-16. As is evident from the diagram, there is a high degree of similarity between the production of incycle and special bills. The production of incycle bills is shown in Figure 11-17. Even though this is part of a physical model, the parallel nature of the lowest level processing to perform the actual computations is retained here—leaving more flexibility to the program designers during the Detailed Design and Implementation phase that follows.

Figure 11-17 indicates that the INCYCLE-BILL may be one of several formats. Most are RESIDENTIAL-BILLs that are printed and sent as postcards, with a stub to be returned with the payment. (See the Case Scenario section of Chapter 12.) Nonresidential customers (that is, commercial, industrial, and institutional customers) and residences that are billed to a landlord rather than to the actual occupant all have bills prepared as invoices and enclosed in envelopes.

The ACCTS-NOT-BILLED report in Figure 11-17 is a control report requested by the user—specifically by the auditor. This report is produced automatically with each incycle billing run. It lists those accounts in the cycle for which there was no balance due and, hence, no bill produced.

As stated earlier, lowest level process bubbles must each have a corresponding process description. A process description expressing the rules for calculating the water charge in bubble 5.2.3 is presented in Chapter 10, Figure 10-21.

Summary

This activity marks a transition from the study of the existing system into the building of the new one. Interviews are used to gather data, including user descriptions of inadequacies of the existing system. Requirements are classified as logical or physical.

The logical model of the existing system and new logical requirements are used to develop a logical model for the new system. Using new physical requirements, a physical model of the new system is prepared. Alternative physical models may be proposed.

A computer-based information system consists of both computer and manual processing. The computer processing is a subsystem within a larger system.

The User Specification document will include an overview narrative, a description of system function, a model of system processing, a data dictionary, process specifications, data access diagrams, an index of outputs for users, an index of inputs, description of user interfaces, user specified physical requirements, and any unresolved policy considerations.

The User Specification provides a means for user verification and approval. It is a starting point for system design and a standard for the Implementation Phase. It sets user expectations and can be used to measure success. The user views the computer processing as a black box and has to know only what goes in and what comes out.

The services rendered by the systems analyst are: analysis of the existing system, criticism of existing methods, innovation, synthesis of solutions, and diplomacy in dealing with user uncertainties.

The logical model of the new system is then evaluated. Tests of mechanical correctness are made. It is checked to be sure that it is an accurate and complete representation of the business. Two important design evaluation criteria are coupling and cohesion. Coupling refers to data interfaces among higher-level processes. Cohesion refers to the singularity of purpose of a process.

A physical model then describes how the logical model will be implemented. Technical, financial, operational, scheduling, and human factor trade-offs are considered. The logical model is marked up to show human-machine boundaries, batch or on-line processes, and timing cycles for batches. Control points for editing and auditing are identified. Performance requirements are specified.

Application software packages are evaluated at this point as a way of reducing costs and lead time. Such packages involve inevitable compromises. These should be evaluated by referring to the model.

The project team for this activity is virtually the same as in Activity 3 and is user oriented.

The resulting project file will include an updated project plan, the Initial Investigation Report, the Feasibility Report, a list of management decision requirements, interview schedules and summaries, the User Specification, and a description of possible new system solutions.

Key Terms

1. black box
2. coupling
3. cohesion
4. balancing

Review/Discussion Questions

1. How does this analysis activity of preparing new system requirements fit in with the activities of studying the existing system and designing the new one?

2. What are the systems analyst's objectives in conducting user interviews in this activity?

3. What is the sequence used in the development of system models used during this activity?

4. What is the concept of a black box and how does this relate to the the User Specification?

5. What are the main objectives of developing the User Specification?

6. What documents are included in the User Specification, and what is the function of each?

7. During preparation of new system requirements, how is the systems analyst involved and what services does he or she render the user organization?

8. What steps are taken in the evolution of logical and physical models for the new system?

9. How are the principles of coupling and cohesion used to evaluate the logical model?

10. What are the objectives of evaluating application software packages and when is it appropriate to do so?

OUTPUT DESIGN 12

LEARNING OBJECTIVES

On completing the reading and learning assignments for this chapter, you should be able to:

☐ Describe how the systems analyst works with users to specify the form, format, and medium for new system output.

☐ Explain the computer output functions of communication, archival storage, and turnaround documents and describe how each of these functions is important to the user organization.

☐ Describe the physical characteristics and trade-offs of commonly used output devices, including: printers, video displays, plotters, audio output, and computer output to microfilm (COM).

☐ Explain the evaluation criteria used to determine whether a proposed output method will do a given job.

☐ Describe the general logical design of output forms.

☐ Give some physical input methods for machine-readable documents, as in the use of turnaround documents.

THE OUTPUT DESIGN TASK

Output design plays a key role in the development of a new computer information system. This is logical. The new system will be developed to satisfy user needs. Users specify needs by describing the results (the outputs) desired.

Output design during Activity 4 is highly interactive. The systems analyst works closely with users to develop a complete under-standing—and ultimate agreement—about what results are to be pro-duced. Designs are kept in rough form—purposely. The purpose at this initial stage is to understand what is wanted and how it is to be delivered. Designs can be tightened up and refined technically during the detailed design and implementation phase.

The end products of output design are rough sketches of the documents and screen displays themselves, a logical representation of the data structures involved, as well as preliminary specifications for the output devices to be used. To arrive at this point, the systems analyst must be able to advise the user about output options and their capabilities, including the devices and methods reviewed in this chapter.

PURPOSES OF SYSTEM OUTPUTS

There are several ways to classify system outputs. Normally, the em-phasis is on end-user outputs—those that appear on a context diagram. In addition to these major outputs, reports and query responses are produced and used by manual processes within the scope of the system. Discussions in this chapter encompass both types of outputs.

Outputs may also be classified as computer-generated or manually prepared. However, even manually prepared outputs are normally based on computer-generated reports. This chapter concentrates on computer-generated outputs.

Perhaps the best way to classify outputs is according to their func-tion. System outputs serve three main purposes, or functions:

- Information delivery. The major purpose of a computer-based in-formation system is to communicate information to users on a timely and accurate basis.
- Archival storage. Computers hold the potential for long-term reten-tion of information in forms and formats that can be retrieved as needed for distribution.

- Turnaround documents. Computers can produce specially encoded outputs that, in turn, can be used to enter data into computers as transactions are completed.

Information Delivery

The main purpose of system output is to communicate data and information to people with the need to know. This output is produced in human-readable form and can be presented in a variety of formats using several types of media.

Informational outputs fall into three general categories:

- Reports
- Query responses
- Transaction records.

Reports.   *Reports* are documents that present information to managers or users. Reports are usually classified according to content and may be grouped in three general categories:

- *Detail reports* present all or nearly all of the data content of one or more files. These kinds of reports are useful to managers watching over the day-to-day activities of a business and to staff people responding to specific customer inquiries. Such reports might be printed weekly or daily to give the operational-level manager the information needed to control the daily work effort.

- *Summary reports* show accumulated totals for detail records—rather than complete file contents. These reports are usually provided to middle-level managers for review of business activity. Normally, summary reports show monthly or weekly figures for the current period along with projections and figures for previous time periods. With this information, the manager can compare current operating results with expected results and with prior operations. Discrepancies between actual and expected results may indicate the need for corrective action to bring the business back on course.

- *Exception reports* are designed to call attention to conditions that can be classified as outside of normal operating limits. For example, a computer might scan an accounts receivable file to identify accounts that are overdue. Rather than a detail report listing all accounts and amounts due on each or a summary report giving the total amount due by sales region, an exception report might list only those accounts that are long overdue (such as more than 90 days), so that managers can take action on them. Another example would be inventory reports that, rather than listing the inventory level for each item, report only on those items for which the quantity falls below predefined limits. Exception reports are normally far more effective than detail reports for day-to-day operational controls.

Query responses. *Query responses* are related to reports in terms of their data content. However, they are dramatically different in their method of presentation, in the currency of the data used, and, perhaps, in the cost of delivery.

A report is normally produced in printed form by a batch run that uses one or more files. The report presents a snapshot of a part of the organization as it existed at the time the report was run.

On the other hand, a query response capability involves on-line terminal output that presents up-to-date information for immediate use. Query-response capabilities are usually developed in response to user needs for current information at a relatively detailed level. Currency demands, in turn, dictate requirements for updating the source files used by the queries. While query responses normally report at a detail level, summary and exception responses are also possible.

Transaction records. A *transaction* is, broadly, an act of doing business. It is an activity associated with the production and distribution of goods and services provided by an organization. Transactions can represent both input to and output from a system. Because of the central role transactions play in many computer information systems, they are worth discussing here.

In the course of doing business, a company generates data representing those transactions. Data provide evidence of transactions, and, by capturing transaction data, the company maintains records of business activity. Most of the data resulting from transactions eventually make their way into company files as documentation on business operations. As described above, reports are produced using these data to provide management with the information needed to control business activity.

Transaction data may be captured on source documents or may be input directly to the computer. Input methods are discussed in Chapter 13. Whatever the method of capture, however, transactions serve other purposes besides collection of data for historical files. One of the most important uses of *transaction records* is to facilitate the flow of work throughout the production and distribution processes of the system. A transaction, which may exist either as a physical document or a computer record, transmits information between people involved in those activities and, in effect, is a process control device. Activities are triggered by the existence of the transactions themselves—and are controlled by the information contained on them.

Consider the following example. In a manufacturing and sales operation, work begins with the arrival of a sales order from a customer. This order transaction triggers the preparation of a production order transaction requesting a manufactured product. In turn, several other transactions are generated to gather together the material required in the production of the item, to specify work orders, and to integrate the materials, people, machines, and manufacturing processes to produce the item. In the meantime, the sales order transaction is used to prepare invoices and statements requesting payment from the customer. These transactions enter the accounting system to be maintained as historical records for reporting and control purposes. Documents sent to customers request and provide evidence of payment for the products. These transactions, in turn, enter the accounting system to be balanced against production and distribution costs and expenses.

As this scenario suggests, transaction records are part of many systems. They provide mechanisms for getting the work done. They represent the key data flows in a system, activating and controlling system processes.

Archival Storage

Archival records, by definition, constitute permanent documentation. In some cases, archival records are the actual business reports and transaction documents themselves. In other cases, copies of these reports and documents are in either human- or machine-readable form and use materials that withstand long-term retention and use.

Extended storage of business records is necessary for three main reasons. First, there are legal requirements for retaining records of business transactions. Certain types of these records must be maintained over the life of the business as documentation of operations for evidence in legal matters. Second, business records provide an historical commentary on business activity. Long-term trends contained in this information can be used to project and plan for future activity. Third, archival records provide backup security. If currently active records are destroyed through fire or other disaster, business files, reports, and turnaround documents can be restored from archival files. Thus, archival records must be accessible when needed without undue difficulty.

Turnaround Documents

Turnaround documents are computer output documents that serve also as input documents to a follow-up processing activity. In its output form, a transaction document triggers some action on the part of its recipient. Usually the action is then indicated on the document itself or accompanies the document on its return. The returned document then activates the next processing step in the system.

A common application for turnaround documents is college class registration. In this case, the outputs are punched cards representing individual seats available for each of the classes. A student registering for a class is given a card. These class cards, together with cards containing student identification information, are then collected and reprocessed through the computer to produce registration records and lists of students enrolled in particular classes.

The principle of turnaround documents is straightforward: An output document is produced to trigger a transaction; then it is returned as evidence of the transaction and becomes input to the next processing phase. Turnaround documents can take physical forms besides punched cards. Several of the options are described in the section that follows.

One of the main benefits of use of the turnaround document is that it assists in automating data entry. In the registration example, class cards are punched with identification information that is already in an input form. Keyboarding of these data is, therefore, unnecessary. The only additional data to be entered are the student identification numbers. Eliminating the need for a person to enter data already known by the system and necessary for the transaction saves time and reduces the possibility for error.

Another benefit is that turnaround documents aid in data collection. For example, in the Central City water billing system, meter reading books serve as turnaround documents. These books can be printed by the computer so that the pages are ordered by the sequence in which the meters will be read and can contain meter location and other information helpful to the meter reader. Usage data are then collected by meter readers who record the data in these books.

OUTPUT MEDIA AND DEVICES

Consideration and selection of the appropriate output medium is an important step in the physical design process. Output options to be considered include:

- Printing Devices
- Video Displays
- Plotters
- Audio Output
- Computer Output to Microfilm (COM).

Printing Devices

Output devices that produce printed documents fall into two categories:

- Impact
- Nonimpact.

Impact printers.   Impact printers create impressions by striking a ribbon that, in turn, transfers images to paper. There are two basic designs for impact printers: serial and line.

A *serial printer* operates one character at a time, with an imprinting device that moves along the line being imprinted. To add speed, many serial printers are *bi-directional*. That is, they accept data and imprint characters while the printing device is traveling either left to right, or right to left. Typically, the first line of a document will be printed from left to right. Then, while the device is in the right-hand position, it will operate backward, printing the next line. Obviously, this eliminates the time needed to return the printing device from one side of the paper to the other.

Printing elements of serial printers include *matrix* and *fixed-type* devices. A matrix print mechanism contains a series of points, usually with wires that are projected forward to cause printing impressions. A typical matrix pattern has a seven-column width and a nine-row height.

The other popular serial printing technique, fixed-type, is to rotate a circular printing device in front of a hammer, which strikes a type element, causing the imprint.

In general, serial units are relatively high in quality but low in speed. Typical production ranges are from 30 to 180 characters per second.

Higher speeds in impact printing are achieved through use of *line printers*. These units imprint a full line at a time. Usually, fixed-type devices move behind the paper on which imprinting is done. One hammer for each column in which printing is done strikes against a ribbon at the front of the paper, causing the imprint. Typeholding devices include moving chains and rotating drums.

Since entire lines are printed in single operations, speeds of line printers are greater than for serial printers. Line printers typically operate at rates of anywhere from 200 to more than 2,000 lines per minute.

Nonimpact printers.   Nonimpact printers are devices that cause images to be imprinted without actual contact between print mechanism and paper. Nonimpact printers fall into three general categories:

- Thermal
- Ink jet
- Electrostatic (laser).

Thermal printers.   Thermal printers use a special paper that develops images under exposure to heat. Matrix points in a print head become hot, causing images to form. The appearance and action of these units is much like that of matrix impact printers, except that heat is used to form the image.

Ink jet printers.   Ink jet printers actually spray images onto the paper. Images are shaped by electromagnetic fields formed behind or within the paper surface by electronic devices. Ferrous particles, small bits of metal that respond to magnetic fields, within the ink are attracted to these image areas. Ink jet printing can be extremely fast and of high quality.

Electrostatic (laser) printers.   Electrostatic, or laser, printers form images on the drums of copier/duplicator units. These machines resemble high speed office copiers internally. Images are formed on light-sensitive drums by high-speed laser beams. Transfer of images is then done in the same general way as in office copiers. Electrostatic printers are the highest speed of document output devices now available. Individual printers have rated capacities of up to 20,000 or more lines per minute. In addition, certain models of electrostatic copiers are among the highest in quality for computer document outputs. Graphic images and typeset forms can be created through laser printers. Many service or training manuals are now created in this manner.

Nonimpact printers run a broad range from relatively slow units that imprint one character at a time to the highest speed devices available for printed output. Similarly, there is a wide range of quality among the devices described above.

Video Display

Video displays utilize CRT terminals. The video tube in these terminals is, in effect, the same as a television picture tube. Thus, depending upon the program and the content of computer files, either alphanumeric or graphic data—or a mixture of both—can be displayed on video tubes.

In most situations, video displays are used for query response only. That is, normally there are no permanent copies. The user asks for desired information. The data are displayed on the CRT terminal, then eliminated when they are no longer needed. In some cases—for example, customer inquires about account transactions—it is helpful to have a serial printer linked to a group of terminals so that a hard copy of the screen image can be obtained.

There are many devices, however, that use video displays to create permanent records. Some Computer Output to Microfilm (COM) devices use cameras that photograph the faces of video displays. (COM devices are discussed in greater depth later in this chapter.) Some *reprographic systems,* such as those that form images for typesetting or printing page makeup applications, also form images on video displays. These are then photographed and used in printing applications.

Video output systems have continually decreased in price as the costs of tubes and accompanying electronic controls have come down. Thus, video display terminals are, today, highly economical methods for providing query response capabilities in either text or graphic form.

Plotters

Plotters are devices that produce documents through computer driven writing devices that create images on paper. Writing is done by a *stylus,* a device that is driven electromechanically in response to a computer-generated signal. Stylus devices can draw in one color or several.

Different techniques are used to achieve bi-directional movement of the stylus. On most plotters, the stylus rides on a track, enabling it to move from side to side. Vertical movement over the image area is either through movement of the track mechanism, or through rotation of the paper sheet on a drum.

A popular application for plotters is to produce business charts and graphs. In such applications, the stylus movements draw the figures needed as well as writing the letters, numbers, or symbols that label the drawings.

Audio

Audio output is through either actual or simulated sounds of a human voice. Under some systems, a collection of syllables actually spoken by people is recorded for reference in output. The computer generates spoken output by referring to this dictionary of syllables, converting data from stored files into audio output. As an alternative, the computer may have a sound generator, or *speech synthesizer*, that simulates human speech or musical instruments.

Applications of audio output are becoming commonplace. For example, many telephone announcements, which were previously prerecorded, are now actually generated by computers at the time messages are needed. Reports of time or weather are commonly being generated by computers and output over telephone lines. Costs of voice synthesizers have come down dramatically in recent years, leading to additional use of audio output.

However, spoken words represent an extremely slow method of getting data out of computers. For this reason, audio output is generally limited to applications involving low volumes of data. Where data volumes are small, however, the universal availability of push-button telephones makes this output option attractive. For example, many banks use audio output systems to provide account balances to tellers. Tellers dial a number that connects the telephone to a computer. Then the push-button dialing system is used to enter an account number. The balance is then received from the computer as audio output over the telephone.

Computer Output To Microfilm (COM)

Archival records, by definition, must be permanent. In practice, archival records usually experience relatively low reference volumes. This combination of conditions—long storage life and low reference volume—is ideal for microfilm. Computers, using laser or video display technology, output data directly onto a film recorder. The film can be either in rolls or in the form of a multi-image sheet called a *fiche*.

In many applications, microfilm is replacing extensive report printouts. For example, banks regularly produce reports on account status. These can be voluminous. In general, these documents are used for reference only when on-line reference capabilities are interrupted. In this situation, microfilm outputs are far less expensive and, in emergencies, more convenient to use because microfilmed records are more compact.

Many publications, such as airline schedule guides, are output regularly on microfilm for use by travel agents, reservation clerks, and others. Parts lists in manufacturing applications also use microfilm outputs.

OUTPUT EVALUATION CRITERIA

Effective design of computer outputs involves evaluation criteria for a number of trade-offs. These criteria include:

- Use
- Volume
- Quality
- Cost.

Use

A starting point for output design lies in classifying the uses of desired outputs. First, it is helpful to distinguish between outputs that remain internal to the organization and those that are prepared for external use.

Outputs generated for internal use include:

- Reports to management summarizing business activities
- Query responses and operational reports on the day-to-day status of the business
- Documents or reports that control active work within an organization, such as job tickets or production schedules
- Business transaction documents that must be maintained for some time, including expense records, payment vouchers, employee time cards, and others.

External outputs generated by the computer include:

- Reports to governmental agencies
- Documents sent to customers, such as invoices, statements, shipping orders, bills of lading, and so forth
- Communications with stockholders
- Paychecks and other documents sent to employees.

The design and ultimate expense of an external output may be impacted by external regulations, desired organizational image, or other factors.

Another dimension affecting output design is the purpose of the output and the ultimate use to which it will be put. In certain applications, for example, printed documents are necessary. In other situations, the same data can be presented on CRT terminals. If an output involves large data volumes that will be referenced only occasionally, microfilm might be a better output technique. In general, the use for the output is a key factor in determining its design and the form in which it will be delivered.

Volume

The volume of printed or displayed material to be generated by an application also affects the selection of output methods. For example, printing devices available for use with computers have speeds ranging from four or five lines per minute up to 20,000 or more lines per minute. In addition, as noted above, microfilm may represent the best choice in very high volume situations. The amount of data to be generated can be a major factor in determining output design and method.

Quality

The use for any given output helps to determine the quality needed. For example, invoices to customers are often produced on multi-color preprinted forms. Such documents are considered to have an advertising value for the company that produces them. Computers can also be used to generate personalized letters to customers. Obviously, the higher the quality of such output documents, the better. On the other hand, while production or status reports to be used internally must have clearly readable information, the quality of the paper, for example, is less critical. Also, to save paper costs, internal documents frequently load more data onto a given sheet of paper than is done with external reports.

Cost

Cost, in general, is most heavily impacted by processing volumes and the desired quality. High output volumes will dictate higher-cost devices. Yet, with any given device, the higher the output volume, the lower the cost per unit or document will be. Similarly, the higher the desired quality, the higher the cost is apt to be. For example, on letter-quality output documents, the cost of impressions from the expensive ribbons used is likely to be greater than the cost of the paper itself.

Output design and selection of output techniques for any given application depend largely on trade-offs among the criteria described above. As with any trade-off decision, however, options are often limited by practical considerations. For example, if an installation does not have an ultra-high-speed printer, it may be impossible to optimize output for a high-volume application. The size of the system and the volume and importance of the output will impose limits on the options that can legitimately be considered.

OUTPUT DESIGN

For design of either output documents or displays, work begins by establishing data content. The systems analyst, working closely with the user, builds a list of data elements to be included in each of the outputs for the system. In effect, this listing leads toward the creation of a data dictionary for the new system. Care should be taken to have users review this list—in several iterations. The point is to be sure that, before you start designing forms, display screens, or report layouts, you know what the content requirements will be.

Once content is established, output requirements should be analyzed and formulated. A number of questions should be addressed by the user and the analyst:

- What is the business purpose of the output?
- Who will use the output and how will it be used?
- Is each data element in the output essential?
- Are any data elements missing, given the intended use?
- Is the same information to be included in other outputs?
- How often should the output be produced?
- How many copies are needed?
- What is the best form and format for presentation of the data?

Answers to these and other, similar questions will help the analyst establish a business understanding of the problems to be solved by the new system. By specifying content, format, and scheduling for output documents, users indicate how important the reports will be and the role they will play in the new system.

Preliminary Output Design

Given a list of data elements to be incorporated in an output document or display, the analyst then works with the user to rough out the appearance of the finished document or display. At this point, design efforts remain informal. It is not yet necessary to use ruled, structured layout forms to delineate the outputs. The rough sketches prepared at this time will provide the basis for completing more formal output specification documents later, during the detailed design and implementation phase.

The rough layouts at this point, nonetheless, should encompass all of the information and appearance factors needed to prepare a final output design. The motivation is to identify the data to be presented and its organization in a form that facilitates communication. Included should be:

- Heading or identification information

- Delineation of the body of the report, form, or screen

- Indication of summary lines and their placement.

Data Content

The informal design of output formats is sufficient to communicate content and appearance to the users. From the standpoint of the designer, however, a precise statement of the data content used in the output is most critical. The data structure notation—using logical constructs of sequences, repetitions, and selections—can be applied in describing output content.

One common output, for example, is a formal report. In general, a formal report has three main sections. Report headings consist of one or more report title and column heading lines. The body of the report is a repetition of detail lines, each containing a sequence of columns of data. The report footing contains one or more summary or total lines.

This general format for a report can be described through use of data structure notations that will become part of the data dictionary for the new system. Figure 12-1 defines the data content for the output form illustrated in Figure 12-2.

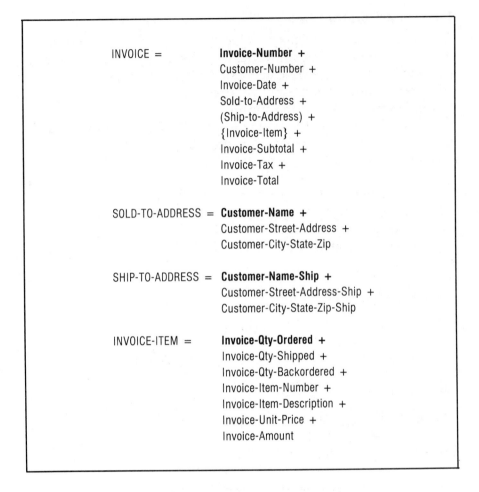

Figure 12-1. Structured syntax describing output content.

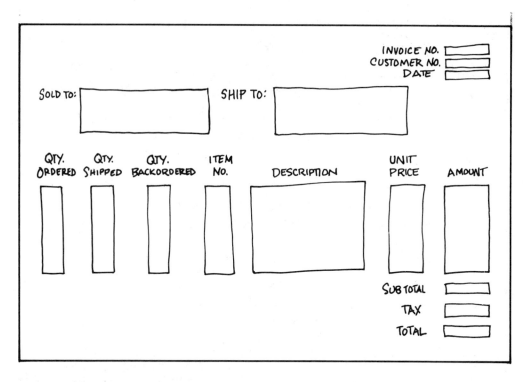

Figure 12-2. Rough design of output form.

Output Documentation

As described in Chapter 11, the user specification for the new system contains a section that defines the system outputs. In general, output descriptions should consist of an index page listing each output by name, followed by a pair of documents for each output. The first of these descriptive items is an output documentation form that communicates the purpose and use of the output and specifies the data content. The second form in this set should be a rough sketch of the output, as described above. These documents are illustrated in Figures 12-3 through 12-6 and in discussions of the case scenario that follows.

CASE SCENARIO

During analysis and general design for the water billing application, a number of implementation options could be identified for each of the

OUTPUT

System: **WATER BILLING**   Date prepared: **NOV 15, 1983**

Output name: **RESIDENTIAL-BILLING**   Prepared by: **JRP**

Output number/id: _____

Design documentation attached: **X** Rough format   ____ Detailed layout

Output media: **X** Printed Report   ____ Screen Display

PURPOSE/USE: **Sent to residential customers who reside at the service address. (Bills for residential service sent to landlords—— see RESIDENTIAL-LANDLORD-BILL). Customer returns stub with payment.**

ORGANIZATION (order, level of detail, totals):
   Mail route order

DISTRIBUTION/ACCESS: **To customer**

SIZE/VOLUME:
5000-7000/cycle

FREQUENCY: **Four cycles-billing run every two weeks. (Individual customer receives bill bimonthly)**

DATA CONTENT:

CUST-NAME
+ADDRESS
+ACCOUNT-NUM
+DATE-LAST-READING
+DATE-CURR-READING
+READING-TYPE
+BILLING-DATE
+DUE-DATE
+WATER-CONSUMPTION
+AMOUNT-DUE

WHERE

AMOUNT DUE =
      WATER-AMT
   +(SAN-DISTR-AMT)
   +(TRASH-COLL-AMT)
   +(ARREARS)
   +(PENALTY)
   +TOTAL-DUE

Figure 12-3. Form specifying residential bill output.

```
┌─────────────────────────────────────────────┬─────────────────────────────┐
│          CENTRAL CITY                          ╎     ⌢⌢⌢⌢⌢⌢⌢⌢⌢             │
│          WATER BILL                            ╎   ⌜Postage⌝  ~~~~~~~       │
│   ACCT.           ADDRESS                      ╎   │ Permit │  ~~~~~~~      │
│   3-27-4625       1403 N 13TH ST               ╎   ⌞_____⌟  ~~~~~~~      │
│                                                ╎                             │
│   SERVICE FROM    TO         READ DATE         ╎  ACCT                       │
│   01- OCT- 84     01- DEC- 84  01-DEC-84        │  3-27-4625                 │
│                                                ╎                             │
│   CONSUMPTION    TYPE        DUE DATE          ╎  JERI JONES                 │
│   17000          ACTUAL      31- DEC-84         │  1403 N. 13TH ST.          │
├────────────────────────────────────────────── ╎  CENTRAL CITY              │
│     WATER            22.75                     ╎                             │
│     TRASH             7.00                     ╎                             │
│     SANITARY DIST     8.42                     ╎  PLEASE PAY 64.68           │
│     ARREARS          24.10                     ╎                             │
│     PENALTY           2.41                     ╎  PLEASE RETURN STUB         │
│     TOTAL            64.68                     ╎      WITH PAYMENT           │
└─────────────────────────────────────────────────────────────────────────────┘
```

Figure 12-4. Rough format for residential bill.

key outputs. The discussion that follows includes a sampling of outputs to illustrate how systems analysis is applied rather than a total listing of every piece of paper or display that could be generated from this system.

The basic document output from a water billing system, obviously, is the customer bill. In the existing system at Central City, water bills are printed on *continuous-form* postcards. That is, preprinted forms are used. These are printed on a heavy card stock that makes it possible for cards to be sent directly through the mail, without having to be inserted in envelopes. This output solution saves both postage and forms handling costs.

Each card, in turn, is perforated so that it can be separated in the middle. The customer returns a stub with each payment. The payment stub includes customer identification and the amount of the bill.

One clear option for the new system is to retain this output form and format, simply modifying it to accommodate the sanitary district

OUTPUT

System: __Water Billing__   Date prepared: __Nov 15, 1983__

Output name: __ACCT-HISTORY__   Prepared by: __JRP__

Output number/id: _____

Design documentation attached: __X__ Rough format   ____ Detailed layout

Output media: ____ Printed Report   __X__ Screen Display

PURPOSE/USE: This is an on-line query capability—to access the transactions on an individual account. ACCOUNT—NUM must be supplied. (Reading/Cash adjustments are included as Reading/Payment transactions.

ORGANIZATION (order, level of detail, totals):
  N/A

DISTRIBUTION/ACCESS:
    Restricted to city finance dept. personnel

SIZE/VOLUME: N/A   FREQUENCY: N/A

DATA CONTENT:

```
    ACCOUNT-NUM              WHERE
  + CUST-NAME               CURR-AMOUNT-DUE = AMOUNT-DUE
  + ADDRESS                   = WATER-AMT
  + CURR-AMOUNT-DUE           + (SAN-DISTR-AMT)
        ⎧ READING-DATE ⎫      + (TRASH-COLL-AMT)
  +    ⎨ + READING-TYPE ⎬     + (ARREARS)
      6 ⎩ + READING-VALUE⎭    + (PENALTY)
        ⎧ BILLING-DATE ⎫      + TOTAL-DUE
  +    ⎨                 ⎬
      6 ⎩ + AMOUNT-DUE   ⎭
        ⎧ PAYMENT-DATE ⎫
  +    ⎨ + PAYMENT-AMT  ⎬
      6 ⎩ + PAYMENT-TYPE⎭
```

Figure 12-5.   Output form for account history screen.

INDIVIDUAL ACCOUNT HISTORY

ACCT: 3-27-4625   ADDR: 1403 N 13TH ST

NAME: JERI JONES   CENTRAL CITY

CURRENT DUE: $64.68

READINGS

DATE	TYPE	VALUE	DATE	TYPE	VALUE
01-APR-84	ACT	8044573	01-JUN-84	EST	8044597
01-AUG-84	ACT	8044650	15-SEP-84	ADJ	-33
01-OCT-84	EST	8044712	01-DEC-84	ACT	8044729

BILLINGS

DATE	WATER	SANITARY	TRASH	ARREARS	PEN.	TOTAL
10-FEB-84	10.26	2.44	7.00	0	0	19.70
11-APR-84	14.50	3.20	12.00	0	2.50	32.20
10-JUN-84	35.42	12.85	7.00	0	0	55.27
9-AUG-84	42.25	15.60	7.00	0	0	64.85
10-OCT-84	14.05	3.05	7.00	0	0	24.10
10-DEC-84	22.75	8.42	7.00	24.10	2.41	64.68

PAYMENTS

DATE	TYPE	AMT	DATE	TYPE	AMT
31-DEC-83	P	24.83	1-MAR-84	P	19.70
27-APR-84	P	29.70	17-MAY-84	ADJ	+ 2.50
25-JUN-84	P	55.27	30-AUG-84	P	64.85

Figure 12-6.   Rough format for account history output screen.

billing. This approach would meet the objective of minimizing expenses for the new system while optimizing the advantages of scale that come from being able to charge the sanitary district a prorated share of the total system cost.

Other options in the design of the billing for the new system center around the possibility of using a turnaround document. That is, the document returned by the customer along with the payment could be machine readable, making it possible to enter customer payment data to the system directly from the bill. In the existing system, the water department uses manual procedures to input payment information.

Turnaround options include use of prepunched cards or the imprinting of bills with optically readable characters. The punched card option would call for creation of a separate punched card for each customer at the time the bill is printed. This card would contain the customer number and amount due. The card would then have to be stuffed into an envelope along with the paper bill. Obviously, output costs would increase with the cost of the envelope, the two documents, and the extra handling. However, the cost of inputting payment information would decrease substantially. The design trade-off, then, would lie in evaluating costs of output against savings through reduced input expenses.

The second option would be to print the data on the bill in special character formats, or *fonts*, that could be read back into computers directly through *Optical Character Reading (OCR)* equipment. Input from OCR bills could either be on machines that read batches of documents at high speeds, entering data directly into the computer, or through the use of *fiberoptics wands* that are operated manually to read data from one imprint at a time. With the wand approach, the reading devices could be attached to point-of-sale registers in the finance department. Data could be entered into the computer on-line or could be stored on diskettes or magnetic tape cassettes for batch entry. In this case, there need not be extra cost for producing and mailing two documents for each bill. The trade-off, clearly, would be between the cost of the OCR equipment, which may be substantial, and the savings resulting from faster and more efficient input of payment data.

Figures 12-3 and 12-4 illustrate the pair of entries that would be included in the output section of the User Specification prepared during

Activity 4, assuming that the first option—modifying the existing bill—is chosen.

Customer bills represent a detailed report-type output. For an example of a summary report, consider a report to provide management control over accounts receivable. Following the processing of each billing cycle, a report is prepared showing the total of payments (accounts receivable) due to the water department. This report shows unpaid balances for each billing cycle, providing a clear-cut tool for evaluating the status of, and progress in, collecting outstanding bills. This type of report is sometimes referred to as an *aged receivables report*. This means, simply, that the report is structured to show the amounts due according to the length of time these receivables have been outstanding.

The existing system contains such a report. For the new system, the report would have to be expanded to include sanitary district receivables. Consideration might also be given to making these data available through on-line inquiry. Even so, however, a decision would probably be made to produce and deliver a report of this type—as the means of assigning and fixing responsibility for monitoring collections.

An example of an exception report for this system would be a listing of all unbilled accounts. This report would be produced at the conclusion of processing for each cycle. This example provides a classic illustration of the value of exception reports in managing a business. Managers don't have to be concerned about accounts that are billed routinely, on their regular cycle dates. They are more concerned with situations in which billing of amounts due to the water department may have been skipped or overlooked—either purposely or accidentally.

A certain number of customers for any utility operation will not receive bills during any given billing period. One common reason is that service has been discontinued because a home has been sold. In other situations, service may have been discontinued while homeowners are on extended vacations. These types of situations can be encoded so that they are immediately apparent to managers. Such exception situations require little attention.

However, there is always the possibility that a meter reader overlooked or was unable to collect current meter data. Or the account may have had a credit balance, resulting in nothing due after charges were computed. Finally, there is the possibility of fraud—a city employee tampering with the system in some way so as to leave the account with zero consumption or zero balance due.

An exception listing of all accounts not billed, automatically produced with each billing cycle, provides a tool for the city financial managers and auditors to monitor potential errors or fraud. Each line on this report should indicate account status and provide some kind of code giving the reason why the account was not billed.

An example of different options for presenting a given output can be seen in the customer account history records to be compiled under the new system. This requirement is cited in Chapter 8, dealing with communications aspects of system design. The situation, briefly: The existing system does not have an adequate way of dealing with customer inquiries or complaints about bills. The solution is to establish either an output report or an on-line display reference to show the account status for each customer. Data on each customer would include current account status and an account history of readings, billings, and payments for at least six months.

For reliable support in processing inquiries about a customer's account status, information would be needed that reflects updates from billings, payments received, adjustments applied, and other service transactions that affect status. A printed report has the advantage of being inexpensive to prepare—on existing equipment. But printed output also has disadvantages. The most notable is the need to produce the report each time accounts are updated so that the printout will be accurate and timely. This can be quite costly if few accounts are changed and few inquires are received.

An on-line query capability can have the advantage of being accurate and up-to-date. However, terminal access will be required and frequent file updates will be necessary to provide current information. Both terminals and the processing costs for file updates involve increased costs.

In this situation, the decision trade-offs involve the costs of producing massive printed reports and the expense of maintaining the on-line disk file and terminals to be used for inquiries. Another trade-off factor is the quality of customer service rendered. Obviously, the city's finance department could be more responsive with an on-line capability. However, the number of inquiries anticipated might not justify the cost of installing the on-line system and maintaining a terminal in the finance department. The specification for this output, assuming a screen layout for an on-line inquiry capability, is illustrated in Figures 12-5 and 12-6.

To round out the output picture for the water billing application, a turn-around document might be used for gathering new meter reading input. In the existing system, the water department uses a computer produced detail report as its meter book. This is a detailed listing of all customers, organized according to the address location in which the meter reader walks a route. Name and address information are included on the report, as are previous readings for each account. Space is provided for the reader to enter the current reading from each meter. The report is formatted to fit into a metal binder used by the meter reader. Options for revision of this form in the new system center around the method of input of the turnaround-captured data. Therefore, data capture alternatives that might lead to revision of this document are covered in the chapter that follows, which deals with input.

Summary

Output design plays a key role in the development of a new computer information system. Users specify needs by describing the outputs desired. Conceptual designs are developed for the outputs to be produced. The end products of output design are rough sketches of the documents or display formats themselves, a logical representation of the data components of the formats, as well as preliminary specifications for the output devices to be used.

Computer outputs provide: information delivery, archival storage, and turnaround documents.

Information delivery outputs fall into three general categories: reports, query responses, and transaction documents. Reports are usually classified according to content and form into three general categories: detail reports, summary reports, and exception reports.

Output devices that produce printed documents fall into two categories: impact and nonimpact. There are two basic designs for impact printers: serial and line.

Video displays utilize CRT terminals. Either alphanumeric or graphic data—or a mixture of both—can be displayed on video tubes. In most situations, video displays are used for reference only. Video display terminals are highly economical methods for referring to computer files and displaying file content.

Plotters are devices that produce documents through computer driven writing devices that create images on paper. Writing is done by a stylus. Stylus devices can draw in one color or several.

Audio output is through either actual or simulated sounds of a human voice. Audio output is generally limited to applications involving low volumes of data. The universal availability of push-button telephones makes this output option attractive for low volume tasks.

Computer Output to Microfilm (COM) is often used for archival storage. Long storage life and low reference volume are appropriate usage characteristics for microfilm output.

Determination of how well computer outputs will do a given job involves evaluation of trade-offs for use, volume, quality, and cost.

Uses fall into two broad categories: internal and external. Outputs generated for internal use include: reports to the management summarizing business activities, operational reports on the day-to-day status of the business, documents or reports that control active work within an organization, and business transaction documents that must be maintained for some time.

External outputs generated by the computer include: reports to governmental agencies, documents sent to customers, communications with stockholders, and paychecks and other documents sent to employees.

The volume of printed or displayed material to be generated by an application affects the selection of output methods. The amount of data to be generated can be a major factor in determining the method used.

The use for any given output helps to determine the quality needed. External documents, particularly those that are customer oriented, must be of high quality. Internal reports generally require less quality and have a higher density of data presentation.

Cost represents a trade-off between the volumes of work at hand and the quality needed. In general, the higher the output volume, the lower the cost per unit or document will be.

For design of either output documents or displays, work begins by establishing data content. The systems analyst works closely with the user to be sure that content requirements are understood before output forms are designed.

Once content is established, document requirements should be analyzed and formulated. The analyst questions the user and establishes a business understanding of the problems to be solved by the new system.

Given a list of data elements to be incorporated in an output document or display, the analyst then works with the user to rough out the appearance of the finished document or display.

From the standpoint of the designer, a formal method of representing the logical design of output forms is desired. The structured syntax used to describe data organization in the data dictionary can be applied in describing output formats. This notation uses the logical constructs of sequences, repetitions, and selections in representing data organization.

Key Terms

1. reports
2. query response
3. detail report
4. summary report
5. exception report
6. transaction record
7. archival storage
8. archival record
9. turnaround document
10. printer
11. video display
12. plotter
13. audio output
14. computer output to microfilm (COM)
15. impact
16. non-impact
17. serial printer
18. bi-directional
19. matrix
20. fixed-type
21. line printer
22. thermal printer
23. ink jet printer
24. electrostatic printer
25. laser printer
26. reprographic system
27. stylus
28. speech synthesizer
29. fiche
30. use
31. volume
32. quality
33. cost
34. internal outputs
35. external outputs
36. font
37. optical character reading (OCR)
38. fiber optic
39. wand
40. aged receivables report

Review/Discussion Questions

1. What procedure does the systems analyst use in working with users to specify output form, format, and medium?

2. What are the three main functions of computer outputs and how is each employed by a business organization?

3. What types of output device options are available and what circumstances would call for the use of each?

4. What trade-offs should be considered in deciding what type of printer is selected to generate a report?

5. How is the output of plotters different from that of printers?

6. What inherent advantages and disadvantages exist in the use of audio output?

7. What characteristics of COM output make it suitable for archival storage?

8. What trade-offs must be considered in evaluating whether an output will do a given job?

9. What is the general logical design of output forms and why is this important to the designer?

10. What output and processing sequences are accomplished by the use of turnaround documents?

11. What specific physical input methods might be employed to input machine-readable turnaround documents?

12. What trade-offs exist between using microfiche versus on-line display as a reference tool for customer inquiries?

Practice Assignments

1. Using the general design in Figure 12-7 for a bank statement, prepare a logical description of the data components identified. Use data dictionary notation.

2. Using the logical descriptions of a sales report shown in Figure 12-8, design the rough format of a printed report to present the information. The two descriptions in Figure 12-8 are logically equivalent and either can be used in designing the report.

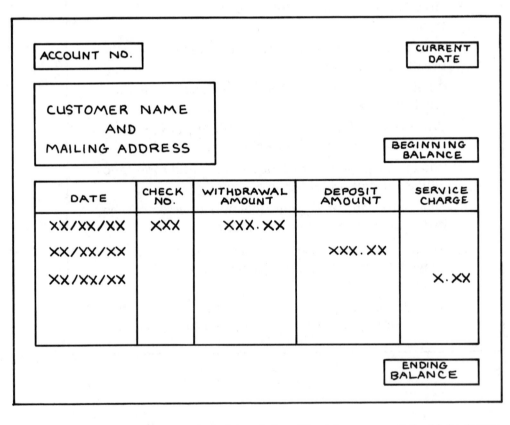

Figure 12-7. Prepare a logical description of the data components for this bank statement output form.

SALES REPORT = **Current-Date +**
    Store-Number +
    $\left\{\begin{array}{l}\left(\begin{array}{l}\text{Department-Number +}\\\text{Gross-Sales +}\\\text{Sales-Returns +}\\\text{Percent-Returns +}\\\text{Net-Sales +}\end{array}\right)\\\text{Store-Net-Sales +}\end{array}\right\}$
    Total-Net-Sales

SALES-REPORT = **Current-Date +**
    {Store-Report} +
    Total-Net-Sales

STORE-REPORT = **Store-Number +**
    {Department-Report} +
    Store-Net-Sales

DEPARTMENT-REPORT = $\left\{\begin{array}{l}\textbf{Department-Number +}\\\text{Gross-Sales +}\\\text{Sales-Returns +}\\\text{Percent-Returns +}\\\text{Net-Sales}\end{array}\right\}$

Figure 12-8. Prepare an output design format that corresponds with this logical description of the data components of a sales report.

13 INPUT DESIGN

LEARNING OBJECTIVES

After completing the reading and other learning assignments in this chapter, you should be able to:

☐ Describe the role of the systems analyst in working with users to define input requirements.

☐ Describe commonly used methods of data capture and tell how these are employed.

☐ Name the kinds of data entry equipment and explain the trade-offs associated with each.

☐ Give selection criteria used to evaluate input methods for a given application.

☐ Describe how physical layouts of input documents are derived.

THE TASK OF INPUT DESIGN

Establishing new system requirements begins with results. Thus, a first step lies in defining and describing the outputs to be produced. Once results are delineated, however, efforts switch back to the beginning of the system. That is, knowing what outputs will be produced, the analyst then works with the user to determine what inputs are needed to produce those outputs—and to identify sources for these inputs.

The analyst should have a general knowledge of input techniques and equipment. With this knowledge, it is possible to suggest and review alternatives for capturing needed data and getting those data into the system.

INPUT ALTERNATIVES

In general, *input* encompasses all activities or tasks needed to acquire data and bring it into a computer for processing. Input tasks encompass *data capture, data entry,* and *data input.* Within this context, data capture refers to the recording of source data as basic events or transactions occur within the system. Data entry is the act of converting or transcribing source data into a form acceptable for computer processing. Data input involves the controlled reading of data into the main memory within a computer's processor.

There are a wide range of alternatives available for capturing, entering, and inputting data into a computer. In general, however, these can be brought under two broad categories:

- Input involving source documents
- Input that does not involve source documents.

Alternative methods are used with each of these approaches.

Source Document Methods

A source document is any piece of paper used for initial recording of data representing a business transaction. Source documents can be prepared manually by having people handwrite or typewrite data onto a form. Alternatively, data can be written onto source documents as a result of computer output. For example, a turnaround document produced by the computer becomes an input source document.

Processing of source documents can be handled in one of three general ways depending on whether the source data are already in a form that can be input into the computer:

- If the data on source documents are handwritten or typewritten, transcription may be necessary. This transcription step involves keyboarding the data onto punched cards, magnetic tape, magnetic disk, or other media acceptable for input into the computer. The input media are then placed in computer input devices that read the coded data into the computer. This three-step method is illustrated in Figure 13-1.

- Data appearing on source documents may already be in a form acceptable for computer processing. In these cases, the documents can be read directly into the computer. This makes it possible for them to become the input media as well as being source documents. For example, turnaround documents such as punched cards already have data coded for input. In other instances, original source documents serve as input media. Input devices using optical character recognition (OCR) are available for reading hand-printed and typewritten documents directly into computers. Other devices read data imprinted from plastic cards, special magnetically encoded data such as those found on bank checks and deposit slips, or forms marked with pencils that can be machine scanned. The common denominator is that the documents themselves are used as input media. In effect, the data capture and data entry tasks are combined into one step, as illustrated in Figure 13-2.

- A third input alternative involving source documents combines the data entry and data input steps. In this case, data are keyboarded through input devices connected directly, or through communication lines, to the computer. This input method is illustrated in Figure 13-3.

Direct Data Input

Increasingly, computer information systems are being designed to capture data as byproducts of source transactions. Original recording of source data is done with devices connected directly to computers. Source documents can be eliminated. Eliminating input activities that require human intervention reduces the prospects of entry errors.

There are two general methods of inputting data into a computer system while avoiding separate data capture and transcription steps:

- Source data can be entered directly into the computer through terminals. For example, an order clerk seated at a computer terminal

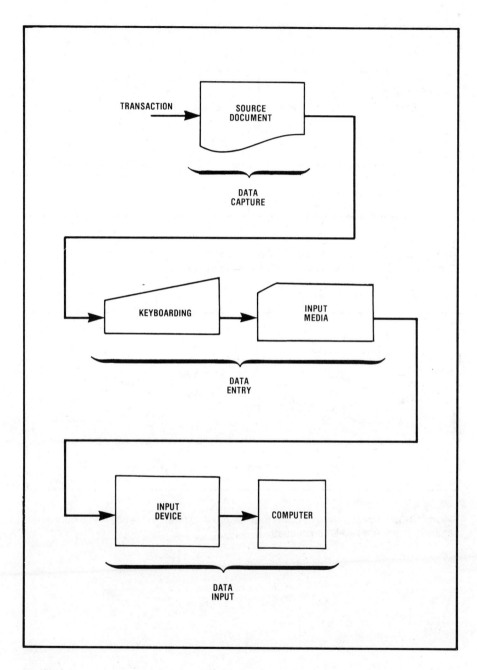

Figure 13-1.   Three-step procedure for input from handwritten or typewritten source documents through keyboarding techniques.

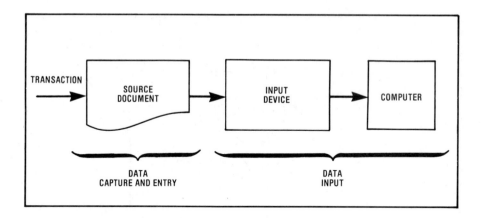

Figure 13-2. If source documents can be used as input media, keyboarding is eliminated and input is completed with a two-step process.

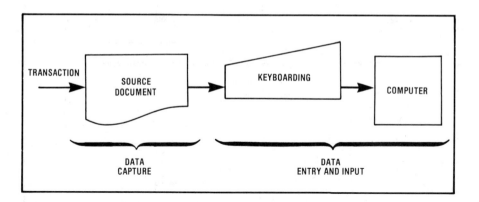

Figure 13-3. Keyboarding of data from source documents directly into a computer achieves input in a two-step process.

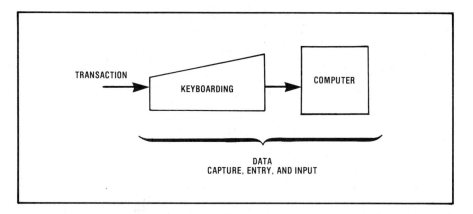

Figure 13-4. When source data are keyboarded directly into a computer from the point of transaction, input is achieved in a single step.

can enter sales requests into the computer in response to telephoned orders. This technique is common in airline or hotel reservation systems. In some instances, a terminal operator is not even involved in the process. This is the principle applied in automated bank teller machines. The same approach is followed also by hospitals that may allow the patient to enter admission information directly into computer terminals. This type of input system is shown in Figure 13-4.

- The final general category of input techniques is called *instrumental input*. There is no keyboarding requirement, since input is accomplished entirely by machines. The most common example of instrumental input is the supermarket checkstand outfitted with a bar code reader. Packages are coded with printed bars of various widths representing product identification data. The codes are read by special scanning devices and transmitted to a computer. The computer, in turn, uses the identification input to look up stored price and product description data that are transmitted to the register and printed on the machine tape. Other forms of instrumental input include use of devices that read garment tags and other product tags in retail stores. This form of input is illustrated in Figure 13-5.

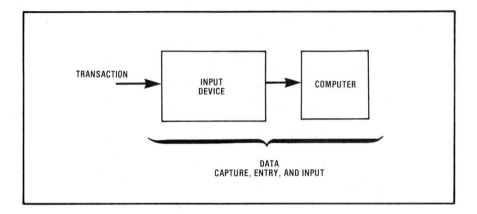

Figure 13-5. Instrumental input involves capture of data generated by another automated device directly into a computer.

These two methods of direct data input combine data capture, data entry, and data input into a single step. In doing so, these methods effectively reduce the amount of effort required to input data into a computer and increase the accuracy of the entire input process.

INPUT EQUIPMENT

The many data capturing and input devices that are available can be grouped into two generalized categories:

- Key-entry devices
- Document reading devices.

Key-Entry Devices

The methods for capturing data through keystroking include:

- Keypunch machines
- Key-to-tape machines
- Key-to-disk machines
- Key-to-diskette machines
- Cathode ray tube (CRT) terminals.

Keypunch machines. A keypunch machine has a keyboard resembling that of a typewriter. Stroking the keys causes holes to be punched in cards. Similar machines, called *verifiers,* are used to reduce the possibility of error in the data entry process. One operator punches cards from a batch of source documents. Another operator places these cards in a verifier and rekeys each source document. The verifier compares the punched card with the data just keyed and signals any differences.

A punched card has historically been referred to as a *unit record.* This is because each card is treated as a separate data record composed of several fields. Keypunch machines, verifiers, and standalone card sorters are referred to as unit record devices.

At one time, punched cards were the predominant method of data capturing and entry. While many of these systems are still operating, use of cards as input media has declined dramatically. Higher costs and much lower data entry rates for cards represent disadvantages that continue the decline in the use of cards.

Key-to-tape machines. Data entry through key-to-tape machines follows the same basic principle as for keypunching. Keyboards used by operators are similar. However, instead of being punched into cards, the data are recorded on magnetic tape. Most key-to-tape devices have switches that convert the device to verifier mode.

Shortly after their introduction in the 1960s, key-to-tape devices became very popular. Since then, use of this input method has declined. Figure 13-6 shows the recording format used for magnetic tape. Since data are recorded on a continuous ribbon of material, tape and other magnetic media eliminate the limitations on the size of records inherent in the 80-column format of punched cards.

Key-to-disk machines. Key-to-disk equipment is usually referred to as an *entry system.* The word *system* signifies that multi-station operations are usually involved. Each operator works at a CRT terminal linked into a recording system that processes entries and places those entries on *disk packs*—multi-surface recording devices on which data can be written and read at random, or directly. Typically, an operator enters a complete data record on the screen of the CRT. This record is then

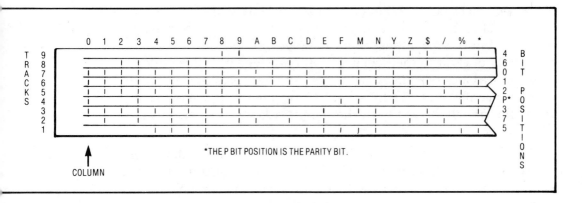

Figure 13-6. Recording format for magnetic tape.

transmitted to the central disk storage unit. Data records can be recorded either sequentially for all stations in the system or separately to segregate the jobs processed by each operator.

In effect, a key-to-disk system has a small, built-in computer that controls a number of work stations. In some systems, this may permit a certain amount of editing at the time of data entry. This method of data capture is highly productive and widely used in CIS departments that handle large volumes of input for multiple applications. The problem, however, is that key-to-disk systems are designed for centralized data entry facilities. The trend in the computer industry however, is to decentralize data capture to the extent possible.

A schematic diagram showing how data are recorded on disks is presented in Figure 13-7.

Key-to-diskette machines. These are usually standalone machines that represent a cross between key-to-disk and keypunch or key-to-tape devices. These units are similar in appearance and function to keypunch or key-to-tape devices, except that they normally include CRT terminals, permitting visual verification of records as they are keyed. Keystroke entries by the operator are recorded on a *diskette,* a small, flexible, circular recording medium. Diskettes measure either 5¼ or 8 inches in diameter. Individual diskettes can hold between 100,000 and 1.2 million characters of data.

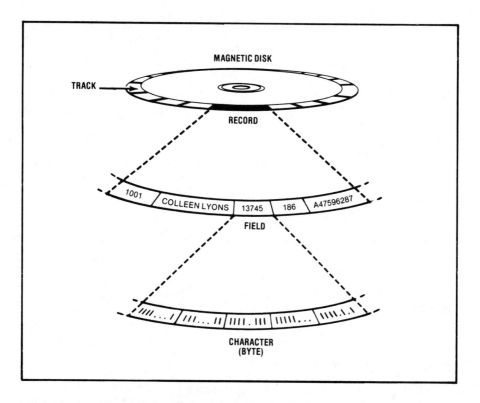

Figure 13-7. Recording format for magnetic disk devices.

Key-to-diskette devices record input records of up to 512 or more characters. The philosophy of capturing and handling input records on diskette is similar to that of punched cards, except that the diskette is far more convenient, compact to handle, and reusable.

Diskettes are the standard storage media for many makes of microcomputer. Therefore, relatively inexpensive microcomputers can often be used, through this approach, as input devices. This makes it possible to process extensive source transactions through microcomputer systems, inputting data directly from the microcomputer to a large system. For example, source documents such as invoices can be entered on a microcomputer at the time transactions are processed. Data entry to a central system can then take place separately, later. This approach can be ideal in such applications as transaction processing in branch offices with data transmitted at the end of the business day to a central facility.

CRT terminals.   Cathode ray tube terminals have become one of the most widely used methods of capturing and entering data. These terminals now come in many types and serve many purposes. Basically, a CRT terminal is any unit that contains a video screen display and also a keyboard for entry of data onto the display and into some recording device or directly to a computer. Thus, modern cash registers, or *point-of-sale terminals,* have CRT features. CRT terminals are also incorporated into automatic teller machines used for many banking transactions.

At one time, keystroking was considered to be a batch data entry method. Data were captured off-line, then entered into computers separately. Now, CRT terminals have made the same basic procedures applicable for either off-line or on-line data entry. CRT input stations can be set up with formats displayed on the screen so that data are entered into clearly defined fields. The other major option is free-form entry: The operator simply types data fields in order, leaving it to the computer to format records.

The method used depends upon the *intelligence,* or lack of it, built into individual terminals. In this sense, intelligence refers to some electronic processing capability that has been installed at point of use—within the terminal. Many terminals include microprocessors and memory units. It is possible to program these units to guide the operator, step-by-step, through a data entry routine. It is also possible, on some units, to retain data in memory or on a diskette for transmission to the main computer in batches. As described above, some intelligent terminal systems even have printing and document originating capabilities.

At the other end of the spectrum, nonintelligent terminals have only limited keyboarding and display capabilities. Typically, however, data are recorded on a memory chip as they are displayed on the video screen. The operator has a chance to review and correct data entries before they are transmitted to the computer system. With nonintelligent input systems, programming of record formats is done at the central computer.

It is also possible, through programming, to add some editing or verification capabilities, right at the point of entry. A special requirement occurs when CRT terminals are used for on-line entry. Some method of recording and logging data entry must be established at the main computer itself. Since on-line terminals do not create input logs or batch control documents, provision must be made to log entries at the computer itself. This is frequently done on dedicated tape or disk drives. By contrast, media created by other keyboard entry systems serve effectively as logs. That is cards, tapes, disk files, or diskettes achieve the logging function.

Document Reading Devices

Increasingly, actual transaction documents are being used to provide their own input to computers. Commonly encountered examples include checks and credit card sales tickets. These documents are part of actual processing transactions. Then, after they are handled at some point of use, the same documents are transported to computer centers and read directly into processing systems. There are two broad categories of document readers in general use:

- Optical character recognition (OCR)
- Magnetic ink character recognition (MICR).

Optical character recognition (OCR). These are devices that read data by sensing the effect upon an intense light beam on printed or marked surfaces. The markings can be in the form of printed or typewritten letters, numbers, or symbols. Also, handwritten entries can be accepted by some systems.

Another method is the *bar code,* a series of bars and spaces printed in a small field on a tag or product label. Bar codes, typically, present numeric data only. The most widely used application of bar codes is the *universal product code (UPC)* used in supermarkets and other retail outlets for automatic sensing of product identification on specially equipped sales registers.

Optical recognition input is also possible with *mark sensing.* A common example of this technique is the automatically scored answer sheet used in many testing programs. The position marked carries the meaning of data. Coding options are limited to multiple choices on tests or digital information in special applications, such as the reading of utility meters. Meter readers have cards with imprinted positions representing digits. Entries on the cards represent the current values read on electric, gas, or water meters.

The common denominator for all of these optical recognition systems is that data can be entered directly from transaction documents into computers through special reading devices that operate either on-line or off-line.

Magnetic ink character recognition (MICR).   MICR uses a special set of numbers and operational codes developed under the sponsorship of the American Bankers Association.

Checks, deposit slips, and other documents using MICR coding are preprinted with customer account numbers. These imprints are in a special ink containing ferrous particles. During input processing on special reader/sorter devices, these imprinted fields pass over a powerful electromagnet. Each character or symbol then develops its own magnetic value that can be sensed by the reading devices.

In addition to the preprinted account numbers, amounts of checks can also be encoded on special machines used in banks. Most of these machines also produce batch totals used in verifying document input.

Other Input Methods

A series of other methods, which are not yet widely used, have become available and do show some promise as input alternatives. These include:

- Voice input
- Touch-screen input
- Light pen input
- Digitizers.

Voice.   Eventually, computers are expected to be able to understand and process many thousands of words of spoken input. At present, there are applications using limited spoken vocabularies for direct input to computers. For example, up to a few dozen commands can be spoken by operators in automated warehouses. The computer recognizes these terms and responds by operating conveyors and/or printing documents.

Touch-screen input.   Computers can be programmed to establish points on the face of special video tubes that are touch- or light-sensitive. Points are recognized where light beams intersect or where portions of a display are sensitized. Data with specific processing meaning can be entered into a system by touching identified points on screens. This application is now being used extensively in *computer-aided instruction (CAI)*. The learner simply touches the screen to enter answers into a computer. The computer program then responds by indicating whether the answer is correct and by providing further information.

Data entered through touch-screen techniques are limited to choices presented by computer programs. That is, persons working at the screens are limited to selecting choices among the formats displayed.

Light pens.   These devices permit users to manipulate data on the face of CRT screens through light sensing devices that resemble pens. Users can actually draw or write on the face of a screen and can also select and move graphic elements offered on a displayed menu. This form of input is used chiefly for engineering and design applications. However, some business uses are being devised.

Digitizers.   A digitizer is another means of entering graphic data into a computer manually. The digitizer is also a pen-like device. However, instead of being used on a video screen, it is moved along a flat surface, or tablet. The movements of the pen on the tablet are also shown as resulting lines and shapes on the video display. Engineering drawings and other types of schematic diagrams and graphics can be traced or created through digitizers. The device gets its name from the fact that the computer assigns digital values to the points traced by the pen.

EVALUATION OF SYSTEM INPUT OPTIONS

The function of data entry is to provide simple, cost effective, and accurate methods for getting data into computer information systems.

Each application should be evaluated to determine the most appropriate input technique to be used. Care should be taken to avoid permitting data entry to become an end in itself. Data entry is not a result. It is a support for application results.

In view of this role, selection of the input method to be used becomes a cost/benefit trade-off. That is, cost is one of several factors to be considered in identifying alternative input techniques. Cost must be balanced against other factors, including:

- Cost
- Timeliness
- Completeness
- Accuracy
- Control
- Auditability.

Cost

Theoretically, all data can be captured instantly, in totally accurate condition—all as transactions take place. However, theoretical performance capabilities can rarely be implemented, as long as cost remains a continuing factor. The economics of two or more methods for capturing and entering data are usually weighed against each other in selecting the data capturing method to be used.

For example, in many applications, immediacy carries a high price tag. As a result, timeliness demands are often modified by the realities of cost. Immediate data entry requires a higher initial investment in equipment. In addition, immediacy can require more complex processing routines and tighter controls.

Within limitations, trade-offs are also possible in connection with the factors of completeness, accuracy, control, and auditability. It is up to the user to establish, for example, the standards for completeness and accuracy of data input. Systems can be devised to assure totality of completeness and accuracy—provided that enough verification steps are included. In many systems, however, standards of acceptability are set at some point below the 100 percent mark as part of cost/benefit trade-offs.

Timeliness

Each computer information system—and each processing step within every system—has its own logical time frame or processing cycle. Timeliness, in a systems sense, is priority related. That is, the system dictates when data are needed. Timeliness specifications are a result of these processing cycles.

To illustrate, an accounting system may be processed once a week or once a month. Given such infrequent cycles, there is little urgency for rapid capture of data. Thus, one of the keyboarding data entry methods described above would probably be adequate.

On the other hand, data entry for an airline reservation request must be completed in a matter of a second or two because the customer is waiting for an answer—and is also waiting to spend money for a ticket. Thus, no matter what the cost, if the system is to be developed, the timeliness requirement must be met. In this case, the choice is not between slower or faster turnaround of input. Rather, if meeting the time requirement is too expensive, the system itself might be curtailed, or perhaps it would include fewer terminals or sales points that could be contacted by telephone.

Completeness

The factor of completeness has two dimensions in the analysis of application requirements. One dimension involves the gathering and presenting of all the appropriate data to the system. The other requirement is at the individual record level. Before a record can be processed as acceptable input, format requirements must be met. Certain fields must be full and complete, only alphabetic entries may be made in alphabetic fields, and so on.

Theoretically, completeness could be assured in both situations. That is, data gathering can be thorough enough to be sure that all available information is presented to every processing cycle of the application. Though this is theoretically possible, it is rarely attainable in the practical world of data processing. The same is true for the completeness for each record being entered. People commit oversights or make mistakes. Provision must be made for handling incomplete, erroneous records.

For example, in an application based upon the reading of water meters, a meter reader might find that a given reading cannot be made on a certain route. Perhaps a gate has been locked, denying the reader access to the yard. Perhaps there is a vicious dog on the property. Theoretically, the customers could be called and arrangements made for the meter reader to return. As a practical reality, however, a procedure would probably be developed under which past usage for the customer would be averaged and carried forward as a current billing amount. Adjustment would be made during the next billing period.

A similar procedure would probably be followed if a meter reader made an obvious data entry error. For example, suppose a meter reading is entered with a value that is lower than for the last meter reading. Obviously, this would show less than zero usage. The system would probably be designed to discard this reading and use averaging techniques in such instances.

The key point to understand is that part of input design involves establishing standards of completeness both at an overall system level and at an individual record level, as well as specifying processing (manual or computer-based) to deal with the unavoidable failures to meet these standards in an operational system. The tightness of the standards will impact the final selection of the input option to be selected.

Accuracy

As is the case with completeness, inaccurate records cannot be processed to produce valid results. Therefore, there must be validation procedures, either as part of manual input preparation or within the computer programs, to monitor accuracy of all records that are entered. Application programs must assure that inaccurate data entries cannot be processed and incorporated in system files and outputs.

Still, there are trade-offs relating to how much validation is done and what level of certainty is applied to input accuracy. There may be situations in which less than total accuracy is acceptable. If so, users may elect, if given options, to forego some of the accuracy potential in exchange for lower costs.

This type of compromise might take place in connection with input entries for a mailing list application. Suppose a company uses its mailing list for nonurgent sampling of new products or for distribution of advertising materials. For such applications, it is common to input mailing list additions without a separate, full verification step. One justification is that, since delivery of end products is not urgent, some reasonable error rate can be tolerated. Further, the Post Office can be employed to advise the using company of incorrect file items through notifications about undeliverable mail. In such instances, users might elect not to pay the cost of full verification. By contrast, such name-and-address files as telephone directories require a high degree of accuracy and full verification of listing entries is common practice.

Control

Input controls are procedures followed to monitor the completeness and accuracy of each individual field, record, and group of transactions. At the individual field level, any of the follow series of controls can be implemented with data entry software or, in some cases, included within data entry devices.

- *Required field.* This control is a check on whether expected data are present in input documents. In effect, people or machines check specified fields for the presence of data characters.

- *Alphabetic/numeric field.* If a field should contain only alphabetic or only numeric characters, controls can be applied that signal the presence of other kinds of characters.

- *Justification.* Justification describes the way in which data are aligned in a field. Typically, alphabetic data are left-justified, meaning that the characters appear beginning in the first position of the field. Numeric data are aligned around decimal points and are usually right-justified.

- *Check digit.* This control applies an arithmetic formula to verify that numeric entries are valid. The result of the calculation is compared against one of the digits (check digit) of the number. The calculated digit must match the check digit. Otherwise, the field contains an invalid number.

- *Limit/reasonableness.* Controls are often built into systems to guard against unusual, nontypical data. For example, a program might check an amount field to determine if the value is within prescribed limits.

During input, data are often collected and processed in batches. To illustrate, suppose 100 transaction records form a control group. Three common types of controls are applied to batches:

- *Item or transaction counts.*   A manually prepared item count is taken and included with each batch. This batch count is written on a transmittal form to accompany the group of records throughout processing. At all stages of processing, item counts are taken and compared with the transaction count.

- *Batch totals.*   Batch, or control, totals may be calculated for amount fields in a group of records. These totals, like the transaction count, are included on a transmittal form and accompany the batch of records through each phase of processing. Subsequent totals for these fields are developed during processing and compared with the batch totals as a means of verifying correct processing.

- *Hash totals.*   ''Hash'' is the name given to a control total field of numeric data that do not contain significant application information. For example, hash totals may be taken on such fields as product number, employee number, customer number, etc. These figures have no monetary or financial significance. Yet they can be used to verify that all transactions in a batch have been processed accurately.

Controls are covered in greater depth in Chapter 17.

Auditability

When business data are processed on computers, the information produced almost inevitably finds its way into operating or accounting reports. These reports, in turn, are subject to verification by both operating managers and outside auditors. This applies for both governmental and private sector organizations.

During the early years of computer processing, auditability posed problems. Auditors were used to dealing with manual, paper-based transaction processing. A transaction could, during the era of paper processing, be traced readily back to its source. Thus, a figure included in a company's financial statements could be spot-checked to be sure that the transactions did, in fact, take place. When computers entered the picture, the recording of data on pieces of paper either disappeared or changed drastically. Conventional auditing techniques did not work when transaction records were represented only on computerized data storage devices. Once the problems became apparent, auditability of computer records attracted considerable attention from managers and computer professionals.

Today, all business data processing systems require *audit trails*. This means, simply, that the system must provide a means by which any given input transaction can be traced through the system—from data entry, through processing, to any affected files, and, as appropriate, to output reports. Audit trails start with input. Input records must identify the sources of all transactions as well as the authorizations that had to be made before the data could be entered into the system. If input records exist on paper, these records may have to be filed or saved according to specific retention cycles. If data are captured at the source of the transaction, there must be *journals*, printed reports or tape or disk files that identify, specifically and exactly, what data were created, by whom, and what controls were applied to assure accuracy and completeness.

Again, the point is that part of input design involves establishing an audit trail capability within the data entry processing that is specified. The level of detail and form required for this audit trail will certainly impact the cost of the input option to be selected.

INPUT DESIGN

In establishing input requirements for a new data processing system, content of actual data records needed to produce the outputs is determined first. Given the volume, frequency, and content of input records, available input methods are evaluated. Alternatives are presented to users and decisions are made according to the criteria described above. Once input methods have been chosen, preliminary designs should go forward for the documents or record formats to be used for input procedures.

At this stage of the systems development life cycle, input documents and formats are designed at a rough draft level only. This means that forms and formats are sketched to show their general appearance. It is unnecessary, at this point, to develop the detailed, character-by-character forms and formats that will be necessary before the system is implemented. This level of planning and designing takes place during the detailed design and implementation phase. Format designs should be developed in any of three appropriate areas, depending on the needs of individual systems. These include:

- Source documents
- Video display screens
- Computer input records.

Source Documents

Sketches should be prepared for all of the manual forms to be used in source data collection or input preparation. For each form to be used manually within the system:

- A title and unique form number should be assigned. This identification will follow the document throughout the systems development life cycle.
- Instructions should be prepared on how the form will be filled out.
- A sketch should be prepared showing the headings, data entries, and any summary or total entries to be made on the form.

In sketching designs for manually prepared forms, the analyst should think about the work to be done. Data fields to be processed manually should be grouped so that clerical workers can make their entries in sequence, logically. All entry items should be labeled. There should be adequate space for all entries. Care should also be taken to be sure that data entry operators will be able to identify and read all handwritten entries clearly.

Video Display Screen

The same procedures are followed in designing formats for video display screens as for source documents. Positions and approximate lengths of all data fields are shown on rough sketches. While it is not essential to do so at this point, special video display features to be used by the application may also be indicated. These could include use of reverse video areas to highlight data entry points. Blinking fields may be designated as a method for identifying errors or improper formats in data entry. Also, error messages to be displayed by the system during entry procedures may blink to call attention to their content. Typically, a number of variations will be reviewed for each form or display format.

Computer Input Records

Source documents and video display screens facilitate data entry by supporting the user's interface with the processing of input to the computer portion of a system. The results of this data entry process are records in computer-readable form—the inputs to the computerized processes in the system. These computer input records must also be defined. The records may be card formats, records on tape or disk, or simply records transmitted from an on-line terminal directly to an application program.

Computer input records are system-oriented rather than user-oriented. That is, computer inputs are designed for use by the system itself, not by the user. Therefore, criteria for design are controlled by the analyst. For this reason, it is not necessary to be concerned with detailed physical design at this point. It is sufficient simply to specify the data content of these computer inputs, leaving physical layouts until the detailed design and implementation phase.

Data Content

The informal design of input formats is sufficient to communicate both content and appearance to the users. From the standpoint of the designer, however, a precise statement of the data content used in the source documents, video display screens, and computer input records is critical. Just as with outputs, the data structure notation—using the logical constructs of sequences, repetitions, and selections—can be applied in describing input content.

The data specifications are entered into the data dictionary, where they can be referenced during detail design of source documents, screens, and input media.

Input Documentation

As described in Chapter 11, the user specification for the new system contains a section that defines the system inputs. In general, this section should consist of an index page listing each source document and screen input by name, followed by a pair of documents for each input. An input documentation form communicates the purpose or use of the input and specifies the data content. This is normally followed by a rough sketch of the input, as described above.

CASE SCENARIO

The water billing application demonstrates how analysis and design of transactions can be important in determining the best method for handling input. Further, this situation also demonstrates that systems applications may be able to make profitable use of two or more input techniques for the same transaction type.

One of the basic input jobs for the water billing application is to collect and enter data on customer payments. No matter what form of billing is chosen, the input application must still be responsive to payment options that are open to the individual customer. The water billing application, for example, must be able to accommodate three clear-cut options.

As one option, the customer can simply walk into City Hall and pay the bill to a finance department cashier. Under the existing system, these items are rung up on cash registers. The finance department then provides a batch total with the billing stubs or substitute receipts prepared by the cashier. When the finance department handles collections, its personnel separate checks from billing stubs and take care of the bank deposits themselves.

A second option is for customers to mail payment checks to the city. These receipts are also handled in the finance department, though not by the cashier. Again, payment data are recorded on the customer billing stubs or receipt forms and forwarded to data processing, with checks separated and deposited by the finance department.

A third option open to customers is to use payment services offered by all local banks. Customers can take their utility bills to the local banks for payment. Payment can be either through checks against customer accounts or through authorized transfer of funds from customer accounts to those of the utilities. The banks then send billing stubs, receipts, and transaction listings to the city finance department along with a record of a deposit to the city's account.

As indicated in the previous chapter, one input option for the payment transactions is to provide the ability to read either punched cards or OCR imprints on billing stubs directly into the system. Another option, used under the current system, is to input payment data manually. In looking at the transaction from a data entry perspective, a new consideration arises: If there are many exceptions—partial payments or payments not accompanied by preprinted or punched billing stubs—the advantage of automatic input could disappear rapidly because payment data will have to be input manually. The analyst would need to find out what percentage of bills produce partial payments, what percentage are paid without having the stubs turned in, and what percentage result in return of the stubs with payments in full.

As a second example, the input of meter reading data represents a classic trade-off between advanced technology and established methods. Traditionally, meter reading has been one of the high cost, labor intensive data gathering jobs that has defied mechanization. Simply stated, it is expensive to have someone go and look at every meter, every month. As the cost of reading meters has increased, the potential for automating this job has become more feasible. Devices and systems have finally been introduced that make it possible to collect data from meters automatically. Meters themselves are built with miniature, low-power radio transmitters that can be activated by radio-transmitted signals. A data collector with a specially equipped vehicle can simply drive through a neighborhood using an automatic *transponder* (transmitter and responder), which activates the radios on the meters and records the transmitted data onto magnetic cassettes. These cassettes can then be used for direct computer input.

The trade-offs in this situation are obvious. Installing the automatic system would involve changing all of the meters in the service area. This would represent a major capital expense. There would also be some cost, though minor by comparison, associated with installing equipment to handle the recorded tapes in the computer center. The new system, however, could continue to use meter books with no additional capital investment. Continuing the present system would involve a continuing expense for the salaries of meter readers—as well as a potential penalty in quality of service associated with the errors of manual meter reading and manual input of data.

A creative option that could be considered in this situation would be to contact the other utilities that provide gas and electric service to the area to see if economies of scale might be realized through a joint venture. That is, the three utilities—gas, electric, and water—could share the cost of collecting meter data.

In the water billing system, systems analysts made a logical decision based on the circumstances in which they found themselves. That is, it turned out that the complexities of developing a system for two separate governmental entities—a city water department and an area sanitary district—were sufficient in themselves, without getting into questions of who would bear the costs of a change in meter reading and how these costs would be prorated. Thus, it was decided to continue the manual meter reading but to design the input subsystems with data formats that would permit easy future conversion to automatic reading techniques.

Summary

Input encompasses all activities or tasks needed to acquire data and bring it into a computer for processing. Input tasks encompass data capture, data entry, and data input. These tasks may be categorized by those that involve source documents and those tasks that do not involve source documents.

Categories of input equipment are key-entry devices and document reading devices.

CRT terminals have become the most widely used method of capturing and entering data. CRT terminals have made input procedures applicable for either off-line or on-line data entry.

Increasingly, actual transaction documents are being used to provide their own input to computers. Two types of document readers used for this purpose are optical character recognition (OCR) and magnetic ink character recognition (MICR) equipment. Other input methods include voice input, touch-screen input, light pen input, and digitizers.

The function of data entry is to provide simple, cost-effective, and accurate methods for getting data into computer information systems. Selection of the input method to be used becomes a cost/benefit trade-off. Cost must be balanced against other factors, including timeliness, completeness, accuracy, and auditability.

Timeliness, in a systems sense, is priority related. The time schedule required by the application becomes a deadline to be incorporated within system design.

The factor of completeness has two dimensions in the analysis of application requirements. One dimension involves the gathering and presentation of all of the appropriate data to the computer. The other requirement is at the individual record level. Before a record can be processed as acceptable input, format requirements must be met.

Accuracy is also important for computer inputs. Inaccurate records cannot be processed to produce valid results.

Input controls monitor completeness and accuracy of each individual field, record, and group of transactions. Controls applied to individual inputs include required field, alphabetic/numeric field, justification, check digit, and limit/reasonableness tests. Controls applied at the batch level include item or transaction counts, batch totals, and hash totals.

All business data processing systems require audit trails. Input records must identify the sources of all transactions as well as the authorizations that had to be made before the data could be entered into the system.

In establishing input requirements for a new data processing system, content of actual data records needed to produce the outputs is determined first. Given the volume and content of input records, available input methods are evaluated. Alternatives are presented to users and decisions are made. Once input methods have been chosen, preliminary designs should go forward for the documents or record formats to be used for input procedures.

At this stage, input documents and formats are designed as rough drafts. Format designs should be developed, as appropriate, for source documents, video display screens, and computer input media.

The structured syntax used in the output design phase is also appropriate for the design of input forms and documents. The data specifications are entered into the data dictionary, where they can be referenced during detail design of source and input media.

Key Terms

1. input
2. data capture
3. data entry
4. data input
5. instrumental input
6. keypunch
7. verifier
8. column
9. unit record
10. key-to-tape
11. key-to-disk
12. key-to-diskette
13. diskette
14. CRT terminal
15. point-of-sale terminal
16. intelligence
17. optical character recognition (OCR)
18. bar code
19. universal product code (UPC)
20. mark sensing
21. magnetic ink character recognition (MICR)
22. voice input
23. touch-screen input
24. computer-aided instruction (CAI)
25. light pen input
26. digitizer
27. cost
28. timeliness
29. completeness
30. accuracy
31. required field check
32. alphabetic field check
33. numeric field check
34. check digit
35. limit check
36. reasonableness check
37. item count
38. transaction count
39. batch total
40. hash total
41. auditability
42. audit trail
43. journal
44. transponder

Review/Discussion Questions

1. What tasks does the function of input encompass?

2. How can input tasks be categorized in terms of source documents?

3. What input methods can be used to capture source documents?

4. What are the main types of data entry equipment and what trade-offs are associated with the use of each?

5. What special requirements are created by the use of nonintelligent terminals?

6. What applications might use OCR? MICR?

7. What other input techniques are available besides key entry?

8. What criteria must be used in evaluating an input method for a given application?

9. Why is the design of input documents more formal at first than the design of outputs?

10. What trade-offs must be considered in evaluating a new on-line data entry system that is intended to replace a manual batch entry system?

14 LOGICAL DATA ANALYSIS

LEARNING OBJECTIVES

On completing reading and other learning assignments for this chapter, you should be able to:

☐ Describe the purposes and features of logical data structures for data stores.

☐ Explain the process of normalization and describe the steps required in carrying out this process.

☐ Explain the role of keys in describing relations among data structures.

☐ Describe the procedures followed in collapsing and combining data structures.

☐ Show how the use of data structure diagrams and the data access diagrams can assist the analyst.

ANALYZING DATA STORES

One of the main tasks of systems analysis is to construct a logical model for the new system. This may be done by defining the data flows, data stores, and data transformations to be applied to data moving through a system to be developed. The modeling techniques capture the processing activities of a system and identify the origins, destinations, processing points, and components of data flows and data stores that support processing. However, in the construction of the new logical model, only the transformation activities and their supporting data flows have come under close scrutiny. No comparably rigorous analysis has been applied to the data stores themselves.

In some cases, the data stores appearing on the data flow diagrams are remnants of the existing system. These data stores have been integrated within the new system because data required to support a transformation happen to be in an existing file. In other cases, new data have been added to existing stores and new data stores have been created to support the production of new or revised system outputs. Finally, entirely new data stores appear within the system to support entirely new transformations that have no precedent in the existing system. The point is, data stores have been created or retained to support the transformations. Yet, the data stores themselves have not been evaluated for content and organization.

The contents of data stores have, up to this point, been defined intuitively by considering the output produced by the transformations that are fed by those data stores. For example, if a report is generated by a particular process, the underlying data that comprise the report must be derivable from the input to that process. If the input source is from a data store, the components of the report must be components of the data store or derivable from them. Further, for data to be extracted from a data store, they must have been put there in the first place. Therefore, data flows into data stores must account for all required elements. Tests of reasonableness are applied throughout data flow analysis to make sure that all data are accounted for and are available at the requisite points within the system.

The motivation for modeling the system and analyzing data flows is to be sure that data are available to carry out the identified transformations to produce the desired outputs. No focused effort is made at this point to assure that the components and organization of the data stores are designed properly. Even if assurance exists that particular data stores support system processing, it does not necessarily follow that the components and organization of those data stores are the best that could be specified. Direct consideration must be given to designing data stores that can be packaged into physical files or databases that most effectively support system processing.

Logical system specification, therefore, includes a means for deriving the *logical data structure* of a system. The logical data structure refers to the organization of system data into data stores that are simplest in structure and minimal in content. These data stores will become the basis for the trade-off decisions in physical database or file design structures.

LOGICAL DATA STRUCTURE CRITERIA

Two main criteria may be applied to data stores to determine whether their components and organization are optimum for the system they support. One criterion is *simplicity*. Organization of and access to data within a data store should be as simple as possible. As a general rule, the goal is to structure a data store so that it can be implemented as a simple sequential or direct-access file. That is, the components of the data store should be referenced only by a primary key and there should be no repeating groups of data within the data store. (A *key* is one or more data elements that identify uniquely the occurrence of a data structure in a data store.) Thus, for example, a data store is simpler if it does not have *alternate keys* or *pointers* to link records, and if it does not require implementation as variable length records. The criterion for logical data organization is always simplicity over complexity. This is true whether the data stores for a particular application will eventually be implemented as conventional files or whether the data stores will be packaged into one or more databases. Just as with systems processing design or software design, the simplest, most straightforward structure is nearly always the best.

The second criterion for logical data design is *nonredundancy*. Redundancy occurs, in part, when the same data element exists within two or more data stores. Redundancy can threaten the integrity of a system: If the value of a data component in one file is changed, the same element must be changed in all other files. Problems arise if files with redundant data are not all processed at the same time. In such cases, special processing runs may be needed to update the redundant components. This, in turn, means that adequate records must be kept to process these special runs. To avoid these problems, it is simpler to attempt to eliminate redundancy.

Redundancy also occurs when the same data appear in different forms within the same data store—when two or more data components within a data store provide the same information. For example, within a student record system at a college, each record within the student file might contain the three data fields: course hours attempted, credits earned, and overall grade point average. There is no reason for including the grade point average. As long as the hours attempted and the credits earned are required as separate data elements, the grade point average can be calculated at any time and is thus unnecessary within the data store. Elimination of redundancy within a data store simplifies the file structure and leaves fewer data elements to be processed and updated.

The task at hand, therefore, is to derive a logical structure for the proposed system. The result will be a set of data stores containing no redundant data elements, organized for simple access, that support the processing functions of the system.

NORMALIZATION OF DATA STORES

Figure 14-1 presents a data flow diagram for a portion of a student registration system. The part of the system shown here contains several data stores, some used to maintain data over a period of time and others used as transitional stores for the production of reports. During the modeling process, each data store was designed to support a particular transformation. The components of these data stores are shown in the partial data dictionary in Figure 14-2. (The data elements that make up the key for each data store are underlined.) Note that each data store is an iteration of a data structure. Thus, the normalization of data stores is essentially equivalent to the normalization of a set of data structures.

Up to this point in systems analysis, the focus has been on the transformations or processes. Data stores have been designed to support that processing. The next step is to derive the best logical design for the set of data stores. The group of existing data stores is replaced in this analysis by its logical equivalent. The result is a set of simple data stores containing no redundant elements. This is the set of stores that will ultimately be packaged into physical files or databases that support processing in the most effective manner.

The procedure used to derive this logical structure is called *normalization*. In general, normalization produces the simplest, most straightforward organization of data elements into component data

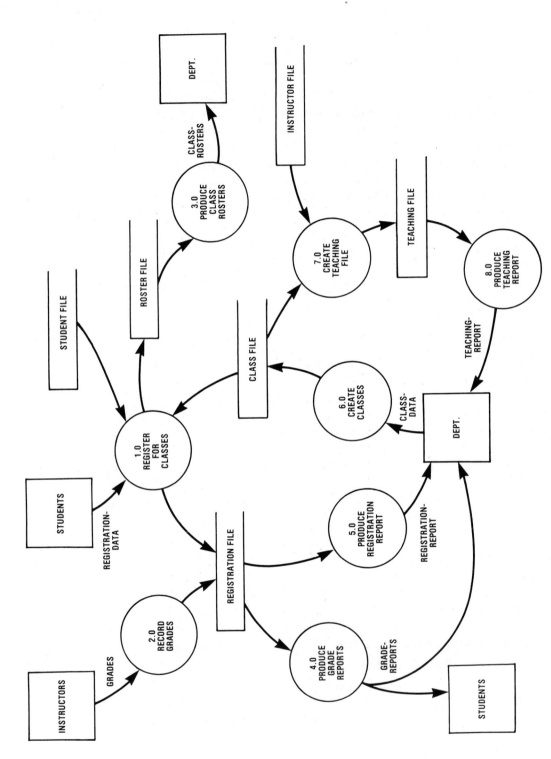

Figure 14-1. Data flow diagram for student registration system.

```
CLASS-FILE                = {CLASS} All classes offered where
CLASS                     = Class-Number +
                            Class-Name +
                            Class-Credits +
                            Class-Room +
                            Class-Time +
                            Class-Instructor +
                            Class-Enrollment +
                            Class-Maximum +
                            Class-Openings

INSTRUCTOR-FILE           = {INSTRUCTOR} All instructors where
INSTRUCTOR                = Instructor-Number +
                            Instructor-Name +
                            Instructor-Dept. +
                            Instructor-Office

REGISTRATION-FILE         = {STUDENT-REGISTRATION} All students where
STUDENT-REGISTRATION      = Student-Number +
                            Student-Name +
                            Student-Address +
                            Student-Credits +
                          ⎧ Class-Number + ⎫
                          ⎨ Class-Name +   ⎬
                          ⎪ Class-Credits +⎪
                          ⎩ Class-Grade    ⎭   All classes for student

ROSTER-FILE               = {ROSTER} All classes where
ROSTER                    = Class-Number +
                            Class-Name +
                            Class-Credits +
                            Class-Room +
                            Class-Time +
                            Class-Instructor +
                            Class-Enrollment +
                          ⎧ Student-Number + ⎫
                          ⎨ Student-Name +   ⎬
                          ⎩ Student-Level    ⎭   All students in class

STUDENT-FILE              = {STUDENT} All students where
STUDENT                   = Student-Number +
                            Student-Name +
                            Student-Address +
                            Student-Major +
                            Student-Level +
                            Student-Credits-Earned +
                            Student-GPA

TEACHING-FILE             = {INSTRUCTOR} All classes where
INSTRUCTOR-ASSIGNMENT     = Instructor-Number +
                            Instructor-Name +
                            Instructor-Dept. +
                            Instructor-Credits +
                          ⎧ Class-Number + ⎫
                          ⎨ Class-Name +   ⎬
                          ⎪ Class-Credits +⎪
                          ⎩ Class-Enrollment ⎭  All classes taught by instructor
```

Figure 14-2. Partial data dictionary for student registration system.

stores. Normalization should produce a set of data stores containing nonredundant data elements accessible through use of unique *primary keys*. The procedure is illustrated below for the student registration system.

Step 1: Partition each data structure that contains repeating groups of data elements. Form two or more data structures without repeating groups that accomplish the same purpose. This step places the set of data structures (or stores) in a state known as the *first normal form*.

Within the data dictionary in the student registration example, there are three current data stores that contain repeating groups. The REGISTRATION-FILE contains, for each student, data on each class taken. The ROSTER-FILE contains, for each class offered, the names of students enrolled in the class. The TEACHING-FILE contains, for each instructor, a list of courses taught.

Each of these data stores is a composite of other stores used in the printing of special reports. For example, the REGISTRATION-FILE combines data elements from both the STUDENT-FILE and the CLASS-FILE. Although the same data are contained in two different data stores, those data have been brought together within the REGISTRATION-FILE as a means of relating classes with students. Also, the ROSTER-FILE relates students with classes and the TEACHING-FILE relates classes with instructors. These composite data stores were created originally to produce relations that did not exist within the set of separate class, instructor, and student files.

Figure 14-3 shows the result of the first step in normalization. For each data structure that contains a repeating group, the repeating group has been removed and set up as a separate data structure. The key for this new structure is formed by *concatenating* (adding) the key for the original data store with the key for the repeating group. The key for the original file is retained as the key for the data structure without its repeating group. For example, consider the two derived structures named REGISTERED-STUDENT and STUDENT-CLASS that are based on the original STUDENT-REGISTRATION structure. REGISTERED-STUDENT is the STUDENT-REGISTRATION structure with the repeating group removed. Its key is the same as for the original structure. The new structure, STUDENT-CLASS, is formed from the

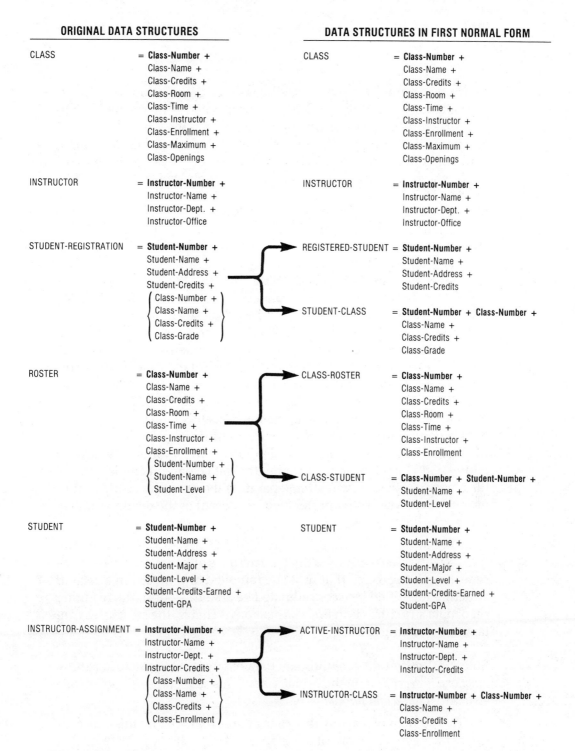

Figure 14-3. Conversion of student registration data structures into first normal form.

repeating group. This structure's key is the combination STUDENT-NUMBER and CLASS-NUMBER. A concatenated key is needed for this new structure because the class data contained in the structure pertains to a particular student. Without the STUDENT-NUMBER appended to the CLASS-NUMBER key, there would be no way of relating a particular class to a particular student, as was implied in the original file.

The fact that the two derived data structures contain the same information as did the original STUDENT-REGISTRATION structure can be verified by the presentation in Figure 14-4. The STUDENT-CLASS structure contains the courses in which each student has enrolled. Each class is uniquely identified by the concatenation of the STUDENT-NUMBER and the CLASS-NUMBER. The REGISTERED-STUDENT structure contains only student-related data on each student enrolled in a class, keyed to the STUDENT-NUMBER. The motivation for having the original REGISTRATION-FILE was to produce a report that lists, by students, all classes for which those students have registered. If such a report is to be generated through use of these new data structures, two data stores must be accessed: First, the store containing the STUDENT-CLASS structures is accessed to locate those classes taken by a particular student. Then, using the STUDENT-NUMBER portion of the concatenated key, the store containing the STUDENT-REGISTERED structures is accessed to locate corresponding names and addresses. The relationships among the data elements in the original file are maintained—even after separating its repeating groups into a file by themselves. The concatenated key describes the relations among these new data stores.

The same procedure is followed for the ROSTER and the INSTRUCTOR-ASSIGNMENT structures. Both structures have repeating data groups that must be removed and placed in a second structure identified by a concatenated key. At this point, the resulting set of data structures is in first normal form. That is, the structures contain no repeating groups.

Step 2:   Verify that each nonkey data element in a structure is fully *functionally dependent* on the primary key. This step places the set of data structures in *second normal form*.

This step involves only those structures that are identified by concatenated keys. The work of this step is accomplished by verifying that

STUDENT-REGISTRATION (*STUDENT-NUMBER* + STUDENT-NAME + STUDENT- ADDRESS +STUDENT-CREDITS +
{CLASS-NUMBER + CLASS-NAME + CLASS-CREDITS + CLASS-GRADE})

10001	JAMES ALLEN	437 MAPLE ST	15	ENG 100	ENGLISH COMP I	3	A
				MAT 100	FINITE MATH I	4	B
				CIS 100	INTRO TO CIS	3	B
				HIS 100	AMER HISTORY I	3	C
10002	FAYE GRAY	JOHNSON AVE	60	CIS 307	SYSTEMS ANALYSIS	3	B
				MGT 300	MANAGEMENT PRIN	3	C
				MKT 300	MARKETING PRIN	3	A
				MAT 210	CALCULUS I	4	B
				MGT 360	QUANT ANALYSIS	3	B
10003	JOE MORRIS	419 W. MAIN	45	BUS 100	INTRO TO BUSINESS	3	A
				ENG 101	ENGLISH COMP II	3	B
				ACC 100	PRIN OF ACC I	3	C
				MAT 101	FINITE MATH II	4	D
10004	JEAN GREEN	13 S. 13TH	75	MGT 300	MANAGEMENT PRIN	3	A
				ACC 101	PRIN OF ACC II	3	B
				BUS 260	BUSINESS LAW	3	B
				CIS 308	SYSTEMS DESIGN	3	B
				CIS 320	DATABASE DESIGN	3	A

REGISTERED-STUDENT (*STUDENT-NUMBER*
+ STUDENT-NAME + STUDENT-ADDRESS
+ STUDENT-CREDITS)

STUDENT-CLASS (*STUDENT-NUMBER* +
CLASS-NUMBER + CLASS-NAME +
CLASS-CREDITS + CLASS-GRADE)

10001	JAMES ALLEN	437 MAPLE	15
10002	FAYE GRAY	JOHNSON AVE	60
10003	JOE MORRIS	419 W. MAIN	45
10004	JEAN GREEN	13 S. 13TH	75

10001ENG100	ENGLISH COMP I	3	A
10001MAT100	FINITE MATH I	4	B
10001CIS100	INTRO TO CIS	3	B
10001HIS100	AMER HISTORY I	3	C
10002CIS307	SYSTEMS ANALYSIS	3	B
10002MGT300	MANAGEMENT PRIN	3	C
10002MKT300	MARKETING PRIN	3	A
10002MAT210	CALCULUS I	4	B
10002MGT360	QUANT ANALYSIS	3	B
10003BUS100	INTRO TO BUSINESS	3	A
10003ENG101	ENGLISH COMP II	3	B
10003ACC100	PRIN OF ACC I	3	C
10003MAT101	FINITE MATH II	4	D
10004MGT300	MANAGEMENT PRIN	3	A
10004ACC101	PRIN OF ACC II	3	B
10004BUS260	BUSINESS LAW	3	B
10004CIS308	SYSTEMS DESIGN	3	B
10004CIS320	DATABASE DESIGN	3	A

Figure 14-4. Components of student registration data structures in first normal form.

each nonkey data element in a data structure is dependent on the full concatenated key, not just on a partial key. That is, each element should require the entire key as a unique identification. If, rather, a data element is determined uniquely by only a part of the key, the element should be removed from the structure and placed in a structure of its own.

For example, consider the STUDENT-CLASS data structure that was identified through first-order normalization of the STUDENT-REGISTRATION structure. As shown in Figure 14-5, this structure consists of a STUDENT-NUMBER + CLASS-NUMBER concatenated key along with the data elements CLASS-NAME, CLASS-CREDITS, and CLASS-GRADE. Neither CLASS-NAME nor CLASS-CREDITS are fully functionally dependent on the key. Both are uniquely determined by the CLASS-NUMBER portion of the key. That is, given the CLASS-NUMBER, the CLASS-NAME and CLASS-CREDITS can be derived. The STUDENT-NUMBER portion of the key is superfluous—it is not necessary to have the STUDENT-NUMBER to find the CLASS-NAME and CLASS-CREDITS. (This example assumes all classes are for fixed credit and that there are no variable-hour classes.) CLASS-GRADE, on the other hand, is fully functionally dependent on the concatenated key. Knowing only the STUDENT-NUMBER, or knowing only the CLASS-NUMBER, is insufficient information for knowing the CLASS-GRADE. The grade relates to the particular student in a particular class and, therefore, both parts of the key are required to define it.

To place data structures in second normal form, the data elements that are not fully functionally dependent on the concatenated key are removed from the relation and are set up in separate data structures with corresponding keys. Thus, in Figures 14-5 and 14-6, the STUDENT-CLASS relation is broken out into two separate structures: CLASS-REGISTERED contains the CLASS-NAME and CLASS-CREDITS data elements that are dependent only on the CLASS-NUMBER portion of the key. The GRADE relation contains the CLASS-GRADE element, which is dependent on the entire key. Similar steps have been taken for the CLASS-STUDENT and INSTRUCTOR-CLASS structures. Note in Figure 14-5 that, in the last two cases, one of the resulting structures contains only key information. This is both permissible and necessary. The CLASS-STUDENT structure establishes the relation between a given class and its students. In other

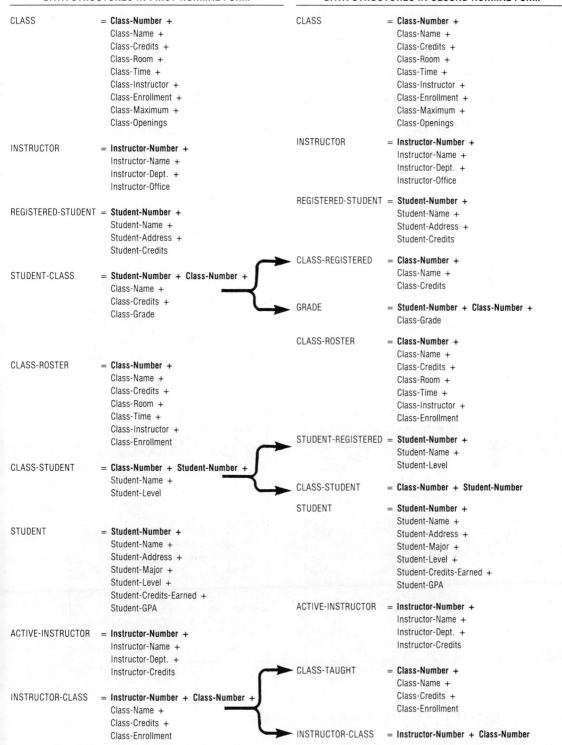

DATA STRUCTURES IN FIRST NORMAL FORM	DATA STRUCTURES IN SECOND NORMAL FORM

DATA STRUCTURES IN FIRST NORMAL FORM

CLASS = **Class-Number +**
Class-Name +
Class-Credits +
Class-Room +
Class-Time +
Class-Instructor +
Class-Enrollment +
Class-Maximum +
Class-Openings

INSTRUCTOR = **Instructor-Number +**
Instructor-Name +
Instructor-Dept. +
Instructor-Office

REGISTERED-STUDENT = **Student-Number +**
Student-Name +
Student-Address +
Student-Credits

STUDENT-CLASS = **Student-Number + Class-Number +**
Class-Name +
Class-Credits +
Class-Grade

CLASS-ROSTER = **Class-Number +**
Class-Name +
Class-Credits +
Class-Room +
Class-Time +
Class-Instructor +
Class-Enrollment

CLASS-STUDENT = **Class-Number + Student-Number +**
Student-Name +
Student-Level

STUDENT = **Student-Number +**
Student-Name +
Student-Address +
Student-Major +
Student-Level +
Student-Credits-Earned +
Student-GPA

ACTIVE-INSTRUCTOR = **Instructor-Number +**
Instructor-Name +
Instructor-Dept. +
Instructor-Credits

INSTRUCTOR-CLASS = **Instructor-Number + Class-Number +**
Class-Name +
Class-Credits +
Class-Enrollment

DATA STRUCTURES IN SECOND NORMAL FORM

CLASS = **Class-Number +**
Class-Name +
Class-Credits +
Class-Room +
Class-Time +
Class-Instructor +
Class-Enrollment +
Class-Maximum +
Class-Openings

INSTRUCTOR = **Instructor-Number +**
Instructor-Name +
Instructor-Dept. +
Instructor-Office

REGISTERED-STUDENT = **Student-Number +**
Student-Name +
Student-Address +
Student-Credits

CLASS-REGISTERED = **Class-Number +**
Class-Name +
Class-Credits

GRADE = **Student-Number + Class-Number +**
Class-Grade

CLASS-ROSTER = **Class-Number +**
Class-Name +
Class-Credits +
Class-Room +
Class-Time +
Class-Instructor +
Class-Enrollment

STUDENT-REGISTERED = **Student-Number +**
Student-Name +
Student-Level

CLASS-STUDENT = **Class-Number + Student-Number**

STUDENT = **Student-Number +**
Student-Name +
Student-Address +
Student-Major +
Student-Level +
Student-Credits-Earned +
Student-GPA

ACTIVE-INSTRUCTOR = **Instructor-Number +**
Instructor-Name +
Instructor-Dept. +
Instructor-Credits

CLASS-TAUGHT = **Class-Number +**
Class-Name +
Class-Credits +
Class-Enrollment

INSTRUCTOR-CLASS = **Instructor-Number + Class-Number**

Figure 14-5. Conversion of student registration data structures into second normal form.

REGISTERED-STUDENT (*STUDENT-NUMBER* + STUDENT-NAME + STUDENT-ADDRESS + STUDENT-CREDITS)

10001	JAMES ALLEN	437 MAPLE	15
10002	FAYE GRAY	JOHNSON AVE	60
10003	JOE MORRIS	419 W. MAIN	45
10004	JEAN GREEN	13 S. 13TH	75

STUDENT-CLASS (*STUDENT-NUMBER* + *CLASS-NUMBER* + CLASS-NAME + CLASS-CREDITS + CLASS-GRADE)

10001ENG100	ENGLISH COMP I	3	A
10001MAT100	FINITE MATH I	4	B
10001CIS100	INTRO TO CIS	3	B
10001HIS100	AMER HISTORY I	3	C
10002CIS307	SYSTEMS ANALYSIS	3	B
10002MGT300	MANAGEMENT PRIN	3	C
10002MKT300	MARKETING PRIN	3	A
10002MAT210	CALCULUS I	4	B
10002MGT360	QUANT ANALYSIS	3	B
10003BUS100	INTRO TO BUSINESS	3	A
10003ENG101	ENGLISH COMP II	3	B
10003ACC100	PRIN OF ACC I	3	C
10003MAT101	FINITE MATH II	4	D
10004MGT300	MANAGEMENT PRIN	3	A
10004ACC101	PRIN OF ACC II	3	B
10004BUS260	BUSINESS LAW	3	B
10004CIS308	SYSTEMS DESIGN	3	B
10004CIS320	DATABASE DESIGN	3	A

GRADE (*STUDENT-NUMBER* + *CLASS-NUMBER* + CLASS-GRADE)

10001ENG100	A
10001MAT100	B
10001CIS100	B
10001HIS100	C
10002CIS307	B
10002MGT300	C
10002MKT300	A
10002MAT210	B
10002MGT360	B
10003BUS100	A
10003ENG101	B
10003ACC100	C
10003MAT101	D
10004MGT300	A
10004ACC101	B
10004BUS260	B
10004CIS308	B
10004CIS320	A

CLASS-REGISTERED (*CLASS-NUMBER* + CLASS-NAME + CLASS-CREDITS)

ACC100	PRIN OF ACC I	3
ACC101	PRIN OF ACC II	3
BUS100	INTRO TO BUSINESS	3
BUS260	BUSINESS LAW	3
CIS100	INTRO TO CIS	3
CIS307	SYSTEMS ANALYSIS	3
CIS308	SYSTEMS DESIGN	3
CIS320	DATABASE DESIGN	3
ENG100	ENGLISH COMP I	3
ENG101	ENGLISH COMP II	3
HIS100	AMER HISTORY I	3
MAT100	FINITE MATH I	4
MAT101	FINITE MATH II	4
MAT210	CALCULUS I	4
MGT300	MANAGEMENT PRIN	3
MGT360	QUANT ANALYSIS	3
MKT300	MARKETING PRIN	3

Figure 14-6.   Components of student registration data structures in second normal form.

words, given a particular class number, the student numbers for the students in that class are available. Similarly, the INSTRUCTOR-CLASS structure relates individual instructors to classes taught.

Step 3: Verify that all nonkey data elements in a data structure are *mutually independent* of one another.

After the data structures have been converted to second normal form, each structure is checked to verify that each nonkey data element is independent of every other nonkey element in the relation. In other words, there is a check for redundancy within the relation. Duplicate data elements or elements that can be derived from other elements are removed to place the relation in *third normal form*.

Within the structure labeled CLASS in Figure 14-7, the data element CLASS-OPENINGS is redundant with the two elements, CLASS-ENROLLMENT and CLASS-MAXIMUM. That is, the number of openings in a class can be derived by subtracting the CLASS-ENROLLMENT value from the CLASS-MAXIMUM value. In effect, CLASS-OPENINGS appears twice in the relation—once explicitly as a named data element and once implicitly as a derived value. Therefore, the element CLASS-OPENINGS has been removed from the data structure.

Within the STUDENT relation, STUDENT-LEVEL is redundant with STUDENT-CREDITS-EARNED. Assuming that class level is given by the number of credits earned by the student, total credit earned is simply another way of representing the class level. Therefore, the data element STUDENT-LEVEL is unnecessary and is removed from the relation.

Step 4: Eliminate redundant data elements among the data structures.

After the set of data structures has been put in third normal form, there are likely to be redundancies among the normalized structures. For example, in Figure 14-7, several data structures share the same data elements. Class data appear in the CLASS relation as well as in the CLASS-REGISTERED, CLASS-ROSTER, and CLASS-TAUGHT relations. Student data are located in the REGISTERED-STUDENT, STUDENT-REGISTERED, and STUDENT relations. Finally, instructor data are found in two different relations—INSTRUCTOR and ACTIVE-INSTRUCTORS. Since one of the primary purposes of logical

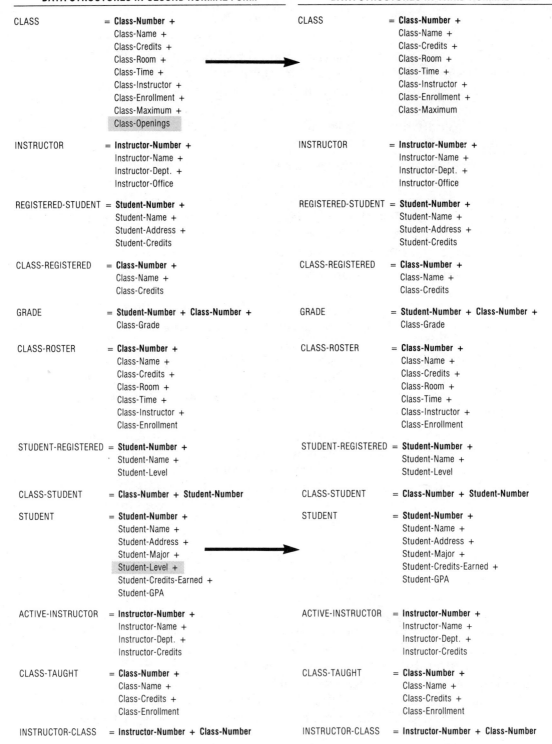

DATA STRUCTURES IN SECOND NORMAL FORM

CLASS = **Class-Number** +
Class-Name +
Class-Credits +
Class-Room +
Class-Time +
Class-Instructor +
Class-Enrollment +
Class-Maximum +
Class-Openings

INSTRUCTOR = **Instructor-Number** +
Instructor-Name +
Instructor-Dept. +
Instructor-Office

REGISTERED-STUDENT = **Student-Number** +
Student-Name +
Student-Address +
Student-Credits

CLASS-REGISTERED = **Class-Number** +
Class-Name +
Class-Credits

GRADE = **Student-Number + Class-Number** +
Class-Grade

CLASS-ROSTER = **Class-Number** +
Class-Name +
Class-Credits +
Class-Room +
Class-Time +
Class-Instructor +
Class-Enrollment

STUDENT-REGISTERED = **Student-Number** +
Student-Name +
Student-Level

CLASS-STUDENT = **Class-Number + Student-Number**

STUDENT = **Student-Number** +
Student-Name +
Student-Address +
Student-Major +
Student-Level +
Student-Credits-Earned +
Student-GPA

ACTIVE-INSTRUCTOR = **Instructor-Number** +
Instructor-Name +
Instructor-Dept. +
Instructor-Credits

CLASS-TAUGHT = **Class-Number** +
Class-Name +
Class-Credits +
Class-Enrollment

INSTRUCTOR-CLASS = **Instructor-Number + Class-Number**

DATA STRUCTURES IN THIRD NORMAL FORM

CLASS = **Class-Number** +
Class-Name +
Class-Credits +
Class-Room +
Class-Time +
Class-Instructor +
Class-Enrollment +
Class-Maximum

INSTRUCTOR = **Instructor-Number** +
Instructor-Name +
Instructor-Dept. +
Instructor-Office

REGISTERED-STUDENT = **Student-Number** +
Student-Name +
Student-Address +
Student-Credits

CLASS-REGISTERED = **Class-Number** +
Class-Name +
Class-Credits

GRADE = **Student-Number + Class-Number** +
Class-Grade

CLASS-ROSTER = **Class-Number** +
Class-Name +
Class-Credits +
Class-Room +
Class-Time +
Class-Instructor +
Class-Enrollment

STUDENT-REGISTERED = **Student-Number** +
Student-Name +
Student-Level

CLASS-STUDENT = **Class-Number + Student-Number**

STUDENT = **Student-Number** +
Student-Name +
Student-Address +
Student-Major +
Student-Credits-Earned +
Student-GPA

ACTIVE-INSTRUCTOR = **Instructor-Number** +
Instructor-Name +
Instructor-Dept. +
Instructor-Credits

CLASS-TAUGHT = **Class-Number** +
Class-Name +
Class-Credits +
Class-Enrollment

INSTRUCTOR-CLASS = **Instructor-Number + Class-Number**

Figure 14-7. Conversion of student registration data structures into third normal form.

file design is to eliminate redundancy, the structures with common data elements should be collapsed into a single structure.

Figure 14-8 shows the components of the data structures after those with common elements have been joined and duplicate elements removed. In making the decision on which structures should be assembled into a composite structure, the analyst is guided by a sense of what the *object* of a structure is and by what the *attributes* of that structure are.

In general, the object of a data structure is the entity to which the structure pertains. The attributes of an object are items of data characterizing that object. Thus, the object of the structure CLASS is classes taught. Its attributes are CLASS-NAME, CLASS-CREDITS, CLASS-ROOM, CLASS-TIME, CLASS-INSTRUCTOR, CLASS-ENROLLMENT, and CLASS-MAXIMUM.

The data structure contains the attributes that pertain to one and only one object. A similar rationale can be applied to the INSTRUCTOR, STUDENT, and GRADE data structures. No superfluous data elements appear in the relations, and no elements appear as attributes in any other relations.

The structures CLASS-STUDENT and INSTRUCTOR-CLASS are special cases in that these structures contain only *key attributes*. These key attributes are primary keys to the other data structures and the attributes of those structures. These special structures are called *correlations*, relating objects identified by the composite data structures. Thus, the structure CLASS-STUDENT is used to relate the attribute CLASS structure with attributes in the STUDENT structure. Similarly, the correlation INSTRUCTOR-CLASS relates INSTRUCTOR with CLASS.

As an example of how such correlative structures are used, recall that the student registration system is to produce class rosters. This report, therefore, combines STUDENT attributes with CLASS attributes. Access to the data stores corresponding to the CLASS and STUDENT data structures alone, however, cannot produce the report. Nothing is in the CLASS structure to indicate which students are enrolled; there are no attributes in the STUDENT structure to point out the classes taken. The independence of these two structures is to be expected and merely indicates the preferred ''single-mindedness'' of these two structures. The relationship between the CLASS and STUDENT structures is given in the correlative structure, CLASS-

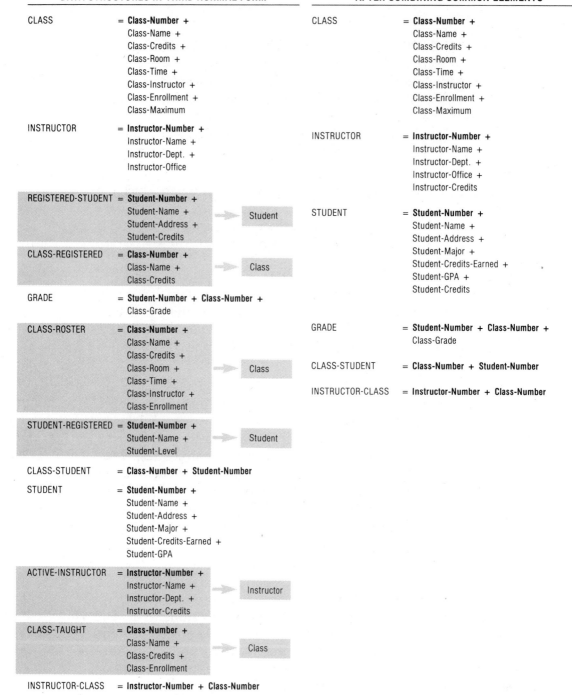

DATA STRUCTURES IN THIRD NORMAL FORM

CLASS = **Class-Number** +
Class-Name +
Class-Credits +
Class-Room +
Class-Time +
Class-Instructor +
Class-Enrollment +
Class-Maximum

INSTRUCTOR = **Instructor-Number** +
Instructor-Name +
Instructor-Dept. +
Instructor-Office

REGISTERED-STUDENT = **Student-Number** +
Student-Name +   → Student
Student-Address +
Student-Credits

CLASS-REGISTERED = **Class-Number** +
Class-Name +   → Class
Class-Credits

GRADE = **Student-Number + Class-Number** +
Class-Grade

CLASS-ROSTER = **Class-Number** +
Class-Name +
Class-Credits +
Class-Room +   → Class
Class-Time +
Class-Instructor +
Class-Enrollment

STUDENT-REGISTERED = **Student-Number** +
Student-Name +   → Student
Student-Level

CLASS-STUDENT = **Class-Number + Student-Number**

STUDENT = **Student-Number** +
Student-Name +
Student-Address +
Student-Major +
Student-Credits-Earned +
Student-GPA

ACTIVE-INSTRUCTOR = **Instructor-Number** +
Instructor-Name +   → Instructor
Instructor-Dept. +
Instructor-Credits

CLASS-TAUGHT = **Class-Number** +
Class-Name +   → Class
Class-Credits +
Class-Enrollment

INSTRUCTOR-CLASS = **Instructor-Number + Class-Number**

**DATA STRUCTURES
AFTER COMBINING COMMON ELEMENTS**

CLASS = **Class-Number** +
Class-Name +
Class-Credits +
Class-Room +
Class-Time +
Class-Instructor +
Class-Enrollment +
Class-Maximum

INSTRUCTOR = **Instructor-Number** +
Instructor-Name +
Instructor-Dept. +
Instructor-Office +
Instructor-Credits

STUDENT = **Student-Number** +
Student-Name +
Student-Address +
Student-Major +
Student-Credits-Earned +
Student-GPA +
Student-Credits

GRADE = **Student-Number + Class-Number** +
Class-Grade

CLASS-STUDENT = **Class-Number + Student-Number**

INSTRUCTOR-CLASS = **Instructor-Number + Class-Number**

Figure 14-8. Data structures of student registration system after combining of common elements from third normal form.

STUDENT. For a given CLASS-NUMBER, the CLASS structure provides information on that class, the CLASS-STUDENT structure provides the STUDENT-NUMBER for each student in the class, and this, in turn, leads to the STUDENT structure.

Another form of redundancy may result when correlations are defined. For example, in the INSTRUCTOR structure shown in Figure 14-9, the attribute INSTRUCTOR-CREDITS is not necessary. This data element gives the total number of credits taught by an instructor. This same information can be derived from the CLASS structure accessed through the INSTRUCTOR-CLASS correlation. The INSTRUCTOR-NUMBER in the INSTRUCTOR data structure can be matched against the INSTRUCTOR-NUMBER in the INSTRUCTOR-CLASS correlation. Then the corresponding CLASS-NUMBERs can be used to access the CLASS-CREDITS attributes in the CLASS structure. INSTRUCTOR-CREDITS, therefore, can be derived by summing the individual class credits for each class taught by the instructor.

In a similar way, STUDENT-CREDITS, recorded in the STUDENT structure, can be derived. The STUDENT-NUMBER is used to access the GRADE structure, and the corresponding CLASS-NUMBER provides access to the CLASS structure containing CLASS-CREDITS. The class credits values are totaled for each class taken by the student. As shown in Figure 14-9, the INSTRUCTOR-CREDITS and STUDENT-CREDITS attributes have been removed from the respective data structures.

Finally, the CLASS-INSTRUCTOR attribute has been removed from the CLASS structure and set up as a separate correlation identified as CLASS-INSTRUCTOR. This situation is a case in which an attribute of one structure, the structure INSTRUCTOR, is an attribute of another structure, CLASS. However, the redundant element cannot simply be dropped from CLASS; if CLASS-INSTRUCTOR were eliminated from CLASS, there would be no direct way of knowing what classes were taught by which instructors. Yet, the information needed would be available if there were a correlation between classes and instructors as there is between instructors and classes. Therefore, the CLASS-INSTRUCTOR correlation is established and replaces the redundant attribute. Another reason for this change is to establish a general correlation between classes and instructors. The correlation provides the same information as does the CLASS-INSTRUCTOR attribute within

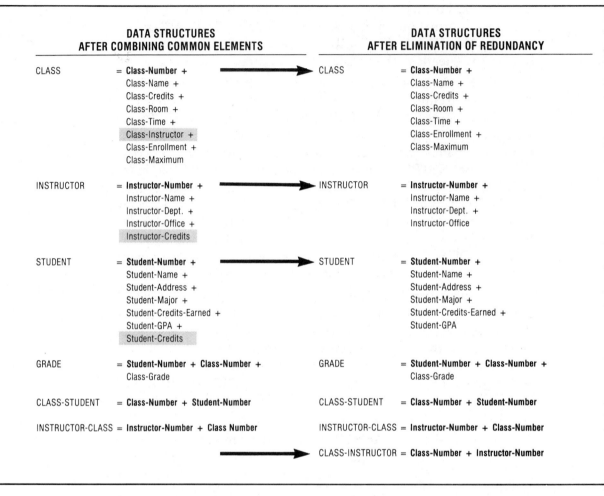

Figure 14-9.   Data structures of student registration system after redundancies among data structures have been eliminated.

CLASS; however, the correlation gives additional information. Now, all of the attributes of INSTRUCTOR can be related to all attributes of CLASS. For example, the information is available and accessible to determine which departments have instructors teaching particular classes. Class numbers can be related to instructor numbers, which, in turn, can be related to instructor attributes that include the department identifier.

DATA STRUCTURE DIAGRAMS

The normalization process results in a set of attribute structures and a set of correlative structures. Each attribute structure relates to one object in the system, has no attributes that it shares with any other structure, and has been designed for simple access. Each correlative structure relates the key attributes from two attribute structures so that all the attributes in one structure can be related to all attributes in another structure. The structures, or relations, are now in the simplest, most logical form.

To document the entire data structure, a *data structure diagram* can be used. The diagram applied to the student registration system is shown in Figure 14-10. Each block on the diagram represents the attribute data structure whose name appears in the block. Along the left side of the block, the access key is written. Arrows between the blocks represent access paths. If the access is made possible through a correlative structure, the name of the structure is written adjacent to the arrowhead pointing in the appropriate direction of the link. If two attribute structures are related because they share the same key, the arrows point to the keys with no notation.

For example, given a particular class number, it is possible to access both STUDENT and GRADE data for each student in the class through the CLASS-STUDENT correlative structure. It is possible to access INSTRUCTOR data through the CLASS-INSTRUCTOR correlative structure.

The data structure diagram presents a new set of data structures—and hence data stores—and access relationships that are functionally equivalent to those in the original data flow diagram. The same data elements exist or can be calculated. The same or more access relationships exist.

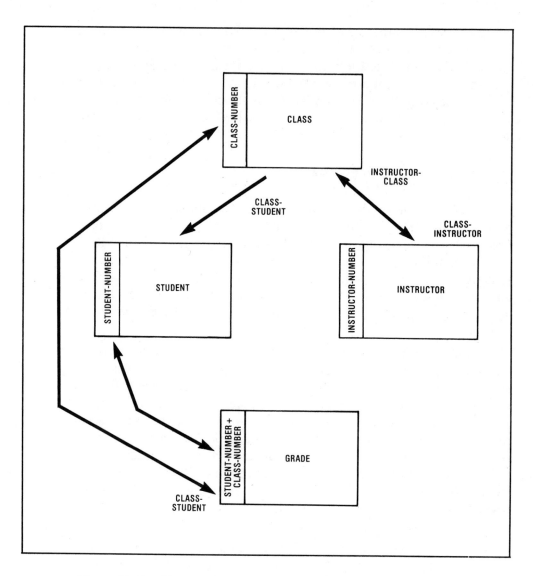

Figure 14-10. Data structure diagram for student registration system.

Two final steps remain. First, the user should verify that the data structure diagram expresses correctly the data needs of the system. Second, the documentation should be put in a form that will facilitate physical file design. These steps are discussed below.

User Verification

As a mechanical step, the revisions that have been made to the set of data stores must be reflected in the data flow diagram and data dictionary. The data flow diagram shown in Figure 14-11 is a redrawing of the original diagram appearing in Figure 14-1 of the student registration system. Note that transformation 7.0 CREATE TEACHING FILE has been eliminated from the system. Also, only the attribute files are presented on the revised data flow diagram. Correlative files are internal to the system and need not be shown for system processing clarification. Figure 14-12 gives the data dictionary entries for the new file structures.

The data structure diagram has some advantages over use of data flow diagrams alone. With data flow diagrams, the emphasis is on the flow and transformation of data. The data stores and access play a background, supporting role. The data structure diagram, on the other hand, allows the user and analyst to concentrate on the ways in which data will have to be accessed in the new system. Theoretically, these accessing relationships, as a product of the normalization process, should be complete. In practice, however, a careful study of the data structure diagram often leads to the specification of new access paths and, as a result, new system outputs that had previously been overlooked.

Transition to Physical File Design

Ultimately, the data stores represented in the data structure diagram will have to be implemented physically to support the desired access relationships. This implementation could involve database management software or traditional files. Traditional file design considerations are reviewed in Chapter 16.

As an illustration, assume the data structures represented by the attribute relations are packaged physically into simple sequential and/or direct-access files. Assume further that the correlative structures are implemented as direct-access files.

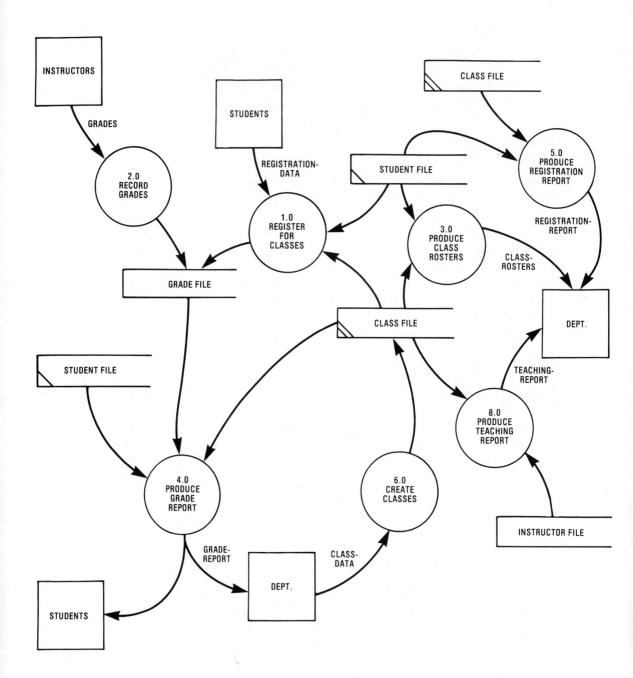

Figure 14-11.   Revised data flow diagram for student registration system.

```
CLASS-FILE              = {CLASS} All classes offered where
CLASS                   = Class-Number +
                          Class-Name +
                          Class-Room +
                          Class-Time +
                          Class-Enrollment +
                          Class-Maximum

INSTRUCTOR-FILE         = {INSTRUCTOR} All instructors where
INSTRUCTOR              = Instructor-Number +
                          Instructor-Name +
                          Instructor-Dept. +
                          Instructor-Office

STUDENT-FILE            = {STUDENT} All students where
STUDENT                 = Student-Number +
                          Student-Name +
                          Student-Address +
                          Student-Major +
                          Student-Credits-Earned +
                          Student-GPA

GRADE-FILE              = {GRADE} Where
GRADE                   = Student-Number + Class-Number +
                          Student-Grade

CLASS-STUDENT-FILE      = *Correlative file relating students with classes*
                        = {Class-Number + Student Number}

INSTRUCTOR-CLASS-FILE   = *Correlative file relating classes with instructors*
                        = {Instructor-Number + Class-Number}

CLASS-INSTRUCTOR-FILE   = *Correlative file relating instructors with classes*
                        = {Class-Number + Instructor-Number}
```

Figure 14-12. Data dictionary entries for revised file structure for student registration system.

Each attribute structure will become an attribute file with records comprised of fields representing each attribute. The attribute key or keys will become key fields within the records. Each correlative structure will be implemented as a direct-access file whose primary key will be the first attribute key in the relation. The correlative file will resemble a table to be searched for matching values.

Figure 14-13 presents a *data access diagram* showing the formats of the files and the corresponding relationships, or access paths, for the student registration system. The arrows indicate the paths from one attribute file to another, either directly through the same key or through the relations established in the correlative files. The data access diagram represents the appropriate documentation format to support the transition from logical to physical file design. It communicates clearly to the designer the precise data and accessing capabilities required.

ADVANTAGES OF THIRD NORMAL FORM

Figure 14-14 summarizes the steps in converting data structures to third normal form. The following list summarizes the advantages of having data in this form.

1. *Ease of understanding.* Third normal form presents data structures in a way that can be understood easily by operational and management users. The structures of data are presented in simple, two-dimensional tables that do not require technical understanding on the part of users and owners of the data.

2. *Ease of use.* Data structures can be partitioned further, or joined together through correlative files, to permit any number of different logical viewpoints to be represented in the structures. Different structures can have different file organizations to allow efficient access for primary applications, yet be accessible for many other secondary applications. That is, attributes from different files can be related with little complexity.

3. *Ease of implementation.* Structures in third normal form can be implemented as simple files set up for either serial or direct access. Additionally, the structures can be implemented within database systems.

4. *Ease of maintenance.* Nonredundancies in the attribute files reduce problems while keeping all files up to date. If an attribute must be

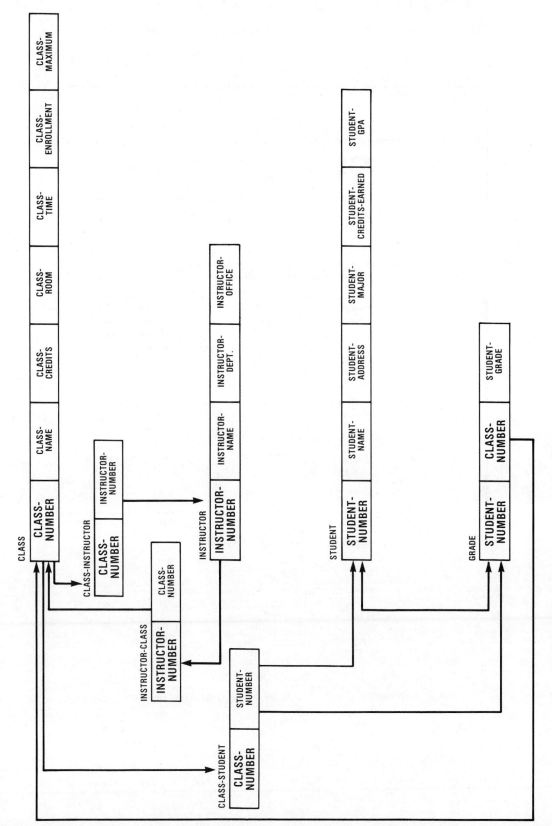

Figure 14-13. Data access diagram for student registration system.

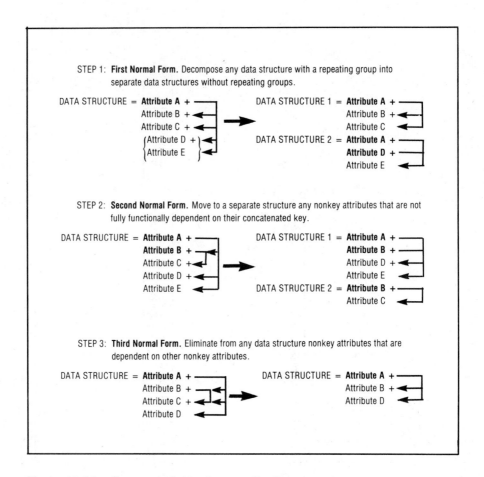

STEP 1: **First Normal Form.** Decompose any data structure with a repeating group into separate data structures without repeating groups.

STEP 2: **Second Normal Form.** Move to a separate structure any nonkey attributes that are not fully functionally dependent on their concatenated key.

STEP 3: **Third Normal Form.** Eliminate from any data structure nonkey attributes that are dependent on other nonkey attributes.

Figure 14-14. Summary of steps in normalization process.

added to, changed, or deleted from a file, there is assurance that no other file will require the same maintenance. All nonkey attributes appear only one at a time in one place within the file structure.

Summary

One of the main tasks of systems analysis is data flow analysis, aimed at assuring that data are available to carry out the processing transformations needed to produce the desired outputs.

The two main criteria applied to data stores are simplicity and nonredundancy. Simplicity relates to the type of file organization and access method that can be used to get to the data. Redundancy refers to the existence of the same data component within two or more data stores. Redundancy also occurs where the same data appear in different forms within the same data store. A proper data structure should contain no redundancy. Each data element should appear only one time within the set of data stores. Another incidence of redundancy occurs when two or more data components within a data store provide the same information.

The procedure used to derive this logical file structure is called normalization, which replaces a set of existing files with an equivalent set containing nonredundant data elements and accessible through only primary keys. Normalization includes four basic steps, which are reviewed and illustrated.

To document the entire data structure, a data structure diagram can be used. Each block on the diagram represents an attribute data structure whose name appears in the block. Alongside the block, the access key is written. Arrows between the blocks represent access paths. If the access is made possible through a correlative structure, the name of the structure is written alongside the arrowhead pointing in the appropriate direction of the link. If two attribute structures are related because they share the same key, then the arrows point to the keys with no notation.

The data structures represented by the attribute and correlative relations can be physically packaged into simple sequential and/or direct-access files. Alternatively, the attribute structures can be implemented within a database with the correlative structures being handled as software links between the attributes.

A data access diagram may also be used to represent access paths among the structures. It is possible in using this type of diagram to be able to visualize and confirm whether or not access paths exist to carry out required processing. The diagram also suggests access and processing capabilities that may be possible beyond the original intent of the system.

The revisions that have been made to the file structure must be reflected in the data flow diagram and data dictionary.

Advantages of placing data structures in third normal form include: ease of understanding, ease of use, ease of implementation, and ease of maintenance.

Key Terms

1. logical data structure
2. simplicity
3. nonredundancy
4. normalization
5. key
6. alternate key
7. pointers
8. first normal form
9. concatenating
10. functionally dependent
11. second normal form
12. mutually independent
13. third normal form
14. object
15. attribute
16. key attribute
17. correlation
18. data structure diagram
19. data access diagram

Review/Discussion Questions

1. Why must the logical data flow diagram be considered preliminary until data stores are analyzed?

2. What is the function of the data store?

3. What two criteria are applied in the analysis of data stores, and why is each desirable?

4. What steps are taken in the normalization of a group of data stores?

5. How are keys formed when creating new structures to eliminate redundancies in an existing one?

6. What is meant by functional dependence on the primary key?

7. In what cases would a new data structure contain only key information and no data elements?

8. What criteria are used to decide which structures should be collapsed into a composite structure?

9. In what cases would an attribute of one structure also be an attribute of another, and how is this apparent redundancy removed?

10. How is the new structure of data stores documented?

11. What are some ways the new data structures may be implemented as files?

12. What is the function of the data access diagram?

13. What are the advantages of the third normal form?

Practice Assignments

1. Figure 14-15 shows data dictionary entries that describe the primary file maintained by a magazine subscription service. Normalize the subscription data structure and derive a file structure to support the application. The existing relations among data items should be retained in the new file structure. Draw a data structure diagram and a data access diagram for the derived structure.

2. The three files identified in Figure 14-16 appear within an invoicing system. The CUSTOMER-FILE contains the names and addresses of persons who have accounts with the company. The ITEM-FILE contains item descriptions and prices per unit for the products sold. Data from these two files, along with sales order data from the customers, are combined within the INVOICE-FILE, which contains all of the information needed to produce sales invoices to be sent to the customers.

   Figure 14-17 presents the data dictionary entries for each of the data structures that make up the files.

   Normalize these structures and determine the appropriate file structure. Draw a data structure diagram and a data access diagram to illustrate the structure of the files. (Note that INVOICE-TAX is always 5 percent of the INVOICE-SUBTOTAL. Therefore, the tax amount does not have to be included in the INVOICE data structure. Also, INVOICE-TOTAL can be calculated as INVOICE-SUBTOTAL + INVOICE-TAX and need not appear in the file. QTY-BACKORDERED is a candidate for elimination from the file, since it can be calculated by subtracting QTY-SHIPPED from QTY-ORDERED. After the files are normalized, ITEM-AMOUNT can also be eliminated. Make sure that, in the final structure of the files, invoice information can be accessed by inputting any particular CUSTOMER-NUMBER. A correlative file will have to be defined to support this access.)

NEW SYSTEM DESIGN 15

LEARNING OBJECTIVES

After completing the reading and other learning assignments in this chapter, you should be able to:

☐ Explain the need for and content of documentation to be used as a basis for a steering committee decision on whether to authorize development of a new system.

☐ Describe the value of updating the feasibility estimate for the new system.

☐ Explain how the cost/benefit analysis is refined by the New System Design activity.

☐ Explain the importance of processing controls and describe how such controls are incorporated into the system design.

☐ Describe the characteristics of and management techniques appropriate for databases.

☐ Describe the use of physical models and system flowcharts in the design of a new system.

☐ Tell how the systems analyst contributes to the evaluation of application software packages as well as proposed computer hardware and system software.

☐ Describe measures for assuring quality in the design of a new system.

ACTIVITY DESCRIPTION

This activity marks the beginning of a transition from analysis to design. That is, the analysis of the existing system has been completed and has served, during Activity 4: New System Requirements, as a basis for development of a user specification—a statement of what the new system should look like. This user specification, based on a physical model for the new system, represents a design of the system from the user's perspective. This design is not sufficiently detailed, however, to meet the objectives of the analysis and general design phase. The key objective of this phase is to provide enough information to allow the steering committee to decide whether to continue or abort the project. The decision of the steering committee will be based on three factors:

- An updated feasibility analysis
- A user commitment that the proposed system will satisfy the specified objectives and that the claimed benefits are achievable
- A commitment from the CIS designers that the proposed system can be delivered within the schedule and budget specified.

The user specification is clearly not detailed enough to support these important commitments. All computer processing has been treated as a black box and options such as batch, on-line, and interactive have been specified in generic terms. Activity 5, then, carries the design to a sufficiently detailed level so that the necessary user and designer commitments can be obtained.

At this point, one of the most significant additions to the design of the new system is the building of controls into the proposed system model. Also incorporated are provisions for security, backup, and recovery procedures.

Proper controls are critical to the success of any system. Such controls require careful, detailed thought and planning. To some degree, controls may have been discussed, or even specified, during Activity 4. However, the level of detailing for controls during Activity 4 was left entirely up to the user's discretion. If the user offered no suggestions about controls, none were included. In Activity 5, however, careful specification of controls and verification that these controls are workable is critically important.

Building on the data modeling done during Activity 4 and expressed in the resulting data access diagrams, basic file design decisions are also made in Activity 5.

If application program packages are to be used within the new system, this is the point at which final, detailed evaluation occurs and the decision must be made.

If the new system will require enhancement or addition of computer hardware or system software, specification of these requirements must be made during Activity 5.

These tasks culminate in the ability to update the feasibility evaluation for the proposed system. Both the computerized and manual processes must be designed in sufficient detail so that technical and operational feasibility are assured. It must also be verified that there will be no difficulties in the areas of human factors or scheduling. Finally, the financial analysis, the weighing of costs and benefits, must now be fine tuned. The goal is to produce a cost/benefit analysis that will be within 10 percent of the final costs and benefits realized by the system. That is, the actual costs should total either 10 percent above or below the estimate, making for a 20 percent range of accuracy. The accuracy of this cost/benefit analysis is achieved by specifying a design that is sufficiently detailed to enable users to commit to operating the system within this range of the costs and benefits and to enable designers to commit to delivering the system within the same parameters.

OBJECTIVES

The general objective of this activity is to:

- Provide sufficient information to serve as a basis for a steering committee decision on whether to proceed with implementation of the system.

This general objective is achieved by meeting the following specific objectives:

- Propose a general design for the new system. This design should implement the user specification.

- Obtain a user sign-off on this general design. By this sign-off, the user is verifying that the predicted operational costs and benefits can be achieved.

- Obtain a CIS sign-off on the general design. The developers are committing, by this sign-off, to produce the system within the specified schedule and development cost budget.

SCOPE

Figure 15-1 is a Gantt chart showing the time-line relationships among the activities of the analysis and general design phase, Activities 3 through 6. The overlap apparent in this chart illustrates the iterative nature of systems analysis. The iterations inherent in the modeling tasks of Activities 3 and 4 have been mentioned several times, but even the design tasks of Activity 5 must overlap these modeling efforts.

The physical model for the new system, developed during Activity 4, must reflect the design considerations that are part of Activity 5. This

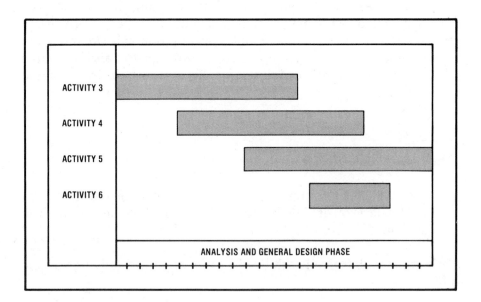

Figure 15-1. Gantt chart shows the heavy overlap among activities of Analysis and General Design phase.

correspondence is necessary because the model developed in Activity 4 represents, in effect, a promise to the user about capabilities of the new system. Without concern for design constraints, it could be possible for the systems analyst to promise capabilities that can't be delivered. Recall that the layering concept plays a prominent role in the iterations that occur during analysis. As successively more detailed understandings of the new system model are achieved, more and more detailed evaluations of technical design options are also being made. In other words, at each level of development of the new system model, design implications are being considered. This is one reason for the overlap of Activities 4 and 5.

There is a special relationship between Activities 5 and 6. Activity 5 actually begins before, and runs longer than, Activity 6: Implementation and Installation Planning. The purpose of Activity 6 is to develop a basic plan and schedule for the next phase. This information is fed into Activity 5 and used to help compute development costs for the new system. By the time Activity 5 is over, a New System Design Specification is developed and ready for implementation pending approval by the steering committee.

It is necessary to apply some constraints to the scope of Activity 5. There is a strong, natural tendency among technical personnel to plunge ahead with detailed design immediately upon beginning design considerations. The life cycle structure precludes full technical design during this activity, partly because this level of commitment has neither been made nor funded. Thus, design activities should be carried only far enough to meet objectives of the activity. In other words, design efforts should fall short of the complete detailing necessary for technical specifications. For example, document and screen display designs for input and output should be in the form of rough sketches, content and access methods should be specified for files, and job streams with major programs identified should document the computer processing.

This level of detail will be sufficient for the objectives of Activity 5. Detailed spacing charts, precise file descriptions and record layouts, and internal program design are usually not necessary for accurate estimates of implementation costs. These more detailed tasks can, and should, be held to the next phase.

END PRODUCTS

This activity produces four principal end products:

- The main result of this activity is the new system design specification.
- A specific recommendation is made concerning the potential for acquiring packaged application programs.
- If new hardware and system software requirements are identified, these requirements are covered by a technical support specification.
- A high level summary is prepared for use by user management and by the steering committee.

New System Design Specification

The New System Design Specification is an extension of the user specification. Some of the elements of the user specification are included, intact, in this later document. Others are updated. To illustrate the relationship between these two documents, the portions of the descriptions below in *italics* indicate content revisions or substantial additions.

The blending of existing documents with new content highlights the cumulative documentation techniques used in systems development projects.

- Overview narrative. This document has three parts. The first covers the goals and objectives of the organization and provides a basis against which system requests are evaluated. *The second describes the system's purpose, goals, and objectives, as well as the basic, logical functions that the system must provide. The third is an overview statement of changes to be made between the existing system and the new one.*
- System function. For the user's benefit, a concise—but processing free—description of what the system will accomplish is prepared. Written in user terminology, it presents a black box description of the computer portion of the system.
- Processing. Processing descriptions include a context diagram and a hierarchical set of data flow diagrams. Diagram 0 should iden-

tify the major subsystems. Lower level diagrams should indicate the physical packaging from the user's perspective. Differentiation should be made between manual and computer processing, batch and on-line processing, timing cycles, and performance requirements. *Computer processing should be defined to the job stream level and should be documented using annotated system flowcharts.*

- Data dictionary. This document supports the data flow diagrams. It is carried forward intact.

- Outputs to the user. This section consists of an index sheet listing all outputs. The index sheet is followed by an output documentation sheet and a rough format for each output. *Additional outputs related to control and security concerns may be added in this activity.*

- Inputs to the system. This section consists of an index sheet listing all inputs. The index sheet is followed by an input documentation sheet and a rough format for each input. *As with outputs, security- and control-related inputs may be added.*

- User interface with the system. Routine aspects of how user personnel work within the system, and how user personnel interface with the computerized portions of the system, are contained in the definition of manual processes. This section may include rough outlines of human/machine interactive conversations. Also included are explanations of the impact upon job descriptions and the number of positions in the user area. *User responsibilities as they relate to security and control processing are added here.*

- *Data Files. This document describes the requirements in terms of files, rather than data stores, highlighting the transition from analysis to general design. File access methods and storage media are specified, along with approximate quantity of stored data and anticipated growth.* (Detailed file layouts or database design will occur in the next phase of the life cycle.

- *Performance criteria. These descriptions of expectations from the new system are critical for both computer and manual processing. Included are required response times, anticipated volumes of transactions, and other performance data.*

- *Security and control. Measures for security and control are discussed as they apply to hardware, computer processing, and manual processing.*

- Policy considerations. This section lists any relevant policy decisions that have not yet been made.
- *Computer operations interface with the new system. These specifications are still at a general level and are not detailed operating instructions. However, descriptions should include hardware, data communication requirements, timing, projected volumes, impact on existing operations, backup and record retention requirements, and recovery procedures.*

Packaged Application Software Recommendation

If application packages are considered, recommendations in this report should include:

- An overview description of each package
- A summary of evaluations of each package
- A summary of modifications that would have to be made, either to the package or to existing software
- Recommendations on the value of each package, including lease/purchase considerations.

Technical Support Specification

If the proposed system involves significant hardware and/or systems software changes, technical specifications should be prepared. These should include:

- A detailed description of requirements for new hardware and software capabilities
- Data communication requirements, if appropriate
- Proposals from vendors, including analyses of these proposals
- Lease/purchase recommendations.

Management Overview

This is a covering document that summarizes the content of the new system design specification at a level that is meaningful to users and to members of the steering committee. Emphasis is on the impact of the proposed changes upon the conduct of the business. Specific contents will vary with each project, but the following sections would normally be included:

- Overview narrative. This is taken directly from the new system design specification.

- System function. This is taken directly from the new system design specification.

- Recommendations. A management-level summary of recommendations is prepared that centers, principally, on three areas: application software (recommended packages and in-house development), major recommended hardware and system software acquisitions, and a recommended development schedule (a calendar for the next two phases at the Activity level).

- Updated feasibility evaluation. A brief summary is presented evaluating the proposed solution in the technical, operational, human factors, and scheduling dimensions of feasibility. In addition, the cost/benefit analysis is updated by summarizing the budgeted and actual development costs to date, revising the cost and time estimates to complete the project, and revising predicted operating costs and benefits.

- Personnel requirements. The key to success in any development project is to have the right people when they are needed. This section should summarize the person-hour requirements by week or month for the remainder of the project. Requirements should be listed by job category (programmer, analyst, user clerical people, and so on) or by name, for key people. Just as a continuing development budget is implicit in Steering Committee approval of the project, so is the availability of personnel as specified in this section.

- Critical policy considerations. These are the policy decisions that the steering committee must deal with for development to continue.

- User acceptance statement. This statement is a formal sign-off by the user that the proposed system will meet the stated needs, that it can be run within the specified cost limits, and that its use will deliver the projected benefits.

- CIS acceptance statement. This statement is a formal sign-off by CIS management that the proposed system can be developed within the established cost and time budgets.

THE PROCESS

The primary goal of this activity is to carry the design of the new system to a point at which an updated feasibility evaluation can be prepared. This includes preparation of accurate estimates for all five dimensions of system feasibility—financial, technical, operational, scheduling, and human factors.

A related goal is to build a clear understanding of the complexity and effort that will be involved in carrying the system forward into the next two phases, involving implementation and installation. Personnel requirements—from both the user and CIS departments—must be clearly specified for these later phases. The key to success in any development project is to have the right people at the right time.

A further goal is to improve the chances of the project's success through close study of any unusually complex or advanced design areas of the new system and by identifying and addressing specifically those areas that might represent high risks.

The process steps within this activity are not sequential or cumulative. Rather, there are a series of somewhat interrelated and overlapping concerns that must be addressed at some time during the activity. These concerns are covered briefly in the sections that follow.

Add Controls

Recall that in Chapter 1 a system was said to contain six major components: input, processing, output, feedback, control, and processing adjustments. In general, the user tends to be most concerned about the first three. While the more obvious controls will have been included in the physical model produced in Activity 4, there will have been no separate and concentrated effort to be certain the controls are complete. The last three system components all involve control processes.

In a systems sense, *controls* are the steps inserted in the processing sequence specifically to assure accuracy, completeness, reliability, and quality of results produced. In any endeavor as extensive as a modern computer information system, it is assumed that the system will be exposed to numerous incidents of human error, software error, machine failure, or even attempted fraud.

Controls must start, therefore, before processing even begins. Controls are established at input. Then, at critical points within the system at which data are transformed or handled, new controls must be applied to verify that results are still valid and reliable. Considerations for designing control and reliability functions into a system are covered in Chapter 17.

One of the key responsibilities of the systems analyst is to be sure that adequate controls are designed into the system. During this activity, the proposed system must be evaluated rigorously with respect to the adequacy of its control processing.

Design the Database

The term *database*, as used here, refers to all of the data resources needed to support a system. During this activity, initial database design—which falls far short of detailed technical design—is completed.

The modeling steps of Activity 4 resulted in a complete identification of required data elements and a set of data stores, all documented in the data dictionary. This identification was refined to some degree through the data analysis and modeling techniques covered in Chapter 14, resulting in a set of data access diagrams. The objective in Activity 5 is to carry the database design far enough to support the updating of the feasibility evaluation—at least far enough to support the high level design of the computer processing. It is not necessary, at this point, to complete final technical specifications such as record layouts, storage formats, and so on. Such specifications can wait until the detailed design and implementation phase.

The actual tasks to be performed in managing system data resources depend on the software support available. In particular, these tasks depend on whether traditional file processing will be done or *database management system (DBMS)* software will be used. In this context, traditional file processing refers to the use of sequential, indexed, and direct file organization methods.

If database management software is to be used, a database specialist will begin to work with the development team. It will be the responsibility of the database administration group to complete the design of the physical database.

If traditional file processing is used, master files will be identified, usually by modifying the data stores contained in the physical model of the new system. These data stores resulted from the normalization process. Modifications to data stores are based, for the most part, on considerations of processing efficiency and newly identified control processing requirements. The modifications are also based on the methods chosen for implementing the required access paths. The choices include use of alternate keys (if supported by the system software), implementation of correlative files as direct files, and extraction of necessary records from the master file for further processing.

For each new proposed master file, the set of data elements to be included, the access keys, and the file organization method will be specified. Backup and recovery procedures for file protection must also be developed. The process of designing the database—given the data access diagrams of the physical model for the new system—is discussed further in Chapter 16.

Database performance requirements for database management are also specified during this activity. These include statistics on the type and amount of database access activity, anticipated growth rates for the database, and required access or response times. Finally, any constraints upon use of the database to meet security or control requirements, or due to limitations in resources, must be spelled out.

Complete the General Design of Computer Processing

General design of computer processing refers to the identification of basic processing jobs or job steps, not to the technical design of computer programs. As with all of the major tasks in Activity 5, the goal is simply to define things specifically enough to support the updating of the feasibility evaluation of the new system.

The physical model of the new system, produced as part of Activity 4 and possibly modified on the basis of database design decisions discussed above, identifies:

- Those processes that are computerized (the human-machine boundary)
- Those computer processes that are batch and those that are on-line
- The cycle and timing requirements for the batch processes.

The design is extended in Activity 5 by first specifying which data and which processes are maintained centrally and which are distributed, either to user areas at the main location or to totally remote sites. Consider, for example, the motel reservation system introduced in Chapter 2. That system was developed by the CIS department at the home office of the motel chain. Portions of the data and some of the processes—such as those involving profitability analysis—were handled centrally at the home office. On the other hand, some data and processing were distributed to the individual motels—for example, those involving specific room assignments and individual billing.

After decisions are made on the portions of the system that are to be distributed, basic computer job streams are defined. In this way, the major computer programs are identified, but are not internally designed. Also, the required communication between programs, or job steps, is defined. The decisions are documented using annotated system flowcharts. To illustrate, consider the abstract physical model, Figure 15-2, that was used as an illustration of the new system requirements activity in Chapter 11. This physical model is a design of the system from the user's point of view. In Figure 15-3, the same model has been modified to show that a portion of the processing and one data store are distributed. In addition, a more detailed look has been taken at the weekly batch processing. Three major programs or job steps have been identified: The first contains process P1. The second contains processes P2 and P3. The third contains process P4.

These basic design decisions may be documented using a *system flowchart* as illustrated in Figure 15-4. Note that the manual input, I1, to process P1 is depicted as card input to STEP #1 and that the outputs, O1 and O2, leaving the computerized portion of the system from the processes P3 and P4, are depicted as printed reports. Note also that temporary files, TF #1 and TF #2, must be created to communicate the results from STEP #1 to STEP #2 and from STEP #2 to STEP #3.

A determination must be made about what guidelines are to be followed by the analyst in deciding how the processes will be packaged as computer programs. In some cases, a single bubble on the data flow diagram will become a single program to carry out a batch job or interactive application. In other cases, a process may be implemented as two or more related programs; or several processes may be integrated into a single program. Such tentative design decisions point out the need

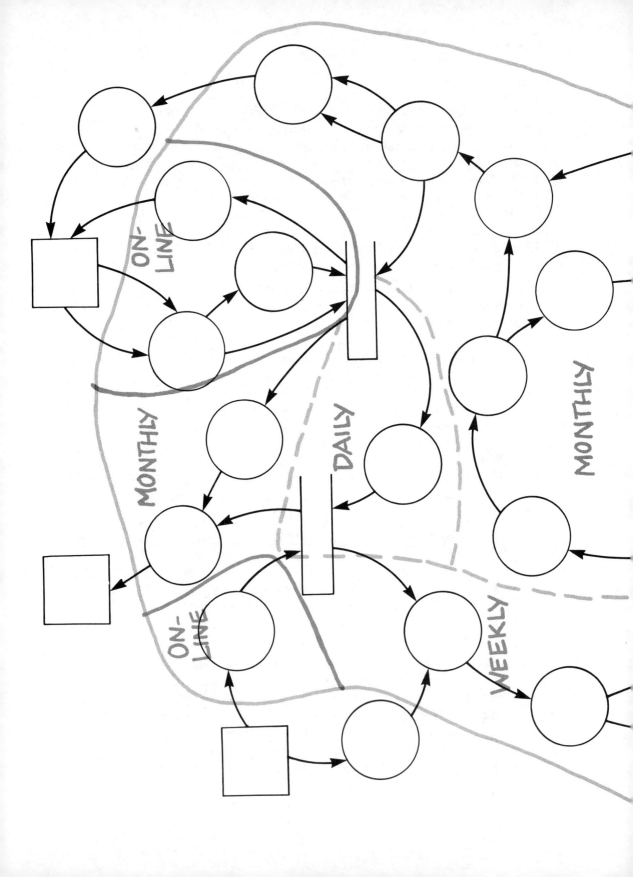

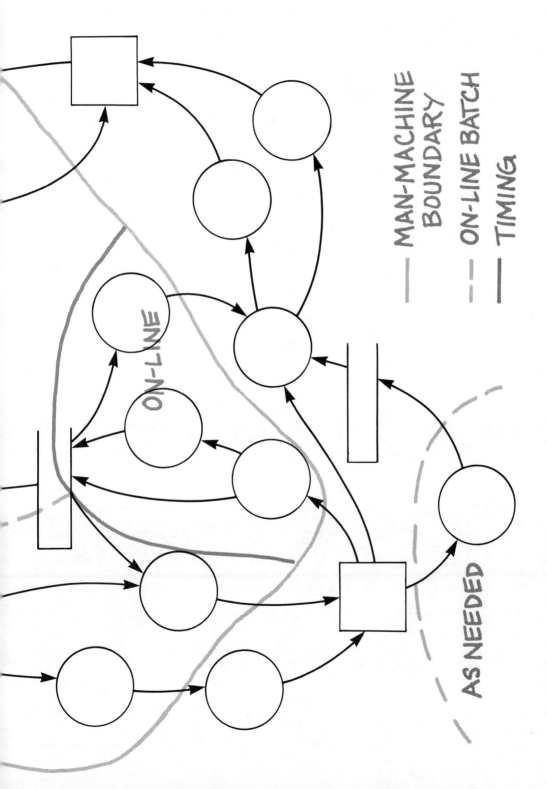

MAN-MACHINE
BOUNDARY

ON-LINE BATCH

TIMING

ON-LINE

AS NEEDED

Figure 15-2. Physical model of new system.

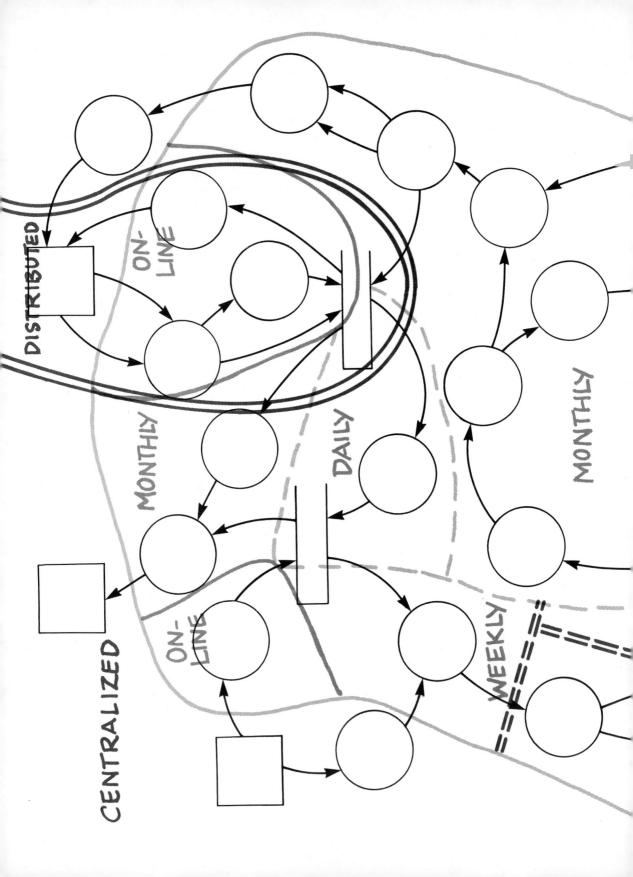

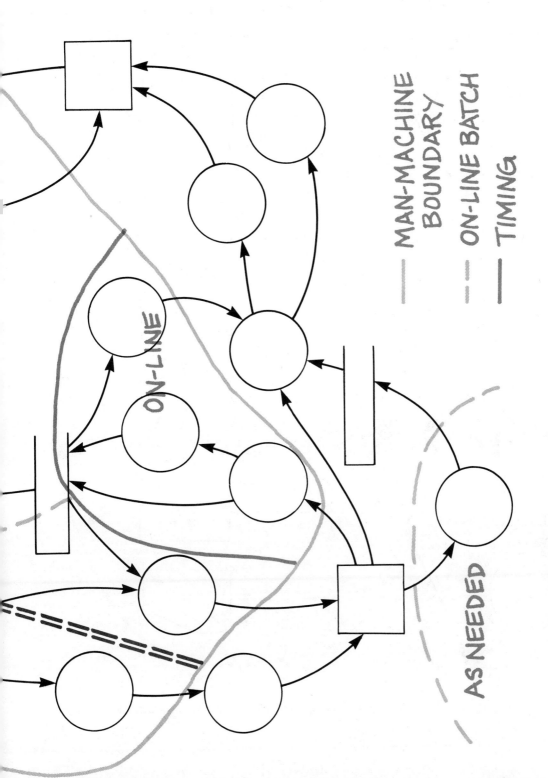

MAN-MACHINE BOUNDARY

ON-LINE BATCH

TIMING

ON-LINE

AS NEEDED

Figure 15-3. Physical model of new system with distributed processing identified and job stream defined for weekly processing.

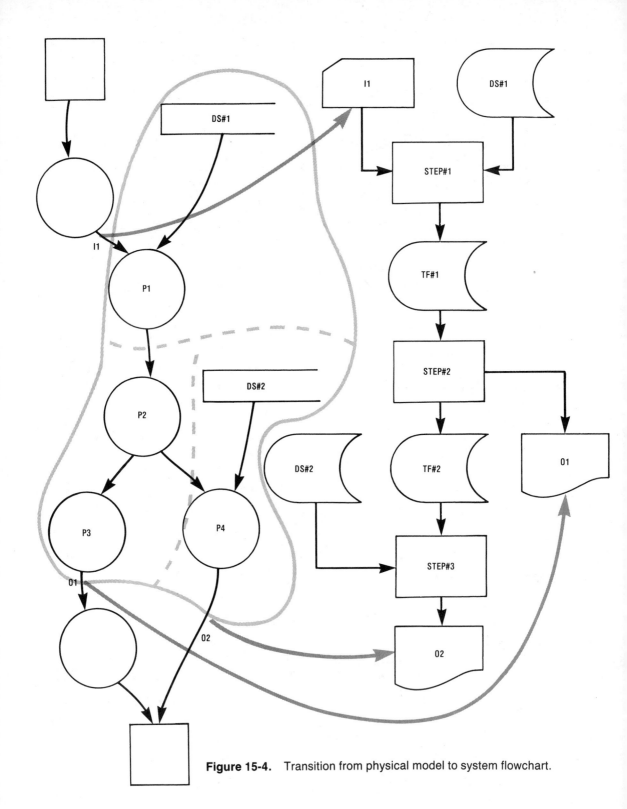

Figure 15-4. Transition from physical model to system flowchart.

474

for the analyst to be familiar with many of the technical aspects of computers and computer processing, as well as being an astute businessperson.

The analyst will be guided in these decisions by an understanding of software capabilities, design methodologies, and availability of packages. In general, there are three ways of acquiring or developing software. Knowing these methods is the basis of the heuristics for packaging the system.

- *Application software packages.* Usually the simplest and quickest way of implementing a system is with the purchase of software packages. The many available packages can generally provide needed data processing capabilities with only minor modification to accommodate specific needs. Regardless of whether acquiring software packages is a viable alternative, the existence of these packages and their capabilities provides guidance in evolving a realistic scheme for implementing a system.

- *Data management, inquiry, and report-writing systems.* Some systems software packages make possible convenient building of business applications without the need to develop original programs. Several of these software tools permit programmers, designers, and even users to perform file creation, file maintenance, report writing, and file inquiry processing through a series of question-and-response operations. Again, these capabilities, even if they are not used, give the analyst ideas on how logical processes can be implemented as hardware/software systems.

- *Original program development.* The third packaging alternative is to develop original programs from scratch. Even though other methods might be available, these other alternatives may impose limitations on flexibility and on the ability to perform specialized processing. In such cases, original programming becomes the only alternative. The particular types of programs to be developed can be determined by considering the general processing capabilities of the existing computer system, the designs used in similar types of systems (either in-house or in other installations), or recommendations from the design and programming staff concerning approaches that have been adopted as organization standards.

System flowcharts.   While not previously covered in this book, system flowcharts should already be familiar to persons with programming experience. System flowcharts, for the purposes of Activity 5, are a graphic technique for depicting computer processing at the job level. Standard symbols, as illustrated in Figure 15-5, are used to represent functions or components of a computer job stream within a system. The system flowchart represents a natural transition from the physical model of the computer processing, as expressed in data flow diagrams, to a set of program specifications that will be prepared at the start of the next phase—detailed design and implementation.

A word of caution is in order here. Don't become confused in making the transition from a data flow diagram to a system flowchart. Remember that a data flow diagram emphasizes the flow and transformation of data. In particular, its arrows depict data flows. A system flowchart, on the other hand, stresses control. Its lines simply show the flow of control from one process to another. Data stores on a high-level data flow diagram translate into files (disks, tapes, cards, or printed reports) on a system flowchart. One or more process bubbles on a data flow diagram are combined into a process box representing a single computer program or job step on the system flowchart.

Hardware and system software acquisition.   If new computer hardware or software are needed to implement the proposed system, these requirements are identified as part of the general design of the computer processing in Activity 5. The actual acquisition tasks—preparing requests for proposal, dealing with vendors, purchasing, and testing— are normally handled by specialists in the technical support area of the CIS department. A representative from this group would begin to work with the project team during Activity 5, using the performance requirements provided. It is necessary for technical services to become involved now, rather than to wait until the next phase, because of the lead time required to purchase and test new hardware and software.

Evaluate Possible Application Software Packages

The evaluation of packaged application software was begun in Activity 4. At the time the logical and physical models of the new system were created, it was possible to evaluate potential software packages in terms of functions provided, completeness of data elements, ease of use, and so on. This evaluation is extended in Activity 5 to the point at which

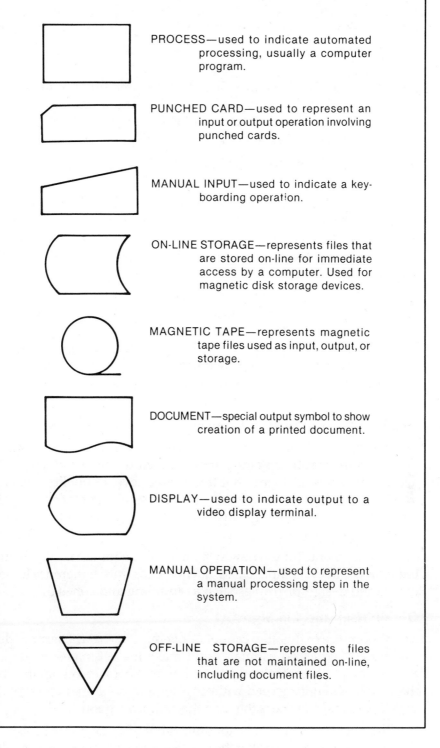

PROCESS—used to indicate automated processing, usually a computer program.

PUNCHED CARD—used to represent an input or output operation involving punched cards.

MANUAL INPUT—used to indicate a keyboarding operation.

ON-LINE STORAGE—represents files that are stored on-line for immediate access by a computer. Used for magnetic disk storage devices.

MAGNETIC TAPE—represents magnetic tape files used as input, output, or storage.

DOCUMENT—special output symbol to show creation of a printed document.

DISPLAY—used to indicate output to a video display terminal.

MANUAL OPERATION—used to represent a manual processing step in the system.

OFF-LINE STORAGE—represents files that are not maintained on-line, including document files.

Figure 15-5. Common system flowcharting symbols.

necessary modifications, interface modules, and other requirements can be identified. These items are needed to update the feasibility analysis. The possible use of application software packages is covered in greater depth in Chapter 21.

Update the Feasibility Analysis

The feasibility analysis is the ultimate basis for a decision whether the new system will be implemented. During this activity, the management steering committee will expect the feasibility analysis to be refined to a level that will make it possible to rely on this report as a basis for committing the extensive funds needed to complete development of the system.

Thus, during this activity, all five dimensions of feasibility must be revised. In particular, for financial feasibility, it is necessary to update the project status to date by comparing budgeted figures with actual time and dollars. Also required to determine financial feasibility are: developmental costs to complete the project, projected operating costs and benefits for the new system, and the opportunity costs that will be lost if the system is not developed.

Evaluate Overall Design Quality

The design specifications for the new system will become the basis for its development and implementation. Therefore, this activity provides a last chance to make sure that the desired level of quality has been designed into the system. If quality is not designed into a computer information system, building it in later can be expensive and frustrating.

Quality analysis is done by a series of walkthroughs using the design documents for the new system. Evaluations are made for such things as accuracy, completeness, adequate controls, adherence to standards, and design principles such as coupling and cohesion.

Obtain User and CIS Sign-Off

The importance of this step cannot be overemphasized. There are dual concerns: Make good estimates and make the estimates good. The analyst can put great time and effort into making good estimates, but the system will not succeed without a commitment on the part of the developers and the users to make the estimates good.

The role of the analyst is not unlike that of a real estate broker, in this case acting as a broker between developers and users. The developers must examine the contract—the new system design specification—to understand exactly what is required. Developers must also come to a conviction that it is possible to develop the system specified within the stated time and dollar limits. Similarly, users must understand what is required of them and come to a conviction that it will be possible for the system to achieve the specified benefits.

PERSONNEL INVOLVED

The makeup of the project team begins to shift somewhat during Activity 5. Normally, additional analysts or designers will be added to the team because of the shift in emphasis toward design.

If appropriate, a database analyst will join the team. If significant changes in hardware or software are contemplated, members of the organization's technical services staff will be called upon.

As the work in this activity moves forward, emphasis shifts away from a user orientation to become increasingly technical. The makeup of the project team shifts accordingly. The role of the user is to keep the project on a correct business course, to confirm appropriateness of products, and to supply necessary input for control processing and manual procedures.

CUMULATIVE PROJECT FILE

The project file assembled at the close of this activity includes some documents produced during Activity 6. The cumulative content encompasses:

- A complete project plan at a task level for the implementation phase of the life cycle that is to follow
- The initial investigation report (of historic interest only)
- The Feasibility Report has been updated to provide a current appraisal. This report will be used in the review phase of the project.
- Documentation of existing systems (to be discarded after the new system has been implemented)
- New system design specification (to be carried forward to Activity 7: Technical Design)
- Data dictionary

- Interview schedules and summaries (to be discarded after implementation of the new system)
- Preliminary test plan (from Activity 6)
- Preliminary installation plan (from Activity 6)
- User training outline (from Activity 6).

CASE SCENARIO

Selected data flow diagrams from the physical model of Central City's water billing system are presented in the case scenario section of Chapter 11. These cover processes for preparing the meter reading book, applying new readings, and preparing bills.

The system flowcharts corresponding to these portions of the physical model are shown in the illustrations that accompany this chapter. The details associated with the process by applying customer payments are presented in Chapter 17.

Refer to Figures 11-12 and 11-13 in Chapter 11 for the context diagram and Diagram 0 of the physical model.

Figure 15-6 presents the annotated system flowchart for the job stream that prepares the meter reading book. This corresponds to Diagram 1 in Figure 11-14.

The annotated flowcharts for the batch and on-line processes that apply new meter readings are given in Figures 15-7 and 15-8. These flowcharts correspond to Diagram 3 in Figure 11-15.

Finally, the system flowchart for the batch processing of incycle bills is given in Figure 15-9. Refer to the data flow diagrams in Figures 11-16 and 11-17.

Summary

The New System Design activity marks the beginning of a transition from analysis to design. The user specification developed in Activity 4 is not sufficiently detailed to meet the objectives of the analysis and general design phase. One of the most significant additions to the design of the new system at this point is the building of controls into

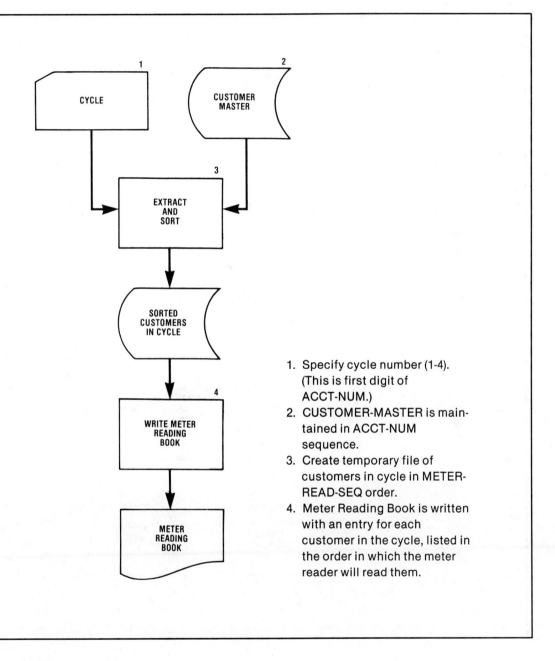

Figure 15-6. System flowchart for EXTRACT METERS TO READ job stream that prepared meter reading books.

1. Readings are keypunched from Meter Reading Book.
2. Sequential update for CUSTOMER-MASTER using only clean transactions.
3. Error report to Billing Clerk, who must prepare Reading Verification Forms as necessary. Any records in error must be resubmitted.
4. New reading is added, oldest is dropped.

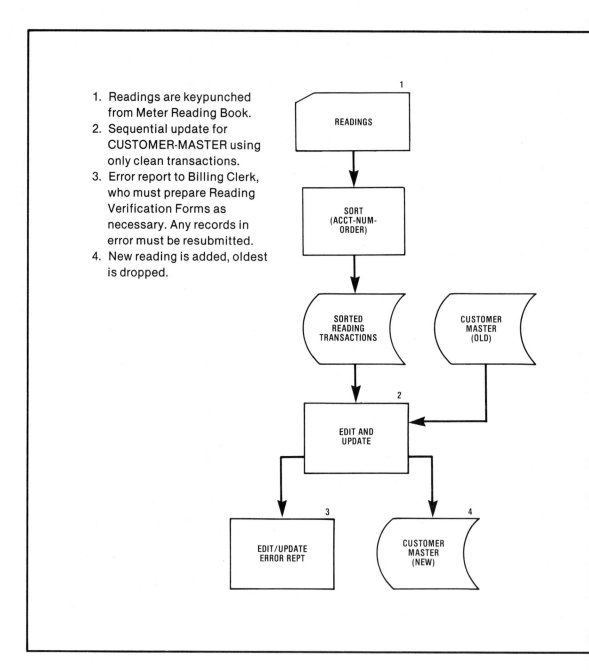

Figure 15-7.   System flowchart for APPLY INCYCLE READINGS job stream.

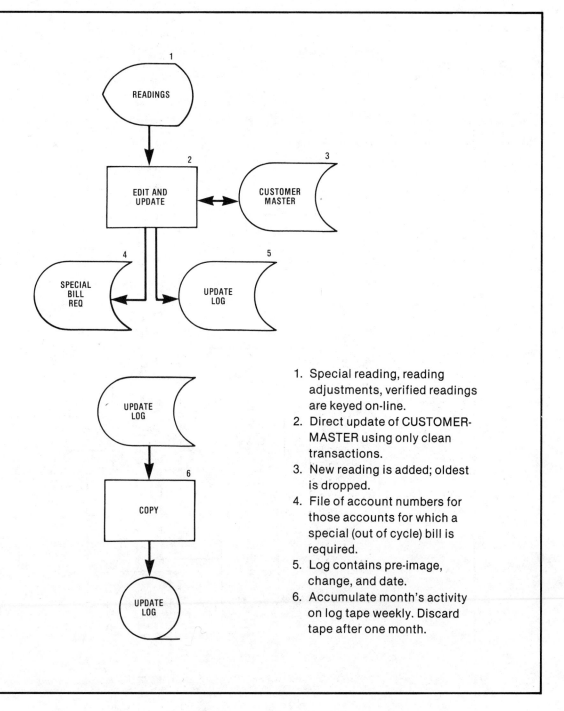

1. Special reading, reading adjustments, verified readings are keyed on-line.
2. Direct update of CUSTOMER-MASTER using only clean transactions.
3. New reading is added; oldest is dropped.
4. File of account numbers for those accounts for which a special (out of cycle) bill is required.
5. Log contains pre-image, change, and date.
6. Accumulate month's activity on log tape weekly. Discard tape after one month.

Figure 15-8. System flowcharts for APPLY SPECIAL READING jobs.

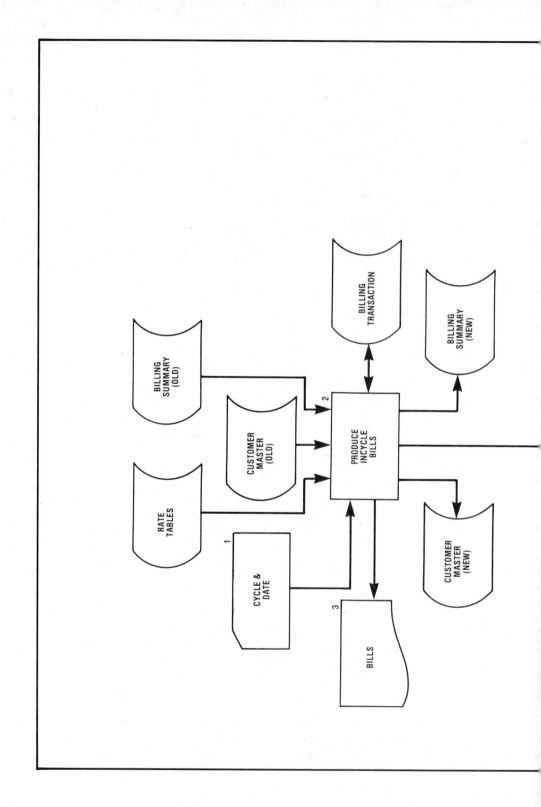

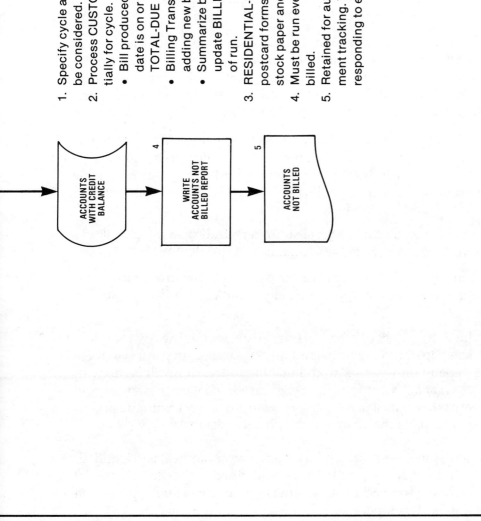

1. Specify cycle and earliest reading date to be considered.
2. Process CUSTOMER-MASTER sequentially for cycle.
   - Bill produced only if current reading date is on or after input date *and* TOTAL-DUE > 0.
   - Billing Transaction record updated by adding new bill and dropping oldest.
   - Summarize bills by user class and update BILLING-SUMMARY at end of run.
3. RESIDENTIAL-BILL outputs printed on postcard forms. All other bills printed on stock paper and mailed in envelopes.
4. Must be run even if all accounts were billed.
5. Retained for audit purposes and management tracking. There must be a report corresponding to each billing cycle.

ACCOUNTS WITH CREDIT BALANCE

4

WRITE ACCOUNTS NOT BILLED REPORT

5

ACCOUNTS NOT BILLED

Figure 15-9. System flowchart for PRODUCE INCYCLE BILL job stream.

the proposed system model. Also incorporated are provisions for security, backup, and recovery procedures.

Final evaluation of any application program packages and any required computer hardware or system software is included in this activity.

An updated feasibility evaluation helps to verify that there will be no difficulties in the areas of human factors or scheduling. The financial analysis is updated to produce a cost/benefit analysis that will be within plus or minus 10 percent (or a range of 20 percent) of the final costs and benefits realized by the system.

This activity produces four principal end products: the new system design specification, a specific recommendation on packaged application programs, a technical support specification (if appropriate), and a high level summary for use by user management and by the Steering Committee.

The primary goal of this activity is to carry the design of the new system to a point at which an updated Feasibility Evaluation can be prepared. This includes preparation of accurate estimates for all five dimensions of system feasibility—financial, technical, operational, scheduling, and human factors.

A related goal is to build a clear understanding of the complexity and effort involved in implementation and installation.

A further goal is to improve the chances of the project's success through close study of any unusually complex or advanced design areas.

The actual tasks to be performed in managing system data resources depend on the software support available. In particular, these tasks depend on whether traditional file processing will be done or database management software will be used. If database management software is to be used, a database specialist will work with the project team to complete the design of the physical database.

If traditional file processing is used, master files will be identified, usually by modifying the data stores contained in the physical model of the new system. Backup and recovery procedures for file protection must also be developed.

Database performance requirements for database management are also specified including statistics on the type and amount of database access activity, anticipated growth rates for the database, and required response times. Any constraints upon use of the database must be spelled out.

The physical model of the new system identifies which processes are computerized, which computer processes are batch and which are on-line, and the timing of batch processes.

The design is extended in Activity 5 by first specifying which data and which processes are maintained centrally and which are distributed, either to user areas at the main location or to totally remote sites. Then, basic computer job streams are defined. Major computer programs are identified, but not internally designed. The required communication between programs, or job steps, is defined. The decisions are documented using annotated system flowcharts.

During this activity, the management steering committee will expect the Feasibility Analysis to be refined to a level that will make it possible for this report to be relied upon as a basis for committing the extensive funds needed to complete development of the system.

Quality analysis is done by a series of walkthroughs using the design documents for the new system. Evaluations are made for accuracy, completeness, adequate controls, adherence to standards, and the design principles of coupling and cohesion.

As the work in this activity moves forward, emphasis shifts away from user orientation and becomes increasingly technical. The makeup of the project team shifts accordingly.

The project file assembled at the close of this activity includes: a complete project plan at a task level for the implementation phase of the life cycle, the initial investigation report, the updated feasibility report, documentation of existing systems, the new system design specification, the data dictionary, interview schedules and summaries, a preliminary test plan, a preliminary installation plan, and an outline for the training of user personnel.

Key Terms

1. controls
2. database
3. database management system
4. system flowcharts

Review/Discussion Questions

1. What is the objective of this activity in relation to the steering committee?

2. What specifically will the steering committee need to render a decision?

3. What is the purpose of updating the feasibility evaluation in this activity?

4. What is the target accuracy of the cost/benefit analysis, and how is this accuracy achieved?

5. What are the principal end products of this activity?

6. How are additional controls incorporated into the system design during this activity?

7. What is the database, and what defines the tasks required to manage the database?

8. What is the difference between traditional file processing and the use of database management software?

9. How is the design of the physical model extended in this activity?

10. How are system flowcharts used in this activity?

11. What are the responsibilities of the analyst relative to application software and to new computer hardware and system software?

12. How is quality analysis applied during this activity?

FILE DESIGN 16

LEARNING OBJECTIVES

After completing the reading and other learning assignments in this chapter, you should be able to:

- [ ] Describe the steps followed in file design.
- [ ] Identify the types of files used to support applications, including master, transaction, reference, archival, backup, and transaction log files.
- [ ] Explain the differences between physical sequential (serial), logical sequential, and direct file access methods.
- [ ] Describe the design trade-offs and appropriate application criteria for selection of sequential, direct, or index-sequential file organization methods.
- [ ] Give the physical characteristics of some secondary storage devices and the trade-offs associated with these devices as they relate to file organization methods.

FILE-RELATED DESIGN DECISIONS

Among the key design decisions that must be made in the development of a new computer information system are those that deal with where and how data will be stored and how those data will be accessed as needed by the new applications.

In the earlier chapter on Logical Data Analysis, attention is paid to analyzing the contents of data stores with a view toward simplifying the overall structure. The resulting set of normalized data stores is part of the physical model for the new system. This physical model forms the basis for the design work done near the end of the analysis and general design phase.

Several file design steps are needed to support the general design. These include:

- Establish the application support files by combining data stores as necessary and adding any required intermediate files to pass data between the processing steps.

- For each file, specify the access method or methods required to support the processing steps.

- For each file, specify the file organization technique required to support the desired access methods.

- Specify the equipment—secondary storage devices—needed to store the identified files.

A final step of specifying the actual physical layout of file records can wait until the detailed design and implementation phase.

This chapter is concerned with the traditional file organizations—sequential, direct, and indexed sequential—supported on virtually all computer systems. Not covered is the database design activity that would be needed if the system were to be implemented using database processing software. In this latter case, personnel from the database administration group within the CIS organization would typically handle the database design for the project team. These specialists would use the set of normalized data stores as a starting point.

APPLICATION SUPPORT FILES

Any given application may require any or all of the types of files described below:

- *Master files* contain basic information about identified entities. For example, there would be separate master files for customers, products, employees, and so on. A master file contains one record for each entity covered, such as a customer account, a part, an employee, and so on. Certain types of fields within master file records tend to be static, or unchanging. For example, a customer name would normally be fairly permanent. On the other hand, some fields within master files change on the basis of transaction data each time an application is processed. For example, year-to-date earnings would be changed each time a payroll is run.

- *Transaction files* are dynamic. Transaction files contain records of source transactions of a business and are used to update master files. Transaction files, thus, reflect specific, timely incidents in the operation of a business. Master files, on the other hand, are cumulative as well as relatively permanent. Examples of transaction files might include current payroll earnings records, invoice detail items, cash receipts, and purchasing records.

- *Reference files* contain constant data used each time an application program is run. These data are used—along with data from transaction files—to update master files. These are relatively stable data—stable enough so that they need not be a part of each transaction record—with sufficient potential for change so that the values should not be coded in the actual programs. An example of a reference file is a data table on federal withholding taxes, indexed according to employee earnings level. Tables of this type are searched each time payroll records are updated.

- *Archival files* are transaction files that have been processed and retained. Such files are used largely for historical reference or special research. For example, a hospital might keep transaction files detailing treatments of patients for many years. These files could then provide a basis for research on the incidence and treatment of specific diseases.

- *Backup files* consist of separate physical copies of transaction files and of historic master files retained for the specific purpose of reconstructing and recovering a company's records in the event of a disaster that interrupts computer services. Typically, for example, copies of last week's payroll earnings records, together with copies of last week's employee master files, would be saved and protected as backup in the event of damage to or loss of current records. Several generations of payroll records would be saved as part of the backup program.

- *Transaction log files* are, in effect, master accounting records that serve as electronic *journals.* Typically, this type of file is kept on a running basis as part of an on-line processing system. All transactions entered into the system are logged—usually on two or more tapes or disks—in sequence, as transactions occur. These logs assure auditability of computer records. In effect, these logs are the starting point on the audit trail for business transactions. The files would also be used for recovery if master or transaction files were inadvertently destroyed.

The first step in designing the files to support a system, then, is to identify the different types of files needed and their basic content. The starting point is a normalized set of data stores prepared as part of the physical model.

Depending on processing requirements, each individual data store may become a separate file or several data stores may be combined into a single file. These decisions are based on how data are to be processed under the computer job steps that emerge during the general design of the new system. A number of questions can be asked:

- Which data are generated or processed together?
- Which data are used as part of a sequential processing of all records?
- Which data are used to support direct queries?
- Which data will be updated as part of a large (sequential) update process?
- Which data will be updated singly, on a direct or random basis?
- Which data are volatile enough to require frequent updating?

These questions help both in selecting the basic files that are needed and also in specifying the type of access required for each file.

FILE ORGANIZATION AND ACCESS

Strictly speaking, file organization and file access are separate concepts. However, the terms tend to be used interchangeably. File access refers to the manner in which an application may need to access or read records on a file. File organization refers to the scheme by which file records are stored on a secondary storage device—the scheme that supports the desired type of access. There are three general options for accessing a file:

- *Physical sequential* or *serial access* is, in a sense, chronological. Records in a file are read or processed in the same order in which the records were initially recorded. An example of a file that is usually accessed serially is a transaction log, or electronic journal, created by an on-line system.

- *Logical sequential access* is conducted in a keyed sequence. That is, records are read in order, according to a logical identifier or key. These keys are generally data fields within the records. Payroll records, commonly accessed successively by employee number, represent a typical example.

- *Direct access* is conducted without regard to sequence, either chronological or keyed. Records are accessed individually according to an identifier, usually a specific value for a key field, that causes the computer to search for and find a single record at a time.

As stated earlier, file organization refers to the physical scheme by which records in a file are actually stored. There are basically three schemes—which support physical and logical sequential access, direct access, and both logical sequential and direct access. File organization options include:

- A *sequential file organization* is one in which records are organized by physical sequence alone. Records are written on the file one after the other in physical sequence. They are read in the same order in which they are written. A sequential file organization obviously supports physical sequential or serial access. It also supports logical sequential access if the records have been written in the desired order according to the particular logical key.

  A typical situation involves the collection of transaction data, say payroll records, in a physical sequential file as they are received. The file is sorted in employee number order for logical sequential access when these transaction records are processed against the employee master file.

  For practical purposes, a sequential file organization does not support direct access. To read the particular record corresponding with a given key value, it would be necessary to begin reading the file from the beginning each time.

- A *direct file organization* is one in which the location or address of a record in the file is determined directly by the value of its key field. Typically, a mathematical formula is applied to the key value to determine an address in the file. Then the record at that address can be read directly, without reading the previous records.

  The entire point of direct file organization is to support rapid, direct access to records in a file. A direct file can also be read in physical sequence. But this physical sequence has absolutely no logical meaning. Thus, logical sequential access is effectively eliminated.

- An *indexed-sequential organization* is one which supports both sequential and direct access to a file. To oversimplify to some extent, records are arranged in sequential order by key. In addition, an index, or table, is established to record the physical location of keys within the file. To access records sequentially, the file can be read in order, by key. Direct access can also be performed on the same file by using the key to reference the index and determine the location of the record on the file.

Each of these file organization methods is explained more fully in later sections of this chapter.

FILE EQUIPMENT AND MEDIA

Many types of secondary storage equipment are available for use with computers. However, the two most commonly used kinds of devices handle magnetic tape and magnetic disks. These devices will be the only kinds of file units discussed below. Even within these limited categories, however, there are many choices to be made. Tape and disk handling units come in a wide range of capacities, storage densities, and data transfer rates. As part of the planning for the design of a new system, the analyst should find out what secondary storage devices are available in the computer installation to be used. The files for the application under development can then be adapted to these available units—unless the units are found to be inadequate. If additional capacities are needed, an equipment study can be initiated. In most situations, however, design of file handling systems is based upon the type of equipment and the capacity of equipment already available.

Separate design approaches and concerns are needed in planning systems to use magnetic tape and magnetic disk files, as discussed below.

Magnetic Tape Devices and Media

Data are recorded on tape in columns, as illustrated in Chapter 13. Bytes are simply recorded next to each other, with bit positions identical from byte to byte. In effect, the recording pattern consists of rows of aligned bit positions known as *channels,* or *tracks.*

Data are recorded on tapes in either seven- or nine-track patterns. One track—or one bit in each character—serves as a parity bit. Data formatted using the six-bit ASCII code use seven-track tape. The eight-bit EBCDIC code requires nine tracks. If even parity is used, each parity bit is set to 0 or 1 to have an even number of 1 bits for that byte. The parity bit is used by the system to identify transmission errors when data are read or written.

Magnetic tape represents the most compact and least expensive method for data storage. Data can be recorded in *densities* of up to 6,250 bits per inch, or *bpi*, on 2,400-foot reels of tape. Since bits are recorded in parallel, this is equivalent to 6,250 bytes, or characters, per inch. This means that a single, relatively compact reel of tape can hold up to 180 million characters of information. With these capacities, tape is characterized as a moderately high-speed, high-density, low-cost storage medium. Further, the peripheral devices, or *tape drives*, that read and write tapes are also relatively inexpensive and highly reliable.

Data are recorded on magnetic tape in a continuous, linear pattern. This means that one record is recorded after the other along the length of the tape. Magnetic tape supports a sequential file organization. However, in general, tape is not practical for handling direct or indexed organizations.

Figure 16-1 diagrams a typical recording pattern for data on magnetic tape. Fields of data are formed into records. Groups of records, in turn, are formed into identifiable files.

Magnetic Disk Devices Media

In disk drives, data are recorded serially—bit by bit—in circular tracks around the hub of a flat, round disk. Disks are coated magnetically, so

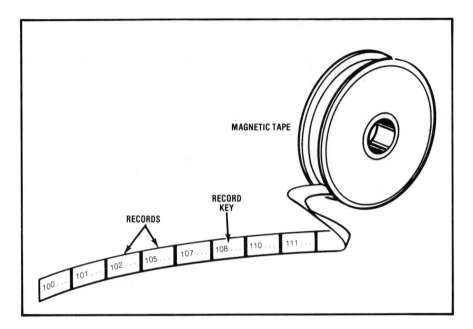

Figure 16-1. Recording format for records on magnetic tape.

that recording can be done by read/write heads similar to those used on tape drives. On some magnetic disk handling devices, there is a separate read/write head for each track of data. On others, heads move on access arms to positions above the tracks to be recorded or read. The disks rotate beneath the read/write heads. In general, access time is determined by three factors: the speed at which disks are rotated, the travel time of the access arm, and the rate at which data are transferred between the disk drive and the computer. On some units, disks are removable. On others disks are fixed. A typical recording pattern for disk files is illustrated in Chapter 13.

In some applications, data records may be written in sequence according to key order on disk surfaces. If this is done, a sequence is followed from track to track in ascending order according to track number.

Disk files can also store and access data on a direct, or random, basis. Nearly all applications requiring direct storage and processing use disk files. Under direct access, data records can be located at any point on a disk surface, or on any surface within a set of disks, or *disk pack.* Placement of, and access to, randomly stored records is through control of record keys. Several different methods are applied by disk system software for automatic access to randomly stored records. These are covered briefly in the discussion that follows.

Both disk and tape present the opportunity for high-density storage. Record access is faster with disk. But tape can be significantly less expensive. The critical difference, however, is in the ability of disk files to support direct access. As a result, use of tape files tends to be limited to archival, backup, log, and some large batch transaction files.

Figure 16-2 diagrams typical sequential and direct recording patterns for disk files.

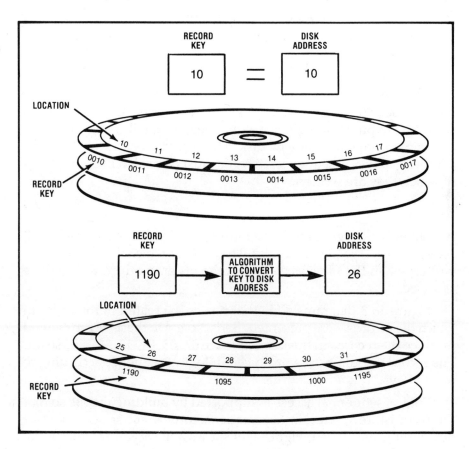

Figure 16-2. Recording patterns for files on disk packs.

The choice of file organization and access method is governed, to a large extent, by the types of devices available. For example, sequential organization can be used with both magnetic tape and magnetic disk. Direct and indexed-sequential organization, however, are limited to disk-based systems.

The sections that follow provide additional information on the file organizations that are commonly available. Further, these presentations describe the relationships among organization methods and device types, providing sufficient information for an understanding of the trade-off decisions involved in choices of file equipment and media.

SEQUENTIAL FILE ORGANIZATION

Planning for and specifying a sequential file organization scheme involves factors of data organization, access methods, and maintenance considerations.

Organization

As described above, sequential files contain records that are organized according to physical sequence alone. Sequential files may be stored on magnetic tape or magnetic disk. The records are written one after another in physical sequence. Records must be read in the same order in which they are written.

Access

A sequential file organization supports either physical sequential (serial) access or logical sequential access. The order in which the records were written when the file was created is the order in which they will be accessed.

Figure 16-3 diagrams a file that has been created in the order in which the records were presented. Serial access to these records would produce the records in the key sequence 07, 03, 01, 12, 10, and so on. The records would not be produced in logical sequence according to record keys.

Logical sequential access is supported by building the file so that the records are written in key sequence order, either ascending or descending, as desired. Figure 16-4 shows a file organized for logical sequential access.

499

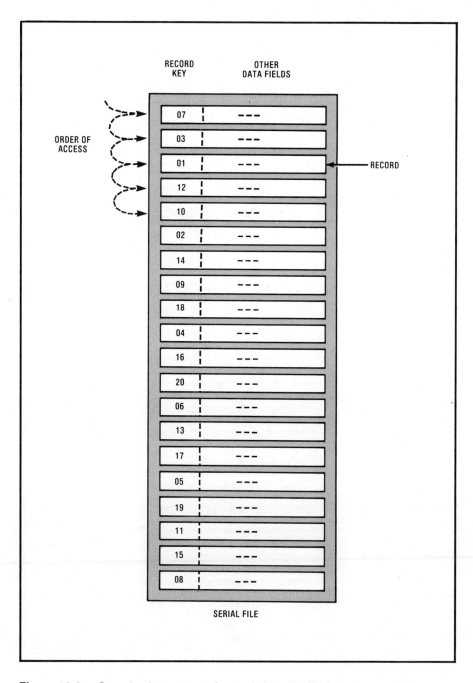

Figure 16-3. Organization pattern of records in serial file for sequential access.

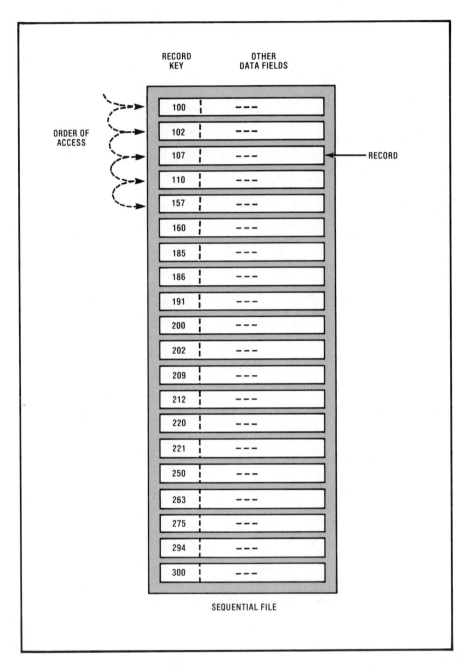

Figure 16-4. Organization pattern of records in sequential file for logical sequential access.

Some processing applications use both serial and sequential files. A master file, for example, is maintained in key sequence. As transactions are captured, they are written to a serial file in the chronological order in which they occur. Prior to posting these transactions to the master file, the serial file is sorted on the record key and a sequential transaction file is created. Since this file is sorted to match the master file sequence, posting of transactions then takes place by matching the transaction and master records on a single pass through the files.

Maintenance

Any time a sequential file is updated, an entirely new file is created. Additions, changes, and deletions are organized in record key sequence in a transaction file. This file is then processed against the original master file. The updating program matches keys between the two files; adds, changes, or deletes the appropriate records; and builds a new sequential master file reflecting the updates. The old master file and the transaction file are saved for use in recreating the new file if it is destroyed.

DIRECT FILE ORGANIZATION

In direct file organization, the location, or address, of a record in the file is often expressed in terms of its position relative to the first record in the file. Although there is a relationship between the record keys and the positions of the records in the file, there is no requirement that these relative addresses correspond with the logical order of keys. When this type of relative addressing is used, direct file organization is also known as *relative file organization*.

Direct files must be maintained on magnetic disk. This is because direct files take advantage of the direct access capabilities of disk drives. While it is possible to process the file serially, in the physical order in which records appear on the device, the file normally is processed directly, without the need to search serially from the beginning to the end. Once the system is provided with a record key, the relative address of the record can be derived and access can be direct.

Organization in Which Key Equals Address

In some cases, it is possible to use the record key itself as the relative address. As an illustration, consider a small file in which the keys of records have been assigned in sequence from 01 through 20. In this instance, each key can be used as the address of the corresponding record. That is, record 01 would appear first in the file, record 02 would appear second, and so on through record 20, which would appear in the twentieth position.

Figure 16-5 illustrates this file organization method. Notice that, if there are missing or unassigned record keys within the sequence, corresponding positions within the file are unused. This is because the records are not written in simple physical sequence, one after another. Instead, the records are assigned to locations in the file area that correspond with their key values.

If the system is provided with a record key, the key can be used as the address for locating the record in the file. Through direct access techniques available to disk files, the record can be accessed directly from the file without the need for a serial search through the file.

Organization in Which Key Does Not Equal Address

In most cases, there will not be a direct correspondence between the record key and the location of the record in the file. Suppose, for example, that the keys range from 1000 to 9999 and that there are large gaps in the key values, such as 1000, 1025, 1050, 1075, and so on. If these keys were used as addresses, there would be large amounts of unused space on the disk. Record locations 0001 through 0999 would be unused. Positions 1001 to 1024 would also be unused, as would positions 1026 through 1049, and so on. Most of the disk space reserved for the file would be empty, wasted.

In cases such as these, in which it is not practical to use the key itself as a record address, a hashing function is used to equate the record key to a corresponding storage position. These hashing functions, or randomizing algorithms, perform a mathematical calculation on the key to convert it to a relative address.

The procedure for calculating addresses is:

1. Determine the number of addresses required to hold all current records in the file.
2. Determine the number of additional addresses needed to handle future file expansion. Usually, about 20 percent additional space over the estimated future size of the file is used.

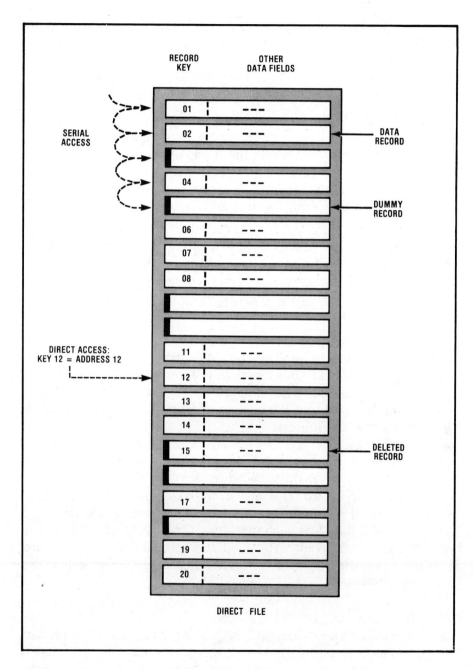

Figure 16-5. Organization pattern of records under direct, or relative, organization method.

3. Choose a hashing function that converts the keys to addresses. This function is then built into the programs that create and access the file.

Several different methods are available for converting record keys to relative addresses. The following algorithm is representative.

Assume a file of 15 records with keys ranging from 1000 to 9999. If it is determined that growth in file size is unlikely, an additional 20 percent of space is added, providing for a total of about 20 storage locations. Thus, each record key should be convertible into a relative address within the range of 1 through 20.

If a record key is divided by a number close to, but not exceeding, the total number of required addresses, the remainder of the division operation plus 1 will be within the range of relative addresses, regardless of the size or range of key values. Commonly, a *prime number*—one that is evenly divisible only by itself and the value 1—is used as the divisor.

To illustrate, assume a record key of 1151. To calculate its relative address, the key value would be divided by the prime number 19—the largest prime number that is less than the total number of addresses required for the file (20). The remainder is 11. The value of 1 is added to the remainder to derive the relative address 12. This hashing function is illustrated in Figure 16-6.

A problem that arises in creating direct files is that two or more record keys may hash to the same address. When this happens a *collision* is said to occur. To illustrate, in the algorithm example above, records 2259 and 9745 both have a calculated address of 18. There are several ways of handling such *synonyms*. One method is to write the synonym in the next available position. In Figure 16-6, therefore, record 2259 appears in the eighteenth position and record 9745 appears in the nineteenth position, the next unused address.

Access

Records in a direct file can be accessed serially or directly. The file can be read from the first through the last record, according to the positions of the records in the file. For situations in which the keys equate directly with the addresses, the records are provided in logical sequence as well.

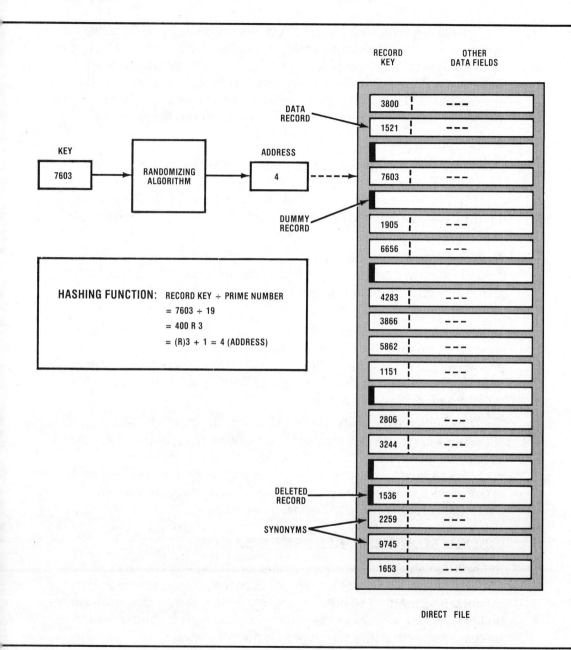

Figure 16-6. Organization pattern of records in a direct file in random order, requiring execution of an algorithm to determine record address.

The main reason for having a direct file, however, is to take advantage of the direct access capabilities of the disk device. The user provides the system with record keys in any order. The system then uses the keys as addresses, or converts them to addresses, and accesses the records directly from these disk locations. Direct files allow the fastest method of accessing file records individually, in random sequence.

Maintenance

Direct files also make it convenient to add to, change, or delete records from a file. When a new record is added, the key is converted to an address and the record is written at that location. If the location is already filled by a synonym record, the new record is written in the next available location.

Records in a direct file are updated "in place." That is, the record is accessed from the disk, its fields are changed, and it is written back to the same relative location in the file. The updated record replaces the old record.

When records are deleted from a direct file, they are not physically removed from the disk. Instead, a special value is written into the first position of the record to indicate that it should be ignored during processing. The address of this "dummy" record then becomes available for adding a new record to the file.

Direct files are normally used for situations in which the overall size of the file will remain fairly stable. The reason is that, as disk space for a file begins to fill up, collisions become more likely. The extra 20 percent of file space was added at the beginning to reduce the likelihood of collisions. If a direct file becomes too full, it is necessary to rebuild the entire file, allocating additional free space.

INDEXED-SEQUENTIAL FILE ORGANIZATION

Indexed-sequential files are appropriate for applications in which there is a need for both logical sequential access and direct access. This organization method maintains records in key sequences and also builds reference indexes to access individual records in random order. Indexed-sequential files are stored on magnetic disk only.

Organization

When the file is created, records are loaded onto disk, in order, by record key. As in the case of sequential files, the records are written in a physical order that matches the logical order of the keys. The disk area that holds this file is called the *data area*. As shown in Figure 16-7, this data area can be visualized as consisting of blocks of records.

An *index area* is established for associating record keys with locations of records in the file. There is an index entry for each block of records in the data area. The entry contains the value of the highest record key in the block and the address of the block. The index area is also diagrammed in Figure 16-7.

Within an indexed-sequential file organization, it is necessary to maintain the sequential order of records in the data area as new records are added. This record order is necessary for continuing support of sequential access capabilities. In practice, there are two basic methods by which record sequences are maintained. One is to establish an overflow area. The second is to distribute free space throughout the file when it is established and to allocate this space as records are added. Each of these methods is covered briefly in the discussions that follow.

Use of overflow for record additions.   Under this method, illustrated in Figure 16-8, the data area—called the *prime data area*—is filled completely when the file is built. A block of records typically corresponds with a disk track.

In addition to this prime data area, an *overflow area* is also defined. This area contains no records initially, but is reserved as space for subsequent addition of records to the file. Use of this area is explained in the section on maintenance, below. Basically, when a record must be added to a track, it is inserted in sequence and the last record on the track is placed in the overflow area—but is associated with its original track.

To support the overflow concept, an additional index is needed. It is necessary to maintain both a track and an overflow index for each disk track in the file. The track index contains the value of the highest record key on the track and the address of the track. The overflow entry contains the value of the highest key appearing in the overflow area associated with the track. When the file is created, the track and overflow entries are the same, since no records appear in the overflow area.

Depending upon the size of the file, there may be other levels of indexes. For a file that spans several disk *cylinders* (the collection of corresponding tracks on each recording surface within a disk pack), there

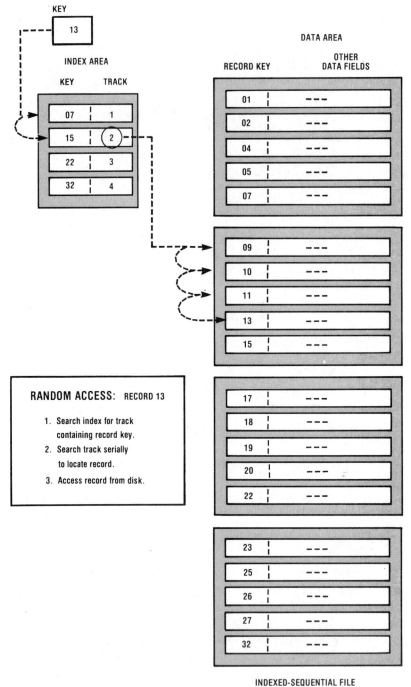

Figure 16-7. Organization pattern of records in an indexed-sequential file for either direct or sequential access and processing.

508

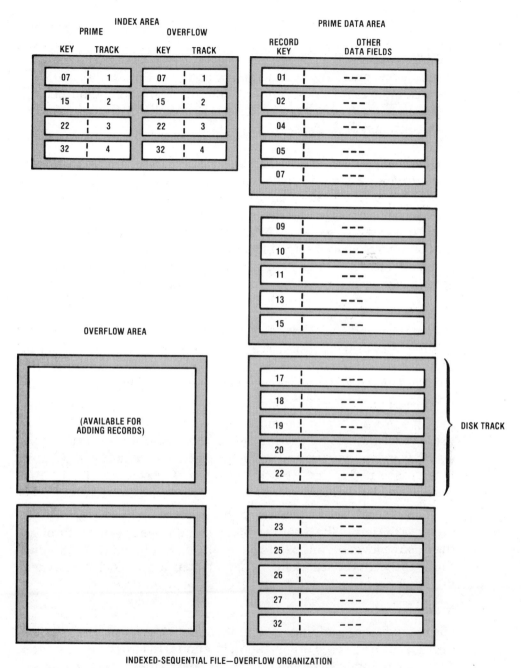

INDEXED-SEQUENTIAL FILE—OVERFLOW ORGANIZATION

Figure 16-8. Organization pattern of records in an indexed-sequential file under the free-space approach.

509

are *cylinder indexes* that give the highest record key associated with each particular cylinder. The cylinder index also gives the address of the set of track indexes for that cylinder. If the file spans a large number of cylinders, a *master index* can be defined to identify the largest keys on each collection of cylinders.

Use of free space for record additions.   Under this method, illustrated in Figure 16-9, a certain percentage of each block of records in the data area is left as free space when the file is built. In addition, a certain number of blocks is left totally free. Then, when a record is added, it may be inserted in sequence in its proper block through use of a portion of the free space in that block. The index area can remain as it is when established initially. For large files, higher-level indexes may be established, as is done in the overflow example described above.

Access

Records in an indexed-sequential file can be accessed either sequentially or directly. For sequential access, the first index record is read to establish the address of the first block of records. The records in this block are then read in sequence. These steps are repeated for each index record in the index area.

This process is slightly more complex when an overflow area is used. After processing each record in the block, the corresponding overflow index gives the address of the first record in the overflow area that is associated with the block. The overflow records are linked and must be read individually.

Direct access is based on use of the indexes. In this case, the user provides the key of the record of interest. The system searches through the existing levels of indexes to locate the block of records containing the record with the search key. Then, the particular block is searched in sequential order to locate and access the desired record.

Maintenance

File maintenance—adding, changing, or deleting records—varies for overflow or free space organization methods. In either case, records added to an indexed-sequential file are maintained in key sequence relative to the block in which they are written. Therefore, whenever a record is inserted into a block, all following records are shifted forward to make room for the insertion.

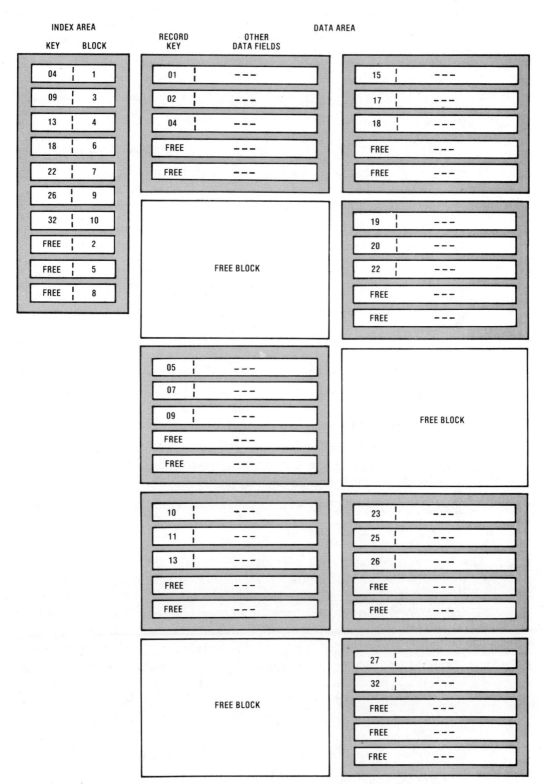

Figure 16-9. Organization pattern of records in an indexed-sequential file under the overflow approach.

When an overflow type of organization is used, the last record on the track is "bumped" into the overflow area. Records that have been displaced to the overflow area are written in the sequence in which they were moved off their original tracks. Address *pointers* within each overflow record are used to *chain* them together in the proper key sequence. Figure 16-10 shows the effects of adding records to an indexed-sequential file using overflow organization.

When a free space type of organization is used, the existing records are shifted forward into the free space to make room for the new records. When there is no longer any free space available in the block, half of the records are first moved to one of the free blocks. This replaces one full block with two blocks that are only half full. The insertion is made in the appropriate new block. The creation of the new block requires the addition of a corresponding index, as shown in Figure 16-11.

When a record is to be deleted from a file with an overflow type of organization, it is marked, or flagged, with a special code. The method is similar to the technique applied for direct files. During subsequent access operations, the system ignores records with these codes, effectively deleting them but not physically removing them from the file.

In the case of a free space type of organization, records following the record to be deleted are shifted backward, physically deleting the record and increasing the free space.

Updating of records occurs in place. The record is read into the computer, fields are changed, and the record is rewritten to the file in the same location.

Over time, additions and deletions to a file with an overflow type of organization create inefficiencies. The occurrence of many records in the overflow area degrades access time because the system has to follow lengthy pointer chains to locate particular records. Also, records marked for deletion take up space that cannot be used for new records, increasing even more the number of records that must be written to the overflow area. Therefore, periodically, indexed-sequential files must be rebuilt. This procedure creates a new file within which overflow records are integrated back into the prime data area and records marked for deletion are dropped from the file.

The deterioration of files with a free space type of organization is less severe. However, the maintenance of the index area is more complex.

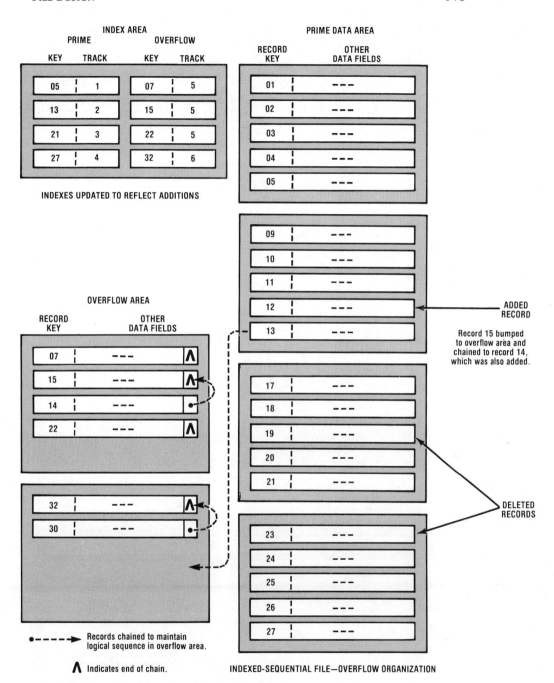

Figure 16-10. Diagram showing the effect of record additions upon an indexed-sequential file with an overflow organization approach.

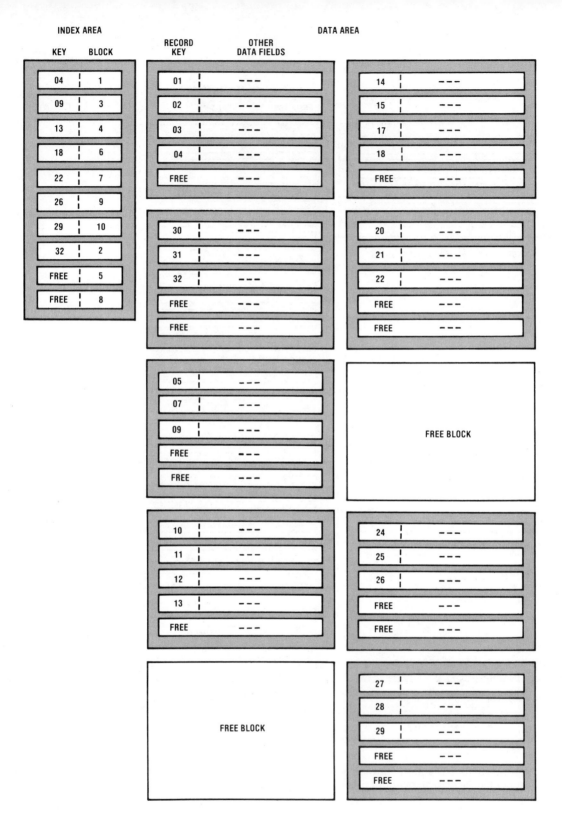

Figure 16-11. Diagram showing the effect of record additions upon an indexed-sequential file with a free-space organization approach.

Indexed-sequential organization provides a compromise to either sequential or direct organization. The indexed-sequential approach makes possible a slightly slower method of sequential access than sequential file organization. It also results in slower direct access than direct organization because of the index searching. However, indexed-sequential files do allow the flexibility of either access technique within the same organization method.

FILE DESIGN TRADE-OFFS

The goal in designing files is to minimize such factors as:

- Data storage costs
- File maintenance costs
- Data processing costs
- Time to access records.

These items are closely interrelated. Minimizing one factor often serves to maximize another. For example, a sequential file organization has the least storage overhead. However, if the particular master file is large and must be updated twice a day with relatively few transactions, file maintenance costs will be unreasonably high.

File design, then, involves some classic trade-offs. There are several available options—sequential, direct, and indexed-sequential organizations—each with strengths and weaknesses. The challenge is to select the option that maximizes the strengths and minimizes the weaknesses for the particular application under consideration. To do this, it is necessary to understand the key characteristics of the application and how they affect the file organization options. These characteristics include:

- Processing method
- Required response time
- Activity rate of the application
- Volatility
- Backup requirements
- File device capacity.

Processing Methods

In general, applications are processed either on a batch or on an interactive basis. Batch processing often involves the accumulation of an entire transaction file that is input as a unit and processed against a master file. In most cases, the most efficient organization method for the files will be sequential. For sequential processing, both the transaction and master files would be in the same order. Matching of the records would be rapid and efficient.

A typical batch application is payroll. Employee time records, which make up the transaction file, may be sorted in employee number sequence. The master file is in the same order. Since almost all employees are paid every pay period, sequential file organization would be best for this batch application.

On the other hand, an interactive application such as airline reservations would require access to information on individual flights on a direct basis. There would be no way to anticipate the order of transactions or to organize transactions so as to correspond with the organization of the file. With this lack of correspondence between transactions and master files, a direct file organization using disk devices is clearly the best answer.

In some instances, application requirements might dictate a mixture of processing methods. Transactions might be processed sequentially against an indexed-sequential file. However, it may also be necessary to support an on-line reference application using the same file. Such a mixture of processing methods is typical of many applications. In a demand deposit system for a bank, for example, checks are sorted by account number key and used for sequential updating of an indexed-sequential master account file. This same file can also be referenced directly, at random, by bank officers and tellers who need status information.

As a general rule, the processing method chosen will dictate the type of file organization and access method that should be chosen. The following criteria present design *heuristics*, or rules of thumb, for evaluating the method that initially seems appropriate for the use.

Response Time

Consideration of *response time* applies to direct access applications only. The volume of inquiries and the response time required must be taken into account in determining what equipment and what organizational approach to use.

For example, an airline reservation system represents a high-volume application in which there is a real, monetary value associated with rapid response time. A direct file organization with direct access provides the fastest method of getting at needed records. By contrast, if an indexed-sequential file were used for airline reservations, access time could be at least twice that for a direct file. This extra time under the indexed-sequential approach is needed because the computer must perform an extensive search of an index before it can even initiate a record access operation.

Activity Rate

The *activity rate* of an application refers to the frequency with which records are accessed by the application. For example, a payroll application would have a high activity rate, or *hit rate*, because most records are processed on every processing run. By comparison, checking account updating applications would have a lower hit rate because only a relatively small percentage of account holders write checks on any given day.

Normally, sequential processing and access methods are appropriate when hit rates are high because sequential processing represents the fastest method for accessing each record in a file. By contrast, occasional reference to records within a file would make on-line, direct access more efficient.

Volatility

The *volatility*, or rate of change and expansion, of master files should be taken into account in determining the organization to be used. If additions to, and deletions from, files are to be relatively great, it is often best to use a sequential organization plan. An excellent example can be seen in billing programs for transient classified advertising in newspapers. These advertisements are called in by telephone. Usually a classified ad runs for a few days and then is dropped. Its customers are one-time or occasional users. When a bill is paid, the customer name is dropped from the accounts receivable file. Thus, there are large volumes of additions to, and deletions from, the file every day. If such a file were organized for direct access, the entire file would have to be restructured almost every day. Under sequential processing, structuring is routine. That is, a sequential file is rewritten every time it is processed. Thus, additions or deletions present no problem; sequential files are volatile by nature.

Special user requirements, of course, can have an overriding effect on the selection of file organization method. To illustrate, highly volatile files are used by law enforcement agencies to record stolen cars or wanted persons. Content of these files changes rapidly. If batch processing were possible, this application would lend itself well to sequential files. However, on-line reference is a must. Therefore, the application itself dictates a direct access capability. Thus, even though greater processing efficiency might be attainable with sequential files, it is virtually necessary to use an indexed-sequential or direct file organization.

Backup Requirements

Every system needs backup and recovery procedures. If master files are destroyed or if an error occurs during update processing, there must be some method for restoring the files to their proper state. Backup files provide a starting point. Recovery procedures specify a plan for restoring the files.

Sequential files have an advantage in that such files automatically create backup files, because a new file is written during each update processing run. Thus, the input file and the transaction file become backup files for each newly created file.

If direct access files are used, special backup procedures must be developed. The protection is needed because master records are updated in place. Transactions are usually logged as they occur, but transaction records are only valuable as related to a current version of the master file. Master records may be written to an update log file before and after updating, providing a basis for file restoration if something goes wrong during the update processing. It is also good practice to make a backup copy of the master file before a direct update is performed.

File Device Capacity

While not a characteristic of the application itself, the proposed file organization should be reviewed to be sure that the file devices available can handle the files to be created. For example, there might be enough room on a disk file to handle a sequential file application. However, it might turn out that there isn't enough room to accommodate the space overhead of a direct or indexed-sequential file. Additional storage capacity—and corresponding additional cost—may be necessary. In general, one of the checkpoints that should be covered is to make sure that the storage devices to be used can accommodate the files to be created.

CASE SCENARIO

The Central City Water Billing System is a fairly straightforward operation, and the files to support it are not very complex. The file structure was developed in a somewhat intuitive manner, grouping together those data elements that most often tend to be processed together. An analysis of the volume and frequency of the system inputs and outputs suggests an overall file structure. This analysis is contained in Figure 16-12. Diagram 0 for the new system is included here in Figure 16-13 for ease of reference.

It is clear from the frequency and volume analysis that there are three key outputs (METER-READING-BOOK, BILL, ACCT-HIST) and two key inputs (READING, PAYMENT) that should influence most heavily the definition of the master files for the system.

The resulting master files, together with the file organization method selected, are shown in Figure 16-14. Other approaches to designing the database are certainly possible. Some of the questions relating to this particular arrangement are discussed below.

Should the data in the BILLING-TRANSACTION file be included in the CUSTOMER-MASTER file? Note that each bill contains eight fields. Saving eight bills for each customer amounts to 64 fields, or about 250 extra bytes. If these data were added to the CUSTOMER-MASTER file, each record would be lengthened significantly. The BILLING-TRANSACTION data are used only for the account history query, while the CUSTOMER-MASTER data are used by three other major processes that do not require billing information. Including billing data in CUSTOMER-MASTER might significantly degrade the performance of these three processes.

A similar question could be raised concerning the data on meter readings. Why are the reading transactions included in CUSTOMER-MASTER? Should the readings be split off in a separate file?

OUTPUT	MEDIUM	VOLUME	FREQUENCY
1. METER-READING-BOOK	PRINTED	HIGH	BIWEEKLY
2. BILL	PRINTED	HIGH	BIWEEKLY
3. ACCT-HIST	ON-LINE QUERY	MED	30 PER DAY AVG
4. SPEC-READING-ORDER	MANUAL	LOW	2 PER DAY AVG
5. ACCTS-NOT-BILLED	PRINTED	LOW	BIWEEKLY
6. CASH&ADJ-JOURNAL	PRINTED	MED	WEEKLY
7. WATER-USAGE-SUMMARY	PRINTED	LOW	ON DEMAND
8. SEWER-USAGE-SUMMARY	PRINTED	LOW	ON DEMAND
9. FINANCIAL-STMT	PRINTED	LOW	MONTHLY
10. DEPOSIT	MANUAL	LOW	DAILY

INPUT	INPUT METHOD	VOLUME	FREQUENCY
1. READING	KEYPUNCH and ON-LINE	HIGH	BIWEEKLY
2. PAYMENT	KEYPUNCH and ON-LINE	HIGH	DAILY
3. SPEC-READ-REQ	MANUAL	LOW	2 PER DAY AVG
4. ACCT-CHANGE	ON-LINE	LOW	3 PER WEEK AVG
5. READ-ADJUSTMENT	ON-LINE	LOW	5 PER MONTH AVG
6. CASH-ADJUSTMENT	ON-LINE	LOW	5 PER MONTH AVG
7. WATER-RATES	ON-LINE	LOW	VERY INFREQUENT
8. SEWER-RATES	ON-LINE	LOW	VERY INFREQUENT
9. UNCOLLECTABLES	MANUAL	LOW	VERY INFREQUENT
10. DEPOSIT-CONFIRM	MANUAL	LOW	DAILY

Figure 16-12.   Analysis of outputs and inputs of Central City water billing system.

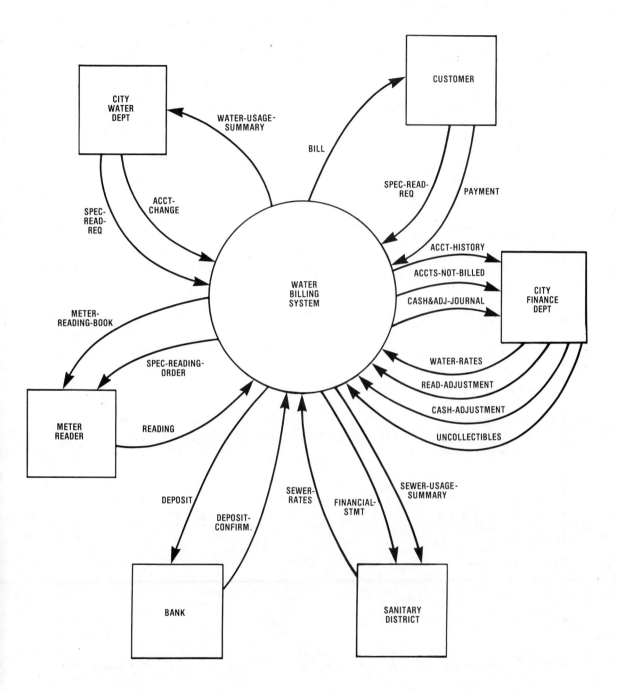

Figure 16-13. Context diagram of the new Central City water billing system—repeated here for ease of reference.

ACCOUNT-JOURNAL (SEQUENTIAL)

$\begin{Bmatrix} \textbf{Acct-Num} \\ + \text{ User-Class} \\ + \text{ Transaction} \end{Bmatrix}$ where   TRANS =   Date

each trans   + Trans-Type

          + Amount

BILLING-SUMMARY (SEQUENTIAL)

$_4\begin{Bmatrix} \textbf{User-Class} \\ + \text{ Water-Consumption} \\ + \text{ Sewer-Usage} \\ + \text{ Water-Amt-Billed} \\ + \text{ Sewer-Amt-Billed} \end{Bmatrix}$ where   USER-CLASS = $\begin{bmatrix} \text{Residential} \\ \text{Commercial} \\ \text{Industrial} \\ \text{Institutional} \end{bmatrix}$

BILLING-TRANSACTIONS (DIRECT)

Acct-Num   BILL-DETAIL =   Bill-Date

+ User-Class   where   + Bill-Water

$+_8\{$ Bill-Detail $\}$ + Bill-San-Dist

                                   + Bill-Trash-Coll

                                   + Arrears-Water

                                   + Arrears-San-Dist

                                   + Arrears-Trash-Coll

all accts   + Penalty

CUSTOMER-MASTER (INDEXES)

$\begin{Bmatrix} \textbf{Acct-Num} \\ + \text{ User-Class} \\ + \text{ Cust-Name} \\ + \text{ Service-Addr} \\ + \text{ Billing-Addr} \\ + \text{ Meter-Read-Seq-Num} \\ + \text{ Meter-Location} \\ + \text{ (Meter-Reader-Msg)} \\ + \text{ Curr-Bal} \\ +_6\{\text{Read-Trans}\} \end{Bmatrix}$

CURR-BAL =   Cur-Water

          + Cur-San-Dist

          + Cur-Trash-Coll

          + Arrears-Water

where   + Arrears-San-Dist

          + Arrears-Trash-Coll

          + Penalty

READ-TRANS =   Date

all accts   + Read-Type

          + Reading-Value

READ-TYPE = $\begin{bmatrix} \text{Actual} \\ \text{Estimated} \\ \text{Self-Read} \end{bmatrix}$

Figure 16-14. Definitions for the master files and access methods for the new Central City water billing system.

522

Note that the BILLING-SUMMARY file contains only four records—each holding the water and sanitary district totals by user class. This file is used to prepare the periodic usage summaries. Is it necessary? No. All of the necessary data is in the BILLING-TRANSACTION file. On the other hand, by summarizing total usage and amount billed by user class each time bills are produced, and by using these subtotals to update the BILLING-SUMMARY file, year-to-date summary reports can be produced quickly and easily.

The final question to be considered here concerns the organization of the BILLING-TRANSACTION file. Should there be one long record for each individual account, as specified? Or should there be a separate record for each bill to each account, perhaps with the key being ACCT-NUM + BILL-DATE. The main advantage of the first option is faster access of billing information for the account history on-line query—the application for which the file was created. The update of the file probably performs better under the first option also. In this case, the overhead consists of rolling the bill occurrences forward each time a new bill is added—a time consuming process. Under the second option, each new billing record would have to be inserted in the file—maintaining the logical order required for the query process. This latter option is probably more time consuming.

Summary

A key systems design decision deals with where data will be stored and how those data will be accessed. Options to be considered include: access method, organization approach, equipment selection, and physical layout of the files on storage media.

Use of files is based upon content of one or more of the fields within a file. These access-control fields are known as record keys. In systems design, trade-offs must be considered for the file structures, devices, and methods available. Any given application may require any or all of the following types of files: master, transaction, reference, archival, backup, and transaction log.

The use of data and the method of data access are closely related within application design. Three broad options are available for accessing data stored within computer systems: physical sequential (serial), logical sequential, and direct.

File organization methods are based upon hardware, software, data content considerations, and access method. Organization alternatives include: sequential, direct, and indexed-sequential.

The two most commonly used kinds of file devices handle magnetic tape and magnetic disks. As part of the planning for the design of a new system, the analyst should find out what secondary storage devices are available in the computer installation to be used. If additional capacities are needed, an equipment study can be initiated.

Methods for organizing, accessing, and maintaining sequential, direct, and indexed-sequential files are reviewed. The choice of file organization method to be used in a given application is based upon these criteria: processing method, required access speed, activity rate of the application, anticipated growth, backup requirements, and file device capacity.

Key Terms

1. file
2. secondary storage device
3. key
4. pointer
5. master file
6. transaction file
7. reference file
8. archival file
9. backup file
10. transaction log file
11. journal
12. serial access
13. physical sequential access
14. logical sequential access
15. direct access
16. serial file
17. sequential file
18. direct file
19. relative file
20. indexed-sequential file
21. table
22. database
23. database management
24. relational value
25. query
26. channel
27. track
28. density
29. bits per inch (bpi)
30. tape drive
31. disk pack
32. relative position
33. relative file organization
34. absolute position
35. algorithm
36. randomizing routine
37. remainder
38. prime number
39. collision
40. synonym
41. data area
42. index area
43. prime data area
44. overflow
45. cylinder
46. cylinder index
47. master index
48. chain
49. heuristic
50. response time
51. activity rate
52. hit rate
53. volatility

Review/Discussion Questions

1. What types of file organization methods are available?
2. What options exist for data access and what are the differences among these access methods?
3. What types of files should be stored on magnetic tape? On disk devices?
4. What different techniques are used to relate keys to records?
5. What are the physical features of magnetic tape devices?
6. What trade-offs are associated with the use of magnetic tape?
7. What are the physical features of disk devices?
8. What trade-offs are associated with the use of disk devices?
9. How does file organization relate to the type of secondary storage device used?
10. What criteria should be used in making a choice of file organization method?
11. How is the choice of secondary storage devices usually made?

Practice Assignment

For each of the following file requirements, determine an appropriate file organization method. Provide a justification for your recommendations.

1. An employee payroll file will be accessed once a week to calculate the company's payroll and to issue paychecks. Records in this file contain employee identification, pay rate, and withholding information. This is a master file against which a transaction file containing data from weekly time cards is processed. The file will be accessed in order by employee number. Between 90 and 95 percent of all records will be processed.

2. An airline reservation file contains passenger flight information used in booking passengers and issuing tickets. It is keyed by the flight numbers of the airline. Rapid access to this file is important so that customers can receive flight information while they wait at reservation counters or on the telephone. Bookings take place immediately. Thus, the flight records are updated as soon as passengers ask for reservations.

3. An inventory file contains product information about all merchandise held in stock. Each record contains product descriptions, prices, quantities on hand, and reorder points. Whenever an item of merchandise is withdrawn from stock or stock is replaced, the record is updated to maintain a current record of product availability. Also, periodic inventory reports are prepared for management. These list, in sequence by product number, the quantities of merchandise in inventory. Also, customer inquiries about the availability of stock require that the product records be accessible immediately through on-line terminals.

4. A file of federal withholding tax tables is used for determining withholding amounts during payroll processing. This file is loaded into program tables when the payroll

program is run. The program then searches the in-memory tables to locate withholding amounts. No maintenance or updating is required of this file. It is a reference file that is built one time, at the beginning of the year.

5. A transaction log file is written as part of the on-line updating procedure for master file maintenance. Additions, changes, and deletions applied against a customer master file are processed interactively, through on-line terminals. These transactions are recorded in a log file and include the date on which the change took place, an identification of the master record that was affected, and a notation about the type of maintenance activity and the field change that was completed. This journalizing technique provides an audit trail through which the transaction can be traced from its point of origin through its appearance in the master file.

CONTROL AND RELIABILITY DESIGN 17

LEARNING OBJECTIVES

After completing the reading and other learning assignments in this chapter, you should be able to:

- ☐ Describe the role of controls in assuring the accuracy, integrity, security, and confidentiality of a system.

- ☐ Identify the points at which controls must be applied throughout the operation of the system.

- ☐ Give types of controls available and techniques used to implement these controls.

- ☐ Describe tests that may be applied during processing to assure the accuracy and validity of data.

- ☐ Define audit trail and tell how auditability of systems can be enhanced.

- ☐ Describe operational procedures that reinforce controls, including documentation and separation of duties.

THE NEED FOR CONTROLS

Controls are functions—applied either by machines or by people—designed to build the needed level of quality into a computer information system. Controls provide assurance that standards of completeness and accuracy are enforced for each individual record or group of business transactions. Thus, controls are needed for quality assurance. Specific needs met by controls include:

- *Accuracy* means that data entered into the system are exactly as the data should be. A commonly used expression describing the need for accuracy is: "Garbage in, garbage out." This means simply that the accuracy of input data controls the quality of the entire system. Thus, accuracy control must be established at input—and must be applied as needed to assure quality of results delivered. In this sense, accuracy means that data entered into the system are exactly the same as those presented in source transactions or on source documents.

- The term *integrity* describes controls to assure that specified processing is applied only to the proper, authorized files. In the course of running applications, files are altered or superseded. Integrity controls assure that the data files processed represent the actual, current status or condition. Integrity controls are also applied to assure that, if any files are inadvertently destroyed, the materials and mechanisms will exist to reconstruct those files and to recover processing capabilities. Integrity also implies the use of security measures to assure that only authorized transactions will be admitted into a system for processing.

- *Confidentiality* controls are designed to protect the rights of privacy of persons or organizations described by, or represented in, data records. Many computer files contain personal or private data about individuals or groups. For example, data such as medical histories or purchasing and credit information about individuals should be available only to authorized users or application systems.

TYPES OF CONTROLS

If a system is to produce accurate, reliable results, controls must be applied at every stage of system operation—including input, processing, output, and file storage. Controls must protect against unauthorized acts and, more frequently, against errors or omissions by persons who operate or use computer information systems. Types of controls that should be considered in the design of computer information systems include:

- Access controls
- Source document controls
- Data entry controls
- Processing controls
- Output controls
- File controls
- Documentation controls
- Organizational controls.

Access Controls

Access controls are designed to limit possession of data resources to authorized persons only. Separate measures are needed to control physical access to computer sites and to limit electronic access to computer systems.

Facilities security is a specialized area about which few systems analysts are consulted. Data access control and security tend to be functions of database management software, communications monitors, and specialized system software. Access control is not normally designed into individual application systems. However, several access controls should be considered during the design of an application system. These include:

- *Unique transaction codes* permit data access security to be implemented at the individual transaction level. For example, in the Central City water billing system, if the display transaction to apply special readings was also used for reading adjustments, there would be no way to restrict (control) the application of special readings to one person or group of persons and the reading adjustments to another.

- *Use of nondisplay fields* should be considered when especially sensitive data are being input from a terminal. Although this type of control is effective only for low volumes, fields requiring this degree of confidentiality should be identified.

- *Restricted functions* that allow select individuals, such as supervisors or auditors, to perform control or audit functions should be identified.

- *Separation of duties* should be planned. If application programs are to contain application-specific authentication and/or verification routines, these requirements should be identified so that allowances can be made from a cost, time, and work-assignment standpoint. Sensitive routines should be designed and programmed in pieces by different people and then joined to make up the whole.

Source Document Control

Before any data can enter a system, an authorization measure should be required. Authorization is usually given in the form of initials or signatures on source documents. Operating controls should assure that these authorizations are applied before data are cleared for input.

Use of prenumbered source documents is an additional, straightforward control procedure. Prenumbering has the effect of controlling physical access to source documents, since all numbered source documents can be accounted for by reference to some type of master list. Transactions whose document numbers fall out of anticipated ranges may be rejected by the system. This control helps assure that source documents are genuine.

Data Entry Controls

Separate types of *data entry controls* are used in batch processing and on-line systems.

For batch systems, a major control technique lies in establishing *control totals* to be carried forward into input and processing functions. These control totals are designed to assure keyboarding accuracy and completeness of records. One type of control total is a count of the number of documents or records in a batch. Other types of totals are applied to data fields within all records within a batch. Included are *hash totals* and *monetary* or *quantity totals*.

Each of these types of controls is applied by adding the values in numeric fields of input documents and records. For example, in processing a batch of orders, all of the controls described above might be applied. The number of documents in the batch would be counted and recorded on a batch *header record* along with a batch identification number and date. Then, the values of the total amount field for each of the orders would be totaled and recorded as a batch control on the header records.

A hash total is the summation of a numeric field that does not contain quantities or values that are normally added together. For example, the customer numbers on the orders might be totaled. Although this total has no meaning in an information processing sense, it can be used to verify accurate entry of the customer numbers.

When all input data for a batch have been captured, the control totals are checked on an edit run before actual processing can take place. During this edit run, the computer develops totals for each control field as it edits the individual records. These totals are then balanced against those entered from the batch header. Unless all controls balance, further processing cannot take place. Failure to balance may indicate that one of the fields was entered incorrectly. (Of course, an out-of-balance condition may also result because an error was made in computing the original control total.) It is then necessary to compare source documents and the entered data manually to search for the error. The same control may be applied after each processing run within the system as long as the batch is kept intact.

Clearly defined manual procedures are critical to the effective batch processing of input transactions. Since batches must be checked document by document if totals do not agree, batch size is usually limited to about 50 to 100 documents. After transactions are counted and batch totals are calculated, the results are written on a batch ticket that accompanies the documents.

Before sending the batch to the data entry operation, the batch identification number and date are entered in a *transaction log*. The main purpose of this log is to improve the physical control of the batches themselves. If there are large numbers of batches, it is all too easy to misplace a batch or even to enter a batch twice. The log provides a method for tracking the physical location and stage of processing for each of the batches.

For systems using on-line input, the types of controls depend on the design of the processing. Basically, the processing may be either batch or real-time. Under a batch processing design, some editing may be done as the transactions are entered on-line. The transactions are then placed in a file for later processing. The physical batching techniques and control totals discussed above also apply to this type of data entry.

Real-time processing refers to a situation in which each input transaction is released immediately for further processing by the system. This, of course, precludes the use of batch control totals. Rather, any input control must be applied to one document at a time. One technique relies on visual verification by the terminal operator. In the order entry example mentioned earlier, the operator might key the customer number, item numbers, and quantities. The system might then respond by adding the customer name and address and item names. The operator could then verify that the computer-supplied entries correspond to those written on the order form.

In addition to visual verification techniques, analysts and designers usually place an even heavier emphasis on processing controls than they might in a batch environment.

Processing Controls

Processing controls are incorporated within individual application programs. These controls are designed to assure accuracy and completeness of records each time a file is processed.

Batch controls.   One type of processing control involves use of batch controls for master file processing. A *trailer record* at the end of a file contains entries covering the number of records and totals for numeric fields in all records. Each time the file is processed, totals are taken of these fields and compared with the totals on the trailer record. Alterations of the fields during processing are documented in the control record to keep it up to date. This technique is similar to the use of batch controls to verify data entry. In this case, verification of the actual processing is accomplished.

Input controls.   Some processing controls are designed to assure accuracy and completeness of input records. These include batch control totals, exception reports, and edit runs. Batch control totals are described in the discussion on input controls. During processing, totals are developed to balance back to these input batch totals. Unless these totals balance, processing will not go forward. *Exception reports* are special, printed outputs identifying either items that cannot be processed or out-of-balance situations.

Edit runs review input transactions for accuracy and completeness. Editing is done at several levels:

- Syntax
- Single-field value
- Cross field
- Cross record.

Syntax checks on fields within a record include numeric, alphabetic, sign, and completeness tests. This latter test verifies that a mandatory field is not all blanks.

Value tests applied to individual fields include:

- *Range test.* This test checks to be sure that the value of entries in a given field fall between high and low levels established by the program. For example, a payroll program might apply a test to be sure that no one is paid for working more than 80 hours per week.

- *Reasonableness test.* This is related to the range test, except that acceptable values are determined individually for each record. Reasonableness is evaluated with respect to master file data and involves matching content of a field with a given file of alternatives. For example, in the water billing system, a reported reading may be judged reasonable by using that reading and the previous reading to calculate a resulting consumption and then comparing that consumption with an average consumption stored in the master file. If the calculated consumption is within, say, 20 percent of the average consumption, it would be considered reasonable.

- *Category test.* These are range or reasonableness tests applied to nonnumeric data. These tests often involve *table lookup* techniques under which tables are searched to find entries to match input data. A common example is a state code table that can be searched to verify the accuracy of a state field in an input record.

- *Check digits.* This is a validity check. A series of calculations is performed on a numeric key field such as an account number. The results of the calculations upon values in certain positions within the field must equal one of the digits in the field.

After individual fields have been checked for correct syntax and values, cross-checking may be done among fields in the record. The values in two fields may be valid individually. But, taken together, the combination may be invalid. One example is the state and ZIP code combination. A table matching ZIP code ranges and the corresponding states could be checked to verify that the combination is correct. A similar check would apply in an order entry application, matching item number with item characteristics, such as size, color, and so on.

A similar cross-checking principle can be applied across records. Consider again an order entry application in which an order consists of multiple records: one with customer information followed by one for each item ordered. Each of the individual records might be complete. But the total value of goods ordered might exceed the customer's credit limit. A cross-record test could be established to trap this condition.

Communication controls.   A specialized control that helps assure the security and confidentiality of data can be applied during processing through techniques of *encryption*. This means that signals representing data are altered, or encoded, when processing involves transmission over communication lines or networks. When the signals are received, the content is recovered through special decoding devices and the signals are put back in original form. Thus, data are unrecognizable while moving over communication lines or networks. This technique is also known as *signal scrambling*. This type of control will be designed by the technical services staff in the CIS organization. The analyst, however, should be aware of the control and request this service if appropriate.

Audit trails.   Integrity, reliability, and accuracy of data can be assured by building in and applying *audit trail* techniques throughout a system. An audit trail is a series of records that can be used for tracking data through a system from the time a transaction originates to the point at which the data are incorporated into master files. Input logs are, typically, used as key parts of audit trails. In addition, each time data items are altered to a level that causes the data to lose their original identity, backup copies of files are retained for reference. If processing output is questioned or verification is needed, results can be traced backward to the point of the original input.

Output Controls

Outputs are the end products of a computer information system. Therefore, output controls are the final, definitive quality assurance measures that can be applied. It should be considered essential that some measure be incorporated in every system for comparing output report totals with input control totals.

Authorization controls are also critical in the handling of computer outputs. Printed documents or displays should be available only to authorized persons. Output reports with sensitive content should be delivered to authorized persons only. Control systems should require signed receipts.

File Controls

Data files, in effect, are the tools and the means by which a company continues to operate. There have been actual cases in which loss of data files has led to business failures. Therefore, there should be no compromise in establishing and applying controls over the handling and use of data resources.

Physical controls are the responsibility of the computer operations group. These controls include procedures for labeling and storing files, as well as releasing file media for processing. The analyst must be aware of these procedures in planning for ways in which to mesh with manual procedures of the system being developed with them.

There are two types of file controls of direct concern to the analyst. The first is to include a grand total, generally monetary, as the last record on the master file. As transactions are processed and new record amounts are developed, the totals of balances and transactions are accumulated. The beginning grand total is then added to the accumulated transaction total. This figure is then compared to the new grand total. These must be equal for processing to continue.

The second concern for the analyst is to identify all files that are necessary to reconstruct the current versions of critical application files. Critical files are those that are necessary to insure continued operation of the application and the business function served. Included are files necessary to recreate business activity and to satisfy business, legal, and regulatory requirements.

Backup files are used to reconstruct critical application files in case original files are destroyed or damaged.

Processing of sequentially organized files produces backup files automatically. Whenever a sequential master file is updated, for example, a completely new master file is created. The old master file then becomes the backup file. If the new master file is inadvertently destroyed, it can be recreated by reprocessing the transaction file against the old master file. Up to three or four *generations* of master files are typically maintained. These generations are called the *son, father, grandfather,* and *great-grandfather* files, from the most recent version to the oldest version of the file.

Direct-access files do not automatically produce backup copies because records are updated in place. The old master record is replaced by the new record following updating. In these cases, special backup procedures are required. Periodically, the master file is copied to a backup file. Frequency of backup will depend on the nature of processing and how much effort will be required to recreate the file. In some cases, a backup file is created for each alteration of the file. In some cases, the transaction record and the old master record are logged to a backup file. In other cases, transaction records are logged to a file and the master file is copied periodically. If the master file or any of its records are destroyed, it can be brought forward to current status by rerunning the transactions against the latest backup copy of the file.

Backup files and recovery procedures should be reviewed and checked periodically. If these reviews are not performed, it is possible that laxity has made the procedures unworkable. The company could actually have a false sense of security rather than a backup and recovery plan.

Documentation Controls

All procedures associated with data processing systems should be documented. There are, basically, four major types of documentation. System and program documentation are maintained within the CIS organization for use in system maintenance. Operations documentation is maintained in the computer operations area to describe all operating procedures. Finally, user documentation guides the users in how to run the system and make use of its results.

All documentation should be updated to reflect current procedures each time changes are made. This book stresses, many times, that computer information systems are dynamic. Change is a regular occurrence during the useful life of a computer information system. If documentation is not updated to reflect changes, it becomes increasingly likely that erroneous processing will take place. People may follow written instructions that are no longer appropriate. Thus, documentation should be current at all times. Current documentation should be distributed and enforced as part of the operational procedures that apply to every system.

System development and maintenance projects are designed to provide the basic documentation essential to computer information systems. Thus, it should be part of every project to make sure that documentation is current. As a tool for achieving this, an historic library of documentation, in all versions, should be maintained. It would be possible, then, to check copies that exist within operations centers to be sure that current versions are in use.

Organizational Controls

A major technique for protecting the integrity and reliability of data processing lies in *separation of duties* for data processing personnel. The principle of separation is straightforward: No one individual should have access to, or know enough about, a system to process data in an unauthorized way. This principle applies both during the development and in the ongoing use of a system. Systems analysis and programming assignments should be divided among a number of individuals. Assignments should be monitored so that combinations of people who have access to major parts of the system do not draw repeated assignments together.

Operationally, no individuals should have full access to an entire system. Thus, it is a common protective measure that programmers are not allowed to run production programs on a computer or to operate the applications they have written. Further, within an operations center, the person who has access to the computer mainframe should, if possible, be restricted from use of the data library or from control over output distribution. These are basic precautions. Computers handle large amounts of assets. An important line of protection lies in separating data resources from the temptations that are basic to human nature.

RESPONSIBILITY FOR DEFINING CONTROLS

Users have a major responsibility for defining controls required in the system. The user is most familiar with the operation of the system and potential problem areas—especially those based on past experience. Since, after the new system has been implemented, the users will be charged with applying many of the controls, it is all the more important to have strong user input in the definition of those controls.

Despite the desirability of heavy user involvement in the definition of controls, as systems have become more sophisticated the control area has become a specialty in its own right. A good systems analyst must be well versed in basic control techniques. The analyst bears ultimate responsibility for designing controls into the new system, calling on specialists when necessary.

Walkthroughs are discussed in an earlier chapter as a means of assuring correctness of system products. Walkthroughs involving users, analysts, and CIS quality assurance specialists provide an effective means of identifying deficiencies in control design. A series of walkthroughs at multiple levels, from overall system flow to detailed manual or computer processes, should be scheduled to evaluate controls.

CASE SCENARIO

Portions of the physical model of Central City's new water billing system are presented in Chapter 11, with corresponding system flowcharts in Chapter 15. One important process, APPLY PAYMENT, was held for this chapter so that the batching of input transactions could be explained more fully.

Figure 17-1 shows the part of Diagram 0 that relates to the APPLY PAYMENT process. The partitioning of this process is shown in Figure 17-2. All cash adjustments for a day are batched together (Process 6.2). Payment transactions are grouped into batches of about 50 to 100 (Process 6.1). An adding machine tape is run on the amount field for each transaction in the batch (Process 6.4). The batch ticket contains the date, batch number and type, and batch total. These data are entered in the DAILY BATCH/DEPOSIT LOG. See Figure 17-3.

After keypunching, all batches for the day enter the edit-update run (Processes 6.6 and 6.7). The annotated system flowchart corresponding

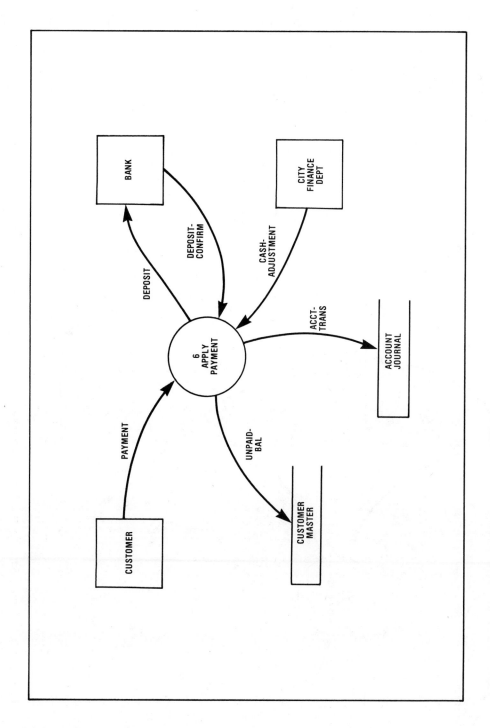

Figure 17-1. Portion of Diagram 0 covering the APPLY PAYMENT process of the new Central City water billing system.

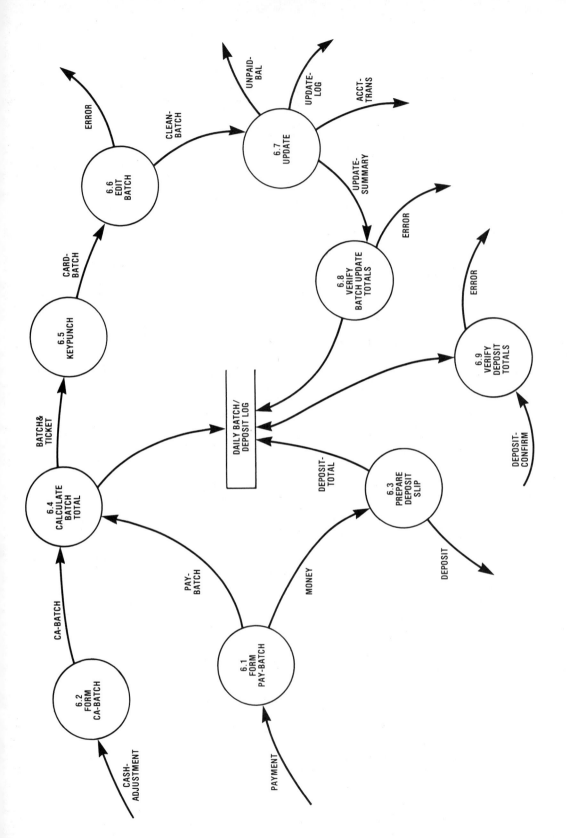

Figure 17-2. Diagram 6 for the new Central City water billing system, covering APPLY PAYMENT processing.

DAILY BATCH/DEPOSIT LOG.

DATE	BATCH NUMBER	BATCH TYPE	BATCH TOTAL	VERIFY UPDATE	VERIFY DEPOSIT	COMMENTS
5-5-84	1	P	2816 43	$\mathcal{R}$		
	2	CA	100 00	$\mathcal{R}$		
	3	P	3039 08	$\mathcal{R}$		
	4	P	1887 76	$\mathcal{R}$		
		TOTAL	7843 27			
		DEPOSIT	7743 27		$\mathcal{R}$	
5-6-84	1	P	3142 18	$\mathcal{R}$		
	2	P	2503 25			Batch total error
	3	P	2792 12	$\mathcal{R}$		
	4	P	2917 63	$\mathcal{R}$		
	5	P	1131 73	$\mathcal{R}$		
	6	CA	76 84			Batch total error
		TOTAL	12563 75			
		DEPOSIT	12486 91			

Figure 17-3. Sample of the document used for control of processed batches and deposits on a daily basis in connection with APPLY PAYMENT processing under the new Central City water billing system.

to this run is shown in Figure 17-4. Note that a batch of transactions is considered to be in error if any of the individual transactions contains an invalid field and/or if the batch total on the card for the batch ticket does not equal the total computed as each of the error report transactions is edited. If the batch is in error, it is rejected. The billing clerk must then locate the error(s) by referring to the transaction documents, adding machine tape, and punched cards. The entire batch must then be resubmitted after all errors have been corrected.

Note that when clean batches complete the update, a brief UPDATE SUMMARY report is produced, showing the total dollars credited, by batch. These totals are verified against the DAILY BATCH/DEPOSIT LOG by the billing clerk (Process 6.8).

Summary

Controls are functions that are designed to build quality into a computer information system. Controls provide assurance that standards of completeness and accuracy are enforced for each individual record or group of business transactions. Specific needs met by controls include: accuracy, integrity, reliability, completeness, and confidentiality.

Controls must be applied at every stage of system operation—including input, processing, output, and file storage. Types of controls include access controls, source document controls, data entry controls, processing controls, output controls, file controls, documentation controls, and oganizational controls. Each of these types of controls is described and illustrated.

Backup files should be maintained for all critical files within the system. Up to three or four generations of master files are typically maintained. These generations are called the son, father, grandfather, and great-grandfather files.

Backup files and recovery procedures should be reviewed and checked periodically.

All procedures associated with data processing systems should be documented. If documentation is not updated to reflect changes, the likelihood increases continually that erroneous processing will take place.

A major technique for protecting the integrity and reliability of data processing lies in separation of duties for data processing personnel. No one individual should have access to, or know enough about, a system to process data in an unauthorized way.

Operationally, no individuals should have full access to an entire system.

Major responsibility for defining controls should be assumed by users, who are most familiar with the operation of the system and the potential problems. Also, once a new system is operational, users will have primary responsibility for applying controls. Systems analysts support control definition efforts with expert advise and by leading walkthroughs that help to assure the acceptability of a system's end products.

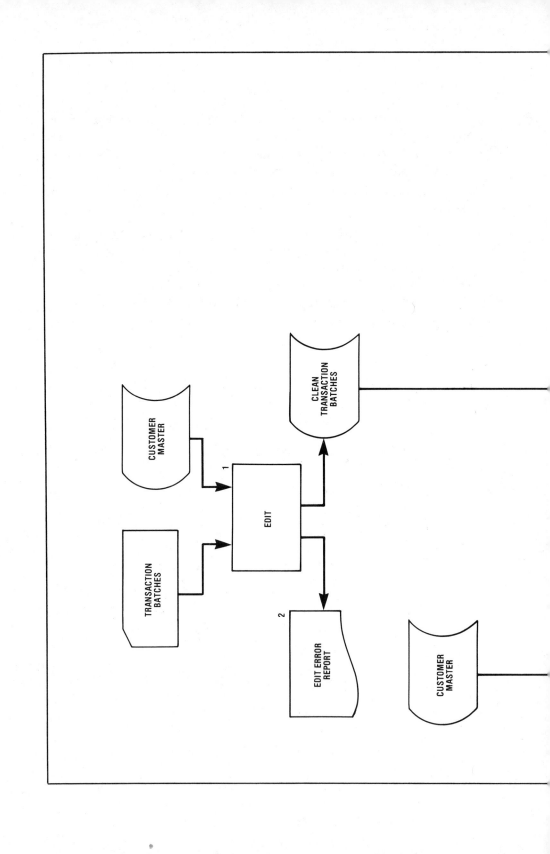

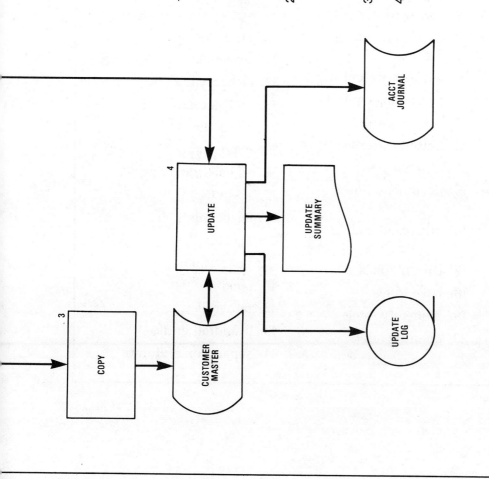

1. Verify that ACCT-NUM is valid, AMOUNT is numeric, and BATCH-TOTAL equals calculated total of amount field on cards in batch. Reject entire batch if error in any transaction or on batch total.

2. For each batch with error(s), list all transactions in batch and note errors. Report sent to billing clerk. Entire batch must be resubmitted.

3. Copy for backup before direct update.

4. Direct update of CUSTOMER-MASTER. Add transactions to ACCT-JOURNAL.

Figure 17-4. System flowchart for APPLY PAYMENT processing under the new Central City water billing system.

Key Terms

1. controls
2. accuracy
3. integrity
4. security
5. confidentiality
6. access control
7. password
8. hardware control
9. source document control
10. data entry controls
11. processing controls
12. batch control
13. output controls
14. file controls
15. documentation controls
16. organizational controls
17. control totals
18. hash totals
19. monetary totals
20. quantity totals
21. header record
22. edit run
23. transaction log
24. trailer record
25. exception reports
26. numeric field test
27. alphabetic field test
28. sign test
29. space (blank) test
30. range test
31. reasonableness test
32. category test
33. table lookup
34. check digits
35. encryption
36. signal scrambling
37. audit trail
38. checkpoints
39. backup files
40. generations
41. son file
42. father file
43. grandfather file
44. separation of duties

Review/Discussion Questions

1. What is the purpose of controls and what specific needs are served by controls?

2. At what stages of system operation should controls be applied?

3. What general types of controls are available?

4. How do input controls differ for batch and on-line applications?

5. What specific controls may be applied to source documents?

6. What processing controls are typically performed on input records?

7. What are some kinds of accuracy and validity controls that may be applied during processing?

8. What control is called for by data transmission?

9. What controls may be applied to files?

10. What is the role of documentation as a control procedure?

11. What organizational controls may be applied to an operational system?

18 IMPLEMENTATION AND INSTALLATION PLANNING

LEARNING OBJECTIVES

After completing the reading and other learning assignments in this chapter, you should be able to:

☐ Discuss the value of a formal planning step in preparation for detailed design and implementation of a new system.

☐ Describe the activities and tasks that must be planned prior to system implementation and tell about the content of those plans.

☐ Describe the content and scope of design plans.

☐ Describe the content and scope of system test plans.

☐ Describe the need for and content of a user training outline.

ACTIVITY DESCRIPTION

During this activity, plans are made in preparation for the two phases that follow: the detailed design and implementation phase and the Installation phase. Careful planning is necessary for two reasons.

First, despite the extensive efforts that have already gone into the project, the steering committee will be asked to make a major commitment in approving the final two phases. This commitment will be based primarily on the updated financial feasibility evaluation produced by Activity 5: New System Design. This updated cost/benefit analysis requires, among other things, reasonably accurate estimates of the cost to complete development of the system. These estimates must be based on work plans for the final phases. Thus, the plans produced in this activity feed the development cost updates produced in Activity 5.

Second, the next phase will have many independent, parallel tasks going on: detailed technical specifications, program design, programming, testing, user training, and so on. To manage these tasks effectively, a detailed work plan is needed right at the start of the phase. The need for this work plan is another example of the layering concept of systems development that has been described throughout this book. Activity 6 bears the same relation to the detailed design and implementation phase that Activity 2: Feasibility Study bears to the analysis and general design phase just being completed. Activity 6 presents an opportunity to estimate and plan the remaining development activities at a more detailed level. Work will then proceed with greater understanding when the next phase begins.

Rather than being buried as part of Activity 5, Activity 6 is established mainly because of the differences in the nature of planning work as compared with analysis and design tasks. Activity 5 still remains user oriented, with heavy interaction among users and systems analysts. Implementation and installation planning, on the other hand, involves different people. In reality, however, the end products of Activity 6 actually feed into Activity 5.

OBJECTIVES

The objectives of this activity are to:

- Establish a preliminary plan for the detailed design and implementation phase. This plan will be defined down to the level of major tasks, working days required, and a schedule for activity and task completions.

- Recommend an installation approach for conversion from the existing system to the new one.

SCOPE

Figure 18-1 shows the time relationships between Activities 3 through 6 in Gantt chart form. This graphic presentation highlights the fact that Activity 6 is both preceded and succeeded by Activity 5. In practice, there will be extensive interaction between Activities 5 and 6.

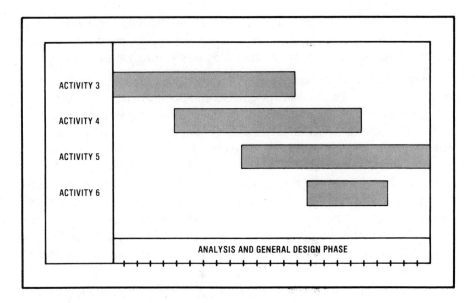

Figure 18-1. Gantt chart for Analysis and General Design phase shows that Activity 5 begins before and ends after Activity 6.

END PRODUCTS

The principal end products of this activity are:

- Preliminary detailed design and implementation plan
- Preliminary system test plan
- User training outline
- Preliminary installation plan.

Preliminary Detailed Design and Implementation Plan

This document contains:

- A list of major tasks to be performed is given. Note the word *major*. This is not a detailed plan, but a preliminary working document.
- At the task level, working day requirements are listed.
- At the task level also, a proposed staffing plan is prepared.

- A proposed timetable is prepared at the activity level (not at the task level). This timetable uses an elapsed-time basis, rather than specific calendar dates. The timetable is simply a planning document.

This preliminary plan will be used, early in the next phase, as a basis for more detailed planning—and also to update estimates of development costs before Activity 5 is completed.

Preliminary System Test Plan

This document contains:

- Criteria for acceptance of the new system are given. These criteria establish expectations of the results to be delivered in the areas of new hardware to be installed, any additional system software to be utilized, application software, user procedures, and operations instructions. All of these are implementation requirements for the new system.

- An initial list is prepared identifying the portions of the system to be tested. This identification is done at the subsystem and program level (without getting into the modules that make up individual programs). This listing covers the major products or functions to be tested and the interrelationships among those products or functions. Actual test data are not yet assembled.

- In addition to system and program test identification, the same type of list is prepared for testing the workability of user procedures.

User Training Outline

This document contains:

- Content outlines are prepared for the manuals to be used for user training.
- Separate manuals are outlined to cover user procedures.
- A list of proposed assignments is prepared covering the activities of users and analysts who will be involved in the writing of the manuals for user training and user procedures.

Preliminary Installation Plan

This document contains:

- The file conversion and system installation approaches to be taken are described at a preliminary level.

- A preliminary list of major files to be created or converted is prepared. This list includes any necessary forms that will be used to collect new data.

- Any computerized file conversion programs that will be needed are identified.

- A preliminary list is prepared covering the installation tasks for the new system. This list includes any special considerations for coordination that may be needed between such areas as file conversion tasks and the overall application programming effort.

Hardware and Software Plan

If the design for the new system calls for installation of new computer hardware or acquisition of new system software, an installation plan to meet these requirements is developed at this time. This work is usually done by the technical support staff and is outside the working area of the members of the project team. Typically, the project leader and the head of the technical support team coordinate this activity and produce the needed plan.

THE PROCESS

At this point, it is not yet possible to review all of the process implications of this activity. The process is devoted to the planning of future phases which have not yet been described. Thus, within the context established so far, it is possible to make only a few general observations about the process followed during this activity:

- The general design that is completed during Activity 5 identifies only the major application programs within the new system. Although an individual program identified at this stage may later be broken down into as many as 15 or 20 individual program modules, the general design is sufficiently detailed to support workable estimates of program development and testing requirements for the next phase.

- At this time, it is also desirable to identify alternatives that can be used in converting from the existing system to the new one and to select one of those alternatives. Conversion alternatives are discussed further in Chapter 20.

- The tasks needed to prepare a preliminary installation plan are completed. Note that during this activity, program development plans for installation are closely integrated with plans from Activity 5. Specifically, any programs that will be required for file conversion are equally as important as the application programs specified in Activity 5. Even though these programs will have only temporary use, the programs should not be treated lightly or casually. Failure to prepare quality conversion programs can result in errors in the new system's master files.

- The preparation of user training and procedures manuals can be particularly critical. When all of the technical activities have been completed, these manuals *are* the system—at least as far as the users are concerned. Therefore, careful consideration should be given to the appointment of user personnel to document procedures and actually write drafts of manuals. Without effective and strong user involvement, the training and procedures manuals may lack the credibility essential for acceptance and effective use.

- Test specifications—and the test data yet to be developed— represent the final criteria to be applied by users in accepting the new system. Therefore, it is important to be sure, during this activity, that users understand what the acceptance criteria are. Users should be asked to sign off on the descriptions of test procedures prepared during this activity.

- Agreement must also be reached with computer operations personnel on the testing and acceptance criteria that will determine when the computerized portions of the new system will be considered operational. In this context, computer operations personnel become users who must sign off and "buy into" the new system before it is considered fully operational. After a new system has been implemented, computer operations personnel will be primarily responsible for service to users. Therefore, it is important that operations personnel understand, at this point, the jobs to be undertaken and the expectations that will be placed upon their staff.

PERSONNEL INVOLVED

In the portions of this activity that deal with planning for user training, systems analysts coordinate closely with carefully selected supervisory and mid-level management personnel from the user areas. Some of the users who join the project team at this point may be entirely new to the systems development effort. Thus, special indoctrination sessions—and special amounts of patience—may be necessary.

The other planning aspects of this activity will be the primary responsibility of the project team leader, since the activity is devoted largely to project management planning.

CUMULATIVE PROJECT FILE

The end results of this activity are incorporated in the final report for Activity 5. Outputs from this activity are included in the description of the cumulative project file for Activity 5, discussed in Chapter 15.

Summary

During this activity, plans are set for the two phases that follow: the detailed design and implementation phase and the installation phase. The next phase will have many independent, parallel tasks going on. To manage these tasks effectively, a detailed work plan is needed right at the start of the phase.

The objectives of this activity are to establish a detailed project plan for the detailed design and implementation phase and to recommend an installation approach for conversion from the existing system to the new one.

The principal end products of this activity are a preliminary detailed design and implementation plan, a preliminary system test plan, a user training outline, and a preliminary installation plan.

If the design for the new system calls for installation of new computer hardware or acquisition of new software, an installation plan to meet these requirements is developed by the technical support staff.

In general, the process followed during this activity identifies a general design of programs—to a depth that makes it possible to estimate program development and testing requirements. It is also important to design and plan for the programs to be used to convert from existing files to new ones.

Careful consideration should be given to the selection of user personnel to document procedures and actually write drafts of manuals.

It is important during this activity to be sure that users understand what the acceptance criteria are. Agreement must be reached on testing and acceptance criteria.

Review/Discussion Questions

1. Why is careful planning necessary at this point in a project?

2. What is the relationship of this activity to Activity 5, and how does this relationship change as these activities proceed?

3. What are the ingredients of an effective detailed design and implementation plan?

4. What are the ingredients of an effective system test plan?

5. What are the ingredients of an effective user training plan?

6. Why is user participation critical to an effective training program for implementation of a new system?

7. Why is user documentation so critical to a successfully implemented system?

8. What personnel are involved in planning for user training?

9. What provisions must be made for training computer operations personnel?

IV IMPLEMENTATION, INSTALLATION, AND REVIEW PHASES

PURPOSE

The four chapters in this final part conclude the book. The chapters are overviews of the final three phases of the systems development life cycle, as well as a concluding chapter that covers some skills, principles, and techniques appropriate for project management. The areas of the life cycle covered in this part of the book are highlighted graphically in Figure IV-1.

Chapter 19 reviews all of the activities involved in the detailed design and implementation phase of the life cycle. This phase begins with the new system design specification prepared at the conclusion of the second phase. In this third phase, the project is carried forward into detailed technical design, programming, testing, and training of users. The purpose of this phase, taken as a whole, is to produce a new system that is ready for installation.

Chapter 20 reviews the installation phase of a project. This phase involves activities in which master files for the new system are prepared and set up for use. Once the files are in place, the new system is actually installed and the old system terminated. At the close of this phase, the project team is dissolved.

Chapter 21 deals with the review phase of the project. This phase involves post-implementation reviews of the development process. One purpose is to evaluate the results of the development project, as compared with the timetables and the cost estimates prepared at several

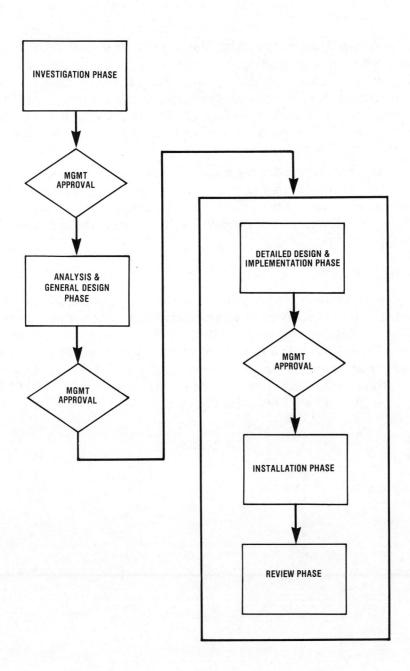

Figure IV-1. Diagram highlights final phases of the systems development life cycle.

stages during development. Also, the new system is reviewed to determine whether it is meeting user needs and achieving the benefit forecasts that were accepted by the user. The purpose of this final phase is to derive lessons from past experience that can be used to direct future efforts. Chapter 21 also reviews several other development approaches that can be used in place of, or in conjunction with, the systems development life cycle.

Chapter 22 concludes the book with a discussion of specific tools that can be helpful in the planning, scheduling, and control of projects—the management dimensions that are particularly critical in dealing with development projects, as distinct from the management of ongoing operations.

ACHIEVEMENTS

On completing work in this part of the book, the student should have the background necessary to understand the relationships between the systems analysis process and skills learned in earlier portions of the book. These skills result from an understanding of the requirements of design and implementation that round out a project. The student will also acquire a working knowledge of such management tools as PERT and the Critical Path Method (CPM).

DETAILED DESIGN AND IMPLEMENTATION PHASE 19

LEARNING OBJECTIVES

After completing the reading and other learning assignments in this chapter, you should be able to:

☐ Describe the tasks involved in detailed technical design, including design of programs, files, input records, and outputs.

☐ Explain the impact on the project of a decision to implement an application software package or new hardware/system software.

☐ State the advantages that can result from implementing the new system in incremental steps, or versions.

☐ Outline the principal activities associated with the detailed design and implementation of a new system.

☐ Identify the members of the project team needed to complete detailed design and implementation of a new system and describe the responsibilities of each member.

PHASE DESCRIPTION

This phase is both highly technical and, hopefully, highly productive. Within this phase, specifications are turned into a developed, ready-to-use system. A flowchart showing the relationship of this phase to the rest of the systems development life cycle, with activities in this phase identified specifically, is shown in Figure 19-1.

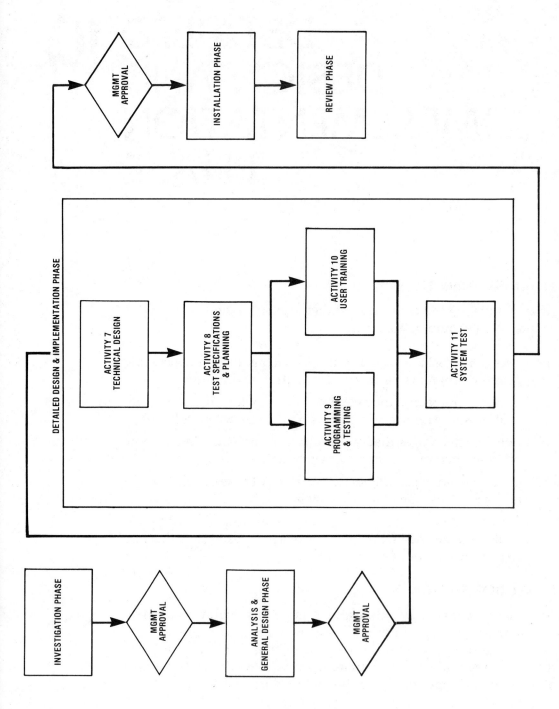

Figure 19-1. Diagram shows activities of the Detailed Design and Implementation phase in relation to the overall systems development life cycle.

Work begins with the new system design specification prepared at the conclusion of the previous phase. This document serves as a basis for detailed technical design, which includes detailed design of programs, specific design of files, input record designs, and output document or display designs. Next, after test specifications have been prepared, individual program modules are written and tested.

During this same period, user training begins. Once trained, users become involved almost immediately in system testing activities. This testing encompasses both computerized and manual procedures. During the system test, the new system is operated under conditions that are as close as possible to normal production conditions, with the project team observing the procedures and results. Any final, fine tuning of the new system takes place during this comprehensive testing activity.

Two strategic decisions can have a great effect on the work that occurs during this phase: the decision to purchase an application software package and the decision on how to install the new system.

In many cases, 50 percent or more of the development resources of a project are expended in this phase. However, the time and resources required for this phase may be reduced significantly if a decision is made to use an application software package rather than developing the programs internally. This option is becoming increasingly viable as large numbers of software houses bring comprehensive and flexible application systems to market. If purchased application software is used, the programming time within this phase may be reduced to a minimum. The only programming normally necessary in this case would be for converting master files, providing special interface functions to meet special needs of specific users, and modifying portions of standard programs for specific needs. No matter where application software originates, however, the user training and system test activities associated with this phase will remain relatively unchanged.

The installation approach can also have a major effect on how this phase progresses. The traditional approach is to design and implement the entire system completely, then to do a massive system test, and finally, to install the system following one of several possible methods. However, in larger systems with reasonably independent components, a far more effective approach can be to implement and install the system in *incremental steps,* or *versions.* In this way, users can learn to use the system effectively, a step at a time, and developers can produce the system with good control over schedules and budgets.

The delineation of the appropriate increments or versions is a complex process and may begin early in this phase or even toward the end of the previous phase. This approach parallels the natural evolution inherent in any business operation: There are short- and long-range plans—with the short-range plans designed to realize certain objectives that fit into a long-range pattern. Similarly, the incremental pieces or versions of a system should realize short-term objectives within a long-range system plan. The net result is an iteration of the detailed design and implementation and the installation phases for each version. Additional remarks concerning version implementation are in Chapter 21 as part of the discussion of other development options.

OBJECTIVES

The objectives of this phase are to:

- Produce a completely documented and fully tested new system (or incremental unit, or version, of a system) that encompasses computer processing, manual procedures, all necessary interfaces between computerized and manual processes, and among multiple computerized processes.

- Secure approval to proceed with system installation from users, from the CIS operations group, and from the management steering committee.

SCOPE

The detailed design and implementation phase begins with a general, high level design for the new system that has been approved by the steering committee. This committee has also approved the necessary resources for proceeding through the phase. Recall that the general design for the new system, for the most part, presents the system from the user's point of view. It includes just enough design of the computer processing to permit a fairly accurate time and cost projection and feasibility evaluation. This general design is documented in a comprehensive new system design specification, described at the close of Chapter 15.

Another starting point for this phase is the preliminary work plan prepared during Activity 6: Implementation and Installation Planning. The content of this document is described in Chapter 18.

Starting from the specification and working plan, development progresses toward a fully tested new system (or version of a system) that includes:

- Writing and testing of a complete set of computer programs
- Preparation of training and procedures manuals
- Completion of training programs for key user personnel
- Full testing of manual procedures
- Complete system test.

At the conclusion of this phase, the system is ready for installation—the next phase of the development life cycle. While less technical in nature, the installation phase requires careful planning and monitoring.

END PRODUCTS

The final end product of this phase is a fully tested and documented system (or version of a system). This product is developed in stages through several activities. These activities overlap one another and must be coordinated closely. For example, while technical design is still proceeding, work has begun on preparation of test data for modules already designed and programming and unit testing has begun on still others. While all this is happening, users are being trained. The need for close coordination is clear. Major end products are described below according to the activities in which the products are produced.

Activity 7: Technical Design

The principle of cumulative documentation and layering of activity levels is particularly apparent during technical design. Designers build on the specifications produced during Activity 5: New System Design, adding detailed technical specifications. The boundary between the general design specifications of Activity 5 and the detailed technical design of Activity 7 is often difficult to delineate. To illustrate this boundary (and also the cumulative nature of the documentation produced), there follows a listing of the state of the documentation at the end of Activity 7. This list shows those products that are newly added, or heavily modified, in *italics*. Note that system documentation and program documentation for the new system are essentially complete—although in rough form—at the end of this activity. These products include:

- An overview narrative describes the system's purpose, goals, and objectives, as well as the basic logical functions that must be performed.

- Processing descriptions include a context diagram and a hierarchical set of data flow diagrams. Diagram 0 should identify the major subsystems. Lower level diagrams should indicate the various physical packaging considerations.

- *Annotated system flowcharts are prepared for each job stream. In the process, program identifications are assigned.*

- *Individual programs are designed and specified through use of structure charts. Structure charts are created for all major job steps in the computerized portion of the system.*

- *A program inventory, or listing, is made for all programs in the system. This inventory is done according to program identification and name, the job stream or streams in which each program occurs, and the external programs (if any) that call this program.*

- *Job Control Language (JCL) description sheets are prepared for each working job stream within the new system. These sheets are used as a basis for operating system instructions in the processing of application programs.*

- *Program specifications are prepared. These include detailed descriptions of modules, of interfaces among modules, as specified on the structure charts, and of inputs and outputs. In addition, processing descriptions for these modules and program components are also prepared. This description is done at the structure chart and pseudocode levels.*

- Specifications are included for backup requirements and recovery procedures.

- A description is prepared of the audit trail and logging requirements to be incorporated in the new system.

- Data dictionary definitions support the data flow diagrams. Previously prepared documentation is updated as data flow diagrams are detailed to include *technical specification details, including edit criteria, data element values, record layouts, storage formats, and so on.*

- A catalog of all output to be delivered to the user—either printed or displayed—together with a description sheet for each output, are included. *Precise layout charts replace the rough outlines of the previous phase. Final designs are prepared for any preprinted forms.*

- A catalog is included listing all inputs, including a descriptive document sheet for each application input. *Layout charts for input records and file designs for any preprinted forms are prepared.*

- User interfaces with the system are specified in the previous phase. Additions at this point reflect the impact of technical designs that may have been added.

- Performance criteria that are critical to either computer or manual processing—including response times, volumes, and other features—are documented.

- Security and control measures aimed at limiting access to either equipment or files are documented. (Security and control measures covering processing are included in the processing specifications themselves.)

- *Computer operations documentation to be used for guidance of computer operators incorporates brief narratives describing the processing of systems and subsystems. Included are estimates of processing volumes and run times. For each job stream, a descriptive sheet is prepared that covers the name, input file requirements, set-up instructions, outputs, data control, backup procedures, recovery and restart instructions, and any special instructions.*

- *Conversion programs incorporating technical specifications for all special file conversion programs identified in the previous phase are prepared.*

- Policy considerations associated with the new system should have been resolved prior to this activity.

Activity 8: Test Specifications and Planning

End products of this activity include:

- Detailed test specifications are prepared. These specifications are applicable at several levels, including individual modules and programs, job streams, subsystems, and for the system as a whole.

- Supporting test data and files are prepared for each of these levels of testing.

Activity 9: Programming and Testing

End products of this activity include:

- A working documentation file is created for each separately compiled program and module. Contents of these files are accumulated in folders that contain the latest source listings for each program module, the specifications for the program module, and a cumulative program test log that builds a history of test activities and results.

Activity 10: User Training

End products of this activity include:

- A user procedures manual will guide the ongoing use of the system after implementation. Contents vary from system to system. However, elements usually include those items listed below.

- A table of contents is prepared, detailed to the level needed for easy reference.

- A narrative overview of the system is prepared for use by managers or for indoctrination of new employees.

- Individual job descriptions and procedures are completed.

- Explanations covering the preparation and use of input forms are written.

- Data entry procedures, controls, error correction methods, and specifications for the handling of exceptions are described.

- Procedures for file maintenance are prepared. These include descriptions of user responsibilities for error correction, backup, and updating. These procedures should encompass the maintenance of tables as well as master files. Authorization procedures for access to these files should also be established carefully and stated clearly.

- Output reports should be covered by explanatory narratives and specifications for distribution and use.

- As required, policy statements should be included.

- Procedures for updating the manual itself should be described.

- Any special learning materials or samples to be used in the training of users are completed during this activity and included in a training manual. Note that the procedures manual is not adequate for training purposes. Rather, the procedures manual is designed to be used as a comprehensive reference book.

Activity 11: System Test

One major end product is prepared during this activity:

- The system test log is initiated. Compilation of this log will continue throughout the life of the system. The log records all activities connected with testing the system and subsystems—for all testing that extends beyond the level of individual programs or modules.

Phase Conclusion

At the close of this phase, a special end product is delivered:

- A post-implementation maintenance list is prepared. This list encompasses all opportunities for change or enhancement that have been identified in the course of technical design and implementation for the new system.

THE PROCESS

A heavy overlapping usually exists for Activities 7 through 10, while Activity 11, dedicated to system testing, cannot begin until the others have been completed. These relationships among activities are shown graphically in the chart in Figure 19-2. These relationships apply to both the full implementation of a system and the incremental, or version implementation, discussed earlier.

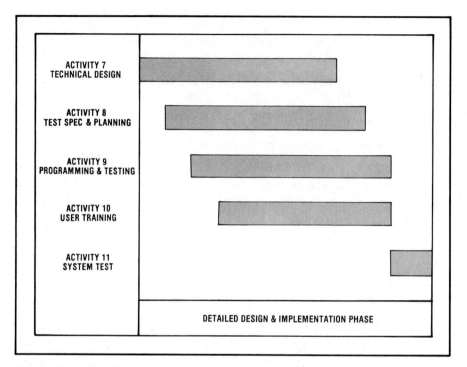

Figure 19-2.   Gantt chart showing interrelationships of activities in the Detailed Design and Implementation phase.

The sections that follow provide a brief overview of the major processes of this phase.

Technical Design

The general design of the previous phase is carried to a deeper level by the precise definition and design of outputs, inputs, and files. Outputs are designed in terms of detailed report layouts, screen layouts, or model dialogs for interactive systems. Input definitions include detailed design of source documents and data entry formats.

In addition, each major processing program to be used in the system is designed. For most business applications, program design is approached through a hierarchical, or top-down, process that results in a set of individual modules. Relationships among the modules that comprise a program are expressed in a *structure chart*. On a structure chart, as shown in Figure 19-3, linkages between individual program

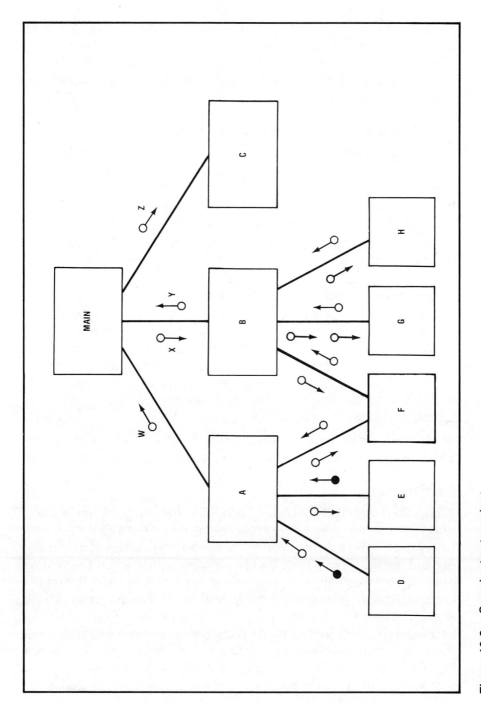

Figure 19-3. Sample structure chart.

modules are defined precisely for each module. Figure 19-3 is an abstract example of a program called MAIN that can call modules A, B, and C. In turn, module A calls D, E, and F; and module B calls F, G, and H. When module B is called, MAIN sends the data structure X and receives Y in return.

Test Planning, Programming, and Testing

Once programs are specified and the interrelationships of modules are understood, test specifications can be written and the actual design, coding and testing of program units or modules can begin. Because of the structured, modular approach, entire programs can be developed and tested in top-down fashion—one module at a time.

If modular design has been executed effectively, it is possible to overlap program development. That is, lower level modules can still be in the design phase, while middle level modules undergo test planning and higher level modules are coded and tested—all within the same time period. Because of the structured approach, overall coordination and management of program development can continue on a module-by-module basis without loss of management control over development of the program as a whole. This overlapping of development tasks makes clear the need for extremely careful and precise definitions of module functions and intermodule linkages during technical design.

In some cases, users should participate in validating test results. This draws on their background and also helps to build confidence.

User Training

While the intensively technical activities for program design and development are being carried out, users and systems analysts—with heavy user involvement—work concurrently on a series of user training and testing tasks. These involve, as described earlier, the writing of procedure manuals, the preparation of training materials, and the conducting of training programs. In addition, all manual procedures are tested thoroughly within the user organization. The training of users and the testing of manual procedures are principally user functions, with systems analysts observing and advising rather than directing. The underlying idea is that the first group of users trained on a new system then proceeds to train the other users who will be involved.

One other topic deserves special consideraton at this point—how to handle change requests from users at this stage of the development process.

Change requests from users. As user personnel undergo final preparation, testing, and training, these users will inevitably begin to identify new opportunities. Frequently, these opportunities will involve modification of the system to encompass new functions or outputs. Basically, the idea that users are discovering increasing potential for the system is healthy and should be encouraged. At the same time, however, it is important that user training programs establish the need to implement the system first, then change it.

Introducing changes into a system while it is in final development and testing can be dangerous. It is not always possible to tell how a seemingly minor change in input, processing, output, or files will impact the system as a whole. It is a safe bet, however, that any change, even a minor change, will result in an interrelated impact elsewhere in the system.

Therefore, a policy should be established about the kinds and extents of changes that are permitted during this phase. For example, the reversing of the positions of two columns on an output report or display might be minor enough to handle. However, the production of an entirely new report would probably be delayed.

Because suggested enhancements to the system will almost surely develop at this point, it is a good policy to establish a post-implementation maintenance list that describes all of these opportunities. Right after the system has been implemented, consideration can begin for the implementation of these new ideas on a maintenance basis.

Of course, mandatory change requirements can come up any time. If such requirements do arise, the situation must be dealt with during this phase, or any other. For example, suppose a new law or government regulation is introduced while the system is still under development. It may be necessary to incorporate this change before implementation. Judgments must be applied continuously. Necessities must be incorporated in the system; enhancements can be deferred for later consideration.

System Test

When a system has had all of its programs and major subsystems tested thoroughly, and when users have been trained, full system testing is carried out—chiefly by users. This involves, first, a series of tests for all subsystems. The subsystems that will be used to build or maintain files are, where possible, tested first. As files are built and used, extensive tests are performed on the backup and recovery procedures for these files. These activities go beyond those that will be performed in the normal use of the system—providing complete assurance that the data resources handled by the system will be protected fully.

As errors are discovered during the system test, those errors are identified specifically and tracked. Severity of processing errors is evaluated to determine whether corrective action in programs or procedures is required immediately or whether noncritical errors can be dealt with through post-implementation maintenance. Any errors that require immediate attention are dealt with during this testing activity. Once these corrections are made, the complete testing cycles are repeated.

As system testing and resulting program modifications begin, this activity must be documented carefully. Program test logs, and similar system test logs, are the means for maintaining this documentation.

Program test log. As systems are tested and brought into use, it is almost inevitable that minor problems will be identified and corrected as part of the system test activity. That is, even after individual program modules and programs themselves have been tested, the system tests conducted by the user will uncover additional needs or opportunities. These can involve modification of modules or of entire programs. As modifications are made, modules and programs are retested, sometimes with the addition of new test data. This process is continuous. Programs are modified throughout the life of the system through maintenance projects that continue until long after a system has been developed and implemented. Any time programs are modified, the appropriate program test log(s) and test files for that program should be updated accordingly. This updating helps to avoid situations in which seemingly minor program modifications create unexpected errors at other points in the system.

Each time a module or program is tested, information on the date, the version of the test file used, and the results should be recorded. The nature of the modifications made should be noted on the test log—or cross-referenced to the original change request or work order.

When a program is modified, it may be necessary to add to or change individual test files for modules or for the entire program. For each change that is made, previously established testing procedures should be applied to insure the continuing reliability of the programs. These procedures should involve running the programs with the previous version of the test files after changes have been made. (Any previous test data made inappropriate by the current change should be removed from the test files prior to this run.) This verifies that the current change does not create any unexpected or unwanted results. After tests with previous test file versions, new test data can be added. Repeated testing like this is one way in which program test files continue to grow. It is a sound practice to maintain at least two or three generations of test files for use in the continual revision of programs.

Technical Support Considerations

Certain projects may require technical support from outside the project team. Two common situations are noted below. These situations are significant because of the coordination that must occur between the project team and technical support areas.

Database considerations. If the computer system on which a new application will run utilizes database management software, there will be special concerns and considerations connected with integrating the data requirements and outputs of the new system with existing databases. In such a situation, a database analyst will typically begin to work with the project team during the general design tasks of the previous phase and continue through this phase. It will be the responsibility of the database administration group to do the physical database design and later handle the creation of the physical database during conversion and installation. The database group will also be involved during testing to oversee program efficiency in terms of database accesses and access paths.

Hardware/system software concerns. Special technical considerations will arise if the system under development requires new items of computer equipment or new system-level software packages. To put this requirement in perspective, there will probably be no special concern unless significant new hardware or system software purchases are being made. However, if the computer installation is being altered to accommodate the new application, a technical specialist would begin to work with the team near the end of the previous phase to oversee the necessary integration. The technical services group would be responsible for the acquisition, testing, and acceptance of new hardware and system software.

PERSONNEL INVOLVED

During Activities 7 through 9, the makeup of the project team becomes heavily technical. Systems analysts are still present, but the analysts' role is shifted. At this point, analysts track progress rather than performing direct development tasks. Numerically, most of the team during these technical activities consists of system designers and programmers. Other technical support personnel may also be present.

During Activity 10, users predominate. Users work with analysts, but this is the point at which users begin to take over responsibility for implementing and utilizing the finished system.

During Activity 11, the transition becomes final. That is, at this point, users and members of the CIS operations group are working together closely. This relationship should continue throughout the life of the system.

Summary

Within the detailed design and implementation phase, specifications are turned into a developed, ready-to-use system. Work initiates with the new system design specification, which serves as a basis for detailed technical design, including detailed design of programs, specific design of files, input record designs, and output documents or display designs.

User training begins. Once trained, users become involved almost immediately in system testing activity. The new system is operated under conditions that are as close as possible to normal, with the project team observing the procedures. Any final, fine tuning of the new system takes place during this comprehensive testing operation.

The time and resources required for this phase may drop drastically if a decision is made to use packaged application programs.

The objectives of this phase are to produce a completely documented and fully tested new system and to secure approvals to proceed with system installation. The final end product of this phase is a fully tested and documented system (or incremental version of a system).

Activity 7: Technical Design, produces an overview narrative and processing specifications.

The end products of Activity 8: Test Specifications and Planning, include detailed test specifications and supporting test data.

The end products of Activity 9: Programming and Testing, include a working document file for each separately compiled program and module.

The end products of Activity 10: User Training, include a user procedures manual and a user training manual.

Activity 11: System Test, initiates the system test log. Compilation of this log will continue throughout the life of the system.

At the close of this phase, a post-implementation maintenance list is prepared. This list encompasses all opportunities for change or enhancement that have been identified in the course of technical design and implementation for the new system.

The major processes of this phase include: technical design; test planning, programming, and testing; user training, including selective handling of change requests; system testing, including maintenance of a program test log; and technical support considerations, including database considerations, and hardware/system software concerns.

During Activities 7 through 9, the makeup of the project team becomes heavily technical. During Activity 10, users predominate. During Activity 11, users and members of the CIS operations group are working together closely. This relationship should continue throughout the life of the system.

Key Terms

1. incremental testing
2. versions
3. Job Control Language (JCL)
4. top-down
5. structure charts
6. program test log

Review/Discussion Questions

1. What major tasks are included in detailed technical design?
2. What strategic decisions affect the work of detailed design and implementation?
3. What alternative exists to installation of a new system in its entirety, and in what circumstances is this alternative feasible?
4. What are processing specifications and what do they include?
5. What are test data files and what do they include?
6. What steps are performed and what is accomplished in program testing?
7. What are the differences and relationships between system reference manuals and user training manuals?
8. Under what circumstances may programs be modified as a result of system testing?
9. What transitions in the makeup of the project team take place as part of detailed design and implementation?
10. Who should be responsible for user training and why?

INSTALLATION 20

LEARNING OBJECTIVES

On completing reading and other learning assignments for this chapter, you should be able to:

☐ Identify the scope and major achievements associated with system installation.

☐ Describe the four basic methods of system installation and explain the advantages and disadvantages of each.

☐ Identify the steps involved in file conversion.

☐ Discuss the transitions to user ownership and system maintenance.

☐ Describe the contents and role of the cumulative project file following system installation.

PHASE DESCRIPTION

Installation is the fourth phase in the systems development life cycle. The position within the life cycle of this phase and the two activities that comprise it are illustrated in the flowchart in Figure 20-1.

This phase is critically important for two reasons. First, it marks the culmination of development efforts and the realization of the proposed new system. Second, it is a critical transition time for the users. Actual, realized—as opposed to projected—benefits will depend on how the user group learns to adapt to the system during the installation phase.

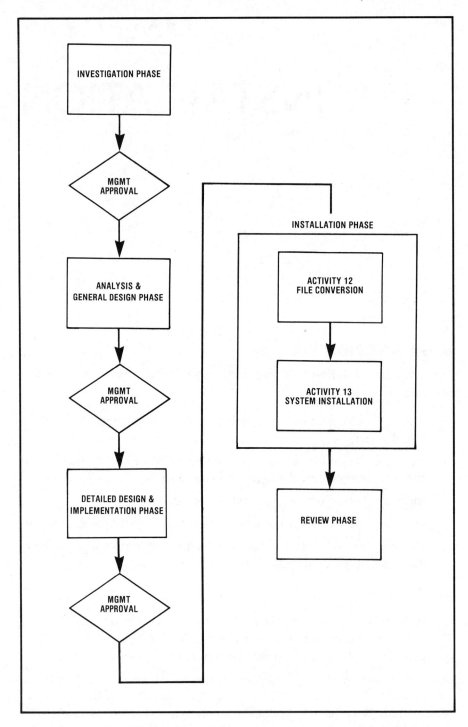

Figure 20-1. Diagram shows activities of the Installation phase in relation to the overall systems development life cycle.

During this phase, users actually take over ownership of the new system. That is, development is complete. The new system is operational. The new files exist and are in day-to-day use. A relationship has begun between users and CIS operations, with systems analysts fading gradually from the picture.

The actual method of installation for the new system will depend upon its design, upon the needs and preferences of user managers, and upon the risks that can be tolerated. Options include:

- Cutover can be abrupt, with the old system simply discontinued and the new one beginning at the same instant.

- The old and new systems can be operated in parallel for some time while results of the two systems are compared.

- There can be a parallel conversion in which the old system is gradually phased out while the new one takes over.

- *Version installation* techniques can be used. Under this approach, the system is divided into a series of functional areas, or incremental steps, called *versions*. These versions can be installed in any of the three ways described above. However, the entire system will not be fully implemented until all of the versions are in place.

These options, and the trade-offs involved, are discussed later in this chapter.

OBJECTIVES

This phase has two principal objectives:

- First, the existing system is replaced with the new, tested, documented system. This replacement assumes user acceptance and ongoing user responsibility for the system. The project team is disbanded, and analysts and programmers are removed from routine involvement with system operation. In connection with system implementation, all files utilized by the old system are converted to the new system, and use of the old system is discontinued.

- Second, to maximize the potential benefits of the new system, the user must be taken beyond simple how-to training to an intimate and detailed understanding of the system that has been installed.

SCOPE

This phase begins with the existence of a complete system—or, if appropriate, a version—that has been completely tested under realistic conditions and is ready for installation. In addition, any needed file conversion programs have been written and tested.

The phase ends with a new system, or version, implemented and in day-to-day operation, with no further intervention or supervision by members of the project team. The conclusion of this phase is also marked by discontinuance of the old system.

END PRODUCTS

No major new end products are produced during this phase. Rather, previously designed and developed products are implemented. New files that have already been created or converted are put into regular use in support of the new system.

In addition, all previously prepared documentation is updated and placed in maintenance status. Copies are distributed to persons who need them, and arrangements are made to update all copies as necessary to reflect modification or maintenance of the system. Processing schedules or calendars to be followed by both users and the CIS operations group are established and put into regular use.

THE PROCESS

This overview of the installation process focuses on three main concerns:

- Strategies for file conversion
- Basic system installation alternatives
- Personnel transitions that must occur as responsibility for the system moves from the development team to the user organization.

File Conversion

File conversion strategies vary with the complexity of the system and with the installation method used. In some cases, file conversion can be completed quickly and with few complications. In other situations, however, the conversion of files can be relatively complex.

Problems, when they arise, center around conversion from the old system to the new one and the possible need to support both systems or parts of both systems concurrently. There is apt to be some delay, or lag time, during which the old system still needs its files while the new one also requires access to files that have already been converted. Thus, one system or the other may be operating with files that are not completely current.

These problems can be avoided if the nature of the system lends itself to an abrupt conversion. For example, changes in general ledger accounting systems are typically made at year-end just to avoid this type of problem. At the end of the fiscal year, the old system begins its closeout routines. The new system then starts up with all balances at zero. If payments or bills are received that should be accounted for in the prior year, these can be processed under the old system. Transactions dated after the first of the year are run through the new system. There are no processing conflicts or file conversion problems because a clean break has been made.

However, this kind of transition is not always possible. For example, suppose a conversion is being made in an accounts receivable system. The existing files represent all unpaid bills owed to the organization. As the new system is implemented, all of the data from the existing files must be captured into the new ones. In the interim while the old system is still in operation, there could be trouble in finding such information as current customer account balances for the purposes of credit authorization. To avoid such problems, arrangements are usually made to maintain and access both files during some interim period while files are being converted.

In general, file conversion involves the following basic procedures:

- Prepare existing computer files for conversion. This means that all master files should be brought up to date. Accuracy should be verified. Errors should be identified and corrected.
- Prepare existing manual files for conversion. Post manual data to new system maintenance input forms, and do data entry of manual data.
- Build new files and validate them as they are created.

- Begin maintenance on the new files. Input data continue to update old files until after implementation, but the converted files must also be updated. The basic procedure is: First, establish a cutoff date for each file to be converted. Then, any input documents that represent transactions after the conversion data are batched and used for periodic updating of the converted file until installation of the new system.

- Make a final check of accuracy, or balancing, between the new files and the old ones.

Installation Alternatives

The methods used in converting files will depend at least in part upon the alternative selected for installation of the new system. The installation technique selected depends chiefly upon the nature of the new system and the trade-offs involved in the various installation alternatives. The basic alternatives are:

- Abrupt cutover
- Parallel operation with a single cutover point
- Parallel operation with a gradual shift from the old system to the new
- Version installation.

Abrupt cutover. As illustrated earlier, an abrupt cutover involves a simultaneous dismantling of the old system and start-up of the new one. It's just that simple. At a predetermined time, the old system no longer exists. The new one handles all transactions.

One advantage of this approach, in situations where it can be used, is that costs are minimized. There are no transition costs because there is no transition.

In some cases, an abrupt cutover may be the most natural, if not the only, way to solve a problem. In addition to the year-end conversion of accounting systems, consider situations in which a new system changes the way a company does business. Consider, for example, what happens when a supermarket installs a checkout system using the universal product code. Under the old system, all prices had to be entered into keyboards by checkers. Checkers needed extensive, manual reference files to look up prices if packages weren't marked clearly. Under the universal product code, store personnel can stop marking individual packages and simply place prices on the shelves where the products are displayed. Pricing is done by an on-line computer. A computer price file replaces the manual reference file. Abrupt cutover represents a natural way to convert to the new system.

The major disadvantage of this approach is that it can carry a high risk. In an abrupt cutover, the old system is stopped. If a major problem develops with the new system, it may be very difficult—perhaps impossible—to return to the old system. Depending on the system and its role in the organization, the ability to carry on the business could be curtailed.

Parallel operation, single cutover.   Under this approach, both systems are operated concurrently for some period of time. Often this parallel operation period coincides with business processing cycles, such as weeks or months. During this interim period, all input transactions are used to update the files that support both the old and the new systems. A balancing between results of the two systems is performed regularly.

An advantage of this approach is that risks are relatively low if problems arise in the start-up of the new system. The corresponding disadvantage is the cost of operating both systems concurrently.

A typical use of this approach occurs when a computerized system is replacing manual procedures. Users already trained in the manual procedures simply carry on for a while, phasing out after the new system has proved itself.

Parallel operation, gradual cutover.   Again, both systems are operated concurrently. However, rather than having a single cutover point between systems, the old system is discontinued gradually. Discontinuance of the old system can be according to geographic location, type of business, or other criteria.

Advantages of this approach, once again, include minimizing the risk associated with any problems that may arise with the new system. Costs are more moderate with a gradual cutover than they are if the old system is continued for a predetermined period of time. With a gradual cutover, the old system can be discontinued as quickly or slowly as management feels comfortable with the new one.

A disadvantage lies in the possible confusion that can result if people are unsure about which system to use.

To illustrate how this approach might work, an order entry system might discontinue the old system for one sales district at a time. Another possible approach would be for cutover to occur according to order processing points. For example, on a given day one warehouse would put all of its orders through the new system, discontinuing the old. In the water billing system used as an example throughout this book, the cutover could be done by billing cycles. That is, the new system could be applied to one cycle of customers at a time.

Version installation. Under this approach, a basic set of capabilities is implemented within the first version of the system, then additional capabilities are added in subsequent versions. Each version goes through a complete implementation and installation cycle of its own. Some time after the first version is operational, procedures, programs, and files are implemented for the second version, which then goes through the installation process. This procedure is repeated for each version. In effect, version installation involves breaking the proposed system into a series of incremental steps, or versions, at the end of the analysis and general design phase and then implementing and installing the system one step at a time.

To illustrate, consider the example of the supermarket that installs a universal product code checkout system. In the first version, files, programs, and procedures would be set up for identifying and pricing products at the checkout counters through use of the computerized system. In the second version, inventory levels could be added to the product file. This would make possible stock control at the individual store level. Then, in a third version, stock replenishment, or requisitioning of merchandise, could be added based on sales histories that are accumulated within the computer files. Thus, each version adds capabilities to a basic system rather than requiring development of an entirely new system each time.

An advantage of version installation is that risks and costs may be lower than if the complete system were installed at one time. Also, the user can learn to utilize major features of the new system, one at a time. A disadvantage is that this approach may not be workable with all systems. The approach works best when the system has clear-cut, separate functions that can be added without penalizing or causing undue disruptions to previously installed versions.

Personnel Transitions

Up to this point in the project, users and systems analysts have, literally formed a team. Close relationships and understandings may have evolved, and friendships may have been built.

Whatever the personal relationships that may exist at this point, installation marks a transition. Once the system is installed and in regular operation, it belongs to the users. Users are the owners of operational systems. Systems analysts have completed their mission; it is time for them to move on to other projects. At this point, it is part of their job to disengage as expeditiously as they can.

Another systems analysis responsibility associated with installation is to avoid making any system changes that are not absolutely necessary at this point. As indicated earlier, a list of maintenance changes to be made following implementation is initiated in the previous phase and continued through installation. What must be avoided is a situation in which a new system remains incomplete—or is permitted to overrun costs exorbitantly—because of a flurry of last-minute modifications and changes. A management nightmare in the systems development field is the system that is 99 percent complete—indefinitely.

One way to be sure that the old system is discontinued is to terminate use of its documentation and programs. The documentation and programs for the old system should be relegated to the archives as part of the installation procedure.

Two special concerns are worthy of additional notice at this point: assuring that the user has the understanding to make the best possible use of the system, and establishing a procedure for moving into the maintenance phase of the system life cycle.

Building use understanding.   Despite the user training activity during the detailed design and implementation phase, the installation of a new system is seldom routine. The problems usually involve the user. Systems analysts can predict ahead of time what the computerized portion of the system will do, but it is very difficult to predict what the user will do. Often users have a much bigger problem adapting to the new system than the developers had building it.

A good user training program is only the first step in building user understanding of the new system. Also, training programs tend to be most effective at the clerical or operational level. This type of program should be followed, during and after installation, by a series of discussions with users at all levels. At the start, these discussions can center around perceived problems with the system. Later, for situations in which several users interact with the system in much the same way, these sessions can emphasize insights gained by individual users in making full use of the system. The point is to encourage the user to go beyond a merely mechanical use of the system to a deeper understanding of its capabilities. The user should learn to exploit the system. It is not at all uncommon for a user who understands how a system works to successfully apply parts of the system in ways that would not have occurred to the original project team.

There are two main requirements for developing user understanding of the new system. The first is that the system work effectively—that it be reliable and easy to use. A system that is straightforward, with clean input requirements and clearly understandable outputs, is far superior to a system with numerous functions, some of which may not always perform reliably, and more complex, unnatural rules for describing inputs and outputs. The second requirement is an alert user management—one that provides the motivation and education required to make effective use of the system.

Transition to maintenance.   Ongoing maintenance of a new system is considered to begin from the time the installation phase ends. To the extent possible, maintenance projects should be held for consideration until after the post-implementation review phase, when it becomes more feasible to consider the results of the system and to put the need for and role of maintenance in perspective.

However, there may be requirements for maintenance that just can't wait until formal reviews have been performed. When maintenance is needed, it should be done following in-place maintenance procedures, rather than as an extension of the development project.

Within each CIS operation, there will usually be one or more staff analysts with maintenance responsibility. Maintenance requests should be routed through these regular channels. Normally, early maintenance requests will involve either correction of errors considered to be important or minor procedural changes that are easy and quick to make. Major enhancements of the system, unless they are mandated by regulatory agencies or changes in corporate policy, should wait until after the review phase is completed.

Whenever maintenance begins, it is important that procedures for updating documentation and keeping all document files current be instituted at the same time. Standards for current, accurate documentation should never be compromised for any kind of maintenance project.

PERSONNEL INVOLVED

File conversion work during this phase is handled by programmers and analysts. Installation responsibilities are coordinated among analysts, key users, and CIS operations personnel.

CUMULATIVE PROJECT FILE

At the end of this phase, the project file should contain:

- *The complete project plan.* This plan now shows both planned and actual hours spent on all activities. It will serve as the main basis for the review phase, after which it can be discarded.

- *The initial investigation report.* At this point, it is of historic interest only.

- *The feasibility report.* This report will be carried into the review phase, after which it is of historic interest only.

- *The new system specification.* This will also be used as a review phase document, then saved for its historic value.

- *A post-implementation maintenance list.* This document will form the basis for ongoing maintenance projects.

The following documents will become permanent support files for the new system:

- Data dictionary
- System documentation
- System test folder
- Program documentation and test logs
- User procedures manuals
- Computer operations manuals.

Summary

The installation phase marks the culmination of development efforts and the realization of the proposed new system. It is also a critical transition time for users, as they take over ownership of the new system.

The method of installation depends on the type of system, the needs and preferences of user managers, and the risks that can be tolerated. Options include an abrupt cutover, parallel operation with a single cutover, parallel operation with a gradual cutover, and version installation.

This phase has two principal objectives. First, the new system must be placed in full day-to-day operation, and the old system discontinued. Second, the user must gain an intimate and detailed understanding of the new system.

The general procedure for file conversion involves the following steps: Prepare existing computer files for conversion by updating, verifying accuracy, and correcting errors. Prepare existing manual files for conversion. Build and validate new files as they are created. Begin maintenance on the new files. Make a final check of accuracy, or balancing, between the new files and the old ones.

Once the system is installed and in regular operation, it belongs to the users. Systems analysts have completed their mission and should disengage as expeditiously as they can. Above all, systems analysts must avoid making any system changes that are not absolutely necessary at this point.

The user training program should be followed up, during and after installation, by a series of discussions with users at all levels.

Ongoing maintenance of a new system is considered to begin from the time that the installation phase ends. To the extent possible, maintenance projects should wait until after the post-implementation review phase has been completed. If maintenance is required, however, it should be handled through normal maintenance channels. Updating of documentation must accompany any maintenance project.

At the end of this phase, the cumulative project file should contain the following documents: the initial investigation report, now of historic interest only; the complete project plan, the feasibility report, and the new system specification, all of which will be used during the review phase; and a post-implementation maintenance list, which will form the basis for ongoing maintenance projects. The following documents will become permanent support files for the new system: data dictionary, system documentation, system test folder, program documentation and test logs, user procedures manuals, and computer operations manuals.

Key Terms

1. version installation   2. version

Review/Discussion Questions

1. What are the most important results of system installation.

2. What are the four basic alternative approaches to system installation?

3. When is system installation considered complete?

4. Under what circumstances are file conversion problems most likely to arise? Why?

5. What are the basic steps involved in file conversion?

6. What are the principal trade-offs between abrupt cutover and parallel operation with a single cutover? Under what circumstances would you be likely to choose one approach over the other?

7. Describe a situation in which parallel operation with a gradual cutover might be the most appropriate installation method. Why?

8. Explain how a version installation might be combined with each of the other three installation methods.

9. What are the main responsibilities of the systems analyst as the installation phase draws to a close?

10. Describe the contents and role of the cumulative project file on completion of system installation?

REVIEW 21

LEARNING OBJECTIVES

After completing the reading and other learning assignments for this chapter, you should be able to:

☐ Describe the scope and objectives of systems development recaps and post-implementation reviews following systems development projects.

☐ Describe the end products and other results of post-implementation reviews.

☐ Describe some systems development options that may be used in conjunction with or in place of the systems development life cycle, including system maintenance, the information center, applications software packages, version installation, and prototyping.

☐ Explain how fundamental systems development techniques may be used for systems maintenance after installation.

☐ Describe the role of an information center as a continuing resource.

PHASE DESCRIPTION

This chapter begins with an overview of the review phase of the systems development life cycle. One purpose of the review phase is to consider how the development project might have been carried out more effectively. Thus, it is natural for the chapter to conclude with a brief overview of other development options—approaches that can be used to modify, or in some cases, substitute for, the basic life cycle.

The position of the review phase within the systems development life cycle—as well as the component activities that make up this phase—are shown graphically in the flowchart in Figure 21-1.

A major characteristic of this phase is that it is completed in a short time span that is devoted to intensive study and analysis of project results.

The phase starts with Activity 14: Development Recap. This activity is devoted to an in-depth study of the developmental activities that have just been completed. The purpose of the recap is to prepare specific suggestions aimed at:

- Helping individual team members to perform more effectively on future project assignments

- Sharpening management skills for the organization as a whole and for the project team leader in particular

- Finding approaches that might enhance or improve the organization's skills and methods in systems development.

Activity 15: Post-Implementation Review is conducted after the new system has been in operation for some time. This time lapse permits the new system to become a regular part of day-to-day operations and the people involved to gain a measure of detachment. The purpose of this review is to:

- Evaluate how well the system has performed in meeting original expectations and projections for cost/benefit improvements.

- Identify any maintenance projects that should be undertaken to enhance or improve the implemented, ongoing system.

This second activity within the phase is particularly useful as a review of projects for which personnel or other cost savings were projected. This activity provides an opportunity to compare actual results with earlier projections.

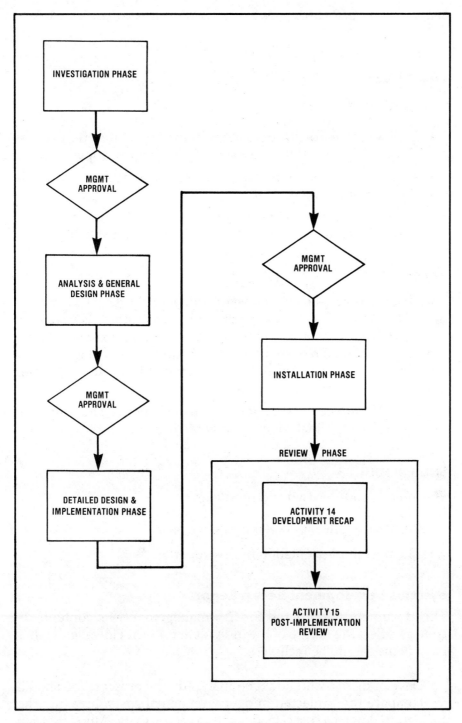

Figure 21-1. Diagram shows activities of the Review phase in relation to the overall systems development life cycle.

OBJECTIVES

Objectives for this phase are:

- Review systems development results in terms of the effectiveness of the life cycle and the management techniques applied.

- Review the new system to determine whether projected benefits have actually been realized.

- Review the new system to determine whether enhancement through maintenance projects is desirable and justifiable.

SCOPE

The development recap should begin immediately after the system is operating routinely. Even if some lingering tasks or details associated with installation remain to be completed, there is no point in delaying the recap activity. On the contrary, it is better to conduct this review while project team members are still available—and while their memories are still relatively fresh.

The post-implementation review is usually performed some four to six months after final completion of the installation phase.

END PRODUCTS

This phase produces two end products:

- The systems development recap report
- The post-implementation review report.

Systems Development Recap Report

This document is prepared for CIS management. Its contents, of course, reflect the nature of the individual project. However, certain basic items should be included:

- Development costs should be analyzed. The presentation should compare the projected budget with actual costs, breaking the figures down by cost category within each activity. Any significant variances should be analyzed and explained.

- Working time on the project should be reported and analyzed. Comparisons should be made between budgeted and actual working hours for each activity. Variances should be analyzed to determine cause, including rework required by user changes; rework required to meet outside mandates, such as rulings from regulatory agencies; rework caused by design errors; rework caused by programming errors; overruns due to failure of development team members to complete work as scheduled; and overruns due to estimating errors.

- Any design errors identified during the review should be described and classified according to their nature and should be related to any required rework.

- Programming errors should be similarly reported and classified.

- Suggested revisions in the systems development methodology should be described and evaluated.

- Any other suggestions or insights should be described.

Post-Implementation Review Report

This report is prepared for review by CIS and user departments. It may also be delivered to the steering committee. The following elements should be covered:

- The original requirements and objectives that led to the systems development project should be listed. This list should be accompanied by an evaluation of the extent to which the original requirements and objectives are being met by the installed system.

- The costs of developing and operating the new system should be reviewed and compared with original cost estimates.

- The originally projected benefits should be compared with the benefits actually realized.

- The new system should be reviewed as a functional entity to determine, first, whether any steps can be taken to realize more of the original or additional benefits, and, second, whether any modifications are needed in the near future.

THE PROCESS

The process approach for each of the activities in this phase is fairly straightforward.

Development Recap

Systems analysis is difficult to structure and do well—largely because it is so people-oriented. Because of these special challenges, a great deal of interest and effort is devoted to developing new techniques and methodologies that can make analysis more effective. But for an organization to incorporate these new ideas and approaches into its own systems development methodology, it is necessary periodically to pause, reflect on past experiences, and suggest modifications based both on these past experiences and on new techniques that have been developed.

The purpose here is to give the project team, and the organization, an opportunity to reflect on the project that has just been completed and to draw lessons and recommendations for improvement from the experience. As a starting point for this activity, the project leader prepares statistical reports that recap the development effort. These include comparisons between projected and actual expenditures, in money and in working time, for each activity. Causes should be assigned to any variances reported. Causes of variances should be readily supportable from statistics gathered during the development project. These may include specification changes that resulted in rework, identifiable errors that led to rework or overruns, inaccurate original projections, or performance by team members that was different from what was expected.

Team participation.   The development recap activity offers professional growth opportunities to each member of the project team. To realize these benefits, a series of meetings should be held to deal with the activities or phases of the project. Persons who were active during each of the phases or activities covered by a meeting should be present. With this level of participation, persons attending the meeting can understand and participate in the reviews and critiques of the work done. Based on their experience, participants can take part in brainstorming sessions aimed at improving project development and administration methods. Active participation in sessions of this type should enhance the professionalism of each of the individual team members.

Skill is needed to keep meetings of this type on track and productive. They must be approached with a positive attitude. The emphasis must be on making positive recommendations for future development work—not on retributions for past mistakes. Otherwise, the activity can degenerate into a forum for finger pointing and excuse making. The meetings themselves should be relatively brief. For example, a recommended schedule might include two one-hour meetings on each of the three key phases of the project.

Importance of the development recap. Many systems development life cycles do not list a development recap as a separately identified activity. This is understandable. First, there is the pressure to "move on." While the recap may be seen as "nice to do," there is normally a backlog of development projects awaiting action, and management sees greater payoff in beginning them with no further delay. Second, without the proper approach and management backing, the recap may be seen as a threat to members of the project team. They may view it only as an exercise in covering past errors and failures.

However, as stated above, without this recap activity it is very difficult for an organization to break out of its old approaches to problems and take advantage of advances being made in the systems development area. With a separately identified development recap activity, and with positive management support and expectations, the stage is set for growth in the ability of an organization to respond to systems development needs.

Post-Implementation Review

This is an actual review of the new system after it has been installed and operating for four to six months. Depending on the size of the system, this review may require the efforts of one or more analysts. These analysts may or may not have been members of the original project team.

Standard systems analysis techniques are used, including interviews with users and operations personnel. Data are collected on processing volumes and operating costs as a basis for analysis and comparison with the projections made during the feasibility study and updated at the end of the analysis and general design phase.

The job of the systems analysts completing this work is, in part, to determine whether user objectives are being met. The results of the new system are compared with the stated objectives. These objectives are contained in the user specification and also in the new system design specification—documents produced during the analysis and general design phase. In addition, the analysts are charged with determining whether projected benefits for the new system are being realized. A comparison is made between existing costs and benefits and those projected during the analysis and general design phase of the development project.

Any problems noted should be analyzed and described. If appropriate, recommendations for corrective action should be submitted.

OTHER SYSTEMS DEVELOPMENT OPTIONS

This entire book has been devoted to the structure and application of analysis and design techniques within the framework of a systems development life cycle. The intent has been to show that the life cycle is not a rigid checklist of tasks to be performed, but rather is a series of guidelines and checkpoints that can be referenced in the process of developing computer information systems.

Within this context, a life cycle structure provides a way for the analyst to organize and keep track of the thousands of specific details that are part of any systems development project. Within the life cycle structure, the experienced analyst is able to keep the principles of systems development clearly in view and to maintain a results-oriented perspective despite inevitable preoccupation with the details of individual activities.

Each project is different, and each is best approached by adapting the systems development process to it. Certainly, different projects will call for varying degrees of emphasis on the several activities of the basic systems development life cycle. The experienced analyst can go beyond this and employ an even broader range of options in modifying the basic structure of the development life cycle to meet the needs of a particular project.

As part of the discussion of the review phase, therefore, it seems appropriate to discuss some of the more prominent options available to the systems analyst. These are:

- System maintenance
- The information center
- Application software packages
- Version installation
- Prototyping.

The experienced analyst—firmly grounded in the principles and processes of systems development—will be able to use these options to modify the basic systems development life cycle as appropriate to fit the particular project.

System Maintenance

Any time a system exists, maintenance should be considered as a possible alternative to the development of an entirely new system. Maintenance can begin almost from the moment a new system is born. It is a normal, expected part of the services associated with a computer information system. Normally, one or more analysts within a CIS department will be assigned to perform maintenance studies and to direct maintenance projects for each system.

The difference between maintenance and full-scale systems development is not clear-cut. Each CIS organization will have its own standards for defining maintenance projects. These are based on the scope or extent of work to be done. All of the principles and techniques described in this book in connection with systems development projects also apply to system maintenance. In other words, a maintenance project can be viewed as a miniature systems development project. Differences lie chiefly in the formality with which the methodology is applied.

Maintenance projects are similar to systems development projects in that there is heavy user involvement in initial problem definition and requirements specification. Furthermore, the analysis, design, and implementation tasks required to complete a maintenance project are very similar to those required to implement an entirely new system. Differences are largely in the degree of change required. Revisions involving correction of errors, minor changes in input methods or output documents, or the addition of reports or capabilities can usually be handled by maintenance. At some point, however, either cumulatively or suddenly, change requirements become so extensive that maintenance is no longer the answer; it is better to commit to the building of an entirely new system.

As indicated, all of the structuring and management principles of the systems development life cycle apply in maintenance, except that they should be tailored to the needs of the individual project. The formal phase and activity checkpoints may be missing in a maintenance project.

No matter how formally the life cycle management structure is applied on a maintenance project, the techniques, processes, and products that have been stressed throughout this book are of paramount importance during maintenance. These analysis processes apply equally well to both maintenance projects and to new system development projects.

In summary, maintenance is always an option. Each organization will normally have criteria, based on time required and extent of change, for choosing this option.

The Information Center

An *information center* is a specialized service and support function within a CIS department. In effect, an information center is a self-service, do-it-yourself facility that can be made available directly to users. User managers with special information needs—such as reports based on data already available in a database—can use powerful, ultra-high-level software tools to write instructions that will access the needed information, assemble the data, and prepare desired reports or displays.

The information center has a number of responsibilities, including:

- Maintaining user-oriented software tools used for special reporting or file management

- Training users to apply special software tools on their own

- Providing some systems analysis support for applications development, operating controls, and the security of data and information

- Maintaining special purpose databases extracted from main production databases or developed and updated directly by the user.

If an information center exists, it may provide either options within or alternatives to systems development projects. For applications involving extensive information retrieval or decision support reporting, the availability of a supporting database may eliminate the need to develop a new system to produce these identified outputs. Instead of a development project, a user can write specifications and, possibly with only minimal help from systems personnel, develop the needed outputs directly and promptly.

Application Software Packages

The term *software package*, when used within a systems development context, usually applies to a specific application. The term can describe anything from a subsystem or routine applicable within large numbers of systems to an entire system that can be applied on an off-the-shelf basis. Hundreds of software suppliers are now offering literally thousands of application packages—with some substantial degree of success.

Application software packages can be either generic or industry-specific. For example, a general ledger accounting package may be appropriate for the financial reporting needs of virtually any business. On the other hand, specialized applications may have limited general applicability. The use of application software packages that are appropriate in a specific industry have great value. Often, these applications support highly complex or regulated portions of an industry. To develop and maintain such applications in-house becomes prohibitive in cost. Further, the knowledgeable professionals and other resources for maintaining such systems are scarce. As an example, packages have been developed for use by common carrier trucks required to report mileage in specific states. Between these two extremes, there are generalized applications, such as job cost analysis, order fulfillment, or accounts payable, that have some industry feature but are fairly general in their applicability.

The possibility of finding and using application software packages is mentioned prominently in earlier chapters of this book, particularly in connection with activities in the analysis and general design phase. This is the point within a project at which a decision should be made on whether application packages are to be used and, if so, which packages should be selected.

The most obvious potential advantage of application packages is that, if they fit, they can save substantial time and money. There is also a degree of assurance, since other users have applied and found success with the package, that the programs are workable and of relatively high quality.

The main disadvantage is that, if the package does not represent an exact fit with identified needs, it may be necessary to modify either the purchased package or the procedures of the user organization. To use the package, the company may find that it has to forego some system features that would have been desirable or to change some of its procedures. If the misfit is great enough, it may be necessary to revise or rewrite portions of programs to tailor them to the specific needs of the company.

Another potential disadvantage of purchased programs is that maintenance may be a problem. Since the programs were not written within the organization where they are being used, different standards may have been applied in designing, coding, or documenting the programs. Program designs may be too inflexible to be changed readily. Even if the package is of generally high quality, time and money will have to be committed to training one or more CIS staff members to maintain it. Typically, it is possible to purchase a maintenance contract that covers error correction and continuing enhancements to the package.

In other words, a packaged application program is not like a piece of furniture. Packaged programs cannot simply be purchased and installed anywhere they seem to fit. Rather, before a decision is made to use packaged application programs, careful study and analysis are necessary.

In evaluating application packages, detailed attention should be given to making sure that the programs being considered will run on existing hardware within a particular CIS facility. The same applies to existing software. Purchased programs, if they are to be used, must be compatible both with system software and with other application programs. The purchased package should also match application requirements in terms of business and CIS processing cycles.

Attention should also be given to installation requirements, including any difficulties that may occur in bringing the purchased system into use; the completeness and quality of documentation; and the flexibility of the design, or architecture, of the programs themselves. Finally, it is critically important to be sure that a package considered for purchase is capable of handling the data and the functions of the system being specified.

The nature of these evaluations highlights the advantages of holding off on decisions concerning application packages until the analysis and general design phase is nearly complete. At this point in the life cycle, the needs of the new system are understood with considerable clarity. The new system has been specified at both a logical and a physical level with such aids as data flow diagrams and supporting documents. Thus, it becomes possible to compare individual data elements, key business processing functions, and even specific process descriptions of software packages with those specified for the new system. At the end of the analysis and general design phase, the tools exist to evaluate with considerable precision whether an available package fits the system and, if the fit is not exact, just what needs to be done to adapt it.

Version Installation

Version installation, as described earlier, breaks a complete system down into a series of parts, identified as versions that can be implemented separately. Typically, a basic version is implemented first. Then, other versions are added to provide additional functions or processing capabilities to enhance the basic system.

Consider, for example, a project to develop a comprehensive student information system at a college or university. This would be a major undertaking, but one which would break apart quite naturally into a series of versions. The initial version could support the basic functions of course registration and grade reporting. After this version was installed and running smoothly, a second version could add the capability to perform degree audits—to verify that students had met degree requirements. Automatic prerequisite checking at the time of course registration could then be added in version three. Finally, a fourth version might add an individualized course planning feature that could be used for student advising and could be summarized for course demand analysis and schedule planning. Successive versions add new capabilities rather than changing those provided by earlier versions.

Version installation represents an option that can modify the steps followed in the later phases of the systems development life cycle. However, the basic project structure and methodologies remain intact. If a version installation option is used, the complete system should still be analyzed as an entity and carried through, again in its entirety, at least to the end of the analysis and general design phase. The system can then be partitioned into versions for performance of the remaining activities of the detailed design and implementation phase and the installation phase.

Some definite advantages accrue from the practice of designing a system as an entity even though it may be implemented and installed in different versions. One of these is that the database can be designed with the total system needs in mind. Thus, the complete system will be supported as each version is implemented and installed. This is because the interrelationships among versions are understood from the outset. Similarly, some of the application programs in the total system may be shared by different versions. If the entire system has been designed in advance, the finished programs will be more appropriate for the final jobs they will be expected to do.

If version installation is used, there will be some modification in the structure of the systems development life cycle. Steering committee decisions at the conclusion of the second and third phases of the project will be limited to one version at a time. This means that the resources allocated in individual decisions will be smaller. On the other hand, financial feasibility may be difficult to justify for the first version because costs may be relatively high and benefits limited. Moreover, changes in cost pictures over time could result in decisions not to implement successive versions after the first one has been installed.

Another possible advantage of implementing the system one version at a time, rather than completing the entire system at once, is the potential for greater responsiveness. Because a part of a system can be implemented in less time, at lower cost, it becomes possible to demonstrate results more quickly and to build credibility for the system as it is unfolding. At the same time, this approach makes it possible to realize some of the benefits of the system at an earlier point than would be possible if the entire system were being implemented at once. This partial completion can be particularly attractive if tight deadlines are involved. For example, it may be possible to implement the version that meets regulatory needs immediately, leaving enhancements to the system for later implementation.

Problems to avoid in connection with version installation involve inconsistencies in overall design that can come with the breaking down of a system into separate versions. Further, version implementation may diminish control over overall system costs.

In summary, version installation can be a potentially valuable option under the right circumstances. However, this methodology requires careful thought and planning to identify proper versions and to provide for tight management control over resources committed to the project over time.

Prototyping

Prototyping is a specialized systems development approach in which operational, working systems are created virtually on a real-time basis. That is, a transition is made directly from user requests to computerized implementation of a system that complies with this request. This is done with powerful application software development tools that make it possible to create all of the files and processing programs needed for a business application in a matter of days, perhaps even hours.

One of the greatest challenges in systems analysis is gaining a sufficiently realistic and detailed understanding of new system requirements that the user can truly evaluate the proposed solution. This understanding is aimed at avoiding the extensive specification changes that can result if users change their minds at later points in a project. Prototyping offers tremendous potential benefit here. The user can actually experience and work with the basic aspects of a proposed solution. The result may be a modification of stated requirements and, hence, a more stable new system design with which to enter the implementation phase. Or the prototype may actually be accepted as the final system, concluding the development project.

Note the difference between prototyping and the services of an information center. The information center provides a setting in which the user can develop reporting services from existing databases. In prototyping, analysts and programmers actually develop operational systems, usually by means of software tools that function as program generators. Typically, inputs to these software tools are in the form of functional parameters used to specify a system. Using these basic functional parameters, the software tools actually generate coding and documentation for programs. Typically, a program generator will produce source coding in a high-level language, such as COBOL. This source coding can then be compiled as though it had been written by a programmer.

A prototype is, in fact, a working system. It can be developed quickly and inexpensively—given the necessary software tools. It may or may not be inexpensive to run. Prototypes are built iteratively. Basic requirements are identified and implemented quickly. Then, the prototype is used, requirements are modified, and the process is repeated. The result may serve as the primary statement of new system requirements in the analysis and general design phase of the systems development life cycle, or it may be accepted as the new system itself.

To put prototyping into perspective, consider a hypothetical situation. Suppose a company wanted to develop a system to prepare shipping orders and invoices. Within a day or so, it would be possible to generate enough programs to produce a few invoices at a time. This would show users and systems people what the initially requested products would actually look like and how inputs could be used to produce those products. The system might not use the computer efficiently enough to be applied for production purposes. However, it would provide a way of evaluating alternatives and specifying desired results.

In the situation described above, the resulting programs would not represent a finished system. On the other hand, if an application required only occasional processing—say, quarterly or semiannually—it might be possible to use a prototype-produced system on a regular basis. For example, suppose management wanted to input industry statistics that became available once each quarter to produce competitive analysis reports and projections. Such a system would require only minimal computer processing time. Although the prototype system might not use the computer as efficiently as one that had been written with conventional techniques, the trade-offs might favor the prototyping approach because of the size of the job and the frequency of use of the system.

Within a systems development project, use of prototyping can change the role and extent of the systems analysis services required. For example, if prototyping is used, it will probably be possible to reduce the number of interviews and other information gathering activities. In effect, the ability to produce and test results directly makes it less necessary to gather opinions on what solutions would be best. Also, the prototyping process brings the user into closer contact with the systems analyst and programmer. The user may wind up spending more time in prototyping than would be the case in traditional systems development. However, users may find that they gain increased control over the development of the systems produced for them.

The main advantages of prototyping are, first, a better understanding of user requirements for the new system through faster feedback and, second, the potential for using the prototype as the final solution—bypassing the time-consuming and expensive implementation activities. The most obvious cost associated with prototyping is the need for sophisticated software tools to support rapid implementation of the necessary computer programs.

There is, however, a second potential cost—more subtle, but clear to anyone who understands the analysis process based on iterative modeling. Prototyping tends to stress only the physical aspects of a system. The entire emphasis is on user statements of (physical) requirements and the rapid realization of a (physical) system that supports those requirements. The prototyping process does not support the logical modeling of requirements and proposed solutions. Thus, system specifications based only on prototypes are likely to carry forward inefficiencies and even errors that were part of the original system. For this reason, prototyping is most effective when used to enhance—rather than replace—the analysis process presented in the earlier chapters of this book.

The five options discussed above, it is worth repeating, are only some of the alternatives and additions that can be identified in connection with the systems development processes covered in this book. Systems analysts should be on the lookout continually for new and improved techniques that can be applied to the analysis, design, and development of computer information systems. At the same time, the basic principles of systems development, supported by an overall life cycle, retain continuing value. These principles provide a basis for assuring that business problems are understood and considered fully, that proposed solutions do address the problems they are supposed to solve, and that technical designs and programs implement the problem solutions that users have accepted and that management has underwritten.

Summary

After a new system is operational, there should be two reviews of results—a recap shortly after implementation and a post-implementation review four to six months later.

The recap should begin as soon as the system is operating routinely. Its purpose is to help individual team members perform more effectively on future project assignments, sharpen management skills, and find approaches that might enhance or improve the organization's skills and methods in future systems development projects.

The systems development recap report prepared for CIS management should compare projected costs, both in money and in working time, against actual costs. Figures should be broken down by category within each activity, and any significant variances should be analyzed and explained. Any design errors or programming errors that may have necessitated reworking should be reported and classified. Finally, any suggested revisions in the systems development methodology should be described and evaluated.

The purpose of the post-implementation review is to evaluate how well the system is meeting original expectations and projections, and to identify any maintenance projects that should be implemented to enhance or improve the system.

The post-implementation review report is prepared for review by CIS and user departments, and may also be delivered to the Steering Committee. This report should include a list of the original requirements and objectives and an evaluation of the extent to which these have been met. Developmental and operational costs of the new system should be reviewed and compared with original cost estimates, and the originally projected benefits should be compared with the benefits actually realized. Finally, the new system should be reviewed as a functional entity to determine, first, whether any steps can be taken to realize more of the original or additional benefits, and, second, whether any modifications are needed in the near future.

This chapter also reviews several other systems development options that may be applied as alternatives or additions to all or part of the basic systems development process outlined in this book. Among these options are system maintenance, the information center, application software packages, version installation, and prototyping.

Key Terms

1. information center
2. software package
3. prototyping

Review/Discussion Questions

1. What reviews should be conducted following implementation of a new system?

2. What information should be gathered and reported during the recap activity that takes place shortly after implementation?

3. What information should be gathered and reported during the post-implementation review activity that takes place four to six months after implementation?

4. What can users gain from review activities that follow implementation of a new system?

5. What can CIS management gain from review activities that follow implementation of a new system?

6. What can top management of a company gain from review activities that follow implementation of a new system?

7. How can procedures for systems development be employed for systems maintenance?

8. What is the function of an information center?

9. What precautions should be taken in the implementation of application software packages?

10. How should a version installation be implemented?

11. What are the potential benefits of and problems that can be associated with prototyping?

PROJECT MANAGEMENT 22

LEARNING OBJECTIVES

On completing the reading and other learning assignments in this chapter, you should be able to:

☐ Describe the role of the systems development life cycle in providing a basis for comparison, measurement, and decision making on CIS projects.

☐ Explain the three functions of project management—planning, scheduling, and control.

☐ Describe the characteristics of a project that make it definable and manageable.

☐ Discuss techniques used in PERT and CPM and tell how these techniques differ.

☐ Show how critical path algorithms are applied.

☐ Demonstrate the use of a Gantt chart.

NATURE OF PROJECT MANAGEMENT

The systems development life cycle is, in effect, a plan, or structure, for a systems development project.

Consider what the life cycle is and what it does for the development of a computer information system: The life cycle establishes standard phases and activities, creating a series of known tasks, activities, phases, and management checkpoints. This structuring makes it possible to communicate uniformly within an organization about the needs of, and progress within, any systems development project. Further, the standardization of phases and activities makes it possible to compare progress and results among a number of systems development projects. Thus, in addition to providing a work structure, the life cycle provides a basis for comparison, measurement, and, ultimately, investment decision making. The life cycle, then, provides a framework for applying analysis, design, and implementation methodologies and also establishes a structure for managing the systems development effort.

If the life cycle is, as indicated, a structure that helps make system projects manageable, it is also true that the life cycle, by itself, falls short of being a project management technique. Putting it another way, the life cycle provides a framework within which each organization must still develop some method for managing individual projects. Also, some means must exist for comparability of reporting to management on plans, schedules, and results. Within this context, the term *project management* refers to a method or combination of techniques to facilitate planning, scheduling, and control—the three components of project management.

Planning

Planning for overall information system support is critically important in any organization. However, the focus of this discussion is on that planning that occurs within the context of a development project. In this setting, planning involves the identification of all of the major segments, or phases, of a project. These phases are then subdivided into specific activities and individual jobs, or tasks. Together, these are the assignments that must be completed in the course of a project. In systems development projects, the standard tasks are fairly well known and established in advance. Thus, while planning and scheduling are critical within the systems development life cycle, planning is done within a fairly structured context. The systems development life cycle itself provides a structure against which an individual project and its goals can be compared to see how well the standard structure matches the specific needs of an individual undertaking. For example, different systems development projects will require varying amounts of technical support, application programming, or user training. In effect, the life cycle provides a matrix against which specific projects can be planned in terms of the end results to be delivered and the interim expectations at managerial checkpoints.

Scheduling

Planning identifies tasks or jobs that must be completed. *Scheduling*, then, relates the tasks in a time sequence. A project scheduling system relates resources, as well as time, in establishing the sequence of events to be followed. Within the project structure itself, provision is made for the sequence in which jobs are done. Provisions are also made for situations in which activities and tasks should overlap and share findings and results. This basic scheduling implicit in the project structure, however, can be no more than a skeleton. Time alone is only one dimension of scheduling.

Resources must be identified and allocated as part of the scheduling operation. Within a systems development project, the primary resources are skilled people. Therefore, part of the scheduling work lies in identifying the personnel who must be available for, and involved in, the project. In some instances, the ready availability of people will facilitate task or activity scheduling, causing jobs to be started or completed ahead of normal expectations. In other cases, a shortage of required people may constrain a project, causing delays or overlaps in scheduling. In the final analysis, then, scheduling is the art of doing the best possible job with the resources available.

Control

Planning and scheduling take place before work is actually done. *Control* involves the monitoring of work to compare plans and schedules with actual performance. Under the control function, results are monitored in terms of time and resources expended and, as necessary, corrective actions are taken. In extreme cases, the control function includes the responsibility for aborting projects as experience proves that the anticipated results cannot be attained. Ultimately, then, management decision making resides in the control function.

APPLYING PROJECT MANAGMENT

A *project* is an extensive job involving multiple, interrelated tasks. But a project has certain other important characteristics that make it manageable—that make it possible to apply project management techniques for planning, scheduling, and control. These characteristics include:

- A project is *finite*. It has a definite beginning and a specific ending point. Before a project is started, its managers should be able to define when it will be concluded. Thus, an ongoing operation, such as management of a computer center or a manufacturing plant, is not a project.
- A project is a one-time effort. It is *nonrepetitive*.
- A project consists of a number of segments that can be broken down into separate phases, activities, and tasks. In other words, a project can be *partitioned* into identifiable parts.
- Because many tasks are involved that require an assortment of knowledge and skills, projects tend to be *complex*.
- Projects are *predictable*. In this respect, a systems development project would differ, for example, from a research program that sets out to discover some previously unknown phenomenon. In a research program, scientists follow their findings. In a project, a predetermined course of task performance is followed.

PROJECT MANAGEMENT TECHNIQUES

The tools of project management must assist in the first two management components—planning and scheduling. These tools will also support the reporting of status that serves as a basis for control decisions. Within the CIS project structure, there are two levels of control decisions. The first is the detailed, day-to-day control of tasks needed to keep the project on track. The second is the decision making authority vested in a top-level steering committee. The project structure assumes that information will be funneled to the steering committee in digestible form. The rest of this chapter talks about some tools available for planning and scheduling, including the feedback of information that will serve as a basis for control.

The challenges in planning and scheduling for projects lie in the interrelationships among activities and tasks. Therefore, the primary tools for supporting the planning and scheduling functions are directed toward dealing with these interrelationships. Two techniques that share many similarities are commonly used for this purpose. These are known as:

- Project Evaluation and Review Technique (PERT)
- Critical Path Method (CPM).

Project Evaluation and Review Technique (PERT)

The *Project Evaluation and Review Technique (PERT)* was developed during the 1950s under the auspices of the United States Navy. The Navy was faced with a major project—development of the Polaris weapon system for firing intermediate range ballistic missles from submarines. All of the characteristic features and problems of project management were present. The computer had just emerged as a tool capable of rapid completion of all of the calculations necessary to interrelate the thousands of identified activities and tasks.

The project structure was classic in that all of the events and tasks were directed toward a specific, single result—putting a weapon into service within a specified time frame. The elements of the project were complex, since multiple components and literally hundreds of manufacturers and other vendors were involved. Special ships had to be designed. Environmental problems had to be overcome in the undersea launching of missiles. Targeting, tracking, warhead, and safety systems all had to be devised and integrated. All of these elements could be identified and broken down into manageable components. But there were so many elements that traditional methods of listing, scheduling, and monitoring simply couldn't do the job. PERT provided a method for project managers to:

- Identify the tasks within the project.
- Order the tasks in time sequence.
- Estimate the time required to complete each task, the relationships among tasks, and the time requirement for the entire project.
- Identify the *critical tasks* that must be performed individually and that, together, account for the total elapsed time of the project.
- Identify noncritical tasks for which some *slack time* could be built into schedules without affecting the duration of the entire project.

Critical Path Method (CPM)

The *Critical Path Method (CPM)* is similar to PERT. It is designed as a planning and scheduling tool for major projects. In addition, CPM incorporates a capability for identifying relationships between the cost and the completion date of a project, as well as the amount and value of resources that must be applied in alternative situations. On certain types of major projects, it is possible to shorten completion dates by applying greater resources to the effort. In other words, by assigning more people and spending more money, the results can be realized sooner. CPM provides a means of predicting and measuring these trade-offs.

CPM was developed in the same general time frame as PERT through a joint effort of the DuPont Company and the Univac Division of Remington Rand.

Comparison of Techniques

The methodologies used in PERT and CPM are essentially similar. These methodologies are described in the discussions that follow. The important differences between PERT and CPM center around the assumptions on which the techniques are based. These assumptions, in turn, deal with time allocations for scheduled tasks.

PERT permits broad estimates about the time durations of tasks. Variations in time allocations do not materially affect use of this technique.

On the other hand, CPM assumes that time requirements for completion of individual tasks are relatively predictable. Within the CPM system also, a relationship is assumed between the time it takes to complete a task and the amount of money an organization is willing to spend by applying resources for its completion.

Because of these basic differences of approach, application areas for PERT and CPM tend to be somewhat different. For the most part, PERT is used for projects involving research and development, situations in which there are apt to be greater variations in time consumed by individual tasks—and in which there are no clear-cut trade-offs between the application of resources and the production of results. Therefore, systems development projects have proved to be ideal candidates for application of PERT techniques. In systems development, it is difficult to relate the allocation of resources to the time required to complete any task.

On the other hand, CPM tends to be used on projects for which direct relationships can be established between time and resources. To illustrate, in building a road, completion can be expedited if more earth moving and grading equipment is assigned to a project. The same is true with other types of construction. Therefore, construction projects—and some manufacturing projects—have been prime application areas for CPM techniques.

There are also some types of systems development projects for which relationships between time and resources can be established. For example, large, sophisticated computer systems have been introduced recently that can expedite systems analysis and design activities. A decision to apply these automated developmental techniques could expedite certain analysis and design activities. On the other hand, simply adding more programmers to an application development assignment would not necessarily guarantee earlier completion. In fact, adding people to certain types of assignments could tend to lengthen the schedule. Because of these features, CPM tends to be used only selectively in the systems development area.

PLANNING AND SCHEDULING NETWORKS

Both PERT and CPM use graphic *networks* as basic tools. Within this context, a network is a flow diagram relating the set of individual tasks, or jobs, that must be completed to the sequence in which they must occur. The network of tasks is presented in a graphic format known as a *project graph*.

To build a visual network, planners usually begin with a list of tasks, or jobs, as shown in Figure 22-1. This example lists the tasks to be completed during the detailed design and implementation phase of a systems development project. The tasks will lead to the design of a file updating system.

A network constructed from the task list for the file updating system is shown in Figure 22-2. In this network, tasks are represented as labeled arrows leading from one circle to another. The circles in scheduling networks are known as *nodes*. The nodes identify the beginning and ending points of a task. The estimated times for completing

SYSTEM DESIGN PROJECT—FILE UPDATING SYSTEM

Job Identification	Alternate Identification	Immediate Predecessor	Job Description	Time Estimate (days)
a	(1,2)	–	Design overall system structure	30
b	(2,3)	a	Develop program specifications	12
c	(3,4)	b	Design control program	8
d	(3,5)	b	Design update program	15
e	(3,6)	b	Design report program	7
f	(4,7)	c	Code control program	2
g	(4,8)	c	Prepare system user guide	5
h	(7,10)	c	Test control program	2
i	(5,9)	d	Code update program	6
j	(9,10)	i	Test update program	4
k	(10,12)	h,j	Test control/update programs	2
l	(6,11)	e	Code report program	3
m	(11,12)	l	Test report program	1
n	(12,13)	k,m	Integration test	4

Figure 22-1. Listing of data for activities of the file updating system project.

the tasks are listed in parenthesis next to the job lines. Each node, or milestone event, is assigned a reference number. These numbers are used as alternate identifications in the basic task list in Figure 22-1. The alternate identifications, obviously, consist of the beginning and ending nodes for the task. These numbers are used as basic identification codes and serve as the basis for scheduling when network data are processed under computer programs.

In effect, Figures 22-1 and 22-2 show the same data in table and graphic form. The data in Figure 22-1 could be used, directly, as computer input for a program that produces a graph like the one shown in Figure 22-2 on a plotter. Using the same data, network graphs can also be developed manually.

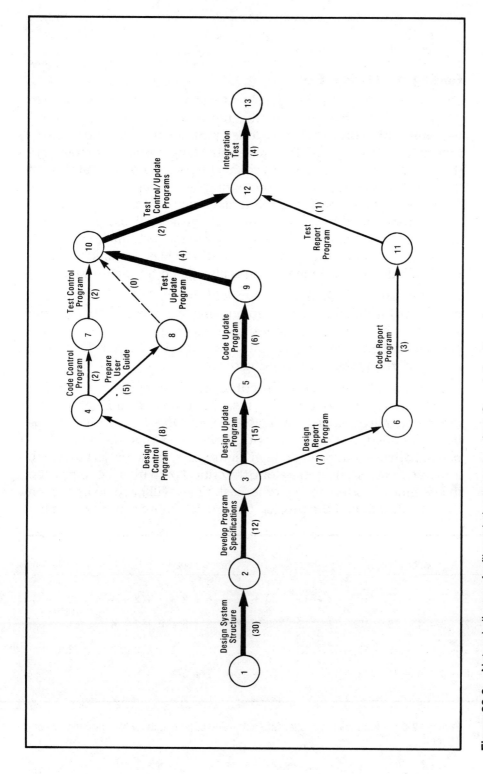

Figure 22-2. Network diagram for file updating system project. Completion times for activities are given in parentheses. Heavy line represents critical path.

Finding the Critical Path

Once a network has been established for project tasks, it is possible to pick a path through the network that represents the projected completion time for the project. This is done by adding together the elapsed-time notations on the task lines to see how long it will take to complete the project. The idea is to form a connecting line, or path, that runs all the way through the project, representing the *minimum* amount of time for project completion. This minimum requirement for the project will actually represent the *longest path* through the tasks. This is because the set, or sequence, of tasks that will take the longest time to complete represents the minimum amount of time that will be required to get the whole job done. This longest path is also called the *critical path*.

To illustrate, look at the network in Figure 22-2. There are four possible paths that can be traced for moving through the network from start to finish. Figure 22-3 identifies these four paths. The longest elapsed time traverses the path through nodes 1-2-3-5-9-10-12-13. This path requires a total of 73 working days.

The tasks, or jobs, along the critical path are referred to as critical tasks. These tasks are critical because the combined completion time determines the duration of the entire project. Once this critical path has been identified, it is drawn in with darker lines than the other alternative paths, as has been done in Figure 22-2. If the project duration is to be shortened, the tasks along the critical path must be completed in less time. Shortening any other task times will have no impact on the total duration of the project. On projects more complex than the

Paths (Nodes)	Times (in days)	Total Time
1 – 2 – 3 – 4 – 7 – 10 – 12 – 13	30 + 12 + 8 + 2 + 2 + 2 + 4	60
1 – 2 – 3 – 4 – 8 – 10 – 12 – 13	30 + 12 + 8 + 5 + 0 + 2 + 4	61
1 – 2 – 3 – 5 – 9 – 10 – 12 – 13	30 + 12 + 15 + 6 + 4 + 2 + 4	73 (Critical Path)
1 – 2 – 3 – 6 – 11 – 12 – 13	30 + 12 + 7 + 3 + 1 + 4	5 7

Figure 22-3.   Identification of alternate paths and critical path for file updating system project.

one shown in Figure 22-3, there may be more than one critical path. If this happens, there will be alternate paths, each taking the same longest time span for completion.

Tasks that are not on the critical path are said to have slack. This means that these tasks can slip either in starting times or in durations without affecting the total running time for the project as a whole. Being able to identify slack tasks can be extremely valuable in project management. Knowing a task is slack, for example, a project manager may divert resources from a slack task to a critical one, helping to keep the entire project on schedule, or reducing overall project duration.

Critical Path Algorithm

For a relatively small project like the one shown in Figure 22-3, the critical path can be located relatively easily and quickly through inspection. On major projects, however, the job can become far more tedious. In these situations, a *critical path algorithm* can be used to help identify the longest sequence of tasks. To illustrate, Figure 22-4 presents a redrawn network for the file updating system based on the same data presented in Figure 22-1. The numbers within brackets in this illustration represent task start and finish times used in applying the critical path algorithm. The source of these numbers is explained below.

Early start and finish times.   To calculate project completion times, it is necessary to develop projected dates on which tasks will start and on which they will be completed. The start and completion dates are relative to the elapsed time from the very beginning of the project. The *start time* for the project, identified by the symbol S, is always zero. The *finish time* for the entire project is identified with the symbol T.

The *early start* of a task is the earliest possible time at which it can begin. The symbol for early start is ES. The *early finish* time for a task, indicated by the symbol EF, is determined by adding its estimated completion time to its early start time. The symbol for the estimated completion time for a task is t_e. The formula for determining the early finish time, then, is:

$$EF = ES + t_e$$

Assuming that the starting time for a project is zero, the finish time for the first task is derived by adding the estimated time to zero. In Figure

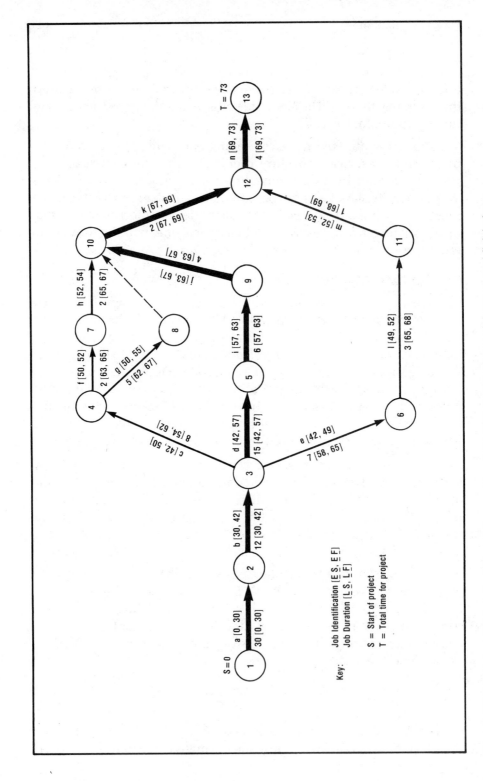

Figure 22-4. Network graph for file updating system project, incorporating activity start and finish times.

22-4, the first task, *a*, has an early start time of zero and an early finish time of 30. These values appear in brackets above the arrow representing this task. Continuing with the example in Figure 22-4, task *b* cannot begin until task *a* is completed. Therefore, its early start time is 30—the same as the early finish time for the previous task. The early finish time for the second task is 42, derived by adding the estimated time to the start time:

$$EF = ES + t_e = 30 + 12 = 42$$

This process is continued for each task on the network. In each instance, the early start time is the latest completion date for the preceding task. This is illustrated in the situation of task *k*. The early start time assigned to this task is 67. This represents the latest of the early finish times for the three jobs that must be completed before task *k* can begin. Task *h* has an early finish time of 54. Task *g* has an early finish time of 55, while task *j* has a finish time of 67. Thus, 67 represents the earliest possible start time for task *k*.

After all tasks along the critical path have been traced in this manner, the early finish time for the last task becomes the total duration time for the project. In the network in Figure 22-4, the early finish time, *T* is 73 days. This means that, unless one or more of the critical path tasks can be shortened, the project will require 73 days to complete.

Late start and late finish times. As noted previously, the tasks not on the critical path offer some slack time. If these tasks delay, the tasks will not slow down the entire project—unless the delays are so long that the delays become part of the critical path. Thus, it may be possible to shift some people or other resources from slack tasks to critical ones to shorten the entire length of the project. If a project manager wishes to consider these possibilities, it can help to identify slack tasks and calculate the amount of slack that actually exists. This is done by calculating late start and finish times for the slack tasks.

The *late start*, or *LS*, of a task is the latest time at which it can begin without extending the total project completion time. The *late finish*, or *LF*, of the task is determined by adding the task duration to its late start time. Thus, to determine the latest possible start time for any task, its elapsed time is deducted from its late finish time:

$$LS = LF - t_e$$

Calculation of late start and late finish times for a network begin at the end of the network and work backward toward the beginning. In Figure 22-4, this has been done with numbers placed in brackets below the task lines. An example of how slack time can be computed for noncritical tasks is shown in the case of task m. This task must be completed before day 69, when task n must begin. The early dates for this task have been computed as 52 to start, 53 for completion, since the task takes only one day. Working backward, the calculations show that, since this task can conclude as late as day 69, it can also begin as late as day 68. Therefore, the potential slack time for task m—derived by deducting the early start date (52) from the late start date (68)—is 16 days. This same slack time, 16 days, applies to the difference between the late and early finish dates. This time is known as the *total slack* for task m.

Time calculations for the tasks in the file updating system are shown in Figure 22-5. The data in this table correspond with all the information in the network in Figure 22-4. Separate columns list time estimates for each task: the early start date, the late start date, the early finish date, the late finish date, and the total slack. Thus, tasks with slack time can be identified quickly and easily by reading the figures in the last column. Any tasks on the critical path will not have any slack time. A listing of this type, clearly, becomes a management tool for the possible reassignment or reallocation of resources within the project.

The time estimating examples cited so far are based upon acceptance of the estimated time for each task as a fixed time for its completion. In reality, time estimating cannot be done with this precision. The completion time for many tasks cannot be pinpointed this closely. Rather, there will be a range of time estimates for each task. These estimated times will usually be represented by low, medium, and high figures. The PERT method provides a means for dealing with these variations in elapsed times for individual tasks.

Job Identification	Job Description	Time Estimate (t_e)	Early Start (ES)	Late Start (LS)	Early Finish (EF)	Late Finish (LF)	Total Slack (days)
a	Design overall system structure	30	0	0	30	30	0
b	Develop program specifications	12	30	30	42	42	0
c	Design control program	8	42	54	50	62	12
d	Design update program	15	42	42	57	57	0
e	Design report program	7	42	58	49	65	16
f	Code control program	2	50	63	52	65	13
g	Prepare system user guide	5	50	62	55	67	12
h	Test control program	2	52	65	54	67	13
i	Code update program	6	57	57	63	63	0
j	Test update program	4	63	63	67	67	0
k	Test control/update programs	2	67	67	69	69	0
l	Code report program	3	49	65	52	68	16
m	Test report program	1	52	68	53	69	16
n	Integration test	4	69	69	73	73	0

Figure 22-5. Calculations and listings of activity and slack times, including total slack, for file updating system project.

PERT Time Estimates

Under the PERT method, three time estimates are made for each task. These estimates are:

- The *optimistic time estimate* (t_o) represents the best guess of the minimum time required to complete the task. This estimate assumes that all conditions will be ideal.
- The *most probable time estimate* (t_m) represents the best guess of the time that will be required to complete a task, assuming a normal number of problems or delays.
- The *pessimistic time estimate* (t_p) allows for the maximum completion time, assuming that everything that can go wrong will go wrong.

The expected duration of a task is then computed as the weighted average of the three time estimates. That is, it is estimated that the optimistic and pessimistic time estimates are equally likely to occur, while the most probable time estimate is four times more likely to occur than either of the other two. Applying these relative weights, the formula for calculating the average, or expected, time to complete a task (t_e) is:

$$t_e = \frac{t_o + 4t_m + t_p}{6}$$

To illustrate application of this formula, refer back to the table in Figure 22-1. This table shows that the initial task in the project, *a*, has been allocated 30 days of elapsed time. This figure was derived from application of the formula given above to an optimistic estimate of 18 days, a most probable time estimate of 28 days, and a pessimistic estimate of 50 days. Applying the formula to these estimates produces the following result:

$$t_e = \frac{t_o + 4t_m + t_p}{6} = \frac{18 + 4(28) + 50}{6} = \frac{180}{6} = 30 \text{ days}$$

The expected time for the first task (t_e) is 30 days. This same figure is calculated, in the same manner, for each of the time estimates appearing in the table in Figure 22-1 and in the network diagrams illustrated in this chapter. The total expected time for the entire project is then estimated by adding together the time estimates for the critical path tasks. As shown in Figure 22-5, the total estimated time for the file updating system project comes to 73 days.

GANTT CHARTS

Networking techniques provide tools for the planning and scheduling of project tasks. To complete the project management picture, some method for monitoring actual project performance and for reaching decisions about changes in project tasks or structures is necessary. A well established, commonly used visual tool for displaying time relationships and monitoring progress of project completion is the *Gantt chart.*

Gantt charts have been standard methods for displaying schedules and work status for production methods since the 1920s. Through the years, they have been adapted to serve the same purposes in multiple-activity projects.

A Gantt chart representing the schedule established in Figure 22-5 is shown in Figure 22-6. This illustration also indicates some of the basic characteristics of Gantt charts:

- Tasks that make up a project are listed vertically, in order of occurrence, starting at the top left of the chart.
- A *time scale* is indicated at either the top or the bottom of the chart. This scale reads from left to right.
- A bar showing the estimated time for each task is drawn in the appropriate time position on the same line as the task listing.
- The current date is indicated on the chart, usually through use of a movable tape or cord.
- An indication of *percentage completion* is given for each task on which work has begun.

In Figure 22-6, dark lines are used to represent the lengths of time between the early start and early finish dates calculated for each task. To illustrate, task *c, Design Control Program,* had an early start day of 42 and an early finish day of 50. A total of eight days had been estimated for this job. However, since this job was not on the critical path and had 12 slack days, it could be completed as late as day 62 without delaying

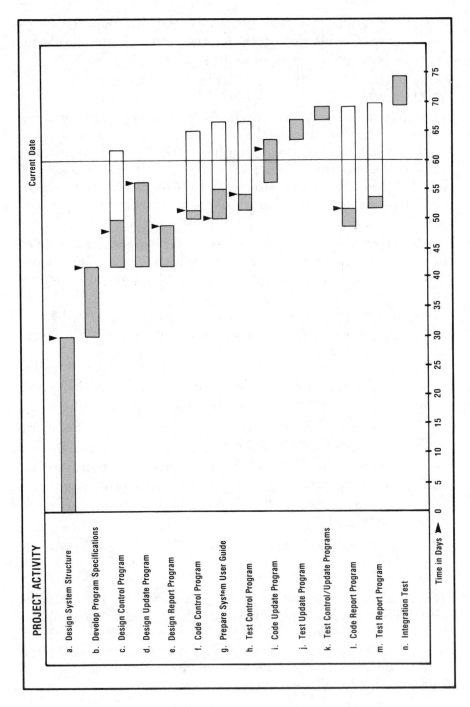

Figure 22-6. Gantt chart for file updating system project.

the project. In Figure 22-6, the available slack days are shown, for tasks on which slack is available, through dotted lines.

Figure 22-6 uses an arrowhead to indicate the percentage of completion for each task. In task *c*, for example, the completion percentage is approximately 75 percent. Although the current date is now past the expected early finish time for this task, the project can still remain on schedule, as long as the work is finished before the slack time elapses.

Note, in the entry for task *i, Code Update Program,* that work is ahead of schedule. Since this is a critical task, it may be possible to advance the schedule for the entire project—even though some jobs not on the critical path are behind schedule.

Gantt charts can be developed directly from task lists and time estimates. It is not necessary to have a critical path network to prepare a Gantt chart. This technique is flexible enough to fit into any project management method.

Summary

The systems development life cycle provides a framework for project management—a method or combination of techniques that facilitates planning, scheduling, and control.

A project is an extensive job involving multiple, interrelated tasks. A project is finite, nonrepetitive, decomposable, complex, and predictable.

The tools of project management must assist in planning and scheduling. Status must be reported as a basis for making control decisions. Two available tools are: Project Evaluation and Review Technique (PERT), and Critical Path Method (CPM).

The methodologies used in PERT and CPM are essentially similar. PERT permits broad estimates about the time durations of tasks.

On the other hand, CPM assumes that time requirements for completion of individual tasks are relatively predictable. A relationship is assumed between the time it takes to complete a task and the amount of money an organization is willing to spend by applying resources for its completion.

PERT is used for projects involving research and development, situations in which there are apt to be greater variations in time consumed by individual tasks. CPM tends to be used on projects for which direct relationships can be established between time and resources. CPM tends to be used only selectively in the systems development area.

Both PERT and CPM use graphic networks, flow diagrams relating the sequence of tasks to the sequence of occurrence. The network of tasks is presented in a project graph. The chapter describes methods for creating and analyzing these networks.

A visual tool for displaying time relationships and monitoring progress of project completion is the Gantt chart. Gantt charts and their users are described.

Key Terms

1. project management
2. planning
3. scheduling
4. control
5. project
6. finite
7. nonrepetitive
8. decomposable
9. complex
10. predictable
11. Project Evaluation and Review Technique (PERT)
12. critical task
13. slack time
14. Critical Path Method (CPM)
15. network
16. project graph
17. node
18. longest path
19. critical path
20. critical path algorithm
21. start time (S)
22. finish time (T)
23. early start (ES)
24. early finish (EF)
25. late start (LS)
26. late finish (LF)
27. total slack
28. optimistic time estimate
29. most probable time estimate
30. pessimistic time estimate
31. Gantt chart
32. time scale
33. percentage completion

Review/Discussion Questions

1. How does the systems development life cycle support the need for project management tools?

2. What are the main functions of production management, and what are the characteristics of each?

3. What are the characteristics of a project?

4. What types of projects generally apply PERT techniques?

5. What types of projects generally apply CPM techniques?

6. What are the basic differences between PERT and CPM techniques?

7. What are the relationships among tasks, nodes, and networks?

8. What is the critical path, and how are critical path algorithms applied?

9. How can identification of slack time assist in project management control?

10. What relationships are shown in Gantt charts?

Practice Assignments

1. Using the network diagram in Figure 22-7 and the activity table in Figure 22-8, determine the critical path tasks and the total slack for each. Redraw the diagram to include the information shown in Figure 22-4.

2. Using the information in Figure 22-9, prepare a Gantt chart showing the early start, early finish, and late finish times as illustrated in Figure 22-6. It is not necessary to show a current date line on your chart.

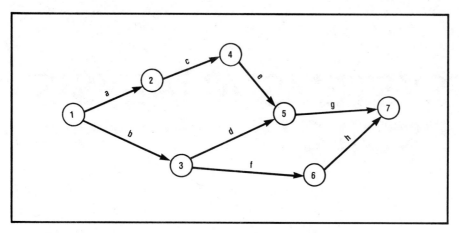

Figure 22-7. Network diagram for use in Practice Assignment.

Job Identification	Alternate Identification	Immediate Predecessor	Time Estimate (Days)
a	(1,2)	–	30
b	(1,3)	—	28
c	(2,4)	a	10
d	(3,5)	b	20
e	(4,5)	c	15
f	(3,6)	b	42
g	(5,7)	d,e	17
h	(6,7)	f	22

Figure 22-8. Project activity table for use in Practice Assignment.

Project Activity	ES	EF	LS	LF	Duration
A	0	5	6	11	5
B	0	3	0	3	3
C	5	9	11	15	4
D	3	10	3	10	7
E	9	11	15	17	2
F	10	15	10	15	5
G	11	14	17	20	3
H	15	20	15	20	5

Figure 22-9. Data for use in preparation of Gantt chart to be completed as Practice Assignment.

A SYSTEMS ANALYSIS PROJECT

INTRODUCTION

This appendix presents a case study in systems analysis that can be used in parallel with the material presented in the text. Assignments within this appendix call for student completion of activities in systems investigation, analysis, and general design. Students can complete these assignments for any case situation that is assigned or selected, under guidance of the instructor. The case can be a real situation with which the individual student is familiar. As another alternative, the student can build a case from readings or reference sources. As yet another option, the student, with approval of the instructor, may apply the assignments in this appendix to the case scenario presented in Appendix B.

The assignments presented here are tailored to academic situations. Some systems development tasks typically followed in industry situations have been deleted to fit the assignments within realistic educational boundaries. However, the essence of systems analysis as an essentially intellectual process has been retained. The basic problem-solving strategies, techniques, and tools of systems analysis are applied within the context of this case project.

The case is divided into four parts, paralleling Activities 2 through 5 of the systems development life cycle. Just as the life cycle activities overlap, so will the parts of the case assignment. While working on any individual activity, the student should be thinking ahead to later consequences and requirements. At the same time, since this case may represent the student's first attempt to apply the systems analysis process, periodic feedback is important. Each part of the assignment structure in this appendix calls for materials to be produced and submitted for evaluation. This evaluation will be necessary for keeping the entire project on track.

The case can be undertaken by students individually or in project teams, as directed by the instructor. If feasible, it is recommended that project groups be used. This arrangement will give students an excellent sense of the pressures, responsibilities, and other interpersonal experiences encountered by systems development professionals. The ability to work as contributing members of project teams can be valuable and, if possible, should be emphasized throughout the case study.

Whether students work through the case scenario in Appendix B or devise their own cases, the series of assignments presented here provides an opportunity to apply the background and skills acquired in working through the content of this text.

PART 1:   SYSTEM SELECTION
AND FEASIBILITY STUDY

The initial assignment is to select a case situation and to perform a feasibility study. The system selected will become the focal point for the case project. Thus, care should be taken to select an appropriate system that can be studied within the time frame of the course.

Approximately three to four weeks within the semester should be allowed for completing this first part. The case assignment can begin as soon as work is completed in *Chapter 5, Feasibility Study*. The case can then continue through the study of the remaining chapters in *Part II, The Investigation Phase*.

Requirements and Guidelines

If possible, choose a system with which you are already familiar or one about which you can become knowledgeable with reasonable effort. Your case should involve some type of operational, management information, or decision support system set in a business or administrative environment. The student is fully responsible for selecting an appropriate system. The instructor may offer advice, suggest references, help in keeping the system within practical boundaries, and give final approval for the case. However, responsibility for system selection should remain with the student.

If the system chosen is a real application that appears too complex to be manageable within the constraints of the course, consider using a subsystem from this larger system. As an alternative, abstract essential elements from the entire system for use in case assignments. If a contrived system is preferred, the school library may have source materials that include system casebooks, directories of accounting systems, or case studies published in professional journals.

The system selected may be manual (nonautomated) or computer-based. If the case uses a manual system, it should be a candidate for automation. It may prove easier to work with a nonautomated system, so a choice of this type of system is recommended. If an automated system is selected, it should have the potential for expansion, modification, or improvement. No matter what system is chosen, the case should offer the opportunity for integrating manual and automated procedures within the final design recommendations.

As a further guideline, the system selected for study should have between five and 10 separate, major processing steps or procedures. It should make use of both master and transaction files and encompass data entry, file creation, file maintenance, report writing, and file inquiry procedures. Ideally, the system should permit development of both batch and interactive techniques. The existing system does not have to include all of these features. But these options should be appropriate for the new system.

Assume use of any available computer system for implementation of the selected case. If the current system is computerized, or an existing computer is available, assume that it will be the basis for the new system. If the current system is not automated and no computer is available, assume the use of any computer system—within realistic, practical limits. In general, the computer system will have slight bearing on the conduct of the case study. It should not impose tight constraints on the requirements to perform analysis and general design. The computer will simply provide a frame of reference for the case study.

Products

A complete description of the system to be studied will be produced. This report is akin to the feasibility study described in Chapter 5.

However, this assignment will not require all of the documentation identified in the text. Rather, the student should produce sufficient documentation to support evaluation of the proposed project in terms of operational, technical, and schedule feasibility.

The student's report should contain the following elements:

1. There should be a narrative overview of the current system. This should include, but not be limited to, explanations of why the project is being considered for study, which areas of the organization are impacted by the system, what major processing functions are being studied, and how the project is expected to contribute to the objectives of the organization or department.

2. An overview description of the current system should include a context diagram and a diagram 0. The student should provide examples of major existing forms, source documents, and other available documentation of major system inputs, outputs, storage, and processing features of the system. If actual forms or documentation are not available, sketches and/or explanations may be used.

3. There should be a description covering problems within the existing system and anticipated benefits from development of a new system. Include explanations of economic, operational, technical, or other benefits as necessary. If possible, provide preliminary cost estimates for development and ongoing operation of the new system.

4. A description should be provided of the actual or assumed hardware/systems software environment. Describe and/or provide systems flowcharts of all pertinent input, output, storage, and processing devices and features. Prepare an impact statement describing any modifications or additions anticipated for the computer system that will handle the proposed information processing system.

Use this list of documents as a guide. But do not be constrained by this list. Include any other pertinent details to provide an understanding of the current system, its problems, its potentials for improvement, its content, and its appropriateness for study.

The materials should be written and organized for ease of reference and reading. They should be included within some type of binder or folder and organized under index tabs. The narrative portions of the report should be typewritten, following standard style formats. Graphic materials should be drawn carefully, labeled, and cross-referenced to the narrative.

PART 2: EXISTING SYSTEM REVIEW

The reason for studying and documenting the existing system is to build an understanding of the business problems and needs behind the technologies in use—either manual or automated. Specialized tools such as data flow diagrams, data dictionaries, and process descriptions assist the analyst in abstracting essential features of the system and isolating them for study. In this assignment, it will be necessary to apply these tools and the processes that use them in building a clear understanding of the system chosen for study. The work in this part of the case study can proceed concurrently with the study of *Chapter 9, Existing System Review* and *Chapter 10, System Modeling Tools*. Approximately three weeks should be allowed for completion of this portion of the case study.

Requirements and Guidelines

From the materials produced in Part 1 of this case study, construct physical and logical models of the current system. Descriptions of documentation requirements follow.

The current physical system should be documented as follows:

1. Prepare a context diagram showing the sources and destinations of net data flows into and out of the system. In this instance, forms and other actual documents will be mentioned on the diagram.

2. A top-level data flow diagram should show the major input and output documents, the major files used in processing, and the major processing procedures—both manual and automated.

3. Samples of all existing forms, source documents, inputs, outputs, file structures, and any existing documentation of systems or procedures should be collected and included.

The current logical system should be documented as follows:

1. Include a context diagram showing the sources and destinations of net logical data flows into and out of the system.

2. Present a top-level data flow diagram showing the logical data flows, data stores, and processes that make up the current system.

3. As appropriate, sets of leveled data flow diagrams describing partitioned bubbles from the diagram 0 should be included.

4. Provide a complete, alphabetized data dictionary describing the components of all data flows and data stores. The entries should be categorized and arranged into sections for input, output, data stores, data elements, and data structures.

5. Prepare a set of process descriptions for all of the transformations appearing on the data flow diagrams. These descriptions may use structured English, decision trees, and/or decision tables, as preferred, or as assigned by the instructor.

On completing this part of the case, the student should have a complete description of the current system. The system will have been defined rigorously, will show underlying business policies and procedures, and will be in a form suitable to analysis of problems and opportunities.

Products

The materials prepared for this part of the assignment should be added to the notebook of materials created during Part 1. An appropriate indexing scheme should be used in organizing the documentation so that there is evidence of progression in producing, identifying, and cross-referencing the cumulative documentation. Graphics should be done with precision and care in penmanship. Data dictionary entries and process descriptions should be typewritten or lettered carefully. If access to a text editing system is available, this equipment could be helpful in preparing documentation, especially in maintaining the data dictionary.

PART 3:   NEW SYSTEM REQUIREMENTS

With completion of the documentation of the existing logical system, analysis proceeds to consideration of system improvements. This activity marks the transition from the study of the existing system into the building of a new one. Effort is at the logical level. The analyst seeks justification for current business policies, practices, and procedures. Also sought are new or replacement policies, practices, and procedures that will be responsive to identified, unmet needs.

The result of this activity should be a specification for a new system—prepared from the user's perspective. The materials presented in Chapters 11 through 14 of this text provide the basis for work on this part of the case study. Approximately three to four weeks should be devoted to this effort.

Requirements and Guidelines

Based on analysis of the current system, additional documentation efforts for the case study project should be as follows:

1. An overview narrative should restate the goals and objectives of the organization as yardsticks against which the new system will be evaluated. State the purposes of the proposed system and the changes to be made between the old and new systems. Describe, in general, what the system will accomplish for the user.

2. A logical system model should encompass business requirements for the new system and the logical model of the existing system. This model should consist of a hierarchical set of data flow diagrams that form the basis for the logical model of the new system. The data dictionary should be updated and new process descriptions should be added as necessary.

3. A physical system model should be created by modifying the logical model of the new system. This physical model should include a context diagram describing net data flows for the proposed system and a diagram 0 supported by necessary leveled diagrams. On these diagrams, indicate the manual and automated procedures that will be implemented, including batch and on-line functions, timing considerations, and performance requirements. To support the physical model, the data dictionary should be revised. The lowest-level bubbles on the data flow diagrams should be supported by process descriptions prepared through use of structured English statements, decision tables, and/or decision trees.

4. Data structure and data access diagrams should be prepared. Start with the data dictionary entries describing the data stores to be supported by the new system. Apply normalization techniques to derive a file structure in third normal form. Then define the attribute and correlative files necessary to meet processing require-

ments. Show the progression of analysis through first, second, and third normal forms and the final data structures to be packaged as files. Prepare both a data structure diagram and data access diagram to document the results.

5. For system outputs, prepare sketches of reports, documents, and displays. cover these with an index identifying all included items.

6. For system inputs, prepare an indexed listing of all source documents and input forms. Include document specification forms and rough format drawings for all inputs. If necessary, include outlines of user-machine dialogs.

7. Where appropriate (and where information is available), describe performance needs, such as response times, transaction volumes, and batch run timing requirements. Special security and control needs should be specified as necessary.

Products

The materials produced in this portion of the case study should constitute a User Specification, as described in this text. These items should be added to the cumulative documentation prepared for the first two parts. As in previous portions of the case, analytical rigor and exactness in approach should be overriding concerns.

PART 4: NEW SYSTEM DESIGN

At this point in the systems development life cycle, complete, user-oriented specifications for the new or replacement system have been prepared. User requirements have been analyzed and this analysis serves as the point of departure for transition into physical design. The broad hardware/software parameters established during analysis can now be elaborated with sufficient detail so that system designers can verify that the proposed system can be delivered within schedule and budget constraints. Both computerized and manual procedures must be brought to a level of detail that provides assurances of technical and operational feasibility.

This part of the case project can begin with the study of *Chapter 15, New System Design*. Approximately one to two weeks should be sufficient to complete this work.

Requirements and Guidelines

Materials produced for this part of the case project represent extensions of the specifications prepared for the previous part. The following activities and results are required:

1. Computer processing requirements should be defined. For batch processing applications, use system flowcharts to document job streams. In an on-line environment, prepare system flowcharts covering application methods. These flowcharts should be annotated to describe timing cycles and performance requirements.

2. A set of files to support the application should be defined and file organization, access methods, and storage media should be specified. Approximate volumes of stored data and anticipated growth patterns should be estimated. If database management systems are to be acquired or used, the specifications should include a description of the package, a summary of modifications necessary to support the new system, and an evaluation of the benefits and costs of the software package.

3. Performance criteria should be delineated. Included should be required response times for on-line processing, transaction volumes, and other meaningful performance requirements.

4. If application packages are to be acquired from software vendors, include a description and evaluation of each system to be considered.

5. If the proposed system involves significant hardware and/or systems software changes, technical specifications should be prepared. Include a detailed description of requirements for new hardware and software capabilities; data communications requirements, if any; and any other modifications or additions to the existing computer system.

Products

The materials produced in this portion of the case constitute a New System Design Specification. The new items are added to the cumulative documentation prepared throughout this case study.

PART 5:   SYSTEM PRESENTATION

The systems analyst is a technical specialist as well as an agent of and salesperson for the system development proposal. In these roles, the analyst must help to convince system users and the steering committee of the viability of the new system. Presentations to these groups must be convincing in terms of both management and technical considerations. Recommendations prepared by an analyst must be presented convincingly enough to warrant allocation of funds that could alternately be used for other capital projects.

The final part in this case study involves presentation of the proposal. Individual students or project teams should give oral presentations to the class, explaining and justifying their approaches to the process and products of analysis.

Specific presentation requirements will be outlined by the instructor. However, it is expected that meticulous care will go into each report. Members of the class will serve as an audience of users and steering committee members. They, along with the instructor, will evaluate the work done in this assignment.

The form on the follow page may be copied or reproduced as a basis for evaluating system presentations.

PROJECT EVALUATION FORM

		Rating	
		High	**Low**

1. The system chosen for study was appropriate in scope and depth for demonstrating analysis techniques. 5 4 3 2 1

2. A clear, substantive rationale was presented for undertaking the systems study. 5 4 3 2 1

3. The presenter was knowledgeable about the system under study and was able to impart that understanding. 5 4 3 2 1

4. The presentation was well organized, with major points emphasized appropriately and minor details subordinated in keeping with their relative importance. 5 4 3 2 1

5. The analysis process proceeded systematically from physical considerations through logical design and finally to physical design. 5 4 3 2 1

6. Appropriate and understandable use was made of data flow diagrams and other graphic tools. . . 5 4 3 2 1

7. The system was analyzed completely, with no logical gaps in the analysis and design process or in the products. 5 4 3 2 1

8. The presentation was clear and understandable. 5 4 3 2 1

9. Visual aids were well prepared, relevant, and used effectively. 5 4 3 2 1

10. The presenter was confident, enthusiastic, and persuasive. 5 4 3 2 1

Name of presenter _____

Name of evaluator _____

Total points _____ ÷ 10 = _____ average.

A CASE $\mathbf{B}$
SCENARIO

This case scenario can be used in conjunction with the project structure in Appendix A.

   The first section provides general background on the existing demand deposit accounting system at a small bank. The material was taken largely from an actual narrative overview. Remarks are incomplete and not always well structured. One of the challenges of modeling the existing system will be to fill in the details. This may be done by contacting a local bank or by identifying issues and constructing responses based on sound business practice.

   The second section is a memo requesting a number of changes in the existing system. These can be used as the main source of input for new system requirements.

EXISTING SYSTEM OVERVIEW

This section provides background information on the demand deposit accounting system at The Alwaystrust Bank (TAB), a small financial institution serving a town of about 100,000 that has a total of three banks. To be competitive, TAB maintains a slim staff; does business from a single, desirable location; and serves about 8,000 checking-account customers. Three types of checking accounts are offered:

- A POWER CHECKING account pays savings-type interest that fluctuates weekly with the price of U. S. Treasury notes (in the range of 9 to 11 percent recently) on balances above $2,000 and 5.25 percent for deposits up to $2,000. Balances and interest are computed daily and credited monthly. Holders of these accounts are entitled to unlimited, free checkwriting privileges.

- Regular checking accounts require a $100 minimum balance. Depositors are charged either 20 cents for each check written or a flat rate of $3 per month, whichever is larger. These accounts are most attractive for persons who don't want to maintain minimum balances and who write comparatively few checks.

- A NOW account pays 5.25 percent interest on all deposits. A $300 minimum balance is required. If the balance falls below this minimum, a service charge of $5 per month is applied.

If a TAB customer also has a loan with the bank—including a mortgage or a personal loan—loan payments can be deducted automatically from his or her checking account with no charge for the transaction. As necessary, transactions are generated by the loan system on the fifth, fifteenth, and thirtieth of the month—until funds in the account are sufficient to cover the loan payment. After a payment for a given month has been deducted from the account, no further loan transactions are processed that month. If the system is unable to deduct the payment in three tries, the loan system generates a collection letter to be sent to the depositor. If a customer has an insufficient balance for three months in any given year, the privilege of automatic loan payment is revoked. Bank management is considering a plan under which free checking would be offered to depositors who authorize automatic loan payments from their accounts.

Another special service, made available to certain preferred, high-quality customers, is overdraft protection. The bank's normal policy in handling overdrafts is to reject any check that cannot be covered in full by the account's available balance. The account number, check number, and amount are noted on an overdraft warning report to bank management. The check is then held and reprocessed the following day. If the balance has been increased to cover the check, it is cleared and no charges are made. However, if a check is rejected a second time, the account is charged a $5 fee.

For accounts that carry a preferred-customer notation on their master files, the policy on overdrafts is more lenient. The check is honored if the amount of the check is for more than the funds available but is covered by the total balance. (The total balance includes both collected and uncollected funds. Uncollected funds are deposited checks that have not yet been paid through the clearinghouse.) Such a transaction results in a negative balance against available funds. However, no overdraft charge is made.

If the check of a special-service customer exceeds the total balance, this condition is noted on the overdraft report and the check is resubmitted the following day. If the check still exceeds the total balance on the second try, one of two actions can be taken. If the overdraft is for less than 10 percent of the face value of the check, the check is cleared and a $5 overdraft charge is made against the account. If the overdraft is more than 10 percent greater than the amount of the check, the check is rejected and a $5 overdraft charge is applied. All rejected checks are returned to the clearinghouse or the depositor. The depositor also receives a letter describing the situation. The rejection is recorded on the overdraft report.

(Checks written on TAB accounts are referred to as ''on-us'' checks. Checks written on accounts at other banks are called ''foreign'' checks. A deposit made by a TAB customer may include both on-us and foreign checks. Foreign checks are sent to the federal clearinghouse each day. In addition, on-us checks are received from the clearinghouse daily. These would be checks written by TAB customers and deposited in accounts at foreign banks.)

TAB operations are fairly straightforward. The bank tellers, who know most of the customers by sight, accept deposits to checking accounts, running a machine tape of each deposit and preparing a ''Cash In'' ticket for deposited cash. Cash may be withdrawn by customers against deposits of checks from recognized organizations and on-us personal checks—as long as the checks are not drawn on TAB's ''DO NOT CASH IMMEDIATELY'' list. If cash is taken against a deposit, a ''Cash Out'' ticket is prepared.

Customers may write their own checks for cash as long as a review of the account status shows that there are sufficient available funds. At several times during the day, teller transactions are picked up for proof machine processing. Deposits are verified, all checks received are encoded with the check amount and separated into ''on-us'' and ''foreign bank'' batches. Totals (batch and daily) are accumulated. Funds from deposits of foreign bank checks are processed with three-day holds on availability. On-us checks have no holds on the availability of funds. To implement the holds, the total for foreign bank checks is encoded on each deposit slip. Checks on foreign banks are then batched and sent to a clearinghouse each evening.

Each day, on-us checks processed by other banks are received from the clearinghouse, along with batch totals. These checks are also processed on proof machines to verify encoded amounts and totals from the clearinghouse. Batch totals are encoded on batch header documents during proofing. These batches are then combined with those from the tellers as input to the nightly checking account update processed on the bank's computer. For each deposit, deposit slips are encoded and processed as credits. Debit entries come from checks, account charges (for the printing of personal checks and from overdrafts), and automatically processed loan payments. Batch totals are developed to make sure that inputs are in balance.

Once input batches balance, the documents are sorted and account updating on the computer begins. Sorted credits, then debits, are applied to the checking account master file. For each account, amounts in float (on hold against use) are advanced a day and eventually are transferred into amounts for collected or available fund balances. The updating of holds in this way is referred to as the "dumping" of funds from three-day hold, to two-day hold, to one-day hold, and finally to available-funds "buckets." The overall process is referred to as "bucket dumping."

Customers may place stop-payment orders on certain checks. Each check processed by the system is compared against any outstanding "stop pays" for the affected account. If a check being processed matches a stop-pay order on three controls—account number, check number, and amount—the check is recorded on a daily stop-pay report and payment is rejected.

If a check matches the stop-pay order on account number and check number but not on the amount, it is processed normally and reported on a stop-pay warning report sheet sent to the customer. A $1 charge is made for each stop-payment request. These charges are processed as debit transactions.

All transactions, including overdrafts, are logged into a transaction file that is used for account audits and for preparation of monthly customer account statements.

At the close of each day's master file update run, a printed account status report is generated. This details the status of each depositor account.

Transaction documents themselves—deposit slips, checks, account charges, and others—are sorted by account number and placed in a physical holding file. The signature on each check is compared with the one on the signature card to verify authenticity of these documents, applying a last control over transaction processing. The holding file—plus the daily account status report—are used in responding to customer questions.

On a monthly basis, statements are sent to each customer. Each statement includes a recap of all account activity since the last statement was sent. Service charges, if any, are calculated and applied to the account. For POWER CHECKING and NOW accounts, interest earned is calculated and added to the account balance. All transactions in the holding file are mailed to depositors with the computer-printed statements.

Each day, management receives an Excessive Change in Balance report that identifies accounts with unusual activity. If a deposit is made that exceeds twice the average monthly total deposit or a check is written for one-half of the average monthly check total, the account number, transaction, and appropriate messages are printed. This report triggers further investigation as account situations warrant. A series of other management reports is prepared to summarize checking account activity and status. Finally, as a part of each day's transaction processing, a summary of the change in net cash position is prepared for the accounting system.

Annually, a 1099 form, a report to the IRS on accountholder interest income, is prepared for each POWER CHECKING and NOW account. A copy is sent to each customer and a machine-readable copy is transmitted to the Internal Revenue Service. The bank retains a printed copy and uses it in filing its own federal tax return.

INPUT FOR NEW SYSTEM REQUIREMENTS

The following memo requests a number of changes in TAB's demand deposit accounting system. The text of the memo can be used as the primary source of information on requirements for the development of a replacement system. As an alternative, a subset of the requested changes can be used as the basis for a maintenance request on the current system.

```
                           Inter-Company Memo
       To:      Flo Bytebaum, DP Manager
       From:    Harvey Pennybuilder, VP Demand Deposit Services
       Date:    March 29
       Re:      Improvements in our Demand Deposit System

       As you know, there have been no requests for major changes in our Demand
       Deposit systems for several years.  Even with the changes going on in the big
       city, it has been business as usual for us.  But no longer!  The newly
       chartered bank that has opened up in the Dry Creek Shopping Mall--North City
       Trust--has been attracting too many of our customers.

       We have to meet competition.  To do so, we are going to need your help to make
       changes in our systems.  After you read this, you may decide to throw out our
       entire system and start over.  That wouldn't disappoint me at all.

       Request 1:  Power Checking
       Too many customers are letting their balances in these accounts drop to a
       level that is unprofitable for the bank.  The account is designed to attract
       and hold large balances.  It is true that interest drops to 5.25 percent for
       balances under $2,000.  However, the unlimited checkwriting feature of this
       account really kills us when balances fall below $300.  So, we want to modify
       this service and charge $5 per month on accounts for which the average balance
       falls below $300.

       Request 2:  Free checking for regular accounts
       We want to offer free checking against regular checking accounts for all
       customers who have their pay or social security checks deposited in their
       accounts automatically.  We also want to extend free checking to customers who
       opt for the automatic loan draft for any loan they carry with us.  (We will
       keep the penalty charges on the NOW and POWER CHECKING accounts, at least for
       the time being.)

       Request 3:  Federal Income Tax Withholding
       As you know, our industry has been successful to date in defeating a law that
       would have required us to withhold a percentage of interest income from our
       depositors and remit these sums to the IRS.  However, as long as we are making
       changes in the system, it seems wise to provide for a tax withholding
       capability against some future need.  In this way, we will be ready for
       whatever happens.

       Request 4:  New Service--Corporate Accounts
       To attract more corporate and other business accounts, we would like the
       ability to set up subaccounts within specially identified accounts.  Business
       customers would be able to establish several different breakdowns, or
       subaccounts, against which checks could be written.  We would cover overdrafts
       on any subaccount as long as the funds in the total account were sufficient to
       cover checks presented for collection.  Also, we will pay 5.25 percent
       interest on the first $1,500 (totaled across all subaccounts) and a higher,
       market-controlled rate for balances of over $1,500.
```

As an added competitive item, we would like to offer corporate customers a
check reconciliation service. Each evening, they can submit a tape file to us
of check numbers, dates, and amounts for all checks written that day. Each
morning, we will report to them the available balance and individual checks
outstanding, by subaccount. This service will make possible advanced money
management techniques for our customers.

Request 5: Change the Deposit Float Procedure
As you know, we now apply an automatic three-day float to hold funds on all
foreign checks deposited in any account. As the geographic origins of the
checks we process continue to spread, we think we may have to extend that
time, at least for some checks. We would like the ability to float a
deposited check for three, four, five, or six days, depending on the bank on
which it is drawn. We can give you a list of bank codes and the number of
days we want.

Request 6: Related Accounts
This is confidential! Mr. Fleece, our president, has asked us to look into
the potential for keeping track of related accounts for our individual POWER
CHECKING customers. The idea is that if several members of a family have
accounts with us, we could total all their balances and treat the total as one
balance within the POWER CHECKING system. This would be a good marketing
feature. It doesn't seem to me that it should be a big deal. Do you see any
problems?

Request 7: Second Location
This is really big news. Next year, we will open a second banking office at
the Dry Creek mall. This gives me some concerns about our account controls.
Will our systems be able to handle everything? I'm afraid that a lot of our
controls work well now because we have only one location and know our
customers so well. What do we need to change?

Well, Flo, that's it. It seems like a lot, I know. But I'm confident that
you and your people can handle it. Let me know when you figure out what's
involved and what we have to do to make these changes.

GLOSSARY

A

absolute position Specific physical point on a disk surface where a record is located. *See also* relative position.

acceptance review Session at which project team presents information to a management group on an activity or phase for which approval is necessary.

access controls Controls that limit physical access to computer sites, and that limit electronic access to computer systems only to authorized persons.

access diagram *See* data access diagram.

access path The correlations or relationships between record keys that establish connections among data items imbedded in file records.

access time The time necessary to locate a data record on disk and read it into memory. Design consideration when choosing access method.

accuracy Conformity to a standard, or true value. Consideration when establishing controls throughout a system, especially where input data are entered.

activity Within the systems development life cycle, a group of logically related tasks that lead to, and are defined by, the accomplishment of a specific objective.

activity rate Frequency of record access by an application. Design consideration when choosing access method.

adjustment Correction or modification generated by feedback within a control process to bring system input or processing back into line with expectations.

administrator (walkthrough) Experienced system analyst who provides organizational or administrative support for a walkthrough.

algorithm A formula, or series of steps, for defining a problem and describing its solution.

alias An alternative name that can be used to represent an identified data structure within a data dictionary notation.

alphabetic field test A test to verify that specific data fields contain only alphabetic characters and blank spaces. Used for specific processing control within a computer program.

analysis The process of breaking situations or problems down into successively smaller elements for individual study and solution. *See also* systems analysis.

analysis and general design phase A major segment (phase) of the systems development life cycle. Includes: establishing definitions and descriptions of existing systems, defining requirements for and designing features of a proposed replacement system, and doing a cost/benefit analysis. The report to management at the conclusion of this phase provides the basis for a go/no go decision on implementation of a new system.

application software package Predesigned software for a specific application, available for purchase and ready for use (possibly with minor modification) in an appropriate CIS; used in place of custom-designed software to reduce overall system costs or shorten development time.

archival file File that has been processed and retained for special research or historic reference.

archival record Permanent records of business activity made for legal requirements, historic perspective, and backup security.

archival storage Storage of archival records in a form that can be easily protected and will not degenerate over time, yet will be accessible when needed.

attribute Data item that characterizes an object. Consideration in choosing which data structures should be assembled into a composite data structure in the process of normalization.

attribute file A file that contains data describing or characterizing an entity about which information is maintained in a CIS.

audio output Data output that is audible and usable—in human language or sound.

auditability Degree to which a system is capable of having a successful and complete audit made to evaluate integrity of data that rely on a system.

audit trail Printed documents and computer-maintained records that can be used by auditors in tracing transactions through a system—from input source, to master file update, to output reports—for purposes of verification.

author Initiator or developer of a specific CIS product. Leader of the walkthrough of that product.

B

backup file Separately retained duplicate physical copy of a transaction file or historic master file, used for reconstruction and recovery of damaged or destroyed files.

balance The correspondence of amounts between an entered control figure and a computer-developed total. Used as a processing control. Also, correlation between parent and child elements of data flow diagrams in terms of flows in and out and functions accomplished.

balancing *See* balance.

bar code Data expressed as a series of bars and spaces printed in a small field on a tag or product label, for capture by optical code reading equipment.

benefit Favorable tangible or intangible result that offsets cost; savings or improvements that can be assigned values (either tangible or intangible) that can be balanced against costs as a basis for decision making. *See also* cost.

bi-directional Capability of a serial printer to print lines of data from left to right, or right to left, in both directions, to eliminate time needed to return to the left side of the paper.

bits per inch (bpi) The number of data bits that can be recorded in an inch of storage space on magnetic media.

black box Processing entity that produces a predictable output for a given input and whose general function is known, but whose internal processing rules are not known.

bubble Circular graphic representation within a data flow diagram of a point within a system at which incoming data flows are processed, or transformed, into outgoing data flows.

C

capital investment Financial resources committed by a business for the purchase of equipment or facilities.

category test Range or reasonableness test applied to non-numeric data that may include table lookup techniques. A processing control.

cathode ray tube (CRT) *See* CRT terminal.

channels Recording patterns on magnetic tape, consisting of bytes recorded next to each other that form rows of aligned bit positions.

check digit Data bit used for a validity check in which a series of calculations is performed on a numeric value in a certain position within a field. The result must equal one of the digits in the field. A processing control.

check point A verification step, usually applied through use of periodic output reports of sampled transactions to verify that processing is proceeding to acceptable standards. A processing control.

child diagram Exploded version of a parent bubble, showing processing or transformation in greater detail. *See also* parent.

cohesion Degree to which a process has a singular business purpose.

collector Symbol for a point within an information system where separate streams of data are merged, repackaged, and forwarded. Indicated on data flow diagram by a half circle.

completeness Control requiring that all appropriate data to be gathered appear on the source transaction. Also, condition of possessing adequate and appropriate data for the processing at hand.

computer-aided-instruction (CAI) Educational and instructional methods using a computer to guide a learner through an instructional program.

computer information system (CIS) A total, coordinated information system that includes computers, people, procedures, and all the resources necessary to handle input, processing, output, and storage of data useful to an aspect of the organization.

computer output to microfilm (COM) The recording of system outputs on microfilm, usually for archival storage.

concatenate To link two or more keys together to form a new, combination key. Used to allow unique identification of records and, at the same time, to permit access to related records in a file.

concatenated key A series of linked keys used for record identification and access.

confidentiality controls Controls designed to protect rights of privacy of persons or organizations described by, or represented in, data records.

context diagram Graphic model of an information system that shows a flow of data and information between the system and external entities with which it interacts, to establish the context, or setting, of the system.

continuous value Data element whose value can vary over a range of optional values. *See also* discrete value.

control Any method or function that monitors input, checks processing, or evaluates feedback to determine if system performance meets expectations.

control (systems development) The organizational activities that govern the systems development process to monitor functions, budgets, schedules, and quality.

control totals Numeric totals used for comparison to assure keyboarding accuracy and completeness of records. Includes count of number of documents or records in a batch, hash totals, and monetary or quantity totals.

correlation Special identifying relationship between objects and composite data structures.

correlative file A special file of relationships between record keys appearing in two separate files. Used to establish access paths among physically separate files.

cost Tangible or intangible expense associated with any system function; encompasses any out-of-book expense associated with any function within a system, as well as human-related intangible costs. *See also* benefit.

cost/benefit analysis Study and evaluation of a course of action, or proposed solution to a problem or need, that compares projected savings and other benefits to projected costs.

cost-effective Course of action that produces maximum relative benefit at minimum relative cost.

coupling Interface on data flow diagram between two higher-level processes, represented by the number of data flows connecting them. Processes with minimum coupling are more independent and more easily maintained. *See also* cohesion.

critical activities Necessary and essential activities that must be performed individually and that, together, account for the total elapsed time of a systems development project. *See* critical path, critical path method.

critical path Sequence representing minimum amount of time necessary for project completion; represented on a critical path method (CPM) visual representation by the longest path through the activities.

critical path algorithm Mathematical formula used to help identify the longest sequence of activities that will lead to a completed project. *See* critical path, critical path method.

critical path method (CPM) Planning and scheduling method for predicting and measuring trade-off relationships between relative costs and alternative completion dates for a project; presented visually on a project graph. *See also* critical activities, critical path.

CRT terminal Unit that contains a video display screen and a keyboard for entry of data. The data may go into a recording device, or directly into a computer.

cumulative documentation Relevant documentation generated during CIS project analysis and design phases to support later developmental stages.

D

data access diagram Graphic representation of data files showing formats of files and corresponding relationships, or access paths, between files.

database Data organized so that multiple files can be accessed through a single reference, based upon relationships among records on the various files rather than through key values or physical position. Also, all data resources needed to support a system.

database management Direction or control of a database through special software that identifies relational values for records, then executes access commands through sequential, direct, or indexed-sequential reference methods, whichever is appropriate to define the relationship specified by the user.

data capture Procedures for initially recording and putting data into a system through keyboarding or other methods.

data dictionary Listing of terms and their definitions for all data items and data stores within an information system.

data element Basic unit of data that has a specific meaning for the system in which it is used.

data entry Converting or transcribing source data into a form acceptable for computer processing.

data flow The movement of data through a system, from an identified point of origin to a specific destination; indicated on data flow diagram by arrow.

data flow diagram Graphic representation and analysis of data movement, processing functions (transformations), and the files (data stores) that are used to support processing in an information system. Used to improve present utilization or planning future changes in the system.

data input Transmission of data into a computer, especially by machine. *See also* data capture, data entry.

data processing system (DPS) Collection of methods, procedures, and resources designed to accept inputs, process data, deliver information and maintain files that provides direct support for an organization's basic transactions and operations.

data store Storage area for collections of data input or generated during processing; indicated on data flow diagram by an open rectangle.

data structure Packet of logically related data that can be decomposed into subordinate data components or data elements.

data structure diagram Graphic representation of relationships among attribute data structures. Indicates: access keys, access paths, access through correlative structures, and relationships among attribute structures sharing the same key.

decision support system (DSS) Type of computer information system that assists management in formulating policies and plans by projecting the likely consequences of decisions.

decision table Representation of decision-making process showing a multidimensional array of conditions and outcomes with points of correspondence at the intersections of these vertical and horizontal elements. Used for description and/or analysis of processing alternatives.

decision tree Graphic representation of conditions or processing alternatives and outcomes that resembles the branches of a tree.

decompose *See* partitioning.

decomposition The process of partitioning a system into increasingly detailed functions that can, separately, be studied in relative isolation.

density Average number of data bits per unit of storage space.

detailed design and implementation phase Portion (phase) during the systems development life cycle that refines hardware and software specifications, establishes programming plans, trains users, and implements extensive testing procedures, to evaluate design and operating specifications and/or provide the basis for further modification.

detail report Report of data content of file records.

developmental benefit One-time benefit resulting from undertaking a systems development project; includes economic benefits, as well as increased experience and competence for systems developers.

developmental costs Costs of establishing a new system and bringing it into use. Depreciable as a capital investment over the anticipated useful life of the system.

Diagram 0 (Zero) Graphic system documentation and specification model that uses a symbol vocabulary to identify main processing functions, data flows, external entities, and data storage points.

digitizer Pen-like device to whose movements, when it is moved along a graphic shape, are assigned digital values by a computer. Used for entering drawings and graphics as data.

direct file A file organized directly, by location key, and also relatively, by position of a record within the entire field. Data can be accessed randomly from a direct file. Serial or sequential access are also possible.

discrete value Noncontinuous, distinct value. Refers to data element that has only specific options, rather than a range of options, for its value. *See also* continuous value.

diskette A small, flexible, circular magnetic recording medium on a plastic base, enclosed in a paper envelope. Most often used as a storage medium with microcomputers. Also called a floppy disk.

disk pack Multi-surface recording device that consists of a set of magnetic disks on which data can be written and read at random, or directly.

documentation controls Control procedures used to assure that correct, updated copies of current processing procedures are available to users and that all previous versions of documentation are maintained.

drum-type plotter Graphic device using a round drum to hold the paper on which lines are plotted.

E

early finish (EF) Earliest time at which a project activity can be finished, determined by adding estimated completion time to early start time. Used in critical path method (CPM).

early start (ES) Earliest possible time (date) at which project activity can begin. Used in critical path method (CPM).

80/20 rule Guideline for systems development costs stating that 80 percent of the benefits of a system can be achieved for 20 percent of the cost of the total system; the remaining 80 percent of the cost provides only an additional 20 percent of benefits. Used as guideline in evaluating system features and capabilities.

electrostatic (laser) printer Highest speed nonimpact printing device. Forms images on a copier drum, then transfers outputs to paper.

encryption Alteration or encoding of signals representing data. Used when processing involves transmission over communication lines or networks. Also known as signal scrambling.

exception Condition outside of the range defined as normal.

exception report Specially produced report indicating exceptions. Used to identify conditions that require human decision, items that cannot be processed or out-of-balance situations.

explode To expand a unit of a Diagram 0 (Zero) representation to a more detailed level for further scrutiny.

external entity Person, organization, or system that supplies data to or receives output from a system being modeled. Indicated on data flow diagram by a rectangle.

external output Documents or reports produced expressly for use outside an organization; includes reports to governmental agencies, documents sent to customers, communications with stockholders, paychecks, etc. *See also* internal output.

F

face validity Appearance of underlying authenticity and purposefulness in an information-gathering questionnaire.

father file *See* generation.

feasibility report End result of a feasibility study. Includes recommendation for a specific course of action, description of the existing problem and anticipated changes, preliminary estimate of costs and benefits, impact statement detailing needed changes in equipment and facilities, proposed schedule for completion, and a list of policy level decisions to be resolved by management.

feasibility study Study that, when completed, will have evaluated initially the relevant factors involved in a problem or need, considered preliminary alternative solutions, recommended a definite course of action, and projected estimated costs and benefits to be derived from the recommended solution.

feedback A specially designed output used for verification, quality control, and evaluation of the results of data processing.

fiber optics wand Hand-held device used with optical character reading equipment to "read," capture, and input data recorded in bar code or a special character set from a printed document or label.

fiche Flat multi-image film sheet. Used with computer output to microfilm (COM) device.

file Collection of records relevant to an application under development.

file controls Procedures and methods used to assure proper and authorized handling, storage, use, and backup duplication, of files.

file conversion Process of changing master and transaction files to meet specifications of new system processing requirements.

fill-in-the-blank Questionnaire item that seeks specific, finite, factual answers not restricted to a given set of choices.

final documentation Detailed report of systems development project after completion. Included are documentation of programs, processing, procedures, forms, and files to assist in solving day-to-day system operational problems or questions when the system is in operation.

financial feasibility Evaluation that results from consideration of the economics of a proposed course of action, to determine potential profitability.

finish time (T) Time at which a project will be completed. Identified on project graph by the symbol *T* . *See also* critical path method, project graph.

finite Having a definite or definable beginning and a specific ending point.

first normal form Preliminary partition of data structures containing repeating groups into two or more relations without repeating groups that accomplish the same purpose.

fixed costs Continuing costs involved in assuring the ongoing existence of a business enterprise that must be considered in any proposed systems development plan. *See also* variable costs.

fixed-type printer Impact printer device that uses a rotating circular printing element in front of a striking device to imprint characters.

flatbed plotter Graphic output device that uses a flat area to hold the paper on which lines are plotted.

floppy disk *See* diskette.

font Format that gives a printed character set its particular "look."

functionally dependent The relation between nonkey data elements and the primary key in the second normal form. Uniquely identified only by a complete concatenated key, not by just a partial key.

G

Gantt chart Graphic representation of a work project showing start, elapsed time, and completion relations of work units in a project. Used to control schedules as part of project management. *See also* project planning sheet, critical path method, project graph.

generation Version of master file produced by processing a transaction file against a master file; the previous master file becomes a backup file. Three generations, known as the son file (most current), father file (previous master file), and grandfather file (predecessor of father file), are typically maintained.

global understanding Understanding of the functioning of a CIS as a complete system by a systems analyst. Represented and documented by high-level physical and logical models.

grandfather file *See* generation.

H

hash function A formula applied to a record key to determine the storage location for the record in a direct file organization.

hash total Summation of a numeric field that does not contain quantities or values normally added together. Used only to verify data entry.

header record Record indicating number of documents in a batch, batch identification number, and date of processing. Input control.

heuristic Method providing aid or direction in the solution of a problem; a "rule of thumb."

hierarchical An ordering and division of problems or functions into successively smaller increments, according to logical and/or functional sequence.

hierarchical partitioning Breaking down a large problem or project into a series of structured, related, manageable parts through iteration, for the purpose of understanding clearly the functions and requirements of individual system parts.

hit rate *See* activity rate.

human factors feasibility Evaluation that results from consideration of human reactions to a proposed course of action, to determine whether such reactions might impede or obstruct systems development or implementation.

I

impact printer Printing device that creates impressions by striking a ribbon that transfers images to paper. *See* serial printer and line printer.

incremental step Implementation and installation of a larger new system with reasonably independent components in increasingly complete stages. Allows users to learn to use the final system effectively, in stages. Makes it possible to develop the final system with good control over schedules and budgets.

indexed sequential file File arranged in sequential order, according to key, and also containing an index, or table, to identify the physical location of each key within the file. File can be searched in ascending order according to key, or a single record can be randomly accessed by reference to a physical location in the index.

information Meaningful data transformed through processing, or knowledge that has resulted from the processing of data.

information center Specialized computer facility that uses sophisticated software tools to generate functional computer applications in direct response to user service requests.

information system The methods, procedures, and resources for developing and delivering information.

initial investigation Activity to handle and evaluate requests for new or improved CIS services. End result is an understanding of the request at a level suffcient to make a preliminary recommendation as to course of action to be followed.

initial investigation report Report documenting the initial investigation activity, findings, and recommendations.

ink jet printer A nonimpact printing device that sprays microscopic ink particles onto paper to form characters.

input Data that serve as the raw material for system processing or that trigger processing steps. Also, to access data and place them into a computer system. Input tasks include data capture, data entry, and input processing.

input controls Controls used to assure that only correct, complete input data are entered into the system. Encompasses control totals for batch processing, video display, and maintenance of a transaction log to produce control totals for on-line systems.

installation phase Portion (phase) during the systems development life cycle during which the new CIS is installed, the conversion to new procedures is fully implemented, and the potential of the new system is explored.

instrumental input Data recorded directly by a machine, without human interpretation; examples are supermarket bar code reading devices and optical character recognition devices.

intangible Real, but not easily assessable. Describes business costs or benefits that are not easily quantifiable in monetary terms. *See also* tangible.

intangible benefit Delivered, identifiable improvement that must be identified, and for which a value not easily quantified must be ascribed.

intangible cost Cost, in most cases readily identified, but not easily quantified, usually attributable to human reactions to changes in the work environment.

integrity Completeness and unimpairedness. Integrity controls assure that: data files processed represent the actual, current status or condition; materials and mechanisms will exist to reconstruct destroyed files and recover processing capabilities in the event of loss; only authorized transactions will be admitted to a system.

intelligence Built-in electronic processing capability within a CRT terminal. May include microprocessors, memory units, printing and document originating capabilities.

interim documentation Documents generated during the analysis and development phase of a systems development life cycle to provide orderly, cumulative records of the development process. *See also* cumulative documentation.

internal output Documents or reports produced for use within an organization, as distinct from documents for use outside of the organization. Includes reports to management, job tickets or production schedules, employee time cards, etc. *See also* external output.

interview Planned interactive meeting between a data gatherer and one or more subjects for the purpose of identifying information souces and collecting information.

investigation phase Portion (phase) at the inception of the systems development life cycle to determine whether a full systems development effort or another course of action is appropriate.

iteration Repetition; indicated on data flow diagram by braces ({ . . . }). Also, partitioning a problem repeatedly to reach increasing levels of understanding.

J

job control language (JCL) Operating system software tool used to identify programs being submitted, and necessary software and equipment support requirements for the processing of application programs.

journal A log or record kept on a daily or regular basis. *See* transaction log file.

K

key Access control field that uniquely identifies a record or classifies it as a member of a category of records within a file.

key attribute Primary key to other data structures and the attributes of those other data structures.

keypunch A machine that punches holes in cards to make a physical data entry. The cards are machine- or human-readable.

key-to-disk machine Keyboard entry device that usually includes a CRT terminal and a recording system that processes entries and places them on disk packs.

key-to-diskette machine A keyboarding device, with or without a CRT, that enters machine-readable data directly onto a diskette.

key-to-tape machine A keyboarding device that enters machine-readable data directly onto magnetic tape.

L

laser *See* electrostatic (laser) printer.

late finish (LF) Latest completion of an activity. Determined by adding the activity duration to the late start time. Used in critical path method (CPM).

late start (LS) Latest time at which an activity can begin without extending the total project completion time. Determined by deducting elapsed time from late finish time for an activity. Used in critical path method (CPM).

layering Iteration of systems analysis studies to produce additional knowledge and/or understanding of problems and system operations.

light pen input An input device, resembling a pen, that allows users to manipulate data on the face of CRT screens. Used chiefly for engineering and design applications.

line printer Impact printing device that prints documents a full line at a time to produce documents faster than a serial printer.

logical model Model of a CIS showing only logically necessary data content and handling to aid in documenting and/or analyzing a system. *See also* physical model.

longest path Minimum time required for project completion, as indicated on a project graph network.

lookup table A program table searched to find entries to match input data. May be used in a category test for processing control.

M

magnetic ink character recognition (MICR) Input method developed and used by banking industry to identify checks, deposit slips, and other documents preprinted with a special magnetic ink.

maintenance Altering or replacing software or hardware of a CIS to meet new or changing processing requirements.

management information system (MIS) Type of computer information system that provides meaningful summarization of data to support organizational management control functions and highlights exception conditions requiring attention or corrective action.

management summary Summary report prepared for management. Recommends a course of action to solve a problem.

mark sensing Optical or electrical document reading method that uses the position of marks to indicate the meaning of data.

master file File containing permanent or semipermanent basic information to be maintained over an extended lifespan. Contains one record for each entity covered.

matrix printing element Impact printing device containing a series of points that are projected forward to cause printing impressions, thus forming characters.

minimodel Individual changes in a proposed CIS, modeled separately.

model Mathematical or logical representation of a system that can be manipulated intellectually to assess hypothetical changes. Also,
to make graphic or written representations of an information system and its functions, to help people understand the system.

monetary total *See* quantity total.

most probable time estimate "Best guess" of the time that will be required to complete an activity, assuming a normal number of problems or delays. Used in project evaluation and review technique (PERT).

multiple-choice Questionnaire item that provides the respondent with a series of finite, specific choices.

mutually independent State when it is verified that each nonkey data element is independent of every other nonkey element in the relation; test for third normal form.

N

net present value (NPV) Present value of benefits, minus present value of investments; can be positive, zero, or negative. Used to compare alternative investment opportunities with a stated benchmark, or standard. *See also* present value.

network Graphic flow diagram relating the sequence of activities to the sequence of occurrence. Used in project evaluation and review technique (PERT) and critical path method (CPM). *See* project graph.

new system design specification Comprehensive proposal for a new CIS, encompassing both user specification and all updated and/or additional detailing of hardware, software, procedures, and documentation needed for actual implementation. Presented to both users and CIS design group for signoff.

node Beginning or ending point of an activity, represented on a project graph by a circle. *See also* network.

nonimpact printer Printing device that causes images to be imprinted without actual contact between print mechanism and paper. *See* thermal printer, ink jet printer, and electrostatic (laser) printer.

nonredundancy Criterion for logical data design, characterized by avoiding inclusion of the same data component within two or more data stores, and/or avoiding inclusion of the same data in different forms within the same data store.

normalization Process of replacing existing files with their logical equivalents, thereby deriving a set of simple files containing no redundant elements.

numeric field test Test to verify that a given field contains only numeric characters. Used for processing control.

O

object Entity, or thing, described by or represented in a data structure. *See also* attribute.

observation Method of gathering information utilizing a highly trained, qualified person who watches firsthand the actual processing associated with a system and records information and impressions of the process.

open-ended question Questionnaire item offering no response directions or specified options. Used to allow a wide variety of potential responses.

operational benefit Recurring benefit that results from the day-to-day use of a system, such as reduced operational costs.

operational costs Variable costs associated with the use and maintenance of a system.

operational feasibility Evaluation that results from consideration of manual processing needs and overhead costs of a given systems operation by an organization.

optical character recognition (OCR) Data input technique that uses reflected light to ''recognize'' printed patterns.

optimistic time estimate ''Best guess'' estimate of minimum time required to complete a project, assuming all conditions will be ideal. Used in project evaluation and review technique (PERT).

optimum Most favorable in terms of cost-benefit analysis. Describes business option that produces greatest benefit for the least relative cost.

organizational controls Methods and techniques for protecting the integrity and reliability of data within a system through patterns of job responsibility. *See* separation of duties.

organizational structure A formal recognition by the management of a business of the subsystems that make up the business organization. Reflects fundamental strategy for achievement of the organization's goals. Often represented on an organization chart.

output A product, or result, of data processing.

owner (system) Upper-level personnel who manage lower-level users of a CIS. *See also* user.

P

parent Single bubble in high-level data flow diagram that can be exploded to produce a more detailed version. *See also* child.

partitioning Division of a complex problem or situation into smaller separate elements for ease of understanding, and/or solution. *See also* hierarchical.

payback *See* payback period.

payback analysis Method for determining period necessary for a new system to generate savings great enough to cover developmental costs.

payback period Length of time necessary to earn an amount equal to the amount required for acquisition of a capital investment.

percentage completion Indication on a Gantt chart of the proportion of a project that has been finished.

pessimistic time estimate Maximum completion time of a project, assuming that everything that can go wrong will go wrong. Used in project evaluation and review technique (PERT).

phase Set of activities and tasks that, when completed, delimits a significant portion of a systems development project.

physical model Graphic representation of the processing activities in an information system, shown in sequence and reflecting all data transformations, file alterations, and outputs.

planning Study and development of projected courses of action for meeting goals or dealing with anticipated problems.

plotter Computer-driven graphic output device that creates images on paper by guiding a pen-like stylus.

pointer *See* key.

point-of-sale terminal Electronic cash register that transmits sales entries into a recording device or computer.

population Total group of persons with a commonality of identification. Information providers identified as potential respondents for a questionnaire.

post-implementation maintenance list List of change requests from users, made during system implementation, and noncritical changes to be made after system test procedures, that are to be handled as maintenance after full system implementation.

post-implementation review report Report prepared for CIS, user departments and steering committee. Covers review, conducted after a new system has been in operation for some time, to evaluate actual system performance against original expectations and projections for cost/benefit improvements. Also identifies maintenance projects to enhance or improve the system.

preliminary detailed design and implementation plan Planning document used as a basis for detailed planning, and also to update estimates of development costs before new system design is completed. Encompasses: activities down to major task level, working days required, proposed staffing plan, and dependable planning schedule for activity and task completions.

preliminary installation plan Document prepared during implementation and installation planning. Contains: file conversion and system installation approaches; preliminary list of major files to be created or converted and forms to collect new data; identification of necessary computerized file conversion programs; and preliminary list of installation tasks for the new systems, including any special coordination considerations.

preliminary system test plan Document prepared during implementation and installation planning that establishes expectations of results to be delivered in each system area. Identifies major system products or functions and interrelationships, modules to be tested, and specifies system, program, and user procedures tests.

present value Current value of money. To determine the value of money in constant dollars, future economic values are discounted backward in time to the present.

present value factor (pvf) Multiplicand used to determine the present value of a sum of money to be received at a certain time in the future.

printing device Output device that produces printed documents.

procedures manual Instructional document written to aid people in performing manual procedures within a computer-based system. *See also* training manual.

process To transform input data into useful information through performance of certain functions: record, classify, sort, calculate, summarize, compare, communicate, store, retrieve. Indicated on data flow diagram by a circle, or bubble.

process description Set of rules, policies, and procedures specifying the transformation of input data flows into output data flows.

processing controls Controls designed to assure accuracy and completeness of records each time a file is processed. *See* trailer record, edit run, batch control, exception report.

programming and testing Detailed design and implementation phase activity encompassing actual development, writing, and testing of program units or modules.

program test log Document describing problems noticed as system was tested and brought into use. Log is updated to provide current information as changes are made to individual program modules and programs themselves.

project Extensive job involving activities that are finite, nonrepetitive, partitionable, complex, and predictable.

project evaluation and review technique (PERT) Project scheduling and control methodology that provides graphic displays to: identify project activities, order activities in time sequence, estimate completion time for each activity, relationships among activities, and time required for the entire project, identify critical activities and identify noncritical activities. *See also* critical path method (CPM)

project graph A graphic network that represents activities as paths between beginning and ending points. Used in project evaluation and review technique (PERT) and critical path method (CPM). *See also* network, node.

project management Method or combination of techniques that facilitates planning, scheduling, and control.

project management review Meeting at which technical or general reports by members of project team are reviewed by team leaders or project managers.

project plan Detailed account of scheduling and staffing—to task level—for the second and succeeding phases of a systems development life cycle.

project planning sheet Worksheet used to identify work units, make personnel assignments, and keep track of planned and actual hours worked and dates of completion. Used for project management. *See also* Gantt chart.

project team A team brought together to carry out a systems development project, representing all user needs and perspectives, usually headed by a senior systems analyst, and including other information system specialists and representatives from each of the functional areas impacted by the system.

prototype A working system that can be developed quickly and inexpensively, given the necessary software tools, to evaluate processing alternatives and specify desired results.

prototyping Specialized systems development technique using powerful application software development tools that make it possible to create all of the files and processing programs needed for a business application in a matter of days or hours, for evaluation purposes.

Q

query A single inquiry sentence that, with a database reference, would seek out and organize all relevant, related records, and present them in a sequence stipulated in the query.

questionnaire A special-purpose document requesting specific information that can be quantitatively tabulated, usually from large populations of source respondents. Used by systems analysts to gather information relating to potential CIS development.

R

random access Disk access technique in which records can be read from, and written directly to, disk media without regard for the order of their record keys.

randomizing routine Algorithm applied for assigning record locations for applications in which keys cannot be used directly as locators.

range test Test to verify that value of entries in a given field fall between high and low limits established by a program. Used for processing control.

ranking scales Questionnaire item that asks the respondent to order a response in terms of preference or importance.

rating scales Questionnaire multiple-choice item that offers a range of responses along a single dimension. Used to assess responses to a given item or situation.

reasonableness test A test applied to determine whether data in a given field fall within a range defined as reasonable, compared with a specified standard. Used for processing control.

reference file File containing constant data to be used each time an application program is run. Used, in conjunction with data from transaction files, to update master files.

relational value The comparison, or ordering, of one record relative to another. Used in database management to identify a record to be accessed through sequential, direct, or indexed-sequential reference methods.

relative position Record position on disk media identified relative to the basing point, or first record, in a given file.

reliability Description of level of confidence that can be placed on probability of performance as expected for a function or device.

repetition *See* iteration.

report Data output from a file in a format that is easily readable and understandable.

reprographic system System that forms graphic images for typesetting, printing page makeup, or displays.

requirements specification *See* user specification.

respondent A person selected as potential information source, who receives and answers a questionnaire.

reviewer (walkthrough) Member of a team appointed to review quality.

review phase Portion (phase) during systems development life cycle that include two activities: the first to evaluate the successes and failures during a systems development project, and the second to measure the results of a new CIS system in terms of benefits and savings projected at the start of the project.

router Point in an information system where a cumulative flow of data are broken down into a series of individual data streams. Indicated on data flow diagram by reverse-facing half-circle. *See also* collector.

S

sample A subset of a population of respondents chosen to represent accurately the population as a whole in an information-gathering process.

sampling Method used to gather information about a large population of people, events, or transactions by studying a subset of the total population that accurately represents the population as a whole. Statistical methods are used to infer characteristics of the entire population.

schedule feasibility Evaluation that results from consideration of time available to complete a proposed course of action, to determine whether or not it can be implemented in the time available.

scheduling Relating project activities that must be completed in a time sequence. *See also* planning.

second normal form Second step in normalization, when it is verified that each nonkey data element in a relation is functionally dependent on a primary key.

secondary storage device Equipment used to write data to, and read data from, magnetic media.

secretary (walkthrough) Member of quality review team who produces a technical report listing identified errors or problems noted.

security controls Controls applied to protect data resources from physical damage, and from intentional misuse or fraudulent use.

selection Group of data structures or data elements out of which one, and only one, item may be selected for use.

separation of duties Policy that no one individual should have access to, or know enough about, a system to process data in an unauthorized way, either during development stages or during ongoing use of the system. Major technique of organizational control.

sequence Linking together of data elements or data structures; indicated by ''+'' sign between units.

sequential access Access technique to read from and write to records and files in an order determined by a logical identifier, or key, that is generally a data field within the record.

sequential file File in which the physical and logical sequences of records match. Records are accessed in an order determined by a key, usually numeric.

serial access Access technique to read from and write to records and files in the same chronological order in which the records were initially recorded.

serial file File in which records are recorded in chronological order, as transactions are entered into a computer.

serial printer Impact printing device that prints one character at a time to produce documents.

service function Function or activity that is initiated in response to, guided by, and aimed at satisfying, user need for information.

sign-off To agree formally and commit to a proposed course of action, for the purpose of proceeding with a project.

sign test Test to identify and verify presence of positive or negative values in fields. Used for processing control.

simulation An imitative representation of the functioning of a system or process. *See also* model.

slack Without tight constraints. Used to describe time spent on subsidiary projects not affecting duration of an entire project.

software package *See* application software package.

son file *See* generation.

source document control Authorization measure that must be applied before data are accepted for input to a system; *See* input controls.

space (blank) test Test to check whether a given field contains some data value or is totally blank. Used for processing control.

speech synthesizer A sound-generating device that can produce sounds understandable by humans as language.

staffing plan Detailed account of personnel assignments, and days or hours to be worked, for a systems development project.

start time Time at which a project begins, indicated on a project graph by the symbol *S*. *See* critical path method (CPM).

starving the process Showing, in a logical model, only the logically necessary elements or steps needed. Distinguished from a physical model's representation of an actual processing sequence.

status review Meeting held to keep user management informed on progress of a project. Participants include project leader, key user manager, and possibly project team members who can make special contributions.

steering committee A committee that sets organizational priorities and policies concerning CIS support. Composed of top management personnel representing all user areas.

structure chart Graphic representation of overall organization, and control logic of processing functions (modules) in a program or system.

structured English Formal English statements using a small, strong, selected vocabulary to communicate processing rules and to represent the structure of a program or system.

structured specification *See* user specification.

stylus Electromechanically driven writing device used on a plotter to produce lines.

subsystem A secondary or subordinate small system within a large system.

summary report Report showing accumulated totals for specific groups of detail records. Used by middle-level managers for review of business activity.

synergistic The way that a system's parts function together, producing results with a greater value than would be produced by the system's separate parts working alone.

synthesis The process of bringing information system component parts together into a remodeled system in which previously existing problems have been eliminated.

system A set of interrelated, interacting components that function together as an entity to achieve specific results.

system flowchart Graphic representation of a system showing flow of control in computer processing at the job level. Represents transition from a physical model of computer processing to a set of program specifications that will be prepared at the start of the detailed design and implementation phase.

system life cycle Activities or conditions common to all computer information systems from inception to replacement: recognition of need, systems development, installation, system operation, maintenance and/or enhancement, and obsolescence.

systems analysis The application of a systems approach to the study and solution of problems, usually involving the application of computers.

systems analyst A problem solving specialist who analyzes functions and problems, using a systems approach, to produce a more efficient and functional system, usually involving application of computers.

systems approach Way of identifying and viewing component parts and functions as integral elements of a whole system.

systems development Process that includes identifying information needs, designing information systems that meet those needs, and putting those systems into practical operation.

systems development life cycle Organized, structured methodology for developing, implementing, and installing a new or revised CIS. Standard phases presented in this book include investigation, analysis and general design, detailed design and implementation, installation, and review.

systems development recap report In-depth review document prepared for CIS management covering completed systems development project. Aimed at enhancing or improving individual members' and the organization's performance on future projects.

systems test Extensive test of full system. Conducted chiefly by users after all programs and major subsystems have been tested. Assures that data resources handled by the system will be processed correctly and protected fully. Careful documentation is maintained through program test logs and system test logs.

T

table An index that records the physical location of each key within an indexed-sequential file, making possible random access to individual records.

tangible A cost or benefit readily quantifiable in monetary terms. *See also* intangible.

tangible benefit A benefit realized when a new system makes or saves money for its organization.

tangible cost Cost of equipment or human factors associated with the operation of a system.

tape drive Peripheral storage unit that performs input and output of data on magnetic tape. Also called a tape unit.

task Smallest unit of work that can be assigned and controlled through normal project management techniques; normally performed by an individual person, usually in a matter of days. *See also* activity.

technical design Activity within detailed design and implementation phase that builds upon specifications produced during new system design, adding detailed technical specifications and documentation.

technical feasibility Evaluation that results from technical consideration of available computer hardware and software capability to carry out a proposed course of action.

test specifications and planning Activity during detailed design and implementation phase activity to prepare detailed test specifications for individual modules and programs, job streams, subsystems, and for the system as a whole.

thermal printer Nonimpact printing device that develops images through exposure of special paper to heat.

third normal form Third stage of normalization process, during which duplicate data elements or elements that can be derived from other elements are removed. *See also* mutually independent.

timeliness Quality factor. Meeting needs of user or process for delivering results when needed to meet service requirements.

time reporting Accounting procedure for reporting work completed and still to be done. Controls are applied at the task level.

time scale Horizontal axis on a Gantt chart reading from left to right, indicating passage of time.

time value Changing value of money as time goes by, assuming inflationary devaluation or investment growth. Money invested at a percentage return will have a value equal to principal plus interest; money left uninvested loses purchasing power as inflation occurs.

top-down Partitioning of functions into successive levels of detail from the top-level module, representing the general system or program function as a whole, down through to lower-level modules that perform actual processing.

total slack Time difference between the early start and late start dates, or early finish and late finish dates, for a noncritical activity. *See also* critical path method (CPM).

touch-screen input Method of inputting data directly through touch contact with specially sensitized locations on the face of CRT terminal video display screens.

track *See* channel.

trade-off Term referring to decision-making consideration that weighs advantages and disadvantages of alternatives as a basis for selection.

trailer record Last record in a file, containing totals for all numeric fields in all records in the file. Compared with field totals each time the file is processed. *See* processing control.

training manual An easy-to-use reference manual that teaches operators how to learn to perform procedures within a computer-based information system. *See also* procedures manual.

transaction A basic act of doing business. The exchange of value for goods or services received.

transaction document Form upon which data generated by transactions are recorded. Used to capture data at source to report on results of transactions, control business activity, and for historic purposes.

transaction file Collection of records containing specific, timely data pertaining to current business activity. Used to update master files.

transaction log file Continuously updated master accounting record that records all transactions of an on-line processing system chronologically. Serves as starting point for an audit trail and can be used for recovery purposes if master or transaction file data are damaged or lost.

transform To process data for conversion (transformation) into information.

turnaround document Computer output documents that also serve as input documents for a follow-up processing activity.

u

unit record A single keypunched card containing an entire data record that may be broken into several fields.

universal product code (UPC) Bar code used extensively in supermarkets and other retail outlets for optical sensing of product identification.

user Term referring both to lower-level personnel who use, and upper-level personnel who own, a CIS. *See also* owner.

user concurrence Agreement by user that capabilities described in the user specification contain a full and complete statement of user needs and that the solution is feasible from operational and human factors standpoints.

user procedures manual *See* procedures manual, training manual.

user specification User-oriented report presenting a complete model of a new CIS for user evaluation and approval. Can include data flow diagrams, description of system inputs and outputs, performance requirements, security and control requirements, design and implementation constraints, and unresolved policy considerations that must be dealt with before the system can be implemented.

user training Activity during detailed design and implementation phase of the systems development life cycle. Encompasses: writing user procedure manuals, preparation of user training materials, conducting training programs, and testing manual procedures.

user training outline Specification document prepared during implementation and installation planning that includes: content outlines for user training manuals, details for preparation of manuals to cover user procedures to be installed, and list of proposed activities and assignments for users and analysts who will write these manuals.

V

validity Description of transaction or data to indicate they are authorized, that transactions actually took place, and that data really exist.

variable costs Costs incurred only when a system is used. *See also* fixed costs, operational costs.

version *See* incremental step.

version installation Technique of installing a new system as a series of functional areas or incremental steps.

video display Visual data display device using a CRT (cathode ray tube).

voice input Method of inputting data directly through voice commands.

volatility Rate of change and expansion of a file. Factor to be considered in determining file organization.

W

walkthrough Technical quality review of a CIS product that can be identified as a separate unit capable of introducing errors into the system.

working papers Documents accumulated during work completion that are useful for project review or for guiding performance of ongoing work.

INDEX

Abstraction, levels of, 18

Acceptance: criteria, 553, 557; reviews, 232, 233. *See also* Sign-off

Access: controls, 531-532; key, 445; paths, 447, 450

Accuracy, 188, 414-415, 529, 530

Acquisition of hardware/software, 476

Activities, defined, 50, 72

Activity rate, 517

Address, of record, 501, 502-503

Adjustments, defined, 13

Algorithms, randomizing, 502, 504

Alphabetic checks, 415, 535

Alternate keys, 518

American Bankers Association, 410

Analysis and general design phase, 44, 57, 238-240; activities, 238, 240; analysis process in, 308, 311; end products, 240; process, 238, 240; purpose, 45; results, 178-179; tasks, 51

Application requirements, and file design, 515-519

Application software development, 475; tools, 607-608

Application software packages, 351, 365, 475, 476, 478, 603-605, 611; compatibility, 604-605; consideration of, 135, 136; decision to purchase, 563; in New System Design specification, 464

Archival: files, 491, 497; storage, 368, 371-372, 377, 391

ASCII (American Standard Code for Information Interchange), 495

Attribute: key, 450; structure, 450

Audience identification, 216-217, 234

Audio output, 376-377, 392

Audit trails, 417, 536

Auditability of input, 70, 416-417

Author, defined, 221

Authorization measures, 532

Backup: files, 372, 491, 537-538; procedures, 518

Balancing, of control totals, 533

Bar code, 409

Batch processing, 350, 370, 469, 516, 532-533

Batch totals, 416

Benefits: developmental, 195-197, 209; intangible, 127, 129, 186-187, 209; operational, 197-199, 209; tangible, 185-186, 198-199, 209. *See also* Cost/benefit analysis

Bits per inch (bpi), 495

Black box, computer system as, 324, 328, 458

Bubbles. *See* Process bubbles

Business, organizational structure, 7, 23. *See also* Organization *headings*

Business systems, 6, 7-14, 23, 25

Case Scenario. *See* Water billing system application (Case Scenario)

Cash flow, 198

Category test, 535

Cathode ray tube (CRT) terminal, 375-376, 392, 408-409, 422

Central processing, 469

Change: impact of, 46; to new system, 573; requests, 333, 335-336, 575

Channels, magnetic tape, 495

Check digit, 415, 535

Checklist: for information gathering, 85-92; of physical documentation, 246-248

Checkpoints, 41

Child diagrams, 282

Cohesion, internal, 346, 349, 365

Collector, symbol, 259

Collision, defined, 504

COM (Computer Output to Microfilm) devices, 376, 377, 392

Commitment, 458

Communication, 37-38, 149, 214-236; accuracy in, 150-151; alternative methods, 149-151; audience identification, 216-217, 234; completeness of, 150-151; controls, 536; costs, 197; documentation and, 142; need for, 215-216, 234; problem-solving sessions, 217-220, 234

Completeness, standards of, 529

Completeness tests, 535

Completion times, 623

Computer-aided instruction (CAI), 411

Computer information systems (CIS): defined, 12, 25; development (see Systems development headings); examples of, 30-34; life cycle (see System life cycle); logical improvements, 36; "packaged," 34; physical improvements, 36; value/cost relationships, 188-193

Computer operations, documentation, 567

Computer Output to Microfilm (COM), 376, 377, 392

Concatenation, 432

Confidentiality: access controls for, 531-532; defined, 530, 531-532

Consultants, 194

Context diagrams, 151, 153, 180-181, 277

Control(s), 13, 14, 25, 90, 466-467, 529-543, 567; access, 531-532; accuracy, 529, 530; budgetary, 41; for confidentiality, 530; defined, 90, 466; file, 537-538; function, 41; input, 415-416; for integrity, 530; output, 537; prenumbering documents, 532; in project management, 615; quality, 41; responsibility for defining, 540; scheduling, 41; specification of, 463; of systems development project, 41, 47-51, 57, 615; types of, 530-539; user-defined, 540

Control totals, 532-533

Conversion: of files, 582-584, 589; programs, 567

Correlative: files, 447; structures, 445, 450

Cost/benefit analysis, 122, 126, 184-210; accuracy of, 459; evaluations in, 193-199; ideal alternatives in, 187-188; and net-present-value (NPV) technique, 205-207, 210; and optimum solution, 190-193; and payback analysis, 200-201, 203-205, 209; and trade-off decisions, 184-185; updated, 550

Costs, 39, 40, 57, 327, 596, 610; administrative, 194-195, 196; developmental, 193-195, 209; fixed, 195; of input, 412; intangible, 185, 186, 209; maintenance, 39-40, 57; operational, 195-197, 209; of output, 379-380; overhead, 194-195, 196; payback analysis, 200-201, 203-205, 209; processing, 194, 196; start-up, 195; tangible, 185, 209; variable, 195. See also Cost/benefit analysis; Investment

Coupling, 346, 349, 365

CPM. See Critical Path Method

Credibility, 125, 555

Criteria: agreement on, 555; performance, 90

Critical path: algorithm, 623, 625; defined, 622; locating, 622

Critical Path Method (CPM), 618-627, 631

Critical tasks, 617

Cross field checks, 535, 536

Cross record checks, 535, 536

CRT (cathode ray tube) terminals, 375-376, 392, 408-409, 422

Cumulative project file, 141, 145, 354, 479-480, 556, 589-591

Cylinder, disk pack, 506; index, 510

Data: access diagram, 329, 450, 467; area, 507; capture, 399, 400; content, 381, 419

Data dictionary, 53, 158, 181, 226, 285-294, 320, 328, 380, 381, 419, 463, 479, 567, 590; building and maintaining control of, 290-294; syntax, 286-287, 290

Data elements, 286, 349, 380, 441; functionally dependent, 434; mutually independent, 439

Data entry, 399, 400; controls, 532-534

Data files, specifications, 463. See also File headings

Data flow diagrams, 53, 57, 151-165, 180-181, 226, 257; balance requirement, 274; construction hints, 262, 264, 265; documentation, 285; expanded, 156, 318; hierarchical partitioning, 158-160, 169, 181, 269-271, 273, 274-275, 320; hierarchical set of, 179, 313; limitations, 158, 160; names, 262; overview, 133; role, 151-183; supporting documentation, 158, 160, 181, 285; symbols, 68, 153, 156, 181, 257, 259, 320; versus system flowcharts, 476; updating, 567

Data management, 475

Data processing systems (DPS), 9, 10, 25, 32-33

Data stores: in relation to data structures, 429; evaluation of, 427; logical analysis of, 427-428; names, 262, 285; nonlogical, 312; normalization, 429, 432-445, 453; symbol, 68, 156, 181, 259

Data structure: 286-287, 290; attributes, 441; correlations, 441; iteration of, 286, 287; logical, 428-448; nonredundancy, 428-429; notation, 381, 393, 419; object, 441; in relation to data stores, 429; and selection, 286, 287; sequence and, 286, 287; simplicity of, 428; syntax rules, 286-287; third normal form presentation of, 450, 454

Data structure diagrams, 339, 445-450, 453

Database, 427, 467, 575

Database administration group, 467, 575

Database analyst, 479, 575

Database management system (DBMS) software, 467

Decision: support systems (DSS), 10, 11-12, 25; tables, 158, 302-305; trees, 158, 297, 299

Decisions, 199; trade-off (*see* Trade-off decisions)

Density, data storage, 495

Departmentalization, 7

Departments, versus systems, 252-253

Design decisions, file-related, 489-490

Design evaluation criteria, 346-349, 365

Design phases. *See* Analysis and general design phase; Detailed design and implementation phase

Design specifications, general, 319, 320

Detailed design and implementation phase, 45, 57, 558; described, 561, 563-564; end products, 565-569, 577; objectives, 564, 577; preliminary, 552, 553; relationships of activities in, 569-570; scope, 564-565

Detail reports, 369, 391

Development Recap, 594, 598-599, 610

Diagrams: child, 273-274, 282, 312; parent, 273-274, 282

Diagram 0 (Zero), 153, 156, 159, 181, 259, 261, 320, 328; developing, 277-285, 320; use, 271, 320

Digitizers, 411

Diminishing returns, point of, 189-190

Direct access: files, 447, 450, 490, 496-498, 501, 506, 516-517, 518; file organization, 493, 494, 501-506, 524

Direct data entry, 400, 403-404

Discounted values, 204, 210

Disk: drive, 495-496; pack, 405, 497

Distributed processing, 469

Document flowchart, 88

Document reading devices, 409-411

Documentation, 245-249, 590, 591; checklists, 246-248; computer operations, 567; controls, 538-539; cumulative, 78, 80, 141, 145 (*see also* Cumulative project file); for data flow diagrams, 158, 160, 181; *80-20* rule applied to, 245-246; end product, 142; of existing system, 244-250, 254, 479; final, 142; in information gathering phase, 94-95; initial investigation, 169; of input, 419-420; interim, 142-143, 145; New System Design, 180; old system, 587; output, 383; permanent, 371-372; preliminary, 141; purpose, 142, 145; system function, 462; Technical Design activity, 565-567, 577

EBCDIC (Extended Binary Coded Decimal Interchange Code), 495

Edit: criteria, 567; runs, 535

80-20 rule, 134-135, 192, 245-246

Electrostatic (laser) printers, 375

Encryption, 536

English, structured, 305-308

Entry system, defined, 405

Errors: design, 597; processing, 574; programming, 597

Exception reports, 11, 369-370, 390, 391, 534-535

Existing system, 45, 167, 181; deficiencies, 249; discontinuance, 587; documentation, 244-250, 254, 479; information-gathering about, 83-115; initial investigation, 74; interface points, 249-250; logical model, 243, 245, 254; maintenance projects, 601-602; physical constraints, 164; and policies, 250; rule of thumb, 66-67

Existing System Review, 141, 240, 242-254, 308; documentation, 141; end products, 245-250; objectives, 243, 254, process, 250-253, 254; scope, 244; walkthrough, 252

External entity, symbol, 68, 181, 257

Face validity, defined, 105

Feasibility: defined, 121; financial, 122-123, 143; human factors, 126, 143-144; and New System Requirements activity, 326-327; operational, 123-124, 143; schedule, 125, 143; technical, 124-125, 143

Feasibility evaluation, 44, 126-127; preliminary, 75, 80; updating, 458, 459, 466, 478, 550

Feasibility report, 127, 132-134, 141, 144, 354, 365, 479, 589, 591; defined, 62; scope and limitations, 129

Feasibility Study, 74, 120-146; activity, 131; cost/benefit decision in, 186-188; description, 121; end products, 132; results, 178; scope, 131

Feedback, 13, 14, 25

Fiberoptics wands, 388

Fiche, 377

Field checks, 415

File: defined, 495; direct access, 447, 450, 490, 494, 496-498, 501, 506, 516-517, 518; generations, 5, 538; sequential access, 447, 490, 496-501

File controls. *See* Control(s)

File Conversion, 582-584, 589

File design, 447, 450, 489-524, 570; in relation to data structure diagram, 447, 450; trade-offs, 515-519

File maintenance: direct files, 506; indexed-sequential files, 510, 512, 515; sequential files, 501

File organization, 490, 492-494

File processing, 468

Financial feasibility, 1, 122-123, 143, 500. *See also* Cost/benefit analysis

Flow diagram, work area, 92

Fonts, 388

Functional units, 86

Gantt charts: of activities, 138, 145, 325, 460, 551; in project mangement, 629, 631

"Garbage in, garbage out," 530

Generations, master file, 538

Glossary of terms, 141, 145

Goals, organizational, 85, 86

Graphic representations, 53, 150, 180. *See also* Models

Hardware, 196, 575-576

Hash totals, 416, 532, 533

Hashing function, 502, 504

Header records, 533

Heuristics, defined, 516

Hierarchical decomposition, 52

Hierarchical structure: of data flow diagrams, 269-275, 320; and partitioning of effort, 18-19; of problem elements, 14, 25; of program design, 570, 572

Hit rate, defined, 517

Human factors, 126, 143-144, 185, 459

Human-machine boundaries, 350

Impact printers, 373-374, 392

Implementation and Installation Planning activity, 240, 550-577; end products, 522-554, 556; objectives, 551; process, 554-555; scope, 511

Index area, 507, 510

Indexed-sequential file, 490; organization, 494, 498, 506-507, 510, 512, 515, 517; overflow type, 507, 510, 512; response time, 517

Information: on authority relationships, 87; categories of, 85-94; incomplete, 124; on interpersonal relations, 87-88; on job duties, 87; about organization, 85-87, 113; quality/value relationship, 188-189; value/cost relationship, 188-193

Information center, 602-603, 611; versus prototyping, 607-608

Information delivery, 368, 369-371, 391

Information gathering: checklist, 85-92; on control mechanisms, 90; on data flow, 88; from external sources, 95; interviews, 95-104, 114; methods, 95-113, 114-115; on methods and procedures, 90; observation, 110-112, 114-115; on performance criteria, 90; questionnaires, 104-110, 114; in systems develop life cycle, 83-115; on work environment, 92-94, 113; about work flow, 88; work sampling, 112-113, 115; on work schedules, 90

Information requirements, 88

Information sources, 94-95, 96

Information systems, 9, 13-14, 25. *See also* Computer information systems (CIS)

Initial investigation. *See* Investigation, initial

Initial Investigation Report, 71, 141, 354, 365, 589, 591

Ink jet printers, 375

Input, 13, 25, 399, 422, 570; accuracy of, 414-415; alternatives, 399-417: alternatives, evaluation of, 411-417; auditability, 416-417; completeness of, 413-414; control, 415-416; cost, 412; design, 398-423, 570; direct, 400-404; documentation form, 419-420, 463; equipment, 404-411, 422; index to, 329; instrumental, 403; layout charts, 567; methods, 399-411, 422; from source documents, 399-400; timeliness, 413

Inquiry systems, 389, 390, 475

Installation, 38, 57; alternatives, 76-77, 581, 584-587, 590; approach to, 563; in increments or versions, 563-564, 581, 605-607, 611; methods, 581, 590

Installation phase, 45-46, 57, 558, 579-591; cumulative project file, 589-590, 591; description, 579; end products, 582; objectives, 581; scope, 582; transition to maintenance, 588-589

Installation planning, 550-577; preliminary, 552, 554 *See also* Implementation and installation planning activity

Installation process, 582-589, 590; abrupt cutover, 584-585; parallel operation with gradual cutover, 585-586; parallel operation with single cutover, 585

Instrumental input, 403

Intangible benefits, 129

Integrity, defined, 530

Interpersonal relationships, 87-88

Interviews, 95-104, 113, 141, 354, 365, 479; advantages and disadvantages, 104; conducting, 97, 100-102; existing systems review, 251-252; follow-up, 102, 104; preparation for, 96-97; on system requirements, 324

Inventory program, 566

Investigation, Initial, 64-81; activity, 72-79; end product, 62; objectives, 65-66; problem definition, 73; recommendations based on, 60, 65, 78; report, 71, 141, 354, 365, 479, 589, 591; results, 169; scope, 66-67

Investigation phase, 44, 57, 60-81; activities, 60, 62; objectives, 60; recommendations based on, 62

Investment: capital, 122, 199-209; credits, 195; evaluation techniques, 200-211; payback period, 122; return on, 122, 132

Item count, 416

Iteration, 52; of data elements or structures, 287; in installation phase, 564; in structured English, 305

Job Control Language (JCL) description sheets, 566

Job duties, 87

Journal, 417, 492

Justification, 415

Key. *See* Record key

Keyboarding, 399-400

Key-entry devices, 404-409

Key fields, 450

Keypunch machines, 405

Key-to-disk machines, 405-406

Key-to-diskette machines, 406-408

Key-to-tape machines, 405

Laser printers, 375

Late finish (LF), 625-626

Late start (LS), 625, 626

Layering concept, 135, 136-137, 144-145, 326, 461, 551

Layout charts, 567

Light pen input, 411

Limit check, 415

Line printers, 374

Logical data analysis, 426-454

Logical data structures, 428-447; criteria, 428-429

Logical model, 160, 164-165, 168-169, 181, 312-316, 338, 426; of existing system, 243, 245, 254; of new system, 324, 338-339, 346, 349, 365; in relation to physical models, 319, 320, 350-351, 365; value of, 311

Magnetic disk, 405-406, 495-498, 501

Magnetic disk devices, 495

Magnetic diskettes, 406-408

Magnetic ink character recognition (MICR) devices, 409, 410, 422

Magnetic tape, 405, 495, 497

Magnetic tape devices, 495

Maintainability of system, 349

Maintenance: contracts, 604; costs, 39-40, 57; of existing system, 601-602; of new system, 588-589; of software packages, 604. *See also* File maintenance

Maintenance list, post-implementation, 569, 573

Management: policy decisions, 250, 354, 365; reports, 224; reviews, 41, 464-466; summaries, 227-228, 235

Mangement information systems (MIS), 9, 10-11, 25, 33

Manual procedures, 168, 533, 572

Manuals: computer operations, 590, 591; procedures, 228-230, 235, 553, 555, 568, 572, 590, 591; user training, 230-231, 236, 553, 555

Mark sensing, 409-410

Master files, 490, 516, 518, 538

Master index, 510

Mechanical checks, of logical model, 339

Microfilm, 376, 377, 392

Modeling, 256-320, 338-351; computerized, 158-160; iterations, 460

Modeling tools, 256-320; application to analysis procedure, 308, 311-313

Models, 12, 53, 57, 150-165, 180-181; logical (*see* Logical models); physical, 160-169, 180-181, 311, 319, 324, 350-351, 365, 468; signing off, 160. *See also* Data flow diagrams

Modular design, 572
Modules, program, 571-572

Names, in data flow diagrams, 262
Narrative descriptions, 149-150
Net present value (NPV), 205-207, 210
Networks, graphic, 619-620
New system, physical model, 350-351, 365, 518
New System Design activity, 141, 180, 240, 311, 319, 457-487; cumulative project file, 479-480; detailed definition of, 468-469, 475-476, 487; documents, 478; end product, 462-466, 486; in relation to Implementation and Installation Planning activity, 461; level of detail necessary, 459, 461; objectives, 459-460; overlap with New System Requirements activity, 461; tasks and goals, 458-459, 466; walkthroughs, 478
New System Design specifications, 168, 179, 180, 181, 240, 462-464, 479, 563, 589, 591
New System Requirements activity, 141, 240, 308, 310, 323-366; description, 323-325; and feasibility, 326-327; objectives, 325; process overview, 333, 346, 349-354, 365; scope, 325-327
Nodes, 619-620
Nondisplay fields, 531
Nonimpact printers, 374-375, 392
Normal form: first, 432; second, 434; third, 439, 450, 454
Normalization of data stores, 429, 432-445, 453
Numeric: field check, 425; tests, 535

Objectives, understanding, 18-19, 51, 54-55, 57
Observation, 110-112, 114-115; advantages and disadvantages, 111-112
Obsolescence, of system, 39, 57
On-line: data entry, 409, 532, 533-534; inquiry, 389, 390; output, 370; processing, 516, 518, 534
Operational: benefits, 197-199; costs, 195-197, 209; feasibility, 123-124, 143
Optical character recognition (OCR) devices, 388, 400, 409-410, 422
Oral presentations, 231-234, 236
Organization chart, 7, 23, 85, 87, 94
Organizational: controls, 538; departmentalization, 7; goals and objectives, 12-13, 15, 17, 18, 34-37, 85-86, 337; policy, 86, 141, 250, 329, 464; structure, 7, 23, 83-86
Output, 13, 25; audio, 376-377, 392; COM, 376, 377, 392; controls, 537; cost, 379-380; definition, 570; evaluation criteria, 378-380, 392; functions, 368-369, 391; layout charts,

567; options, 368; purposes, 368-373; use, 378-379; volume, 379
Output design, 367-393, 570; end products, 368; preliminary, 381; tasks, 367
Output documents/displays, 383, 385; content, 380, 381; continuous-form postcards, 385; formats, 381-383, 393; index to, 329, 383; and user needs, 380
Output media and devices, 373-377, 392
Overflow area, 507
Overview narrative, 328, 462

Parity, 495
Partitioning: of effort, 18-19; hierarchical decomposition, 52
Payback/payback period, 200-201, 203-205, 209
Performance criteria, 90, 351, 463
Personnel, 87-88, 324, 576; in conversion phases, 186; and costs, 196; and file conversion, 589; indoctrination sessions, 556; and initial investigation, 77-78; in installation phase, 587-589; and intangible costs and benefits, 186-187; new opportunities, 573, in New Systems Requirements activities, 354; and organizational controls, 539; requirements, 465, 466; separation of duties, 532, 539. See also Human factors; Project team; User headings
PERT. See Project Evaluation and Review Technique (PERT)
Phases, defined, 51
Physical model, 160-169, 180-181, 311, 319, 324, 350-351, 365, 468; and design considerations, 461; in relation to logical model, 312, 313, 319, 320, 350-351, 365; trade-off decisions, 350
Planning: long- and short-range, 564; of systems development project, 614-615
Plotters, 376, 392
Point-of-sale terminals, 408
Policy, organizational, 86, 141, 250, 329, 464
Population, defined, 106
Post-Implementation maintenance list, 589, 591
Post-Implementation Review, 588, 594, 599-600, 610; report, 597, 610
Presentations, oral, 231-234, 236
Present value, 204-205, 210
Present value factor (pvf), 205
Prime data area, 507
Prime number, 504
Printers, 373-375, 392
Problem identification, 34-37, 38, 57, 73-74

Problem solving: sessions, 217-220, 234; strategies, 18-19, 23-25

Procedures: information on, 90; manuals, 228-230, 235, 568, 590, 591

Process bubble, 68, 158, 181, 259, 262, 320; child, 273; parent, 273, 282, 312, 346; partitioning of, 271, 320

Process descriptions, 53, 158, 181, 329, 462, 566; defined, 294-295; tools for communication of, 294-308

Process narratives, 295, 297

Process specification, 226; tools, 158

Processes: nonlogical, 312; starved, 313

Processing, 13, 25; costs, 194, 196

Processing methods: in relation to applications, 516; file design trade-offs, 516-517; in new system, 328; physical model, 350-351

Processing rules, 294-308

Program: design, 570; development, 475; documentation, 590; generators, 608; modules, 571-572; specification, 566; test log, 568, 574-575

Programming, 124-125

Programming and Testing activity, 568

Programs. *See* Application software *headings*

Project: characteristics, 616; completion times, 623; defined, 615-616; early start, 623; file (*see* Cumulative project file); graphs, 619; layering (*see* Layering); start time, 623

Project Evaluation and Review Technique (PERT), 617, 618, 626, 631; time estimates, 628-629; project management, 45, 613-632; components, 614-615

Project management: components, 614-615; reviews, 231; and system development life cycle, 613-614, 631; techniques, 616-632; tools, 135, 137-138, 145

Project plan, 44-45, 133, 137, 144, 145; complete, 589, 591

Project planning sheet, 138, 145

Project team, 30, 56, 138, 141, 145, 479, 576; dissolution of, 558; in review phase, 598-599; user orientation, 354

Prototyping, 607-609, 611

Punched cards, 405

Quality analysis, 478

Quality control. *See* Control(s)

Quality of information: versus cost, 188-190; versus value, 188-189

Questionnaires, 95, 104-110, 113, 114; administration and scoring, 105; advantages and disadvantages, 110; fill-in-the-blank, 107; multiple-choice, 108; planning, 106; ranking scales, 108; rating scales, 108; reliability, 105; types of questions and responses, 106-108; validity, 105

Randomizing algorithms, 502, 504

Range tests, 535

Read/write heads, 496

Real-time processing, 516, 518, 534

Reasonableness checks, 415, 427, 535

Recognition processing, 124

Record: defined, 495; header, 533; key, 432, 501-504, 518; layout, 567; trailer, 534

Recovery procedures, 538

Redundancy, elimination of, 428-429; 432, 439

Reference files, defined, 491

Relative address, 501, 502-503, 504

Relative file organization. *See* Direct file organization

Reliability: design, 529-545; of questionnaires, 105

Reports, 225-233, 235-236; aged receivables, 389; detail, 369, 391; exception, 369-370, 390, 391; formats, 381; management, 224; oral, 231-234, 236; steps in preparation, 225-226, 235; summary, 369, 389, 391; walkthrough, 223-224; written, 226-228, 235

Report-writing systems, 475

Reprographic systems, 376

Respondents, defined, 106

Response time, 516-517

Restricted functions, 532

Review phase, 46-47, 57, 558, 560, 588, 593-611; description, 593, 594; development recap, 594, 610; objectives, 594, 610; post-implementation, 594, 610; purpose, 593

Router, symbol, 259

Schedule feasibility, 125, 143

Scheduling, 459, 615; of interviews, 141; in project management, 615; time reporting system, 137, 145; tools, 618; of work, 90

Secondary storage, 518-519; equipment and media, 494-498

Security measures, 463, 530, 567. *See also* Control(s)

Separation of duties, 532, 539

Sequential access, 493, 498, 501

Sequential files, 447, 490, 498, 501; backup procedures, 518, 538; maintenance, 501; organization, 493-494, 496-501

Serial printers, 373-374

Sign-off: CIS, 460, 466, 478-479; defined, 168; securing, 327; user, 460, 465, 478-479, 555

Sign tests, 535

Simulation. *See* Modeling *headings*; Models

Slack: tasks, 623, 625; time, 617, 625, 626

Software: costs, 196; modification of, 125. *See also* Application software *headings*

Source coding, 608

Source documents, 399-400, 418, 532

Space (blank) test, 535

Specifications: new system design, 179, 180, 181, 240, 462-464, 486; user, 179, 181, 240

Spoken output, 376-377, 392

Staffing plan, 137, 145

Standards, performance, 90

Start-up costs, 195

"Starving" of processes, 182, 313

Status reporting, 138, 145

Status reviews, 231-232

Steering committee, 41, 44, 45; decisions, 30, 62, 132, 458, 459, 550; oral presentations to, 234

Storage capacity, 518-519. *See also* Secondary storage

Structure chart, 226, 570, 572

Structured English, 305-308; constructs, 305-306; sequence in, 305

Subsystems, 6, 7, 23, 574

Summary reports, 369, 389, 391

Supplies, costs of, 194, 196

Symbols, data flow diagrams, 153, 156, 181, 257, 259, 320

Synergism of systems, 5

Synonyms, 504

Syntax checks, 535

System flowchart, 469, 476

System function description, 328

System life cycle, 38-40, 57

System output. *See* Output *headings*

System Test: activity, 569, 574; logs, 569, 574, 590, 591; preliminary plan, 552, 553

Systems, 5, 6, 23, 36, 38-39, 57, 252-253

Systems analysis, 51-56, 57; characteristics of, 52-56, 57; communication in, 37-38, 56, 149, 180; defined, 29, 36, 56; goal, 148-149, 180; iterated steps in, 167-168, 181; process, 167-169, 178-179, 181

Systems analysts: and communications, 216; and computer programming, 124-125; judgmental skills, 246; and project team

leader, 141, 145; and prototyping, 609; responsibilities, 336-337; role, 29, 34-38, 56, 156, 473, 475, 478-479, 609-610; role, in control design, 540, 545; role, in detailed design and implementation phase, 576; role, in installation phase, 581, 587; role, in New System Requirements activity, 332-333; understanding of, 336; as walk-through administrators, 222

Systems approach, 14, 25

Systems designer, commitments, 458

Systems development, 29-30, 38, 56, 57; *80-20 rule*, 134-135

Systems development life cycle, 40-41, 57; optional modifications, 600-602; phases and activities, 44-47, 50-51, 57; and project management, 613-614, 631; structuring, 41, 44, 57

Systems development project team. *See* Project team

Systems development recap, 594, 596-597, 610; report, 596-597, 610

Table lookup techniques, 535

Tape drives, 495

Tasks, defined, 48, 72

Tax deductions, 195

Technical design, 570, 571

Technical Design activity: documentation, 565-567, 577

Technical reviews. *See* Walkthroughs

Technical services group, 576

Technical support, 575-576; specifications, 464; staff, 554

Terminals. *See* Cathode ray tube (CRT) terminals

Test: criteria, 555; data, 568; files, 568; logs, 590, 591

Test specifications, 553, 555, 563, 572; detailed, 567, 568

Test Specifications and Planning activity, end products, 568

Thermal printers, 375

Third normal form, 439, 450, 454

Time estimates: Critical Path Method, 623-627; PERT, 628

Time reporting system, 137, 145

Time scale, Gantt chart, 629

Time table, 553. *See also* Scheduling

Time value of money, 204-205

Top-down: development, 570, 572; partitioning of data flow diagrams, 269-275, 320

Track, magnetic tape, 495; index, 507

Trade-off decisions, 76-77, 80, 184-188, 337, 388; Case Scenario, 390-391; and cost/benefit analysis, 184-185; in feasibility considerations, 125; in file design, 515-519; optimum solution and, 190-193; in physical model construction, 350; prototyping, 608-609. *See also* Cost/benefit analysis

Trailer records, 534

Training: manuals, 230-231, 236; programs, 230-231, 588

Transaction: codes, 531; count, 416; defined, 370; files, 490, 492, 516; logs, 492, 536; records, 368, 370-371, 391

Transponder, 421

Turnaround documents, 369, 372-373, 388, 391, 400

"User friendly" systems, 230

User interface, 329, 350, 463

User needs. *See* User requirements; Users

User procedure manuals, 568. *See also* Procedures: manuals

User requirements, 29, 88, 329, 368, 391; identification of, 167, 181, 225, 235, 318

User sign-off, 460, 465, 478-479, 555

User specification: Case Scenario, 354-368; value of, 329, 332

User specification document, 179, 181, 240, 319, 325, 327, 328-332, 364-365, 458, 459

User training, 45, 46, 555, 556, 563, 572-573; end products of activity, 568; manuals, 230-231, 236; outline, 553; programs, 588

Users, 555, 576; acceptance of, 588 (*see also* User sign-off); in analysis and general design phase, 45; change requests from, 353, 573; commitment of, 458; communication with, 37, 215-216, 234; complaints or problems, 252; and control design, 540; expectations of, 332; information gathering from, 95; in installation phase, 579-580; orientation of, 324, 325, 354; participation of, 327, 337, 555, 572; requests of, 74-75, 353, 373

Validation procedures, 414-416, 535

Validity, of questionnaires, 105

Value/cost relationships, 188-193

Value test, 535-536

Verifier, 405

Verifier mode, 405

Version installation, 581, 586, 605-607, 611

Video displays, 375-376, 392, 408-409, 422

Voice input, 410-411

Volatility, and file design, 517-518

Walkthroughs: administrators, 222; control design, 540, 545; defined, 221; of existing system, 252; of logical model, 339; of new system design, 478; participants, 221-222, 235; pitfalls, 224-225; reports, 223-224, 225-236; structure, 222-223

Water billing system application (Case Scenario), 67-71; context diagram, 151, 153, 363; controls, 540-544; Diagram 0 (Zero), 279; feasibility study, 130-131; file design trade-offs, 519, 523; input options, 420-422; output requirements, 383-391; user specification, 354-368

Work environment: flow diagram, 92; information about, 92-94, 113; physical arrangement, 92

Work flow, 88

Work plan, layering concept applied to, 551

Work sampling, 112-113, 115

Work schedules, 90

Working papers, 133, 144